Enterprise Law

Enterprise Law

Contracts, Markets, and Laws in the US and Japan

Edited by

Zenichi Shishido

Hitotsubashi University, Japan

Edward Elgar

Cheltenham, UK • Northampton, MA, USA

Published by
Edward Elgar Publishing Limited
The Lypiatts
15 Lansdown Road
Cheltenham
Glos GL50 2JA
UK

Edward Elgar Publishing, Inc.
William Pratt House
9 Dewey Court
Northampton
Massachusetts 01060
USA

A catalogue record for this book
is available from the British Library

Library of Congress Control Number: 2013949806

This book is available electronically in the ElgarOnline.com
Law Subject Collection, E-ISBN 978 1 78100 445 6

MIX
Paper from responsible sources
FSC® C013056
FSC www.fsc.org

ISBN 978 1 78100 444 9

Typeset by Servis Filmsetting Ltd, Stockport, Cheshire
Printed and bound in Great Britain by T.J. International Ltd, Padstow

Contents

List of contributors viii
Preface x

Introduction: the incentive bargain of the firm and enterprise law: a nexus of contracts, markets, and laws 1
Zenichi Shishido

PART I THE INCENTIVE BARGAIN BETWEEN EMPLOYEES AND MANAGEMENT

1 What we know (and don't know) about how employment protection law affects employment 53
J.H. Verkerke

2 Complementarity among the abusive dismissal rule, company community norms, and an illiquid external labor market: transformation of directors' fiduciary duty under Japanese corporate law 70
Toru Kitagawa

3 The relative bargaining power of employers and unions in the global information age: a comparative analysis of the United States and Japan 81
Kenneth G. Dau-Schmidt and Benjamin C. Ellis

4 Employee stock purchase plans in Japan 100
Yohsuke Higashi

Comments on Part I: complementarity 118
Hideshi Itoh

PART II THE INCENTIVE BARGAIN BETWEEN CREDITORS AND MANAGEMENT

5 The role of debt in the governance of US business corporations 125
George Triantis

6 Senior creditor control in Chapter 11 137
Kenneth M. Ayotte and Edward R. Morrison

7 Cramdown versus extinguishing security interests: secured claims in bankruptcy in the United States and Japan 150
Wataru Tanaka

8 Reduction of retirees' benefits upon the reorganization of a company 161
Gen Goto

Comments on Part II: unsolved aspects of corporate governance problems 172
Noriyuki Yanagawa

PART III THE INCENTIVE BARGAIN BETWEEN SHAREHOLDERS AND MANAGEMENT

9 Takeover law and managerial incentives in the United States and Japan 177
Curtis J. Milhaupt

10 Management–shareholder relations in Japan: what's next after cross-shareholdings? 191
Takaaki Eguchi

11 Regulation of bank shareholding: a functional and historical analysis 205
Akira Tokutsu

12 Reappraising the role of the appraisal remedy 222
Hidefusa Iida and Kenichi Sekiguchi

13 Appraisal or injunction? Corporate takeovers under uncertain judicial valuation 237
Akio Hoshi

14 Stagnant Japan? Why outside (independent) directors have been rare in Japanese companies 252
Kenichi Osugi

Comments on Part III: the diversification of corporate governance arrangements: ownership structure and the board of directors 267
Hideaki Miyajima

PART IV THE ROLES OF GOVERNMENTS

15 Taxation and incentives in the business enterprise 277
David Gamage and Shruti Rana

16 Income tax and incentives for corporate transactions: a Japanese perspective 289
Tetsuya Watanabe

17 Tax law influences on the form and substance of equity compensation in the United States 302
Mark P. Gergen

18 Public enforcement: an update of the literature on resource-based evidence 317
Howell E. Jackson

19 Transparency and corporate governance 342
Benjamin E. Hermalin

20 Reverse engineering SOX versus J-SOX: a lesson in legislative policy 349
Zenichi Shishido and Sadakazu Osaki

21 Regulating in the dark 367
Roberta Romano

Comments on Part IV: the political economy of legislation 377
Noriyuki Yanagawa

General comments: afterword 381
J. Mark Ramseyer

Table of references 386
Index 419

Contributors

Kenneth M. Ayotte, Northwestern University, US

Kenneth G. Dau-Schmidt, Indiana University – Bloomington, US

Takaaki Eguchi, Doctorate Program, Hitotsubashi University, Japan

Benjamin C. Ellis, Betz & Associates, US

David Gamage, UC Berkeley, US

Mark P. Gergen, UC Berkeley, US

Gen Goto, University of Tokyo, Japan

Benjamin E. Hermalin, UC Berkeley, US

Yohsuke Higashi, Mori Hamada & Matsumoto, Japan

Akio Hoshi, Nishimura & Asahi, Japan

Hidefusa Iida, Kobe University, Japan

Hideshi Itoh, Hitotsubashi University, Japan

Howell E. Jackson, Harvard University, US

Toru Kitagawa, Seikei University, Japan

Curtis J. Milhaupt, Columbia University, US

Hideaki Miyajima, Waseda University, Japan

Edward R. Morrison, University of Chicago, US

Sadakazu Osaki, Nomura Research Institute, Japan

Kenichi Osugi, Chuo University, Japan

J. Mark Ramseyer, Harvard University, US

Shruti Rana, University of Maryland, US

Roberta Romano, Yale University, US

Kenichi Sekiguchi, Mori Hamada & Matsumoto, Japan

Zenichi Shishido, Hitotsubashi University, Japan

Wataru Tanaka, University of Tokyo, Japan

Akira Tokutsu, Tohoku University, Japan

George Triantis, Stanford University, US

J.H. Verkerke, University of Virginia, US

Tetsuya Watanabe, Waseda University, Japan

Noriyuki Yanagawa, University of Tokyo, Japan

Preface

"How does law matter?" is a tough question for lawyers to answer, although they are experts in answering the question, "What is the cause and effect of this particular law?" A few attempts to answer the first question have been made by economists, even without having any expertise on the second question.

Thousands of comparative law studies which focus on specific subjects of law have been conducted by academic lawyers, particularly with respect to Japanese and United States laws. However, very few of them have argued about how different laws affect practices in different environments, such as markets and social norms. Also very few of them have taken into consideration the interrelationship between different areas of law.

This book grew out of an attempt to gain a better understanding of how law as a whole matters to enterprise. The title of this book, *Enterprise Law*, covers many areas of law that affect the practice of business enterprises. The challenge of our attempt is to draw the whole picture of enterprise law and to show how enterprise law affects practice together with the markets and social norms of each region.

As an analytical framework, we choose the incentive analysis of economics. We take the enterprise (or firm) as an incentive mechanism between the four indispensable capital providers of the firm: management and employees as the human capital providers, and creditors and shareholders as the monetary capital providers (the "four players"). Our view is that the four players bargain with each other to give other players incentives to provide their capital to their joint project (that is, the enterprise) for maximizing their own payoff ("incentive bargain"). Enterprise law is a part of the infrastructure of the incentive bargain of the firm, together with markets and social norms.

Because the incentive bargain among the four players is always negotiated via management, the first three parts of this book are organized along the lines of the three bargaining relationships in the firm: between employees and management (Part I); between creditors and management (Part II); and between shareholders and management (Part III). Part IV describes how governments affect the incentive bargain of the firm.

Such an attempt is indispensably a group effort. No one in the world can be an expert on all legal areas, even if they focus on enterprise law.

Very few have the same level of expertise in both law and economics. Fortunately, we can successfully organize an ideal group of people: academic lawyers in different fields of enterprise law, such as corporate law, securities regulation, bankruptcy law, employment law, labor law, and tax law; economists who are interested in organizational economics and the economic analysis of law; and practitioners who provide a sense of the practice of law and business.

Our group's work already has a substantial history. It started from April 2007 as a project at RIETI (the Research Institute of Economy, Trade and Industry) and held 38 workshops including US speakers over three and half years. Since 2011, it has continued on a monthly basis as a workshop at Hitotsubashi Graduate School of International Corporate Strategy (ICS) sponsored by the Zengin Foundation for Studies on Economics and Finance.

The result of the RIETI project was published in Japanese by contributing Japanese members (ZENICHI SHISHIDO ED., "KIGYOU-HO" KAIKAKU NO RONRI: INSENTHIBU SHISUTEMU NO SEIDO SEKKEI [THE LOGIC OF "ENTERPRISE LAW" REFORMATIONS: INSTITUTIONAL DESIGN OF THE INCENTIVE SYSTEM] (Nikkei Book, 2011)). This book is the second release of our project, this time with US members. We held an international conference in Tokyo in January 2014 with most of the contributors to this book for presenting our achievement so far and discussing further development of the enterprise law project. Our project is still ongoing, particularly with respect to combining detailed arguments concerning each part and the whole picture of enterprise law, and developing a theory of legislative policy which stimulates efficient enterprise.

Participants in the conferences and workshops provided us with valuable comments. The able research assistance of Anthony Bertero, Alexander Coley and Aaron Ferner contributed to this publication. We are indebted to RIETI and the Zengin Foundation for Studies on Economics and Finance for sponsoring this project.

Zenichi Shishido

Introduction: the incentive bargain of the firm and enterprise law: a nexus of contracts, markets, and laws

Zenichi Shishido

I.1 INTRODUCTION

The firm is an ongoing joint project requiring both financial and human capital. Like other joint projects, the firm cannot maximize its value added without achieving an efficient "incentive bargain" between its indispensable capital providers, that is, the shareholders and creditors that act as monetary capital providers, along with the management and employees that act as human capital providers ("the four capital providers").[1] The incentive bargains can be defined as the bargain between the indispensable capital providers of the firm which motivates each actor to provide the capital they own to the joint project, including the bargains for sharing control and the bargains for sharing the firm's value added. The result of a successful incentive bargain is that each capital provider has the optimal incentive to maximize the firm's value added.

To understand how law influences the firm's practices, we need an account and theory of "enterprise law," broadly defined to include the entire range of private contracts and public regulations governing the relationship of these different capital providers. This chapter will illustrate the incentive bargain of the firm by focusing on the interrelationships and complementarities between different institutions, such as markets, social norms and laws. I will also consider some related legislative policy implications.

The legal system is an important infrastructural element of the firm's incentive bargain. Those parts of the legal system that affect the bargaining between the participants in the firm we call "enterprise law."

---

[1] Zenichi Shishido, Dokizuke no Shikumi toshiteno Kigyo: Insenthibu Shisutemu no Hoseido Ron [The Firm as an Incentive Mechanism: The Role of Legal Institutions] 1 (2006).

Enterprise law specifically includes corporate law, securities regulation, bankruptcy law, labor law, tax law, and other areas of law (intellectual property law, antitrust law, etc.). In general, each part of enterprise law works complementarily with other parts of enterprise law, including in respect to enforcement systems.

Enterprise law affects bargaining between the four capital providers in three ways. First, it may directly affect the incentive of a specific player.[2] Second, it may affect the relative bargaining power between two players and consequently increase or decrease the risk borne by each player.[3] And third, it may affect the coalition between two players.[4]

The important point to understand is that law is not always effective in its attempt to affect the incentive bargain between the four capital providers by itself, but instead works to affect the incentive bargain by interacting complementarily with markets and social norms. In order to elucidate the interaction between markets, social norms, and laws, this chapter focuses on the United States and Japan, and comparatively analyzes the way these infrastructures complement each other in both regions; brief references to other jurisdictions are also made. The object of this chapter is to answer the question of how to structure a legal system in a way that stimulates efficient incentive bargaining at the firm level by indicating the right direction for legislative policy, and consequently, enhancing the efficiency of the whole economy.

In section I.2, a framework is introduced to facilitate viewing the firm as an incentive mechanism between the four capital providers and the government as a given infrastructural component. Additionally, three basic "incentive patterns" are set forth and each of the four capital providers are further divided into two subcategories for the purpose of analyzing the effects of the relevant market on each provider. Section I.3 describes issues related to the incentive bargain between employees and management and demonstrates how the liquidity of the external labor market, social norms, and employment protection laws complementarily

---

[2] For example, subjecting management to strict liability will give management an incentive to take less risk. *See infra* notes 111–112, 169 and their accompanying text.

[3] For example, shareholders' voting rights provided for by corporate law strengthen shareholders' bargaining power with management and decrease the risk of providing monetary capital to corporations. *See infra* note 85 and its accompanying text.

[4] For example, strong employment protection laws encourage employees and management to create a coalition. *See infra* notes 28–29 and their accompanying text. *See, also*, John C. Coffee, Jr., *Unstable Coalitions: Corporate Governance as a Multiple-Player Game*, 78 Geo. L. J. 1495 (1990).

affect the other bargaining relationships, particularly as between shareholders and management; the roles of labor unions during renegotiations in the US and Japan are also compared. In section I.4, issues related to the incentive bargain between creditors and management are described. The most important issue here is renegotiation in insolvency-related scenarios. This section demonstrates why laws matter in both private and legal reorganization processes and how laws affect the *ex ante* incentives of the relevant providers. In section I.5, issues related to the incentive bargain between shareholders and management are described by dividing the wide range of issues into three parts: laws which encourage or discourage shareholder activism, particularly by institutional investors; legal regulations applicable to control transactions in respect of both buyers and sellers; and the problem of cross-shareholding in Japan and the potential for its regulation via the Japanese legal system. Section I.6 describes the role of government and its incentive effects, particularly its role in taxation and regulation, as an exogenous factor on the incentive bargain of the firm. Finally, in section I.7, as a conclusion, an overview of this chapter is provided where the incentive bargain of the firm is thought of as a repeated game. The chapter also proposes an approach to legislative policy that may lead to increased efficiency of the incentive bargain of the firm.

I.2 THE FIRM AS AN INCENTIVE MECHANISM

I.2.1 The Incentive Bargain

The firm can be understood as an incentive mechanism between those who provide human capital (management and employees) and those who provide monetary capital (shareholders and creditors). Each of the four groups provides capital that is crucial to their collective enterprise. Should one group fail to provide that capital, the enterprise will suffer. According to contracts negotiated from the outset, the four groups of participants also share the returns that arise out of the activity of the firm. Therefore, the groups try to use the firm structure to give each other incentives to invest in a way that maximizes the firm's value added and consequently maximizes their own payoff.

There are conflicting interests between the four players and each player will face certain risks based on such conflicting interests. If the players leave those risks (that is, both their own risks and other players' risks) as they are, the incentive of the players to provide their own capital to the joint project will be distorted. As such, the four players try to incentivize each other through bargaining over sharing control to decrease risk, and sharing value added as a positive incentive.

The most fundamental conflicting interests, the one that represents the largest risk for all four players, is the conflict between the autonomy of the human capital providers and the monitoring power of the monetary capital providers. The human capital providers use the funds provided by the monetary capital providers to create value. Therefore, the human capital providers seek more autonomy while the monetary capital providers want more monitoring power in respect of how their funds are used.[5] The risk to the monetary capital providers is that the human capital providers may waste the money that was provided; the risk to the human capital providers is that the monetary capital providers may retrieve the control right of assets of the firm. It is important to reach a bargain that sets up a good balance between the autonomy of the human capital providers and the monitoring power of the monetary capital providers (hereinafter, I will call this "the balance between autonomy and monitoring").[6]

The incentive bargain of the firm is always negotiated via management, which functions as the sole bargaining window, although a coalition may be formed between some of the four players. Therefore, there are three bargaining relationships in the firm: that between employees and management; that between creditors and management; and that between shareholders and management (see Figure I.1). We can observe various interactions among these bargaining relationships.

I.2.2 Three Incentive Patterns and Divergence of Internalized Governance

The differences between the "functional corporate governance" practices of different countries will be revealed as resulting from differences in the "incentive bargaining" practices between the four players in these countries, particularly in the way coalitions are constructed among the four players. There are three different incentive patterns in publicly held companies, specifically: the balancing image, monitoring image, and bargaining image incentive patterns.[7]

---

5 *See* SHISHIDO, *supra* note 1, at 38; Zenichi Shishido, *Reform in Japanese Corporate Law and Corporate Governance: Current Changes in Historical Perspective*, 49 AM. J. COMP. L. 653, 654 (2001).

6 Such balancing is inevitable in many issues of legislative policies. *See e.g.*, Benjamin E. Hermalin, Chapter 19 in this volume: "Presumably, an optimal amount of transparency exists that balances benefits and costs."

7 *See* SHISHIDO, *supra* note 1, at 169.

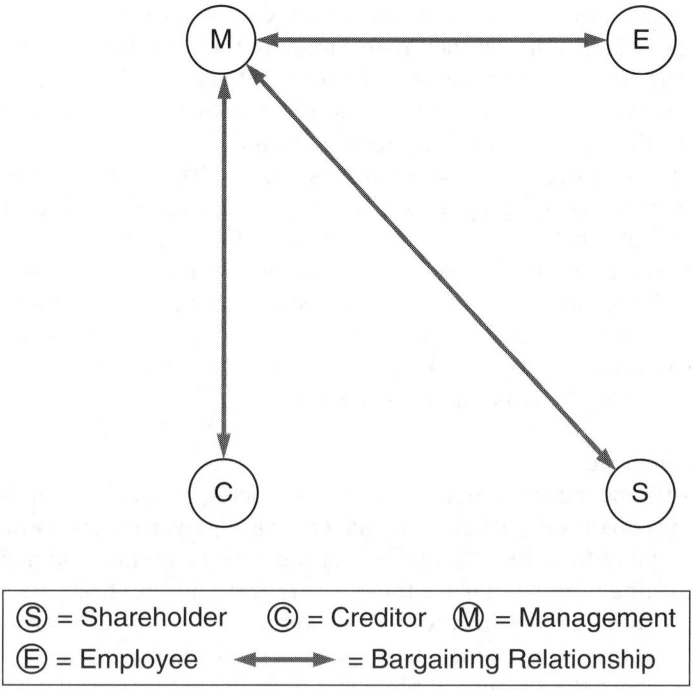

Figure I.1 The four players and three bargaining relationships in the firm

In the convergence of corporate governance debate,[8] diversity of stock ownership is generally regarded as a criterion for functional convergence.[9] However, the most fundamental aspect of a functional corporate governance system, which can be chosen by the players under certain exogenous

---

[8] *See* Lucian Bebchuck & Mark Roe, *A Theory of Path Dependence in Corporate Governance and Ownership*, 52 Stan. L. Rev. 127 (1999); J. Mark Ramseyer, *Are Corporate Governance Systems Converging?* (Working Paper, 1998); Ronald Gilson, *Globalizing Corporate Governance: Convergence of Form or Function*, 49 Am. J. Comp. L. 329 (2001); John Coffee, Jr., *The Future as History: The Prospects for Global Convergence and Its Implications*, 93 Nw. U. L. Rev. 641 (1999); Henry Hansmann & Reinier Kraakman, *The End of History for Corporate Law*, 89 Geo. L. J. 439 (2001). Contrary to the prediction of and the recognition by these knowledgeable convergence theorists (*see id.*), however, "there is little sign that Japanese corporate governance practices are being fundamentally transformed or rapidly 'converging' with those of the United States." *See* Curtis Milhaupt, The Lost Decade for Japanese Corporate Governance Reform?: What's Changed, What Hasn't, and Why (Working Paper 2003).

[9] *See* Bebchuck & Roe, *supra* note 8, at 127.

conditions, is how to motivate monetary capital providers and human capital providers to invest their own capital in the firm; this aspect is hereinafter referred to as an "incentive pattern." Diversity of stock ownership (and liquidity of stock markets) is simply one of the exogenous factors which restricts the choice of incentive pattern.[10]

The optimal internalized governance system – that is, incentive patterns – will diverge depending upon exogenous factors, namely markets (capital, labor, and product), social norms, and laws. There is also the possibility of the coexistence of multiple internalized governance systems in a single country, depending upon the industry sector and the growth stage of the company. Different degrees of significance of firm-specific investment in each industry sector will be particularly influential on the choice of optimal internalized governance system.

Balancing image

The most basic incentive pattern is the "balancing image," in which, while there is no coalition between the players, each player monitors management to ensure that their "promises" to the players are met. Management will accordingly try to balance the pressure from different players and, as a consequence, run the firm toward the direction in which the compound vectors of monitoring points (see Figure I.2).[11] The length of each vector, which indicates the amount of pressure, depends on the overall bargaining power of the relevant player, which is in large part determined by markets, social norms, and laws.[12]

The number of players and the complexity of the conflicting interests that arise among them increases as the size of the firm increases. It will also be costly to create and maintain coalitions between different types of players as a firm grows. In this sense, the balancing image is the basic incentive pattern utilized by listed companies and is well adapted for flexibly balancing various interests on an ongoing basis. In many

---

[10] *See* Zenichi Shishido, *The Turnaround of 1997: Changes in Japanese Corporate Law and Governance*, *in* CORPORATE GOVERNANCE IN JAPAN: INSTITUTIONAL CHANGE AND ORGANIZATIONAL DIVERSITY 310, 323 (Masahiko Aoki et al. eds., 2007). Although diversity of stock ownership in each jurisdiction is an exogenous condition, management can still generally change the ownership structure of companies. In this sense, diversity of stock ownership has endogenous aspects.

[11] *See* Zenichi Shishido, *Japanese Corporate Governance: The Hidden Problems of the Corporate Law and Their Solutions*, 25 DEL. J. CORP. L. 189, 194 (2000).

[12] Corporate law makes the vector representing shareholders longer by giving them voting rights, which collectively can be used to replace management. *See id.*, at 194.

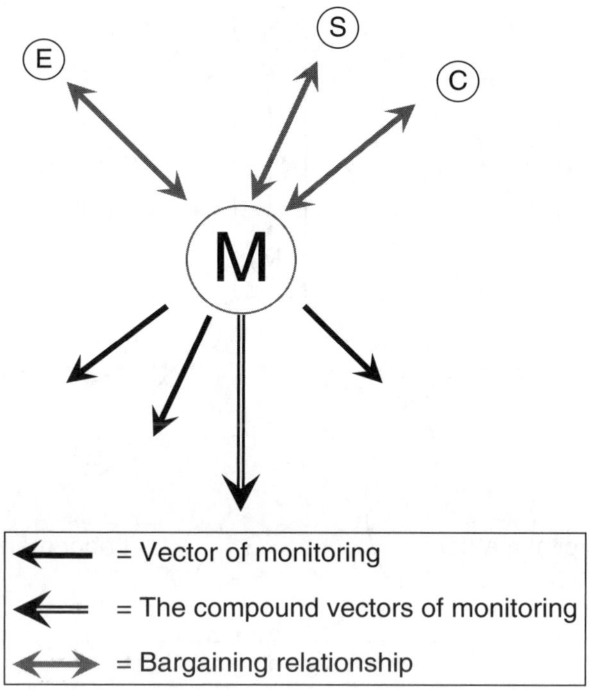

Figure I.2 Balancing image

respects, this is similar to Berle and Means's "management control" company.[13]

A problem with the balancing image is that management is not necessary neutral but has its own private benefit. Although corporate law provides procedural regulations to combat conflict-of-interest transactions, such as limitations imposed on managerial compensation, and the fiduciary duty imposed on management in general, it remains difficult to prevent management from empire building.

Monitoring image

The second incentive pattern is the "monitoring image," in which shareholders and management create a coalition, while the other players, that is, creditors and employees, are motivated through markets and not involved in corporate governance (see Figure I.3).

---

[13] *See* ADOLF A. BERLE & GERDINER C. MEANS, THE MODERN CORPORATION AND PRIVATE PROPERTY (1932).

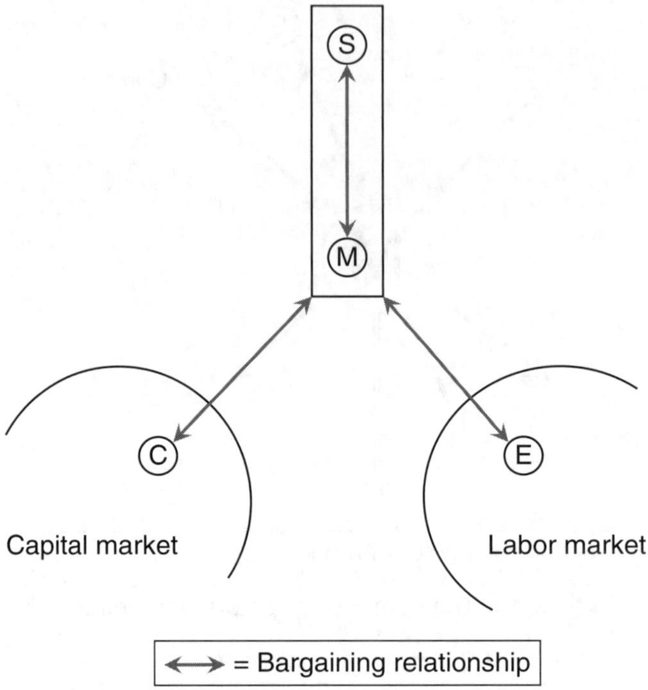

Figure I.3 Monitoring image

In most listed companies in the US, the incentive bargain seems to be in line with the monitoring image (the A-model).[14] In the US, the so called "agency model," in which shareholders, as owners, monitor their agent, management, in an effort to ensure that the firm is being run in the best interest of the shareholders, turns into a social norm, which in turn sustains the coalition between shareholders and management.[15] Incentive pay systems, such as stock options,[16] are attempts to align management's inter-

[14] *See* Michael C. Jensen & William H. Meckling, *Theory of the Firm: Managerial Behavior, Agency Costs and Ownership Structure*, 3 J. FIN. ECON. 305 (1976); FRANK H. EASTERBROOK & DANIEL R. FISCHEL, THE ECONOMIC STRUCTURE OF CORPORATE LAW 69 (1991); Jonathan R. Macey, *An Economic Analysis of the Various Rationales for Making Shareholders the Exclusive Beneficiaries of Corporate Fiduciary Duties*, 21 STETSON L. REV. 23 (1991); Manuel A. Utset, *Towards a Bargaining Theory of the Firm*, 80 CORNELL L. REV. 540, 550 (1995).

[15] *See* Kenneth G. Dau-Schmidt & Benjamin C. Ellis, Chapter 3 in this volume.

[16] As a result of tax law, management will generally prefer compensation packages based on stock options and other incentive compensation rather than guaranteed salaries. *See* David Gamage & Shruti Rana, Chapter 15 in this volume.

ests with shareholders' interests.[17] The existence of liquid capital markets and liquid external labor markets are necessary for the monitoring image to work efficiently.[18] The monitoring image seems to suit those businesses in which firm-specific investments are not very important, such as those in the financial industries.[19]

Bargaining image

The third incentive pattern is the "bargaining image," in which monetary capital providers and human capital providers organize into two teams, and these two teams bargain with each other via their representatives in an attempt to motivate each other to invest their respective monetary and human capital (see Figure I.4).

The typical bargaining image can be found in venture capital investments in Silicon Valley (the Silicon Valley model). In the Silicon Valley model, the lead venture capitalist, as the representative of the monetary capital providers, bargains with the founder of the start-up company, as the representative of the human capital providers.[20]

Another typical bargaining model is the Japanese main bank model (the J-model).[21] In the J-model, the chief executive officer (CEO) of the main

---

[17] Even with liquid external labor markets for executives, executive compensation is a controversial issue and considered by many to not accurately reflect the ability of CEOs in the US. *See* LUCIAN A. BEBCHUK & JESSE M. FRIED, PAY WITHOUT PERFORMANCE: THE UNFULFILLED PROMISE OF EXECUTIVE COMPENSATION (2004).

[18] In countries with liquid external labor markets, such as the US, the social norm of maximizing shareholder value is accepted relatively easily. *See* JEAN TIROLE, THE THEORY OF CORPORATE FINANCE, Ch. 1 (2006).

[19] A typical example is the American investment bank. Particularly, the existence of liquid labor markets for investment bankers is a key factor to the success of American investment banks. It is difficult for Japanese investment banks to follow the monitoring image incentive pattern because external labor markets for investment bankers are not sufficiently liquid in Japan.

[20] *See* Zenichi Shishido, *The Law and Practice of the Venture Industry in Japan: A Period of Transition, in* THE JAPANESE LEGAL SYSTEM: AN ERA OF TRANSITION 193, 194 (Tom Ginsburg & Harry N. Scheiber eds, 2012).

[21] *See* Tetsuji Okazaki, *Nihon niokeru Koporeto Gabanansu no Hatten* [*The Development of Corporate Governance in Japan*], *in* SHISUTEMU TOSHITENO NIHON KIGYO [JAPANESE ENTERPRISES AS A SYSTEM] 456 (Masahiko Aoki & Ronald Dore eds., 1995); Shishido, *supra* note 5, at 663. *But see* Yoshiro Miwa & J. Mark Ramseyer, *The Myth of the Main Bank*, 27 LAW & SOC. INQUIRY 401 (2002). Although the significance of the main bank system has been decreasing since its heyday in 1960s and 1970s, it still plays an important role particularly for companies which have no access to the bond market. See Yasuhiro Arikawa & Hideaki Miyajima, *Relational Banking in Post-Bubble Japan: Co-existence of Soft-*

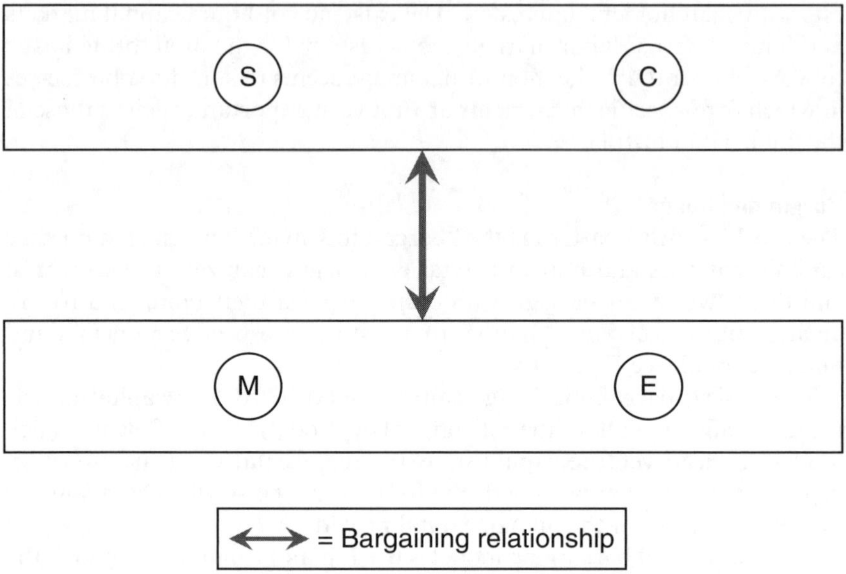

Figure I.4 Bargaining image

bank, as the representative of the monetary capital providers, bargains with the CEO of the borrower company, as the representative of the human capital providers.

The bargaining image incentive pattern cannot be maintained when the cost of creating and maintaining a coalition between human capital providers and between monetary capital providers becomes too expensive. In Japan, illiquid external labor markets for both employees and management, strong employment protection laws, and the "company community" social norm have complementarily contributed to the prevalence of coalitions between management and employees.[22] Cross-shareholding can also be seen as a scheme to strengthen coalitions between monetary capital providers.[23] The bargaining image seems to suit those industries in which firm-specific investments are important, such as the car manufacturing industry.[24]

---

and Hard Budget Constraint, in CORPORATE GOVERNANCE IN JAPAN: INSTITUTIONAL CHANGE AND ORGANIZATIONAL DIVERSITY 51 (Masahiko Aoki et al. eds, 2007).

[22] *See infra* notes 32–33 and their accompanying text.

[23] *See infra* notes 34–35, 128–129 and their accompanying text.

[24] Typical examples are Japanese car makers, such as Toyota, Nissan, and Honda. It would be difficult for GM and Ford to choose the bargaining image

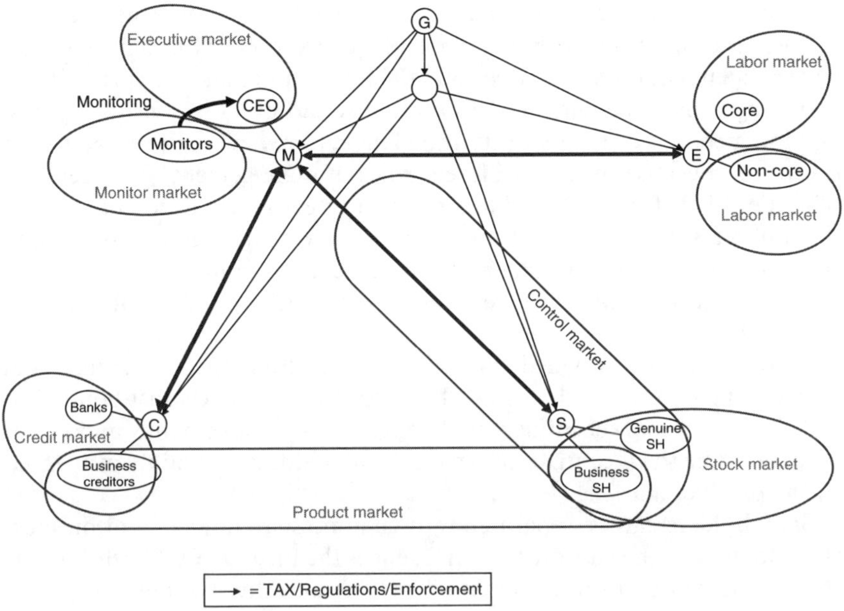

Figure I.5 Government, two categories for each of the four players and their relevant markets

I.2.3 Government, Categories of Each Player, and Relevant Markets

In addition to the four players, the government also provides crucial foundational services (not only physical infrastructure, but also the legal system including public enforcement), and has an interest in the returns on firms' activities through its tax regime. Therefore, we should also consider government as the fifth participant in the incentive bargain of the firm. In this analysis, however, the government does not act as a fifth player in the game. Instead I will treat taxation, regulations, and enforcement, which are provided by the government, as given foundational components of the incentive bargain between the four players.

Although I have already identified the four indispensable capital providers of the firm – that is, management, employees, shareholders, and creditors – it is necessary to further divide each player into two subcategories, at least for the purpose of analyzing the effects of the relevant market on each player (see Figure I.5).

---

incentive pattern because of the adversarial labor management relationships commonly found in the US.

Specifically, management can be divided into executives, particularly CEOs, and monitors, such as independent directors. Although the CEO and independent directors constitute the board and make important business judgments together, the CEO initiates and executes business plans, and independent directors ratify the plans and review the results of their execution. Because of these different roles of management, the incentives of and markets for CEOs and independent directors are different.

Employees can be divided into core employees and non-core employees.[25] The labor market, which influences employee incentives, can also be divided into the labor market for core employees and that for non-core employees.

Creditors can be divided into secured creditors, such as banks, and unsecured creditors, such as most business creditors and most bondholders. The credit market influences the incentives of both banks and bondholders, while the incentives of the business creditor are mainly influenced by the product market.

Shareholders can be separated into genuine shareholders and business shareholders.[26] The stock market influences the incentives of both genuine shareholders and business shareholders. The incentives of business shareholders are also influenced by the product market. Both types of shareholders create the control market, which influences the incentives of both types of shareholders.

I.3 INCENTIVE BARGAIN BETWEEN EMPLOYEES AND MANAGEMENT

I.3.1 Coalition between Employees and Management

Although the media often focuses on the adversarial relationship between employees and management, such as can be seen during labor disputes, it is in fact more common for management and employees to create a coalition because they share the same interest in their role as human capital

---

[25] Core employees have their own value in the labor market. Non-core employees are provided by the labor market as commodities.

[26] Genuine shareholders, such as institutional investors, buy and sell stocks, and exercise their voting rights solely in consideration of maximizing their investment return. Business shareholders place a higher priority on their business relationship with the issuing company rather than on maximizing their investment return. Most business shareholders are cross-holding shareholders in Japan. *See infra* notes 141–143 and their accompanying text.

providers, that is, to maintain their autonomy from monetary capital providers, particularly "genuine shareholders."[27] Long-term employment contracts effectively transform employees into a "shark repellent"[28] and employees will frequently act as "white squires" to the extent that they are not protected by long-term contracts against the risk of wage cuts by corporate raiders.[29] Management also has an incentive to set up an employee share ownership plan (ESOP) as a defensive device.[30] Employees may deter hostile takeovers, not only by being stable shareholders, but also by lobbying against the raider.[31]

---

27 *See* Martin Hellwig, *On the Economics and Politics of Corporate Finance and Corporate Control, in* CORPORATE GOVERNANCE: THEORETICAL AND EMPIRICAL PERSPECTIVES (Xavier Vives ed., 2000); Marco Pagano & Paolo Volpin, *Managers, Workers, and Corporate Governance*, 60 J. FIN. 841, 842 (2005).

28 The abusive dismissal rule not only strengthens the management's bargaining power against shareholders (*see infra* notes 41–45 and their accompanying text), but also makes the existence of full-time employees a shark repellent because even new management cannot discharge surplus labor easily. In addition to the abusive dismissal rule, other Japanese labor law rules have similar shark repellent effects. It is not easy for new management to change the salary system in a way which is unfavorable for employees (Labor Union Act Article 16; *In re* Asahi Fire Marine Insurance, 713 ROHAN 27 (Sup. Ct., Mar. 27, 1997); *In re* Daiyon Bank, 51-2 MINSHU 705 (Sup. Ct., Feb. 28, 1997)), or make employees work overtime (Labor Standards Act Article 36), if labor unions do not agree. As a result, labor unions are able to exert bargaining power against corporate raiders.

29 Pagano & Volpin, *supra* note 27, at 842. Although Japanese employment protection and labor law rules strongly protect employees against the risk of wage cuts by the raider, Japanese employees almost always act as white squires. Particularly in cases of hostile takeovers, Japanese enterprise unions almost always declare their support for incumbent management and against the raider. *See e.g.* NIKKEI, Aug. 3, 2006, at 3 (Hokuetsu Paper case).

30 In the US, ESOPs have grown dramatically in number, from 1601 in 1974 to 11 500 in 2000. The Business Combination Statute implemented in Delaware in 1987 enhanced the anti-takeover effect of ESOPs. *See* Pagano & Volpin, *supra* note 27, at 859.

Also in Japan, a broad-based employee stock purchase plan (ESPP) is prevalent among listed companies. Although employee shareholders have private benefits in their employer corporation and are stable shareholders for management, it may improve productivity complementary with certain corporate culture or employment practices. The current Japanese legal framework, which shows a favorable attitude towards ESPPs by providing specific regulatory exemptions without providing tax advantages, is probably a realistic and reasonable choice. *See* Yohsuke Higashi, Chapter 4 in this volume.

31 Pagano & Volpin, *supra* note 27, at 859, 863.

Particularly in Japan, the practice of lifetime employment,[32] the lack of liquid external labor markets, and the existence of strong employment protection laws complementarily support the coalition between employees and management, which has become known as the "company community."[33] In addition to the coalition between employees and management, the coalition between business shareholders,[34] who are mostly cross-holding shareholders,[35]and management is well organized in many Japanese companies, and both types of coalitions act as an alliance against genuine shareholders.

I.3.2 Liquidity of External Labor Markets and Choice of Incentive Patterns

Japanese labor markets are unique in two ways. First is the illiquidity of external labor markets both for core employees and for management. Second is the combination of internal labor markets for core employees and for management. In other words, the turnover rate of core employees is low and management is usually chosen from among core employees via in-house promotion.[36] As a result, incumbent management and core employees share the same identity and both groups invest their energies to maintain a good reputation within the firm. It is also understandable that these groups would try to prevent raiders' interventions in order to preserve the human capital they have invested and the implicit contracts between them. Illiquid external labor markets and the company community norm affect each other and complementarily support the choice of the bargaining image incentive pattern.[37]

In the United States, liquid external labor markets and the shareholder value maximization norm affect each other and complementarily support

---

32 Although the prevalence of lifetime employment is decreasing, various studies show that it is still the norm at a majority of Japanese companies, which are often reluctant to lay off employees in times of economic downturn when compared to companies in other countries. *See* Takashi Araki, Labor and Employment Law in Japan 21 (2002).

33 *See* Shishido, *supra* note 11, at 201.

34 In general, long-term contracts with suppliers can serve as anti-takeover devices. *See* Pagano & Volpin, *supra* note 27, at 843.

35 *See infra* notes 128–129 and their accompanying text.

36 To administer such an internal labor market, the human resources department of each Japanese company plays an important role. *See* Sanford M. Jacoby, The Embedded Corporation: Corporate Governance and Employment Relations in Japan and the United States 21–40 (2005).

37 *See supra* notes 22–23 and their accompanying text.

the choice of the monitoring image incentive pattern.[38] The negative externalities exerted by shareholder control on employees are smaller in countries with liquid external labor markets, where the norm of shareholder value maximization is less controversial.[39]

I.3.3 Dismissal Rules and their Spillover Effects

Rules relating to dismissal of employees are some of the most divergent when comparing US law and Japanese law. In the United States, the general position is that management can discharge employees without cause (the employment-at-will rule).[40] In Japan, management cannot discharge employees without good cause, which has been strictly interpreted by the courts (the abusive dismissal doctrine).[41]

Rules relating to dismissal will affect the incentive bargain of the firm, not only between employees and management, but also between all four players.[42] Strong employment protection will also have spillover effects on corporate governance.

Although the abusive dismissal rule was originally created to protect employees and has supported the practice of so-called "lifetime employment,"[43] it not only strengthens employees' bargaining power with management, but also strengthens management's bargaining power with shareholders because it gives management a good excuse to decrease dividends during company's downturns rather than laying off employees.[44] In fact, the abusive dismissal rule, company community norms, and the lack of a liquid external labor market have complementarily transformed directors' fiduciary duties under Japanese corporate law.[45]

---

38 *See supra* notes 14–18 and their accompanying text.

39 *See* TIROLE, *supra* note 18.

40 Even in the US, however, it is a risky event for employers to dismiss employees because there are statutory and common law exceptions to the employment-at-will rule, particularly, termination based on racial or gender discrimination is prohibited. *See* J.H. Verkerke, Chapter 1 in this volume.

41 *See* Ryuichi Yamakawa, *Changing Aspects of Japanese Dismissal Law, in* LAW IN JAPAN: A TURNING POINT 483 (Daniel H. Foote ed., 2007).

42 *See* Toru Kitagawa, Chapter 2 in this volume.

43 The abusive dismissal rule was originally based in case law. It became statutory law in 2004. *See* Labor Contract Act Article 16.

44 *See* Kitagawa, *supra* note 42.

45 *See id.*

I.3.4 Renegotiations and the Role of Labor Unions

From the outset, some renegotiation is expected between employees and management. Labor law provides rules for such renegotiations, for example the "collective bargaining" rule, in which labor unions play an important role.

When renegotiation is expected, the hold-up problem occurs.[46] Parties with less bargaining power, employees in this case, expect that they will be forced to accept unfavorable changes to their current contracts, and as a result, their incentive to continue to invest human capital becomes distorted. Mandatory legal regulation is necessary not only for protecting employees but also for providing an infrastructure that facilitates efficient incentive bargaining, by making it possible for management to commit to not breaching their agreements.

In the United States and in EU countries, labor unions are industry-wide unions organized on a national basis, while Japanese labor unions are typically enterprise-specific unions.[47] It is much easier to create a coalition between employees and management when enterprise-specific unions, rather than industry-wide unions, are present.[48]

Another distinction between the labor union systems in both countries is the difference between the US's exclusive unionism and Japan's plural unionism. While it is the case that in the US a union is considered the "exclusive representative" for the "appropriate bargaining unit," multiple unions may represent workers from a single class within a single workplace in Japan.[49]

If we compare the relative bargaining power of employees and management in the US and Japan, Japanese labor law appears to give Japanese unions greater bargaining power than US labor law gives to

---

46 *See* Oliver Hart, Firms, Contracts, and Financial Structure 26–27 (1995).

47 *See* Nobuhiro Hiwatari, *Employment Practice and Enterprise Unionism in Japan, in* Employees and Corporate Governance 275 (Margaret M. Blair & Mark J. Roe eds, 1999); Dau-Schmidt & Ellis, *supra* note 15.

48 While Japanese enterprise unions share basic interests with management, American industry unions do not generally share a strong common interest with any particular employers. *See* Dau-Schmidt & Ellis, *supra* note 15.

49 "[T]he doctrine of exclusive representation probably undermines the bargaining power of American unions in the early stages of labor organization in a region or industry, although it may enhance union bargaining power for well-established unions." *Id.*

US unions;[50] US management can therefore impose greater costs on their employees for refusing to agree to management's proposals and thus exert greater bargaining power, relative to Japanese management.[51] However, the adversarial nature of negotiations in the US favors union power, while the structure of negotiations in Japan limits the desire of Japanese employees to exercise their legal rights. Such differences in the structure of negotiations between employees and management can be considered a result of the existence of different incentive patterns in the two countries.[52]

Questions relating to which set of legal rules for renegotiation is more flexible, and whether Japanese wages are more flexible than US wages,[53] are hard to answer. In both countries, the law permits unilateral changes to employment contracts by management in cases of deadlock after a proper bargaining process, if no collective agreement is reached.[54] In practice, however, flexibility is more essential to management in Japan, which has strong employment protection, than in the US, which follows employment-at-will. The relatively large percentage of incentive pay, called a bonus, in employees' wages is a managerial effort to maintain wage flexibility in Japan. In both countries, the questions of which

---

50 Partial work stoppage, slowdowns, and secondary boycotts are justifiable in Japan. Whereas American management can permanently replace economic strikers and undertake offensive lockouts in advance of employees collective action. *See id.*

51 *See id.*

52 "American management is strongly allied with the interests of shareholders," and "Japanese management is more likely to identify their interests with those of their employees." *Id.*

53 *See* Ronald J. Gilson & Mark J. Roe, *Lifetime Employment: Labor Peace and the Evolution of Japanese Corporate Governance*, 99 COLUM. L. REV. 508, 512 (1999).

54 Japanese labor law states that wages can be decreased as long as the change is reasonable (Labor Contract Act Articles 9 and 10), and case law considers the renegotiation process with labor unions as a criterion of such reasonableness, which does not resolve the resultant ambiguity. *See* Masato Hara, *Rodo Joken Henkoji niokeru Jugyoin-Keieisha kan Kosho no Igi [The Significance of Bargaining between Employees and Management in Determining the Fairness of Modified Labor Agreements] in* "KIGYO-HO" KAIKAKU NO RONRI: INSENTHIBU SHISUTEMU NO SEIDO SEKKEI [THE LOGIC OF "ENTERPRISE LAW" REFORMATIONS: INSTITUTIONAL DESIGN OF THE INCENTIVE SYSTEM]102 (Zenichi Shishido ed., 2011). From the economics point of view, however, strategic ambiguity may produce positive effects and prevention of disputes is not necessarily efficient. *See* Hideshi Itoh, *Kosho niokeru Kachi no Soshutsu-Bunpai to Hoseido no Hokansei [Value Creation and Allocation by Bargaining and Complementarities of Law], in* THE LOGIC OF "ENTERPRISE LAW" REFORMATIONS, at 132, 134.

organization should represent the diverse interests of employees and how to provide optimal rules for efficient incentive bargaining in renegotiations between employees and management are difficult to answer.[55]

I.4 INCENTIVE BARGAIN BETWEEN CREDITORS AND MANAGEMENT

I.4.1 Creditors as Monetary Capital Providers

Creditors share common interests with shareholders as monetary capital providers and demand that human capital providers be monitored, particularly management. In that sense, creditors and shareholders form into a continuum rather than two distinct sets. Their conflicting interests, however, come from the fact that creditors are fixed claimants and shareholders are residual claimants. As a result, creditors prefer risk-averse management and shareholders prefer risk-neutral management.[56]

Creditors have their own control rights. On one hand, creditors have a contingent right to remove assets and possibly to initiate liquidation proceedings in the event that a borrower corporation defaults, an operation which requires active monitoring. On the other hand, creditors control the borrower's access to capital in two ways. First is the periodic repayments made to the creditor which effectively reduce the cash available for use by the borrower. Second is the priority of debt claims, which can impede the borrower's future ability to raise capital from outside investors.[57] Although in general creditors have no vote for so long as the corporation is solvent, major creditors, typically banks, will have a voice and play an important monitoring role.[58]

---

55 *See* Hara, *supra* note 54, at 110.

56 Shareholders even prefer risk-seeking management in near insolvency situations.

57 *See* George Triantis, Chapter 5 in this volume.

58 A typical example is the main bank system, or the relationship banking system in Japan in its heyday (1960s–1970s). Main banks played an important role in monitoring the management of their client companies in a contingent way. Although main banks did not intervene in the management of well-performing clients, they dispatched representatives to troubled clients, and on occasion took control of restructuring efforts. *See* Arikawa & Miyajima, *supra* note 21, at 51. A good example is the main bank role played by Sumitomo Bank in the case of the Mazda turnaround in the middle of the 1970s. *See* Richard Pascale & Thomas P. Rohlen, *The Mazda Turnaround*, 9 J. JAPANESE STUD. 219 (1983). *But see* Miwa & Ramseyer, supra note 21. After financial deregulation and the banking crisis in the

Although the active role of a creditor in corporate governance depends on the creditor's incentives (which rest on its economic interests in the corporation), the recent increase in the use of risk-spreading instruments, such as credit default swaps and securitization, make it easy for creditors to diversify and transfer the economic risk of their investment in corporate borrowers. The incentive of creditors may be so distorted by hedging that it results in negative exposure, leading the creditor to prefer a borrower's failure over its success.[59] This is a major challenge posed to lawmakers by financial engineering, in line with "empty voting,"[60] an issue that may require a reconsideration in regard to what corporate governance structure is appropriate.

I.4.2 Contracts, Laws, and Taking Risks

The risk-taking of management is relevant to the incentives of the other three players in the incentive bargain, particularly shareholders and creditors. Creditors have an incentive to push management to adopt a risk-averse management policy, while shareholders have an incentive to push management to adopt a risk-neutral management policy. Management is put in a position of balancing such conflicting interests.[61] In this we can observe the interrelationship between the two bargaining relationships. Several contracts and laws interrelationally affect the risk-taking of management.

Creditors, particularly banks and bondholders, who feel exposed to the risk of opportunistic behavior by shareholders and management, often try to insert covenants in lending contracts to prevent management from taking too much risk, such as restrictions on providing collateral, requirements to maintain a certain level of profitability, requirements to retain certain amounts of equity or certain equity ratios, restrictions on dividends, and so on.

Besides including restrictive provisions in such contracts, several different laws encourage management to take less risk. Robust disclosure

---

late 1990s, the main bank system has grown more heterogeneous. Although main banks became less important to those firms with bond ratings of single A or higher, other firms continued to depend on bank borrowing. A statistical study shows that main bank commitments imposed soft-budget constraints on firms with poor performance. *See* Arikawa & Miyajima, *supra* note 21, at 75.

59 *See* Triantis, *supra* note 57.

60 *See infra* note 143.

61 While the role that balances conflicting interests appears to have shifted from the CEO to independent directors in the US, the role is still played by the CEO in Japan. *See infra* notes 97–98 and their accompanying text.

regulations, such as the Sarbanes–Oxley Act of 2002 (SOX) and the Financial Instruments and Exchange Act of 2006 (J-SOX),[62] contrary to the original intention of the lawmakers, may lead management to be overly risk-averse.[63] Comparatively, Japanese corporate law has stricter dividend restrictions than most jurisdictions in the US.[64] Japanese corporate law also has a unique statute providing for director responsibility to third parties, who are mostly creditors.[65] Members of management at Japanese companies are at risk of being held personally liable to creditors in cases of corporate bankruptcy as Japanese bankruptcy law has procedural statutes to enforce liability against the management of a company.[66] The structure of shareholder derivative actions will also affect the risk preference of management. Japanese corporate law has no rule which allows courts to respect a board decision, which is contrary to a shareholder derivative action.[67] These aspects of Japanese law lead management to take less risk, relative to management at a US company.

On the other hand, both in Japan and in the US, tax laws that let companies deduct interest payments from their profits lead management to take more risk.[68] This is in addition to bankruptcy laws that favor the debtor-in-possession and allow management more room for renegotiation, which also leads management to take more risk.

I.4.3 Insolvency and Bankruptcy Regime

Theoretically, once insolvency has occurred, the corporate law regime ceases to be relevant and the bankruptcy law regime becomes relevant. Creditors become new residual claimants and have a vote, instead of shareholders. It is the end-game norm, which is a source of the monitoring effect of debt. After this point, all four players formally participate

---

[62] On SOX and J-SOX, *see* Zenichi Shishido & Sadakazu Osaki, Chapter 20 in this volume.

[63] *See infra* notes 169–171 and their accompanying text.

[64] In Japan, however, shareholders can propose that a firm pays more dividends and/or repurchases shares at shareholder meetings (Companies Act Articles 454, 156). This practice is impossible in the United States. This part of Japanese corporate law therefore gives shareholders more bargaining power to push management to take more risk.

[65] Companies Act Article 429.

[66] Bankruptcy Act Articles 177, 178.

[67] In the United States, *see* American Law Institute, Principles of Corporate Governance: Analysis and Recommendations, §§ 7.08, 7.09, 7.10 (1992).

[68] *See* Gamage & Rana, *supra* note 16.

in the new incentive bargain under the umbrella of the bankruptcy law regime.

The problem is, however, the ambiguity in determining when insolvency exists; practically speaking, it is not easy to identify when a company is insolvent. Although insolvency should in theory be a definite boundary in respect of the autonomy of management, its ambiguity allows management room for renegotiation and incentivizes management to misrepresent the actual financial situation of the corporation.

I.4.4 Renegotiations under the Shadow of Law

The scope for renegotiation in the insolvency stage of a corporation depends on the type of creditors and the type of insolvency resolution systems that apply. Management can renegotiate with banks and long-term trading partners for postponement of payments of interest and/or principal, and sometimes even for a decrease in the amount of principal outstanding, particularly when creditors have committed a lot to the borrower corporation,[69] and therefore have an incentive to make short-term sacrifices in exchange for future benefits from the corporation, as long as its rehabilitation is possible. On the other hand, it is very hard for management to renegotiate with bondholders and promissory note holders, who are typically anonymous, in cases of default or potential default.

Retirees are a special type of creditor with whom renegotiation in the insolvency stage can be difficult. Renegotiations for the reduction of a company's payment obligations, which normally take the form of healthcare benefits in the US and defined benefit pension plans in Japan, is a bargain made under the shadow of laws relating to the priority of the claims of the retirees in the bankruptcy procedure and the modification of those claims.[70] Although more flexible legal rules allowing for unilateral

[69] Japanese banks have an incentive to continue making credit available even to weak corporations because it is in the self-interest of troubled banks to follow a policy of forbearance in order to avoid pressure on them to increase their own loan-loss reserves, and the government also has an incentive to allow banks to continue their forbearance policy. *See* Joe Peek and Eric S. Rosengren, *Unnatural Selection: Perverse Incentives and the Misallocation of Credit in Japan*, 95 AM. ECON. REV. 1144 (2005).

[70] *See e.g.*, William J. Holstein, *Who's to Blame for GM's Bankruptcy?*, Bloomberg Businessweek (June 1, 2009), http://www.businessweek.com/lifestyle/content/jun2009/bw2009061_332081.htm; The Bankruptcy of General Motors: A Giant Falls, The Economist (June 4, 2009), http://www.economist.com/node/13782942?fsrc=scn/tw_ec/a_giant_falls; Chikafumi Hodo, *Japan Airlines Survival Hinges on Pension Cuts*, Reuters.Com (Nov. 6, 2009), http://www.reuters.

modification of these claims and/or the downgrading of their priority will make it easier to get a compromise from the retirees and may lead to a successful reorganization, such legal rules have unfavorable effects on the *ex ante* incentive of employees.[71]

Management is normally able to choose between several systems of insolvency resolution. In most cases, management first attempts private reorganization in order to avoid reputational damage to the corporation. Although renegotiation in the private reorganization scenario is more flexible than that in legal reorganizations, management must obtain agreement from all creditors in order to proceed. If private reorganization is not successful, the corporation is forced to initiate legal reorganization proceedings. In this sense, even private reorganizations are proceedings conducted under the shadow of law.

The legal rules relating to reorganizations affect the incentives of the players and their relative bargaining power. Strict legal rules give management an incentive to avoid legal reorganization and, as such, interested parties may lose the opportunity to restore the value of the company. Traditional strict rules relating to legal reorganizations in Japan have opened the door to various types of private reorganization.[72] On the other hand, flexible rules for legal reorganizations strengthen management's bargaining power against creditors.

I.4.5 Principles of Legal Reorganizations

Legal reorganizations, such as reorganizations under "Chapter 11" in the US, are schemes designed to allow for the sharing of the rights to the future going-concern value of the borrower corporation after the reorganization among the players (interested parties), without liquidating the corporation's assets. Amending the original rights of most players is requisite because the corporate value after reorganization is usually less than the sum of the original rights. The requirements for confirming a reorganization plan are based on several principles, including liquidation

com/article/2009/11/06/us-jal-pension-idUSTRE5A517U20091106; *Japan Airlines Files for Bankruptcy*, New York Times (Jan. 19, 2010), http://dealbook.nytimes.com/2010/01/19/japan-airlines-set-to-file-for-bankruptcy/?_r=0.

[71] *See* Gen Goto, Chapter 8 in this volume. This is a typical issue for management that shows the overlap between the incentive bargain with employees and that with creditors.

[72] *See* Kentaro Suzuki, *DIP-gata Kaisha Kosei to Jigyo Saisei ADR* [*Debtor-in-Possession Type Reorganization and Business Rehabilitation ADR*], *in* The Logic of "Enterprise Law" Reformations, *supra* note 54, at 176.

value guarantee, equal among same rights, and fair and equitable differences among different rights.

Although the basic scheme for legal reorganizations mentioned above is the same in the US and Japan, interpretation of the third principle – that is, "fair and equitable differences" – is not necessarily shared by both countries. While the absolute priority theory is established in the US, the relative priority theory is influential in Japan.[73] While the absolute priority system does not allow for distribution to lower seniority claims, unless more senior claims are fully satisfied from the going-concern value of the corporation, the relative priority system allows some distribution to lower class claims, even though upper class claims may be subject to a deduction, provided that the deduction rate applicable to the less senior claims is larger than that applied to more senior claims.

I.4.6 Deviations from Absolute Priority

It is not easy to adhere to the absolute priority rule, even in the US. In practice, valuing the future going-concern value of the corporation, which is indispensable in applying the rule, is costly and difficult. To avoid the cost, an exemption to the absolute priority rule is permitted as long as the plan is ratified by all classes upon the legally required majority votes and only the liquidation value needs to be guaranteed.[74]

Incentive effects of deviations from the absolute priority rule are controversial. Although the deviation may not only distort the *ex ante* incentive of creditors and lead to an increase in interest rates, but may also induce some moral hazard for management, deviation may nonetheless have some positive incentive effects. First, relaxing the absolute priority of creditors over shareholders may give shareholders an incentive to make firm-specific human capital investments.[75] Second, relaxing the absolute priority of secured creditors over unsecured creditors may give secured creditors the incentive to monitor management more closely.[76]

---

[73] *See* Keiko Yamamoto, *Saikosho niyoru Kigyo no Saiken: Kaisha Kosei Tetsuzuki niokeru Saikenshakan no "Kosei-Kohei" na Kenri Bunpai no Arikata wo Fumaete* [*Restructuring of Companies by Renegotiation: "Fair and Equitable" Sharing of Interest among Creditors in Corporate Reorganization Procedure*], *in* The Logic of "Enterprise Law" Reformations, *supra* note 54, at 159.

[74] 11 U.S.C. §1129(a)(8).

[75] *See* Lucian A. Bebchuk & Randal Picker, Bankruptcy Rules, Management Entrenchment, and Firm Specific Human Capital (Working Paper 1993).

[76] *See* Lucian A. Bebchuk & Jesse Fried, *The Uneasy Case for the Priority of Secured Claims in Bankruptcy*, 105 Yale L. J. 857 (1996).

A recent statistical study shows, however, that few reorganization plans deviate from the absolute priority rule and senior creditor control is pervasive in Chapter 11 proceedings.[77] The same study points out that the bargain between secured and unsecured creditors can distort the reorganization process.[78]

I.4.7 Renegotiation with Secured Creditors

Secured creditors may be able to hold up the bargaining process by using their right of foreclosure as a threat to obtain some share of the going-concern surplus. Both US and Japanese bankruptcy laws provide debtors with an "exit option" from such costly negotiations with secured creditors by recapturing the collateral, but in a different manner. In the US, the Chapter 11 procedure known as "cramdown" permits debtors to make deferred cash payments with a present value equal to the collateral, and the court has to estimate not only the value of the collateral but also the value of the deferred cash payments promised in the plan, a process which is complicated and time-consuming. In Japan, the Civil Rehabilitation Act procedure for extinguishing security interests permits debtors to cancel security interests by making a one-time cash payment equal to the liquidation value of the collateral; this involves a court appraisal procedure which is much simpler than in the US cramdown procedure.[79]

I.5 INCENTIVE BARGAIN BETWEEN SHAREHOLDERS AND MANAGEMENT

I.5.1 Shareholders as Monetary Capital Providers

Shareholders share a basic interest with creditors as both are monetary capital providers. The method of providing money used by shareholders is, however, different from that of creditors. Shareholders have residual claims, which are not legally enforceable, but they do have voting rights and certain minority protections.[80] Therefore, the way shareholders monitor management is also different from the way creditors monitor management. Shareholders prefer risk-neutral management and have an

77 *See* Kenneth M. Ayotte & Edward R. Morrison, Chapter 6 in this volume.
78 *See id.*
79 *See* Wataru Tanaka, Chapter 7 in this volume.
80 Most *ex post* bargaining power of shareholders with management is created by corporate law.

interest in free cash flow being distributed as dividends.[81] They monitor management by exit (selling stock) and voice (voting, proposing, and litigating). The latter form of monitoring has recently turned out to be important as "shareholder activism," and is increasingly exerted to influence management.[82]

I.5.2 Relative Bargaining Power and Laws

Although it is reasonable for shareholders to monitor management either by exit or by voice to maximize their interest, overly aggressive monitoring will distort the incentive of management. From the view of the incentive bargain, a good balance between the autonomy of management and monitoring by shareholders is important for maximizing corporate value.[83] Laws significantly affect the relative bargaining power of shareholders and management.[84]

Voting rights and the stock majority rule

The strength of shareholders' bargaining power with management is based on their voting rights because aggregate voting rights can be used to veto an important proposal from management, such as a mergers and acquisitions (M&A) transaction, and could even replace incumbent management if their aggregated voting rights amount to an overall majority. Although this basic rule is shared among most major jurisdictions, legal rules regarding the decision-making power of the shareholders in shareholder meetings, shareholders' rights to elect directors, and shareholders' rights to dismiss directors are different, particularly between the US and most other major jurisdictions including Japan. These differences affect the relative bargaining power between management and shareholders. [85]

On the opposite side, however, the stock majority rule supports

---

[81] Shareholders even have an incentive to push management to gamble with regard to the cost of creditors in near insolvency.

[82] *See* Sanford M. Jacoby, *Convergence by Design: The Case of CalPERS in Japan*, 55 AM. J. COMP. L. 239 (2007); Takaya Seki, *Legal Reform and Shareholder Activism by Institutional Investors in Japan*, 13-3 CORP. GOVERNANCE 377 (2005).

[83] *See supra* note 6 and its accompanying text.

[84] In general, the relative bargaining power will affect the incentive of each player by either increasing or decreasing risk. The relative bargaining power between shareholders and management, in particular, directly affects the balance of autonomy and monitoring.

[85] The US adopts as the default a plurality standard for director appointment. In most major jurisdictions other than the US, proxy access is granted to dissenters' nominees, and shareholders are granted the irrevocable right to dismiss

management control. If the stock ownership of a corporation is dispersed and no single shareholder owns a significant block, the incumbent management position is quite stable, a situation that is also supported by the proxy machinery.[86]

Takeover bid (TOB) regulations, particularly the rule that requires mandatory bids for all stocks, can discourage hostile takeovers by increasing the associated costs. Reporting requirements for those holding a large volume of stocks (the so-called 5 percent rule[87]) not only discourage institutional investors from acquiring stock over the threshold amount, but also discourage shareholder activism,[88] by raising the risk of misrepresentation to possible criminal sanctions.[89] Case law, which allows management to use certain defensive measures, also discourages hostile takeovers.[90]

---

directors without cause, and the irrevocable right to initiate a shareholder meeting. *See* Takaaki Eguchi, Chapter 10 in this volume.

[86] *See* BERLE & MEANS, *supra* note 13; MELVIN A. EISENBERG, THE STRUCTURE OF THE CORPORATION: A LEGAL ANALYSIS 97 (1976).

[87] This 5 percent rule was implemented as an early-warning system, in order to prevent the so-called "Saturday night special" and to promote auctions and increase takeover premiums. *See* WILLIAM A. KLEIN & JOHN C. COFFEE, JR., BUSINESS ORGANIZATION AND FINANCE 193 (10th ed, 2007).

[88] The reporting obligations for joint ownership (Financial Instruments and Exchange Act Article 27-23 (4) (5)) weaken the incentive of institutional investors to solicit other institutional investors against voting. The disclosure obligation of the purpose of holding shares (Financial Instruments and Exchange Act Article 27-23 (1)) will discourage institutional investors from making informal proposals to management. *See* Sadakazu Osaki, *Tairyo Hoyu Houkoku-seido no Haseikoka to Kinofuzen* [*Spillover Effects and Malfunction of the Large Stockholding Report Regulation*], *in* THE LOGIC OF "ENTERPRISE LAW" REFORMATIONS, *supra* note 54, at 272.

[89] In the United States, the proxy solicitation rule and the 5 percent rule (Rule 13D) have complementarily discouraged shareholder activism. *See* Bernard S. Black, *Shareholder Passivity Reexamined*, 89 MICH. L. REV. 520 (1990). American law makers, however, reformed the proxy solicitation rule in 1992 and in 1999, and the 5 percent rule in 1998 to get rid of such negative effects on shareholder activism. *See* Thomas W. Briggs, *Corporate Governance and the New Hedge Fund Activism: An Empirical Analysis*, Summer 2007 J. CORP. L. 681, 686–694. *But see* Stephen Choi, *Proxy Issue Proposals: Impact of the 1992 SEC Proxy Reforms*, 16 J. L. ECON. & ORG. 233 (2000); STEPHEN M. BAINBRIDGE, CORPORATE GOVERNANCE AFTER THE FINANCIAL CRISIS 208 (2012) (explaining that even after the SEC's 1992 reforms, the proxy rules still impede shareholder communication).

[90] On comparing the case law in the US and Japan, *see infra* notes 144–147 and their accompanying text.

Fiduciary duty of management

The fiduciary duty of management to shareholders[91] and its private enforcement mechanism – that is, shareholder derivative and class actions – strengthens shareholders' bargaining power against management. On the other hand, the business judgment rule supports the autonomy of management by guaranteeing management discretion provided there are neither conflicts of interest nor bad faith behavior.[92]

Board systems

Indirect ways for shareholders to monitor management, via delegated monitors such as independent directors,[93] play a more significant role than direct monitoring by shareholders, such as voting and litigation, under normal circumstances.[94] Therefore, the method of regulating such monitors and the board of directors affects the relative bargaining power between shareholders and management.

Strong requirements relating to independence, and the majority independent director requirement, strengthen shareholders' bargaining power against management in general,[95] and at the same time provide management with a set of legal protections against hostile takeovers and shareholder litigation in the US, but not in Japan.[96]

---

[91] Although Japanese corporate law statute stipulates "fiduciary duty to the company" (Companies Act Article 355), it is generally interpreted by leading commentators and recent court cases as "duty to the shareholder." *See* MISAO TATSUTA, KAISHA HO TAIYO [BUSINESS CORPORATION LAW] 74 (2007); KENJIRO EGASHIRA, KABUSIKI KAISHA HO [LAWS OF STOCK CORPORATIONS] 20 (4th ed. 2011); *In re* Nireko, 1219 KINHAN 8 (Tokyo High Ct., June 15, 2007); *In re* Rex Holdings Shareholder Litigation, 1363 KINHAN 48 (Tokyo District Ct., Feb. 18, 2011). On the other hand, many states in the US, not including Delaware, have so-called "stakeholder statutes" that allow management to balance the interests of stakeholders, particularly in the case of a hostile takeover. *See* Richard A. Booth, *Stockholders, Stakeholders, and Bagholders (or How Investor Diversification Affects Fiduciary Duty)*, 53 BUS.LAW. 429 (1998). *See also* Kitagawa, *supra* note 42.

[92] *See* J. MARK RAMSEYER, BUSINESS ORGANIZATION, Ch. 4 (2012).

[93] Additionally, in Japan, statutory auditors (*kansayaku*) may play the role of "incomplete substitute" to independent directors. *See* Kenichi Osugi, Chapter 14 in this volume.

[94] In other words, it is not in an end-game scenario, such as a hostile takeover or bankruptcy.

[95] In the US, in particular, independent directors occupy the majority of the boards of most listed companies and often vote to replace management who have failed. *See* Jeffrey Gordon, *The Rise of Independent Directors in the United States*, 59 STAN. L. REV. 1465 (2007).

[96] Such difference, whether privileging the decision of independent directors or

The board system, which serves as a method for sharing the role of managing the firm between executives and monitors, is totally different in the US and Japan. In the US, the power and the role of monitors – that is, independent directors – has been steadily increasing for several decades[97] and it now seems that the role of balancing the interests of the other three players is not being played so much by CEOs, but instead by independent directors. In Japan, the power and the role of monitors, including statutory auditors and independent directors, is still limited,[98] and the CEO and inside directors still hold the real decision-making power and balance the interests of the other three players.

Minority shareholder rights

Although there are a variety of minority shareholder rights, most of them do not have an impact on shareholder bargaining power.[99] Among them, the minority shareholders' right of proposal[100] may be important and appears to be complementary with the decision-making power of shareholder meetings,[101] the proxy voting system,[102] and the practice of

---

not, creates different legal incentives for adopting independent directors in the US and Japan. *See* Curtis J. Milhaupt, Chapter 9 in this volume.

[97] *See* Gordon, *supra* note 95.

[98] The major reasons that there are so few outside directors in Japan are the lack of well-developed external labor markets and the robust "company community" social norm. *See* Osugi, *supra* note 93.

[99] Although a series of studies by La Porta et al. see minority shareholders' rights as the key to an efficient capital market (Rafael La Porta, Florencio Lopez-De-Silanes, Andrei Shleifer, & Robert W. Vishny, *Legal Determinants and External Finance*, 52 J. Fin. 1131 (1997)), few of them have any substantial effect on strengthening shareholder bargaining power with management. *See* John C. Coffee, Jr., *The Rise of Dispersed Ownership: The Role of Law and the State in the Separation of Ownership and Control*, 111 Yale L. J. 1, 8 (2001). *See also* Sofie Cools, *The Real Difference in Corporate Law between the United States and Continental Europe: Distribution of Powers*, 30 Del. J. Corp. L. 697 (2005); Holger Spamann, *The "Antidirector Rights Index" Revisited*, 23 Rev. Fin. Stud. 467 (2010).

[100] *See* Companies Act Articles 303, 304, 305. In Japan, shareholders can propose amendments to the articles of incorporation without board approval, while this is impossible in the US. *See* Bainbridge, *supra* note 89, at 204.

[101] In Japan, the shareholder meeting is able to make decisions on a wider range of matters than the US shareholder meeting, such as dividends, repurchase of shares, and directors' salaries. In 2011, a non-binding vote on executive compensation ("say on pay") was given to shareholders of listed companies by the Dodd–Frank Act in the US (Securities Exchange Act §14A).

[102] Whether proxy access is granted or not, and whether coalition-forming among institutional investors is admitted or not, are particularly influential.

shareholder activism by institutional investors.[103] Appraisal rights in cases of M&A transactions may also be influential, depending on the case law relating to fair value, and may work to discourage M&A transactions.[104]

Disclosure regulations and information rights

Information asymmetry is the biggest barrier to shareholders' monitoring of management.[105] Stronger disclosure regulations strengthen shareholder bargaining power. Disclosure regulations that are too strong will, however, distort management's incentives to take adequate risk, increase managerial compensation, and may even give management an incentive to manipulate information.[106]

Shareholders' information rights to inspect books and records, as well as to obtain the shareholders' list are valuable adjutants to enforce fiduciary duties in litigation or proxy fights. Apart from shareholders' information rights provided by corporate law and securities regulation, the strong pre-trial discovery system, complementarily with a system that allows for wide range of injunctive relief, strengthens shareholder bargaining power with management in the US.[107]

I.5.3 Legal Liabilities of Management and Shareholder Suits

The legal liability of management is a major restriction on the autonomy of management in addition to the possibility of hostile takeovers as a market restriction. Management, both directors and officers, owe fiduciary duties

---

103 *See* Roberta Romano, Foundations of Corporate Law 411 (2nd ed 2011).

104 In the US, besides the appraisal remedy and fiduciary fairness actions (which provide the same measure of damages as appraisal), injunctive relief accompanied by shareholder suits based on a violation of directors' fiduciary duty plays an important role. The appraisal system and the injunction system may have different deterrent effects depending on the court's valuation of company stock. If courts create the public impression that they tend to overvalue a target's shares, the appraisal system will have a substantial deterrent effect on takeovers. On the other hand, although the injunction system does not have such a general deterrent effect, it may individually frustrate efficient corporate takeovers if the realized value of the court's valuation exceeds the target's potential enterprise value. *See* Akio Hoshi, Chapter 13 in this volume.

105 Besides the problem with information asymmetry, the "rational apathy" and "collective action" problems are other barriers to effective monitoring by shareholders.

106 *See* Hermalin, *supra* note 6.

107 The weak discovery system in Japan discourages the use of injunctions against management activities (Companies Act Articles 360, 422) and the raising of shareholder derivative actions.

to shareholders, which consist of the duty of loyalty and the duty of care.[108] If management breach their duties, they will owe legal liability in respect of the resulting damage to the corporation and shareholders. Accordingly, the shareholder derivative and representative class actions play an important role as an enforcement mechanism. In Japan, although there is no class action system yet, a part of the US's shareholder direct actions is covered by Japan's unique corporate law statute providing for director responsibility to third parties (so called "Article 429 actions").

As an enforcement scheme in respect of legal liabilities of management, however, the shareholder derivative action has a serious problem with its incentive structure. There is no monetary incentive for the plaintiff shareholder,[109] who may be a minimum-amount holder, to raise a derivative action that will have a strong impact on management which is disproportionate to the amount of their residual claim.[110]

The risk of having to pay damages from their own pockets, which is determined by both substantive rules (including directors' and officers' – D&O – insurance contracts) and enforcement mechanisms, affects the incentive of management and monitors.[111] It is important but not easy to maintain a sufficient deterrent effect while avoiding too much of a chilling effect on management.[112]

---

[108] While US case law distinguishes the duty of loyalty and the duty of care from a conflict-of-interest point of view, Japanese case law denies such a distinction and takes the fiduciary duty as a whole. *See* Hideki Kanda and Curtis J. Milhaupt, *Re-examining Legal Transplants: The Director's Fiduciary Duty in Japanese Corporate Law*, 51 AM. J. COMP. L. 887 (2003).

[109] Plaintiff attorneys have an incentive to organize shareholder derivative actions because of the ability to collect under the contingency fee system in the US. Although in Japan the fee system does not give attorneys enough monetary incentive, they receive gains in the form of advertising, rewarding work, or altruistic gains; derivative litigations occur with relative frequency even without the same level of monetary incentives seen in the US. *See* Mark D. West, *Why Shareholders Sue: The Evidence from Japan*, 30 J. L. STUD. 351 (2001).

[110] That is also the rationale for the use of class rather than individual shareholder action. Some commentators argue that even purely irrational behavior has played more than a marginal role in driving shareholder litigation in Japan. *See* Dan W. Puchniak & Masafumi Nakahigashi, *Japan's Love for Derivative Actions: Irrational Behavior and Non-Economic Motives as Rational Explanations for Shareholder Litigation*, 45 VAND. J. TRANSNAT'L L. 1 (2012).

[111] *See* Roberta Romano, *The Shareholder Suit: Litigation without Foundation?*, 7 J. L. ECON. & ORG. 55 (1991) (arguing that the risk to directors of having to pay from their own pockets is rare and the shareholder derivative action has almost no deterrent effect in the US).

[112] It is obvious that shareholder derivative action has been significantly affecting the incentive of management and monitors in Japan since the legisla-

In order to decrease the chilling effect from the shareholder derivative action on management, the law provides several schemes in the US and Japan. First, the business judgment rule basically prevents non-interested management and directors from being liable for their business decisions, provided they are made pursuant to adequate procedure.[113] Second, the law permits corporations to set a cap on the maximum amount of damages its directors may be required to pay,[114] in addition to permitting the purchase of D&O insurance.[115] And third, the law provides ways of screening shareholder suits, such as the demand requirement and litigation committees in the US[116] and security for expense awards by the court in Japan.[117]

I.5.4 Control Transactions

Hostile takeovers as a source of shareholders' monitoring power

Hostile takeovers are phenomena via which shareholders replace inefficient management who are not successful in maximizing shareholder value

---

tive reduction of the filing fee in 1993, which increased the number of actions dramatically, and particularly since the 2000 Daiwa Bank decision (*In re* Daiwa Bank Derivative Litigation, 1271 HANJI 3 (Tokyo District Ct. Sep. 20, 2000)), which awarded $775 million – an award 66 times higher than the previous record (*see* Bruce E. Aronson, *Reconsidering the Importance of Law in Japanese Corporate Governance: Evidence from the Daiwa Bank Shareholder Derivative Case*, 36 CORNELL INT'L L. J. 11, 50 (2003–2004)), although it is arguable whether the current system provides an optimal deterrent effect or too much of a chilling effect.

[113] The business judgment rule is, however, not perfectly clear even in the US (*see* Melvin A. Eisenberg, *The Divergence of Standards of Conduct and Standards of Review in Corporate Law*, 62 FORDHAM L. REV. 437 (1993); William T. Allen, *The Corporate Director's Fiduciary Duties of Care and the Business Judgment Rule Under US Corporate Law, in* COMPARATIVE CORPORATE GOVERNANCE: THE STATE OF THE ART AND EMERGING RESEARCH 307 (Klaus J. Hopt et al. eds., 1998)), and the court has been reviewing the reasonableness of management decisions in Japan (*see in re* Nomura Securities Co., 1760 HANJI 144 (Tokyo District Ct. Jan. 25, 2001)). In addition, the business judgment rule does not necessarily protect directors that fail to exercise their duty to monitor management. *See in re* Caremark Int'l Inc. Derivative Litigation, 698 A. 2d 1156 (De. Ch. 1996); *in re* Daiwa Bank, 1721 HANJI 3 (Osaka District Ct. Sep. 20, 2003).

[114] Neither US nor Japanese law permit an *ex ante* cap on maximum damage for executives; both permit it only for monitors, such as outside directors.

[115] D&O insurance contracts give both defendant directors and plaintiff attorneys the incentive to settle in the US. *See* Romano, *supra* note 111, at 57.

[116] *See* WILLIAM A. KLEIN & JOHN C. COFFEE, JR., BUSINESS ORGANIZATION AND FINANCE: LEGAL AND ECONOMIC PRINCIPLES 2010, 2011 (10th ed. 2007).

[117] *See* Puchniak & Nakahigashi, *supra* note 110, at 49.

by using the resources of the corporation.[118] Although hostile takeovers do not occur frequently, the possibility of their occurrence, in other words the existence of the market for corporate control, provides shareholders with a source of monitoring power over management.

The possibility of hostile takeovers is particularly effective at solving the agency problem related to free cash flow.[119] How much free cash flow should be distributed to shareholders or retained in the corporation is an issue of sharing control, rather than an issue of sharing value added, between management and shareholders, because it is a matter of degree of management discretion in operating monetary capital. If a corporation retains too much free cash flow, management is not only likely to be idle as a result of escaping the monitoring effects of debt, but also likely to waste free cash flow on empire building. Stock markets will discount the value of the stock of companies with a lot of free cash flow, and the possibility of such companies facing a hostile takeover will increase. This increase in the risk of a hostile takeover exerts pressure on management to distribute free cash flow to shareholders.

There are conflicting interests between shareholders and the other three players when it comes to the choice between distributing dividends or retaining earnings. Employees and management share the same interest as human capital providers: to retain control over monetary capital. Creditors also have an interest in maintaining free cash flow in the company as it minimizes their risk in a corporate bankruptcy scenario. Such interests encourage management, employees, and creditors, including banks and trading partners, to create a coalition against shareholders who insist that the company should distribute free cash flow.[120]

---

[118] From an economic point of view, the hostile takeover is a scheme for efficient resource allocation and the market for corporate control enables resources to move more quickly to their highest-value use. *See* Michael C. Jensen, *Takeovers: Their Causes and Consequences*, 2 J. ECON. PERSP. 21 (1988).

[119] *See* Michael C. Jensen, *Agency Costs of Free Cash Flow, Corporate Finance, and Takeovers*, 76 AM. ECON. REV. 323 (1986); George G. Triantis & Ronald J. Daniels, *The Role of Debt in Interactive Corporate Governance*, 83 CAL. L. REV. 1073 (1995). *See also* Ronald Gilson & Mark J. Roe, *Understanding the Japanese Keiretsu: Overlaps Between Corporate Governance and Industrial Organization*, 102 YALE L. J. 871 (1993) (pointing out that Japanese main bank monitoring, without a corporate control market, failed to monitor the use of free cash flow).

[120] On the general coalition between employees and management, *see supra* notes 27–31 and their accompanying text. Such a general coalition is strengthened by cross-shareholding and turns into an alliance against genuine shareholders in Japan. *See infra* notes 141–142 and their accompanying text.

Balancing autonomy and monitoring

The optimal level of potential for a hostile takeover is a typical issue of balancing autonomy and monitoring. Although a certain level of potential for a hostile takeover is indispensable in monitoring management, if there is too much potential it will distort the incentive of human capital providers to make firm-specific investments.

Therefore, several mechanisms have been invented to reduce shareholder ability to disrupt management, typically through staggered boards, "poison pills," and "shark repellent" provisions in charters or bylaws in the US; and cross-shareholdings, issuing new stocks to "white squires," and Japanese-style "poison pills" in Japan.[121]

Regulations of buyers and sellers

Most countries with a market for corporate control have regulations in respect of control transactions, including both hostile and friendly takeovers, because control transactions inevitably give rise to serious conflicting interests between all players. Such regulations usually include regulations on both buyers (acquirers) and sellers (management and boards of target companies).

Regulations on buyers are basically TOB regulations and disclosure regulations applicable to large shareholders (the 5 percent rule). These regulations discourage control transactions to a certain degree.[122] In particular, requiring mandatory bids forces controlling shareholders to share their controlling premium with minority shareholders and discourages controlling shareholders from selling their controlling blocks.[123] Requiring mandatory bids for all shares increases the cost of takeovers and discourages raiders from buying companies. Therefore, although strong TOB regulations may effectively protect minority shareholders, particularly against coercive bids, they support management autonomy, rather than shareholder monitoring, from the point of view of balancing autonomy and monitoring.

Regulations on sellers are basically defense regulations. Case law has been developed on how to regulate defensive measures in both the US and Japan. The difficulty of solving specific cases of takeover battles is that raiders do not necessarily maximize shareholder value, and instead may destroy corporate value, although management and the board of directors

---

[121] Most Japanese poison pills are "pre-warning rights plans," which lack legal effect. *See* Milhaupt, *supra* note 96.

[122] *See supra* notes 87–89 and their accompanying text.

[123] *See* Easterbrook & Fischel, *supra* note 14, at 109.

will not be free from conflicts of interest in implementing and exercising defensive measures.[124]

It is important to consider these regulations on buyers and sellers as a whole in order to maintain a good balance between autonomy and monitoring. The UK system maintains a good balance by enforcing strong regulations on both buyers and sellers; that is, requiring buyers to make mandatory bids for all shares and by prohibiting incumbents from initiating any defense. The US system is another example of a well-struck balance, reached by putting weak regulations on both buyers and sellers; that is, not requiring buyers to make mandatory all-share bids but allowing boards to implement defenses. Japan's system follows a UK-like takeover rule and a US-like defense rule. As a result, the balance is too much in favor of management autonomy.[125]

Appraisal remedy and minority protections

Control transactions may give rise not only to conflicting interests between shareholders and human capital providers, but also to conflicting interests among shareholders. In particular, minority shareholders are susceptible to economic damage. Therefore, most countries with a market for corporate control have minority shareholder protection laws, such as fiduciary duty claims and the appraisal remedy available to dissenting shareholders.[126]

Historically, the appraisal remedy was developed to make mergers and other types of reorganizations possible by way of a majority vote, so that a unanimous vote was not required. As such, the appraisal remedy has basically played a role in expanding management discretion. The appraisal

---

[124] Jesse H. Choper, John C. Coffee, Jr., Ronald J. Gilson, Cases and Material on Corporations 945 (7th ed. 2008).

[125] Zenichi Shishido, *A Response to John Armour, Jack B. Jacobs and Curtis J. Milhaupt*, Harv. Int'l L. J. (Feb. 10, 2011), http://opiniojuris.org/2011/02/10/hilj_shishido-response-to-armour-jacobs-milhaupt/.

[126] While in the US, fiduciary duty claims play a more important role than appraisal rights, the appraisal right is in practice the exclusive remedy in Japan because neither the Companies Act nor the case law stipulate the existence of directors' fiduciary duty to specific shareholders who suffer damage because of a board decision, such as damage suffered due to a merger. Certain Japanese commentators argue that for the purpose of providing a stronger incentive to management and directors to make the term of mergers more fair, fiduciary duty claims would be more effective than appraisal rights. *See* Hidefusa Iida & Kenichi Sekiguchi, Chapter 12 in this volume. A reason why fiduciary claims are more important than appraisal actions in the US is the collective action problem: they can take the form of representative actions, whereas appraisal cases are individual claims, and courts need not award attorney's fees.

remedy may, however, give minority shareholders an incentive for opportunistic behavior and discourage reorganizations, depending on how case law interprets the concept of "fair value."[127]

I.5.5 Cross-Shareholding and Schemes to Reduce Shareholder Disruption to Management

The mechanism and its reasoning

Each cross-shareholding is made between two companies, with each holding stock in the other company. The reasoning behind such an arrangement is to create a business alliance. Cross-shareholding may be useful to maintain a long-term trading relationship. Cross-shareholding between trading partners, typically between supplier and manufacturer, so called vertical *keiretsu*, has been positively evaluated as a mechanism to discourage opportunistic behavior by trading partners and encourage companies to make relation-specific investments.[128]

Another purpose of cross-shareholding is to defend against hostile takeovers. Management of cross-shareholding partners implicitly agree to support each other in the exercise of their voting rights. Since the 1950s, defensive web-like circles of cross-shareholding have been established and maintained among the pre-war *zaibatsu* companies as loose-knit, bank-centered groups and communities of equals, so called horizontal *keiretsu*.[129] Horizontal *keiretsu* can be viewed as a mechanism by which the corporation becomes an owner of itself.[130]

---

[127] The Companies Act of 2005 revised the original Japanese appraisal right provision that, similar to the Delaware General Corporation Law, did not include synergies arising from the merger. This revision enabled the courts to include such synergies in the stock price valued through appraisal, which may have in turn deterred certain mergers from occurring. Other important differences between the Japanese appraisal remedy and its American counterpart are the reliance of the Japanese courts on the market price to determine the appraisal price and the lack of any exception, such as the "market out" exception, in granting appraisal rights in Japan. *See* Iida & Sekiguchi, *supra* note 126. *See also* Hoshi, *supra* note 104.

[128] *See* Gilson & Roe, *supra* note 119, at 886, 891–895.

[129] *See* James R. Lincoln & Masahiro Shimotani, Whither the Keiretsu, Japan's Business Network: How Were They Structured? What Did They Do? Why Are They Gone? (Working Paper 2009). *But see* Yoshiro Miwa & Mark Ramseyer, *The Fable of Keiretsu*, 11 J. ECON. & MGMT. STRATEGY 169 (2002).

[130] *See* Eguchi, *supra* note 85.

The unwinding and reconstructing of cross-shareholding

Following the financial crisis of 1997, the rate of cross-shareholding, particularly bank ownership, steadily decreased until 2004. Banks reduced their shareholdings mainly by selling those shares with higher liquidity and higher expected rates of return, while holding on to the shares of those firms with which they had long-term relationships. Such investment behavior not only undermined the corporate governance of their portfolio companies, but also led to the degradation of their own portfolios.[131]

From the point of view of cross-shareholding, one can observe heterogeneity among Japanese listed companies. Profitable companies with easy access to capital markets and a high percentage of foreign ownership have tended to unwind their cross-shareholdings, while low-profit companies without easy access to capital markets and a low percentage of foreign ownership have tended to keep their cross-shareholding relationships with banks in place.[132]

Cross-shareholding has even started to increase among the latter type of companies since 2005, the year the market for corporate control in Japan opened.[133] It would therefore seem that the benefit of cross-shareholding to the management of companies that are subject to a high risk of takeover must be larger than the risk of a bad reputation in the stock market.

The cost of cross-shareholding

Beyond the business logic of maintaining long-term trading relationships, the defense purpose of cross-shareholding should not be evaluated only in a negative light. In every country, some scheme to reduce shareholder disruption to management is indispensable in order to balance management autonomy and shareholder monitoring.[134] In the US, corporate law follows the principle of director primacy and restricts the decision-making power of shareholder meetings, and case law has allowed certain "poison

---

131 *See* Hideakai Miyajima and Fumiaki Kuroki, *The Unwinding of Cross-Shareholding in Japan: Causes, Effects, and Implications*, *in* CORPORATE GOVERNANCE IN JAPAN: INSTITUTIONAL CHANGE AND ORGANIZATIONAL DIVERSITY 79 (Masahiko Aoki et al. eds, 2007).

132 *See id.* For a discussion of a new pattern of management-shareholders relation and a possible role for institutional investors, *see* Zenichi Shishido & Takaaki Eguchi, *The Future of Japanese Corporate Governance: Internal Governance and the Development of Japanese-Style External Governance through Engagement*, *in* RESEARCH HANDBOOK ON SHAREHOLDER POWER (Randall Thomas & Jennifer Hill eds., forthcoming).

133 *See id.*

134 *See* Eguchi, *supra* note 85.

pills" to stand as defenses.[135] In the UK, although corporate law respects shareholder choice as it does in Japan, shareholder intervention occurs mainly through collective engagement by major domestic investment managers who have historically formed a close-knit community.[136] Cross-shareholdings have played a major role in reducing shareholder ability to disrupt management in Japan.

The problem is that the cost of cross-shareholding often turns out to be too high. This cost is twofold: first is the cost of implementing and maintaining the scheme, and second is the cost of entrenchment.

The first cost of cross-shareholding, which will accrue to shareholders, is higher than that of a poison pill, particularly when stock prices decrease. Such a cost could theoretically function as soft market monitoring: if cross-shareholding partners sell off underperforming stock that they cannot tolerate to hold, the underperforming company may become the target of hostile takeovers. The reality is that after the financial crisis in 1997, however, the opposite occurred, as previously noted.[137]

The second cost, that associated with the entrenchment of cross-shareholding, has only become obvious with the passage of time. After the control market was created and the trend of shareholder activism emerged in 2005, the management of listed companies vulnerable to hostile takeovers started to re-establish cross-shareholdings, which had been decreasing during the 1990s. A statistical study shows that firms with poison pill defenses also tended to organize more cross-shareholdings. This suggests that cross-shareholdings and poison pills are not substitutive but instead are complementary, which indicates the entrenchment of management. [138]

In the US, poison pills seldom block hostile bids. Independent directors, the Delaware courts, and the capital markets complementarily cause poison pills to operate largely as a negotiation tool, rather than as a means of entrenchment.[139] In Japan, the combination of cross-shareholdings and poison pills can in fact block hostile takeovers.[140]

In some Japanese listed companies, at least, there are conflicting inter-

---

135 *See id.*

136 On engagement in the UK, *see id.*

137 *See supra* note 131 and its accompanying text.

138 *See* Miho Takizawa, Kotaro Tsuru & Kaoru Hosono, Baishu Boeisaku Donyu no Doki: Keiei Hoshin Kasetsu no Kensho [Takeover Defense Measures: Testing of Entrenchment Hypothesis for Corporate Managers] (RIETI Discussion Paper, 2007).

139 *See* Ronald J. Gilson, *The Poison Pill in Japan: The Missing Infrastructure*, 2004 COLUM. BUS. L. REV. 21 (2004).

140 *See Steel Partners v. Bulldog Sauce*, 61-5 MINSHU 221 (Sup. Ct., Aug. 7, 2007).

ests between genuine shareholders who vote for maximizing shareholder value[141] and cross-holding shareholders who vote for other purposes, such as maintaining their trading relationships; there is a possibility that as a result, the interests of genuine shareholders may be damaged. Generally speaking, if a substantial percentage of shareholders exercise their voting right in a way which does not maximize shareholder value, the preposition of corporate law, which gives voting rights exclusively to shareholders, will collapse.[142] This issue is related to "empty voting."[143]

Law and cross-shareholding

Regulations affecting defense mechanisms set out in Japanese takeover law, which have been developed since 2005, encourage management to organize defensive cross-shareholdings by encouraging *ex ante* shareholder approval of defensive plans.[144] In particular, the Supreme Court decision in the Bulldog Sauce case in 2007,[145] which held that the exercise of the poison pill by Bulldog Sauce was legitimate because it was supported by a majority of the shareholders, gives management an incentive to create cross-shareholdings between companies which are vulnerable to hostile takeovers, even incentivizing the creation of inefficient business alliances as an excuse for such cross-shareholdings.[146] The business

141 Although some genuine shareholders may not exercise their voting rights because of "rational apathy," if they vote, they will always vote for maximizing shareholder value.

142 In this regard, the reinterpretation of a Japan's corporate law statute which prohibits the giving of a benefit in exchange for the exercise of shareholder rights (Companies Act Article 120) is suggested. Although the statute was originally made to prohibit management from bribing professional shareholders (*sokaiya*), it may be utilized for aligning the incentive structure of shareholders in the context of cross-shareholding. *See* Takahito Kato, Riekikyoyo Kinshi Kitei to Kabushiki Mochiai: Kabunushi no Insenthibu Kozo no Kanten kara [*Corporate Law Statute to Prohibit Giving Benefit for the Exercise of Shareholder Rights and Cross-shareholding: From the Point of View of the Shareholders' Incentive Structure*], *in* THE LOGIC OF "ENTERPRISE LAW" REFORMATIONS, *supra* note 54, at 227.

143 *See* Henry T.C. Hu & Bernard Black, *Hedge Funds, Insiders, and the Decoupling of Economic and Voting Ownership: Empty Voting and Hidden (Morphable) Ownership*, 13 J. CORP. FIN. 343 (2007).

144 The Takeover Guidelines of 2005 and the Bulldog Sauce case encourage acquiring shareholder approval, which is effectively required by the Tokyo Stock Exchange rules. *See* Milhaupt, *supra* note 96.

145 *Steel Partners v. Bulldog Sauce*, 61-5 MINSHU 221 (Sup. Ct., Aug. 7, 2007). *See* Milhaupt, *supra* note 96.

146 *See* Peng Xu & Wataru Tanaka, *Baishu Boeisaku in za Shado obu Mochiai: Jirei Kenkyu* [*Anti-Takeover Measures in the Shadow of Cross-Shareholding: A Case Study*], 1885 SHOJIHOMU 4 (2009).

judgment rule protects management's discretion to organize defensive cross-shareholdings, which can then serve as an excuse for creating business alliances.[147]

On the other hand, various laws can be effective in discouraging management from establishing defensive cross-shareholdings and encouraging management to instead dissolve existing cross-shareholdings.

The Bank for International Settlements (BIS) regulation of banks' equity capital has had the effect of decreasing cross-shareholding by banks, particularly after the financial crisis of 1997.[148] Although the Banking Act and Anti-Monopoly Act cap bank ownership of the voting rights of a business corporation at 5 percent, this is not a meaningful deterrent against cross-shareholding. Nor is it an adequate reason for distinguishing banks' shareholdings from business corporations' shareholdings.[149]

Mark-to-market accounting, which has applied to cross-shareholding stocks since the fiscal year beginning April 2001,[150] may have some effect in discouraging management from creating and maintaining cross-shareholdings. Similarly, further disclosure requirements related to cross-shareholding situations would have a disincentivizing effect on cross-shareholdings via stock market monitoring.

It is arguable whether or not strong regulation, such as denying voting rights connected to cross-shareholding stocks, is required. A milder alternative would be either to require agreement from a shareholder meeting which consists only of genuine shareholders, or allowing genuine shareholders to sue for injunctive relief upon the exercise of any voting rights by cross-holding shareholders and for the annulment of any resolutions taken at the relevant shareholder meeting.[151]

---

[147] The different approaches taken by US and Japanese takeover laws on shareholder approval provide contrasting incentive effects on the independent director system. The US takeover law, which gives the board of directors the exclusive gatekeeper role, without any participation by shareholders, generates strong incentives for boards to be comprised of truly independent directors in order to establish the reasonableness of board decisions. On the other hand, the Japanese takeover law, which focuses on shareholder approval and does not privilege the decisions of independent directors or committees, creates few incentives for the adoption of independent directors. *See* Milhaupt, *supra* note 96.

[148] Banks choosing to sell off stocks was, however, not based on performance, but on relationship with portfolio companies. *See supra* note 131 and its accompanying text.

[149] *See* Akira Tokutsu, Chapter 11 in this volume.

[150] Enterprise Accounting Committee, Financial Instruments Accounting Guideline of 1999.

[151] *See* Kato, *supra* note 142.

I.6 ROLES OF GOVERNMENT

Government is the provider of indispensable infrastructure for business activities, both physical infrastructures and legal infrastructures. Legal infrastructure includes both legislation and public enforcement of laws.[152] As compensation for these services, government levies taxes on the firm and the four players. Government is also the regulator of each industry, as the delegate of consumers. In each of these aspects, as the legislature, the enforcer of laws, the taxing authority, and the regulator of industries, the government affects nearly all aspects of the incentive bargain of the firm.

I.6.1 Taxation and Incentives

The four players provide the corporation with capital that is indispensable in running its business, either human capital or monetary capital. The corporation pays some form of compensation to all capital providers. Compensation paid to human capital providers is treated differently when it comes to corporate-level tax, depending on the identity of the payees: salary paid to employees is fully deductible as a cost, whereas salary paid to management is not fully deductible in Japan.[153] Compensation paid to monetary capital providers is treated even more differently, depending on the identity of the payees: interest paid to creditors is fully deductible as a cost, whereas dividends paid to shareholders are not deductible but instead are taxed at both the corporate level and the shareholder level, under a system known as "double taxation."[154] Such differences in tax treatment may have incentive effects on management.

---

[152] The two fundamental elements of legal infrastructure which are indispensable for making the incentive bargain of the firm efficient and developing the market economy, are those for protecting private property and for enforcing contracts. Without such elements, people's incentive to invest and incentive to trade would be distorted. Although in most emerging economies these basic elements may not yet be in place, this chapter takes them as given in the US and Japan.

[153] Although US law also placed a limitation on tax deductions for compensation received by corporate executives, the limitation depends not on the category of human capital provider but on the amount of compensation. *See* Tetsuya Watanabe, Chapter 16 in this volume.

[154] Most countries have some adjustment system aimed at double taxation when the payee is a corporation. A part of dividends received is not recognized as income of the payee corporation depending on how much of the payer corporation's stock is owned by the payee corporation. The difference of such non-recognition rules in different countries may impact corporate group planning. *See* Randal Morck, How to Eliminate Pyramidal Business Groups: The

Double taxation may incentivize management to choose debt financing as long as the resulting debt–equity ratio is within a reasonable level. Double taxation also encourages retained earnings,[155] and may facilitate managerial empire building. The cost of double taxation is not necessarily carried by shareholders, as management has an incentive to transfer the cost of corporate income tax to the player with the weakest bargaining power, which may be the employees.[156]

Individual income tax law gives human capital providers, particularly management, an incentive to shift from taxable monetary compensation to non-taxable non-monetary compensations, such as fringe benefits, and the use of tax deferral through incentive compensation schemes.[157] There is no strong evidence that tax law significantly influences the substance of equity compensation – that is, the mix between equity and cash and the risk and term structure – but it is possible that tax law has had an impact on the form of equity compensation, particularly in regard to start-up companies and venture capital funds.[158]

Another area of corporate income tax law, which significantly affects corporate behavior by influencing the incentives of management, is the non-recognition rule of corporate reorganizations. Although reorganizing transactions, such as mergers, are basically taxable because they are realization events, if the transactions are qualified reorganizations under the law, no gain or loss will be recognized at both corporate and shareholder levels, and the basis of the assets or stock transferred will be carried over. Japanese reorganization tax law, compared with the US law, is prohibitive against corporate spin-offs and encourages the creation of wholly owned subsidiaries.[159] It is also important to note that the record-keeping requirements of corporate income tax law may facilitate stronger corporate governance and support monetary capital providers as a result.

Double Taxation of Inter-Corporate Dividends and Other Incentive Uses of Tax Policy (Working Paper 2004). *But see* Steven A. Bank & Brian R. Cheffins, The Corporate Pyramid Fable (Working Paper 2011).

[155] The reason why the corporation pays dividends despite the cost of double taxation is usually explained by the signaling theory.

[156] The cost-bearer of double taxation may be trading partners or consumers, depending on the market. *See* Watanabe, *supra* note 153.

[157] *See* Gamage & Rana, *supra* note 16.

[158] *See* Mark P. Gergen, Chapter 17 in this volume.

[159] *See* Tetsuya Watanabe, Tax-Free Treatment for Corporate Reorganizations in Japan (Sho Sato Conference Paper 2009). Japanese law also provides a "continuity of employees" requirement and a "no boot" requirement for qualified reorganizations. *See id.*

I.6.2 Public Monitoring and Enforcement

The government also plays an important role in monitoring and enforcing substantive legal rules. This subsection focuses on anti-competition regulations and securities regulations, which are two typical areas where public monitoring and enforcement are indispensable for maintaining efficient markets.[160]

Human capital providers, both management and employees, have an incentive to collude with competitors in order to avoid robust market competition. It is widely recognized that such collusions damage consumer interests and product market efficiency.[161] Therefore, public monitoring and enforcement is indispensable when it comes to combating anti-competitive activities. Product markets with little room for collusion give management an incentive to encourage employees to produce better products at a cheaper price.

Regarding anti-competition regulations, every jurisdiction's enforcement system has its own characteristics rather than in its substantive rules. The form of sanctions under US law is criminal; it is administrative under European Union (EU) law; and a hybrid of both under Japanese law. Some commentators think that the Japanese enforcement system does not have enough of a deterrent effect because the administrative surcharge is aimed only at collecting gain, the amount is automatically calculated, and cannot reflect the culpability and gravity of the subject conduct, and imprisonment without suspension of the term has not yet occurred.[162]

Securities regulations and their enforcement contribute to the efficiency of capital markets. Unfair trading regulations create capital markets with little room for insider trading and manipulation, and encourage investor participation. Disclosure regulations create capital markets which efficiently reflect accurate information.[163] The existence of an efficient capital market encourages monitoring based on the market price of stocks[164] and gives management an incentive to run the company's business with a view toward increasing stock price.

---

160 *See* Howell E. Jackson, Chapter 18 in this volume.

161 *See* Robert S. Pindyck & Daniel L. Rubinfeld, Microeconomics §12.7 (7th ed. 2008); Philip Areeda & Louis Kaplow, Antitrust Analysis §201 (6th ed. 2004).

162 *See* Shigeki Kusunoki, *Shaping an Anti-Monopoly Law Sanction Regime Against Cartels or Bid Collusion: A Perspective on Japan's Choice*, 79 U. Det. Mercy L. Rev. 399 (2001–2002).

163 *But see infra* note 170 and its accompanying text.

164 *See* Gordon, *supra* note 95, at 1541.

Although the substantive rules of securities regulations are not particularly different between the US, the EU, and Japan, their enforcement systems are substantially different. While *ex post* monitoring via litigation initiated by the Securities Exchange Committee and private parties has played an important role in the US,[165] *ex ante* monitoring by the Ministry of Finance (currently the Financial Services Agency, FSA) played the dominant role with almost no private enforcement actions in Japan until 1990.[166] In 1991, following several securities scandals, the Securities and Exchange Surveillance Commission (SESC) was founded and has since been active in *ex post* enforcement of securities regulation. Besides the SESC, the Tokyo Stock Exchange also plays an important role in monitoring. Private enforcement attempts still rarely occur in Japan.[167]

I.6.3 Disclosure Regulations and SOX

Government is the major monitor and enforcer of disclosure regulations not only via securities regulation, but also via corporate law, industry regulation, and so on. Disclosure regulation is an example of an area of law that requires a good balance, which is not the general perception; that is, the stricter, the better. I will focus on the SOX law in the US as a good example of this.

The SOX law in the US constitutes governmental intervention into the internal control of listed companies and provides a good example of the way in which the government can significantly affect the incentive bargain of the corporation as a monitor and an enforcer; examining SOX also raises the legislative policy question regarding what is the optimal approach to disclosure regulation.

---

165 Although private enforcement has the potential to offer important contributions to the robustness of a capital market, public enforcement has a more major role to play and is a necessary complement to private enforcement. *See* Jackson, *supra* note 160; Howell E. Jackson & Mark J. Roe, *Public and Private Enforcement of Securities Laws: Resource-Based Evidence*, 93 J. FIN. ECON. 207 (2009).

166 Corporate cross-shareholding patterns in post-war Japan and the relative low priority traditionally placed on formal securities regulation and its enforcement are probably interrelated. *See* Curtis J. Milhaupt, *Managing the Market: The Ministry of Finance and Securities Regulation in Japan*, 30 STAN. J. INT'L L. 423 (1994).

167 A reason for the scarcity of private litigations in Japan may be the lack of a class action mechanism. The potential for collective actions through use of the internet and new legislation on no-fault liability and presumptive damage (the Financial Instruments and Exchange Act Article 21-2) may encourage private litigation in misrepresentation cases in Japan in the future.

Because the SOX law is a regulation not on the corporation itself, but on the specific players[168] – that is, management and auditors – and because it includes criminal sanctions among its enforcement tools, it has a significant influence on the incentive of the players, for better or worse.

Although the SOX law probably strengthens shareholder bargaining power with management in respect of better disclosure, negative side effects have also been noted. In addition to the significant increase in the cost of maintaining sufficient internal controls, the SOX law discourages management from taking risks by strengthening the bargaining power of monitors, such as auditors and independent directors.[169]

Generally speaking, as a result of too much transparency, management is induced to behave in ways that merely look good rather than in ways that are truly good. Overly aggressive disclosure regulations may lead management to become too timid and may even lead management to manipulate information.[170]

Four years after SOX was implemented, the Japanese legislature implemented internal control regulations similar to those that make up the SOX law, often cited as the J-SOX law. The impact of the SOX law and the J-SOX law, however, appear to be totally different. Although the J-SOX law did not successfully strengthen shareholders' bargaining power with management in respect of better disclosure, it did not lead to an increase in defensive management. No direct reporting requirements by auditors, weak public enforcement, and an insufficient independent director system complementarily prevent any increase in the bargaining power of monitors, and as a result, management does not need to be defensive.[171]

---

168 Usually, the government exercises its influence over the incentive bargain among the four players through the corporate personality of the firm, through either taxation or industrial regulation. Sometimes, however, governmental regulations directly address a specific player. The latter mode of regulation strongly impacts the incentive bargain among the four players, although even the former mode of regulation cannot be said to be neutral to the incentive bargain.

169 *See* Leonce L. Bargeron et al., *Sarbanes–Oxley and Corporate Risk-Taking*, 49 J. ACCT. & ECON. 34 (2010); Kate Litvak, Defensive Management: Does the Sarbanes–Oxley Act Discourage Corporate Risk-Taking? (Working Paper 2008); Qiang Kang et al., *The Sarbanes–Oxley Act and Corporate Investment: A Structural Assessment*, 96 J. FIN. ECON. 291 (2010); Shishido & Osaki, *supra* note 62.

170 Overly aggressive disclosure regulations also may lead management to excessive risk-taking. *See* Hermalin, *supra* note 6.

171 *See* Shishido & Osaki, *supra* note 62. However, the fact that the documentation requirement of J-SOX decreases the autonomy of each sector's employees and discourages their creativity has been criticized.

I.6.4 Industry Regulations and Informality

Besides taxation and public enforcement of laws, the government also monitors corporations that belong to a certain industry via industry regulation. The government, as the delegate of consumers, monitors and negotiates with industry associations and their member corporations. The four players of each corporation in a certain industry are subject to such pressure from the government as a given infrastructural component of the incentive bargain.[172]

The government negotiates with an industry not always based on specific laws but often in informal ways. Such negotiations seldom take a coercive form, but are usually a request for voluntary cooperation in pursuit of statutory or extra-statutory policy goals. Administrative informality does not only exist in Japan. Negotiation efforts during US administrative processes are substantially similar to Japanese administrative guidance in pursuit of statutory policy goals.[173]

I.7 CONCLUSIONS

In conclusion, the previous discussions are summarized from the perspective of the incentive bargain of the firm as a repeated game; a legislative policy is then proposed for enhancing the efficiency of the incentive bargain of the firm, which this chapter refers to as legislating through backward induction.

I.7.1 Repeated Game

The incentive bargain of the firm is a repeated game (see Table I.1). In stage 0, the four players design contracts establishing incentive patterns. They also agree on methods for sharing control and sharing value added. In stage 1, each player provides their own capital and management executes the business plan. In stage 2, the players monitor each other and share the realized value added. Management also proposes financing and

---

172 Although politically there is room for negotiation, this chapter does not take it into consideration.

173 *See* Takehisa Nakagawa, *Administrative Informality in Japan: Governmental Activities Outside Statutory Authorization*, 52 ADMIN. L. REV. 175 (2000). This observation related to administrative informality may lead one to see government as a fifth player in the bargain, a topic which I intended to address in the future.

Table I.1 Stages of the game

- Stage 0
  - Design contracts establishing incentive patterns
  - Agreements for sharing control and sharing value added
- Stage 1
  - Each player provides capital
  - Execution and monitoring
- Stage 2
  - Players share value added
  - Management proposes plan for next stage
- Stage 3
  - Usually, start again from stage 1
  - Possibly, return to stage 0 (end-game)

business plans for the next stage. And in stage 3, the players usually start again from stage 1, but in end-game scenarios they return to stage 0.

Stage 0 is the bargaining stage before contracts are entered into. As with the choice of incentive patterns,[174] the importance of firm-specific investments in the industry,[175] the liquidity of the external labor markets,[176] social norms,[177] and laws and practices which encourage or discourage coalitions among the players[178] are particularly influential. Sharing control among the players in a way which reduces the risk to each player is particularly influenced by corporate law,[179] bankruptcy law,[180] and labor law.[181] Sharing value added in a way which creates positive incentives between each of the players is influenced by each player's market power and characteristics prior to contract formation.

Stage 1 is the execution stage. Each player provides capital to the firm based on the agreements made in stage 0. The potential for renegotiation in the future will, however, distort the incentive of the players, particularly employees, when they provide their capital.[182] Management then executes the business plan.

---

174 *See supra* notes 7–24 and their accompanying text.
175 *See supra* notes 19, 24 and their accompanying text.
176 *See supra* notes 18, 22, 36–39 and their accompanying text.
177 *See supra* notes 15, 22, 37–39 and their accompanying text.
178 *See supra* notes 16–17, 23, 28–39, 47–48 and their accompanying text.
179 *See supra* notes 84–117 and their accompanying text.
180 *See supra* notes 57, 72 and their accompanying text.
181 *See supra* notes 42–45, 49–52 and their accompanying text.
182 *See supra* note 46 and its accompanying text.

Stage 2 is the after-contract stage of bargaining, including both monitoring and renegotiation. The provision of human capital needs to be monitored; employees are monitored by management, and management is monitored by shareholders and creditors. Overly aggressive monitoring, however, discourages human capital providers from making firm-specific investments. Furthermore, balancing autonomy and monitoring is important,[183] and renegotiations are frequently necessary. Changing employment contracts is a typical form of renegotiation.[184] Financing decisions also involve an aspect of renegotiation, including the choice between debt finance or equity finance and the choice between distributing dividends or retaining earnings.[185]

Stage 3 is possibly the end-game stage between human capital providers and monetary capital providers. Legal regulation is indispensable here because serious conflicting interests will occur at this stage. Legislation needs to maintain a good balance between buyers and sellers in takeover regulations,[186] and between the *ex ante* and *ex post* incentives of the players in bankruptcy regulations.[187]

I.7.2 Legislating through Backward Induction

New legislation in the field of enterprise law not only directly affects the actual practice of the firm, but also indirectly affects the incentive bargain between the four players.[188] Therefore, if the legislature alters enterprise law in an attempt to change the practice of the firm, the new law may cause unpredictable effects to the current practice as legal reforms can change the premises of the incentive bargain.[189]

When drafting new legislation, there are two complementarities that need to be taken into account. First are the complementarities between relevant laws; particularly, substantive rules and enforcement systems

---

183 *See supra* notes 5–6, 83–84, 125, 134–136 and their accompanying text.

184 *See supra* notes 46–55 and their accompanying text.

185 *See supra* notes 81, 119–120 and their accompanying text.

186 *See supra* notes 122–125 and their accompanying text.

187 *See supra* notes 69–79 and their accompanying text.

188 If enterprise law is too restrictive for the players to make an efficient incentive bargain, affected players will push the legislature to change the law towards deregulation. This type of reformation of law is termed "demand pull legislation". *See* Shishido, *supra* note 5, at 656.

189 Unintended consequences often arise, particularly due to crisis-driven financial legislation. Inclusion of a sunset provision is useful in mitigating such legislative failures. *See* Roberta Romano, Chapter 21 in this volume.

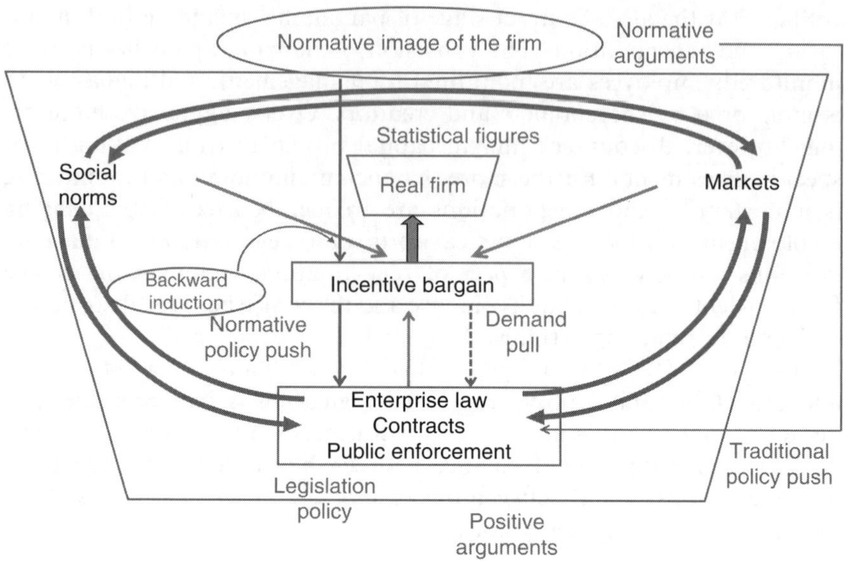

Figure I.6 Legislating through backward induction

complementarily affect reality.[190] Second are the complementarities between different infrastructures; it is important to note that enterprise law is only one of the infrastructures related to the incentive bargain and that it affects the incentive bargain complementarily with other infrastructures, such as markets and social norms.

Legislatures need to engage in backward induction simulations when trying to create law that aims to change the practice of the firm from the actual practice to a desired practice. This can be called "policy push legislation."[191] A traditional argument for policy push legislation is that enterprise law should be adapted to influence the firm to conform to what is considered desirable practice. Enterprise law itself, however, does not have the ability to recreate the firm into an entity that matches the desired normative image. If one has a normative image of the desired practice of the firm, one must also consider the incentive bargain between the four players, as the only way to alter the actual practice of the firm is by changing the bargains made between the players. Following this, one must consider what legal infrastructure is necessary to make such an incentive bargain possible (see Figure I.6).

---

190 *See* Hoshi, *supra* note 104.

191 *See* Shishido, *supra* note 5, at 656.

I.7.3 Incentive, Complementarities, and Optimal Balance

In response to the question of how to create a legal system which stimulates an efficient incentive bargain at the firm level and enhances the efficiency of the whole economy, the general answer is simple, although detailed answers on specific points become complicated. First, focus on the incentives of the indispensable capital providers of the firm and the incentive bargain between such providers. Second, take into consideration complementarities between markets, social norms, and laws that affect the incentive bargain of the firm. And third, try to maintain an optimal balance between competing interests, particularly between the autonomy of management and monitoring by shareholders.

PART I

The incentive bargain between employees and management

1. What we know (and don't know) about how employment protection law affects employment

J.H. Verkerke

1.1 INTRODUCTION

This book aims to describe and theorize "enterprise law," a concept that encompasses all of the private contracts and public regulations that affect shareholders, creditors, management, and employees as they participate in a business enterprise. Each chapter explores how markets, contracts, social norms, and legislation interact to create incentives for these various actors. The resulting incentives influence market behavior and play a crucial role in determining the optimal configuration of enterprise law. I focus in this chapter on how the constellation of legal rules known as "employment protection law" (EPL) affects the incentive bargain between workers and their employer.

Section 1.2 compares the many specific legal constraints on discharge in the US to the more general just-cause standards that prevail elsewhere in the world. Section 1.3 highlights several prominent theoretical and empirical analyses of EPL and identifies the limitations that make those studies ultimately inconclusive. Section 1.4 uses a comparatively simple principal–agent framework to illustrate the fundamental tension between incentives and insurance. Section 1.5 critically reviews some of the most intriguing arguments for adopting a general "just-cause" requirement. Section 1.6 focuses more narrowly on the descriptive flaws and analytical contradictions that undermine one scholar's behavioral economic approach to employment termination law. Finally, I conclude, in section 1.7, that existing theoretical and empirical work can offer at best tentative and equivocal conclusions – far short of the confidence that might reliably predict how legal innovations will affect worker and firm behavior or whether any specific legal change will increase or decrease social welfare.

1.2 THE LEGAL LANDSCAPE AND COMPARATIVE FIRING COSTS

Elsewhere, I have developed a detailed typology of laws regulating employment termination that distinguishes individual from collective rights, statute from common law, voluntary from involuntary termination, stringent from lax requirements of business justification for discharge, and subjective from objective legal standards.[1] For my present purposes, I simplify this classification scheme and focus, as most scholars do, on any rules that penalize employers who discharge workers without some legally adequate justification. This "firing cost" interpretation of EPL is convenient shorthand that captures the essence of most theoretical and empirical work on the subject. I will draw more precise distinctions as necessary in the discussion that follows.

According to conventional wisdom, EPL in the United States provides very modest protection and largely preserves management's prerogative to terminate unwanted workers "at will," whereas European and Japanese EPL is extremely restrictive. Most observers thus conclude that firing costs outside the US are substantially higher. These assessments contain more than a grain of truth because labor laws in most European countries and in Japan require employers to justify discharges. Under US law, by contrast, the prevailing contractual default of "employment at will" ostensibly permits employers to terminate workers for "for good cause, bad cause or no cause at all."[2] At the very highest level of abstraction, the US legal regime establishes a presumption that employment termination is permissible. In contrast, legal systems outside the US presume that employers bear a burden of justification for every discharge.

Beyond these broad differences, however, the comparative picture becomes more complicated and suggests substantial convergence of expected firing costs and termination practices. At least a quarter, and perhaps slightly more than a third, of US workers have some form of generally applicable legal right against unjust termination because they are union members, civil service employees, or protected under an individual contract.[3] Moreover federal, state, and even local laws establish a

---

1 J.H. Verkerke, *Discharge*, in LABOR AND EMPLOYMENT LAW AND ECONOMICS (Kenneth G. Dau-Schmidt, Seth Harris, & Orly Lobel eds, 2009).

2 *See, e.g., Clanton v. Cain-Sloan Co.*, 677 S.W.2d 441 (Tenn. 1984), citing *Payne v. Railroad Company*, 81 Tenn. 507 (1884).

3 See Verkerke, *Discharge, supra* note 1, at 450. This rough estimate includes the 16 percent of all workers who have civil service protection, plus 8.2 percent of private sector workers who are protected under a collective bargaining agreement, plus the 15

vast array of more specific protections against various "bad" reasons for termination. These laws prohibit firing based on race, color, sex, religion, national origin, age, disability, and various other characteristics. They also protect against retaliation for a wide variety of protected activities, including – among many other categories – whistleblowing, refusing to engage in unlawful conduct, filing a claim for or assisting in the investigation of myriad federal or state statutory violations, and engaging in collective action for "mutual aid or protection."[4]

Such patchwork protection offers far less certainty for workers than a general requirement of business justification, but the availability of these claims unquestionably raises employers' firing costs and significantly constrains their termination decisions. Although not every US employer acts as though the firm must affirmatively justify each discharge, the extensive laundry list of potential grounds for challenging a firing makes well-counseled managers quite careful to document the basis for their actions. This potential legal exposure also encourages companies to design multi-layered review processes and to establish internal grievance procedures in an effort to forestall wrongful-discharge litigation.[5]

Outside the US, national legislation ordinarily requires firms to justify employment termination, but those statutes also exclude wide swaths of workers from their coverage. Employees working for small employers or under fixed-term contracts, temporary or casual workers, and non-citizen guest workers commonly receive little or no protection against discharge. The distribution of non-covered workers varies by country, but on average, perhaps a third of all employees fall into one of these categories of contingent work. Even for covered workers, standards of justification vary widely in stringency, and damages for successful claimants tend to be much lower than in the US.[6] Nevertheless, employers of legally protected

---

percent of non-union private sector workers with a just-cause contract, plus roughly 2 percent who work under a definite term contract. The final calculation is 0.16 civil service employees plus 0.082*0.84 private sector union contracts plus 0.15*0.918*0.84 just cause contracts plus 0.02*0.918*0.84 definite term contracts equals approximately 36 percent protected. However, the estimate above for the incidence of non-union just-cause contracts extrapolates from a relatively small sample, and thus a more conservative calculation suggests that somewhere between 24.4 percent and 36 percent of all workers have a generally applicable legal right against unjust termination.

4 National Labor Relations Act § 7, 29 U.S.C. § 157 (2012).

5 *See, e.g.*, Lauren B. Edelman, Howard S. Erlanger, & John Lande, *Internal Dispute Resolution: The Transformation of Civil Rights in the Workplace*, 27 LAW & SOCIETY REV. 497–534 (1993).

6 See Jeffrey M. Hirsch, *A Comparative Perspective on Unjust Dismissal Laws, in* GLOBAL LABOR AND EMPLOYMENT LAW: REPORTS FROM LAW OFFICES

workers outside the US likely face higher expected firing costs – even though judicial and administrative damage awards tend to be smaller – because severance pay obligations and legal restrictions on termination are more certain. Several efforts to quantify the restrictiveness of labor laws in various countries have reached the same conclusion.[7]

Comparing the treatment of business-related reductions in force (RIFs) in the US and Japan illustrates both the structural difference between the legal regimes and the practical convergence of employment practices that I have hypothesized. First, even express "just-cause" contracts in the US ordinarily permit temporary layoffs or permanent discharge in connection with a RIF. And, of course, "at-will" employees enjoy no legal protection against layoff or termination caused by a business downturn. Japanese law is more restrictive. As Toru Kitagawa explains in his contribution to this volume (Chapter 2), Japanese courts demand: (1) a legitimate need; (2) efforts to avoid dismissal; (3) reasonable criteria for selection; and (4) a fair process including consultation.[8] This approach surely raises employers' costs in these situations and constrains their freedom to shed employees as readily as US employers may lay off or terminate workers in response to reduced demand. Thus, a RIF is easier to execute in the US than in Japan.

Other factors, however, make this contrast less stark than it first appears. Japanese employers have responded to these legal constraints by expanding use of non-regular workers, temporary contracts, and other arrangements that do not trigger the legal protections afforded to regular full-time workers. Thus, Japanese employers adapt to fluctuations in product demand by adjusting their use of these non-covered workers, who make up an increasing minority of all employed individuals.[9] Many commentators have also suggested that, in recent years, Japanese courts have become more lenient in assessing employers' showing of a legitimate need for a RIF.[10] Thus, Japanese law constrains employers less stringently than the formal rules would imply.

On the other side of the comparison, US federal and state laws prohibit many specific illegitimate reasons for discharge. This body of wrongful-termination law makes employers much more careful about any

---

WORLDWIDE (Samuel Estreicher ed., 2012); Samuel Estreicher, *Unjust Dismissal Laws: Some Cautionary Notes*, 33 AM. J. COMP. L. 310, 313 (1985).

[7] *See, e.g.*, World Bank, DOING BUSINESS IN 2007: HOW TO REFORM (2007).

[8] Toru Kitagawa, Chapter 2 in this volume.

[9] Masanori Kuroki, *The Deregulation of Temporary Employment and Workers' Perceptions of Job Insecurity*, 65 ILR REV. 560 (2012).

[10] *See* Kitagawa, Chapter 2 in this volume.

termination decision, including those connected with a RIF. Companies contemplating a RIF particularly fear being sued under one of the many laws barring age, sex, and race discrimination. As a result, employment attorneys in the US spend considerable time counseling employers about how to design their RIFs to prevent discrimination claims. Their advice often involves at least the first three factors Kitagawa cites as requirements under Japanese law. Similar precautions also extend to routine discharge decisions. Companies carefully document legitimate reasons for termination and use internal review procedures in an attempt to weed out unlawful motivations for firings or discipline. Moreover, an informal social norm requiring good cause for termination makes most employers eager to maintain a reputation for treating workers fairly.[11] The combined effect of these legal rules and workplace norms makes most US firms act as if every termination decision requires a solid business justification.

It would be foolish, however, to overstate the case for convergence. Instead, I offer this revisionist comparative analysis as a corrective to the facile notion that employment practices in the US and in non-US countries are as polarized as the formal differences between their employment protection laws would suggest. Despite this tendency towards convergence, we can be reasonably confident that non-US employers face higher firing costs than their US counterparts.

1.3 THEORETICAL AND EMPIRICAL ANALYSIS OF EPL

A substantial economic literature investigates how these differences in expected firing costs affect the labor market. Scholars usually ask whether EPL within a particular jurisdiction affects employment levels, unemployment, wages, or other aggregate measures of labor market performance. An early example of this approach is also one of the most frequently cited papers on the subject of EPL.[12] In this article, Edward Lazear presents a simple static model of wage determination and investigates how imposing a mandatory severance pay obligation will affect the employment

[11] *See* Edward B. Rock & Michael L. Wachter, *The Enforceability of Norms and the Employment Relationship*, 144 U. PENN. L. REV. 1913 (1996); Michael L. Wachter, *Theories of the Employment Relationship: Choosing between Norms and Contracts, in* THEORETICAL PERSPECTIVES ON WORK AND THE EMPLOYMENT RELATIONSHIP (Bruce E. Kaufman ed., 2004).

[12] Edward Lazear, *Job Security Provisions and Employment*, 105 Q. J. ECON. 699 (1990).

contract. Commentators most often cite Lazear's paper for a Coasean invariance result – "[a]ny severance pay arrangement can be offset by an optimal contract that should evolve in a competitive labor market"[13] – that Lazear treats as a mere theoretical curiosity. He acknowledges that liquidity constraints, cross-subsidies, and the possibility of "bankruptcy" are likely to eliminate the efficient equilibrium on which this invariance result depends. In addition to these acknowledged problems, Lazear's model also fails to specify the employment contract with sufficient specificity to support the "optimal contract" he derives. Lazear omits any mention of contract provisions or statutory requirements governing discharge. The model assumes, however, that workers continue employment from period to period with an exogenously fixed probability. Such an assumption is incompatible with the rules of any known employment law regime, and thus the proposed equilibrium contract could not be sustained under existing law.[14]

The paper's empirical results have fared no better than its theoretical conclusions. Lazear reports the results of cross-country comparisons purportedly showing that more stringent legal requirements for severance pay and notice before termination increase the unemployment rate and reduce employment levels, labor force participation, and hours worked. Although we should credit Lazear with pioneering a line of research that continues today, subsequent work has raised serious doubts about his empirical conclusions. A careful effort to replicate his study and investigate the robustness of its results to alternative econometric methods and model specifications failed to confirm Lazear's finding that greater severance pay and notice obligations cause adverse labor market consequences.[15]

If firing costs rise, all theoretical models predict fewer discharges and thus a reduced flow from the employed to the unemployed state. These models also agree that higher expected firing costs will decrease firms' willingness to hire, and thus they predict that EPL will depress the flow into employment. However, no model can resolve *a priori* whether the first or second of these effects on worker flows will dominate. Thus, the net effect of EPL on employment is surely an empirical question. But measuring the

---

[13] *Id.*, at 702.

[14] For a more detailed critical analysis of Lazear's famous paper, *see* Verkerke, *Discharge, supra* note 1, at 455–457, 461–462.

[15] John Addison, Paulino Teixeira, & Jean-Luc Grosso, *The Effect of Dismissals Protection on Employment: More on a Vexed Theme*, 67 SOUTHERN ECON. J. 105 (2000). *See also* the superb technical review of the early empirical literature in John Addison and Paulino Teixeira, *The Economics of Employment Protection*, 24 J. LAB. RES. 85 (2003).

stringency of different EPL regimes and modeling the likely effect of these laws on employer behavior is fraught with difficulty. It is thus perhaps unsurprising that studies designed to estimate these employment effects have produced decidedly mixed results.

More recent empirical work on the effects of EPL divides broadly into cross-country comparisons, firm-level or industry-level analyses, event studies of legal change, and efforts to identify the effects of US state laws. In each of these categories, estimates of the impact of EPL on employment range from no effect to large negative effects. James Heckman and Carmen Pagés-Serra, for example, estimate that job security mandates reduce youth employment rates in their sample of Latin American countries by nearly ten percentage points.[16] Oliver Blanchard and Justin Wolfers creatively extend the conventional causal model to investigate interactions between EPL and macroeconomic shocks.[17] They find preliminary evidence that more restrictive policies may significantly impede dynamic adjustment to those shocks. David Autor, John Donohue and Stewart Schwab study whether states suffer lower employment levels when they recognize certain legal exceptions to the US at-will rule.[18] These authors take unusual care to investigate the robustness of their results to alternative specifications and estimation methods. They find modest but statistically significant negative employment effects for states that recognize an "implied contract" exception to at-will employment, but two other categories of exceptions appear to be uncorrelated with employment levels.

Even the best of these studies, however, suffer from severe measurement and modeling issues. Errors of legal classification and interpretation have been common in cross-country comparisons.[19] Moreover, a widely used measure of legal stringency produced by the World Bank focuses solely on statutory provisions and thus dramatically understates legal constraints on termination that arise from the judicial development of common law

---

16 James J. Heckman & Carmen Pagés-Serra, *The Cost of Job Security Regulation: Evidence from Latin American Labor Markets*, 1 ECONOMIA 109 (2000).

17 Oliver Blanchard & Justin Wolfers, *The Role of Shocks and Institutions in the Rise of European Unemployment: A First Pass*, 6 J. EUROPEAN ECON. ASSOC. 45 (2008).

18 David Autor, John Donohue, & Stewart Schwab, *The Employment Consequences of Wrongful Dismissal Laws: Large, Small or None at All?*, 94 AM. ECON. REV. PAPERS & PROCEEDINGS 440 (2004); David Autor, John Donohue, & Stewart Schwab, *The Costs of Wrongful-Discharge Laws*, 88 REV. ECON. & STAT. 211 (2006).

19 *See* John T. Addison & Jean-Luc Grosso, *Job Security Provisions and Employment: Revised Estimates*, 35 INDUS. REL. 585 (1996).

rules. Nearly all cross-country comparisons also depend on the heroic assumption that the law in action matches the law on the books. Even in industrialized countries, however, statutory labor rights need not translate into effective worker protection in practice.[20]

Among the studies of US states, Autor, Donohue and Schwab most thoroughly explore alternative indices of legal stringency. Their efforts produce the best currently available estimates, but they still neglect important spillover effects. Large employers ordinarily maintain uniform human resource practices nationwide. Their contract practices and internal review of disciplinary actions often follow a single corporate policy and draw no distinction among employees in different states. Thus, more restrictive decisions in states where an employer has a significant presence may cause the company to alter its behavior nationwide.

In addition, leading decisions from a handful of influential jurisdictions give companies and their legal counsel valuable information about the future direction of the law in other jurisdictions. We can also identify broad groups of jurisdictions that pursue permissive, restrictive, or centrist approaches to the judicial regulation of the employment relationship. Most existing empirical studies, however, rely on classifications that use "on/off" coding for each category of legal protection – or more rarely "broad/narrow/off" categories. Finally, many existing coding schemes equate jurisdictions that have not spoken about a particular doctrinal innovation with those that have considered and rejected that same theory of liability. An employment attorney who advised clients without attending to this distinction would surely be guilty of legal malpractice. Pooling these two groups of states for the purposes of estimation grossly mismeasures the prevailing legal standard.

It is difficult to say whether the combined effect of these measurement and modeling problems tends to bias estimates of the employment effects of EPL upward or downward. Of course, randomly distributed measurement error would bias estimated coefficients towards zero. But the misclassification of legal decisions and the direction of spillover effects could be systematically related to the underlying pattern of EPL stringency and employment outcomes. Non-random measurement errors might inflate some estimated coefficients and reduce others. We thus should treat even the best of the existing estimates as highly provisional indicators that are subject to significant doubt and residual uncertainty.

These inconclusive empirical results have caused many commentators

---

[20] *See, e.g.*, Alvaro Santos, *Labor Flexibility, Legal Reform, and Economic Development*, 50 VA. J. INT. L. 43 (2009).

to rely instead on theoretical arguments grounded in empirical speculation. In order to understand these arguments, we must first shift our focus from estimating the effects of EPL on aggregate labor market variables to analyzing the incentive bargain between workers and firms.

1.4 REFRAMING THE ECONOMIC ANALYSIS OF EPL

So what is the correct economic approach to this issue? The theory of principal–agent relationships offers a useful theoretical starting point. An employer, as principal, wishes to design incentives that will induce employees, as agents, to perform in a way that maximizes the company's profit from the enterprise. Performance is costly for the employees. Managers can observe employees' level of effort only imperfectly and at some cost. More complicated versions of this basic model incorporate additional features such as asymmetric information about employee skill, exogenous shocks to productivity and demand, or complex strategic interactions between internal and external labor markets.[21]

To analyze EPL, however, a comparatively simple approach illuminates the most significant influences on worker and firm behavior. Economic analysts routinely understand involuntary termination as a penalty that employers use to deter employees from shirking. Management spends resources to monitor employee performance and terminates those workers who fall short of some standard of effort or quality. In reaction to the threat of discharge, employees work harder in order to retain their job. Legal protection against discharge – whether imposed by statute or pursuant to a contract – constrains these termination decisions. Severance pay requirements impose a direct cost on every discharge. And protecting workers against termination without cause forces employers to bear the cost of justifying challenged decisions before a third-party adjudicator. Thus, EPL in any form increases employers' firing costs and offers workers a form of "insurance" against termination.

According to this analysis, EPL interferes with employers' ability to police shirking. Like any insurance policy, these legal restrictions potentially give rise to a problem of moral hazard among protected workers. How then could laws that mandate firing constraints ever do anything other than impair labor market efficiency? The scholarly debate over

---

21 *See, e.g.*, Gary Charness, Peter Kuhn, & Marie Claire Villeval, *Competition and the Ratchet Effect*, 29 J. Lab. Econ. 513 (2011).

"just-cause" protection in the US has produced a rich collection of proposed answers to this question.

1.5 THE "JUST-CAUSE" DEBATE IN THE US

Academic commentators have felled forests and spilled oceans of ink debating whether lawmakers should abandon the prevailing employment-at-will default and adopt instead a legal rule that requires employers to justify every employment termination decision. Scholars have shown similar industry theorizing market failures that afflict employment contract formation. I have engaged many of these theories in prior work,[22] but a few examples will illustrate why these creative speculations are a dubious guide for making legal policy.

I can still recall the excitement I felt when I first encountered the idea that asymmetric information about worker quality might justify imposing legal constraints on employment termination. One version of this argument hinges on the idea that, in an at-will regime, job applicants who seek just-cause protection signal to employers that they value insurance against termination more than those who remain silent and accept the at-will default.[23] Workers have private information about their skills and abilities and may also vary in their tendency to shirk. Employers thus may worry that someone who wishes to opt out of the default will perform poorly. Anticipating this "bad worker signal," employment applicants are unwilling to negotiate for job security, even if its value to them far exceeds the cost employers would incur to provide that legal protection. In theory at least, the resulting market failure could justify adopting a mandatory rule requiring just cause for termination.

This clever signaling argument resonates with our common intuition that a job applicant should put his or her best foot forward and scrupulously avoid doing anything from which an employer might infer a lack of skill or motivation. Despite its intuitive plausibility, however, widespread employment practices raise doubts about the signaling story's practical

---

[22] *See* J. Hoult Verkerke, *An Empirical Perspective on Indefinite Term Employment Contracts: Resolving the Just Cause Debate*, 1995 Wisc. L. Rev. 837; J.H. Verkerke, *Employment Contract Law, in* The New Palgrave Dictionary of Economics and the Law (1998); J.H. Verkerke, *The Story of Woolley v. Hoffmann-La Roche: Finding a Way to Enforce Employee Handbook Promises, in* Employment Law Stories (Samuel Estreicher & Gillian Lester eds, 2007).

[23] For a more detailed discussion of this argument, *see* Verkerke, *Empirical Perspective, supra* note 22, at 902–905.

significance. For reasons of administrative convenience, firms routinely maintain standardized and identical terms of employment for all but their senior executive management. Thus, employers' need for uniformity rather than workers' fears about signaling probably explain why terms governing discharge only rarely become the subject of individual negotiation.

Nevertheless, asymmetric information might still give rise to a problem of adverse selection.[24] According to this argument, companies that offer better job security terms will tend to attract workers who particularly value legal protection against discharge. If these workers are more likely to be "lemons," as the bad-worker-signaling argument presumed, then firms will hesitate to offer just-cause protection in the first place. Once again, a market failure could prevent employees from receiving the job security that they value. However, the available empirical evidence casts doubt on this theoretical speculation. Almost all union workers enjoy a form of just-cause protection and still maintain levels of productivity that equal or exceed non-union, at-will employees. Even in industries like construction, in which union and non-union firms compete for work and for employees, the available empirical evidence shows no signs of adverse selection against companies that offer greater job security. Moreover, a modest fraction of private employers voluntarily offer legally enforceable just-cause protection evidently without suffering the predicted productivity penalty.[25] In the absence of empirical confirmation that fears of adverse selection deter employers from offering better job security terms, the case for legal change is weak.

Other theoretical speculations fare no better when we examine their empirical implications closely. In some cases, the problem is symmetric and thus yields no clear prediction about behavior. The bad-worker-signaling argument already considered above, for example, has a counterpart bad-employer-signaling problem that could make firms reluctant to refuse an applicant's request for just-cause protection because doing so would signal that the firm wants the freedom to discharge workers for arbitrary reasons. Signaling thus might impede or facilitate employees' efforts to contract for job security. Similarly, some have argued that workers are unduly optimistic in assessing the risk of unjust discharge.[26] This excessive optimism could depress demand for contractual job security. But the very same optimism would lead workers to underestimate the likelihood that

---

[24] David I. Levine, *Just-Cause Employment Policies in the Presence of Worker Adverse Selection*, 9 J. Lab. Econ. 294 (1991).

[25] *See* Verkerke, *Empirical Perspective, supra* note 22.

[26] For more detailed discussion, see *id.*, at 898–902.

their own job performance might justify a future termination, and thus those same workers would tend to overvalue legally enforceable just-cause protection. It is impossible to determine *a priori* which of these misperceptions of risk will dominate.

My empirical study of employment contract practices confirms that at-will contracts predominate in the private sector workplace.[27] This observation arguably reveals the preferences of market participants and establishes a prima facie case for adopting the at-will rule as a majoritarian default. As I acknowledge in that article, however, lack of information about prevailing legal rules could distort workers' choices. If workers mistakenly assume that they enjoy just-cause protection, for example, they will perceive no need to demand contract terms requiring good cause for termination. Even more perniciously, employers' informal assurances might mislead workers into believing that they have a legal right to challenge any unjust discharge decision.

In response to this latter problem, I proposed that courts should protect workers – who might otherwise misunderstand informal assurances of job security – by construing any ambiguity against the employer.[28] Such a "legal-information-forcing" default rule places a duty on the comparatively sophisticated employer to clarify the terms of employment for the benefit of workers who will ordinarily be far less legally sophisticated than the firm that employs them. Indeed, most US courts already require employers to bear the burden of clarifying any ambiguous terms governing discharge.[29] This information-forcing approach particularly encourages firms to use clear written disclaimers to confirm employees' at-will status. In my sample of employers, for example, express at-will contracts were roughly three times more common than any other terms governing discharge. Under an information-forcing rule, employers thus confirm an at-will relationship by bearing the relatively small cost of clarifying workers' legal status.

Subsequent work confirms that the optimal legal policy for employment contracts may depend on how the law affects workers' beliefs about job security. In a now widely cited pair of articles, Pauline Kim presents survey results tending to show that individual workers are poorly informed about their legal rights upon termination.[30] Her subjects overwhelmingly assume

---

27 *Id.*, at 867.

28 *Id.*, at 889–890.

29 For further elaboration of this descriptive story, *see* Verkerke, *The Story of Woolley, supra* note 22.

30 Pauline Kim, *Bargaining With Imperfect Information: A Study of Worker Perceptions of Legal Protection in an At-Will World*, 83 CORNELL L. REV. 105

that they enjoy much broader protection against arbitrary termination decisions than the prevailing legal rules provide. Although Kim identifies an important fact about employee beliefs, she acknowledges that workers will likely struggle to draw a distinction between the constraints of legal rules and the force of informal social norms that also constrain employer behavior.[31]

Other scholars reinforce the importance of workplace norms and question the value of legal protection against discharge. As we have already seen, Edward Rock and Michael Wachter argue that an informal just-cause norm exists in non-union workplaces.[32] Workers and firms use this social norm to solve a challenging contracting problem at the lowest possible cost. Because employers find it difficult and costly to verify to a third-party decision maker that a good reason supports each termination, the informal just-cause norm allows firms and workers in an internal labor market to police their own implicit bargain using the tools of repeat play and reputation.

As I suggested earlier, legal policymakers might try to remedy workers' chronic optimism about their legal rights by requiring employers to bear the burden of clarifying the terms governing discharge. Kim's study also investigates the most common method used to convey this information – contractual confirmations of at-will status – and finds that these disclaimers do nothing to alleviate her subjects' misconceptions.[33] The design of Kim's survey, however, raises doubt about the significance of this finding. Her survey instrument asked participants whether they would have legal protection against discharge in each of several scenarios. It then instructed them to read hypothetical contract language confirming the subjects' at-will status. Finally, the survey asked them to evaluate the same scenarios again. This within-subjects comparison cannot rule out the possibility that study participants ignored the simulated disclaimer and responded instead to the equivalence of the pre- and post-disclaimer scenarios.

Assuming for the sake of argument that disclaimers fail to alleviate workers' legal misconceptions, we should also consider what benefits would flow from acquiring and processing more information about the contract terms governing discharge. Does the expected value of formal legal protections make those terms worth considering carefully? As Jesse Rudy has argued, employees may be rationally ignorant about discharge

---

(1997); Pauline Kim, *Norms, Learning, and Law: Explaining the Influences on Workers' Legal Knowledge*, 1999 Ill. L. Rev. 447.

31 Kim, *Norms*, *supra* note 30.

32 Rock & Wachter, *Enforceability of Norms, supra* note 11.

33 Kim, *Imperfect Information, supra* note 30.

terms because the odds of suffering an unjust termination and being able to secure counsel, prove a wrongful termination, and recover damages for that discharge, are extremely remote.[34] The existence of many specific legal protections against termination for bad reasons – such as discrimination, whistleblowing, and the like – further vitiates the marginal value of a more general right to challenge an unjust discharge. If this assessment of their situation is accurate, then workers have little reason to focus on legally enforceable just-cause protection.

Far from making the choice of legal rule irrelevant, however, this argument offers a potential explanation for the prevalence of express at-will contracts. Employers' behavior implies a strong desire to avoid the cost of defending contractual discharge claims, even if they ultimately expect to prevail or to settle the vast majority of those claims for nuisance value. We cannot know for certain whether a fully informed worker would place a value on a general just-cause term greater than the cost an employer incurs to offer that protection. Nevertheless, all of the law firms in my sample contracted expressly for an at-will relationship with all of their employees. Although far from conclusive, this empirical pattern suggests that even attorneys – who are presumably the most knowledgeable and sophisticated of all employees concerning both contract terms and background rules – acquiesce in their employers' preference for an at-will relationship.

1.6 AN UNSUCCESSFUL BEHAVIORAL TURN

During the last two decades, many scholars have applied the insights of cognitive psychologists and behavioral economists to legal policy analysis. Cass Sunstein, one of the foremost proponents of "behavioral law and economics," has brought this approach to the debate over the employment-at-will doctrine.[35] Sunstein's article draws on key findings from the behavioral literature concerning loss aversion, bounded rationality, optimism bias, reciprocal fairness, framing effects, status quo bias, and the endowment effect. He argues that a behavioral perspective corrects the "many blunders" to which "traditional understandings of employee behavior and employment law" are prone.[36] Although space constraints

---

[34] Jesse Rudy, *What They Don't Know Won't Hurt Them: Defending Employment-At-Will in Light of Findings that Employees Believe They Possess Just Cause Protection*, 23 BERKLEY J. EMP. & LAB. L. 307 (2002).

[35] Cass R. Sunstein, *Human Behavior and the Law of Work*, 87 VA. L. REV. 205 (2001).

[36] *Id.*, at 206.

prevent me from offering a detailed critique of Sunstein's analysis here, a couple of examples will illustrate why his behavioral turn sheds surprisingly little light on the law of discharge.

First, any effort to justify or criticize existing employment law doctrine requires an accurate description of that complex body of law. Sunstein relies heavily on Stewart Schwab's article defending a "life-cycle just cause" default rule.[37] Schwab argues that courts tend to protect late-career employees from opportunistic firings (and recent hires who reasonably rely on a job offer) while leaving mid-career workers subject to at-will termination.[38] Schwab also argues that this life-cycle just-cause default is a normatively desirable remedy for the danger of opportunism that plagues career employment relationships in internal labor markets. I have demonstrated elsewhere, however, that Schwab's descriptive account relies on a handful of judicial decisions that are unrepresentative of the broader pattern of employment contract law.[39] Sunstein hopefully asserts that we can see "an implicit behavioral foundation" for innovations found in "a number of [good faith and fair dealing] cases."[40] Like Schwab, however, he succumbs to a form of confirmation bias. The broader pattern of judicial decisions contradicts these speculative theories and thus renders suspect Sunstein's project of relating his behavioral theories to contemporary judicial developments.

A second example shows how Sunstein's approach overstates the force of behavioral arguments and selectively ignores inconvenient empirical facts. Sunstein firmly embraces Pauline Kim's finding that "workers [wrongly] believe that they have legal protection against arbitrary discharge."[41] He also claims that "if for-cause protection is initially given to the employee, it is reasonable to predict that the employee will demand more to relinquish job security than he would be willing to pay to obtain it in the first instance." According to this endowment effect theory, switching the default rule from at-will to just-cause would likely alter the labor market equilibrium contract. Sunstein concludes: "Under the conventional view, the default rule does not matter . . . [T]he conventional view is wrong, and a behavioral approach does much better."[42]

Sunstein's story ultimately founders, however, because it neglects an

---

37 *Id.*, at 216–217.

38 Stewart J. Schwab, *Life-Cycle Justice: Accommodating Just Cause and Employment At Will*, 92 MICH. L. REV. 8 (1993).

39 Verkerke, *Empirical Perspective, supra* note 22, at 844–862.

40 Sunstein, *supra* note 35, at 217.

41 *Id.*, at 231.

42 *Id.*, at 219.

important empirical fact about contemporary employment contract practices. My prior work demonstrates that an express at-will contract governs the overwhelming majority of employment relationships. According to Kim's survey results, an even greater majority of workers believe that they enjoy broad legal protection against termination without good cause. The logic of the endowment effect turns not on the law itself but rather on how workers perceive their legal rights. Kim's findings, on which Sunstein relies heavily, imply that workers already believe that they are endowed with a robust legal right against unjust termination. It is this perception rather than the prevailing at-will default that should determine their willingness to accept an express term disclaiming just-cause protection and confirming their at-will status. However, Sunstein's endowment effect argument proceeds as if workers instead were perfectly informed about their lack of legally enforceable job security. My study shows that they routinely waive the legal protection that Kim's results suggest they wrongly believe they have. On this interpretation of the evidence, any alleged endowment effect appears to have little or no effect on workers' willingness to accept an at-will contract. Thus, shifting the default rule would do no more than reinforce the existing tendency of employers to contract expressly for an at-will relationship.

Sunstein's behavioral analysis undoubtedly offers useful insights and some valuable correctives for the most strident defenders of a neoclassical approach to analyzing the employment relationship. A promising avenue for future research would be to explore whether integrating existing knowledge and behavioral theory in a more disciplined way could shed new light on old controversies. For example, I suspect that applying the literature on reciprocal fairness might be far more productive than relying on the comparatively controversial endowment effect.[43] Sunstein ultimately proposes that courts should adopt a rule of construction identical to the legal-information-forcing default that I discussed above. And he suggests that some jurisdictions should consider experimenting with a

---

[43] *See* Gregory Klass & Kathryn Zeiler, *Against Endowment Theory: Experimental Economics and Legal Scholarship*, Georgetown Public Law and Legal Theory Research Paper No. 13-013 (2013); Russell Korobkin, *Wrestling with the Endowment Effect, or How to Do Law and Economics without the Coase Theorem*, in OXFORD HANDBOOK OF BEHAVIORAL ECONOMICS AND THE LAW (Oxford University Press, forthcoming); Kathryn Zeiler & Charles R. Plott, *Exchange Asymmetries Incorrectly Interpreted as Evidence of Endowment Effect Theory and Prospect Theory?*, 97 AM. ECON. REV. 1449 (2007); Kathryn Zeiler & Charles R. Plott, *The Willingness to Pay – Willingness to Accept Gap, the "Endowment Effect," Subject Misconceptions, and Experimental Procedures for Eliciting Valuations*, 95 AM. ECON. REV. 530–545 (2005).

waivable just-cause default. Whatever the merits of these modest proposals, Sunstein's analysis of the controversy over the at-will rule falls far short of showing that traditional analysis has blundered and fallen into serious error.

1.7 CONCLUSIONS

I began this chapter by asking what we know (and do not know) about how EPL affects employment. Despite a large body of both theoretical and empirical work on the subject, scholars can offer only tentative and equivocal conclusions, or quite commonly they make bold claims that collapse on closer examination. None of this work comes close to providing legal policymakers with definitive guidance about the net social welfare effects of adopting or repealing particular employment protection laws. Indeed, our knowledge also falls short of being able to predict how legal innovations are likely to affect worker and firm behavior.

More refined coding of legal variables and more subtle modeling of spillover effects could allow us to estimate with greater confidence the employment effects of particular regulatory interventions. The rapidly maturing field of behavioral economics also may produce work that can point us toward a better understanding of how both statutory and contractual job security provisions influence the incentive bargain between employers and their employees. For the moment, however, this literature offers useful metaphors and hypotheses but no reliable basis for prescribing policy. To be sure, legal reformers in Europe and Latin America have cited empirical studies in support of calls for more flexible labor market policies. But political influences predominate, and the pattern of EPL adoption around the world almost surely owes more to path-dependency than to any meaningful economic analysis of its effects.[44]

---

44 *See* Björn Brügeman, *Employment Protection: Tough to Scrap or Tough to Get?* 117 Econ. J. F386 (2007).

2. Complementarity among the abusive dismissal rule, company community norms, and an illiquid external labor market: transformation of directors' fiduciary duty under Japanese corporate law

Toru Kitagawa*

2.1 INTRODUCTION

Decisions on whether to dismiss employees involve not only negotiations between management and employees but also, to a large extent, negotiations between management and shareholders. When a company experiences a downturn in earnings, its management often faces a choice about whether to pay dividends to shareholders by laying off employees or place precedence on maintaining employment at the cost of reducing dividends to shareholders. Even companies with strong earnings may lay off workers in conjunction with proactive restructuring undertaken at the behest of shareholders. When companies make such business decisions, on what norms do they base their decisions? This chapter discusses from a comparative law standpoint differences in Japanese and US norms underlying management decision-making vis-à-vis these issues.

As a rule, employers in the US can freely dismiss employees based on business necessity in accordance with the employment-at-will doctrine. In Japan, employee dismissal is substantially restricted by case law dating back to the 1970s.

Meanwhile, fiduciary duty rules have an important function in both

* This work was supported by a Grant-in-Aid (2009-2010 academic year) from Seikei University.

Japan and the US as a code of conduct for corporate directors in pursuit of maximizing shareholder value. In other words, directors in both countries have a duty to maximize shareholder value. They may not subordinate shareholders' interests to other stakeholders' interests. Business decisions that prioritize maintaining employment over shareholders' interests should accordingly be impermissible even under Japanese corporate law. However, Japanese directors' fiduciary duty has been substantially transformed by the complementary effects of Japan's abusive dismissal doctrine, an illiquid external labor market, and company community norms peculiar to Japan.

Rules regarding directors' fiduciary duty under corporate law should theoretically function identically in Japan and the US, but the substance of the relevant Japanese rules has changed significantly as a result of the complementary effect of Japanese labor law, social norms, and the market environment. This change has had a major impact on how corporate management exercises discretionary authority when making business decisions.

Section 2.2 below provides an overview of the Japanese law related to employee dismissal, particularly the abusive dismissal doctrine, and analyzes its incentive effects on both human capital providers and monetary capital providers. Section 2.3 presents the hypothesis that the abusive dismissal doctrine has transformed Japanese directors' fiduciary duty to pursue maximization of shareholder value. Section 2.4 expands upon this hypothesis and suggests that the abusive dismissal doctrine's transformation of directors' fiduciary duty may have been amplified by complementarity between the abusive dismissal doctrine and Japan's social norms and labor market. Section 2.5 compares the Japanese abusive dismissal doctrine and the stakeholder statutes of the US, which are also intended to preserve jobs, particularly in terms of their influence on directors' fiduciary duty. In conclusion, section 2.6 emphasizes the significance of institutional complementarity among laws, markets, and social norms in terms of the abusive dismissal doctrine's transformative effect on directors' fiduciary duty in Japan.

2.2 DISTINCTIVE FEATURES OF JAPANESE EMPLOYEE DISMISSAL LAW

2.2.1 Abusive Dismissal Doctrine

Under Japan's Labor Standards Act, employers may freely dismiss employees (terminate indefinite employment contracts) by furnishing 30 days' advance notice of dismissal. However, the abusive dismissal doctrine established by Japanese courts in the 1970s[1] is widely regarded as a significant impediment to dismissal of regular employees.[2] The abusive dismissal doctrine holds that a dismissal is invalid[3] if it lacks objectively reasonable justification and is deemed to contravene prevailing social norms.[4]

Dismissal of employees based on no fault of their own but on the grounds of business necessity is called a "reorganizational dismissal" or "dismissal for economic reasons." Such dismissals are judged strictly under the abusive dismissal doctrine.[5] Japan has established a legal doctrine that requires reorganizational dismissals to meet four requirements (or to possess four factors[6]) to avoid invalidation as an abusive dismissal. The four factors are: (1) a legitimate need to reduce the employee headcount; (2) a duty to endeavor to avoid dismissing employees;[7] (3) rational justification in the selection of the employees to be dismissed; and (4) a fair dismissal process, including consultation with the employees subject to dismissal or their labor union.[8] With respect to the first of these factors, the only one requiring substantial judgment, Japanese courts have recently tended to be more flexible in respecting the business decisions of management in response to prevailing circumstances.[9] The other three factors, however, are now subject to greater judicial scrutiny than in the past,

---

1 The Nihon Shokuen Co. case, 29 MINSHU 456 (Sup. Ct., Apr. 25, 1975).

2 The abusive dismissal doctrine is now codified in Article 16 of the Labor Contract Act (enacted 2007).

3 While in many other countries unjust dismissal results in the payment of damages, employers in Japan are obliged not only to pay back wages in full but also to reinstate the dismissed employees, as the dismissal is invalid. TAKASHI ARAKI, LABOR AND EMPLOYMENT LAW IN JAPAN 27 (2002).

4 The Kochi Hoso Co. case, 268 ROHAN 17 (Sup. Ct., Jan. 31, 1977).

5 *See* KAZUO SUGENO (translated by Leo Kanowitz), JAPANESE EMPLOYMENT AND LABOR LAW 486 (2002); ARAKI, *supra* note 3, at 25.

6 When the four requirements for reorganizational dismissal are construed as four factors, courts may consider the elements in aggregate when determining the legality of a reorganizational dismissal. This interpretation thus serves to ease restrictions on dismissal in comparison to when the four factors are construed as requirements that must all be met to avoid invalidation of a dismissal. *See* ARAKI, *supra* note 3, at 26.

7 For example, reduction in overtime, reduction in mid-term recruitment, implementation of transfer or farming out, non-renewal of fixed-term contracts, curtailment of regular hiring, reduction in salaries of executives and managers, temporary stoppage of operation with reduced pay, and solicitation of voluntary retirement. *See* Araki, *supra* note 3, at 26.

8 *See* The Toyo Sanso Co. case, 30 ROMINSHU 1002 (Tokyo High Ct., Oct. 29, 1979).

9 *See* The National Westminster Bank case (3rd Provisional Disposition), 782 ROHAN 23 (Tokyo District Court, January 21, 2000); Takashi Araki, *Corporate*

according to some labor law practitioners. On balance, the reorganizational dismissal doctrine's constraint on corporate management's prerogative to dismiss employees remains unchanged.

The US has adopted the employment-at-will doctrine with respect to employee dismissal. Employers in almost every state can freely dismiss employees on the grounds of business necessity.[10] The employment-at-will doctrine is predicated on a liquid external labor market. In Japan, by contrast, employers cannot easily dismiss employees for business reasons due to the judicially established doctrine of abusive dismissal, as explained above. While Japanese regular employees have a high level of job security, a liquid external labor market for regular employees has yet to develop in Japan.[11]

2.2.2 Incentive Effects of Abusive Dismissal Doctrine

Japan's abusive dismissal doctrine has a wide range of incentive effects on all four players: management, employees, shareholders, and creditors.[12] From management's point of view, the abusive dismissal doctrine means that headcounts and labor costs are fixed once a company employs regular workers. To compensate for being unable to adjust regular-employee headcounts, management has an incentive to react to changes in economic conditions by adjusting wages[13] or working hours, or by exercising their broad prerogative to change employees' working conditions through such

---

Governance Reforms, Labor Law Developments, and the Future of Japan's Practice-Dependent Stakeholder Model, 2-1 JAPAN LABOR REVIEW 26, 38 (2005).

[10] *But see* J.H. Verkerke, Chapter 1 in this volume (arguing that although business-related reductions in workforce in the US are easier to execute than the same action in Japan, patchwork protection against "bad" reasons for termination by federal, state, and local laws raises employers' firing costs and significantly constrains their termination decisions). *See also* Jeffrey M. Hirsch, *A Comparative Perspective on Unjust Dismissal Laws* (Working Paper 2006).

[11] In terms of distribution of the burden of worker dislocation, the Japanese and US systems are polar opposites. The British, German, and Swedish systems lie between the US and Japan's. *See* Clyde W. Summers, *Worker Dislocation: Who Bears The Burden? A Comparative Study of Social Value in Five Countries*, 70 NOTRE DAME L. REV. 1033, 1058 (1994–1995).

[12] The following analysis of incentive effects is based on Takashi Toichi, *Kaikoken Ranyo Hori no Motarasu Insenthibu Koka to Hasei Mondai* [*Incentive Effects of the Abusive Dismissal Doctrine and Their Spill-over Effects*] *in* "KIGYO HO" KAIKAKU NO RONRI [Logics of "Enterprise Law" Reform] 59, 66–74 (Zenichi Shishido ed., 2011).

[13] The bonus system is a typical scheme used to adjust labor costs in response to market fluctuations. More than 20 percent of employees' wages have typically been paid as bonuses (i.e., variable costs). *See* ARAKI, *supra* note 3, at 74.

means as workplace reassignment and secondment.[14] In this sense, management is able to flexibly utilize its own intracompany[15] and intragroup labor markets.[16] Even the courts, which have historically taken a hardline stance toward dismissal of regular employees, tend to be relatively permissive with respect to the legal validity of employers' reassignment and secondment of regular employees without the employees' prior consent.[17]

It is also argued that the abusive dismissal doctrine gives management an incentive to invest in educating and training their employees, not only for firm-specific skills but also for general skills. Some scholars disagree, however, arguing that the abusive dismissal doctrine of itself is unlikely to induce employers to invest in their workforces' human capital. In these scholars' view, the absence of an external labor market is what gives employers such an incentive.[18]

From the employees' point of view, the abusive dismissal doctrine means long-term employment protection. It is widely believed that such employment protection enhances employees' incentive to build firm-specific human capital by deterring management's opportunistic behaviors such as using dismissal as a threat to induce employee acceptance of retroactive wage cuts.[19] Some scholars disagree, however, arguing that courts cannot retrospectively verify that workers are assured of receiving wages commensurate with their efforts, and that employees protected by the abusive dismissal doctrine have no incentive to exert their best efforts because their jobs are protected regardless.[20]

---

[14] *See* Ronald J. Gilson & Mark J. Roe, *Lifetime Employment: Labor Peace and the Evolution of Japanese Corporate Governance*, 99 COLUM. L. REV. 508 (1999).

[15] *See* Sanford M. Jacoby, THE EMBEDDED CORPORATION: CORPORATE GOVERNANCE AND EMPLOYMENT RELATIONS IN JAPAN AND THE UNITED STATES 21–40 (2005).

[16] A major reason why Japanese companies have many wholly owned subsidiaries is because it acts as an incentive for management to differentiate wage standards between the parent company and its subsidiaries. Management also has an incentive to choose M&A schemes that enable them to select which employees are to be transferred, such as company splits. To protect employee interests in the event of a company split, the Act on the Succession to Labor Contracts upon Company Split was enacted with effect from April 1, 2001. *See* ARAKI, *supra* note 3, at 39.

[17] *See e.g.*, The Toa Paint Co. case, 1198 Hanrei Jiho 149 (Sup. Ct. July 14, 1986). *See also* ARAKI, *supra* note 3, at 132.

[18] *See* Gilson & Roe, *supra* note 14, at 540.

[19] *See* Hiroyuki Chuma, *"Kaikoken Ranyo Hori" no Keizai Bunseki* [*Economic Analysis of the "Doctrine of Abusive Dismissal"*], *in* KAISHAHO NO KEIZAIGAKU [THE ECONOMICS OF CORPORATE LAW] 425, 444 (Yoshiro Miwa et al. eds, 1998).

[20] *See* Atsushi Tsuneki & Manabu Matsunaka, *Labor Relations and Labor Law in Japan*, 20 PAC. RIM L. & POL'Y J. 529, 557 (2011).

While this debate remains ongoing, the rapid growth in the number of non-regular employees (i.e., workers other than permanent full-time employees)[21] in combination with limited employment opportunities for new graduates has created a major social problem in recent years.[22] Large distortions have arisen in the overall labor market, including in regard to non-regular workers and inactive jobseekers.[23] Japanese dismissal law, which was developed based on the premise of single-employer lifetime employment, is now being called into question.[24]

From the shareholders' point of view, the abusive dismissal doctrine poses a risk of reducing firm value and increasing the cost of merger and acquisition (M&A) transactions.[25] It deters corporate raiders and potential shareholders from acquiring companies with surplus workers.

Finally, from the creditors' point of view, the abusive dismissal doctrine may have a negative effect on debt repayment. It gives creditors an incentive to evaluate debtor companies' debt service capacity conservatively by assuming that current labor costs are a given.

2.3 TRANSFORMATION OF DIRECTORS' FIDUCIARY DUTY

2.3.1 Directors' Fiduciary Duty and Principle of Maximization of Shareholder Value

In the US, corporate directors owe a fiduciary duty to shareholders. The US directors' code of conduct is clearly aimed at the maximization of shareholder value.

Japan's Companies Act likewise imposes a fiduciary duty on directors, but it merely stipulates that, "Directors shall perform their duties for the Stock Company in a loyal manner." However, recent court

---

21 In 2006, the proportion of non-regular workers in non-agricultural sectors was 30.3 percent. *See* TADASHI A. HANAMI & FUMITO KOYAMA, LABOUR LAW IN JAPAN 71 (2011).

22 *See* Tsuneki & Matsunaka, *supra* note 20, at 558.

23 "In Japan, the heavy burden of dislocation and unemployment is placed on those outside the lifetime employment system – the temporary and part-time employees who serve as a buffer to protect the job security of lifetime employees." Summers, *supra* note 11, at 1059.

24 *See* ARAKI, *supra* note 3, at 36.

25 The abusive dismissal doctrine may, however, benefit shareholder interests by making management and controlling shareholders' commitment to lifetime employment credible and sustaining a good relationship between labor and management.

decisions[26] and influential commentators[27] have interpreted the phrase "for the Stock Company" to mean "for the shareholders." A company is a for-profit legal person whose purpose is to distribute profits to its owners, and directors owe a fiduciary duty to the company to realize the company's purpose. Their fiduciary duty can therefore be construed as a fiduciary duty to the company's shareholders.[28] Accordingly, directors' fiduciary duty means that directors' code of conduct is maximization of shareholder value in both Japan and the US.

2.3.2 Transformation of Directors' Fiduciary Duty in Japan

Under Japanese corporate law, directors' fiduciary duty functions as a legal standard that promotes maximization of shareholder value, but from the broader standpoint of enterprise law, including labor law, the abusive dismissal doctrine's existence substantially transforms fiduciary duty under corporate law.

Economists have conducted a number of empirical research studies on the question of whether companies undergoing a downturn in earnings maintain or reduce shareholder dividends or employee headcounts. A recent study shows that most "traditional Japanese companies" reduce shareholder dividends while maintaining employment, while "revolutionary Japanese companies" are more likely to reduce both dividends and employment.[29] Norms underlying management decision-making are discussed below from the standpoint of how differences in legal systems

---

[26] *See* The Nireko Co. case, 1219 KINYU SHOJI HANREI [The Financial and Business Law Precedents] 8 (Tokyo High Ct., June 15, 2005); The Rex Holdings Shareholder Damage Suit case, 1363 KINYU SHOJI HANREI [The Financial and Business Law Precedents] 48 (Tokyo District Ct., Feb. 18, 2011).

[27] *See* MISAO TATSUTA, KAISHA HO TAIYO [BUSINESS CORPORATION LAW] 74 (2007); KENJIRO EGASHIRA, KABUSHIKI KAISHA HO [LAWS OF STOCK CORPORATIONS] 20 (4th ed. 2011).

[28] This is based on Article 105(2) of the Companies Act, which states that provisions in articles of incorporation that do not entirely grant shareholders the right to receive dividends of earned surplus and the right to receive distributions of residual assets are invalid. *See* Seiichi Ochiai, *Kigyo Ho no Mokuteki: Kabunushi Rieki Saidaika Gensoku no Kento* [*The Object of Corporate Law: Consideration of the Shareholder Value Maximization Rule*], *in* KIGYO TO HO (GENDAI NO HO 7) [ENTERPRISE AND LAW (CONTEMPORARY LAWS, vol. 7)] 23 (Masahiko Iwamura et al. eds, 1998).

[29] *See* Katsuyuki Kubo, *Haito Seisaku to Koyo Chosei* [*Dividend Policy and Employment Adjustment*], *in* NIHON NO COPORETO GABANANSU [JAPANESE CORPORATE GOVERNANCE] 409, 434 (Hideaki Miyajima ed., 2011). In this paper, "revolutionary Japanese companies" are defined as companies that have a high

influence whether management prioritizes shareholders over employees or vice versa.

US corporate management's answer to this question is clear-cut. One reason for this clarity is that the US legal system allows companies to freely dismiss employees. A second reason is that directors owe shareholders a fiduciary duty to pursue maximization of shareholder value. For Japanese corporate management (directors), this question is more difficult to answer, reflecting the fact that, although Japanese directors ow shareholders a fiduciary duty under the Companies Act, the labor law doctrine of abusive dismissal severely restricts dismissal of regular employees.

The abusive dismissal doctrine is undoubtedly a constraint on Japanese corporate management's free exercise of business judgment on reducing workforce. However, it is a misconception to regard the abusive dismissal doctrine as a one-sided constraint on management's discretionary authority. When management and shareholders' respective interests conflict, management can gain a bargaining-power advantage over shareholders by allying with employees under the pretext of the abusive dismissal doctrine.[30] When faced with shareholder demands for increased dividends, management can use the abusive dismissal doctrine as justification for business decisions that compromise shareholders' interests. In this respect, the abusive dismissal doctrine can be construed as paradoxically contributing to the expansion of management's discretionary authority in making business decisions.

2.4 COMPLEMENTARITY BETWEEN SOCIAL NORMS AND EXTERNAL LABOR MARKET

It would be misleading to claim that it is the abusive dismissal doctrine alone that has transformed directors' fiduciary duty by expanding management's discretionary authority. More accurately, the abusive dismissal doctrine contributed to the expansion of management's discretionary authority in concert with two other contributing factors. The first is a Japanese company community norm that places priority on maintaining employment.[31] The second is Japan's illiquid external labor market.

The case law doctrine related to abusive dismissal is widely regarded

---

percentage of foreign-ownership and have reformed their boards of directors; "traditional Japanese companies" are defined as all other companies.

[30] *See* Marco Pagano & Paolo Volpin, *Managers, Workers, and Corporate Control*, 60 J. FIN. 841 (2005).

[31] On company community, *see* Shishido, "Introduction" to this volume.

as having been predicated on the long-standing Japanese employment practice known as lifetime employment.[32] Even today, when corporate management is faced with the choice between maintaining dividends and maintaining employment, business decisions that give precedence to maintaining employment have wide social acceptance.[33] This acceptance reflects not only the legal restrictions on dismissal, but also a deeply rooted company community norm that places utmost priority on preserving employee jobs.

Another major reason that Japanese corporate management is reluctant to dismiss employees is that human capital is not easily sourced externally. In other words, Japan's external labor market is relatively illiquid. Based on the assumption of lifetime employment, Japanese companies have historically invested in on-the-job training while workers have likewise actively invested in building firm-specific human capital; consequently. formation of an external labor market has been impeded to some extent. Mutual complementarity is also evident as between the abusive dismissal doctrine and the illiquid external labor market. Even within the same industry, human resources are not readily interchangeable between companies that have amassed firm-specific human capital. Japanese corporate management's reluctance to dismiss employees is more often attributable to fear of losing irreplaceable human capital than it is to the legal restrictions on dismissal.

Nonetheless, the abusive dismissal doctrine has undeniably played an important role in expanding management's discretionary authority and increasing management's bargaining power over shareholders. While overseas institutional investors who regard maximization of shareholder value as an inviolable norm may be skeptical of the importance of the aforementioned company community norm and firm-specific human capital, the assertion that legal restrictions prevent companies from laying off workers for the sake of shareholder interests, even where such companies desire to do so, is highly persuasive.

In sum, institutional complementarity between social norms and the external labor market can be observed as a derivative effect of Japanese dismissal law.

---

[32] On life-time employment, *see* ARAKI, *supra* note 3, at 18. *See also* Gilson & Roe, *supra* note 14.

[33] Government has also contributed to the establishment of the social norm concerning employment security, particularly by mandating an Employment Adjustment Allowance for employers compelled to temporarily shut down operations due to an economic downturn. *See* ARAKI, *supra* note 3, at 30.

2.5 COMPARISON OF JAPANESE ABUSIVE DISMISSAL DOCTRINE AND US STAKEHOLDER STATUTES

Even in the US, worker demands for job preservation are having an influence on directors' fiduciary duty. One example are the so-called stakeholder statutes that have been adopted by many US states.[34] However, these stakeholder statutes differ from Japan's abusive dismissal doctrine in two major respects in terms of their impact on directors' fiduciary duty.

The first difference is that stakeholder statutes regulate corporate takeovers by explicitly permitting directors to take job preservation into consideration when a company has been targeted by a hostile takeover attempt. The abusive dismissal doctrine, however, applies not only to a company's existing management but also to a prospective acquirer. It is therefore theoretically neutral with respect to takeover defense. Whether the abusive dismissal doctrine operates to the advantage of existing management or the acquirer, if either, is unclear.[35]

The second difference is that stakeholder statutes have had little effect in terms of transforming directors' fiduciary duty, largely because Delaware, the state in which most publicly traded US companies are incorporated, has not adopted a stakeholder statute. In Japan, the abusive dismissal doctrine has had a substantial nationwide transformational effect. This difference is arguably attributable to institutional complementarity among the legal system, the market, and social norms in Japan, and the absence of such complementarity in the US. In Japan, the abusive dismissal doctrine, complemented by company community norms and an illiquid external labor market, has had a strong substantive effect. The absence of such institutional complementarity in the US could account for the stakeholder statutes having a limited effect on directors' fiduciary duty.

---

34 *See* James, J. Hanks, Jr., *Playing with Fire: Nonshareholder Constituency Statutes in the 1990s*, 21 STETSON L. REV. 97 (1991); Eric W. Orts, *Beyond Shareholders: Interpreting Corporate Constituency Statutes*, 61 GEO. WASH. L. REV. 14 (1992); Roberta S. Karmel, *Implications of the Stakeholder Model*, 61 GEO. WASH. L. REV. 1156 (1993); Richard A. Booth, *Stockholders, Stakeholders, and Bagholders (or How Investor Diversification Affects Fiduciary Duty)*, 53 BUS. LAW. 429 (1998); Jonathan D. Springer, *Corporate Constituency Statutes: Hollow Hopes and False Fears*, 1999 ANN. SURV. AM. L. 85 (1999); JESSE H. CHOPER, JOHN C. COFFEE, JR., & RONALD J. GILSON, CASES AND MATERIALS ON CORPORATIONS 40–48 (7th edn 2008).

35 In practice, however, enterprise unions in Japan are almost always opposed to hostile takeover attempts and play the role of a white squire.

2.6 CONCLUSIONS

When companies are faced with a typical conflict between their shareholders' and employees' respective interests, such as a choice between maintaining employment or maintaining dividends, their management presumably makes business decisions based on legal norms. However, in such situations, Japanese and US corporate management tend to make distinctly different business decisions despite there being no substantive difference between the two countries' statutory provisions regarding directors' fiduciary duty. What accounts for this difference?

In response to this question, I have presented the hypothesis that the Japanese labor law doctrine of abusive dismissal, in concert with an illiquid external labor market and the company community norm that places priority on maintaining employment, has transformed directors' fiduciary duty and expanded management's discretionary authority.

The interrelationship between Japan's labor law doctrine of abusive dismissal and directors' fiduciary duty under the Companies Act not only offers an important case study from the standpoint of enterprise law, but it is also a very interesting example of institutional complementarity among the law, the relevant markets, and social norms.

3. The relative bargaining power of employers and unions in the global information age: a comparative analysis of the United States and Japan

Kenneth G. Dau-Schmidt and Benjamin C. Ellis

3.1 INTRODUCTION

Although implicit or explicit bargaining is a common means for resolving differences among the various stakeholders of the modern corporation, perhaps the quintessential expression of this phenomenon is collective bargaining between representatives of employees and management over the terms and conditions of employment. The resolution of disputes through private bargaining has the great benefit of being a decentralized method of problem solving in which the parties who are directly affected by the problem, and know the most about it, determine the solution. Although bargaining solutions are undoubtedly influenced by information and the parties' conceptions of "fairness," bargaining is not a detached inquiry into either "truth" or "justice." Instead, the determination of issues through bargaining is largely determined by the relative "bargaining power" of the two parties, or their ability to force the other side to accept an agreement on their terms.[1]

Law can influence the relative bargaining power of labor and management. The law can raise labor's bargaining power relative to management's by: facilitating broad organization across industries or the economy; allowing unions a broad array of economic weapons against employers such as strikes, secondary strikes, and consumer boycotts; or limiting employers'

[1] Kenneth G. Dau-Schmidt, *A Bargaining Analysis of American Labor Law and the Search for Bargaining Equity and Industrial Peace*, 91 MICH. L. REV. 419 (1992).

ability to respond to a strike by prohibiting discharges and permanent replacements.[2] Alternatively, the law might lower union bargaining power relative to that of employers by limiting employee organization and economic weapons or allowing greater employer response or economic weapons.[3] American (i.e., US) and Japanese labor laws have their roots in the same New Deal principles of the US Wagner Act; however, these laws have developed in significantly different ways that influence the parties' relative bargaining power with the adoption of the Taft–Hartley amendments in the United States and various amendments and doctrines in Japan.[4]

The rise of the global economy based on information technology has also done much to shift the relative bargaining power of labor and management. New information technology has allowed the organization of firms on a global basis for production, subcontracting, and sales. In the United States, "outsourcing" work to lower-paid foreign workers has become "good business" as well as a necessary strategy to compete with producers in lower-wage countries.[5] In this new economic environment, employers place a high premium on flexibility in production and employment, and the employment relationship is subject to the market in ways that have not previously been experienced. This decreases union bargaining power by putting downward pressure on wages and limiting the parties' ability to make long-term contractual commitments.[6]

In this chapter, we examine how the relative bargaining power of organized labor and employers has changed under the labor laws of the United States and Japan in the new global economy. In section 3.2, we discuss the economic concept of bargaining power, and how bargaining power might predictably shift between employees and employers with changes in the employment relationship. In section 3.3 we conduct a comparative analysis of the relative bargaining power of unions and employers in the United States and Japan, taking account of the differences in each country's labor laws concerning the definition of an employee, the American doctrine of exclusive representation, the permitted employee and employer weapons

---

[2] Kenneth G. Dau-Schmidt & Arthur R. Traynor, *Regulating Unions and Collective Bargaining*, *in* LABOR AND EMPLOYMENT LAW AND ECONOMICS (K.G. DAU-SCHMIDT ET AL. EDS, 2009).

[3] *Id.*

[4] THE DEVELOPING LABOR LAW: THE BOARD, THE COURTS, AND THE NATIONAL LABOR RELATIONS ACT, VOL. 1 (JOHN E. HIGGINS ED., 2006); KAZUO SUGENO, JAPANESE LABOR LAW (LEO KANOWITZ TRANS., 1992).

[5] PETER CAPPELLI, THE NEW DEAL AT WORK: MANAGING THE MARKET DRIVEN WORKFORCE 74 (1999) (hereinafter "Cappelli").

[6] Kenneth G. Dau-Schmidt, *Employment in the New Age of Trade and Technology: Implications for Labor and Employment Law*, 76 IND. L.J. 1 (2001).

in collective bargaining, and the structure of collective negotiations. In section 3.4, we discuss the general decline in union bargaining power in developed countries like the United States and Japan with the rise of information technology and the global economy and with the increased competition of labor from low-wage developing countries.

We conclude that various features of Japanese labor law, including its broader coverage, generous definition of "justifiable" collective action and restrictions on employer economic weapons, probably insure that Japanese workers will have superior bargaining power to that of similar American workers, although the context of Japanese collective bargaining on a firm by firm basis with an expectation of life-time employment with that same firm means that the Japanese workers will be less likely to engage in costly collective action. We also conclude that the rise of the global economy has decreased the importance of collective bargaining in the accommodation of employee interests in the United States and Japan, and that in Japan collective bargaining is becoming relatively less important than the complementary institution of the employees' coalition with management in determining the incentive bargain of the firm.

3.2 BARGAINING POWER

Although bargaining is a very complex phenomenon depending on the underlying cost structures, information, and strategy, economists have sought to develop simple yet useful models of collective bargaining.[7] Almost all of these models focus on bilateral negotiations between the union and an employer over the single facet of wages. Although these models are limited in scope, they offer insights into the process of collective bargaining and the concept of bargaining power that are relevant to the impact of legal doctrines and changes in economic conditions on collective bargaining.

"Bargaining power" has been defined as the ability to induce an opponent to accept an agreement on one's own terms.[8] In economic terms, a party's bargaining power depends on that party's ability to impose costs on the other side for failure to reach agreement, while minimizing the party's own costs of disagreement.[9] In collective bargaining, the union's

---

7 BRUCE E. KAUFMAN & JULIE L. HOTCHKISS, THE ECONOMICS OF LABOR MARKETS (7th edn 2006).

8 NEAL CHAMBERLAIN, A GENERAL THEORY OF ECONOMIC PROCESS 81 (1955).

9 BRUCE E. KAUFMAN & JULIE L. HOTCHKISS, *supra* note 7.

bargaining power depends on its ability to inflict costs on the employer through lost sales from a strike or other collective action, while minimizing the costs of the collective action to their membership in lost wages and jobs. The employer's bargaining power depends on its ability to minimize its costs from the employees' collective action while maximizing the costs of the collective action on the employees.

Accordingly, the parties' relative bargaining power in collective bargaining depends on economic factors such as the nature of the firm's product, the firm's technology of production, general economic conditions, the structure of bargaining, and the employees' commitment to collective action. If these factors favor the union and it has relatively greater bargaining power, the union will have a greater ability to negotiate terms and conditions of employment that favor its members. However, if these factors favor the employer and it has relatively greater bargaining power, the employer will have a greater ability to determine the terms and conditions of employment in negotiations.

However, the relative bargaining power of parties in collective bargaining is also dependent upon the laws that govern a country's system of labor relations. A government might enact legislation to impact the relative bargaining power of unions and employers in order to raise or lower negotiated wages and achieve a more equitable distribution of the proceeds from production.[10] For example, a government might limit or prohibit the use of permanent replacements if it wants to lower the potential costs of strikes to employees and raise union bargaining power and wages. Alternatively, a government might outlaw secondary boycotts to lower the unions' ability to impose costs on employers for not agreeing, and lower union bargaining power and wages. This was, in fact, one of the purposes behind the prohibition on secondary boycotts enacted in the Taft–Hartley amendments to the National Labor Relations Act (NLRA).[11] To the extent that a nation's labor laws raise or lower union bargaining power relative to employer bargaining power, such regulation will also encourage or discourage employee organizing as it raises and lowers the expected benefits of organization relative to its costs.[12] Thus, it

---

10 Kenneth G. Dau-Schmidt & Arthur R. Traynor, *supra* note 2.

11 K.G. Dau-Schmidt, M.H. Malin, R.L. Corrada, C.D. Ruiz Cameron, & C.L. Fisk, Labor Law in the Contemporary Workplace 67 (2009). A "secondary boycott" is an attempt by the union to influence the actions of the "primary employer," with whom the employees have a dispute, by exerting economic pressure on other businesses that deal with the primary employer and causing them to no longer deal with the primary employer. *Id.*

12 Kenneth G. Dau-Schmidt and Arthur R. Traynor, *supra* note 2.

is inevitable that differences in American and Japanese labor law and the recent changes in the global economy would have an impact on the relative bargaining power of labor and management in these countries.

3.3 A COMPARATIVE ANALYSIS OF THE IMPACT OF AMERICAN AND JAPANESE LABOR LAW ON THE RELATIVE BARGAINING POWER OF THE PARTIES TO COLLECTIVE BARGAINING

Despite their common heritage, there are several significant differences between American and Japanese labor law and the practice of labor relations in each country that would logically have an impact on the relative bargaining power of labor and management.

3.3.1 The Definition of "Employee"

In the United States, the NLRA uses the term "employee" to describe the people who enjoy the right to organize and bargain collectively under that statute. Although the NLRA's definition of employee includes "any employee," it expressly exempts "independent contractors," "supervisors," and employees covered by the Railway Labor Act.[13] The United States National Labor Relations Board and courts have narrowly interpreted the term "employee,"[14] broadly interpreting the exceptions,[15] and adding additional exceptions for "managerial" and "confidential" employees.[16] Under United States law, many professionals, and even employees with only minimal supervisory responsibilities, are excluded from coverage under the Act.[17]

---

13 29 U.S.C. § 152(3) (2009).

14 For employees covered by the Railway Labor Act, see 45 U.S.C § 151 (2009). The NLRA defines supervisors at 29 U.S.C. § 152(11) (2009). The independent contractor exemption was added with the Taft–Hartley Amendments of 1947, overruling *NLRB v. Hearst Publ'n, Inc.*, 322 U.S. 111, 131 (1944).

15 *NLRB v. Babcock & Wilcox Co.*, 351 U.S. 105, 113 (1956).

16 *NLRB v. Yeshiva*, 444 U.S. 672, 682 (1980). This case exempted employees who "formulate and effectuate management policies by expressing and making operative the decisions of their employer"; *Oakwood Healthcare, Inc.*, 348 N.L.R.B. 686, 694 (2006), exempted certain charge nurses under the "supervisor" exception.

17 *NLRB v. Bell Aerospace Co. Division*, 416 U.S. 267 (1974), exempted managerial employees, while *NLRB v. Hendricks County Rural Electric Membership Corp.*, 454 U.S. 170 (1981), exempted confidential employees.

In contrast, Japanese labor law covers a broader array of economically dependent people. In Japan, the term "workers" is used to describe persons protected by the Labor Union Act (LUA), Japan's primary body of labor laws. The Act defines "workers" as "those persons who live on their wages, salaries, or other equivalent income, regardless of the kind of occupation."[18] Because this standard is not particularly effective in differentiating workers from non-workers, legal commentators and courts often use a substitute standard, asking whether an individual has a "subordinate relationship to an employer."[19] A commission established by the Minister of Labor determined that identifying a worker under this definition includes two factors: "(1) the rendering of service under the direction and supervision of another party; and (2) the receipt of remuneration in return for the service rendered."[20] Sugeno identifies four factors: (1) that the persons perform indispensable work for the enterprise and that they are an essential component of the enterprise; (2) that the content of their contracts are unilaterally decided; (3) that they are supervised with regard to such matters as the date, time and hour, the place, and the method of accomplishing their work; and (4) that they are not free to accept or refuse contracts relating to their employer's business that are tendered by third persons.[21] Though supervisors are excluded from membership in certified unions, they are nonetheless considered to be "workers" under the Act.[22] Supervisors are simultaneously considered to be "employers." Additionally, temporary workers are typically not admitted to unions.[23]

Japanese labor law's broader coverage of economically dependent people favors greater union bargaining power in Japan. With greater coverage, Japanese unions would have a better opportunity to organize a larger percentage of employees in a given firm, industry, and the nation as a whole. Organizing a greater share of a given firm's workers gives the union a more credible threat that it can cease production through a strike. Greater union density also helps protect union workers from non-union competition, at least within the country's borders. With the changes in production methods wrought by the information technology in the new global economy, production is more decentralized, and more employees

---

[18] Labor Union Act, Law No. 174 of 1949.

[19] *Id.*

[20] Kazuo Sugeno, *supra* note 4, at 425.

[21] Ryuichi Yamakawa, *New Wine in Old Bottles: Employee/Independent Contractor Distinction Under Japanese Labor Law*, 21 Comp. Labor L. & Pol. J. 99, 104, 107 (1999).

[22] Kazuo Sugeno, *supra* note 4, at 426.

[23] T.A. Hanami, Labour Law and Industrial Relations in Japan 37 (1979).

work for subcontractors and exercise some degree of managerial or supervisory skill. In the United States, the narrow NLRA definition of an employee has led to an increased share of the workforce that are either excluded from coverage under the NLRA, or left working for "employers" with no economic leverage with the ultimate producer or retailer. Alternately, with increased international trade, national borders have proven less important in collective bargaining. Even if Japanese workers are protected under Japanese labor law, they must still bargain with employers who can shift production to low-wage workers overseas.

3.3.2 Exclusive Representation

A major difference between US and Japanese unions is the set of individuals the union is authorized and obligated to represent. In the United States, a union is considered the "exclusive representative" for all of the employees in the "bargaining unit" for which it has been certified.[24] This position as "exclusive representative" carries various responsibilities and rights for the union. First, the union is authorized and obligated to bargain on behalf of all employees whose positions fall within the bargaining unit, whether or not the employee is a member of the union.[25] A union that fails to fairly represent any employees in its bargaining unit is liable under federal law for any damages caused by the "failure to fairly represent."[26] However, with this responsibility comes the power of exclusive representation; no other organization may represent the unit or bargain with the employer on their behalf while the union remains certified.[27] Any other union seeking to represent a unit covered by a certified union will be in violation of NLRA section 8(b)(4)(C).[28] Furthermore, at least in states that have not passed a "right to work" law, a lawfully recognized union is free to bargain for a union security agreement, which requires the payment of union agency fees as a condition of continued employment.[29]

Conversely, Japanese unions are authorized to bargain only on behalf

---

[24] *Id.* at 103.

[25] 29 U.S.C. § 159(a) (2009).

[26] *Steele v. Louisville & Nashville R.R.*, 323 U.S. 192, 203 (1944). This case explains that the bargaining representative has "the duty to exercise fairly the power conferred upon it in behalf of all those for whom it acts, without hostile discrimination against them."

[27] *Breininger v. Sheet Metal Workers Int'l Ass'n Local Union No. 6*, 493 U.S. 67, 84 (1989).

[28] 29 U.S.C. § 158(b)(4)(C) (2009).

[29] 29 U.S.C. § 158(a)(3) (2009).

of their members.[30] Additionally, the LUA contains only a limited exclusivity provision, which provides: "When three-fourths or more of the workers of the same kind regularly employed in a particular factory or workplace come under application of a particular collective agreement, the agreement concerned shall also apply to the remaining workers of the same kind employed in the factory concerned or workplace."[31] Similarly:

> [w]hen a majority of the workers of the same kind in a particular locality come under application of a particular collective agreement, the Minister of Health, Labor, and Welfare or the prefectural governor may, at the request of either one or both of the parties to the collective agreement concerned and, pursuant to a resolution of the Labor Relations Commission, decide that the collective agreement . . . should apply to the remaining workers of the same kind employed in the same locality and to their employers.[32]

The absence of an exclusivity or appropriate bargaining unit provision in Japanese labor law allows for the possibility of plural unions. This means that, unlike in the United States, multiple organizations may arise to represent workers from a single class within a single workplace.

Exclusive representation has proven to be both a blessing and a curse for American unions. Exclusivity simplifies representation and bargaining issues and provides insulation from competitive unions entering the bargaining unit. However, the election procedure which the United States has adopted to determine representation in bargaining units has proven to be a significant burden on employee organization.[33] As a result, it is more difficult for US unions to achieve a high level of union density in an industry and "take wages out of competition." This is particularly true given Japan's rule that non-union employees in the same locality or industry are governed by the terms of relevant collective bargaining agreements if the relevant unions achieve majority or two-thirds representation. As a result, the doctrine of exclusive representation probably undermines the bargaining power of American unions in the early stages of labor organization in a region or industry, although it may enhance union bargaining power for well-established unions.

---

30 Alvin L. Goldman, Labor and Employment Law in the United States 176 (1996).

31 Labor Union Act, Law No. 174 of 1949, art. 6.

32 Labor Union Act, Law No. 174 of 1949, art. 17.

33 Kenneth G. Dau-Schmidt, *supra* note 1, at 503.

3.3.3 Employee Collective Action

In the United States, the employees' right to organize and engage in collective action to pressure their employer to address their demands and grievances is set forth in the NLRA's section 7.[34] This section of the law guarantees the employees' right to: (1) "self-organization, to form, join, or assist labor organizations;" (2) "bargain collectively through representatives of their own choosing;" and (3) "engage in other concerted activities for the purpose of collective bargaining or other mutual aid or protection."[35]

These broad rights are explicitly bounded by sections 8(b) through (g).[36] Prohibited tactics include: restraint or coercion of employees' section 7 rights; causing an employer to discriminate against an employee on the basis of his non-union status; refusal to bargain collectively and in good faith; and undertaking a "secondary boycott" aimed at inducing a "secondary employer" to pressure the "primary employer" to recognize or negotiate with a union.[37] In addition to this broad prohibition on secondary boycotts, the NLRB has held that partial work-stoppages or slowdowns are unprotected activities under the NLRA and employees who engage in them can be fired. [38]

In Japan, many labor rights stem from Constitutional provisions. While both the US and Japanese Constitutions guarantee a right to free association, the Japanese Constitution further provides "the right and obligation to work," and "[t]he right of workers to organize and bargain and act collectively."[39] Although Japanese law contains no similar set of express limitations on union activity like NLRA section 8, the Japanese limit employee collective action to "justifiable acts" judged in context.[40] Under the doctrine of justifiable acts, the Japanese courts rule for union conduct.

The propriety of disputed acts is generally determined on a case-by-case basis in Japan. Four elements will be examined in determining whether collection action is justifiable: "(1) their parties, (2) their objectives, (3) their procedures, and (4) their means."[41] The employees' dispute rights

---

34 29 U.S.C. § 157 (2009).
35 *Id.*
36 29 U.S.C. § 158(b)–(g) (2009).
37 *Id.*
38 *Elk Lumber Co.*, 91 N.L.R.B. 333, 338 (1950).
39 Meiji Kenp, art. 27, no. 1.
40 *Id.* at art. 28.
41 Kazuo Sugeno, *supra* note 4, at 548–554.

must be balanced against the employer's property rights, and violence is always improper. Moreover, a dispute is only justifiable if it has collective bargaining as its object. As a result, political strikes are unjustifiable, as are sympathy strikes. Unions must wait until negotiations have begun before initiating a dispute. Similarly, unions are required to give notice before initiating a dispute. Although Sugeno believes that dispute acts in violation of a no-strike or similar agreement are generally unjustifiable, he acknowledges a case-by-case basis, and that there are opposing views.[42]

Although secondary actions are suspect, the Japanese have a broad definition of what constitutes a primary action. If in the course of an industrial dispute workers appeal to customers and the public not to purchase the products of the struck employer, the action is considered a primary product boycott. Such conduct is proper and justifiable because it is within the scope of the protection accorded by the dispute right.[43]

A dispute act is generally justifiable if it involves the total or partial withholding of work.[44] Among the acts Sugeno mentions as being generally permissible are full strikes, partial strikes, "designated strikes," rolling strikes, and limited-duration strikes.[45] This includes concerted vacation or sick leave, and refusals to come to or leave work at designated times, or refuse overtime. In addition, slowdowns that do not involve destruction or damage are permissible.

American labor law provides workers with a smaller array of economic weapons for collective bargaining than Japanese labor law. American workers are unprotected in partial work stoppages or slowdowns, while secondary boycotts are prohibited. In Japan, workers can undertake such collective actions as long as they are "justifiable" under Japan's Constitution and laws.[46] As a result, American workers have fewer options for effectively imposing costs on their employers for failure to agree with them in collective bargaining, and thus less bargaining power than comparable workers under Japanese law. This advantage in bargaining power for Japanese workers has probably declined with the advent of the global economy. In the global economy, where an employer can subcontract work abroad, employee collective action of any sort becomes more risky. However, consumer boycotts may be a viable union weapon even in the global economy.

---

42 *Id.*, at 554.
43 *Id.*, at 544.
44 *Fukui Shinbunsha*, 19 Lab. Civ. Cases 714 (Fukui Dist. Ct., May 15, 1968).
45 KAZUO SUGENO, *supra* note 4, at 555.
46 *Id.*

3.3.4 Employers' Economic Weapons

Employers in the United States have considerably more freedom to use "economic weapons" as compared with their Japanese counterparts. In the United States, employers are prohibited from firing striking employees. However, under the "MacKay doctrine" economic strikers can be "permanently replaced."[47] Although strikers who have been permanently replaced have a right to recall if openings occur and a right to vote in unit elections for up to one year, permanent replacement has proven to be a very powerful weapon for American employers in resisting and breaking unions. Although permanent replacements were rarely employed in the years immediately after the adoption of the MacKay doctrine, American employers have shown an increased willingness to resort to permanent replacements since the 1980s.[48] In addition, US employers are permitted to resort to offensive lockouts as a means of pressuring their employees to accept a collective bargaining agreement on the employer's terms. [49] It is currently unclear whether the US courts will allow employers to lock out their employees and replace them.

In Japan, employers have the "freedom to conduct operations" during dispute acts, which grants a limited right to replace striking workers. The Japanese Supreme Court is often quoted on the matter as saying, "Even during a strike . . . an employer is not required to suspend the operation of its business, and can take measures that are necessary to continue its operations in response to the workers' dispute acts that seek to obstruct those operations."[50] However, while this principle permits employers to hire replacements, they may only do so temporarily; even those Japanese workers who would be considered "economic strikers" in the United States are entitled to reinstatement at the conclusion of the strike.[51]

In addition to this limited replacement right, Japanese employers may

---

47 *NLRB v. MacKay Radio & Tel. Co.*, 304 U.S. 333 (1938). "Economic strikers" are workers who are engaged in collective action for economic reasons, for instance seeking higher wages or benefits, as opposed to workers who are engaged in collective action to redress unfair labor practices or other violations of the law by the employer.

48 James Brudney, *To Strike or Not to Strike*, WISC. L. REV. 65, at 80–81 (1999).

49 *Am. Ship Bldg. Co. v. NLRB*, 380 U.S. 300, 310 (1965) states that "we cannot see that the employer's use of a lockout solely in support of a legitimate bargaining position is in any way inconsistent with the right to bargain collectively or with the right to strike."

50 KAZUO SUGENO, *supra* note 4, at 585

51 *Id.* Sugeno also notes that some collective bargaining agreements contain

have the right to lock out employees under certain circumstances. In *Marushima Suimon*, the Japanese Supreme Court stated that:

> [I]n a particular labor dispute, the power balance between workers and their employer collapses because of the workers' dispute acts, and the employer is subjected to extraordinarily disadvantageous pressures, the employer can prevent such pressures in light of the fairness principle. The employer's opposing defensive measures which are limited to restoring the power balance between the workers and the employer will be recognized . . . They will also be approved as an employer's proper dispute acts.[52]

Sugeno's position on the lockout is that it is a purely defensive right allowing employers to mitigate the financial burden created by extraordinary adverse pressures produced by the worker conduct that hinders their business. As a result, the principal requirement for recognizing a lockout's propriety is that there be worker obstruction of the business, which causes unusual harm to an employer, so that the employer will be in an extraordinarily disadvantageous position if it cannot refuse to accept the work of the disputing workers.[53]

Because American employers are allowed greater resort to economic weapons, they should have greater bargaining power than similarly situated employers under Japanese law. The ability of American employers to permanently replace economic strikers and undertake offensive lockouts in advance of employee collective action affords the imposition of costs on employees for failure to come to an agreement during negotiations, thereby allowing the employers to wield greater bargaining power in negotiations. An employer's ability to resort to international outsourcing in the new global economy has, if anything, probably increased American employers' power in this regard.

3.3.5 The Structure of Negotiations

Although most of the factors we have discussed so far suggest that Japanese unions should have greater bargaining power than similarly situated American unions, the structure of negotiations in the United States probably favors union power, while the structure of negotiations in Japan probably limits the desire of Japanese employees to exercise the economic power they have over their employers.

---

scab-prohibition provisions that would prohibit the employer from hiring replacements at all.

52 *Id.*, at 585–587.

53 *Id.*

American collective bargaining tends to be conducted on an adversarial basis in which labor has achieved some organization across a regional or national market. Under American law, corporate managers owe stockholders a fiduciary duty and generally have strong financial rewards for maximizing returns to shareholders. American management is strongly allied with the interests of shareholders and conducts collective bargaining through arm's-length negotiations with the employees.[54] Therefore, it is common for American corporate management to identify with shareholder interests and view employee interests with some hostility as an impediment to achieving corporate goals.[55] Moreover, American unions tend to organize by trade or industry on a regional or national basis.

As a result of these structural characteristics of American industrial relations, American unions do not share a strong community of interest with any particular employer. Although American unions certainly have no interest in bankrupting viable employers, since their interests are less often tied to the interests of a single employer, the unions have no problem employing strikes in whipsawing strategies to bid up wages, or even driving out inefficient low-wage employers for the benefit of the majority of employees in the union. Moreover, American labor unions tend to be sizeable organizations with resources to maintain local unions in conflicts with individual employers.

By contrast, Japanese collective bargaining takes place on a less adversarial footing and is organized on the basis of a single firm. Although there has been some erosion in Japan's system of "life-time employment" in recent years, it is still true that "core" Japanese employees have strong protections against discharge without cause and generally expect to work their entire lives for the same firm.[56] As a result, Japanese employees tend to strongly identify with the interests of their firm. Moreover, under the Japanese system of corporate governance, shareholders exercise less control over management and management tends to be promoted from within the ranks of the firm's employees. As a result, Japanese management is more likely to identify with the interests of their employees than the interests of their shareholders.[57] The coincidence of employee and

---

[54] K.G. DAU-SCHMIDT ET AL., *supra* note 11, at 1–80.

[55] Kenneth G. Dau-Schmidt, *Promoting Employee Voice in the American Economy: A Call for Comprehensive Reform*, 94 MARQ. L. REV. 765, 769–773 (2011).

[56] Takashi Araki, LABOR AND EMPLOYMENT LAW IN JAPAN 18 (2002); Ronald J. Gilson & Mark J. Roe, *Lifetime Employment: Labor Peace and the Evolution of Japanese Corporate Governance*, 99 COLUM. L. REV. 508 (1999).

[57] This alignment of management interests with employees, rather than shareholders, may account for a few differences in American and Japanese managerial

management interest in the running of Japanese firms gives rise to the "employee/management coalition" in the governance of the firm identified by Professor Shishido in the introduction to this volume. Finally, Japanese unions typically organize on the enterprise level. To the extent that industrial organizations exist, they are typically federations of enterprise unions, rather than industry-wide unions.[58] These organizations are relatively informal and have little or no power to control their affiliated unions.[59]

As a result, Japanese managers and employees negotiate in a "community of shared fate" and generally conduct collective bargaining on a firm-by-firm basis.[60] The alignment of interests between labor and management within Japanese firms means that collective bargaining is conducted on a less adversarial basis. Moreover, the fact that Japanese labor unions are organized on a smaller enterprise basis, suggests that they will exercise less bargaining power relative to their employers than similarly situated American workers because they will not have a larger organization to financially support them in their disputes. Furthermore, Japanese employees who are organized on an enterprise basis certainly have no incentive to engage in whipsawing strikes among employers to bid up wages or to drive inefficient low-wage employers out of the market. Thus, even if Japanese workers do have greater access to economic weapons than American workers, they are less likely to use them to resolve disputes. However, the relative bargaining power of Japanese and American workers in collective bargaining has become less important in corporate governance with the decline of collective action in industrialized countries and the rise of the global economy of the information age.

---

practices, such as the dramatically higher levels of executive compensation in the United States and American management's tendency to focus on short-run profits, even to the long-run detriment of the firm. Kenneth G. Dau-Schmidt, *supra* note 55, at 815–819 (2011).

[58] T.A. HANAMI, *supra* note 23 at 105. The All Japan Seamen's Union (JSU) stands in contrast as a true industrial union that had 150 000 members in 1979.

[59] There are a few large national organizations as well. Hanami identified four very large organizations ranging from 500 000 to 2 million workers in 1979 that had been coordinating smaller unions in a 'spring offensive' for two decades. The tactics of these organizations varied, but they typically coordinated strategy and planed actions on a national scale. *Id.*

[60] Yasuo Kuwahara, *Employment Relations in Japan*, *in* INTERNATIONAL AND COMPARATIVE EMPLOYMENT RELATIONS 249, 257 (GREG J. BAMBER & RUSSELL D. LANSBURY EDS., 1998).

3.4 THE GENERAL DECLINE IN RELATIVE BARGAINING POWER OF EMPLOYEES IN DEVELOPED COUNTRIES IN THE NEW GLOBAL ECONOMY OF THE INFORMATION AGE

During the 1970s, the post-war system of trade and technology that served as the foundation for the system of industrial unionism began to change.[61] With the rebuilding of Europe and the rise of the "Asian tigers," international trade began to make serious inroads into the US economy. The impact of international trade was first felt in low-capital industries such as textiles and shoes, but the 1970s oil crisis facilitated significant inroads into even the capital-intensive automotive and steel industries.[62] After the quadrupling of oil prices in the 1973 OPEC (Organization of Petroleum Exporting Countries) embargo, the automotive and steel manufacturers in Europe and Asia enjoyed competitive advantages through fuel-efficient designs, up-to-date production facilities, superior management, and lower wages. Manufacturing jobs began to migrate to low-wage countries or disappear entirely as industry strived to become more efficient. As a result, global trade played a more important role in the economies of all industrialized countries.

During the 1980s, new information technology accelerated globalization and allowed for the efficient horizontal organization of firms. Information technology allowed employers to coordinate production among various suppliers and subcontractors around the world. Employers no longer had to be large and vertically integrated to ensure efficient production; they just had to be sufficiently wired to reliable subcontractors.[63] The "best business practices" became those of horizontal organization, outsourcing, and subcontracting, as firms concentrated on their "core competencies" – or that portion of production or retailing that they did best. In this economic environment, employers sought flexibility in employment; the number of "contingent employees" who work part-time or are leased or subcontracted reached new heights in the American economy.[64] The new horizontal organization of firms broke down the job ladders and administrative rules of the internal labor market, and firms became more market

---

[61] Cappelli, *supra* note 5, at 4.

[62] Kenneth G. Dau-Schmidt, *The Changing Face of Collective Representation: The Future of Collective Bargaining*, 82 CHI. KENT L. REV. 903, 912 (2007).

[63] Cappelli, *supra* note 5, at 99.

[64] Karen Winegardner, *Who Are Your Employees? Contingent Workers on the Rise*, THE CAPITAL 10, Apr. 1, 2001.

driven. New technology allowed "bench-marking," or the checking of the efficiency of a division of a firm against external suppliers, thus bringing the market inside the firm in a way not previously experienced.[65]

New information technology also facilitated the rise of the "big box" retailers to a position of unprecedented worldwide economic power.[66] The simple bar code allowed Wal-Mart to master inventory control, coordinate sources of product supply worldwide, and grow into an international economic powerhouse with unprecedented power to determine wholesale prices and employment. This power allows the "big box" retailers to determine the wages and employment of production employees, even without legal relation to those employees. For example, in 1995 when the US firm Rubbermaid sought to raise its prices to cover an increase in the cost of plastic resin, Wal-Mart's refusal to comply resulted in wage cuts and layoffs for Rubbermaid's production workers. Moreover, these retailers provide an extensive retailing network for foreign producers, facilitating the inroads of foreign production into the American economy and across the world. In the case of Rubbermaid, important parts of the firm's production process were eventually sold to China for employment there.

Finally, in the 1990s, the global labor market experienced a near doubling of the relevant labor force with a concomitant downward pressure on wages and benefits that is yet to be fully felt in the industrialized world. Since 1990, the collapse of communism, India's turn from autarky, and China's adoption of market capitalism have led to an increase in the global economy's available labor force from 3.3 billion to 6 billion.[67] Because these countries were relatively capital-poor, their entry into the global economy has brought no corresponding increase in global capital. As a result, the capital-to-labor ratio in the global economy has dropped approximately 40 percent.[68] This abrupt change in the ratio of available labor and capital in the global economy has put tremendous downward pressure on wages and benefits in global competition. Low-wage competition from elsewhere in the world has contributed to US employers' desire to subcontract work to low-wage countries and to encourage the immigration of low-wage employees from Central and South America. The downward pressure on wages and benefits exists not only in manufacturing, but in any service in which work can be digitalized and sent to qualified people elsewhere in the world.

---

65 Cappelli, *supra* note 5, at 104.

66 Kenneth G. Dau-Schmidt, *supra* note 62, at 914.

67 Richard B. Freeman, America Works: Critical Thought On The Exceptional US Labor Market 128 (2007).

68 *Id.*

As a consequence of these changes, unions in developed countries such as the United States and Japan have generally suffered a significant decline in their bargaining power relative to their employers. The efficient organization of firms across the globe has decreased unions' ability to impose costs on recalcitrant employers through collective action, and increased the potential costs of such action to employees. If American or Japanese workers go on strike and their work can be subcontracted to low-wage workers in other countries, American and Japanese workers can lose their jobs even if they are more productive and produce higher-quality output. Moreover, as firms have adopted a leaner, more horizontal, form of organization that is more subject to market discipline, and put a higher premium on flexibility in production, there has been less for employees and employers to gain through collective bargaining. In the new economic environment, employers are less interested in supporting a long-term employment relationship, so there are less benefits and administrative rules for unions to achieve and administer through collective bargaining. The result has been a precipitous decline in union bargaining power and activity in both the United States and Japan. In the United States, between 1980 and 2012, the number of work stoppages involving 1000 or more employees a year has declined from 187 to 19 while the percent of total work time lost to these strikes has declined from 9 percent to less than 0.5 percent.[69] In Japan, the number of work days lost to strikes has declined from over 8 million days in 1975 to just 7492 days in 2009.[70] With collective bargaining in decline, workers are left to seek accommodation of their interests within the firm through the complementary institutions described by Professor Shishido in the introduction to this volume. American workers are left to accommodate their interests within the firm through an ever softening global labor market while Japanese workers can rely to some extent on their historic coalition with management in negotiating the incentive bargain of the firm.

3.5 CONCLUSION

The balance of bargaining power between labor and management varies according to underlying economic parameters and the laws governing the

---

[69] U.S. Bureau of Labor Statistics News Release, *Major Work Stoppages in 2012*, Table 1, Friday, February 8, 2013.

[70] Hiroyuki Fujimura, *Japan's Labor Unions: Past, Present, Future*, 9 JAPAN LAB. REV. 6, 7 (2012).

conduct of collective bargaining. A party's bargaining power, or its ability to induce the other side to accept an agreement on its terms, depends on that party's ability to impose costs on the other side for failing to agree, and to avoid or absorb its own costs from failing to agree. Each party's ability to impose and avoid costs depends on economic factors, such as the nature of the firm's product, the firm's technology of production, general economic conditions, the structure of bargaining, and the employees' commitment to collective action. However, the parties' ability to impose and avoid costs also depends on the legal framework for collective bargaining, the legal structure of bargaining and the economic weapons that each side is allowed under the law.

The labor laws of the United States and Japan create differences in the relative bargaining power of unions and management. It seems clear that Japan's system of plural unionism facilitates the organization of employees by increasing union density and bargaining power. However, in industries where unions are well established, the United States system of exclusive representation simplifies representation and bargaining issues and insulates unions from competition. With respect to economic weapons, the United States restricts employee collective action while allowing employers greater latitude in economic warfare. American employees are prohibited from engaging in secondary boycotts and are unprotected in partial work stoppages or slowdowns, while American employers can permanently replace economic strikers and undertake offensive lockouts. In Japan, employees are protected in undertaking "justified" collective action, including boycotts and partial strikes or slowdowns, and employers are constrained from making permanent replacements or offensive lockouts. This imbalance in economic weapons suggests that, relative to Japanese employers, American employers can impose greater costs on their employees for refusing to agree and thus enjoy greater relative bargaining power. Finally, in the structure of bargaining, American employees enjoy larger labor organizations that tend to bargain on a multi-enterprise basis. As a result they can better support local unions in disputes with individual employers. Moreover, the organization of Japanese unions on an enterprise basis and the greater community of interest between labor and management in Japan mean that even if Japanese workers enjoy greater legal access to economic weapons, they are less likely to need or want to resort to those weapons to resolve disputes.

However, the rise of the global economy and new information technology has significantly decreased the bargaining power of unions relative to employers in developed countries. New information technology has allowed the organization and distribution of production on a global basis, subjecting all facets of the firm to market discipline and low-wage competition in the global economy. This fundamental change facilitates the relocation of production to low-wage countries, putting downward pressure on wages in the industrialized countries and raising the possible costs of employee collective action. As a result, collective bargaining and the possibility of collective action has taken a significant decline in importance in accommodating employees' interests within the firm, raising the relative importance of the complementary institutions of the market in the United States and the coalition of management and employees in Japan for negotiating the incentive bargain of the firm.

4. Employee stock purchase plans in Japan

Yohsuke Higashi[1]

4.1 INTRODUCTION

Employee ownership is widespread across the globe. Japan represents a good example of a country where employee ownership enjoys great popularity. A broad-based employee stock purchase plan (ESPP) called *jūgyōin mochikabu seido*[2] is prevalent among Japanese listed corporations. As of March 31, 2013, 2,109 out of 2,306 (or 91.5 percent) Japanese corporations listed on the Tokyo Stock Exchange (TSE), have adopted ESPPs.[3]

The appeal of employee ownership is that it benefits everyone. By adopting it, employees will be able to share in the upside of the corporate business through the rise in its stock price and thus be motivated to work harder and more efficiently, which in turn results in improved productivity, better corporate performance and higher returns for shareholders. This is how the story goes.

However, this may seem optimistic when analyzed from the traditional viewpoint of corporate governance: that the value of a corporation will

---

[1] The opinions expressed in this chapter are solely those of the author and do not reflect the opinions of the firm or of any organization to which the author belongs.

[2] In some literature, *jūgyōin mochikabu seido* has been used interchangeably with *jūgyōin mochikabu kai*. Specifically, the former refers to the scheme as a whole, and the latter refers to the association of participants in the plan, while it can also refer to the scheme as a whole.

[3] The number of listed corporations that have adopted employee ownership plans by entering into contracts with one of five major securities companies is 2109, i.e., Daiwa Securities Co., Ltd.; SMBC Nikko Securities Inc.; Nomura Securities Co., Ltd.; Mizuho Securities Co., Ltd; and Mitsubishi UFJ Morgan Stanley Securities Co., Ltd. *Heisei 24 Nendo Jūgyōin Mochikabu Kai Jōkyō Chōsa Kekka no Gaiyō ni tsuite* [*Outline of Research Results on the Status of Employee Stock Purchase Plans in Fiscal Year 2012*], TOKYO STOCK EXCHANGE (Oct. 9, 2013) http://www.tse.or.jp/market/data/examination/b7gje600000050b5-att/employee_2012.pdf.

be maximized when shareholders act to maximize their residual claims, which, in turn, justifies shareholders in monopolizing voting rights.[4] If shareholders have private benefits (fixed contractual claims as opposed to residual claims) and act to increase the former rather than the latter, it may compromise corporate governance and generate inefficiency. Employee shareholders have private benefits in their employer corporation, such as job security, salaries, and promotions. Employee shareholders may exercise their voting rights to maximize the sum of investment returns on the stock and their private benefits rather than to maximize investment returns only,[5] or can team up with the management to fend off hostile buyers,[6] both of which may result in a decrease in the value of the corporation. As a result, such decrease may offset the productivity effect and other benefits of employee ownership, if not surpass it. Questions also remain as to whether low-profile employees can really affect overall corporate performance and whether it is a good idea for employees to invest both their human resources and their capital resources in one corporation (e.g. Enron, Worldcom).

Nevertheless, Japanese law seems to recognize the potential positive value of employee ownership. The purpose of this chapter is to consider whether the current Japanese legal framework provides the right incentive structure.

In section 4.2, I will first briefly look at some literature on employee ownership and show that there is yet no clear consensus on the effect of employee ownership, while its proponents generally agree that certain complementary factors are necessary for increased productivity. In section 4.3, I will summarize specific features of Japanese ESPPs in comparison to US employee stock ownership plans (ESOPs) and ESPPs. In section 4.4, I will describe certain special treatments for ESPPs under Japanese law to show that Japanese law recognizes the potential positive value of employee ownership. Certain legal regulations relevant to ESPPs will also be explained to show that they actually provide management with ample discretion. Lastly, in section 4.5, I will conclude that the current Japanese legal framework represents a realistic and reasonable choice under the present circumstances.

---

4 Frank H. Easterbrook & Daniel R. Fischel, The Economic Structure of Corporate Law 67–68 (1991).

5 Olubunmi Faleye et al., *When Labor Has a Voice in Corporate Governance*, 41 J. Fin. & Quan. Anal. 489 (2006).

6 Marco Pagano & Paolo F. Volpin, *Managers, Workers, and Corporate Control*, 60 J. Fin. 841 (2005).

4.2 IS EMPLOYEE OWNERSHIP BENEFICIAL FOR EVERYONE?

There are a number of empirical studies on employee ownership. Some support the productivity effect of employee ownership and others find no such effect. Among proponents of employee ownership, however, there appears to be a consensus that certain complementary factors are necessary for employee ownership to contribute to productivity.

For example, with respect to ESPPs in Japan, Jones and Kato studied Japanese ESPPs and found that ESPPs led to a 4–5 percent increase in productivity and also that the productivity effect of bonuses is enhanced by the existence of ESPPs.[7] Ohkusa and Ohtake later found that ESPPs do not increase productivity if they are introduced without profit-sharing (profit-sharing bonuses) in large firms, but that the productivity effect of profit-sharing is enhanced by the existence of ESPPs.[8] Ohkusa and Ohtake suggest that the Japanese bonuses are often linked to individual performance and can help combat the free-rider problem pertaining to employee ownership (i.e., because the upside for employees is linked to the overall corporate performance and not to the efforts of individual employees, employees tend to shirk and free-ride on others' efforts).[9] They explain that the difference between their results and the findings by Jones and Kato is caused by the difference in samples: theirs contained only large firms, as opposed to those of Jones and Kato.[10] These studies when combined suggest that ESPPs in Japan do have a productivity effect, although at least for large Japanese firms, some profit-sharing system may be necessary for ESPPs to contribute to productivity. US studies supporting employee ownership have also suggested that complementary factors such as corporate culture or employment practices are a prerequisite.[11] The National Center for Employee Ownership, one of the most powerful

---

[7] Derek C. Jones & Takao Kato, *The Productivity Effects of Employee Stock-Ownership Plans and Bonuses: Evidence from Japanese Panel Data*, 85 AM. ECON. REV. 391 (1995).

[8] Yasushi Ohkusa & Fumio Ohtake, *The Productivity Effects of Information Sharing, Profit Sharing, and ESOPs*, 11 J. JAP. & INT'L ECON. 385 (1997).

[9] Ohkusa and Ohtake *supra* note 8, at 388, 401.

[10] Ohkusa and Ohtake *supra* note 8, at 399–400.

[11] *E.g.*, Douglas Kruse et al., *Motivating Employee-Owners in ESOP Firms: Human Resource Policies and Company Performance* (Nat'l Bureau of Econ. Research, Working Paper No. 10177, 2003), *available at* http://www.nber.org/papers/w10177.pdf, and Joseph R. Blasi et al., *Creating a Bigger Pie? The Effects of Employee Ownership, Profit Sharing, and Stock Options on Workplace Performance, in* SHARED CAPITALISM AT WORK: EMPLOYEE OWNERSHIP, PROFIT

supporters of employee ownership, also recognizes that ownership alone and participation alone have, at best, spotty or short-lived results.[12]

On the other hand, there have been several empirical studies which argue that there is no evidence that employee ownership improves productivity or corporate performance.[13] Faleye et al. found that employee-owned public firms in the US (with at least 5 percent of outstanding shares owned by employees) led to lower productivity and lower corporate performance when compared to other firms.[14] This study reasons that because employees exercise their rights as shareholders to maximize the total value of the fixed salary claim and the residual equity-based claim, and because the former is usually much larger than the latter, employees tend to focus on securing their fixed salaries, become risk-averse and forgo otherwise high net present value projects.

Judge Posner, in his opinion in a case related to the bankruptcy of United Airlines,[15] summarized skepticism about employee ownership well:

> The time may have come to rethink the concept of an ESOP, a seemingly inefficient method of wealth accumulation by employees because of the under diversification to which it conduces (though remember that what is important is the diversification of the employee's entire asset portfolio, including his earning capacity, rather than whether an individual asset is diversified). The tax advantages of the form do not represent a social benefit, but merely a shift of tax burdens to other taxpayers. Nor are we aware of an argument for subsidizing the ESOP form, as the tax law does, rather than letting the market decide whether it has economic advantages over alternative forms of business structure. As for the notion that having a stake in one's employer will induce one to be more productive, the evidence for such an effect – see "Motivating Employees with Stock and Involvement," NBER Website, Apr. 25, 2006, http://www.nber.org/digest/may04/w10177.html; Joseph Blasi, Michael Conte & Douglas Kruse, "Employee Stock Ownership and Corporate Performance Among Public Companies," 50 Indus. & Lab. Rel. Rev. 60 (1996) – is weak and makes no theoretical sense. An employee has no incentive to work harder just

---

AND GAIN SHARING, AND BROAD-BASED STOCK OPTIONS 139 (Douglas L. Kruse et al. eds, 2010).

[12] *Research on Employee Ownership, Corporate Performance, and Employee Compensation*, NAT'L CENTER FOR EMPLOYEE OWNERSHIP, http://www.nceo.org/articles/research-employee-ownership-corporate-performance (last visited Apr. 10, 2013).

[13] *E.g.*, Faleye et al., *supra* note 5 and William N. Pugh et al., *The Effect of ESOP Adoptions on Corporate Performance: Are There Really Performance Changes?*, 21 MANAGE. DECIS. ECON. 167 (2000).

[14] Faleye et al., *supra* note 5.

[15] Summers v. State St. Bank & Trust Co., 453 F.3d 404, 411–412 (7th Cir. 2006).

> because he owns stock in his employer, since his efforts, unless he is a senior executive, are unlikely to move the price of the stock. Nor is employee stock ownership likely to forge sentimental ties between employees and employers that might cause the former to work harder, although it may alleviate union pressures for wages or benefits that would jeopardize solvency.

Posner's criticism on the weakness of existing studies should be tested by empirical results offered by the proponents and skeptics. While there are studies finding no effect of employee ownership as mentioned above, there are also a number of studies showing a positive correlation between corporate performance and employee ownership.[16] Studies on public-company employee ownership are relatively few, but there are still some empirical studies[17] showing the positive effect of employee ownership, in addition to the 1996 study by Blasi, Conte and Kruse, which is criticized by Posner above. Also, Blasi and Kruse counterargue that, at the time of the 1996 study, although they already predicted the complementarity of employee ownership and corporate culture or employment practices in that study, they had yet to prove it, which might have led Posner to misunderstand their point of view.[18] In the other study Posner also referenced, Blasi and Kruse (with co-authors) had already concluded that, in order to combat the free-rider problem, ownership must be combined with employee involvement and other policies that give workers the power to act on the

---

[16] In addition to literature cited herein, see Steven F. Freeman, *Effects of ESOP Adoption and Employee Ownership: Thirty Years of Research and Experience* (Organizational Dynamics Programs, University of Pennsylvania, Working Paper #07-01, 2007), *available at* http://repository.upenn.edu/cgi/viewcontent.cgi?article=1001&context=od_working_papers, which gives a general view about employee ownership studies conducted for the past decades.

[17] For example, E. Han Kim & Paige Ouimet, *Employee Capitalism or Corporate Socialism? Broad-Based Employee Stock Ownership*, AFA 2010 Atlanta Meetings Paper (2008), *available at* http://ssrn.com/abstract=1107974 shows that ESOPs controlling less than 5 percent of outstanding shares benefits both workers and shareholders, which implies positive productivity gains (on the other hand, the effects of large ESOPs on worker compensation and shareholder value are more or less neutral, suggesting slight productivity gains). Robert Stretcher et al., *The ESOP Performance Puzzle in Public Companies*, 18 J. Emp. Ownership L. & Fin. 3 (2006) shows that ESOPs have positive effects on return on assets (ROA), net profit margins, and operating cash flows, and Hewitt Associates LLC, Unleashing the Power of Employee Ownership a Research Report (1998) shows that the ESOPs had a positive correlation to ROA.

[18] John Blasi & Douglas Kruse, *The Court's Views On Employee Ownership Research*, Ohio Employee Ownership Center, http://www.oeockent.org/library/doc/304/raw (last modified Jul. 16, 2009).

incentives,[19] and they further confirmed this need for complementary factors in another study, in which they also suggested that the "corporate culture" could be the latent variable underlying such complementarities.[20] It seems that the results of empirical studies are not clear enough to deny the productivity effect as easily as Posner does (to the contrary, the combined results seem rather supportive). Also, with respect to the diversification risk mentioned by Posner, Blasi and Kruse argue that employees could prudently hold reasonable proportions of their assets in employee stock ownership of their firm with only a modest loss in utility due to risk.[21] These criticisms remain questions to be answered by further studies.

On the other hand, the argument that if employee ownership is really beneficial the market will decide by itself, and there is no good reason to grant employee ownership a tax advantage, seems persuasive. Tax subsidies may be justifiable when the market participants, the corporations, are overlooking the benefit of employee ownership, resulting in underuse of employee ownership and loss of otherwise achievable social wealth, and tax subsidies can induce them to adopt employee ownership. Indeed, given the mixed views on the effect of employee ownership, it may not be easy for corporations to precisely evaluate the effect of employee ownership and thus corporations may be prone to overlooking its positive effect. However, if there is any other factor which induces adoption of employee ownership, tax subsidies should not be necessary even when corporations overlook its benefit, because they will adopt it in any case due to that different factor. Actually, there may be such a factor pertaining to employee ownership: management's motive to prevent takeovers and secure their positions.[22] Part of the criticism by the skeptics of employee ownership derives precisely from the concern that management is abusing it for their own entrenchment; the concern here is overuse rather than underuse. There seems to be only a weak case to justify tax subsidies.

In sum, there is no consensus on the question of whether employee

---

19 Kruse et al., *supra* note 11.

20 Blasi et al., *supra* note 11.

21 Joseph R. Blasi et al., *Risk and Lack of Diversification under Employee Ownership and Shared Capitalism*, *in* SHARED CAPITALISM AT WORK: EMPLOYEE OWNERSHIP, PROFIT AND GAIN SHARING, AND BROAD-BASED STOCK OPTIONS, *supra* note 11, at 105.

22 *E.g.*, Myron S. Scholes & Mark A. Wolfson, *Employee Stock Ownership Plans and Corporate Restructuring: Myths and Realities*, 19 FIN. MANAGE. 12 (1990) concluded that, particularly for large companies, taxes do not seem to be the motivation for adopting ESOPs; that the case is also weak for employee incentives being the driving force; and that the main motivation for the growth of ESOPs resides in their anti-takeover characteristics.

ownership generates net social wealth. If there is nothing good about employee ownership, the law should flatly prohibit it. Conversely, if employee ownership always improves social wealth under any circumstances, the law should always promote it. In reality, however, studies suggest that even if we are to assume that employee ownership does have positive effects on productivity and other corporate performance, certain complementary factors are necessary to solve the free-rider problem among employees. The ideal law, therefore, may be one that makes such factors prerequisites for the adoption of employee ownership. However, it is difficult for a statute to precisely define something as vague as corporate culture or employment practices. Also, imposing a uniform culture or practice may not be a good idea given that each corporation operates its business under different circumstances. As a result, employee ownership seems to be one of the many items that should be left to the business judgment of management, who are most familiar with the corporate culture and employment practices, and most likely to make the right decision. Of course, however, attention should be paid to prevent management from placing their own interests before those of shareholders, especially considering the fact that employee ownership could affect the ownership structure. Lastly, because tax subsidies seemingly lead to inefficiency by creating overuse, they should not be granted, unless the government has a separate policy to make a wealth transfer to employees and corporations adopting employee ownership from other taxpayers, when such transfer cannot be accomplished more efficiently by other means (which is unlikely).

4.3 JAPANESE ESPPs AND THE US COUNTERPARTS

4.3.1 ESPPs in Japan

As stated at the beginning of this chapter, ESPPs (*jūgyōin mochikabu seido*) have been widely adopted as a form of broad-based employee ownership and have been available for rank-and-file employees in many Japanese listed corporations. (In earlier literature about Japanese employee ownership, *jūgyōin mochikabu seido* was sometimes translated as an ESOP rather than ESPP.[23] However, *jūgyōin mochikabu seido* is not a retirement plan,

[23] Jones & Kato, *supra* note 7, and Ohkusa & Ohtake, *supra* note 8 also use this terminology.

but an employee stock purchase plan where the employer corporation provides subsidies for the purchases and the employees have an option to participate;[24] this is more similar to an ESPP in the US.[25] For this reason, I choose ESPP as the translation for *jūgyōin mochikabu seido* in this chapter, even though I am dealing with the same legal framework as in earlier literature.)

Under typical Japanese ESPPs in listed corporations,[26] employees have the choice whether or not to participate in the plan. Once enrolled, participants make a monthly contribution, through a payroll deduction, to an acquisition vehicle (*jūgyōin mochikabu kai*), which is a general partnership consisting of the plan's participants. In the meantime, employer corporations make employer contributions as subsidies for ESPPs. They typically contribute to the acquisition vehicle on behalf of each participant, 5–10 percent[27] of his or her contribution (this effectively works as a discount on the stock price) and bear the administrative costs of the ESPP.

The acquisition vehicle purchases shares of the corporation every month on the market using the combined contributions from the participants and the corporation. The administrator (*rijichō*) of the vehicle holds the purchased shares in trust on behalf of the participants and receives dividends on them. The number of shares accumulated by the vehicle is limited due to the fact that the stock purchases are composed mainly of employees' contributions which are a small part of their salaries.

Participants can withdraw the shares allocable to them, but only in trading unit increments. They can also terminate their enrollment in the plan and withdraw all the shares purchased using their contributions (the enrollment will be automatically terminated when the participants cease to be employed by the corporations). In that case, however, this

---

24 I will provide detailed comparison later in this section.

25 Hiroshi Osano, Kōporēto Gabanansu to Jinteki Shihon [Corporate Governance and Human Capital], 158 (2005). Ohtake and Ohkusa point out the same (Ohtake & Ohkusa, *supra* note 8, at 387 & n. 2), but used "ESOP" as the translation in their article.

26 Description of an ESPP structure in this chapter assumes that the ESPP is operated by retaining a security company and is structured as an "indirect investment type" pursuant to a guideline provided by the Japan Securities Dealers Association, which is the most typical design of an ESPP in Japan. *Mochikabu Seido ni Kansuru Gaidorain* [*Guideline for Stock Purchase Plans*], Japan Securities Dealers Ass'n (June, 2008), http://www.jsda.or.jp/shiryo/houkokusyo/h20/files/mochikabu01.pdf.

27 According to the TSE survey (*supra* note 3), 41.1 percent of the sample companies contributed 4 percent or more and less than 6 percent, and 33.5 percent contributed 10 percent or more and less than 15 percent.

participant will not be allowed to enroll in the same corporation's ESPP again. Therefore, despite the fact that they can dispose of the shares freely, ESPPs have the function of creating long-term shareholding by employees, albeit in a limited manner.

With respect to the shares held in ESPPs, the administrator exercises the voting rights. The administrator must let the participants know of the content of convocation notices and provide them with the opportunity to give specific instructions as to the voting of shares allocable to them. In practice, the head of the Human Resources Department or Department of General Affairs is often appointed the administrator, and specific instructions regarding the exercise of voting rights from the participants are rarely seen. ESPPs are generally viewed as a friendly shareholder for the corporation.

There is no tax benefit specifically provided for ESPPs in Japan. Participating employees make employee contributions from their after-tax salaries, and because employer contributions are treated as salaries for tax purposes, employees are taxed with respect to them as well.[28] Participants will be taxed on the capital gain when they withdraw and sell the shares purchased.[29] Employer corporations recognize normal tax losses when they pay salaries and employer contributions. The tax consequences would be the same if employer corporations paid additional salaries in the amount equal to employer contributions, and participating employees purchased and sold the same amount of shares in the corporations using their salaries.

4.3.2 The US Counterparts

ESPPs in the US[30]

The ESPP in the US is similar to the Japanese one in that it is not a retirement plan, but an optional plan for employees with a certain discount

---

[28] JAPAN SECURITIES DEALERS ASS'N, *supra* note 26.

[29] Because here we assume a public company ESPP which purchases the stock in market, no income will be recognized upon the purchase of stock through an ESPP. On the other hand, in the case that ESPPs purchase the stock directly from corporations through issuance of new shares, the difference (if any) between the market value and issue price may be recognized as taxable income. YO OTA ET AL., ATARASHĪ MOCHIKABU KAI SETSURITSU UN'EI NO JITSUMU [PRACTICE OF ADOPTION AND OPERATION OF NEW EMPLOYEE STOCK PURCHASE PLANS], 224 (2011). This situation is more similar to the taxation of ESPPs in the US, but there is no special treatment in Japan to defer the taxation of income recognized upon the purchase through an ESPP.

[30] Unless otherwise noted, the description is based on SANTA CLARA UNIV.

on the purchase price. Still, the structure is somewhat different. Under a typical tax-qualified ESPP, the contributions of a participating employee to the plan are accumulated by payroll deduction over a designated offering period (e.g. six months). At the end of the offering period, the employer corporation issues new shares at a discount (e.g. 15 percent) off the market price at either the beginning or the end of the offering period, whichever is lower, and participating employees purchase such shares at this price, using the accumulated contributions.

Other notable differences between ESPPs in the US and their Japanese counterparts include their special tax treatment, more freedom on participants' resale of the shares, and (for tax-qualified ESPPs) the requirement of shareholders' approval of adoption.[31] Under non-tax-qualified plans, participants will be subject to ordinary income taxation with respect to the difference between the stock's fair market value and its actual purchase price on the purchase date pursuant to I.R.C. §83, whereas participants in tax-qualified plans can defer such taxation to the time they sell the stock.[32] While ESPPs in Japan have some function to (albeit limitedly) encourage long-term shareholding by employees, ESPPs in the US often offer a feature called "quick sale" which allows employees to sell the shares acquired through the ESPPs immediately upon purchase and reap the discount offered ("flipping"). Unlike tax-qualified US ESPPs, no shareholders' approval is required for adoption of ESPPs in Japan.

ESOPs in the US[33]

Unlike the ESPP in the US and Japan, the ESOP in the US is a defined contribution retirement plan, which has to cover, with limited exceptions,

---

Certified Equity Professional Institute, GPS: ESPP (Employee Stock Purchase Plans), 7 (2012).

[31] I.R.C. §423(b)(2)

[32] I.R.C. §423. If the sale is a qualified disposition (i.e. the participant holds the stock at least for two years from the grant date and one year from the purchase date, and the participant remains an employee from the grant date to three months before the purchase date), ordinary income will be recognized in an amount which is the lesser of: (a) the difference between the fair market value of the stock at grant and the purchase price as if it were calculated on the grant date (e.g. 85 percent of the grant date fair market value); or (b) the actual gain (sale price minus the purchase price). On the other hand, for a disqualifying disposition, ordinary income is recognized upon sale to the extent the fair market value at the purchase date exceeds the purchase price, even if no actual gain is realized upon the sale. Santa Clara Univ. Certified Equity Professional Institute, *supra* note 30, at 35, 36.

[33] Unless otherwise noted, the description is based on Corey Rosen, *An Overview of How ESOPs Work*, *in* Understanding ESOPs, 1 (Corey Rosen & Scott Rodrick eds, 2010).

all general employees. A US corporation adopting an ESOP establishes a trust as a vehicle to acquire its own stock on behalf of its employees. There are a variety of ways for the corporation to have the trust acquire the company's stock, but the corporation often borrows money from a lender and reloans it to the trust; the trust then uses the money to purchase the corporation's stock (a structure called "leveraged ESOP"). The purchase is made using the corporation's money and employees do not make any contribution. The acquired shares are initially put in a suspense account and subsequently released to employee accounts as the repayment of the loan progresses. The corporation makes tax-deductible contributions to the trust and the trust repays the loan using the contribution.

Shares allocated to employees remain held in trust until employees leave the corporation, and are subject to vesting (with various vesting schedules). In listed corporations, employees have the right to direct the ESOP as to the voting of shares allocated to their employee account on all issues.[34]

The corporation and employees both enjoy tax benefits. When a loan is used to fund the ESOP, the trust will repay the loan (the secondary loan from the corporation) by using the contributions from the corporation, which are tax-deductible;[35] as a result, the corporation can, in effect, deduct both principal and interest with respect to the money it borrowed from the lender. The corporation can deduct reasonable dividends that are passed on to the participants, used to repay a loan, or reinvested in the corporation's stock at the participant's election.[36] On the other hand, employees will not be subject to taxation while the stock is held in the ESOP. The taxation occurs only upon the termination of employment and the accompanying distributions. Even then, employees can roll over the distributions into an Individual Retirement Account and further defer taxation.[37]

4.3.3 Introduction of Debt Leverage into ESPPs in Japan

The incentive effects of Japanese ESPPs in creating long-term shareholding by employees may be somewhere in between the US ESPPs and

[34] Employees of closely held corporations also have voting rights on major corporate issues, but not necessarily on all issues. I.R.C. §409(e).

[35] Deductibility limit applies. For a C corporation, contributions to be used for repayment of the principal of the loan are deductible up to 25 percent of the covered payroll separately from other defined contribution plans, while contributions to be used for interest payments are unlimitedly deductible. I.R.C. §404(a)(9).

[36] I.R.C. §404(k).

[37] I.R.C. §402(c)(1).

ESOPs, because they allow participants to withdraw the stock before termination of employment unlike the US ESOPs, while they may not offer the same flexibility in selling stock as in the US ESPPs. Also, being funded mainly by employee contributions, the size of stock purchased under Japanese ESPPs is generally limited. These facts led to the idea of creating new forms of employee ownership[38] more similar to ESOPs in the US, forms which can have a more direct effect in realizing long-term and more significant shareholding with the use of debt leverage.

Many Japanese listed corporations have already adopted such new forms, in particular after the Ministry of Economy, Trade and Industry of Japan (METI) published a report in 2008, which discusses accounting, legal, and tax issues of the new forms.[39] Broadly speaking, there are two different types in the new forms. One is a retirement benefit plan similar to US ESOPs, where a newly established trust purchases and holds the corporation's stock, and distributes it to employees upon their retirement (but without any US-like tax benefits such as deductibility of principal repayments).

The other form,[40] which is much more prevalent, is unique to the Japanese system. This form is not a retirement plan and the underlying idea is to "leverage" an existing ESPP, and thus the adopting corporation must have a conventional ESPP. Typically, the corporation establishes a trust (or an alternate vehicle), and then has the trust borrow money directly from a lender to purchase the corporation's stock (either on the market or from the corporation). The corporation provides a guaranty for such a loan. The existing ESPP continues to operate in the same way it did before the trust was established, except that the ESPP now purchases the stock from the trust, instead of buying from the public on the market. The trust sells the stock to the ESPP and uses the proceeds for repayment of the loan; the corporation does not provide the trust with other sources of repayment. The amount of shares the trust purchases at the outset is usually determined to be such that the trust can continue the sale for at least several years. If the trust retains some profits when the trust has sold

---

38 These forms are often referred to as "Japanese versions of ESOPs" in Japan. However, as discussed later, the most popular form is quite different from an actual ESOP. I intentionally avoid using that expression in this chapter.

39 Aratana Jishakabu Hoyū Sukīmu Kentō Kai [Research Committee of New Equity Ownership Scheme], *Aratana Jishakabu Hoyū Sukīmu ni Kansuru Hōkokusho [Report on New Equity Ownership Scheme]*, MINISTRY OF ECONOMY, TRADE AND INDUSTRY (Nov. 17, 2008), http://www.meti.go.jp/policy/economy/keiei_innovation/keizaihousei/esop_houkoku.pdf.

40 For more details, see OTA ET AL., *supra* note 29, at 251–260.

all the shares, the profits will be distributed to the participants in the ESPP. Conversely, if the trust cannot repay the loan in full by then, the corporation must fulfill its guaranty and repay the balance. The trustee usually votes the shares unsold and held in trust either in a way proportionately mirroring the voting of the ESPP or pursuant to a prescribed guideline (in either case voting must be independent of the corporation). By creating such a pool of stock which lasts for years (if the scheme is continuously renewed, it can be always in place), the new scheme realizes long-term and significant shareholding by employees. No specific tax benefits are given to this new form either.

4.4 HOW JAPANESE LAW SEES ESPPs

While not granting any specific tax benefits for ESPPs, Japanese law provides some special treatments for ESPPs; in particular, in the area of securities regulation. The exemption from the insider trading regulation under the Financial Instruments and Exchange Act of Japan (FIEA) is one good example. Stock purchases through ESPPs are in essence joint purchases of stock by participating employees, who are general partners of the acquisition vehicle. If the insider trading regulations were applicable to such purchases, all participating employees would have to be scrutinized upon each purchase as to whether they were in possession of any insider information. It would make the operation of ESPPs impossible in practice. The FIEA and its ancillary regulations, therefore, provide an exemption specifically available for ESPPs;[41] stock purchases through ESPPs will be exempted from insider regulations as long as the purchases are carried out continuously pursuant to a specified plan and not based on individual investment decisions, and certain other conditions are met. Japanese ESPPs are designed to be eligible for this exemption.

Another example is the exclusion of the ESPP interest from the definition of securities under the FIEA. When ESSP participants form an association, which is a general partnership, to jointly acquire the employer's stock, the partnership interest in such an ESPP partnership would be deemed "securities" under the FIEA.[42] As a result, certain regulations

---

[41] Kin'yū shōhin torihikihō [Kinshōhō][Financial Instruments and Exchange Act], Law No. 25 of 1948, art. 166, para. 6, item 8, and art. 167, para. 5, item 8, and Yūkashōken no torihiki tō no kisei ni kansuru naikaku furei [Cabinet Office Ordinance on Restrictions on Securities Transactions, etc.], Cabinet Office Ordinance No. 59 of 2007, art. 59, para. 1, item 4 and art. 63, para. 1, item 4.

[42] Kinshōhō, art. 2, para. 2, item 5.

such as disclosure and registration requirements could apply to the operation of the ESPPs. This would make the cost of adoption and operation of ESPPs prohibitive in practice. Accordingly, the partnership interest in an ESPP partnership has been excluded from the definition of securities when certain conditions similar to those required for the above-mentioned exemption from insider regulations are met.[43] This special treatment frees the adoption and operation of ESPPs from a variety of cumbersome securities regulations.

This is not a comprehensive illustration of special legal treatments granted for ESPPs under the Japanese law. Nonetheless, if the government were to abolish either of the two treatments, the operation of ESPPs in Japan would be impossible in practice. This means that Japanese law takes a more than neutral position toward the ESPPs and recognizes their potentially positive effect. If the Japanese law had recognized nothing good in ESPPs, there would have been no reason to give up regulatory interests and provide these special treatments, and open the way for ESPPs.

On the other hand, there are certain regulations that may affect the adoption and design of ESPPs in Japan. Among others, there are two significant provisions in the Companies Act of Japan (hereafter: Companies Act): (1) Article 120, which prohibits corporations from providing property benefits to their shareholders in connection with their exercise of shareholders' rights including voting rights (the "Prohibition on Property Benefits"); and (2) Article 156 et seq., which makes it a general rule that corporations must perform certain procedures including obtaining shareholders' approval before they repurchase their own shares (the "Repurchase Regulations"). Because the employer corporation provides employer contributions to the ESPP, such subsidies may be seen as property benefits in connection with the exercise of shareholders' rights, which are prohibited by the Prohibition on Property Benefits. While the Repurchase Regulations are interpreted as regulating purchases of the corporation's stock by the corporation or by a third party on account thereof, because the corporation provides part of the funds for stock purchases by ESPPs, they may be seen as being carried out on the corporation's account. However, ESPPs in Japan are operated assuming that the Repurchase Regulations do not apply. Actually, these seemingly

---

43 Kinshōhō, art. 2, para. 2, item 5, *in*, Kin'yū shōhin torihikihō shikōrei [Order for Enforcement of the Financial Instruments and Exchange Act], Cabinet Order No. 321 of 1965, art. 1-3-3, item 5 and Kin'yū shōhin torihikihō ni kitei suru teigi ni kansuru naikaku furei [Cabinet Office Ordinance on Definitions under Article 2 of the Financial Instruments and Exchange Act], Ordinance of the Ministry of Finance No. 14 of 1993, art. 6.

troublesome regulations do not really limit the adoption or operation of ESPPs, because they have been interpreted to allow for the management's discretion.

There is one lower court case[44] that discussed the application of the Prohibition on Property Benefits to an ESPP. The court reasoned that the presumption[45] that the employer contribution was made in connection with the exercise of shareholders' rights had been rebutted because the employer contributions were made for other purposes such as part of the operation of the corporate welfare program. The ruling was based on the findings that: (1) there was no unreasonable restriction on enrolling in or quitting the plan; (2) independence of the participants' voting of shares was structurally secured; (3) the participants could freely dispose of their shares after a certain volume of shares had accumulated; and (4) the amount or ratio of the employer contribution did not show any purposes for the employer contribution other than those of the ESPP. Because (1) through (3) are features an ESPP always has, and (4) does not give any strict guidance as to how much or what ratio may suggest purposes other than those of an ESPP, it does not seem very difficult for a normal ESPP to rebut the presumption. With respect to (4), while a typical level of employer contribution is 5–10 percent of the employee contribution, there are also examples of much higher contributions including 100 percent (i.e., an employee can purchase two shares for the price of one). The court and practitioners' application of the Prohibition on Property Benefits to ESPPs are quite deferential to management.

The situation for the Repurchase Regulations is quite similar. In judging whether a purchase of a corporation's stock is being conducted on account of the corporation itself, evaluation of several factors is considered necessary: (1) who provided the money for the purchase; (2) who decided the purchase; and (3) who holds the control of the stock after the purchase.[46] Some factors overlap those for the Prohibition on Property Benefits, and similarly, there is no clear line as to what should and should not be done. With respect to employer contributions, it has been argued that if employee ownership improves the employees' welfare and motivates them,

---

44 Fukui Chihō Saibansho [Fukui Dist. Ct.] Mar. 29, 1985, Showa 59 (wa) no. 53, 559 Hanrei taimuzu 275.

45 Article 120, Paragraph 2 of the Companies Act stipulates that when a corporation gratuitously provides a specific shareholder with a property benefit, it shall be presumed to be made in connection with the exercise of a shareholder's right. Because employer contributions are gratuitous, this presumption applies here.

46 Research Committee of New Equity Ownership Scheme, *supra* note 39, at 14–15.

and if the resulting benefits the corporation enjoys match the expenses the corporation bears, employer contributions can be treated as if they were costs to realize such benefits and will not provoke the Repurchase Regulations.[47] Although it is quite interesting to see part of the Japanese legal framework of ESPPs being rooted in the productivity argument, this does not give any guidance as to how high a level of employer contribution is permissible, partly because of the practical impossibility of evaluating whether the level of employer contribution matches that of the productivity effect. As a result, the Repurchase Regulations are not interpreted in a restrictive manner, resulting in deference to management.

4.5 CONCLUSION

Is it good for Japanese law to provide special treatments and open the way for ESPPs while not granting any tax advantages, and to allow management ample discretion over the adoption and design of ESPPs? First, there is as yet no consensus on the question of whether employee ownership generates net social wealth. Nevertheless, Japanese law shows a favorable attitude towards ESPPs by providing specific regulatory exemptions, which is a judgment that cannot be proven either right or wrong based on studies to date. On the other hand, Japanese law does not go as far as US law, which provides tax advantages for employee ownership. Instead, Japanese law solely lifts regulations and leaves the choice to the respective corporations, or to the market. This makes Japanese law immune from the criticism that tax subsidies cannot be justified and are resulting in a mere shift of tax burdens among taxpayers.

However, the positive studies do not praise employee ownership unreservedly. They require accompanying corporate culture or employment practices to solve the free-rider problem among employees. Accordingly, if the law is to promote employee ownership, the ideal law should make such factors prerequisites for the adoption of employee ownership. Having said that, it is difficult for a statute to precisely define these vague factors in reality. Also, such factors may vary from corporation to corporation. As a result, when assuming that ESPPs can contribute to corporate performance, the realistic choice will be to trust in the business judgment of the management, who are most familiar with the corporate culture or employment practices, and most likely to make the right decision. The Companies

---

47 Osamu Mimura, *Jugyōin Mochikabu Seido* <Jō> [*Employee stock purchase plans* <Vol. 1>], 430 SHŌJI HŌMU KENKYŪ 2, 5 (1967).

Act regulations affecting ESPPs are interpreted in such a manner that management have ample discretion in adopting and designing the plan. This seems in line with the abovementioned position that the judgment should be deferred to management.

Considering the above, the current Japanese legal framework is a realistic and reasonable choice based on the assumption that ESPPs can contribute to corporate performance, which, in itself, is a judgment that cannot be either verified or refuted under the present circumstances.

On the other hand, because of the ever-present doubt that management will abuse employee ownership for their own entrenchment, attention should be paid to prevent management from placing their own interests ahead of those of shareholders. In a situation where a battle over corporate control is present, because of the obviousness of the conflict of interest, shareholders are likely to take actions which may prevent the abuse. Actually, the Tokyo High Court recently heard the first case involving the new scheme of a "leveraged" ESPP[48] adopted pending a corporate control dispute.[49] However, unlike this new scheme, traditional ESPPs do not have a feature to instantly create a large shareholder, and cannot be used as a takeover defense with immediate effect. Instead, the effect of ESPPs may be more continuous and long-term, an effect that we cannot expect shareholders to detect. Therefore, the real challenge is how we can address such a quiet conflict of interest when no takeover threat exists. One extreme is to always require shareholders' approval before adopting an ESPP, in the same way that shareholders' approval is required for a US ESPP to be tax-qualified. However, this approach contradicts the idea that management is in a better position to know the corporate culture or employment practices, and may lead to another inefficient outcome by prohibiting management from adopting an ESPP which would otherwise improve corporate performance. Also, because Japanese ESPPs are so widespread among Japanese corporations, as a practical matter, the transition cost of introducing such a new requirement will likely become prohibitive. A more modest, but realistic measure may be to encourage management to conduct a more detailed analysis of employee owner-

---

48 See section 4.3.

49 The court ruled for the corporation and rejected the appeal seeking an injunction of the stock issuance to the acquisition vehicle. The court applied the primary purpose rule, which has been long adopted by Japanese lower courts, and concluded that the primary purpose of the stock issuance accompanying the adoption of the new scheme was not to dilute the hostile shareholder's influence over the company. Tōkyō Kōtō Saibansho [Tōkyō High Ct.] Jul. 12, 2012, Heisei 24 (ra) no. 1457, 341 SHIRYŌBAN SHŌJI HŌMU 27.

ship and to hold them accountable for such analysis. While it does not seem possible or preferable to create a uniform statute to incorporate the complementarity issue, management should be encouraged to consider it when adopting or operating an ESPP or deciding to leverage the existing ESPP through the adoption of a new scheme. It seems that management, and Japanese legal society as a whole, have not paid enough attention to this issue (or accumulation of empirical studies in general) when thinking of employee ownership.[50] ESPPs in Japan represent one of the many areas where empirical studies can contribute to improvement of the legal system.

---

50 For example, the METI report (*supra* note 39) on the new schemes took the productivity effect of ESPPs somewhat for granted, and did not closely examine empirical studies.

Comments on Part I: complementarity

Hideshi Itoh

Complementarity is an important concept in my field of specialization, organizational economics (see Brynjolfsson and Milgrom, 2012, for an up-to-date overview of complementarity in organizations). It should be important for the study of "enterprise law" as defined as the entire range of private contracts and public regulations governing the relationship of different capital providers (see the 'Introduction' to this volume by Shishido). It is in particular relevant for Part I: complementarities among various employment, personnel and workplace practices have been extensively examined in the economics and management literature.

The theme of Part I, incentive bargaining between employees and management, is also closely related to complementarities between various practices for employees and corporate governance (Aoki, 1994). Pagano and Volpin (2005), cited in Chapters 2 and 4, point out theoretically a possibility of alliance between employees and incumbent managers against potential raiders, and show that labor–management alliance is formed if the managers' incentive to maximize shareholder value is weak, and under that condition employment policy is likely to be used by the managers only if employees are sufficiently well protected by law. Tirole (2006, Chapter 1) conjectures that one reason why shareholder-value maximization is less controversial in Anglo-Saxon countries than in continental Europe and Japan is that negative externalities imposed by shareholder control on other stakeholders – in particular, employees – are smaller in the former countries, due to general training and flexible labor markets. Hirota and Kawamura (2007) rigorously analyze internal governance mechanisms by employees as a substitute for external mechanisms by shareholders.

Furthermore, complementarity is relevant to each chapter of Part I. As the title shows, it is obviously a core concept in Chapter 2 by Kitagawa, who studies complementarities among employment protection law, informal norms, and labor markets. Chapter 4 by Higashi mentions the importance of complementarities between the employee stock purchase plan (ESPP), stock ownership plan (ESOP) and other employment and workplace features (such as employment protection, information sharing, teams, internal training, and so forth) in order for ESPP and ESOP to have significant productivity effects. While the term "complementarity" does not appear in the other chapters, I think it still has some relevance. Chapter 3 by Dau-Schmidt and Ellis suggests that the differences in relative bargaining power of unions and management between the United States and Japan generated by the labor laws complement their differences in factors related to outside options of labor and management, which in turn are affected by information technology. Chapter 1 by Verkerke suggests that employment protection law (EPL) is a system that consists of complementary legal rules and constraints.

My modest purpose here is to complement these chapters by offering an accessible formal definition of complementarity. Suppose there are two institutions denoted by Y and Z. For example, Y could be an employee stock purchase plan (ESPP), and Z a rule protecting employee dismissal I denote by y and z the "levels" of Y and Z: here I assume for simplicity that these variables take either 0 or 1. For example, $y = 0$ means "Y does not exist" and $y = 1$ means "Y exists." I can then draw the following table consisting of four cells:

	$y = 0$	$y = 1$
$z = 1$	b	d
$z = 0$	a	c

The letter in each cell represents the numerical "performance measure" of the combination of institutions corresponding to the cell. For example, if neither institution exists, that is, $(y,z) = (0,0)$, then performance is a; if only institution Y exists, that is, $(y,z) = (1,0)$, performance is c.

Here is one example of complementarity, based on this table. The statement of complementarity "ESPP does not generate any positive effect unless it is combined with some other practice, such as employment protection" corresponds to $b = 0$, $c = 0$, and $d > 0$, with normalization of performance under neither institution by $a = 0$, That is, institutional change has a positive performance effect only if both institutions Y and Z are introduced together. I think this pattern of complementarity is easiest to understand intuitively.

It is an extreme pattern, however. Here is a precise definition of complementarity. Two institutions Y and Z exhibit complementarity if:

$$a + d > b + c$$

holds. This inequality can be rewritten as:

$$d - b > c - a,$$

or

$$d - c > b - a.$$

The first rewritten inequality ($d - b > c - a$) means that performance change from introducing institution Y is larger when Z already exists ($d - b$) than when Z does not exist ($c - a$). Similarly, the last inequality means that performance changes more with the introduction of institution Z when Y already exists ($d - c$) than when Y does not exist ($b - a$). If any one of the three inequalities holds, then the other inequalities are satisfied as well.

As another example, if $a > 0$, $d > 0$, $b \leq 0$, and $c \leq 0$ hold, the left-hand side of each of the last two inequalities is positive, and the right-hand side is negative. The inequalities are thus satisfied, and Y and Z exhibit complementarity. Note that in this example, performance is highest at $(y,z) = (0,0)$ or $(y,z) = (1,1)$: introducing either no institution or both institutions is optimal. If no institution is currently introduced and $d > a$ holds, moving from (0,0) to (1,1) is desirable. However, such a move is difficult because performance is decreased by introducing only one of the institutions. Furthermore, uncertainty concerning which of d and a is larger makes institutional change even harder.

Hirota and Kawamura (2007) are interested in comparative analysis of governance of managers by employees (internal governance) and that by shareholders (external governance). In the table, suppose Y represents internal governance and Z external governance. Their comparison is then between b and c, and having both is inferior, implying that these governance mechanisms are unlikely to exhibit complementarity.

One can analyze complementarities among various legal rules by regarding Y and Z as distinct rules, and by examining four possible patterns (0,0), (0,1), (1,0), and (1,1) explicitly. When more than two laws interact with each other, more patterns have to be analyzed. Comparative analysis of laws, while it remains to be seen, looks very promising.

REFERENCES

Aoki, Masahiko, *The Japanese Firm as a System of Attributes: A Survey and Research Agenda, in* Masahiko Aoki and Ronald Dore (eds), THE JAPANESE FIRM: SOURCES OF COMPETITIVE STRENGTH, 1994, pp. 11–40, Oxford University Press.

Brynjolfsson, Erik and Paul Milgrom, *Complementarity in Organizations, in* Robert Gibbons and John Roberts (eds), THE HANDBOOK OF ORGANIZATIONAL ECONOMICS, 2012, pp. 11–55, Princeton University Press.

Hirota, Shinichi and Kohei Kawamura, *Managerial Control inside the Firm*, JOURNAL OF THE JAPANESE AND INTERNATIONAL ECONOMIES, vol. 21, 2007, pp. 324–335.

Pagano, M. and P.F. Volpin, *Managers, Workers, and Corporate Governance*, JOURNAL OF FINANCE vol. 60, 2005, pp. 841–868.

Tirole, Jean, THE THEORY OF CORPORATE FINANCE, Princeton University Press, 2006.

PART II

The incentive bargain between creditors and management

5. The role of debt in the governance of US business corporations

George Triantis

5.1 INTRODUCTION

For the most part, the study of corporate governance in the US has focused on the control mechanisms of shareholders: particularly their right to vote for and replace directors, to solicit proxies, and to acquire voting control through takeover bids. Yet, debtholders have their own control rights that should be incorporated in analyses of corporate governance. The essence of a debt contract gives the debtholder a contingent right to remove assets and possibly to force liquidation in the event of the borrower's default. The contract lists the obligations and covenants whose violation constitutes an event of default. In addition, debtholders control the firm's access to capital in two ways. First, debt contracts typically require the borrower to make periodic payments of interest and principal, which removes internal capital and thereby might compel the borrower to seek external financing for new projects. Second, the priority of debt claims (particularly secured or senior claims) can impede the future ability of the firm to raise capital from outside investors.

Insolvency lawyers (and scholars) are more closely familiar with the levers of creditor control than their corporate law counterparts, because these levers are more significant when the corporation is financially distressed. Debtholder control assumes different forms depending on whether the distressed firm is also in bankruptcy proceedings. Outside of bankruptcy, distressed debtors may be in default or in imminent danger of default, and they are either insolvent or on the verge of insolvency. As a result, creditors may either exercise their rights to remove assets or threaten to do so in order to influence corporate decisions. Although creditors should be careful in exercising their governance levers so as not to assume liability for the civil or regulatory debts of the corporation, the law allows debt contracts to provide for a broad scope for creditor control.

Creditor control in bankruptcy is quite different. In some ways, creditors have more influence inside bankruptcy than outside because shareholder control rights are limited and eventually eliminated. Yet, bankruptcy freezes the ability of pre-bankruptcy creditors to enforce their contractual rights and to seek satisfaction from the debtor's assets. In place of these rights, bankruptcy law places the decisions of the debtor under the oversight of the bankruptcy judge. Creditors have the right to appear before the judge on any issue relating to the debtor, and they are entitled to vote for or against a plan of reorganization. Over the past 20 years, however, the bankruptcy process has become far more contractual, allowing creditors to recover many of the control levers they enjoy outside of bankruptcy. In particular, lenders who provide new capital to debtors in bankruptcy do so under new agreements that convey to the lenders the same type of rights they enjoy in deals outside of bankruptcy.

At the same time, developments in financial markets have witnessed the growing separation of the economic and control rights of debtholdings. Some parties hold formal debt claims and control rights, while they have transferred away the economic risk through techniques such as securitizations or swaps. This poses a fundamental challenge to the traditional paradigm of debtholder governance, and a new one has yet to emerge to replace it. Moreover, bankruptcy law's reliance on representation through committees, judicial hearings, and voting needs to be reconsidered in light of this market transformation.

This chapter begins by describing in section 5.2 the conventional paradigm of creditor control, which historically has been exemplified by bank lending, and the more elaborate model of interactive governance. Section 5.3 discusses the role of priority in corporate decision making, both out of and in bankruptcy. Section 5.4 discusses the emergence of contractual instruments of creditor control in bankruptcy cases. Section 5.5 identifies some of the fundamental issues stemming from the rise in the fragmentation of debt over the past decade.

5.2 THE CONVENTIONAL PARADIGM: RELATIONAL LENDER CONTROL

The paradigmatic relational creditor through the 1980s was the bank lender who extended a term loan and a revolving line of credit. The bank screened its borrower and then monitored its operations and financial condition. Many of the terms of loan agreements could be traced to these functions. Periodic repayments withdrew cash from the borrower, thereby removing internal capital with which managers could pursue inefficient projects in their self-interest, and compelling them to raise necessary funds through their bank or in external capital markets. Covenants – such as limitations on future borrowing, asset sales or mergers – restricted the borrower's freedom to act in ways that enriched managers or shareholders at the expense of the creditors. Violations of these covenants were events of default that accelerated the maturity of the loans. When covenants were tight, the borrower was often compelled to seek lender approval in order to pursue opportunities outside the ordinary course of business, such as significant asset sales or acquisitions. Finally, banks often held security interests over a large portion of their borrowers' assets, which further enhanced their leverage over corporate decisions.

Armed with these contractual rights, banks would police their debtors in order to reduce the risks of their loans. These institutions thereby played important governance roles. To a large degree, this influence was benign because other creditors benefitted from the discipline that banks imposed on self-interested managerial or shareholder actions (interdependent governance). Even if a bank decided to call in a loan because of a default or to demand more collateral, its actions in so doing communicated valuable information to other constituencies, so that they could intervene to rectify problematic management (interactive governance[1]). For its contribution to corporate governance, the bank received an implicit premium in the contractual rate of interest or fees (above the rates that public debtholders would be offered). The benefit of bank monitoring spread to other constituencies such as suppliers, employees, and even shareholders. The announcement of a new bank financing agreement or a renewal often enhanced the borrower's ability to raise capital from other sources and produced even abnormal increases in the price of the borrower's stock.

Of course, the bank's influence over corporate decision making was not always benign. In particular, the bank's self-interest conflicted with those of other constituencies when the borrower was in financial distress. For example, a secured bank lender could threaten acceleration to induce the borrower to transfer value to collateral assets (such as inventory) by selling other assets in which the bank has no security interest. Various legal rules provided some (but not full) protection to the more passive constituencies. This is discussed in some detail elsewhere, but one example is the rule against preferential transfers under bankruptcy law.[2] Under this rule, the bankruptcy trustee can reverse increases in the value of the bank's

---

1 George G. Triantis & Ronald J. Daniels, *The Role of Debt in Interactive Corporate Governance*, 83 CALIF. L. REV. 1073 (1994); George G. Triantis, *Debt Financing, Corporate Decision Making and Security Design*, 26 CAN. BUS. L. J. 93 (1995).

2 *Id.*

collateral that occur while the borrower is insolvent and within 90 days before bankruptcy.

5.3 CREDITOR PRIORITY AND GOVERNANCE

A significant feature of a firm's debt is its hierarchical structure: a debt claim may have priority over others either because the former is secured by collateral or because the latter is contractually subordinated. The motivation for this hierarchical structure is more complicated than it might seem at first blush and, over the past 30 years, a number of scholars have sought to explain the presence of secured credit. One theory, for example, is that some creditors take security interest in assets in which they enjoy comparative monitoring advantages.[3] Another theory is that firms can exploit less sophisticated or non-consensual creditors whose claims are compromised by the debtor's issuance of security interests to other creditors.[4]

In the mid-1990s, a different explanation emerged.[5] Secured debt restricts the availability of external financing because its principal and interest has priority over liabilities incurred to later investors whether they are unsecured or secured. The resulting impediment to new financing can be efficient or inefficient, depending on the future cash flow and investment opportunities of the borrower. If the borrower has few profitable opportunities, existing priority debt makes it difficult for managers to pursue inefficient projects that serve their selfish interests or those of their shareholders. In the language of finance theory, priority debt mitigates the problem of overinvestment. However, priority debt also restricts the borrower's ability to raise new capital for profitable projects. Depending on the amount of the prior debt, either these projects must be very profitable or the firm must renegotiate with the priority debtholder. In the language of finance theory, priority debt exacerbates the problem of underinvestment or debt overhang.

---

3 *E.g.* Alan Schwartz, *Security Interests and Bankruptcy Priorities: A Review of Current Theories*, 10 J. LEGAL STUDIES 1 (1981); Saul Levmore, *Monitors and Freeriders in Commercial and Corporate Settings*, 92 YALE L. J. 49 (1982); George G. Triantis, *Secured Debt under Conditions of Imperfect Information*, 21 J. LEGAL STUDIES 225 (1992).

4 *E.g.*, Schwartz, *supra* note 3.

5 George G. Triantis, *A Free Cash-Flow Theory of Secured Debt and Creditor Priorities*, 80 VA. L. REV. 2155 (1994); George G. Triantis, *Financial Slack and the Laws of Secured Transactions*, 29 J. LEGAL STUDIES 35 (2000). See also Oliver Hart & John Moore, *Debt and Seniority: An Analysis of the Role of Hard Claims in Constraining Management*, 85 AM. ECON. REV. 567 (1995).

The delicate balance between correcting for overinvestment and minimizing the underinvestment problem is illustrated in the following simple example. Suppose that a firm has assets worth $100 and owes $80 to its initial lender (Cl) who enjoys the highest priority as a first-in-time lender. Lender Cl holds a perfected blanket lien over all the firm's current and after-acquired assets. One year from today, the firm has equal chances of being in one of two possible states. In the good state, the firm's current assets would be worth $150; in the bad state, they would be worth $50 (that is, the firm is insolvent in the bad state). The firm now has an opportunity to invest in project A, which is a risk-free, profitable project that requires an investment of $20 and will yield $30 a year from now (a certain return of 50 percent). Assume that the firm cannot capture the value of this venture by transferring it to another entity because, for example, it has no property right protection in the opportunity. It also has no available liquid assets to invest.

Suppose for the moment that Cl cannot finance the investment. Shareholders will not invest $20 in new equity because the debt overhang from Cl's priority claim in the bad state would absorb their investment, and their payoff from the good state is $30, which yields an expected payoff of only $15. Given Cl's first-in-time priority, a new creditor C2 would also recover nothing in the insolvent state and, therefore, C2 would lend only if the firm promised it at least $40 in the good state (an expected value of $20) to compensate for the effect of debt overhang in the bad state. The project pays only $30 in the good state, however, and the balance must come out of the value currently owned by the shareholders. Therefore, the shareholders and C2 would not reach an agreement to finance the project. If, however, C2 were given priority, the debt could be paid in full in both states. The shareholders and C2 could therefore agree to split the gains from project A in the good state. In this example, therefore, later-in-time priority for C2 is necessary to exploit the profitable project.

In contrast, suppose that the firm has the opportunity to invest in project B, which has a negative expected value. Project B requires an investment of $20 and yields $30 in the good state and nothing in the bad state. Although they are not willing to finance the project, the shareholders would encourage the firm to take the gamble because it improves their payoff in the good state without making them worse off in the bad state. If Cl has priority over all subsequent lenders, its priority effectively precludes the firm from obtaining financing to fund the gamble. However, if the new investor C2 enjoyed priority, it would be paid in full in either state and can be enticed into the coalition by the promise of a portion of the shareholders' gain in the good state. Similarly, given later-in-time priority, C2 would also be prepared to finance other forms of misbehavior, such as distributions to shareholders, perquisites to managers, or a reserve pool of cash that insulates managers from the discipline of product or factor markets. In each case, C2 facilitates and participates in the inefficient transfer of wealth from C1.

Thus, the granting of a priority to a lender has a significant effect on the future decisions of the borrower. In this regard, it is worthwhile to contrast the operation of covenants and events of default, on the one hand, and debt priority on the other. They are similar in the sense that they restrict managerial discretion: in one case, by threatening acceleration and liquidation; and in the other case, by impeding access to external capital. Therefore, one might view these instruments as substitutes: low-priority debt may have tighter covenants than high-priority debt. This prediction, however, is not borne out in practice. Secured bank loans often have strict restrictions across a range of corporate decisions so that covenants and security interests work together, particularly where the borrower has either a thin or problematic track record. Conversely, business enterprises with abundant opportunities or other effective sources of discipline on managerial misbehavior are both less likely to have priority debt and less likely to be subject to significant restrictive covenants.

As governance tools, covenants and priority differ in an important respect. The behavior being proscribed must be described in covenants, in more or less precise terms. Even vague language must be construed eventually by a court in the event of dispute. In contrast, as suggested above, the first-in-time priority of security interests lets the market decide what types of investments to allow. This discipline is self-executing (unlike that of covenants and events of default) in the sense that it does not require active monitoring by any party. Moreover, the priority of a secured party is a property interest that can be enforced against third parties (such as future creditors and transferees outside the ordinary course of business), while covenants cannot. Therefore, a future lender who finances a breach of covenant cannot be sanctioned under that contract, but it would bear the cost of being subordinate to an earlier security interest.[6]

The problems of both overinvestment and debt overhang are more severe when the debtor is insolvent. Bankruptcy law addresses overinvestment by giving the court powers to oversee the activities of the debtor. The court has the authority to determine whether the debtor should be reorganized or liquidated, and if the debtor continues to operate, the

---

6 George Triantis, *Exploring the Limits of Contract Design in Debt Financing*, 161 U.Pa.L.Rev. 2041 (2013).

court must authorize decisions made outside the debtor's ordinary course of business. It is relatively more difficult for a court to compel investment in positive net present value opportunities than to block unprofitable projects. Therefore, the overhang problem is addressed by creating financial slack under judicial intervention. Bankruptcy courts have the authority to increase the availability of cash flow and the ability of the debtor to issue secured or senior debt to postpetition lenders. The justification for making a broader later-in-time priority available in bankruptcy is that: (1) the debt overhang problem is more severe when the firm is insolvent; and (2) the affairs of the debtor are being overseen by the court and by creditor committees, which signals a shift in emphasis from *ex ante* constraints in the capital structure to *ex post* discipline under the bankruptcy process.[7]

The main way that the bankruptcy judge can allow later-in-time priority is by authorizing debtor-in-possession (DIP) financing. Under §364 of the US Bankruptcy Code, a firm in bankruptcy can finance its ongoing operations and investments by issuing new debt that enjoys higher priority than the firm's pre-petition unsecured debt. Moreover, under §364(d), the court may authorize later-in-time priority that is senior even to a pre-petition security interest in the debtor's assets. In order to "prime" pre-petition security interests in this manner, the debtor must show not only that the firm is unable to obtain credit otherwise but also that the interest of the pre-petition secured party is adequately protected.

Adequate protection requires that the pre-petition secured party's economic position is somehow preserved. A debtor who applies for DIP financing is unlikely to have either the liquid or unencumbered assets with which to provide adequate protection. Rather, the debtor often asserts that the secured party will realize the indubitable equivalent of its interest in the collateral because of the profitability of the proposed investment of new capital. The debtor then proposes that the primed creditor either can be paid periodically from the value created or will continue to enjoy a substantial equity cushion in its collateral as a result. Consequently, the court's assessment of the profitability of the proposed use of new funds and continuation of the firm has been pivotal in many cases. Thus, the requirement of adequate protection calls on the bankruptcy court to ensure that the new funds will finance only value-creating (positive net present value) investments.

---

7 George G. Triantis, *A Theory of the Regulation of Debtor-in-Possession Financing*, 46 Vand. L. Rev. 901 (1993); Triantis, *Financial Slack*, *supra* note 5.

5.4 ACTIVE LENDER CONTROL IN BANKRUPTCY

The Bankruptcy Code was designed to replace the contract rights of creditors with the oversight of the bankruptcy judge. The bankruptcy stay prohibits creditors from taking steps to enforce their rights against the debtor, in accelerating the maturity, suing for judgment, or executing a judgment against the debtor's assets. The set of covenants, events of default, acceleration and enforcement rights in debt contracts cease to be relevant. Instead, the debtor must obtain authorization from the bankruptcy judge of any decision outside the ordinary course of its business. In addition, the judge will review even decisions in the ordinary course, upon a motion by a creditor.

As noted above, the judge may authorize the debtor to issue priority debt, even if such action is prohibited by covenants in the firm's outstanding debt. The judge also has discretion to authorize priority that primes a pre-petition secured claim, an action that could not occur outside of bankruptcy without the consent of the secured creditor. The court also may be inclined to permit priority financing in a wider range of cases in bankruptcy than are available outside of bankruptcy because it has other means at its disposal to sanction misbehavior and control managerial discretion. In the past, the motions and judicial orders authorizing DIP financing were relatively simple and short.

DIP financing became increasingly common through the 1990s, rising from about 30 percent to over 50 percent of bankruptcy reorganization cases at the end of the decade. The DIP lenders fell largely into three groups: (1) significant pre-petition creditors (the majority of DIP lenders); (2) new lenders seeking high return and low risk, which might also provide exit financing; and (3) potential acquirers or future equity partners. Most DIP lenders received security interests in virtually all the debtor's assets and contracted for the right to enforce these interests in the event of default without further judicial permission. Over the course of the 1990s and into the first decade of this century, DIP agreements contained significant affirmative and negative covenants, many of which controlled the path of the bankruptcy case. For example, they would specify deadlines and prescribe procedures for asset sales or plan confirmation. They would often impose cash flow requirements, budgets and performance targets; the failure to comply would trigger default. These developments are widely regarded as having restored lender control in the governance of debtors in bankruptcy, after a couple of decades in which observers deemed debtors to be in control.

There is some evidence that DIP lending promotes successful bankruptcy outcomes: that reorganization is more likely and that bond prices enjoy positive returns. However, this evidence is relatively weak. A darker side of DIP financing is also plausible and calls for further empirical examination. DIP financing agreements are authorized with considerable urgency, so that other creditors have little time and limited information with which to object. Courts are usually not presented with alternative financing proposals and seem averse to the risk of undermining restructuring efforts. Two systematic patterns of authorizations should raise some concern about the process.

First, where a pre-petition lender also provides the DIP financing, the courts generally allow the lender to "roll up" its pre-petition debt with its postpetition DIP financing agreement. As a result, the lender can bootstrap its pre-petition undersecured debt to the higher priority of its DIP loan, which must be paid in full in a confirmed reorganization. In the two major business bankruptcy jurisdictions in the US (Delaware and New York), the courts generally permit this as long as there has been full disclosure. For reasons I have explored elsewhere, the roll-up (or its cousin, cross-collateralization) is unnecessary to correct the problem of debt overhang. Instead, it redistributes value to the DIP lender from the next level of priority creditors and it may well cause wasteful overinvestment. It appears that half of the pre-petition lenders who contributed a DIP loan in these jurisdictions enjoyed a roll-up of their pre-petition debt, and that ratio is increasing.

Second, some DIP lenders end up purchasing assets in subsequent sales. In fact, it is an increasingly well-traveled path, particularly for private equity firms, to the acquisition of liquidated assets or equity interests in the reorganized company. As noted above, the terms of the DIP loan often set the procedure and timetable for the sale or reorganization. Two well-known examples occurred in airline bankruptcies. The DIP lender to US Airways, Retirement Systems of Alabama, subsequently acquired 37.5 percent of the postpetition stock and five of 13 seats on the board. American Airlines' DIP arrangement with TWA required an auction of TWA's assets. As expected, American Airlines was the purchaser. Courts are aware of these patterns. Yet, the fact that DIP lenders are prospective purchasers raises concerns about their conflicts of interest, particularly when they have hedged their default risks, as discussed briefly in the next section.

5.5 FRAGMENTATION OF DEBT

Legal ownership is characterized by two fundamental attributes: (1) an economic interest in the value of the subject property and (2) control rights. For example, common stock comprises a residual interest in the value of the corporation as well as dividends, after fixed debt claims have been satisfied, and the right to vote for directors and to enforce fiduciary obligations. The holder of a debt instrument has an economic interest in the collection of principal and interest from the corporation, and the right to enforce that claim against its assets. Under non-bankruptcy law, the creditor can sue and enforce its judgment against corporate assets. Under bankruptcy law, it has the right to participate in the bankruptcy process and to share in the distributions under liquidation or a reorganization plan.

The active role of a debtholder in corporate governance depends on a debtholder's incentives which, in turn, rest on its economic interest in the firm. In the conventional paradigm of the relational bank described in Section 5.2, the lender had the incentive to monitor for signs of financial distress or inefficient decisions, in order to be able to reduce its exposure or induce a change of strategy in the firm. Moreover, the bank also benefitted from the profitable growth of the borrower's enterprise, which could bring more business for the bank. The broader, interactive governance paradigm integrated the monitoring and governance activities of many diverse constituencies, including smaller trade creditors, employees, customers, and so on. Each one of these actors had an economic interest in the profitability of the firm, and would decide to exit or exercise voice if it witnessed signs of distress.

Driven by risk-spreading objectives over the past decade or more, debtholders have fragmented and transferred the economic risk of their investment in corporate borrowers. Loan syndications and participations were followed by the evolution of collateralized loans and debt obligations, and by credit default swaps (CDS). A considerable body of literature has been focused on the manner in and extent to which credit risk has been shifted away from banks in the vast markets for these instruments. In particular, if a lender has transferred away its economic interest in the borrower through loan participations, securitization or CDS, how can it be relied on to monitor the borrower and intervene to correct mismanagement? The incentives of the holder of naked control are at least to shirk, and they may be even swayed further by ulterior motives or interests (such as an interest in acquiring the assets of the distressed borrower).

The puzzle at stake can be divided into three layers. The first layer concerns the contract between the initial lender, who is in privity with the borrower, and the subsequent transferees of portions of the risk of the borrower's enterprise. Why do these investors accept such risk and yet leave the control levers of debt in the hands of a party who retains little if any economic interest in the borrower? One might imagine that the risk bearer might require the holder of the naked control rights to exercise them with loyalty and due care. But how effective can we expect a contractual duty of loyalty or care to be in these circumstances?

Where the risk is fragmented into such small pieces, is there any other party or institution that might be in a position to exercise the governance levers of debt? In the past, indenture trustees have been notoriously lax in monitoring on behalf of their debenture holders. Under the paradigm of interdependent governance, however, at least the investors could rely on a bank walking the beat on their behalf. The issuance of dispersed debt instruments under an indenture had another significant feature: they were very difficult to modify or restructure. Then again, under the traditional paradigm, it was the bank (along with other creditors) which led the restructuring. So, the second layer asks how the separation of the economic interest and control rights of debt affects other investors who might rely on the monitoring of lenders or who interact with them along the lines of the interactive model outlined in Section 5.2.

A third question is how the legal process of bankruptcy needs to be adjusted to this reality. As noted earlier, bankruptcy substitutes the right to appear before the judge and to vote, for the debtholder's contractual right outside of bankruptcy to enforce the covenants of the debt agreement. The bankruptcy mechanism relies on representation. For example, a creditor's committee is typically comprised of the creditors who hold the largest claims against the debtor. When a reorganization plan is put to a vote, the plan must receive a supermajority of two-thirds in amount of the claims in each class of creditors. Accordingly, if a debtholder holds more than one-third of the nominal amount, it can block or delay a plan, even if it has no economic interest in the debtor.

For example, a creditor holding a $400 million claim may have bought credit protection, through a swap or otherwise. This may dramatically reduce its economic exposure. Is it likely to be a good representative of other creditors, either in adversarial hearings before the court relating to decisions of the debtor during bankruptcy or in the voting for the exit of the debtor under a reorganization plan? The lender with naked control may have a range of ulterior motives. As noted in the previous section, a hedge fund may purchase the distressed debt of a firm and use its resulting influence in bankruptcy proceedings to purchase the firm's assets at favorable prices. The incentives could be even more distorted. For example, a creditor may be hedged to such an extent that it is left with a "negative" exposure, leading the creditor to prefer the failure over the success of the borrower. The Bankruptcy Code and its rules do not mandate disclosure of hedging activity. Some judges have applied their discretion to require it. Disclosure, however, is only the first step toward a solution to the underlying governance process. A new institution may well emerge, or an old one re-emerge, to restore the lost discipline on corporate decision making. In the meantime, Congress and bankruptcy judges might reconsider the reliance on representation that lies at the core of the governance structure in bankruptcy.

5.6 CONCLUSION

Debt has long enjoyed a prominent role in US corporate governance, but the configuration of this role has been in flux over the past 25 years or so. The conventional paradigm of relational bank lending in the US is not as common today. Patterns of the essential governance tools of covenants and security interests have fluctuated over time, as covenant-lite structures wax and wane, seemingly in response to market forces that are unconnected to governance parameters.[8] As Professors Ayotte and Morrison describe in the next chapter, secured DIP lenders now exercise significant control over the process, which in turn is more focused on the sale of assets and less on the reorganization of the liabilities of the debtor. Further attention in law and finance scholarship will be warranted as debtholders continue to play a critical governance role and we evolve toward a new model of interactive corporate governance.

[8] Albert Choi and George Triantis, *Market Conditions and Contract Design: Variations in Debt Contracting*, 88 N.Y.U.L.Rev. 51 (2013).

6. Senior creditor control in Chapter 11

Kenneth M. Ayotte and Edward R. Morrison*

6.1 INTRODUCTION

Two themes dominate traditional accounts of Chapter 11 bankruptcy reorganization in the United States. First, managers or equity holders, or both, control the reorganization process.[1] This is made possible by debtor-friendly features of the US Bankruptcy Code and judges who are passive or biased in favor of continuation. Exploiting the court's protection, managers can entrench themselves and equity holders can extract concessions from creditors in the form of deviations from absolute priority. As a result, courts may permit reorganizations of firms that should liquidate. The second theme, usually implicit in the literature, is that creditors act as a unified constituency, usually in agitating for a quick liquidation. Together, these traditional themes continue to influence the academic literature in many areas related to financial distress.

A recent wave of literature by academics[2] and practitioners [3] suggests

* This chapter is a condensed version of Kenneth M. Ayotte & Edward R. Morrison, *Creditor Control and Conflict in Chapter 11*, 1 J. LEGAL ANALYSIS 511 (2009).

[1] Classic references are Michael Bradley & Michael Rosenzweig, *The Untenable Case for Chapter 11*, 101 YALE L. J. 1043 (1992); Lucian Arye Bebchuk & Howard F. Chang, *Bargaining and the Division of Value in Corporate Reorganizations*, 8 J. L. ECON. & ORG. 253 (1992); Alan Schwartz, *A Contract Theory Approach to Business Bankruptcy*, 107 YALE L. J. 127, 183 n.60 (1997); Barry E. Adler, *Financial and Political Theories of American Corporate Bankruptcy*, 45 STAN. L. REV. 311, 315–316 (1993).

[2] Douglas G. Baird & Robert K. Rasmussen, *The End of Bankruptcy*, 55 STAN. L. REV. 751 (2002); David Skeel, *Creditor's Ball: The "New" New Corporate Governance in Chapter 11*, 152 U. PENN. L. REV. 917 (2003); Elizabeth Warren & Jay Westbrook, *Secured Party in Possession*, 2003 AM. BANKR. INST. J. 150 (Sept. 2003); Barry E. Adler, Vedran Capkun, & Lawrence A. Weiss, *Destruction of Value in the New Era of Chapter 11*, working paper (2008).

[3] Harvey R. Miller & Shay Y. Waisman, *Does Chapter 11 Reorganization*

that these themes – at least in large corporate bankruptcies – are outdated. During the past decade, creditors with senior, secured claims have come to dominate the Chapter 11 process. Much of this creditor control is exercised through pre- and post-petition secured lines of credit, which limit the debtor's access to cash and impose strict requirements on business activity.[4] Because of this control, it is argued, we have seen a dramatic increase in the proportion of Chapter 11 cases that result in piecemeal liquidation or a going-concern sale.[5] Among large, publicly traded firms in Chapter 11, going-concern sales accounted for less than 20 percent of cases filed during the 1980s.[6] In 2002, they accounted for about 75 percent of the cases.[7]

In addition to shifting the focus away from equity and managerial control in Chapter 11, the recent literature also directs attention away from the unified, single-creditor framework. The onset of senior, secured creditor control raises issues of potential creditor conflict between senior and junior classes of debt. As senior lenders have obtained control through pre- and post-petition financing, junior lenders have used claims trading, committees, and other tactics to gain leverage over the reorganization process.[8] Junior lender activism has increased as hedge funds and other investors have purchased the claims of bondholders and similarly dispersed creditors who, in the past, did not participate actively in the bankruptcy process.[9, 10]

Remain a Viable Option for Distressed Businesses For the Twenty-First Century?, 78 Am. Bankr. L. J. 153 (2004).

[4] David A. Skeel, *The Past, Present and Future of Debtor-in-Possession Financing*, 25 Card. L. Rev. 1905 (2004); Douglas G. Baird and Robert K. Rasmussen, *Private Debt and the Missing Lever of Corporate Governance*, 154 U. Penn. L. Rev. 1209 (2006).

[5] Douglas G. Baird and Robert K. Rasmussen, *Chapter 11 at Twilight*, 56 Stan. L. Rev. 673 (2003). *See also* Lynn LoPucki, *The Nature of the Bankrupt Firm: A Response to Baird and Rasmussen's* The End of Bankruptcy, 56 Stan. L. Rev. 645 (2003).

[6] LoPucki, *supra*, at 648.

[7] *Id.*

[8] Chaim J. Fortgang & Thomas M. Mayer, *Trading Claims and Taking Control of Corporations in Chapter 11*, 12 Cardozo L. Rev. 1 (1990); Frederick Tung, *Confirmation and Claims Trading*, 90 Nw. L. Rev. 1684 (1996); Frank Partnoy and David Skeel, *The Promise and Perils of Credit Derivatives*, 75 U. Cinn. L. Rev. 1019 (2007).

[9] Paul M. Goldschmid, *Note, More Phoenix than Vulture: The Case for Distressed Investor Presence in the Bankruptcy Reorganization Process*, 2005 Colum. L. Rev. 191 (2005); Eric B. Fisher & Andrew L. Buck, *Hedge Funds and the Changing Face of Corporate Bankruptcy Practice*, 25 Am. Bankr. Inst. J. 24 (Dec.–Jan. 2007).

[10] It is not obvious a priori whether these developments are helpful or harmful to *ex post* efficiency of bankruptcy outcomes; that is, whether the value of the

Our chapter has two main objectives. The first is to provide systematic evidence on the validity of these new themes – creditor control and creditor conflict – in large, corporate Chapter 11 cases. Most of the existing evidence is anecdotal, raising doubts whether a new perspective on the bankruptcy process is necessary. Our second objective is to identify the effects of creditor control and conflict on bankruptcy outcomes, such as the decision to reorganize or sell the firm. Prior theoretical literature shows that manager–creditor and equity–creditor conflict can lead to asset misallocation during the reorganization process. We use our database to investigate whether a different kind of conflict – senior creditors versus junior creditors – distorts outcomes in bankruptcy cases.

The chapter will proceed as follows. Sections 6.2 and 6.3 describe our data and some basic summary statistics. Section 6.4 generates some simple measures of creditor control and conflict. Section 6.5 generates hypotheses about how creditor control and conflict should affect bankruptcy case outcomes using the theory of real options. Section 6.6 finds evidence in support of our hypotheses. Section 6.7 concludes.

6.2 DATA

We collected data on all corporate bankruptcies listed in the Bankruptcy Datasource "Public and Major Company Database" during the latter half of 2001. Our sample includes 153 cases. For each case, we gathered information about the parent company and all of its subsidiaries in bankruptcy. Our data sources were PACER, SEC filings, and the Bankruptcy Datasource. PACER is our primary resource. Every bankruptcy court maintains a PACER website, which contains the docket sheet for and, often, images of all documents filed in a bankruptcy case. Because document images were unavailable on a number of websites, our data are more complete for some cases than others. Indeed, we focused on cases filed during the second half of 2001 because the Bankruptcy Court for the District of Delaware began posting images in July 2001.

In most of the analysis that follows, we will rely on information contained in the court schedules, because they offer up-to-date information

---

estate is maximized. We simply note here that junior creditors – like all other claims – have objectives that are different from estate value maximization. They might, for example, favor delay when a quick sale is efficient, particularly when their claims are "out of the money." We discuss these ideas in section 6.4.

about the firm's capital structure when it files, including data on secured debt. Comparable information is not available in SEC filings.

6.3 SUMMARY STATISTICS

Table 6.1 presents information about the bankruptcy cases. Ninety-five percent of the cases were filed voluntarily by the debtors' owners. All but 3 percent of the cases were filed under Chapter 11. Among these cases, 75 percent resulted in a confirmed plan of reorganization; most of the remaining cases resulted in dismissal or conversion to Chapter 7. Because we do not have direct indicators of whether a plan was prepackaged, we assume that a case involved a prepack if confirmation occurred within four months.[11] Eight percent of the Chapter 11 cases were prepacks.

The fourth section of Table 6.1 illustrates the frequency with which Chapter 11 cases resulted in the sale or liquidation of the business. Across all filings, sale or liquidation occurred in 66 percent of the cases. A traditional reorganization – in which the distressed firm's creditors retain stakes in the firm and, often, become its new owners – occurred in 32 percent of the cases.

The fifth section of Table 6.1 summarizes case duration. Across all Chapter 11 cases, the median duration to confirmation, dismissal, or conversion to Chapter 7 was 13 months. This figure is somewhat misleading, however, because many plans are "liquidating plans" that merely distribute the proceeds from a going-concern sale that occurred months before.[12] In these cases, the fate of the firm (whether it would be reorganized or sold off) was decided long before a plan was confirmed. The fifth section of Table 6.1 illustrates this phenomenon. Although we do not have the dates on which sales occurred, we do have the dates when motions to conduct a sale were filed. Among firms that were sold off, a motion to sell the firm was typically filed within the first two to three months of the case.

---

[11] This cut-off captures all but two of the cases identified as "prenegotiated" in Lynn LoPucki's WebBRD database. The two exceptions were cases with durations of seven and nine months, respectively.

[12] As with our discussion of junior lender activism above, it is unclear a priori whether or not the trend toward faster, going-concern sales is consistent with efficiency. The main concern, as we describe in section 6.4, is that the firm might be sold quickly (as a going concern or as a piecemeal liquidation) for less than its fundamental value. This "fire sale" problem reduces creditor recoveries in the aggregate, which can have negative *ex ante* consequences. If aggregate creditor recoveries are expected to be lower inside bankruptcy, healthy firms will be less able to raise funding for potentially valuable projects.

Table 6.1 Filings and outcomes

Variable	Mean	SD	Median	Min	Max
Types of filings (n = 153)					
Chapter 7 filings	0.03				
Chapter 11 filings	0.97				
Prepackaged Chapter 11 case	0.08				
Involuntary filings	0.05				
Venue (n = 153)					
Filed in Delaware	0.22				
Filed in SDNY	0.10				
Legal outcomes in Chapter 11 (n = 149)					
Confirmed Chapter 11	0.75				
Chapter 11 converted to Chapter 7	0.13				
Chapter 11 dismissed	0.09				
Case ongoing	0.03				
Economic outcomes in Chapter 11					
Traditional reorganization (n = 148)	0.32				
Entire firm sold off (n = 148)	0.66				
Any asset sales (n = 149)	0.85				
Case duration in Chapter 11					
To legal outcome (n = 145)	15.63	11.91	13.10	1.13	74.30
To motion for sale of firm (n = 25)	2.87	3.92	0.90	0.00	16.20
To motion for first sale (n = 106)	2.26	3.07	1.33	0.00	16.57
CEO turnover (n = 136)					
Turnover within one year preceding filing	0.40				
Turnover within two years preceding filing	0.70				
Equity payoffs (n = 115)					
Equity holders received payment	0.13				
APR deviation	0.09				

6.4 SIMPLE MEASURES OF CREDITOR CONTROL AND CONFLICT

We can measure creditor control directly and indirectly. Direct measures of creditor control appear in Tables 6.1 and 6.2. Statistics on CEO turnover appear in Table 6.1, which shows that 70 percent of chief executive officers (CEOs) were replaced within two years of the bankruptcy filing. This turnover rate is markedly higher than the rate (45 percent) among all

Fortune 500 firms during a comparable two-year period (1999–2000).[13] It is also significantly higher than the rate (about 55 percent) observed among firms that entered bankruptcy during the 1980s. The frequency of turnover in our data rises further, to about 80 percent, when we include CEO replacements that occurred during the two years after the case commenced. Table 6.1 also shows that deviations from the absolute priority rule (APR) – payments to shareholders when creditors have not been paid in full – were rare, occurring in only 9 percent of the cases. This is a dramatic shift from the frequency of APR violations during the 1980s. In a study of publicly traded corporations that entered Chapter 11 between 1979 and 1986, for example, Weiss[14] found APR violations in 78 percent of the cases. He also found that equity holders received some payment in 80 percent of the cases. That was true in only 13 percent of the cases in our sample. If APR deviations measure the degree of control exercised by managers and equity holders, as is commonly thought, the patterns in Table 6.1 show that these groups exercise little influence over the modern Chapter 11 process.

Table 6.2 focuses on the frequency and terms of pre- and post-petition financing. Prior to entering bankruptcy, 75 percent of the businesses obtained financing through a revolving pre-petition credit facility (PCF). Seventy-eight percent of these facilities were secured by all or nearly all of the firm's assets. This is a strong measure of senior creditor control. If all of a firm's assets are encumbered by liens, it cannot obtain additional secured financing in bankruptcy without obtaining permission from or offering adequate protection to the pre-petition secured lender.[15]

Upon entering bankruptcy, 50 percent of the firms obtained post-petition debtor-in-possession (DIP) financing. Another 26 percent obtained liquidity by filing motions to use cash collateral. These motions differ little from those for DIP financing; in either case, the debtor hopes to finance its operations using funds over which a lender has control. Indeed, cash collateral motions frequently contain the same terms found in motions for DIP financing. In 76 percent of the cases, the firm obtained financing through a DIP loan or an order permitting it to use cash collateral. This, in

---

[13] Steven N. Kaplan & Bernadette A. Minton, *How Has CEO Turnover Changed? Increasingly Performance Sensitive Boards and Increasingly Uneasy CEOs*, NBER Working Paper No. 12465 (August 2006) (the 45 percent figure was computed based on Table 6.2; the average number of firms during 1999 and 2000 was 733; the total number of turnovers was 328, which is about 45 percent of 733).

[14] Lawrence A. Weiss, *Bankruptcy Resolution: Direct Costs and Violation of Priority of Claims*, 27 J. FIN. ECON. 285 (1990).

[15] *See* 11 U.S.C. 364(c), (d).

Table 6.2 Terms of financing

	N	Mean	SD	Median	Min	Max
Pre-petition financing						
All firms:						
Had pre-petition credit facility (PCF)	107	0.75				
Firms with PCF:						
PCF secured	77	0.97				
PCF secured by all assets	77	0.78				
Post-petition DIP Financing						
All firms:						
Had DIP loan	153	0.50				
Used cash collateral	153	0.26				
Used DIP loan or cash collateral	153	0.76				
Firms with DIP loan:						
DIP lender is also PCF lender	63	0.54				
Size of DIP loan						
Maximum DIP loan	66	93.42	249.82	20.00	0.20	1743.00
DIP loan ÷ assets	51	0.89	3.70	0.15	0.01	26.28
DIP loan ÷ unencumbered assets	51	−0.72	12.14	0.15	−82.55	17.23
Priority of DIP loan						
Firms with DIP loan:						
DIP secured by all assets	62	0.92				
DIP with priming security interest	62	0.65				
DIP with admin. expense superpriority	63	0.95				
Firms with priming security interest:						
DIP lender is also PCF lender	40	0.80				
Financial covenants in DIP loan						
Budget limits	60	0.72				
Capital expenditure limits	60	0.50				
EBITDA targets	60	0.42				
Any financial covenants	60	0.90				
Other covenants in DIP loan						
Automatic stay terminates in event of default	60	0.85				
Power of attorney	60	0.20				
Deadlines for disclosure statement or plan	60	0.18				
Sale requirements	63	0.17				

turn, suggests that the providers of the firms' credit lines have substantial control over, at a minimum, the timing of the bankruptcy filings. These results are important, because they provide confirmation that a primary justification for the bankruptcy filing is the debtor's need to access cash that is not available outside bankruptcy.

The remaining sections of Table 6.2 dissect the terms of DIP loans. Ninety-five percent of these loans give the lender administrative expense superpriority. This is a potent form of control because it gives the lender the right to demand repayment in cash before any plan of reorganization can be confirmed. Ninety-two percent of the loans give the lender a security interest in all of the firm's assets. This too is an important mechanism of control when combined with covenants permitting the lender to seize the collateral – without petitioning for court authorization – in the event of default. These covenants ("Automatic stay terminates in event of default") are present in 90 percent of DIP loans.

Other covenants enhance creditor control. Perhaps our most surprising result, and the strongest evidence of senior creditor control, is the large percentage of loans that impose specific line-item budgets on the firm (72 percent of loans). These budgets obligate the firm to submit detailed evidence of cash receipts and expenditures; an event of default occurs if the firm deviates from any given line-item by a significant margin (usually 5–15 percent). Other covenants are of the more standard variety and restrict capital expenditures (50 percent) or require the firm to achieve certain profitability or EBITDA (earnings before interest, tax, depreciation, and amortization) targets (42 percent). Ninety percent of loans contained at least one of these provisions ("Any financial limits").

Table 6.2 also shows that 65 percent of DIP loans contain provisions giving the lender a "priming lien," that is, a security interest with priority over pre-existing security interests. This phenomenon could be seen as a means by which DIP lenders divert value from pre-existing lenders. Most DIP lenders, however, are the same banks that extended PCFs to the debtor. A priming lien typically primes only the DIP lender's own pre-existing security interest. There is no diversion of value. As Table 6.2 illustrates, 80 percent of priming liens involve the DIP lender priming itself; in the remaining 20 percent, the DIP lender obtained a priming lien at the expense of another secured lender. We cannot say, however, whether the DIP lender adequately compensated the pre-existing secured lender for the priming lien.

Senior creditor control, then, appears to be pervasive in a large number of corporate bankruptcies. The majority of firms will sign loan agreements that give lenders significant control over the course of the Chapter 11 process. Evidence on PCFs indicates that, for most firms, the senior lender has effective control over the debtor's access to cash and thus determines the timing of the bankruptcy filing. Our analysis of DIP covenants suggests that this control extends beyond the filing and continues throughout the bankruptcy case in the form of line-item budgetary control over the debtor's operations.

6.5 HYPOTHESIS TESTS

Our primary question is whether (and to what extent) creditor conflict affects the ultimate allocation of the bankrupt firm's assets. This question is important because creditor control and conflict can lead to suboptimal sales or reorganizations.[16] An intuitive sketch of this idea is provided below.

Consider, first, the incentives of a secured lender whose claim is oversecured, meaning that the firm's assets, if sold immediately, would yield more than the lender's claim. This implies that the lender will be paid in full, even if the sale occurs at a "fire sale" price that could be avoided by waiting, and perhaps reorganizing.

Relative to a strategy that maximizes the value of the bankruptcy estate, the oversecured lender is always biased toward an immediate resolution of the case. If asset value is volatile, the delay caused by the reorganization process can only harm the lender. Any increase in value will offer no benefit, because the lender's payoff is capped by its claim. Decrease in value can be costly, because it may reduce the lender's payoff.

While the oversecured creditor will always prefer an immediate sale, the ability to realize his preferred outcome should depend on the extent to which it is oversecured. When a creditor is substantially oversecured, the bankruptcy judge is likely to be less sympathetic to actions that would force an immediate sale (such as covenants in the DIP loan that force a sale, or motions to lift the automatic stay). When the value of the firm greatly exceeds the secured creditor's claim, it is very likely that the creditor will be paid in full, even in a reorganization. As the secured creditor becomes only slightly oversecured, we expect that the judge is more likely to approve attempts by the secured creditor to move for a quick sale, since its claim is more at risk.

Now consider a secured lender whose claim is undersecured, that

---

16 LoPucki and Doherty, for example, argue that bankruptcy sales generate significantly less value for creditors than traditional reorganizations. Lynn M. LoPucki & Joseph W. Doherty, *Bankruptcy Fire Sales*, 106 MICH. L. REV. 1 (2007).

is, its claim exceeds the sale value of the firm's assets. In this case, the secured lender will not be paid in full in a sale. If the creditor is slightly undersecured, its incentives are similar to those of the slightly oversecured creditor, since reorganization can increase its payoff only slightly, while a decline in firm value can hurt its payoff substantially. As the secured creditor becomes substantially undersecured, it will have incentives that are better aligned with maximizing the value of the estate, since it will capture nearly all the upside from a successful reorganization. The substantially undersecured creditor will be the firm's approximate residual claimant and entitled to the entire value of the firm.[17] Thus, if an illiquidity problem makes reorganization socially optimal, the lender will prefer to reorganize the firm in order to improve its payoff.

Finally, consider unsecured creditors. They will generally exhibit a bias toward lengthy cases, especially reorganizations, when the firm enters bankruptcy with senior secured debt. Longer delay adds to the risk of their eventual payoff, and junior claimants typically exhibit a preference toward greater risk.[18] When the firm has no secured debt, however, unsecured creditors will prefer to make the reorganization-versus-sale decision in a way that is consistent with the maximization of firm value.

This simple analysis of creditor conflict predicts that a bankrupt firm's creditors will make the value-maximizing decision when secured creditors are substantially undersecured or when there is no secured debt.[19] If the capital structure is a mix of oversecured and unsecured debt, then a bias toward sale will result. The intensity of the bias will depend on which party exerts more control over the outcome. We expect that senior creditors will have greater influence over the outcome when their claims

---

[17] The undersecured creditor's incentives are not exactly consistent with social efficiency. It will still have a slight bias toward a quick sale, all else equal, because unsecured creditors may capture some of the upside risk to a high-value reorganization.

[18] Here, we are employing standard logic that is normally used to describe equity-versus-debt conflicts. Unsecured creditors expect to share most of the gains from a successful (high-value) reorganization, but they expect to avoid most of the losses from a low-value reorganization or liquidation. These losses are borne primarily by senior secured creditors. Because of this asymmetry in payoffs, unsecured creditors prefer risk, all else equal. *See* Michael C. Jensen and William H. Meckling, *Theory of the Firm: Managerial Behavior, Agency Costs, and Ownership Structure*, 3 J. FIN. ECON. 305 (1976).

[19] There are a few important assumptions that are implicit in this argument. For instance, it assumes that secured creditors have full control when they are oversecured. It also assumes that equity will be extinguished with certainty (which is approximately true in our data).

are large relative to the value of the firm. Thus, a capital structure with slightly oversecured senior creditors will produce relatively quick cases and yield sales more often than traditional reorganizations. As the power of unsecured creditors increases relative to secured creditors, the reverse should be true.

These observations point to the following hypothesis: because time to resolution is generally longer when a firm is reorganized than when it is sold off, a traditional reorganization is more likely among firms with no secured debt and those with undersecured lenders, than among firms with oversecured lenders.

6.6 RESULTS

Table 6.3 compares the capital structures and bankruptcy outcomes of firms with different levels of secured debt. The most important pattern in Table 6.3, for our purposes, is the relationship between the probability of reorganization and the ratio of secured debt to assets. We see the hypothesized non-monotonic relationship. The likelihood of reorganization is higher among unsecured firms (44 percent) and undersecured firms (47 percent) than it is among those with oversecured debt (between 21 and 34 percent).[20] Among oversecured firms, the probability of reorganization is declining in the ratio of secured debt to assets, but the difference is only marginally significant.[21]

Overall, however, these patterns are consistent with the hypothesis that secured lender preferences distort real economic outcomes. But if secured lenders can distort economic outcomes, we should see a response from the unsecured creditors' committee (UCC)[22] when lenders propose outcomes that will reduce payoffs to unsecured creditors. Objections to sales, for example, should be more common in cases involving oversecured firms than in those involving unsecured or undersecured firms. Objections should be less common among unsecured firms, because unsecured creditors should have greater influence over the bankruptcy process when

---

[20] The difference between undersecured and slightly oversecured firms (50–100 percent) is statistically significant at the 5 percent level. The difference between unsecured and highly oversecured firms (0–50 percent) is not significant, probably due to small sample size.

[21] The difference is significant at the 10 percent level.

[22] The UCC is the official committee appointed in Chapter 11 cases to represent the interests of unsecured creditors. It typically consists of creditors holding the seven largest unsecured claims against the debtor.

Table 6.3 Firm characteristics by secured debt level

	Secured debt/assets			
	0 (N = 9)	0–0.50 (N = 35)	0.50–1.0 (N = 25)	> 1.0 (N = 20)
Traditional reorganization	0.44	0.34	0.21	0.47
UCC objected to sale	0.11	0.29	0.48	0.20
UCC objected to sale, conditional on sale	0.20	0.41	0.55	0.33
CEO turnover, 2 years	0.67	0.81	0.72	0.70
Public	0.67	0.74	0.80	0.95
Prepack	0.11	0.09	0.04	0.05
Assets, mean (median)	28.19 (4.34)	1093.16 (195.52)	187.84 (97.92)	105.95 (18.56)
Compustat assets, mean (median)	79.20 (18.86)	1795.15 (668.67)	463.07 (158.29)	610.15 (151.2)
Sec. debt, mean (median)	0.00 (0.00)	238.46 (32.31)	153.85 (87.73)	238.69 (70.87)

there are no secured creditors. Objections should be less common among undersecured firms for two reasons. First, undersecured lenders are less likely to agitate for a quick sale. Second, when these lenders do agitate for a sale, a court is unlikely to grant the UCC's objection (relative to a case where the lenders are oversecured) because these lenders are effectively the firm's residual claimants and will tend to advocate the socially efficient bankruptcy outcome. Knowing that objections will be denied, the UCC will not object to the sale.

These predictions are borne out in the data, as Table 6.3 shows. Objections to sale occurred in 29–48 percent of cases involving oversecured firms. The percentages are much lower (11 percent and 20 percent, respectively) in cases involving unsecured and undersecured firms. A similar non-monotonic pattern emerges when we restrict attention to cases that ended in a sale.[23]

[23] In the longer version of this chapter, we confirm this non-monotonic pattern in a regression analysis that controls for variables such as size, industry, and whether the firm is public or private. *See* Ayotte & Morrison, *supra note* *, at 535.

6.7 DISCUSSION AND CONCLUSIONS

The data presented here show that, among large privately and publicly held businesses, creditor control is pervasive. Equity holders and managers exercise little or no leverage during the reorganization process. Seventy percent of CEOs are replaced in the two years before a bankruptcy filing. Sixty-six percent of firms are sold off. Very few reorganization plans (at most 9 percent) deviate from the absolute priority rule in order to distribute value to equity holders.

Creditors dictate the dynamics of the reorganization process. Senior lenders exercise significant control through stringent covenants contained in DIP loans. Bargaining between secured and unsecured creditors can distort the reorganization process. A Chapter 11 case is significantly more likely to result in a sale if secured lenders are oversecured; it is much less likely when these lenders are undersecured or when the firm has no secured debt at all.

We draw two conclusions from these patterns. First, the advent of creditor control has not eliminated the fundamental inefficiency of Chapter 11: resource allocation questions (whether to sell or reorganize a firm) are confused with distributional questions (how much each creditor will receive). Instead of separating the two questions, Chapter 11 gives senior lenders, unsecured creditors, and equity holders leverage over resource allocation issues. Because these parties have distinct preferences, the bargaining process can yield a misallocation of assets. During the 1980s, this problem was noted by Baird and Jackson, who emphasized the conflict between creditors and equity holders.[24] Today, as our data show, the problem persists, but now the conflict is between senior and junior lenders.

---

[24] Douglas G. Baird & Thomas H. Jackson, *Corporate Reorganizations and the Treatment of Diverse Ownership Interests: A Comment on Adequate Protection of Secured Creditors in Bankruptcy*, 51 U. Chi. L. Rev. 97, 121 (1984).

7. Cramdown versus extinguishing security interests: secured claims in bankruptcy in the United States and Japan[1]

Wataru Tanaka

7.1 INTRODUCTION

A challenging legal task in bankruptcy is how to treat different kinds of claims and interests. Claimants with different priorities in a bankrupt firm have different interests, which can cause serious coordination problems. In an ideal Coasean world with no transaction costs, conflicts of interest could be resolved by voluntary negotiations.[2] As long as the going-concern value of a bankrupt firm is greater than its liquidation value, all claimholders would agree to refrain from enforcing their claims and share the going-concern surplus. More often than not, however, negotiation costs and/or information asymmetries prevent efficient transactions from taking place. Carefully designed bankruptcy law can mitigate the coordination problem and help the firm reorganize when it is worthwhile to do so.[3] Designing an efficient bankruptcy system is a difficult task, however, and the law may cause, rather than solve, a problem. Specifically, a prolonged reorganization procedure may let an inefficient firm survive at the expense of creditors.

[1] This chapter is based mainly on my research developed while I was a visiting scholar at Yale Law School in 2002–2004. For more detailed analysis on the theme, *see* Wataru Tanaka, *Extinguishing Security Interests: Secured Claims in Japanese Business Reorganization Law and Some Policy Implications for US Law*, 22 EMORY BANK. DEV. J. 427 (2006).

[2] *See* Ronald Coase, *The Problem of Social Cost*, 3 J. LAW & ECON. 1, 15 (1960).

[3] *See* Thomas H. Jackson, *Bankruptcy, Non-bankruptcy Entitlements, and the Creditors' Bargain*, 91 YALE L. J. 857 (1982) (proposing the view that bankruptcy law can be regarded as the product of hypothetical bargaining where all creditors could negotiate *ex ante*).

Among other claims and interests, it is especially difficult to tell how to treat secured claims in bankruptcy. On one hand, the interests of secured creditors often diverge from the interests of other claimants and shareholders of the debtor firm, as well as from social interests. Since secured creditors enjoy priority on the proceeds coming from the foreclosure sale of the asset used as collateral, they may choose to foreclose on the asset even if it is indispensable for continuation of the debtor's business. In this case, the foreclosure could cause inefficient liquidation. This possibility provides a reason to restrict the secured creditors' rights in bankruptcy. On the other hand, secured lending offers various social benefits,[4] such as mitigating the problem of the debtor's moral hazard, whereas restriction on the rights of secured creditors in bankruptcy may decrease those benefits. Since determining proper legal treatment of secured claims in bankruptcy requires the subtle balancing of costs and benefits, it is no wonder that various jurisdictions treat secured claims in different ways.

This chapter examines how secured claims are treated in bankruptcy in the United States and Japan. In particular, this chapter focuses on the treatment of secured claims in the Civil Rehabilitation Act (*Minji saisei ho*) of Japan (CRA).[5] The CRA provides reorganization proceedings available to any type of business entity[6] and has been used by both large, small and mid-sized companies.[7] Generally, the CRA provides a debtor-in-possession (DIP) proceeding[8] and enables modification of unsecured

---

[4] *See, e.g.*, Thomas H. Jackson & Anthony T. Kronman, *Secured Financing and Priorities Among Creditors*, 88 YALE L.J. 1143 (1979); Saul Levmore, *Monitors and Freeriders in Commercial and Corporate Settings*, 92 YALE L. J. 49 (1982); Ronald J. Mann, *The Role of Secured Credit in Small-Business Lending*, 86 GEO. L. J. 1 (1997); Clifford W. Smith, Jr & Jerold B. Warner, *Bankruptcy, Secured Debt, and Optimal Capital Structure: Comment*, 34 J. FIN. 247 (1979); Rene M. Stulz & Herb Johnson, *An Analysis of Secured Debt*, 14 J. FIN. ECON. 501 (1985); George G. Triantis, *Secured Debt Under Conditions of Imperfect Information*, 21 J. LEGAL STUD. 225 (1992).

[5] Civil Rehabilitation Act, Law No.225, Dec. 22, 1999 [*hereinafter* CRA].

[6] *See id.* §2 (ii).

[7] According to the survey of Teikoku Databank, Ltd, a private company engaging in corporate credit research and market research, during ten years from April 1, 2000 to March 31, 2010, 7754 firms the amount of whose debts were JPY 10 million (about US$125 000) or more applied for the Civil Rehabilitation proceedings, of which 103 firms were listed firms. *See* Teikoku Databank, Ltd, *Minji saisei ho seko 10 nenkan no shinsei doko chosa* [Research on Filings During the 4 Years Since the Enforcement of the Civil Rehabilitation Act] 1-3 (2010), available at: http://www.tdb.co.jp/report/watching/press/pdf/p100401.pdf.

[8] *See id.* 38(1) (a debtor continues operating her own business even after commencement of the Civil Rehabilitation procedure).

claims to the debtor by a rehabilitation plan approved by a majority of unsecured creditors (in both amount and number of claims) and is then confirmed by the court.[9] In this respect, the CRA is similar to Chapter 11 of the Bankruptcy Code of the United States.[10] In contrast to Chapter 11, however, the CRA does not have an automatic stay on secured claims, nor does it permit secured claims to be modified by a rehabilitation plan.[11] Nevertheless, the CRA has a unique procedure to restrict the rights of secured creditors which is called "the procedure of extinguishing security interests (*tanpo-ken shometsu seikyu tetsuzuki*)."[12] This procedure permits a debtor to cancel security interests in any owned property necessary for continuation of the business by paying the secured creditors the liquidation value of such property. This chapter analyzes how this procedure can reduce the transaction costs that arise when the debtor has to bargain with the secured creditors in order to avoid foreclosure sales, and also compares the procedure with the "cramdown" procedure in Chapter 11.[13]

The rest of this chapter is organized as follows: section 7.2 briefly explains how secured claims are treated in a Chapter 11 proceeding, section 7.3 introduces the CRA's treatment of secured claims (especially the procedure of extinguishing security interest), and section 7.4 discusses the potential social benefit of this procedure. Section 7.5 then compares this procedure with the "cramdown" procedure in Chapter 11, followed by section 7.6 which concludes by mentioning the potential cost of the procedure of extinguishing security interests.

---

[9] *See id.* §§172–3(1), 174 & 179.

[10] As for the bankruptcy law in the United States, this chapter focuses on Chapter 11 of the Bankruptcy Code. *See* 11 U.S.C. §§1101–1174.

[11] *See* section 7.3, *infra*.

[12] *See* section 7.3, *infra*.

[13] There is another reorganization procedure in Japan named the Corporate Reorganization proceeding (*Kaisha kosei tetsuzuki*). *See* Corporate Reorganization Act (*Kaisha kosei ho*), Law No. 154 of Dec. 13, 2002. Like Chapter 11, the Corporate Reorganization proceeding "captures" secured as well as unsecured creditors. *See id.* §§50(1), 167 & 203(1). The number of uses of the Corporate Reorganization Act has been small, at most dozens each year. One important reason for this is that the Corporate Reorganization Act does not employ a DIP procedure, *see id.* §67 (1) (the court must appoint administrators to operate the debtor company's business), discouraging debtor corporations petitioning for the proceedings. *See* Tanaka, *supra* note 1, at 435–436.

7.2 SECURED CLAIMS IN THE UNITED STATES

Bankruptcy law in the United States imposes substantial restrictions on the rights of secured creditors. First of all, secured creditors are prohibited from enforcing their rights at the time a debtor files for bankruptcy (automatic stay).[14] Second, each secured creditor's claim is bifurcated into two parts: the part covered by the value of collateral and the part not covered.[15] Only the first part of the creditor's claim is treated as a secured claim in the bankruptcy proceeding (bifurcation).[16] Third, terms of each secured claim can be modified notwithstanding the claimholder's objection. In particular, if the debtor promises to make deferred payments to each objecting secured creditor in a reorganization plan, with value at least equal to the value of the collateral, and the plan satisfies other requirements of the statute, then the plan will be confirmed by the court and each claim will be modified accordingly (cramdown).[17]

7.3 SECURED CLAIMS IN THE CIVIL REHABILITATION ACT OF JAPAN

In contrast to US law, secured creditors can freely enforce their rights even after commencement of the Civil Rehabilitation proceeding.[18] In other words, there is no "automatic stay" on secured claims in the CRA. It is true that the CRA has a procedure which allows the court to order a stay on enforcement of specific security interests in a specified time period (temporary stay – *tanoken no jikko tetetsuzuki no chusi meirei*).[19] Nevertheless, requirements for the stay order are rigid[20] and, even if the petition for stay is permitted, the stay period is rather short (typically

---

[14] *See* 11 U.S.C. §362(a)(4).

[15] *See id.* §506(a).

[16] *See id.* For a more specific explanation of bifurcation, *see* David Gray Carlson, *Bifurcation of Undersecured Claims in Bankruptcy*, 70 AM. BANKR. L.J. 1 (1996).

[17] *See id.* § 1129(b)(1)&(2)(A). For more discussion on cramdown, *see* section 7.5, *infra*, and 7 COLLIER ON BANKRUPTCY 1129.03-05 (Alan N. Resnick & Henry J. Sommer eds, 16th edn 2012).

[18] *See* CRA §53(2).

[19] *See id.* §31.

[20] The court may order the temporary stay only if: (a) it is in the general interests of creditors; and (b) there is no likelihood of causing unreasonable loss to the secured creditor. *See id.* §31(1).

several months).[21] Thus, the effect of temporary stay on the interests of secured creditors is arguably limited.[22] Also, while unsecured claims can be modified by a rehabilitation plan that is accepted by the majority of unsecured creditors and confirmed by the court,[23] secured claims cannot be modified by the plan.[24]

However, the CRA has a unique procedure to restrict the rights of secured creditors, which is the procedure of extinguishing security interests.[25] In essence, this procedure permits a debtor in the Civil Rehabilitation proceeding to cancel security interests in any of the debtor's property that is necessary for continuation of her[26] business by simply paying the secured creditors the amount of cash equal to the liquidation value of such property (the value realized if the property were disposed of).[27] The debtor cannot pay this value in installments or by securities. Only a one-time cash payment is acceptable.[28] When parties do not agree on the liquidation value of the property, the court will assess it in an appraisal proceeding.[29]

For example, suppose a debtor owes a creditor $150 and has pledged, as collateral, a property with a liquidation value of $120. Outside of the bankruptcy procedure, secured interest can be cancelled only when the debtor pays the full amount of the secured debt or when the property is sold by the foreclosure sale. In contrast, in the Civil Rehabilitation proceeding, the debtor can apply to the court for permission to cancel the creditor's security interest by paying just $120, not $150. The difference between the face value of the secured claim and the value of the collateral,

---

21 For explanation of practices in the Tokyo District Court, where the period of temporary stay is usually three months, *see* Ryuji Sonoo, *Minji Saisei Tetsuzuki to Saisei Keikaku no Jitsujo to Kadai* [Real State and Issues of the Civil Rehabilitation Proceedings and Rehabilitation Plans], 736 NBL 8, 20-21 (2002); Jin Mimori, *Annotation to §31, in* SHIN CHUSHAKU MINJI SAISEI HO JO [1 New Annotation to Civil Rehabilitation Act] 145, 160 (Chiharu Saiguchi & Makoto Ito eds, 2011).

22 For more discussion on temporary stay, *see* Tanaka, *supra* note 1, at 441–443.

23 See *supra* note 9 and accompanying text.

24 *See* CRA §177 (2).

25 *See id.* §§148–152.

26 This chapter uses "she" to refer to a debtor and "he" to refer to a creditor.

27 *See* Civil Rehabilitation Rules §79(1), Supreme Court of Rule No. 3, Jan. 31, 2000.

28 *See* CRA §152(1) (requiring the debtor to pay the value of the collateral in cash to the court).

29 *See id.* §§149–151.

$30, becomes an unsecured claim. The creditor can participate in the Civil Rehabilitation proceeding with this claim.[30]

For another example, suppose there are three creditors, to be referred to as C1, C2, and C3. Each has a $100 claim secured by the same asset but with different priorities. C1 has first priority, C2 has second priority, and C3 has third priority. The asset is now worth $120. If there were no procedure to extinguish security interests and the debtor paid $100 to C1, then C2's second-priority interest would be promoted to the first, and C3's third priority interest would be promoted to the second. Thus, the debtor eventually would have to pay all of the debts to extinguish these security interests. In contrast, when the debtor uses the procedure of security interests, $100 can be paid to C1, $20 to C2, nothing to C3, and all of these security interests are extinguished. C2 will make a claim of $80, and C3 will make a claim of $100 as unsecured creditors in the Civil Rehabilitation proceeding.[31]

7.4 SOCIAL BENEFIT OF EXTINGUISHING SECURITY INTERESTS

This section examines what social benefit the procedure of extinguishing security interests may have. Simply put, it argues that this procedure can enhance efficiency by giving a debtor an exit option from potentially costly negotiations with secured creditors.

If there are no obstacles inhibiting a debtor and secured creditors from bargaining with one another, restrictions on secured claims are not necessary for a successful reorganization. In such an ideal world, the parties would agree to avoid foreclosure sales if and only if such sales would be inefficient. For example, suppose a debtor owes a creditor $150 and has collateralized some real property whose liquidation value is $120. If going-concern value of the property[32] is $130, then it is better to use the property

---

[30] *See id.* §88 (a secured creditor can make a claim in the Civil Rehabilitation proceeding if and to the extent his claim is no longer secured).

[31] *See id.*

[32] Some may wonder how we can define "going-concern value" of a property. Usually, we discuss "going-concern value" of a business, not a property. For the analysis in this chapter, however, we can define going-concern value of a property owned by a debtor as "the difference between the value of the debtor's business (i.e., the present value of expected cash flows the debtor's business will produce in the future) if she can continue using the property for her business and the value of her business without the property." If the going-concern value of the property so defined is greater than its liquidation value, then it is worthwhile for the property to continue being used for the debtor's business, rather than being disposed of.

for the debtor's business than to sell it by foreclosure. In this case, the debtor will promise to pay the secured creditor some price ($\$p$) which is between \$120 and \$130 and ask him not to foreclose on the collateral. Such a bargain would leave both parties better off; the debtor (and unsecured creditors, whose interests are represented by the debtor) will obtain the value equal to $\$130–p$, which is positive, and the secured creditor will obtain p, which exceeds what he would receive by the foreclosure sale (\$120). Therefore, as long as there is no obstacle in the bargaining process, inefficient foreclosure could be avoided by a voluntary agreement.

More often than not, however, a variety of obstacles may prevent the parties from negotiating smoothly. A secured creditor may hold up the bargaining process by requiring as large a share of the going-concern surplus (the difference between the going-concern value of the collateral and its liquidation value) as possible by using their rights to foreclose as a threat. Such a hold-up problem may become more serious when a debtor must negotiate with multiple secured creditors in order to realize the going-concern surplus (for example, when several creditors have security interests with different rankings of priority in the same asset).[33] Furthermore, the going-concern value of the collateral is likely to be uncertain and, through the daily management of her own business, the debtor may have acquired private information on it. Such asymmetric information may also hinder the parties from bargaining efficiently.[34]

The procedure of extinguishing security interests may enhance efficiency in those circumstances. With this procedure, the debtor can end costly negotiations by recapturing the collateral by paying its liquidation value to the secured creditors. This exit option of the debtor can prevent each secured creditor from holding up the bargaining process to obtain a larger share of the going-concern surplus. It can also prevent any delay in the bargain because of uncertainty on the going-concern value of the collateral.

Of course, for the procedure of extinguishing security interests to function well, the court must be able to assess the liquidation value of the collateral in a fairly accurate and foreseeable way. If not, disputes

---

[33] Economic literature analyzing bargaining among multiple parties with non-cooperative game theory predicts that bargaining may be delayed even under perfect information. Hongbin Cai, *Delay in Multilateral Bargaining Under Complete Information*, 93 J. ECON. THEORY 260 (2000); Hongbin Cai, *Inefficient Markov Perfect Equilibria in Multilateral Bargaining*, 22 ECON. THEORY 583 (2003).

[34] For a review of economic literature on bargaining under asymmetric information, *see* John Kennan & Robert Wilson, *Bargaining with Private Information*, 31 J. ECON. LITERATURE 45, 53–63 (1993).

over the liquidation value may have to be settled in a time-consuming appraisal proceeding. Such a proceeding's cost may be even higher than the negotiation cost that would arise if the procedure of extinguishing security interests did not exist. Still, it appears to be reasonable to assume that the court can estimate the liquidation value of the collateral fairly easily, at least more easily than the court can estimate the going-concern value of the collateral. While estimating the latter value requires the court to predict future cash flows that the debtor's business will earn using the collateral, estimation of the former value only requires prediction of a price of an individual asset. In predicting such a price, the court can often refer to a market price of the same or similar kind of asset in the neighborhood.[35]

7.5 COMPARISON TO "CRAMDOWN" IN THE US CHAPTER 11 PROCEEDING

One may better appreciate the procedure of extinguishing security interests by comparing it to the treatment of secured claims in Chapter 11, especially with the procedure known as "cramdown."[36] Cramdown can also be viewed as an exit option of the debtor to recapture the collateral by paying the value of the collateral to the objecting secured creditor. There is, however, an important difference between these two procedures. While extinguishing security interests requires that the debtor make a one-time payment of the value of the collateral, cramdown permits the debtor to make deferred cash payments with a present value, in the court's estimation, equal to that of the collateral.[37]

A possible advantage of cramdown is that the debtor can exercise an exit option even in a position of being too liquidity-constrained to prepare the amount of cash equal to the value of the collateral. This apparent benefit is not, however, without cost. Cramdown imposes a much heavier burden on the court than the procedure of extinguishing security interests. To determine whether the requirements of cramdown are satisfied, the court has to estimate not only the value of the collateral but also the value of deferred cash payments promised in the plan.[38] To estimate the latter

---

[35] For more discussion when the procedure of extinguishing security interests is likely to produce social benefit, *see* Tanaka, *supra* note 1, at 452–455.

[36] *See* section 7.2, *supra*.

[37] *See* 11 U.S.C. §1129(b)(2)(A)(i)(II).

[38] *See id.* (for a plan to be crammed down, each holder of a claim of a dissenting class must receive "deferred cash payments totaling at least the allowed

value, the court must first examine the feasibility of the plan,[39] consider a variety of risks involved in the reorganized business, and then determine a proper interest rate by which to discount the deferred payments.[40] These tasks are close to estimating the going-concern value of the debtor's business as a whole, which is arguably much more difficult than estimating the liquidation value of an individual asset (or assets) used as collateral.

In the procedure of extinguishing security interests, the task of the court is restricted to estimating the liquidation value of the collateral. It is up to the debtor to prepare this value by obtaining new money in the financial market. Judging from statistics showing that many Chapter 11 debtors fail to reorganize after time-consuming proceedings,[41] there seems to be a good reason for the Civil Rehabilitation Act to require that the debtor make a one-time payment, though this requirement sometimes makes it difficult for some liquidity-constrained debtors to prepare the necessary amount of cash.[42]

---

amount of such claim, of a value, as of the effective date of the plan, of at least the value of such holder's interest in the estate's interest in such property").

[39] *See id.* §1129(a)(11) (confirmation of the plan must be denied if it is not feasible; that is, if it is likely to be followed by the liquidation or the need for further reorganization).

[40] To determine a proper interest rate, the United States Supreme Court has accepted the "formula" approach, which employs the national prime rate as a base rate and adjusts it to account for the greater nonpayment risk that bankrupt debtors pose. See Till v. SCS Credit Corp., 541 U.S. 465, 477–480 (2004). Courts have difficulty in determining what is an appropriate size of risk premium, especially because they often do not find a market for a loan to a reorganizing firm with terms similar to those provided in the plan, *see* Tanaka, *supra* note 1, at 464 n.201 (citing cases). For more specific discussion on determining interest rates, *see* 7 Collier on Bankruptcy, *supra* note 17, 1129.05[2][c].

[41] *See* Gordon Bermant & Ed Flynn, *Bankruptcy by the Numbers: Outcomes of Chapter 11 Cases: US Trustee Database Sheds New Light on Old Questions*, Am. Bankr. Inst. J., Feb. 1998, at 8 (reporting confirmation rate of Chapter 11 proceedings was 26 percent based on 131 089 filings between January 1, 1989 and December 31, 1995). For the confirmation rate of the Civil Rehabilitation proceedings, *see infra* note 47.

[42] There is another difference between the procedure of extinguishing security interest in CRA and the cramdown procedure in Chapter 11: how to determine the value of the collateral. While CRA employs the liquidation value standard, *see supra* note 27 and accompanying text, the collateral is evaluated by the "replacement value" standard (i.e., what the debtor would have to pay for comparable property) in the cramdown procedure, according to the US Supreme Court decision, *see* Associates Commercial Corp. v. Rash, 520 U.S. 953 (1997). In this respect, the cramdown procedure is more favorable to secured creditors than the procedure of extinguishing security interests.

7.6 POTENTIAL COST OF EXTINGUISHING SECURITY INTERESTS

Although allowing a debtor to extinguish security interests by paying the liquidation value of the collateral can be beneficial for the purpose of efficient reorganization, it can also involve costs. Since this procedure gives a debtor an option to recapture the collateral by paying its liquidation value, it tends to reduce the return on secured credit in bankruptcy. If the procedure of extinguishing security interests did not exist and the secured creditor could enforce his lien, the debtor would have to bargain with the secured creditor to obtain his consent to stop foreclosure. As compensation for his consent, the secured creditor could obtain some share of the going-concern surplus. In contrast, when the procedure of extinguishing security interests exists, the secured creditor only receives the liquidation value of the collateral. Such reduction on the return of secured credit is, by itself, only a matter of transfer of income. To the extent that the return of the secured creditor decreases, the joint returns of the unsecured creditors and the debtor's equity-holders will increase. As has already been discussed in the literature, however, the priority of secured credit is likely to create some social benefits.[43] Thus, to the extent that it curtails such priority, the procedure of extinguishing security interests may diminish net social benefits.

In particular, a debtor may have an incentive to do additional borrowing and invest in an overly risky business at the expense of existing (original) creditors. Securing the original claim in advance can prevent such overborrowing and overinvestment by the debtor.[44] If the priority of a secured claim is curtailed by the procedure of extinguishing security interests, however, secured credit may not be enough to prevent the debtor from doing such borrowing and investment. In this case, the procedure of extinguishing security interests can produce inefficiency *ex ante*.[45]

7.7 CONCLUSION

Considering the difficulties mentioned in the previous section, the procedure of extinguishing security interests may not always enhance efficiency.

---

[43] *See* the literature cited in *supra* note 4.

[44] *See* Mann, *supra* note 4, at 25–26; Triantis, *supra* note 4, at 255.

[45] For more discussion on the matter in this section using a specific example, *see* Tanaka, *supra* note 1, at 467–473.

Still, it is worth noting that hundreds of firms each year, including dozens of publicly held corporations, file for the Civil Rehabilitation proceedings[46] and a considerable percentage of these firms succeed in rehabilitation.[47] The evidence suggests that such a simple procedure as the CRA, with no automatic stay on secured claims, no cramdown, and rather limited intervention of the court, can work fairly effectively. Hopefully, this chapter will enhance our understanding of how the law should treat secured creditors in a reorganization procedure and will contribute to the improvement of our bankruptcy systems.

---

46 *See supra* note 7.

47 Of 7754 firms that petitioned for the Civil Rehabilitation proceedings from April 1, 2000 to March 31, 2010, 5394 firms (69.6 percent) obtained confirmation of the rehabilitation plan by the end of March 2010. *See* Teikoku Databank, *supra* note 7, at 4. For more statistics on the Civil Rehabilitation proceedings, *see* Tanaka, *supra* note 1, at 440–441.

8. Reduction of retirees' benefits upon the reorganization of a company

Gen Goto*

8.1 INTRODUCTION

In the wake of the global financial crisis of 2008, both the United States and Japan have experienced the collapse and subsequent reorganization of some of their largest companies, including General Motors (GM) in the United States and Japan Airlines (JAL) in Japan.[1]

In the reorganization processes of both GM and JAL, one of the key issues to be resolved was the reduction of retiree benefit payment obligations of the companies (the "legacy cost"). The legacy cost took the form of healthcare and life insurance benefits in the case of GM and a defined-benefit pension plan in the case of JAL.[2]

The negotiation for the reduction of these payment obligations took place under the shadow of laws regarding the priority of claims of retirees in a bankruptcy scenario and the modification of such claims. In both

* I would like to express my gratitude to Aaron Ferner for his excellent editorial assistance. This work was supported by the Grant-in-Aid for the Global COE Program "Soft Law and the State-Market Relationship: Forming a Base for Education and Research of Private Ordering" from the Ministry of Education, Culture, Sports, Science and Technology of Japan.

1 For materials regarding the reorganization process of JAL, *see* http://www.jal.com/en/corporate/houkoku_backno.html (last visited 2012/10/3).

2 As all citizens of Japan have public medical care insurance, a reduction in the healthcare benefits provided by private companies is not a serious problem in Japanese reorganization processes. For an overview of the Japanese health insurance system, *see* http://www.mhlw.go.jp/english/org/pamphlet/dl/pamphlet-about_mhlw.pdf#page=30 (last visited 2012/10/3). By contrast, defined contribution pension plans are still uncommon in Japan, which makes a reduction in defined benefit pension plans an important issue for the success of Japanese reorganization processes. For an overview of the Japanese pension system, *see* http://www.mhlw.go.jp/english/wp/wp-hw4/dl/pension_security/2011072501.pdf and http://www.mhlw.go.jp/english/wp/wp-hw4/dl/pension_security/2011071912.pdf (last visited 2012/10/3).

cases, the companies were able to reach an agreement with the majority of the relevant retirees or the unions representing them. Once agreement had been reached, the reorganization processes went fairly smoothly with governmental support. Taking the favorable performance of GM and JAL as of the time of writing in November 2013 into consideration, it might be said that we should celebrate the US and Japanese laws which have enabled the reduction of the relevant legacy costs and subsequent reorganization of companies which are important to the US and Japanese economies.

On the other hand, the fate of the retired employees of GM and JAL reminds current employees (including those working for other companies) that the promises of their employers regarding post-retirement benefits are not absolutely certain, and that if their employers become insolvent, such benefits may be subject to reductions and they may be forced to agree to such reductions in negotiations with their employer. This possibility is likely to have consequential effects on incentives of employees of companies which are not insolvent, which in turn might affect the value of those companies.

First, employees who think that their future benefits may be subject to reductions in case of insolvency might undervalue the benefits offered by their employers. This will diminish the incentive effect[3] of after-retirement benefits. Second, since future payments will be undervalued because of the risk of reduction, employees might prefer immediate payments rather than deferred payments. Third, if it is correct that the potential for reductions is higher where the after-retirement benefits are overcompensating employees, employees might stop requesting after-retirement benefits where there is a risk that they might be judged as such,[4] or conversely the employees might be overly aggressive when they negotiate their original after-retirement benefits package in order to ensure that they are in the best possible position. This is a type of moral hazard for the employees.

Law reforms such as downgrading the priority of claims of retired employees in a bankruptcy scenario or allowing unilateral modification of these claims will reduce the benefit of the retirees if the company and the retirees are not able to reach an agreement, and thus make it easier for the company to get a compromise from the retirees. However, we should remember that these reforms may effect incentives as mentioned above.

---

[3] By offering after-retirement benefits to employees, companies might be expecting to induce employees to refrain from moving to other companies and to invest in firm-specific human capital.

[4] Richard A. Ippolito, *Bankruptcy and Workers: Risks, Compensation and Pension Contracts*, 82 Wash. U. L. Q. 1251, 1259 (2004).

The degree of these effects will depend on the ability of the employees to predict the likelihood of reductions in the event of bankruptcy.

When we take all of these factors into consideration, it is clearly quite difficult, if not impossible, to determine the optimal rules for the priority of and modification of retirees' claims in a bankruptcy scenario, both theoretically and empirically. Rather than trying to answer this question, this chapter deals with the actual rules of the US and Japan that are relevant to these topics from the viewpoint of a comparative analysis. After describing the US rules regarding healthcare benefits and defined-benefit pension plans in section 8.2, and the Japanese rules regarding defined-benefit pension plans in section 8.3, a comparative analysis follows in section 8.4. A short conclusion is provided in section 8.5.

8.2 THE CASE OF THE UNITED STATES

8.2.1 Reduction of Healthcare Benefits for Retirees

For the modification of the healthcare benefits of retirees, there is a special provision in the Bankruptcy Code of the United States: Section 1114. Section 1114 protects retirees receiving healthcare benefits from a company subject to Chapter 11 bankruptcy proceedings by requiring the company to pay healthcare benefits to retirees in a timely manner,[5] and granting an administrative expense status, which is of second priority,[6] to payments in respect of healthcare benefits to be made before the confirmation of the reorganization plan.[7]

On the other hand, modification of these benefits is permitted when the court orders such modification according to Section 1114 or the authorized representative[8] of the retirees agrees to such modification.[9] The court will also order such modification in circumstances where the modification proposed by the company is necessary to permit the reorganization of the

---

5 11 U.S.C. §1114(e)(1).

6 11 U.S.C. §507(a)(2).

7 11 U.S.C. §1114(e)(2).

8 When the healthcare benefits of retirees are covered by a collective bargaining agreement, the labor organization, which is the signatory for such agreement, becomes the authorized representative of the retirees (11 U.S.C. §1114(c)(1)). However, since there may be a conflict of interest between the retirees and the current employees of the company, the court may appoint a committee of retired employees to act as the authorized representative upon a motion by any party in interest (11 U.S.C. §1114(c)(2)).

9 11 U.S.C. §1114(e)(1).

company and it is assured that all creditors, the company, and all of the affected parties will be treated fairly and equitably, and it is clearly favored by the balance of equities[10] and the authorized representative of the retirees refuses to accept the company's proposal without good cause.[11] When the healthcare benefits of retirees are modified in compliance with Section 1114, the retirees' claim for the part of the benefits that will not be paid as a result of the modification is treated as an unsecured pre-petition claim, except to the extent that it is granted an administrative expense status by the court.[12]

Section 1114 is based on Section 1113, which relates to collective bargaining agreements[13] and was enacted to protect employees and reverse a Supreme Court decision[14] which allowed companies to reject collective bargaining agreements on the same basis as other executory contracts. If Congress wished to protect the benefits of employees and retirees more effectively, it could simply have prohibited rejection or modification of collective bargaining agreements and retirees' healthcare benefits. Such a rule, however, could turn the negotiation between the company and the labor union into a "game of chicken" and disrupt the whole reorganization

---

10 11 U.S.C. §1114 (g)(3).

11 11 U.S.C. §1114(g)(2). In addition to the substantive requirements described above, there are also some procedural requirements to be met (11 U.S.C. §1114(f)(1)(2)).

12 7 COLLIER ON BANKRUPTCY 1114.09[1] (Alan N. Resnick & Henry J. Sommer eds, 16th edn 2012).

13 In contrast to Section 1113, the Japanese Corporate Reorganization Act completely prohibits a trustee from rejecting collective bargaining agreements in connection with corporate reorganization procedures (see Article 61 paragraph 3 of Kaisha-Kosei-Ho, Law No.154/2002). Although one prominent bankruptcy practitioner has mentioned this point as a major difference between the US and Japan (Shinjiro Takagi, Bei-GM-Mondai kara kangaeru jigyou-saisei no houkou (Thinking the Way of Business Restructuring from the case of GM in the United States), NIHON KEIZAI SHINBUN, 2009/4/7, p. 25), there were no serious requests for reform of the Article 61 paragraph 3 during the reform project of Corporate Reorganization Act leading to the enactment of the New Act in 2002. This suggests that there are no major difficulties in Japan with modifying working conditions even without an Article equivalent to Section 1113 in the US. One possible explanation is that in Japan, working conditions tend to be determined by rules of employment (*syugyo kisoku*) rather than by collective bargaining agreements (*rodo kyoyaku*), and the employers can modify the rules of employment unilaterally if the modifications are "reasonable" in light of several factors, (Rodo Keiyaku Ho (Labor Contract Act) Law No.128/2007, article 10). *See*, Hisashi Ikeda, Saiken-gata Tosan Tetsuduki ni okeru Rodoho Kihan no Tekiyou (Go) (The Application of Labor Law in Corporate Reorganization and Rehabilitation (5)), 128 HOGAKU KYOKAI ZASSHI 2837, 2903–2904, 2909–2911 (2011).

14 *NLRB v. Bildisco & Bildisco*, 465 U.S. 513 (1984).

process. Sections 1113 and 1114, which allow the court to act as an objective third party in order to make the necessary rejections or modifications, can be seen as a reasonable way to avoid this destructive scenario.[15]

In the Chapter 11 proceedings of GM, however, the procedures and requirements of Section 1114 were bypassed by selling all of the assets of the company to a new entity in accordance with Section 363.[16] This strategy enabled the new entity to choose whether or not to assume the obligations of the company regarding the retirees' healthcare benefits, which in turn made it easier for the company to negotiate with the representatives of the retirees.[17]

Regarding the healthcare benefits of retirees, it should also be noted that in the US there is a trend away from the defined-benefit model and towards the defined-contribution model by using the Voluntary Employee's Beneficiary Association (VEBA) trust, which is similar to the trend in corporate pensions in the US.[18] As a result of this change, employers hope to remove large future liabilities from their balance sheets and retirees hope to attain some protection against the possible bankruptcy of their employer.[19] It would seem that retirees' receptiveness to this change is due, at least in part, to the potential for their defined-benefit model healthcare benefits to be modified in the future in a bankruptcy scenario.

8.2.2 Reduction of Defined-Benefit Pension Plans

In contrast to healthcare benefits, the reduction of corporate pensions is not a material issue in the US today, as most corporate pension plans are defined-contribution pension plans which do not involve an ongoing

---

[15] On Section 1113, *see* Daniel Keating, *Why the Bankruptcy Reform Act Left Labor Legacy Costs Alone*, 71 Mo. L. Rev. 985, 999 (2006).

[16] Daniel Keating, *Automobile Bankruptcies, Retiree Benefits, and the Futility of Springing Priorities in Chapter 11 Reorganization*, 96 Iowa L. Rev. 261, 274–277 (2010). For critiques against the bankruptcy practice using section 363 sale, see Mark J. Roe & David Skeel, *Assessing the Chrysler Bankruptcy*, 108 Mich. L. Rev. 727 (2010) and Ralph Brubaker & Charles Jordan Tabb, *Bankruptcy Reorganizations and the Troubling Legacy of Chrysler and GM*, 2010 U. Ill. L. Rev. 1375.

[17] The outcome of such negotiations will depend on the bargaining power of the retirees. If the retirees are represented by a union which covers current employees who are important for the continuation of the business at the new entity, those retirees may benefit from the bargaining power of such union, provided that there is no conflict of interest between retirees and current employees within that union. Keating, *supra* note 16 at 282–285. *See also, In re General Motors Corp.*, 407 B.R. 463, 509–512 (Bankr. S.D.N.Y. 2009).

[18] Keating, *supra* note 16 at 265–267.

[19] Keating, *supra* note 16 at 263–264.

payment obligation from the company which may be subject to a reduction. This section provides a brief overview of the rules regarding defined-benefit pension plans in the US as a comparison with the situation in Japan.

Under the Employee Retirement Income Security Act, or ERISA, an employer is free, within the range permitted by ERISA, to amend an employee's future benefits under a defined-benefit pension plan.[20] but is prohibited from decreasing the accrued benefit, which corresponds to the past period, by an amendment of the plan[21] (the "anti-cutback rule"). The anti-cutback rule, however, does not apply to a plan which is unfunded and is maintained by an employer primarily for the purposes of providing deferred compensation to a select group of management or highly compensated employees.[22]

If the employer is insolvent and has an underfunded defined-benefit pension plan, there exists a payment guarantee in the form of the Public Benefit Guarantee Corporation (the PBGC),[23] but there are certain limitations on what plans are covered by this guarantee[24] and on the amount of guarantee.[25]

Beyond the scope of the payment guarantee by the PBGC, unsecured claims for contributions to an employee benefit plan arising from services rendered within 180 days before the date of the filing of the bankruptcy petition are granted fifth priority in the bankruptcy proceedings up to a certain amount.[26]

8.3 THE CASE OF JAPAN: REDUCTION OF DEFINED-BENEFIT CORPORATE PENSION PLANS

Japanese rules regarding reductions in defined-benefit corporate pension plans[27] are substantially different to those in the US in that reductions are

---

[20] *Cf.* 29 U.S.C. 1054(b)(1).

[21] 29 U.S.C. §1054(g)(1).

[22] 29 U.S.C. §1051(2). A highly compensated employee means, in general, any employee who received compensation from the employer in excess of $80 000 in the preceding year (26 U.S.C. §416(q)(1)(B)).

[23] 29 U.S.C. §1322, 29 U.S.C. §1322a.

[24] 29 U.S.C. §1321(b).

[25] 29 C.F.R. 4022, subpart B.

[26] The amount of the claims with the priority is capped at an amount equal to number of employees covered by the plan multiplied by US$11 725, less the aggregate amount paid as wages, salaries, and so on (11 U.S.C. §507(a)(4)(5)).

[27] There are several different systems for corporate pensions in Japan. For an

possible upon the conditions described below even where the payment corresponds to a past period.

In order to reduce the payment to retirees under a fund-type defined-benefit corporate pension plan, the employer needs to modify the Articles of Association for the defined-benefit corporate pension plan fund. For this modification, the employer needs to obtain the approval of the Minister of Health, Labor and Welfare,[28] regardless of whether the employer is in reorganization proceedings or not. To obtain this approval, certain substantive and procedural requirements must be met.[29]

As substantive requirement, there must be one of following situations: (1) there are difficulties in maintaining the defined-benefit corporate pension plan without the modification; (2) a reduction in payments to retirees is inevitable because the management condition of the employer has worsened; or (3) a reduction in payments to retirees is inevitable because it is difficult for the employer to pay the contribution to the fund without such reduction.[30]

---

overview, see the websites cited *supra* in note 2. Hideyuki Morito, Jigyo Saisei to Kigyo Nenkin (Business Restructuring and Corporate Pensions), 1401 JYURISUTO 38 (2010) is a more detailed explanation in Japanese. The type described here, *kikin-gata kakutei kyufu kigyo nenkin* (fund-type defined benefit corporate pension plan), is the one which was used in the case of JAL.

[28] Defined Benefit Corporate Pension Plan Act (Kakutei Kyufu Kigyo Nenkin Ho, Law No.50/2001), Article 16.

[29] Government Ordinance to Enforce the Defined Benefit Corporate Pension Plan Act (Kakutei Kyufu Kigyo Nenkin Ho Seko Rei, Government Ordinance No.424/2001), Article 4 Nr.2 and Article 7.

[30] Order of the Ministry of Health, Labor and Welfare to Enforce the Defined Benefit Corporate Pension Plan Act (Kakutei Kyufu Kigyo Nenkin Ho Seko Kisoku, Order of the Ministry of Health, Labor and Welfare, No.22/2002) Article 5 Nr.2 and 3, Article 12. The Ministry of Health, Labor and Welfare and the courts have interpreted this requirement, particularly the second alternative (inevitability of the reduction of payment to retirees because the management condition of the employer have worsened), quite strictly. See for example, Tokyo High Court, July 9, 2002, 964 Rodo Hanrei 5 (admitting the Ministry's refusal to approve reduction). Recently, however, it has been reported that the Ministry is going to abolish the second alternative in order to clarify that it is possible to reduce the payments to retirees even if the employer is not insolvent. (For press release of the Ministry in Japanese, *see* http://www.mhlw.go.jp/stf/houdou/2r9852000002gbjw.html, last visited 2012/10/3). The direct reason for this reform is the AIJ case, a case similar to the fraud committed by Bernard Madoff, in which many corporate pension funds entrusted and lost a large portion of their money to an investment advisory company which was reporting false investment returns. It has been reported that a part of the background to this case is the difficulty in Japan of reducing payments under defined-benefit pension plans, which in turn encouraged pension funds (which were running large deficits) to make high-risk investment decisions.

Procedurally, the employer is required to obtain consent for the reduction from more than two-thirds of the retirees receiving pensions under the plan, and to pay a minimum accumulation, calculated without taking the reduction into account, as a lump sum to those retirees who choose such payment rather than receiving the pension with the reduction.[31] This procedural requirement means that it is impossible to reduce payments to retirees unless two-thirds of them consent to the reduction, even if the reduction meets the substantive requirements set out above. Thus, the negotiations to obtain the consent of the retirees are crucial.

In the negotiations, the priority of the claims of the pension fund against the employer regarding contributions for the deficit in the reorganization procedure is particularly important. The priority of such claims depends on whether these claims are granted general statutory liens for employer–employee relationships under the Civil Code.[32]

Article 308 of the Japanese Civil Code grants general statutory liens for employer–employee relationships to claims that arise under employer–employee relationships such as salaries or retirement payments paid directly by the employer to retirees. In liquidation proceedings, claims with general statutory liens for employer–employee relationships are treated as preferred bankruptcy claims,[33] and are therefore granted a second-rank priority regarding distributions from the bankruptcy estate, after expenses payable for the common benefit of all creditors.[34] In corporate reorganization proceedings, claims with general statutory liens for employer–employee relationships are granted second-rank priority in the reorganization plan, after claims made by creditors with security interests in a specific asset of the debtor.[35]

There is no commonly accepted view or court decision, as of the time of writing in November 2013, on whether the claims of a pension fund against an employer for contributions in respect of a pension deficit can be classified as a "claim that arose under the employer–employee relationship between the obligor and his/her employee."[36] One leading bankruptcy-law professor has taken a negative view on this point on the

---

31 Order of the Ministry of Health, Labor and Welfare to Enforce the Defined Benefit Corporate Pension Plan Act, Article 6 Para.1 Nr.1, Article 13.

32 Min Po, Law No.89/1896.

33 Bankruptcy Act (Hasan Ho), Law No.75/2004, Article 98 paragraph 1.

34 Bankruptcy Act, Article 194 paragraph 1 Nr.1, Article 98 paragraph 2, Civil Code, Article 306.

35 Corporate Reorganization Act, Article 168 paragraph 1 Nr.2 and paragraph 3.

36 Civil Code, Article 308.

basis that the claim of the pension fund is not based on individual labor contracts.[37] It seems quite unnatural, however, to deny that claims regarding the corporate pensions of former employees are "claims that arose under the employer–employee relationship." Also, it seems quite difficult to interpret Article 308 as excluding from its scope of application claims regarding pension plans which might be considered to be overcompensating[38] when we take the legislative history of the Civil Code reform of 2003 (i.e. the abolishment of the limitation of general statutory liens for employer–employee relationships to claims regarding salaries for last six month) into consideration.

Thus, there is a substantial possibility that claims of a pension fund against an employer for contributions in respect of a pension deficit will be granted high priority in corporate reorganization proceedings. This priority might make it difficult for an employer to obtain the necessary level of consent from its retirees in connection with a reduction in pension payments.

8.4 COMPARISON

From the observations above, the law of the US can be summarized as enabling a reduction of overcompensating retiree benefits, for it permits the modification of healthcare plans for retirees by a court order without the consent of the retirees, excludes pension payments to highly compensated employees from the application of the anti-cutback rule, and limits the amount of claims for pension contributions which are granted a high priority. This might mean that US law takes seriously the success of the negotiations for reorganization and the moral hazard of the employees mentioned in section 8.1 above.

On the other hand, Japanese law requires employers seeking a reduction in payments in respect of defined-benefit pensions to obtain consent from more than two-thirds of the relevant retirees and to offer such retirees a lump sum payment as an option. Thus, even though Japanese law does not adopt the anti-cutback rule for pensions corresponding to

---

[37] Kazuhiko Yamamoto, Nihon ni okeru Honkakuteki na Jizen Chosei Gata Kaisya Kosei Tetsuduki no Makuaki he (The Beginning of a Full-Scale Prepackaged Corporate Reorganization Procedure in Japan), 128 JIGYO SAISEI TO SAIKEN KANRI 4, 7–8 (2010).

[38] Such a view by one of the leading law firms in Japan is introduced in Shingo Miyake, Nikko Saiken to Hoteki Seiri (Restructuring of JAL and Statutory Reorganization Procedure), NIHON KEIZAI SHINBUN, Nov. 10, 2009, p. 15.

past periods, it is not easy to fulfill the necessary procedural requirements. Also, Japanese law seems to grant a high priority to the claims of pension funds against employers regarding contributions for pension deficits in corporate reorganization proceedings, without a limitation on the amount of such claims. It is arguable, therefore, that Japanese law does not pay enough attention to the success of the negotiations for reorganization and the moral hazard of the employees, when compared to the US law.

Considering that employers are not able to use dismissal as a threat against retirees in the negotiations regarding the reduction since they are already retired, it might be sensible for Japanese law to make the reduction of pension plans over a certain amount easier. Although more than two-thirds of the retirees finally agreed to the reduction in the case of JAL, the number of the retirees who agreed by the deadline to obtain consent was 67 percent,[39] only slightly above the required percentage.[40]

Assuming that it is more difficult to reduce retirees' benefits in Japan, the next question is what effect this has on the incentives of employees mentioned in section 8.1 above. Unfortunately, it is difficult to compare the effects in Japan and the US, as there are many differences regarding labor relationships between both countries which may affect the incentives of employees.

As anecdotal evidence, it is worth noting that, in comparison with the US, most corporate pension plans in Japan are still defined-benefit plans and that the defined-contribution plans (the "Japanese 401k") are not yet particularly popular.[41] This might seem strange, since employers should prefer defined-benefit pension plans to defined-contribution pension plans given that the reduction of payments for pensions is difficult. If the slow pace of transition to defined-contribution pension plans in Japan can be attributed to some extent to the reluctance of employees and labor unions

---

39 NIHON KEIZAI SHINBUN, 2010/1/13, p. 1. After the deadline, this rate rose to 72.4 percent in the end. NIHON KEIZAI SHINBUN, 2010/1/23, page 13.

40 There are several cases besides JAL in which the employers have succeeded in obtaining consents from more than two-thirds of the retirees. *See*, for example, NIHON KEIZAI SHINBUN, 2005/9/9, p. 19 (NTT) and NIHON KEIZAI SHINBUN, 2010/1/27, p. 11 (Kinki Nippon Tourist). Some might wonder why the retirees ever agree to reduction when they have nothing to lose. One of the reasons might be that the retirees feel obliged to agree to a reduction for the benefit of the current employees, since it is customary in Japan for employees to work for the same company for their whole life and they have a sense of belonging to the society of their company even after their retirement.

41 *See*, websites of the Ministry of Health, Labor and Welfare cited in *supra* note 2.

to adopt the Japanese 401k[42] due to the poor performance of the stock market over the last 20 years or so, it might be construed as one form of the moral hazard of the employees to request too much as after-retirement benefits.

8.5 CONCLUSION

This chapter has compared certain rules relating to the reduction of retirees' benefits in reorganization procedures in both the US and Japan, and has found that there is a significant difference between the two countries regarding how difficult it is for employers to obtain such a reduction, particularly a reduction of the benefits which can be regarded as overcompensating. Unfortunately, however, it was not possible to compare the effect of these rules on the incentives of employees. It is possible to argue that, as the effect of the rules regarding the reduction of retirees' benefits are unclear, these rules are designed solely from the viewpoint of efficiency and protection of retirees in reorganization procedures. It would be a valuable research topic for the future to explore whether there has been a change in the way employees view their after-retirement benefits following the reductions made to such benefits in connection with the reorganization of companies such as GM and JAL.

---

42 The Japanese Trade Union Confederation (JTUC), the national-level association of labor unions in Japan, takes a negative position to the International Financial Reporting Standards (IFRS). One of the reasons for such a position is the fear that the disclosure of the obligation regarding post-retirement benefits required by the IFRS might push employers to abolish defined-benefit pension plans. *See*, the statement of Mr Naoto Omi, the Vice Secretary General of the JTUC, in the minute for the General Meeting of the Corporate Accounting Council on 2011/6/30 (available at http://www.fsa.go.jp/singi/singi_kigyou/gijiroku/soukai/20110630.html (last visited 2012/10/3).

Comments on Part II: unsolved aspects of corporate governance problems

Noriyuki Yanagawa

Part II mainly focuses on certain corporate governance problems that occur during periods of financial distress or reorganization processes. For the market mechanism to work properly, appropriate entry into and exit from the market are necessary. Hence, bankruptcy procedures are an important element for corporate governance, and the relationship between corporate law and bankruptcy law is a crucial point that must be examined rigorously. All four of the chapters in this section examine important aspects of this relationship.

Chapter 5, "The role of debt in the governance of US business corporations" by George Triantis, focuses on the role of debt in corporate governance problems. In short, a debt contract gives the debtholder a contingent right to remove assets and possibly force liquidation in the event a borrower defaults. This chapter stresses that the connection between corporate law and bankruptcy law is a key factor in understanding the role of debt. Certain issues come to light, such as the fact that debtholder control assumes different forms depending on whether the distressed firm is also in bankruptcy proceedings, and that bankruptcy law places the decision-making debtor under the oversight of a bankruptcy judge. The chapter also stresses the fact that developments in financial markets are promoting the separation of economic and the control rights of debtholders. The technological changes in financial markets may change the governance structure in drastic ways, which might in turn require amendments to the relevant legal rules in the near future.

Chapter 6, "Senior creditor control in Chapter 11" by Kenneth M. Ayotte and Edward R. Morrison, points out that during the past decade in the United States, creditors with senior, secured claims have come to dominate the Chapter 11 process. Traditionally, managers or equity holders control the Chapter 11 reorganization process because of the debtor-friendly features of the US Bankruptcy Code and judges who are passive or biased in favor of continuation. This chapter explains why this is not true these days; data has clearly shown that, among large privately and publicly held businesses, creditor control is pervasive. This finding is very interesting and it may be valuable to thoroughly examine the reasons why creditor control is now pervasive.

This chapter insists that the disparate treatment of senior creditors versus junior creditor distorts outcomes in bankruptcy cases. Because these parties have distinct preferences, the bargaining process can often lead to a misallocation of assets. During the 1980s, this problem was evident in the conflict between creditors and equity holders. Today, as the data shows, the problem persists, but now the conflict tends to arise between senior and junior lenders.

Chapter 7, "Cramdown versus extinguishing security interests: secured claims in bankruptcy in the United States and Japan" by Wataru Tanaka, looks at the treatment of secured claims under the Civil Rehabilitation Act (CRA; *Minji saisei ho*) of Japan. In contrast to the Chapter 11 process in the United States, secured creditors can freely enforce their rights even after commencement of Civil Rehabilitation proceedings under the CRA. However, this chapter clearly shows that the CRA has a unique procedure that restricts the rights of secured creditors: the procedure for extinguishing security interests. This procedure permits a debtor undergoing Civil Rehabilitation proceedings to cancel security interests in any of the debtor's property, as is necessary for the continuation of their business. This can be achieved simply by paying an amount of cash equal to the liquidation value of the subject property to the secured creditors. If the parties cannot agree on the liquidation value of the property, the court will assess the value through an appraisal proceeding.

The chapter sets forth the idea that the procedure for extinguishing security interests may have some social benefit, and further argues that this procedure can enhance overall efficiency by giving the debtor an exit option, thereby avoiding potentially costly negotiations with secured creditors. Although the chapter is restricted to Japanese situations, this result might provide interesting information for understanding the conflict in the United States which is explained in Chapter 6.

Chapter 8, "Reduction of retirees' benefits upon the reorganization of a company" by Gen Goto, addresses another aspect of the conflicts of interest that occur during a reorganization process. This chapter mainly focuses on the negotiations involved in reducing retiree benefit payment obligations, comparing the actual rules of the US and Japan that are relevant to such negotiations. Furthermore, the chapter suggests that US law might be able to realize the success of the negotiations for reorganization and to avoid the moral hazard of the employees. On the other hand, even though Japanese law has not adopted the anti-cutback rule for pensions corresponding to past periods, it is not easy to fulfill the necessary procedural requirements. It seems that Japanese law does not pay enough attention to the negotiations for reorganization and the moral hazard of the employees, when compared to US law. As the reduction of retiree benefit payment obligations is a very crucial matter for the actual reorganization process, examination of this chapter is useful and indicates that there is significant need to gather more empirical evidence on this matter.

All four chapters examine interesting topics and explore important aspects of the relationship between corporate law and bankruptcy law; however, there are still many questions about this relationship. One of the most fundamental questions is whether or not the two separate bodies of law are needed. Even more practically, as explained by Triantis, the power of each stakeholder is quite dependent on whether the distressed firm is undergoing bankruptcy proceedings. Hence, it may be meaningful to empirically examine how such dependence affects each stakeholder.

Furthermore, in understanding the corporate governance system of a distressed firm, a review of court behavior may be necessary. In particular, the fact that Japanese judges' discretion is relatively large means the predictability of judgments is relatively low. Of course, this fact not only affects the behavior and decision-making process of each agent, but also affects the understanding of researchers. In order to more deeply understand the corporate governance mechanism, it seems necessary to investigate the decision process of judges, both theoretically and empirically, which may improve researchers' ability to predict the outcomes of judgments.

PART III

The incentive bargain between shareholders and management

9. Takeover law and managerial incentives in the United States and Japan

Curtis J. Milhaupt*

9.1 INTRODUCTION

In their seminal work *The Corporate Contract*,[1] Frank H. Easterbrook and Daniel R. Fischel conceptualized the interaction among corporate actors as a series of contractual agreements. Easterbrook and Fischel argued that through these contractual agreements, "managers and certain other participants exercise a great deal of discretion that is 'reviewed' by interactions with other self-interested actors."[2] In this conception of corporate law, formal legal rules function as gap-fillers in the contracts between corporate participants.[3] Three types of formal rules relevant to corporate governance in most countries are: (1) corporate statutes enacted by legislators; (2) fiduciary principles defined by courts; and (3) regulations promulgated by securities regulators and stock exchanges. In every economy, informal (non-binding) gap fillers, such as codes of best practice, also play an important role in fleshing out the corporate contract.

Managerial discretion is "reviewed" by other self-interested actors in many ways, creating competitive pressures that shape corporate contracts. Investors decide whether to purchase shares in the company (capital market competition), customers decide whether to buy the company's products or services (product market competition), and – the focus of this chapter – potential acquirers decide whether to try and wrest control of the

* Geoffrey Walter provided valuable research assistance. Portions of this chapter are drawn from John Armour, Jack B. Jacobs, & Curtis J. Milhaupt, *The Evolution of Hostile Takeover Regimes in Developed and Emerging Markets: An Analytical Framework*, 52 HARV. INT'L L. J. 219 (2011).

1 Frank H. Easterbrook & Daniel R. Fischel, *The Corporate Contract*, 89 COLUM. L. REV. 1416 (1989).

2 *Id*., at 1418.

3 *Id*., at 1446.

firm away from existing management (the market for corporate control). When the market for corporate control, or takeover market, is operating efficiently, the threat of ouster at the hands of a potential acquirer serves as an important check on managerial performance.

In view of potential abuses and conflicts of interest, the market for corporate control is subject to legal regulation in all developed and many developing economies.[4] In theory, one might assume that legal regulation of the takeover market would be relatively uniform around the world. After all, this basic form of transaction is found, with varying degrees of frequency, in every economy in which shares of public companies are sufficiently dispersed to facilitate changes in control without the consent of the target company's board.

In fact, legal regimes for hostile takeovers vary considerably from country to country. Returning to the contractual conception of corporate law, with respect to this crucial term in the corporate contract – who decides whether an unsolicited bid should go forward, the shareholders or the board of the target company? – the answer varies greatly from one legal system to the next. Cross-country variation in this important contract term has major potential consequences for managerial incentives.

The United States and Japan, the focus of this book, both have mature economies with highly developed capital markets. Yet the legal regimes governing hostile takeover activity evolved at different times through very different processes of institutional development, and with rather different results. Naturally, these different regimes generate quite different incentives for managers of US and Japanese firms, respectively. This short chapter will briefly describe the evolution and legal "bottom line" of the regulatory regimes governing hostile takeovers in the United States and Japan, and analyze the managerial incentives created by each regime. Section 9.2 analyzes the development of laws governing hostile mergers and acquisitions in the United States and Japan. Section 9.3 examines the managerial incentives generated by these two different regimes. Section 9.4 concludes.

---

4 Hostile bids, whether in the form of tender offers or proxy contests, are open to many forms of abuse and potential for coercion of the target company shareholders. Moreover, such bids generally pit the interests of target company shareholders (maximizing financial returns on their investment) against those of target company managers (retaining their positions in the firm).

9.2 HOSTILE TAKEOVER REGIMES IN THE US AND JAPAN

9.2.1 United States

There are two primary methods for an acquirer to obtain control of a publicly held corporation without the consent and cooperation of the target company board. The first is a proxy contest, to obtain control of the board. The second is a tender offer, to obtain a majority of the outstanding shares. Recently in the United States, both methods have been combined as part of a unified takeover strategy.

Until the 1960s, the primary method to force a change of corporate control in the US was to wage a proxy contest to replace the target board. In that setting, the lawmakers were the Securities and Exchange Commission (SEC) and the federal courts applying Section 14(a) of the Securities Exchange Act of 1934 and implementing SEC proxy rules. Beginning in the mid-1960s, the hostile tender offer gradually displaced the proxy contest as the preferred mechanism for acquiring corporate control. This change came about because of the relatively greater speed with which the acquisition could be consummated, the hostile acquirer's ability to bypass the board and deal directly with target shareholders, the unsuccessful acquirer's ability to recoup the expenses of a failed offer by selling its target company stock, and most importantly, the comparatively lower transaction costs in a tender offer as compared to a proxy contest.

Until 1968, tender offers were often strategically abusive, to the detriment of target-company shareholders. In 1968, the US Congress responded to these abuses by adopting the Williams Act, a statute that imposed important disclosure and procedural requirements for tender offers. But the Williams Act did not require a bidder obtaining control by means of a block purchase to make a "mandatory bid" for all shares so as to give the minority shareholders a chance to exit their investment. Nor did the Williams Act regulate the conduct of target company boards in responding to and resisting hostile takeover bids.[5]

The consequence was to leave the regulation of board anti-takeover defensive conduct to the states. Because Delaware was, and continues

---

[5] For a detailed analysis of the evolution of hostile takeover regulation in the United States, Japan and the United Kindom, see John Armour, Jack B. Jacobs, & Curtis J. Milhaupt, *The Evolution of Hostile Takeover Regimes in Developed and Emerging Markets: An Analytical Framework*, 52 HARV. INT'L L. J. 219 (2011). The discussion of the US and Japanese regimes in this chapter draws heavily on that prior work.

to be, the state where a majority of large public US companies are incorporated, the conduct of corporations' directors became the subject of regulation under Delaware law, administered by the courts on a case-by-case basis. However, the Delaware General Corporation Law does not answer the fundamental question of who should decide whether an unsolicited takeover bid can go forward: the shareholders or the target company board. Because the statute provides no explicit guidance on this fundamental issue, by default the Delaware courts were left to develop rules to determine the circumstances under which a target board can take measures to frustrate an unsolicited bid.

In *Unocal v. Mesa Petroleum Co.*,[6] the Delaware Supreme Court held that, as a matter of fiduciary law, where a target board has reason to regard a hostile bid as a threat to legitimate corporate policy and shareholder interests, the board has the authority and the duty to interpose itself between the offeror and the shareholders and, where necessary, take defensive measures that are not disproportionate to the threat.[7] Thus, while formally establishing the right of a corporation's board to employ defensive mechanisms, *Unocal* does not grant target boards unfettered discretion; they must be able to establish that their defensive actions were objectively reasonable. Under *Unocal*, the board must prove that the hostile offer was reasonably perceived as a threat to corporate value and policy, and that the board's selected defense was not disproportionate to the threat. This standard, by its very nature, lends itself to objective judicial application. As elaborated below, it also provides incentives for corporations to have independent directors. Independent directors do not face, at least as acutely, the potential conflict of executive directors in evaluating the threat posed by a hostile bid, because their principal employment is not with the target corporation.

One year after *Unocal*, the Delaware Supreme Court confronted a different kind of takeover defense that called for a different formulation of the reasonableness standard: a board decision either to sell the company or to cause it to engage in a change of control transaction, rather than keep the company independent. In *Revlon, Inc. v. McAndrews & Forbes*

---

6 493 A.2d 946 (Del. 1985).

7 Note a critical difference on this point between Delaware law and that of the UK. The UK City Code prohibits target boards from employing defensive mechanisms without shareholder approval. As we will see, Japan's takeover regime represents a middle position between that of Delaware and the UK. In Japan, shareholder approval of defensive measures is technically not mandatory, but it is strongly encouraged and significantly enhances the probability that the measures will be upheld in the face of a challenge.

Holdings, Inc.[8], the court held that in these circumstances, the board's fiduciary duty is to sell the company to the bidder that offers to the shareholders the highest value reasonably available. In this setting the court must review the reasonableness of the board's choice of transaction and transaction partner as to both process and prices, with the board having the burden of proving that its decision was reasonable in both respects.

In the 1980s, public corporations in the United States faced an unprecedented rise in the number of hostile takeover bids. In response, boards of directors adopted a number of defensive mechanisms to deter potential hostile bidders. By far the most important of these was the shareholder rights plan or "poison pill."[9] If the rights were exercised, the bidder's ownership percentage in the target would be massively diluted, thereby making economically suicidal any such acquisition or announcement without the target board's approval. This novel and extremely potent defensive mechanism was unsuccessfully challenged in *Moran v. Household Inc.*[10] The court upheld the adoption of a poison pill as a pre-planned defense, and held that where the pill is used as a defense against an actual hostile bid, the defense is subject to the *Unocal* standard of review. This and other challenges to the pill proved unsuccessful because, in most cases, allowing the pill to be kept in place often results in higher bids and superior transaction terms compared with the bidder's initial offer. As a result, the poison pill became the defensive mechanism of choice in the United States.

Delaware courts have consistently allowed a target board to "just say no" to an unwanted bidder – that is, keep the pill in place so that shareholders cannot decide for themselves whether to sell their shares in the offer – as long as the board is pursuing a long-term stand-alone corporate strategy in good faith.[11] But director discretion to deploy defenses is not unlimited; it must be couched in terms of shareholder wealth maximization. A recent poison pill dispute illustrates the point. In *eBay*,[12] the directors (co-founders) of the online marketing company craigslist Inc. adopted a poison pill that prevented an outside minority shareholder (eBay) from

---

[8] 506 A.2d 173 (Del. 1986).

[9] The poison pill is essentially an option created unilaterally by board resolution that is distributed to target-company shareholders if a hostile bidder acquires shares exceeding the trigger threshold or announces that it will acquire all non-tendered shares in a second-step merger. When exercised, the rights typically entitle the holder of each right – except the hostile bidder – to acquire two shares of the target company for the price of one share.

[10] 500 A.2d 1346 (Del. 1985).

[11] *See e.g. Air Products & Chemicals, Inc. v. Airgas, Inc.*, 16 A.3d 48 (Del Ch. 2011).

[12] *eBay Domestic Holdings, Inc. v. Newmark*, 16 A.3d 1 (Del. Ch. 2010).

gaining control of the firm or transferring its stake to a third party without board approval. The craigslist founder-directors argued that this measure was necessary to protect their public-service-oriented (i.e. not maximally profitable) business model for classified advertising against the possibility that one day the firm might be controlled by a more profit-oriented shareholder such as eBay. The Delaware Court of Chancery, applying the *Unocal* standard discussed above, held that the protection of corporate culture – particularly one that "seeks *not* to maximize the economic value of a for-profit Delaware corporation for the benefit of its stockholders"[13] – oversteps the permissible range of discretion afforded to directors. In so ruling, the court was clear about the legally required objective of directors of Delaware corporations: "Having chosen the for-profit form, the craigslist directors are bound by the fiduciary duties and standards that accompany that form. Those standards include acting to promote the value of the corporation for the benefit of its stockholders."[14]

9.2.2 Japan

The market for corporate control was not active during Japan's post-war high-growth period. In the post-war corporate governance regime, publicly traded firms were typically affiliated with a corporate group (*keiretsu*) with a major bank at the center. Group-affiliated firms cross-held shares of their affiliates, forming stable, friendly investor relationships involving significant percentages of the public float. Investor activism was rare and hostile takeover activity was condemned as antithetical to Japanese business norms, which conceptualizes the firm as a community of employees rather than an assemblage of financial assets to be bought and sold. But the situation began to change in the 2000s, as patterns of share ownership, the composition of corporate shareholders, and investor activism all began to change. Given the dearth of market activity, it is not surprising that until this period the legal regime for takeover regulation was minimalist. Indeed, Japan's relatively blank institutional slate as hostile takeovers began to occur in the early 2000s is loosely equivalent to the situation just described in the United States in the early 1980s, before the development of Delaware takeover doctrine in the hands of the courts.[15]

In 2005, two simultaneous developments significantly altered this

---

[13] *Id.*, at 34.

[14] *Id.*

[15] Kenichi Osugi, *Transplanting Poison Pills in Foreign Soil: Japan's Experiment*, *in* TRANSFORMING CORPORATE GOVERNANCE IN EAST ASIA 36 (Hideki Kanda, Kon-Sik Kim, & Curtis J. Milhaupt eds, 2008).

institutional landscape. In the spring of that year, a hostile bid involving two Japanese firms transfixed the public. The target company, Nippon Broadcasting, took defensive measures to defeat a hostile tender offer from Livedoor Corporation. Livedoor sued, and the courts ruled that the defensive measures were "grossly unfair" and thus invalid. In affirming the lower court's decision to enjoin the defenses, the Tokyo High Court ruled that where a hostile bidder has an "abusive motive," defensive measures may be used to protect the interests of shareholders if they are necessary and proportionate.[16] (Notice the parallels to the Delaware court's *Unocal* ruling.)

A second development in Japanese takeover policy was culminating just as the *Livedoor* ruling was issued. In 2004, "in light of concerns about the steady rise of hostile bids,"[17] the Ministry of Economy, Trade, and Industry (METI) and the Ministry of Justice (MOJ) jointly established the Corporate Value Study Group (CVSG) composed of legal and policy experts to consider an appropriate policy response to hostile takeover activity. The CVSG conducted extensive research on Anglo-American takeover defenses and legal precedents and issued a report in March 2005, in the midst of the Livedoor bid. The report noted that the establishment of defensive measures in Japan had been hampered by uncertainty over their legal effect, a paucity of precedents and experience, and a lack of consensus on what should constitute reasonable defensive measures. The report exhaustively analyzed Delaware's experience with defensive measures, in particular the poison pill, focusing on the *Unocal* rule and its progeny. The report suggested that if adjusted for local circumstances, most defensive measures recognized in the United States could be implemented in Japan.

Significantly, however, the report emphasized that defensive measures should be implemented to protect corporate value, a concept that, in the words of one member of the CVSG, is "ambiguous enough to be

---

[16] The court enumerated four examples of an abusive motive: (a) greenmail; (b) "scorched earth" practices involving stripping the target of assets after the acquisition; (c) liquidation of the target's assets to pay down debt of the acquirer; and (d) selling off assets unrelated to the core business of the target in order to pay a high one-time dividend.

[17] KIGYŌ KACHI KENKYŪ KAI [CORPORATE VALUE STUDY GROUP], TEKITAITEKI BAISHŪ BŌEISAKU (KIGYŌ KACHI BŌEISAKU) NO SEIBI [PREPARING DEFENSIVE MEASURES TOWARD HOSTILE TAKEOVERS (MEASURES TO DEFEND CORPORATE VALUE)] 2 (2005) [hereinafter CVSG 2005 REPORT], *available at* http://www.meti.go.jp/committee/materials/downloadfiles/g50307a11j.pdf. An English summary is available at http://meti.go.jp/policy/economic_oganization/pdf/ shishin_hontai.pdf.

interpreted either as shareholder interests or as wider interests of the entire body of stakeholders, such as the employees."[18] Thus, although the CVSG borrowed heavily from Delaware takeover doctrine in formulating its policy recommendations, it also adroitly straddled the conceptual divide between the shareholder orientation of US corporate law and the more stakeholder- (particularly employee-) oriented approach of post-war Japanese corporate governance practices.

Based on the report, non-binding Takeover Guidelines were jointly issued by METI and MOJ in May 2005.[19] The Takeover Guidelines embrace three fundamental principles. First, adoption, activation, and removal of defensive measures should be undertaken to maintain or improve corporate value.[20] Second, defensive measures should be adequately disclosed when adopted, and should be based upon the reasonable will of the shareholders.[21] Third, defensive measures should be necessary and reasonable.[22] The guidelines explicitly endorse the use of a shareholder rights plan as a defensive measure under Japanese corporate law. But, in a major departure from US law and practice, the Takeover Guidelines strongly recommend (but do not require) advance shareholder approval of defensive measures as a means of ensuring their fairness.

With the guidelines and the emergence of new judicial doctrine, Japan suddenly had a new, if still incomplete, institutional framework for hostile acquisitions. In 2006 the CVSG observed, "We can say that Japan is changing from [a] situation without rules [for hostile takeovers] to [a] situation with formulated rules."[23]

As noted, a key element of the Takeover Guidelines is their endorsement

---

18 Osugi, *supra* note 15, at 51.

19 KEIZAI SANGŌYSHŌ [Ministry of Economy, Trade and Industry (METI)] & HŌMUSHŌ [Ministry of Justice], Kigyō kachi, kabunushi kyōdō no rieki no kakuho mata wa kōjō no tame no baishō bōeisaku ni kansuru shishin [Takeover Defense Guidelines for Protecting and Enhancing Corporate Value and the Common Interests of Shareholders] (May 2005) [hereinafter JAPANESE TAKEOVER GUIDELINES], *available at* http://www.meti.go.jp/press/20050527005/3-shishinn-honntai-set.pdf. An English translation is available at http://www.meti.go.jp/policy/economy/ keiei_innovation/keizaihousei/pdf/shishinn_honntai.pdf.

20 *Id.*, at 3.

21 *Id.*

22 *Id.*, at 4.

23 CORPORATE VALUE STUDY GROUP, CORPORATE VALUE REPORT: TOWARD THE FIRM ESTABLISHMENT OF FAIR RULES IN THE CORPORATE COMMUNITY 59 (2006), *available at* www.meti.go.jp/policy/economic_organization/pdf/houkoku06_eng.pdf.

of the shareholder rights plan, a distinctly American takeover defense. Promulgation of the guidelines sparked a small stampede by Japanese firms to adopt defensive measures. By 2011, 465 public companies, approximately 20 percent of companies traded on the Tokyo Stock Exchange (TSE), had adopted a pill-like defense plan.[24]

However, unlike the US shareholder rights plan, in Japan the overwhelming majority of defensive mechanisms are "pre-warning rights plans." This is not a legal instrument; it is a public statement in the form of a press release by the board setting forth the procedures to be followed should an acquirer contemplate a large-scale acquisition of the company's shares. The statement declares that if an acquirer starts an acquisition or takeover bid that would result in the acquirer holding a specified percentage (typically 20 percent) of the target company's outstanding shares, the target board will establish a special committee to evaluate the bid. If the committee determines that the bid would damage "corporate value of the company or the common interests of shareholders" (the typical formulation of the press release), it will recommend that the board issue warrants to shareholders other than the bidder so as to dilute the bidder's holdings.

Japanese defensive measures took on this distinctive, and highly uniform, cast due to the influence of another important actor in the takeover landscape: the Tokyo Stock Exchange. After the publication of the CVSG 2005 Report and Takeover Guidelines, the TSE published policy statements and listing standards formally incorporating the non-binding principles of the Takeover Guidelines. To ensure the effectiveness of the listing standards, the TSE requires that firms consult with it before adopting defensive measures. Firms that fail to do so, or whose defensive measures are deemed by the TSE to violate the listing standards, are subject to public criticism by the exchange, and ultimately to delisting if corrective action is not taken. Thus, the TSE's listing rules and policy statements have become the de facto mandatory rules governing takeover defenses for Japanese listed companies.

Importantly, promulgation of the Takeover Guidelines and the TSE's involvement in the adoption of takeover defenses did not eliminate the role of Japanese courts in takeover-related disputes. Because the prewarning plan adopted by most Japanese firms lacks legal effect (as it is

---

24 Tokyo Stock Exchange, Inc., TSE Listed Companies: White Paper on Corporate Governance (2011) at 78, available at http://www.tse.or.jp/english/listing/cg/b7gje60000003y6y-att/20110613.pdf. The TSE notes, however, that in 2011 only five new companies reported adopting defensive measures, while 23 companies abolished them, suggesting that adoption of takeover defenses in Japan may have peaked, at least for the time being.

simply a press release issued before the appearance of any bidders), questions of legal validity may arise when the plan is actually triggered and warrants are actually issued in response to an unsolicited bid, as well as when a company without a pre-warning plan adopts a defensive measure in response to a particular unsolicited bid. The latter scenario generated an important, and highly controversial, set of judicial decisions: the *Bull-Dog Sauce* case.

In May 2007, US private equity fund Steel Partners launched a tender offer for a small, publicly listed Japanese condiment maker called Bull-Dog Sauce.[25] The board of directors of Bull-Dog Sauce, with the support of employees, opposed the tender offer and sought to defeat it by issuing warrants to shareholders exercisable into additional common shares. Although as a shareholder Steel Partners would also receive warrants, they could be exercised only for cash, not shares. The proposal was approved by over 80 percent of the outstanding shares – virtually all shares other than those held by Steel Partners.

Steel Partners sued to enjoin the warrant issuance. The case made its way to the Supreme Court after the District Court's dismissal of the request for a preliminary injunction was affirmed on appeal.[26] The Supreme Court also affirmed, concluding that the warrant issuance was necessary and reasonable.[27] Like the District Court, the Supreme Court reasoned that it is for the shareholders to determine whether damage would arise upon acquisition of control by a particular shareholder. Accordingly, the court should respect the determination of shareholders unless there is a material defect in their decision-making process.[28] Given the overwhelming shareholder approval, almost all shareholders other than Steel Partners had agreed that the defensive measure was necessary to prevent damage to corporate value. Thus, the allocation of warrants under the circumstances was not unreasonable or unfair under the corporate law.[29] As a result, the Steel Partners bid was defeated, but it was entitled to a cash payment of just over ¥2.3 billion (about $19 million at then prevailing exchange rates).

This ruling was met with jeers by the foreign investment community, which viewed the decision as confirmation that corporate Japan

---

25 *See* Saikō Saibansho [Sup. Ct.] Aug. 7, 2007, Hei 19 (kyo) no. 30, 1809 SAIKŌ SAIBANSHO HANREISHŪ [SAIBANREI JŌHŌ] 16, 16 (Japan).
26 *Id.*, at 17.
27 *See id.*
28 *See id.*, at 17–18.
29 *Id.*, at 18–19.

remained insular and unwelcoming to foreign investment.[30] Some domestic commentators, including the CVSG, also appeared to disapprove of at least the larger implications of the case. In June 2008, the CVSG issued a supplemental report taking stock of developments since the adoption of the Takeover Guidelines in 2005. With an understated but unmistakable tone of concern that the Takeover Guidelines had been (mis)interpreted by management and even by the courts as approving any defensive step so long as shareholder approval were obtained, the 2008 report notes that "adopting defensive measures in accordance with the Guidelines does not mean that their implementation is permitted unconditionally."[31] The 2008 report discourages payoffs to bidders by target management of the kind made in the Bull-Dog Sauce contest. More pointedly, the CVSG opines, "[t]akeover defensive measures that are . . . exploited for the purpose of managerial entrenchment should not be allowed."[32]

As this brief review indicates, Japan's modest exposure to hostile takeovers in recent years prompted a burst of institutional development to fill a major gap in the Japanese corporate contract. Although uncertainties about the exact scope of permissible defensive measures inevitably remain, at least some observers believe that the upshot of these developments, capped by the *Bull-Dog Sauce* ruling, is clear: in Japan, "a company [is] a community that need[s] to be defended from abusive forces."[33]

9.3 MANAGERIAL INCENTIVES

Having traced the evolution and substance of the takeover rules in the United States and Japan, I now turn to the question of how the different rules may affect managerial incentives in the two countries. The rules for hostile takeovers in the US and Japan reinforce pre-existing corporate governance structures and resulting incentives in the two countries. In the

---

30 *See, e.g.*, David Makman, *Japanese Market Reform Sputters*, 31 NAT'L L. J. 13 (2008) (highlighting the *Bull-Dog Sauce* ruling in arguing that Japan permits "arbitrary or discriminatory" dilution of shareholders).

31 CORPORATE VALUE STUDY GROUP, TAKEOVER DEFENSIVE MEASURES IN LIGHT OF RECENT ENVIRONMENTAL CHANGES 6 (June 30, 2008) [hereinafter CVSG 2008 REPORT], *available at* http://www.meti.go.jp/english/report/data/080630TakeoverDefenseMeasures.pdf.

32 *Id.*, at 3.

33 JOHN BUCHANAN ET AL., HEDGE FUND ACTIVISM IN JAPAN: THE LIMITS OF SHAREHOLDER PRIMACY 224 (2012).

US, the corporate contract is deeply imbued with principal–agent theory: directors are the agents of shareholder "owners." As such, directors receive a high degree of discretion in formulating and executing business strategy,[34] but the objective of their efforts is narrowly focused on advancing the interests of their shareholder-principals. In Japan, traditionally the corporation has been viewed "as consisting first and foremost of its workforce, up to and including those responsible for its management at the board level, rather than as a collection of assets ultimately owned by its shareholders."[35] The result is that Japanese corporate governance is extremely managerialist in its orientation. The key constraint on directors' discretion is not the shareholder wealth maximization imperative, but the need to explain corporate policies in terms of employee welfare and the long-term viability of the firm.

Parenthetically, it bears noting that this result was not foreordained; the emergence of hostile takeovers and an ensuing regulatory framework could have disrupted, rather than reinforced, the status quo. Specifically, a very different form of hostile takeover regulation could have emerged in either country if a different "gap-filling institution" had taken control of the rule-making process. In the US, the key institutional moment was the emergence of the Delaware courts, by default, as the gap-filling institution. Not surprisingly, that institution relied upon its existing bedrock principles in fashioning a standard for the validity of takeover defenses. Those standards unambiguously place the board of directors in the position of gatekeeper over hostile bids and give a large measure of discretion to the board in crafting a defensive response, without any participation by shareholders.[36] The overriding consideration in taking action, however, is the directors' fiduciary obligation to protect shareholder interests. Other potential gap-filling institutions, most prominently the SEC, might have chosen a very different set of rules that gave an active role to shareholders in responding to unsolicited bids. In Japan, multiple gap-filling institutions emerged in the form of the CVSG, the TSE, and the courts. As a result, the rules have a rather diluted "drafted by committee" feel to them: there is something in them for everyone. But this quality reinforces

---

[34] DGCL §141(a) provides that the business of a Delaware corporation is carried out by or under the direction of the board (and by implication, *not* by the shareholders).

[35] Buchanan et al., *supra* note 33, at 108.

[36] In *Unocal*, the Delaware Supreme Court explicitly rejected the idea that board's response to a takeover bid should be passive, because DGCL §141(a) and the directors' fiduciary duties require the board to defend the firm from bids that threaten shareholder interests. 493 A.2d 946, 955 n. 10 (Del. 1985).

the status quo in Japanese corporate governance. *Ex ante* shareholder approval of a defensive plan is encouraged by the Guidelines and the *Bull-Dog Sauce* case and effectively required by the TSE rules. But the ambiguous concepts of "corporate value" and "abusive acquirer" work to the distinct advantage of directors in wielding those defensive plans to fend off unwelcome bidders for reasons much broader than, or even in conflict with, shareholders' financial interests.

In the United States, one of the principal mechanisms for retaining director control while advancing the interests of shareholders is the independent director. As it has developed in the hands of the Delaware judiciary, the US hostile takeover regime generates strong incentives for boards to be comprised of a majority of truly independent directors. Applying Delaware takeover doctrine, the courts focus intently on the process through which decisions are made in response to an unsolicited bid. Decisions by independent committees of the board receive far more deference than decisions of executive directors, who the court fears may be acting in their own rather than the shareholders' best interests in resisting a bid. The widespread presence of independent directors in the United States, partially incentivized by the hostile takeover doctrine, has had a major impact on corporate governance in the United States. All of its manifestations cannot be mentioned here. Suffice it to say that the independent-director movement has led to the concept of the "monitoring board," and accelerated the outward, capital markets-oriented focus of US boards of directors.[37]

By contrast, the Japanese takeover regime, focused on shareholder approval, ironically has served to reinforce the inward orientation of the board of directors. The current rules do not privilege the decisions of independent directors or committees, thus creating few legal incentives for their adoption. The effect of the Supreme Court's *Bull Dog Sauce* opinion, which emphasizes shareholder approval as validating a defensive measure, may be to encourage the re-establishment of corporate ties to stable, long-term shareholders, so that management can more easily obtain shareholder approval of defensive measures in response to hostile takeover attempts. A full-scale return to group-oriented, stable and cross-shareholding patterns among Japanese firms, however, would once again virtually shut down the market for corporate control in Japan.[38] Incentives

---

37 *See* Jeffrey Gordon, *The Rise of Independent Directors in the United States, 1950–2005: Of Shareholder Value and Stock Market Prices*, 59 STAN. L. REV. 1465 (2007).

38 *See* KIGYŌ KACHI KENKYŪ KAI [CORPORATE VALUE STUDY GROUP], DAI 23 KAI KIGYŌ GIJI YŌSHI [SUMMARY OF 23 MEETING] (2007), *available at* http://www.meti.go.jp/policy/economic_industrial/gather/eig0000050/index23.html.

generated by the Japanese hostile takeover regime turn principal–agent theory on its head: boards of directors choose their shareholders, rather than the other way around.

9.4 CONCLUSION

Within the contractual conception of corporate law, formal legal rules and judicial decisions serve to fill gaps in the bargains made by corporate actors. As demonstrated by hostile takeovers in the United States and Japan, gap-filling institutions and the rules they generate can vary considerably even as between two advanced, market-oriented economies with highly developed legal systems. The divergence in rules that have evolved to govern responses to hostile takeover bids in the two countries has major implications for the market for corporate control, and consequently, for the implicit shareholder–manager bargain and corporate governance in the US and Japan.

10. Management–shareholder relations in Japan: what's next after cross-shareholdings?*

Takaaki Eguchi

10.1 INTRODUCTION

In Japan, corporate law endows shareholders with strong voting rights. In reality, though, the practice of cross-shareholding has "blocked" the effective exercise of these rights. This situation is now in flux. The sluggish stock market since the 1990s has caused significant losses on cross-held stock positions. Corporations, particularly banks, have found it increasingly difficult to justify the practice of holding each other's shares.

The goal of this chapter is to shed light on the direction in which management–shareholder relations in Japan are likely to evolve in the new era. The starting point is the understanding of historical patterns elsewhere in the world. Three distinctive patterns of management–shareholder relations are identified as "model" cases. These are the board primacy model of the US, the reference shareholder model still prevalent in continental Europe, and the collective engagement model that arose in the United Kingdom. I will describe their features and discuss the patterns in Japan from a comparative perspective.

This chapter is organized as follows. Section 10.2 sets the stage for subsequent discussions. The three sections that follow then present the three models. Section 10.3 highlights American (that is, US state) corporate

* The opinions expressed in this chapter are solely those of the author and do not represent the views of the companies and organizations that the author has been affiliated with. I would like to thank Nicholas E. Benes (Board Director Training Institute of Japan) and Zenichi Shishido (editor of this volume), as well as the members of the corporate law workshop led by the editor, for helpful discussions and comments. Nicholas Benes generously gave his time to help edit and improve the manuscript. For his friendship, I owe him special gratitude. Needless to say, any errors or omissions are entirely my responsibility.

law's cautiousness about giving shareholders power;[1] sections 10.4 and 10.5 discuss the mechanism of shareholders' influence in continental Europe and Britain (that is, the United Kingdom) respectively. The next two sections discuss management–shareholder relations in Japan. Section 10.6 reviews their historical evolution and discusses the post-war pattern based on cross-shareholdings. This post-war pattern is likely to evolve into a new pattern emphasizing engagement between management and institutional investors. Section 10.7 discusses the transition of the old pattern and gives a sketch of the new pattern. Section 10.8 concludes.

10.2 FRAMEWORK OF ANALYSIS

In this chapter, I will solely focus on public corporations that need external equity finance from time to time. Private corporations are outside the scope of discussion. According to the economic theory of the firm, centralized decision-making authority is the cornerstone feature of the firm as distinguished from the market.[2] In public corporations, this decision-making authority resides with the board of directors.[3] The board appoints managers and delegates to them the task of running the corporation on a day-to-day basis. I will refer to the board and the managers collectively as "management."

Though management takes the helm of running the corporation and controls most of its decision-making based on its authority, shareholders also retain their share of control by use of their statutory voting rights that

---

[1] The reference to American corporate law is based on the provisions in either the Delaware General Corporation Law (DGCL) or the Model Business Corporation Act (MBCA) as drafted by the Committee on Corporate Laws of the American Bar Association, or both.

[2] Benjamin E. Hermalin, *The Firm as a Noneconomy: Some Comments on Holmstrom*, 15 J. L. Econ. & Org. 104 (Mar. 1999).

[3] In major jurisdictions other than Britain, corporate law provides that important management decisions, except for those related to certain fundamental corporate matters, are to be taken by the board of directors or the management board. Luca Enriques, Henry Hansmann, & Reinier Kraakman, *The Basic Governance Structure: The Interests of Shareholders as a Class*, Reinier Kraakman et al. (eds), The Anatomy of Corporate Law, Chapter 3, 73 (2nd edn 2009). In Britain, the corporation's Articles of Association, rather than the Companies Act, specify the division of powers between the shareholder meeting and the board, but the default rule set forth in the Model Articles for Public Companies is that the directors have all the powers of management. Paul Davies, Introduction to Company Law 109 (2nd edn 2010). Also, see Mathias M. Siems, Convergence in Shareholder Law 152–154 (2008).

are exercisable at shareholder meetings. They may exercise these rights directly, or they may use the rights indirectly in the form of threats, to intervene in and influence managerial decision-making.

The extent and ways by which shareholders intervene and exert influence vary depending on countries. As will be discussed below, the allocation of legal entitlements, stock ownership structures, and social institutions affecting the use of given entitlements are the key factors that determine the reach of shareholders' power.

10.3 THE BOARD PRIMACY MODEL

The traditional pattern of management–shareholder relations in the US, which I call the board primacy model, is founded on the board-centric allocation of legal authority by means of entitlements. These entitlements stipulate what the board can decide on its own, and what requires shareholder approval. They also specify what decisions shareholders can initiate on their own without the board's consent. Bebchuk (2005) observes that the US stands out among the major jurisdictions for its allocation of entitlements that limit the scope of shareholders' intervention and initiative.[4]

American law has not only constrained shareholders' power, but it has also expressly buttressed management's authority in court cases. A case in point is the role of directors as fiduciaries. Court cases clarify that directors are required to ignore the express wishes of specific shareholders in situations where, they believe, doing so better serves shareholders as a whole.[5] Because of such strong authority granted by law to boards, managerial decision-making can occur in a manner that it is substantially unaffected by the voices of specific shareholders.

American corporate law's board-centric bias is exhibited in shareholders' rights to remove directors. Two statutory rights are relevant. One is the appointment right, which may be used to remove incumbents at the end of their terms. The other is the dismissal right, which may be used to remove incumbents in mid-term. American law's cautiousness about empowering shareholders is evident especially with respect to the latter.

That is, corporate laws in all major jurisdictions except the US confer on shareholders the irrevocable statutory right to dismiss directors

---

[4] Lucian Bebchuk, *The Case for Increasing Shareholder Power*, 118 HARV. L. REV. 848 (Jan. 2005).

[5] Robert S. Saunders, *Why Majority Voting in Director Elections Is a Bad Idea*, 1 VA. L. & BUS. REV. 117–118 (Spr. 2006).

without cause. In Britain, France, Italy and Japan, the statutory requirement for dismissal is a simple majority of votes cast in favor; in Germany the requirement is a supermajority of three-quarters of votes. On the other hand, in the US, even in the cases where state law sets forth the right to dismiss "at-will," this statutory default is often revocable or subject to exceptions.[6]

The dismissal right is most effectively exercised by requesting an extraordinary meeting called specifically for the purpose of dismissal. Here again, in all major jurisdictions except the US, shareholders are provided with the irrevocable right to initiate such a meeting.[7] This stands in contrast with the US where a provision allowing shareholders to call such a meeting is frequently limited or eliminated by subsequent amendments to the company's Articles of Incorporation or bylaws.[8]

10.4 THE REFERENCE SHAREHOLDER MODEL

In continental Europe, the ownership of even the large public corporations has concentrated in the hands of families, corporations, and banks.[9] Cools

---

[6] Enriques, Hansmann, & Kraakman, *supra* note 3, at 61–62. In Japan, the threshold for dismissal was raised from a simple majority to a super-majority of two-thirds of votes in the 1950 revision of the Commercial Code, but it was brought back to a simple majority in the new Companies Act of 2005 (Art. 341). In the US, under MBCA, the right to dismiss directors without cause may be overruled in the company's Articles of Incorporation (§8.08(a)), and under Delaware corporate law, dismissal without cause is disallowed for classified boards unless stipulated otherwise in the company's Articles of Incorporation (§141(k)(1)).

[7] Generally, see SIEMS, *supra* note 3, at 92–96. Christoph Van der Elst & Gulsum Aslan, *Economic Consequences of Large Shareholder Activism*, Report Prepared for the European Parliament, Directorate-General for Internal Policies, Table 1 (2009) gives a convenient overview, across major European jurisdictions, of the percentage thresholds for exercise of various shareholders' rights that are related to convocation of shareholder meetings.

[8] Bonnie Buchanan, Jeffry M. Netter, Annette B. Poulsen, & Tina Yang, *Shareholder Proposal Rules and Practice: Evidence from a Comparison of the US and UK*, 49 AM. BUS. L. J. 756–757 (Win. 2012). In Delaware, the default caller of an extraordinary meeting is the board of directors, and the shareholders are not allowed to call meetings unless authorized by the company's Articles of Incorporation or bylaws (DGCL §211(d)).

[9] For analysis of the ownership structure, *see* Jeremy Grant & Thomas Kirchmaier, Who Governs? Corporate Ownership and Control Structures in Europe, Tables 3, 5 & 7 (working paper, June 2004) (http://ssrn.com/abstract=555877). According to the authors, the largest shareholder has the legal control (i.e., holds more than 50 percent of all voting rights) in 35–45 percent of

(2005) points out that concentrated ownership does not by itself subject management to the control of large shareholders. Management can be quite immune from interventions of shareholders if their power to intervene is legally constrained as in the US.[10] In continental Europe, unlike the US, corporate law generally empowers shareholders with substantive statutory rights. In this case, managerial control will not stabilize unless large shareholders are in support of management, explicitly or implicitly endorsing its decisions.

Relating to this point, it should be noted that empowering shareholders tends to destabilize managerial control. This is because differing views and opinions of intervening shareholders can cause dispersion in managerial decision-making. For this reason, in the jurisdictions where shareholders are empowered, some form of institutional mechanism usually limits the extent of shareholders' influence by narrowing the source of influence to certain types or groups of shareholders.

In continental Europe, such a mechanism is implicit in the concentration of ownership. Cools observes that the presence of reference shareholders that are in support of management holds off the influence of other shareholders. In her terminology, "reference shareholder" is a generic term used to make reference to a large blockholder that has a sufficient amount of votes at hand to determine the outcome of a shareholder meeting.[11] The pattern of management–shareholder relations in which the reference shareholder stabilizes managerial control by the exclusion of other shareholders' influence is referred to as the reference shareholder model.

10.5 THE COLLECTIVE ENGAGEMENT MODEL

Engagement is a dialogue between management and minority (or more precisely, relatively large but still minority) shareholders that takes place when the latter wish to intervene in and influence managerial decision-making. In Britain, institutional investors with a stake in the corporation's

---

the large public corporations in France, Germany, and Italy. The percentage goes up to more than 50 percent if other corporations in which the largest shareholder has *de facto* control (i.e., holds more than the percentage threshold for the mandatory tender offer) are also counted. Also see Van der Elst & Aslan, *supra* note 7, at 15–17 for a useful survey on the literature.

[10] Sofie Cools, *The Real Difference in Corporate Law between the United States and Continental Europe: Distribution of Powers*, 30 DEL. J. CORP. L. 755–756 (2005).

[11] Cools, *supra* note 10, at 756, 766 & 737–738.

equity have occasionally formed coalitions in order to engage collectively with management. I refer to the pattern of management–shareholder relations that is characterized by British-style engagement as the collective engagement model.

The presence of several conditions made British-style collective engagement possible. Foremost was the distinctive ownership structure of large British public corporations that prevailed in the 1980s and 1990s. During that period, a major portion of the typical British corporation's equities was in the hands of a small group of domestic institutional investors.[12] As a result, it was often the case that, except in the very largest public corporations, a collection of five or six institutional investors, or investment managers managing institutional assets, could comprise as much as one-quarter of the total voting rights among themselves.[13]

Cheffins (2008) describes three other conditions that facilitated coalition formation in Britain.[14] First, because of the relatively large size of their individual stakes, the domestic institutional investors had incentives to engage rather than remain completely passive. Second, the small number of investors in each group held down the coordination cost for organizing coalitions. Last, domestic investment managers of institutional assets formed a close-knit community. Their affinity with each other made it easier to share common viewpoints and build consensus.

In addition to these market conditions, it should be pointed out that, in Britain, the relevant regulations do not obstruct coalition formation.[15]

---

[12] BRIAN R. CHEFFINS, CORPORATE OWNERSHIP AND CONTROL: BRITISH BUSINESS TRANSFORMED, 86–88 & 371 (2008) describes this ownership structure using statistics and citations. By the 1980s, individuals were replaced by institutions (pension funds, insurance companies and unit and investment trusts) as the dominant owners of British equities. According to a study cited, by the 1990s, the 20 top domestic investment managers managed just over one-third of the equity of all listed corporations.

[13] DAVIES, *supra* note 3, at 133–134. Marc Goegen & Luc Renneboog, *Strong Managers and Passive Institutional Investors in the UK*, FABRIZIO BARCA & MARCO BECHT (EDS), THE CONTROL OF CORPORATE EUROPE, Table 10.4 (2001) shows that, in 1992, the insurance companies and investment and pension funds that individually had more than 3 percent stakes together controlled roughly 20 percent of all voting rights of listed corporations. This calculation is based on the ownership data from a sample of 200 randomly selected listed corporations.

[14] CHEFFINS, *supra* note 12, at 371–372.

[15] Bernard S. Black & John C. Coffee, Jr, *Hail Britannia?: Institutional Investor Behavior under Limited Regulation*, 92 MICH. L. REV. 2002 & 2024–2025 (Jun. 1994), and CHEFFINS, *supra* note 12, at 45–46. Also see Paolo Santella, Enrico Baffi, Carlo Drago, & Dino Lattuca, *A Comparative Analysis of the Legal Obstacles to*

The legal issue in this regard is whether such a conduct of corporate governance is to be considered a case of acting in concert, which is subject to regulation. On this issue both the Takeover Panel and the Financial Services Authority (FSA) have explicitly indicated that the standard acts of collective engagement such as joint conferences and voting together on a particular resolution would not constitute acting in concert for the purpose of takeover regulation.[16] Moreover, although shareholders are subject to aggregate disclosure under the Disclosure and Transparency Rules if they are in agreement to a lasting common voting policy, FSA has clarified that this requirement does not typically apply to normal acts of collective engagement.[17]

Commentators have remarked on the "behind-the-closed-door" nature of British-style engagement.[18] In large part, this tendency is a natural consequence of the recognition that reputational damage might be incurred by both sides of the negotiation if their confrontation were made public. But more importantly, "closed-door" negotiations reflect perceived credibility of the threat that the institutional investors could pose as a group in an "open-door" voting contest. While most of engagements did not reach the coalition formation stage, institutional investors in Britain could still wield influence over management because of several instances where coalitions had formed.

10.6 MANAGEMENT–SHAREHOLDER RELATIONS BASED ON CROSS-SHAREHOLDINGS

A useful way of understanding horizontal cross-shareholding as it occurs in Japan[19] is to view it as a mechanism for turning the corporation into the

---

Institutional Investor Activism in the EU and in the US, 22–23 & 26–27 (working paper, 2009) (http://ssrn.com/abstract=113791), published as *Legal Obstacles to Institutional Investor Activism in the EU and in the US*, 23 Eur. Bus. L. Rev. 257 (2012).

[16] Panel on Takeover and Mergers, The Takeover Code, Notes on Rule 2.1, F_2 (11th edn, May 20, 2013). Prudential Regulation Authority Handbook, SUP 11, Annex 6G, Q9 (April 1, 2013).

[17] Financial Services Authority, Letter to the Institutional Shareholder's Committee (Aug. 19, 2009).

[18] For instance, Black & Coffee, *supra* note 15, at 2033; Davies, *supra* note 3, at 134; and Jill Solomon & Aris Solomon, Corporate Governance and Accountability, 112 (2004).

[19] It is worth pointing out that the scheme of horizontal cross-shareholding as practiced in post-war Japan is different from, for instance, the scheme in Korea

de facto owner of itself. For instance, suppose that two corporations, say A and B, cross-hold each other's shares. If they implicitly agree to always support each other's management at shareholder meetings, then A and B will be essentially swapping the voting rights each holds as the owner of stock back to the other. If this process is repeated between multiple corporations, the outcome will be an arrangement where each corporation assumes substantial control of the voting rights in itself.

Viewed from this perspective, it is possible to analytically position the practice of cross-shareholding as a variation of management–shareholder relationship that develops when shareholders are empowered as is the case in Japan. As noted earlier, in the jurisdictions where shareholders are granted substantial statutory rights for intervention, some form of institutional mechanism usually limits the extent of shareholders' influence. During much of the post-war period in Japan, the practice of horizontal cross-shareholding served this purpose. By turning the corporation into the owner of itself, cross-shareholding shielded management from the influence of all other shareholders. Naturally, in this case, management became entrenched.

The structure of management–shareholder relations was totally different in pre-war Japan. In that period, even for the largest corporations, stock ownership was concentrated in the hands of a small group of legally empowered capitalist shareholders.[20] This pattern, which is congruent with the reference shareholder model, was totally overturned by the late 1940s. What emerged from its remains was the post-war pattern of cross-shareholdings. Several major upheavals caused this drastic regime shift.

The first major cause was Japan's wartime policy. The government and military bureaucrats who were charged with the urgent task of mobilizing

---

that is practiced as part of a vertical ownership structure. In the latter, a controlling minority shareholder effectively controls the whole group of corporations using various ownership schemes including cross-shareholding.

[20] In the sample of 20 largest corporations, 40 percent of the equity was held by the ten largest shareholders in 1935. In the *zaibatsu* (defined to include Mitsubishi, Mitsui, and Sumitomo), the group holding company (headquarters) owned around 40 percent of the equity of its group corporations. In the other conglomerates, the founders and their families as well as their asset management companies held around 20 percent of the equity of the group corporations. Tetsuji Okazaki, *Development of Corporate Governance in Japan: A Historical Perspective (in Japanese)*, 13 Bank of Japan Monetary & Econ. Stud. 62-63 & 65, particularly Table 1 (Sep. 1994). For an account of the pre-war ownership structure that is available in English, *see* Tetsuji Okazaki, *The Japanese Firm under the Wartime Planned Economy*, Masahiko Aoki & Ronald Dore (eds), The Japanese Firm: Sources of Competitive Strength, Chap. 13 (1994).

resources for the war effort found the influence of profit-motivated shareholders over corporate decision-making undesirable. They implemented policies that downplayed the interests of shareholders and protected management's autonomy.[21] Another major cause was the occupation policy of the General Headquarters (GHQ) serving the Supreme Commander of the Allied Power. As part of its broad goal of democratizing Japan, GHQ implemented policies aimed at eliminating the hierarchical control of Japanese corporations by the *zaibatsu* and other major conglomerates.[22]

Thus, by the end of the 1940s, a new landscape took shape in the Japanese stock market. On one hand, the ownership structure and the board composition of public corporations were both different. Instead of large blockholders, individuals as a class emerged as the largest owner of the equity.[23] Additionally, unlike their pre-war predecessors, the post-war boards of large public corporations were composed entirely of former employees and did not include any members that represented shareholders' interests.[24] On the other hand, shareholders continued to remain legally empowered. While under the 1950 revision of the Commercial Code of 1899, the shareholder meeting lost its all-powerful status conferred by the original Code, shareholders still enjoyed strong appointment and dismissal rights over board membership.[25]

Against the backdrop of this post-war landscape, corporations, especially former *zaibatsu* members, started re-huddling around their banks by holding each other's shares. An initial factor stimulating the move was the high-profile share buy-ups led by legendary "greenmail"

---

[21] For more detail, *see* Okazaki, *supra* note 20, at 74–75.

[22] To eliminate the influence of capitalist ownership, *zaibatsu* holding companies were dissolved, and the shares held by them or the families were placed under public ownership. Furthermore, *zaibatsu* family members and their designees were purged out of the corporations' boardrooms. Okazaki, *supra* note 20, at 81–82 & 83–84, also Table 2.

[23] The government started selling the shares that had been temporarily placed under public ownership. Individuals including company employees took up these shares. By the end of FY1949, they held 69.1 percent of shares of listed corporations. Tokyo Stock Exchange et al., 2012 Share Ownership Survey, mimeo, Reference-Table 2 (Jun. 20, 2013).

[24] Okazaki, *supra* note 20, at 65–66 & 83–84, also Table 2.

[25] The 1899 Code conferred on the shareholder meeting the authority to resolve on any matters. Under the revised Code of 1950, the shareholder meeting could resolve only on the agenda items that are stipulated by law or by the company's Articles of Incorporation to be within its purview. Masahiro Kitazawa, *Ownership/Management/Control of Business Corporation (in Japanese)*, Makoto Yazawa (ed.) Gendai ho to kigyo [Contemporary Law and Firm], Part I, Chap. 2, 67–68 & 77–80 (1966).

artists in the mid-1950s.[26] Re-huddling progressed further during and after a major market downturn of the mid-1960s, as financially vulnerable individual investors pulled out and were replaced by banks and other corporations as the owners of the equity.[27] Formation of cross-holding networks gained further momentum when concerns about foreign takeovers mounted in view of government plans to liberalize the securities markets for foreign investors by the early 1970s.[28]

10.7 MANAGEMENT–SHAREHOLDER RELATIONS IN THE NEW ERA

The practice of cross-shareholding persisted throughout the stock market boom of the 1980s because corporations considered stock ownership as a source of profit. But once the boom was over and the bubble had burst, the proportion of total outstanding shares held as cross-holdings started declining in the mid-1990s and has generally continued to decline ever since.[29] The practice of cross-shareholding is certainly not a relic of the past, but the direction of change appears to be toward further unwinding.

The impact of unwinding shows in the percentage of disapproval

---

[26] Hidetaka Kawakita, Nihon gata Kabushiki Shijo no Kozo henka: Kinyu Shisutemu no Saihensei to Gabanansu [Structural Change of the Japanese-Style Stock Market: Restructuring of the Financial System and Corporate Governance] 38–40 (1995).

[27] In the universe of large listed corporations, the percentage of the equity held by banks and other corporations increased from the low level of 16.0 percent in 1953 to 33.2 percent in 1962. The percentage rose further to 41.5 percent in 1974. *See* Julian Franks, Colin Mayer, & Hideaki Miyajima, Equity Markets and Institutions: The Case of Japan, Table 2 (RIETI Discussion Paper Series 90-E-039, 2009).

[28] Kawakita, *supra* note 26, at 66–68.

[29] Banks' holdings of corporate shares, and corporate holdings of bank and corporate shares, comprise the broadly defined cross-holdings. Their total as a percentage of the value of all listed stocks declined from 34.61 percent in FY1991 to 12.75 percent in FY2009. Of this broad category, those confirmed as being part of cross-ownership arrangements fell from 24.69 percent to 5.70 percent as a percentage of the value of all listed stocks during the same period. Masaharu Ito, *Cross-Shareholdings Being Unwound Especially by Banks (in Japanese)*, Daiwa Research Institute Quarterly Report, vol. 1, Tables 5 & 7 (Spr. 2011). Nomura Securities reports that the percentage value of the broadly defined cross-shareholdings hit the lowest point since 1990 in three years in a row in FY2010 through FY2012 (an analyst report by Kengo Nishiyama dated August 29, 2013).

votes at shareholder meetings.[30] Driving the change in voting pattern from the previous mutual acquiescence are the reform-minded foreign investors that have drastically increased their presence as the owners of Japanese equities.[31] Also pertinent is the changed stance of domestic investment managers who no longer feel hesitant about openly opposing management if deemed necessary.[32] Faced with this change in the wind, executives at progressive companies have started having active dialogues with institutional investors. Given the dispersed and institutional ownership structure of large Japanese public corporations, it is likely that these active dialogues will play a pivotal role in shaping management-shareholder relations in the post-cross-shareholding era.[33] Will the management–shareholder relationship in Japan evolve into a pattern similar to the classic British model?

The answer is most likely no. On this point, the reader is reminded that British collective engagement was made possible by the presence of a small, close-knit community of domestic institutional investors managing

---

[30] For instance, the percentage of votes cast against the reappointment of the top executive of Canon was as high as 28 percent at the shareholder meeting held in March, 2013. While Toyota introduced outside directors to the board in that year, this leading manufacturer did not appoint any outsiders to the board. (Disclosure of the detail of the voting outcome at the shareholder meeting is mandatory under the Financial Instruments and Exchange Act.)

[31] In the universe of listed corporations, the percentage of the equity held by foreigners increased from 4.3 percent in FY1988 to 28.0 percent in FY2012. Tokyo Stock Exchange et al., *supra* note 23, Table 3. The California Public Employees' Retirement System (CalPERS) decided to start the systematic proxy voting in Japan as early as in 1990. For more detail, *see* Sanford M. Jacoby, *Convergence by Design: The Case of CalPERS in Japan*, 15 Am. J. Comp. L. 256 (2007).

[32] Fund management firms (i.e., investment advisory companies and investment trust management companies) disclose their voting results pursuant to the internal rules of their respective industry associations.

[33] Rafael La Porta, Florencio Lopez-de-Silanes, & Andrei Shleifer, *Corporate Ownership around the World*, 95 J. Fin. 471 (Apr. 1999) compares the ownership structure of the 20 largest corporations by capitalization in 27 different countries. Of these countries, Japan is only behind Britain in the degree of dispersion of the equity ownership (Table II). Tokyo Stock Exchange et al., *supra* note 23, Table 3 provides the source data for estimating the extent of institutional ownership. According to the data, the percentage of the equity held by domestic institutional investors (including trust banks, insurance companies and other financial institutions excluding banks and securities companies) was 24.2 percent in FY2012. Since the percentage of the equity held by foreigners was 28 percent in FY2012, summing these figures gives an estimate of the total institutional holding as 52 percent of all listed stocks.

major portions of British equities. In fact, this condition no longer holds even for Britain. As the portion of British equities held by domestic institutional investors has shrunk, the once close-knit community of investment managers has become fragmented.[34] In this context, it is quite understandable that a recent review of the British stock market, the Kay Review,[35] called for the establishment of an investors' forum to facilitate coalition formation. Because spontaneous formation of sizable coalitions could no longer be taken for granted, the Kay Review suggested government involvement in the forum as means of effectively rallying key players and revitalizing collective engagement.[36]

In Japan, the situation is even more challenging. Japan lacks not only affinities and coherence of views in its investor community, but also does not even have any history of collective engagement itself. Compared with the case of Britain, the hurdles for forming a coalition will be substantially higher, if not insurmountable, for institutional investors. Moreover, unlike Britain, both the rules of Large Shareholding Reports and the takeover bid (TOB) rules under the Financial Instruments and Exchange Act (FIEA) do not distinguish corporate governance activism from other concerted activities.[37] Institutional investors are likely to show reluctance

---

[34] In the mid-1990s, domestic pension funds and insurance companies together held about one-half of the equity of all public corporations. The ratio started dropping around the turn of the century, and the aggregate stake of these domestic investors is reduced to around one-quarter of the equity. Replacing them are foreign investors. Brian Cheffins, *The Stewardship Code's Achilles' Heel*, 73 Mod. L. Rev. 1017-1020 (2010).

[35] John Kay, *The Kay Review of UK Equity Markets and Long-Term Decision-Making – Final Report*, (July 23, 2012). This review was commissioned by the Secretary of State for Business, Innovation and Skills.

[36] Kay, *supra* note 35, at Chap. 7, Para. 7.3, 51.

[37] Under the rules for Reports of Possession of Large Volume, the aggregate interests including those of Joint Holders will need to be reported if the stock ownership exceeds the 5 percent threshold (FIEA Art. 27-23(1)(3)(5)(6)). Those that are deemed as "Joint Holders" due to their motive (FIEA Art. 27-23(5)) include, among others, parties to voting agreements, written or verbal, and parties to joint shareholder proposals. The Financial Services Agency (FSA) has clarified the definition of such Joint Holder. FSA, Q&A Regarding Reports of Possession of Large Volume *(in Japanese)*, mimeo, especially Q20, 22 and 23 (Mar. 31, 2010).

Institutional investors are only required to file a simplified report if their ownership does not exceed the 10 percent threshold. The additional condition for qualifying for this preferential status is that the motive of ownership is not for "Act of Making Important Suggestion, etc" (FIEA Art 27-26(1)). The "Important Suggestion, etc." includes proposals, made at a shareholder meeting or to the corporate officials, regarding appointment and dismissal of representative direc-

even to respond to open calls for vote alignment because of concerns about triggering the regulation.

If transplanting the British-style engagement to Japan appears challenging, what other approaches can Japan take to build a new pattern of management–shareholder relations? The Kay Review provides us with a hint.

In Britain, the bargaining power of those investors that engage with management was substantiated by the credible threat of coalition formation. If coalition formation is not realistic, at least in the near term, in Japan, the source of the bargaining power will need to be found elsewhere. A forum that builds and sets the views of institutional investors at large could be such a source. In this scheme, the forum plays the role of an "opinion leader" that develops themes and priorities for engagement. Actual engagement activities will be conducted individually by those that follow the framework developed by the forum. To the extent that management finds its influence over the investor community pervasive, the forum can play a role similar to that of a coalition. There might be multiple forums that compete for a status of the leader. Those with a sufficient number of followers would win the race.

An example of how such an "opinion leader" might develop is found in the activity of several investment managers that have started working with executives at progressive Japanese companies. Their engagement style is that of a catalyst, with a focus on inducing internal initiatives, rather than pressuring management to make desired changes. Whether they can extend their success within a select group to a broader set of companies will depend on their capability to win the support of other institutional investors, who would then assimilate their agenda and approach and use these for engagement. Forming a forum would help. The government could play a supportive role by facilitating the formation of such a forum.[38]

---

tors and important changes in dividend policy (The Ordinance for Enforcement of FIEA Art. 14-8-2).

Under the TOB rules, a tender offer will be required if the sum of voting rights held by all related parties exceeds the percentage threshold. The parties that are deemed to be in "Special Relationship" with the Tender Offerer due to their motive essentially match with the Joint Holders explained above (FIEA Art. 27-2(7)).

[38] An example of the government's facilitating role is the Corporate Reporting Lab (CRL) under the auspices of the Ministry of Economy, Trade and Industry. CRL's initial-year project focused on better dialogue between management and shareholders. Members of both the business and investor community participated in the project. For more information, visit CRL's official website. http://www.meti.go.jp/policy/economy/corporate_accounting/index.html.

Engagement in Japan would develop as more and more institutional investors recognize the importance of constructive dialogue with management. Clarifying regulations that might otherwise cause unnecessary fears of concerted activities would send a clear message to the investor public that smooth management–shareholder communications are desired.

10.8 CONCLUDING REMARKS

In all major jurisdictions, decision-making authority within the corporation resides with management. This chapter analyzes different patterns of management–shareholder relations by focusing on shareholders' influence over managerial decision-making. In the US, legislators and courts were cautious about empowering shareholders, and the resulting traditional pattern was that boards remained largely independent of the voices of specific shareholders. In other major jurisdictions, corporate law empowered shareholders more, and variations in the pattern of management–shareholder relations reflected the difference in the mechanism of shareholders' influence. In continental Europe, for instance, the ownership of large public corporations was concentrated in the hands of large shareholders. The resulting pattern was a sponsorship relationship where large shareholders that were in support of management excluded the influence of other shareholders. In Britain, institutional shareholders formed coalitions. Their aggregate voting power was the basis of the distinctive pattern of management–shareholder relations that featured collective engagement. And last, in post-war Japan, corporations formed intricate networks of cross-shareholdings. These networks turned the corporation into a *de facto* owner of itself and excluded the influence of all other shareholders.

Looking forward, because of the strong shareholder rights set forth in Japanese corporate law, combined with the dispersed ownership structure of large public corporations, management–shareholder relations in Japan are likely to evolve into a pattern emphasizing engagement by institutional investors. Like the classic engagement model in Britain, engagement in Japan will facilitate inputs and influence from institutional shareholders. But reflecting the market conditions in Japan, the style of engagement will be quite different from that in Britain.

11. Regulation of bank shareholding: a functional and historical analysis

Akira Tokutsu

11.1 INTRODUCTION

In this chapter, I explore regulations related to bank stock ownership. Specifically, I focus on bank shareholding as an activity that serves to render a financial institution as both equity holder and debtholder. In Japan, legislation related to this issue is housed under two types of law: banking law and antitrust law. This chapter analyzes these regulations from two perspectives. First, in line with the rest of this volume, I explicate the laws with a focus on legislative intent. Second, I adopt a historical perspective to inspect the laws.

Generally speaking, banking laws are intended to ensure that banks operate in a fair and appropriate manner.[1] Antitrust laws, on the other hand, are meant to respond to issues related to market power,[2] particularly those associated with market competition.[3] Superficially, the regulations related to bank shareholding in each area seem to align with that respective area's purpose. The goal of this chapter, however, is to demonstrate that the regulations related to bank shareholding deviate from their traditional intentions. I will ultimately demonstrate, both functionally and historically, that bank shareholding regulation has truly served to control private benefits.

In section 11.2, I will apply functional analysis to regulations related to bank shareholding to show that the regulations do not serve the typical purposes of banking or antitrust legislation. Following the functional analysis, I will provide a historical analysis in section 11.3 to elucidate the original intentions of banking and antitrust laws. This will be performed by reviewing the documents written at the time the legislation was

---

1 Banking Act § 1 (1) (1981).

2 Louis Kaplow, *Why (Ever) Define Markets?*, 124 Harv. L. Rev. 437–517 (2010).

3 Tadashi Shiraishi, Dokusenkinshiho (Anti-monopoly Law) 7 (2006).

formed. My review of these documents will be centered on the premise of "economic democracy" in the context of the original antitrust law, which can facilitate the emergence of the private benefit problem. Section 11.4 will explicate "private benefit," which has typically been treated as an issue for controlling shareholders. Section 11.5 will look at implications, and section 11.6 will offer a tentative solution to respond to bank shareholding.

11.2 FUNCTIONAL ANALYSIS

In this section, I aim to demonstrate that the regulations related to bank shareholding under banking and antitrust law do not serve the purposes for which they were originally intended.

11.2.1 Banking Act

In the Japanese banking field, there are two types of regulations related to shareholding. The first relates to the ratio of the gross amount of all stocks to the total assets of each bank. Neither a bank nor its subsidiaries can hold stocks of other companies that exceed the bank's stated capital,[4] thus limiting the total amount of stocks that each bank can hold. Given its similarity to legislation related to risk-based capital standards, this rule is clearly intended to promote sound banking practices.[5] This aligns with the declared goal of banking law in Japan.[6]

The second type of regulation related to shareholding, which concerns limitations on the amount of each company's stock, is the focus of this chapter. The Japanese Banking Act prohibits any bank or bank subsidiary

---

4 ACT ON LIMITATION ON SHAREHOLDING BY BANKS & OTHER FIN. INSTITUTIONS § 3 (2001).

5 International Convergence of Capital Measurement and Capital Standards (commonly known as the Basel Accord) emphasizes sound banking in regard to financial regulations.

6 Shinsaku Iwahara, *Ginko no Kessaikino to Kawase Gyomu no Haitasei (The Finality Function of Banks and the Exclusiveness of the Business of the Money Order)*, *in* GENDAIKIGYORIPPO NO KISEKI TO TENBO (THE ORBIT AND THE HORIZON OF THE MODERN LEGISLATION OF THE ENTERPRISE LAW) 529, 566 (Seiichi Ochiai, Kenjiro Egashira, & Tomonobu Yamashita eds, 1995); SHINSAKU IWAHARA, DENSHIKESSAI TO HO (ELECTRONIC CLEARING AND LAW) 537 (2003); Shigeyuki Maeda, *Wagakuni ni okeru Ginkokantokuho to sono Ripporontekikadai – Jorontekikousatsu (The Law of Supervising Banking and the Issue of its Legislation in Japan–Isagogics)*, *in* Ochiai et al., *supra*, at 469, 482.

from holding more than 5 percent of the voting rights (i.e., stocks) of any non-finance company.[7] This law applies not only to individual banks but also to banking groups that can hold no more than 15 percent of a non-finance company's voting rights.[8]

Many explications of banking law have argued that the second rule was developed to promote sound business practice in the banking industry.[9] The 1997 Reform of Banking Act introduced this rule to prevent a bank from holding the majority rights of a non-finance subsidiary.[10] The stipulations related to subsidiary ownership originally specified that they may possess 50 percent of the voting rights,[11] but the 1997 Reform assumed that a bank could effectively and substantially control non-finance companies with even less than 50 percent of the voting rights in those companies. To avoid this problem, the 1997 Reform reduced the amount of stock a bank could hold.[12]

In addition to the limitations imposed upon banks, there were also restrictions on the amount of stock that bank subsidiaries could hold. The purpose of this regulation is to balance business through subsidiaries with the prohibition against non-banking business. Although bank subsidiary companies are generally weaker than their parent bank, banking legislation prohibited them from aggressively broadening their business through extensive stock ownership in non-finance companies.[13] The original aim of the legislation was to protect the soundness of banking business

---

7 BANKING ACT § 16-3 (1) (1981). This rule has an exception: when a bank and/or its subsidiary companies comes to hold voting rights of a domestic company through the exercise of security rights or another means specified by a Cabinet Office Ordinance, if the total number of the voting rights held by the bank and/or its subsidiary companies exceeds the voting right holding threshold within one year (at most), the rule does not apply. BANKING ACT § 16-3 (2) (1981).

8 BANKING ACT § 52-24 (1) (1981).

9 YOSHIAKI KOYAMA, GINKOHO (BANKING ACT) 352 (2nd edn 2012).

10 BANKING ACT § 16-2 (1981).

11 BANKING ACT § 2 (8) (1981).

12 KOYAMA, *supra* note 9, at 352.

13 KOYAMA, *supra* note 9, at 339. However, Dependent Business, which BANKING ACT § 16-2 (1) (xi) permits for subsidiary companies of a bank, includes administrative business related to benefit packages (Ordinance for Enforcement of the BANKING ACT § 17-3 (ii) (1982)), buying and managing goods in offices (iii), printing and bookbinding documents, voucher and other papers (iv), advertisement (v), and driving, maintaining and checking cars (vi). BANKING ACT § 216-2 (2) (i) (1981); Ordinance for Enforcement of the BANKING ACT § 17-3 (1982). They can be interpreted broadly.

practice through the removal of systemic risk associated with owning other businesses.[14]

However, this stated purpose seems nonsensical. It is important to promote stability in the banking industry, and keeping a bank away from the risks associated with stock ownership in non-finance businesses could be one method for doing so.[15] In this regard, limitations on the total amount of non-finance company stocks a bank may own could be reasonable. However, limitations on shareholding do not reduce systemic risk faced by the bank holding the stocks. Because limited liability is one of the most important elements of incorporation,[16] non-finance businesses that issue stock in the bank are typically partitioned from the bank itself.

Of course, piercing the corporate veil can render shareholders liable for the owned company's debt. However, the corporate veil is pierced only when the legal personality of a corporation has served as an "abuse" or "façade."[17] In the case of the above-mentioned "abuse," control takes the form of a shareholder using the corporation as an instrument for illegal or inadequate aims.[18] When the corporation serves as a "façade," the respective businesses of the shareholder and company are confounded.[19] This means that piercing the corporate veil requires that shareholders engage in some form of malicious control in addition to holding the majority of stocks.

---

14 Iwahara, *supra* note 6 (1995), at 566; IWAHARA, *supra* note 6 (2003), at 537; Maeda, *supra* note 6, at 482.

15 *See, supra* note 14.

16 REINIER KRAAKMAN ET AL., THE ANATOMY OF CORPORATE LAW: A FUNCTIONAL AND COMPARATIVE ANALYSIS 5, 9–11 (2nd edn 2009); KENJIRO EGASHIRA, KABUSHIKIGAISYAHO (LAWS OF STOCK CORPORATIONS) 31 (4th edn 2011).

17 Saikō Saibansho [Sup. Ct.] Feb. 27, 1969, Sho 43 (ne) no. 193, 23 SAIKŌ SAIBANSHO MINJI HANREISHŪ [MINSHŪ] 511 (Japan). The dual classification has been criticized because it does not address the interest where the corporate veil is pierced. EGASHIRA, *supra* note 16, at 44; KENJIRO EGASHIRA, KAISHAHŌJINKAKUHININ NO HŌRI (PIERCING THE CORPORATE VEIL) (1980). In the US, the corporate veil is also pierced, although it occurs only in limited situations. ROBERT CLARK, CORPORATE LAW 71–85 (1986); WILLIAM ALLEN ET AL., COMMENTARIES AND CASES ON THE LAW OF BUSINESS ORGANIZATION 151–168 (3rd edn 2009).

18 Saikō Saibansho [Sup. Ct.] Oct. 26, 1973, Sho 43 (ne) no. 469, 27 SAIKŌ SAIBANSHO MINJI HANREISHŪ [MINSHŪ] 1240 (Japan).

19 EGASHIRA, *supra* note 16, at 43.

These events happen so rarely (particularly when a shareholder does not possess a controlling share) that the corporate veil is seldom lifted.[20] Possession of about 5 percent of voting rights, for example, would not lift the corporate veil. Given these cases, it seems illogical to suggest that holding a small amount of stock in each company should render shareholders responsible for the debts of the corporation.

I can imagine that limitations on stock ownership could serve to protect the solvency of an individual bank. The protection of individual banks means defending the clearing system from systemic risk. However, the second type of regulation outlined above does not play any role in this context. In contrast to the stock ownership limitations related to total assets, the second type of regulation hinges on the percentage of voting rights held by the bank for each non-finance company in which it owns stock. Whereas the percentage of risk assets (e.g., stocks of non-finance companies) owned by a bank is an important component of a bank's total assets, the percentage of a company's stocks owned by the bank is not. The degree to which stocks are risky is dependent on the size of the company that issued them relative to the size of the bank that holds them. Therefore, the second type of limitation is unable to protect the security of banking business.

As outlined above, it is clear that limitations on shareholding are unrelated to the promotion of sound banking. They can, however, prevent a bank from doubling as a shareholder and creditor.

11.2.2 Antitrust Law

Japanese antitrust law also contains regulations related to bank shareholding. Similar to the Japanese Banking Act, one antitrust law stipulates that no corporation engaged in banking business shall acquire or hold more than 5 percent of voting rights in another Japanese corporation.[21]

---

20 EGASHIRA, *supra* note 16, at 41 describes piercing the corporate veil as a last resort.

21 ACT ON PROHIBITION OF PRIVATE MONOPOLIZATION & MAINTENANCE OF FAIR TRADE § 11 (1) (1947). This statute also regulates insurance companies, for which the threshold is 10 percent. There are some cases in which finance companies are permitted to hold a greater percentage of voting rights than legislated thresholds stipulate. These include: cases in which approval from the Fair Trade Commission is obtained in advance; cases in which voting rights are acquired or held in the interest of security; cases in which the ratio of the voting rights related to already-held stocks to voting rights of all stockholders increases as a result of another Japanese corporation's acquisitions; cases in

Generally, the purpose of antitrust law is to address issues related to competition in a particular field of trade. Therefore, the development and implementation of effective antitrust law requires clear definition of the relevant market.[22] This, like most antitrust regulation, is designed to respond to market concentration. However, regulations that respond to bank shareholdings are not due to their failure to define any type of market. Instead, bank shareholdings fall under the other type of Japanese antitrust regulation: general concentration.[23]

One of the unique characteristics of Japanese antitrust law is its inclusion of legislation related to general concentration. While antitrust law typically regulates the concentration within a specific market, general concentration, which is considered exceptional to traditional antitrust law, relates to excessive concentration within an industry or national economy.[24] In antitrust law, legislation associated with general concentration was designed for two purposes with respect to bank shareholding. First, it prevents excessive concentration of a bank's (or insurance company's) economic power obtained through shareholding. By lending money, banks and insurance companies can leverage their substantial financial power

---

which voting rights are acquired or held in the form of trust property pertaining to monetary or security trusts; cases where voting rights are acquired or held by a limited liability partner in an investment limited partnership; cases in which voting rights are acquired or held by a member of a partnership that was established through a contract allowed by paragraph 1 of Article 667 of the Civil Code; and cases provided for in the Rules of the Fair Trade Commission in which there is no danger of restriction on the business activities of another company in Japan.

[22] SHIRAISHI, *supra* note 3, at 7. While "Abuse of Dominant Bargaining Position" (mainly in the ACT ON PROHIBITION OF PRIVATE MONOPOLIZATION & MAINTENANCE OF FAIR TRADE, § 2 (9) (v) (1947)) can be interpreted as a regulation related to an indirect inhibition of competition in the defined market (DOKUSEN-KINSHIHO-KENKYUKAI, HOKOKU (REPORT OF THE FORUM OF ANTI-MONOPOLY LAW), FUKOSEI-NA TORIHIKI-HOHO NI KANSURU KIHONTEKI-NA KANGAE-KATA (THE FUNDAMENTAL POLICY OF UNFAIR TRADE PRACTICE) JULY 2 1982 Part I 2 (5)) can be interpreted as a regulation which prohibits exploitation from monopolists (SHIGEKAZU IMAMURA, DOKUSENKINSHIHO (ANTI-MONOPOLY LAW), 285 (2nd edn 1985); SHIRAISHI, *supra* note 3, at 79). The former interpretation is referred to as indirect competition inhibition theory and argues that the purpose of antitrust law is to respond to problems related to market power in the defined relevant market. However, the latter interpretation, which is called exploitation theory, is considered another exception to the traditional purpose of antitrust law.

[23] TOSHIFUMI YAMABE, CHUSHAKU DOKUSENKINSHIHO (A COMMENRARY ON THE ANTIMONOPOLY LAW OF JAPAN) 247 (Akira Negishi ed., 2009)

[24] *Id.*, at 247.

to influence non-finance companies. In addition, banks can increase their control over a company by holding a large number of stocks, thus increasing their voting rights. Both strategies can cause the bank to have an excessive concentration of economic power.[25]

Second, the legislation is useful for preventing improper relationships between banks and non-finance companies. If strong financial entities develop relationships with non-financial partners, competition between non-finance companies can be distorted.[26] Despite this, a question remains: why do relationships between financial institutions and non-financial companies distort market competition? Of course, some business relationships can be useful for gaining a legal advantage in a specific market. In this case, market competition is not altered. Some banking regulations, such as government-mandated deposit insurance,[27] can support not only the banking industry but also businesses that possess a close relationship to the bank. However, the benefits garnered through these means are too far removed and can thus be regulated by another form of regulation (i.e., the arm's-length principle).[28]

It follows that antitrust legislation related to bank shareholding is justified not by the traditional motivations of antitrust law (to prevent the inhibition of the market), but by the concept of general concentration. Despite this, general concentration and its effects have not been satisfactorily conceptualized. Some researchers have posited that general concentration causes an excessive concentration of economic power, but this description seems tautologous. It does not explain why general concentration requires legal intervention. Therefore, the nature of general concentration must be conceptualized in more concrete terms, thus allowing for an examination of why legal intervention to prevent it is justified. To offer such a conceptualization, I analyze general concentration from a historical perspective in the next section.

---

25 *Id.*, at 274.

26 *Id.*, at 274; Noboru Kawahama, *Beikoku ni okeru Ginko no Kabushikihoyukisei no Hensen (The Transformation of the Regulation Related to Bank Shareholding)*, 152 Hogaku-Ronso 21, 237 (2003).

27 Deposit Insurance Act (1971).

28 Banking Act § 13-2 (1981).

11.3 HISTORICAL ANALYSIS

In this section, I leverage historical analysis to evaluate regulations related to bank shareholding for two reasons. First, the legislative intent approach is a common and validated methodology within Japanese legal studies.[29] Second, regulations related to bank shareholding seem outdated. Although an outdated legislation is not necessarily inappropriate, it is useful to periodically revisit laws to interpret their applicability in the context of contemporary events.[30]

11.3.1 Banking Law

As mentioned in section 11.2.1 above, the regulation related to bank shareholding in banking law was designed to prohibit improper non-banking business[31] as a means to maintain sound banking practices within the industry. When evaluated historically, however, there seems to have been another motivation for the law's implementation.

Although Japanese banking legislation dates as far back as the Banking Ordinance of 1890, its early iterations did not have provisions prohibiting non-banking business. The prohibition of non-banking business was first enacted by the Banking Act of 1927[32] in response to the Showa Financial Crisis in which the Tokyo Watanabe Bank went bankrupt. Following the collapse of the Tokyo Watanabe Bank, many other banks fell into bankruptcy, resulting in a loss of public trust in the banking sector. The act was established to restore the public's confidence in banks, which serves as the foundation of reliable banking. According to the act, maintenance of the public's faith in the banking system was its primary motivation.[33]

In addition, the rule was also intended to prevent the confusion that resulted from divisions among banks. There were, and are, three types of banks in Japan: hypothec banks, industrial banks, and commercial banks.

---

29 Kenjiro Ume, *Horitsu no Kaishaku (The Interpretation of Law)* 9 Taiyo 61 (1903); Ei-ichi Hoshino, *Minpo-Kaisyakuron Josetsu (Isagogics of the Interpretation of Civil Law)*, *in* EI-ICHI HOSHINO MINPO RONSHU (THE COLLECTION OF PAPERS ABOUT CIVIL LAW) VOL.1. 11 (1970); Tatsuaki Maeda, *Ho-Kaishaku ni tsuite (On the Interpretation of Law)*, 64 HOSO-JIHO 1, 4 (2012).

30 Kawahama, *supra* note 26, at 216–217.

31 BANKING ACT § 12 (1981).

32 BANKING ACT § 5 (1927).

33 GOTARO OGAWA, SHIN-GINKOHORIYU GE (THE LEGISLATIVE PURPOSE OF NEW BANK ACT) 165–170 (1930).

Prior to the Showa Financial Crisis, commercial banks principally supplied long-term loans with mortgage collateral, and hypothec and industrial banks collected money from depositors. This dynamic confounded business operations among banks because, originally, banking business was to be conducted solely by commercial banks. This, in turn, led to delinquency or laziness on the part of the managers of banks. Therefore, the Banking Act of 1927 was designed, in part, to delineate banking responsibilities and mitigate the delinquencies of bank managers.[34]

The Imperial Diet considered the financial crisis while the act was being developed and determined that prohibiting non-banking business would promote reliable banking. However, stipulations within the act that prohibited non-banking business were not originally designed as a response to the Showa Financial Crisis. The soundness of banking justification, therefore, emerged after the crisis. As a result, prohibition plays a limited role in maintaining sound banking practices.[35]

This historical analysis lends support to the conclusions of the functional analysis in section 11.2.1 above. Legislation related to bank shareholding was originally unrelated to the soundness of banking. Given this, the true aim of the laws related to general concentrations remains unclear. To explore further, the following section features a historical analysis of antitrust law.

11.3.2 Antitrust Law

Although general concentration is contemporarily regarded as an exception to antitrust law, it was considered an integral part of antitrust law after World War II. The first antitrust law related to general concentration was the Antitrust Act of 1947, which completely prohibited non-banking companies from holding large amounts of stock in any other company.[36] The Antitrust Act permitted banks to own a maximum of 5 percent of another company.[37] In this way, original antitrust law was more generous to banks relative to non-banking companies. In 1949, the Antitrust

---

[34] *Id.*, at 7.

[35] OSAKA KOTO SHOGYO GAKKO GINKO-GYMU KENKYUSHITSU. (OSAKA HIGH COMMERCIAL SCHOOL RESEARCH CHAMBER OF BANKING BUSINESS), HUTSU GINKO SEIDO KAIZEN TO SHIN-GINKOHO (REFORM OF THE SYSTEM OF COMMERCIAL BANKS AND NEW BANKING ACT) (1928).

[36] ACT ON PROHIBITION OF PRIVATE MONOPOLIZATION & MAINTENANCE OF FAIR TRADE § 10 (1) (1947) (in original form).

[37] ACT ON PROHIBITION OF PRIVATE MONOPOLIZATION & MAINTENANCE OF FAIR TRADE § 11 (1) (1947) (in original form).

Act was amended such that: (1) the prohibition of non-bank company shareholding was limited to the stock of the competitive companies;[38] (2) shareholding was prohibited if it precluded competition among companies in a particular field of trade;[39] and (3) regulations related to non-finance company shareholding shifted from general concentration to concentration in a specific market. At the time of the revisions to the Antitrust Act, however, regulations within banking law related to shareholding were not revised.

A second reform to the Antitrust Act was implemented in 1953. This reform stipulated that regulation of non-finance company shareholding was limited to cases in which shareholding may restrain competition in a particular field of trade.[40] In essence, shareholding regulation was crystallized to protect competition within a particular market. Although the 1953 reform changed the bank shareholding limit from 5 percent to 10 percent,[41] its purpose remained focused on general concentration.

When the original antitrust laws were enacted in Japan, they were said to regulate general concentration "to promote the democratic and wholesome development of the national economy."[42] Legislators cited "monopolies," "control by companies," or "concentration" as justifications for legal intervention without logical elaboration.[43] Citing economic democ-

---

38 ACT ON PROHIBITION OF PRIVATE MONOPOLIZATION & MAINTENANCE OF FAIR TRADE § 10 (2) (1947) (in 1949 form).

39 ACT ON PROHIBITION OF PRIVATE MONOPOLIZATION & MAINTENANCE OF FAIR TRADE § 10 (1) (1947) (in 1949 form).

40 ACT ON PROHIBITION OF PRIVATE MONOPOLIZATION & MAINTENANCE OF FAIR TRADE § 10 (1) (1947).

41 ACT ON PROHIBITION OF PRIVATE MONOPOLIZATION & MAINTENANCE OF FAIR TRADE § 11 (1) (1947) (in 1953 form). This criterion was reverted to 5 percent in 1977. The 1972 reform was designed and implemented at the same time that controls were placed on total volume of bank shareholding (ACT ON PROHIBITION OF PRIVATE MONOPOLIZATION & MAINTENANCE OF FAIR TRADE § 9-2 (1947) (in 1953 form)). These reforms were designed to respond to increases in shareholding by companies, particularly financial institutions. SHIGEKAZU IMAMURA, DOKUSENKINSHIHO (ANTI-MONOPOLY LAW), 338 (2nd edn 1978).

42 ACT ON PROHIBITION OF PRIVATE MONOPOLIZATION & MAINTENANCE OF FAIR TRADE § 1 (1947).

43 SHOKOSHO KIKAKU-SHITSU (MINISTRY OF COMMERCE AND INDUSTRY, DEPARTMENT OF PLANNING), DOKUSENKINSHIHO NO KAISETSU (COMMENT ON ANTI-MONOPOLY LAW) 4 (1947); RYUGO HASHIMOTO, DOKUSENKINSHIHO TO WAGA KOKUMINKEIZAI (ANTI-MONOPOLY LAW AND OUR NATIONAL ECONOMY) 7 (1947); RYOZO ISHII, DOKUSENKINSHIHO-KEIZAISHUCHUHAIJOHO (ANTI-MONOPOLY LAW AND ECONOMIC DECENTRALIZATION LAW) 2 (1947); IZUMOI MASAO,

racy as a justification for the antitrust laws related to bank shareholding seems insufficient. The idea, however, can be divided into concepts that respond to potential harms.[44]

Economic democracy is described as the maintenance of competition "to prevent the arbitrary expansion of political power, to realize the democratic order related to economy by decentralizing private economic power and by keeping the freedom of consumers' choices and the freedom of the companies, and, thereby, to form the foundation for the liberal society."[45] This conception suggests that the economic system can be used to facilitate the realization of democracy in the political context.[46] Even at the time that the original Antitrust Act was developed, economic democracy was perceived as separate from the idea that economic power should be determined on the basis of majority rule or that employees' participation in management should be increased.[47] Stated differently, economic democracy champions the economic power of the minority, even in an environment in which excessive economic power via general concentration can influence the executive and legislative branches of government through lobbying.[48] Although a full explication of lobbying is beyond the scope of this chapter, it is evident that some lobbying yields inefficient results in agency problems within companies.[49]

Specific articles of legislation in the statute related to general concentration specified that shareholdings by companies, holding companies,[50]

SHINDOKUSENKINSHIHO NO KAISETSU (COMMENT ON NEW ANTI-MONOPOLY LAW) 16 (1953). Hashimoto and Ishii drafted the original antitrust law.

44 Kawahama, *supra* note 26, at 216–217, emphasizes the need to delineate the concept of economic democracy into reasonable principles to respond effectively to emergent problems.

45 AKIRA NEGISHI ET AL., DOKUSENKINSHIHO NYUMON (THE INTRODUCTION OF ANTI-MONOPOLY LAW) 4 (1983).

46 HASHIMOTO, *supra* note 43, at 8.

47 8 *id.*

48 Ichiro Sugiura, *Kyodai-na Keizaikenryoku no Shakaitekiseigyo toshiteno Mochikabugaishakisei (The Regulation for Holding Companies as a Social Control Giant Economic Power)*, 17 KEIZAIHO GAKKAI NENPO 30, 33 (1983); Akira Tokutsu, *Mochiaikabushiki no Hoteki-chii, vol.1. (The Legal Status of the Stock in the Cross-shareholding, Vol.1.)*, 125 HOGAKU KYOKAI ZASSHI 455, 539 (2008).

49 Lucian A. Bebchuk & Zvika Neeman, *Investor Protection and Interest Group Politics*, 23 REV. OF FIN. STUD. 1089, 1100 (2010).

50 Japanese antitrust law prohibited companies whose sole purpose was to hold the stocks of other companies (ACT ON PROHIBITION OF PRIVATE MONOPOLIZATION & MAINTENANCE OF FAIR TRADE § 9 (1947)), but this prohibition was removed in 1997.

and stock pyramids were geared towards "saving the controlling capital," or "saving contributions."[51] Even bank shareholding was considered, as its legislation was meant to contribute to "saving controlling capital."[52] Because the concept of "capital" is ambiguous in the Antitrust Act, the nature of the "saving controlling capital" function of the law is unclear. In the context of this chapter, "capital" refers to the consideration paid to the company for issued stock. The value of the stock can be appraised as the form embodied from the stream of cash flow from the company. Therefore, capital can be regarded as a stream of future cash flow.

"Saving controlling capital" relates to the procurement of control through undercapitalization and focuses on the disparity between controlling rights and cash flow.[53] The disparity suggests the possibility for the private benefit of control to increase. There is a direct relationship between private benefits of control and the possibility that managers will make inefficient decisions.[54] Originally, "private benefits of control" accounted for only one majority shareholder.[55] However, the Antitrust Act only prohibits more than 5 percent of bank shareholding. Thus, the theory of private benefit does not seem to explain the justification for regulation. That said, the theory can be expanded to include non-controlling shareholders.

11.4 EXPANSION OF THE PRIVATE BENEFIT THEORY

The "saving capital" strategy can lead to disparities between cash flow and control rights. For companies in which the disparity occurs, controlling shareholders manage corporations with less cash flow. Therefore, they are likely to set their private benefits, which consist of all benefits other than dividends and liquidation distributions cash

---

[51] SHOKOSHO, *supra* note 43, at 27; HASHIMOTO, *supra* note 43, at 78; ISHII, *supra* note 43, at 199, 202.

[52] SHOKOSHO, *supra* note 43, at 32; IZUMOI, *supra* note 43, at 149.

[53] Akira Tokutsu, *Mochiaikabushiki no Hoteki-chii, vol.5. (The Legal Status of the Stock in the Cross-shareholding, Vol.5.)*, 126 HOGAKU KYOKAI ZASSHI 2027 (2009).

[54] Lucian Bebchuk et al., *Stock Pyramids, Cross-Ownership and Dual Class Equity: The Mechanism and Agency Costs of Separating Control From Cash-Flow Rights*, in CONCENTRATED CORPORATE OWNERSHIP 295–315 (Randall Morck ed., 2000).

[55] Sanford Grossman & Oliver Hart, *Takeover Bids, the Free Rider Problem, and the Theory of the Corporation*, 11 BELL J. OF ECON. 42–69 (1980).

flow (hereafter, "public benefits"), above the cash flow value for those companies. This leads to an agency cost.[56] If controlling shareholders retain all stocks in a company, the choice between private benefit and public benefit is moot. If controlling shareholders do not retain all the stocks, however, increased public benefit increases the benefits of not only controlling shareholders but also other shareholders. In contrast, an increase in private benefits only assists controlling shareholders. Therefore, a reduced stake in the company for controlling shareholders yields a lesser degree of social welfare among all shareholders. As a result, inefficiency increases.

For a company issuing only common stock, a controlling shareholder's cash flow ratio (α) must be greater than or equal to 0.5. In companies with the disparity (e.g., stock pyramids), I use the term n (greater than or equal to 2) to refer to the number of the sequence of the controlled companies. The term "S_1" refers to controlling shareholders' portion of the cash flow for company 1. Assume that company $i - 1$ retains $s_i(\geq \frac{1}{2})$ of the shares in company i. In this assumption, controlling shareholders have

$$\alpha = \left(\prod_{i=1}^{n} s_i\right)$$

of the cash flow of company i. For example, if $i = 3$ and $s_i = \frac{1}{2}$, then $\alpha = 0.125$.

Let V_X equal the total value of Project X that is performed by the controlled company, S_X (the total cash flow contributed to all shareholders), and B_X (the total value of private benefits of control). Then, $V_X = S_X + B_X$.

Similarly, let V_Y equal the total value of Project Y performed by controlled company, S_Y (the total cash flow contributed to all shareholders), and B_Y (the total value of private benefits of control). The controller will select Project X when $\alpha S_X + B_X > \alpha S_Y + B_Y$. In contrast, even if project Y is more efficient than X in terms of social welfare ($V_Y > V_X$), the controller will still select X when $B_X > B_Y$. Because $\alpha \in [0.5, 1)$, the condition is

$$V_Y - V_X < \left(\frac{1 - \alpha}{\alpha}\right)(B_X - B_Y)$$

When the right side of this inequality is differentiated with respect to α, it becomes $-(\alpha^{-2})(B_X - B_Y)$. This indicates that there exists an inverse relationship between α and the likelihood that Project X is selected, regardless

56 Bebchuk et al., *supra* note 54, at 455–460.

of its inefficiency. In other words, a lower portion of cash flow for controlling shareholders yields a greater agency cost.

Although this format emphasizes a controller that possesses more than 50 percent of a company's cash flow, the inefficiency described above is common to non-controlling shareholders as well. Despite their minority ownership, non-controlling shareholders still retain voting rights. If there is no majority shareholder in the company, non-controlling shareholders may determine whether to retain incumbent managers or apply the tender offer bid or proxy solicitation. Given this, as pure investors, all shareholders consider not only future cash flow but also private benefit. Therefore, regardless of ownership structure, decisions about the company may be distorted because of the influence of private benefit.

This agency problem is also common among non-finance companies.[57] Therefore, this regulation is couched in general corporate law.[58] Based on the theory of the main bank in Japan, however, banks maintain a variety of relationships with non-financial entities. Some of these relationships include lending via checking account agreements, cross-shareholding, attaching a bank employee to a company as a director or general auditor, among others.[59] By definition, the output produced by each of these relationships relates to private benefit. Main Bank theory supposes that banks provide private benefits to companies whose stocks they hold. Therefore, regulations related to bank shareholding seem to have been developed to respond to the "typical" private benefit problem.

11.5 IMPLICATIONS

As outlined in section 11.4, the private benefit model can theoretically be applied to bank shareholding. However, there is no empirical data to support this assertion. That said, there are some empirical data that apply to the provision of private benefits for a bank. In East Asia, for example, companies with controlling shareholders that did not have equivalent cash

---

57 Bebchuk et al., *supra* note 54; Tokutsu, *supra* note 53.

58 MAKOTO YAZAWA, KIGYOHO NO SHOMONDAI (PROBLEMS ABOUT ENTERPRISE LAW), 354 (1981); Michiyo Hamada, *Kaishaho to Mochikabugaishkisei (Corporate Law and the Regulation for Holding Companies)*, 17 KEIZAIGAKKAI NENPO 48, 54 (1996).

59 Shin-ichi Hirota, *Nihon no Main Bank Kankei (The Relationship of Main Bank in Japan)* 6-10 (RIETI Discussion Paper 09-J-023, 2009) *available at*, http://www.rieti.go.jp/jp/publications/dp/09j023.pdf.

flow rights to control were more likely to be exploited by controlling shareholders during times of financial crisis.[60] This empirical study revealed the influence of legal intervention on private benefits. Additionally, the main bank's monitoring activities were shown to be ineffectual with respect to performance (as measured by the company's stock value).[61] Other empirical research has demonstrated that when banks hold only a small quantity of stocks, there is an inverse relationship between the quantity of stocks held and firm value.[62] These results provided justifications for the regulation of bank shareholding.

Contrarily, there have also been a number of empirical studies that offered different conclusions. According to main bank theory, banks that maintain a number of relationships with non-finance companies substitute the market of corporate control by compelling them to change inefficient management practices and restructure corporate assets. This contributes to social welfare among companies.[63] Because of the relationships possessed by main banks, they tend to succeed in monitoring non-finance companies.[64]

Some individuals have invested money into companies that had dual stock systems. This suggests that the market has accepted the disparity between cash flow and control.[65] From this evidence, it seems as though the regulation of bank shareholding should not be compulsory. On the contrary, bank shareholding should be encouraged.

Despite the numerous findings offered by past empirical work in this

---

[60] Dennis P. Lemmon & Karl V. Lins, *Ownership Structure, Corporate Governance, and Firm Value: Evidence from the East Asian Financial Crisis*, 58 J. OF FIN. 1445–1468 (2003). Though useful, the evidence produced here excluded Japan from the analysis.

[61] Randall Morck & Masao Nakamura, *Banks and Corporate Control in Japan*, 54 J. OF FIN. 319–339 (1999).

[62] Randall Morck et al., *Banks, Ownership Structure, and Firm Value in Japan*, 73 J. OF BUS. 539–567 (2000). However, some criticized this study because of its methods. Hans Degryse et al., *Corporate Governance: A Review of the Role of Banks* 15 (Working Paper, 2008).

[63] Paul Sheard, *The Main Bank System and Corporate Monitoring and Control in Japan*, 11 J. OF ECON. BEHAVIOR & ORG. 399–422 (1989).

[64] Sheard, *supra* note 63; Paul Sheard, *Reciprocal Delegated Monitoring among Delegated Monitors: Principal–Agent Aspects of the Japanese Main Bank System*, 8 J. OF JAPANESE & INT'L ECON. 1–21 (1994); Masahiko Aoki, *Monitoring Characteristics of the Main Bank System: An Analysis and Development View*, *in* THE JAPANESE MAIN BANK SYSTEM: ITS RELEVANCE FOR DEVELOPING AND TRANSFORMING ECONOMICS (Masahiko Aoki & Hugh Patrick eds, 1994).

[65] Dennis P. Sheehan, *Comment*, *in* CONCENTRATED CORPORATE OWNERSHIP 315 (Randall Morck ed., 2000).

domain, researchers have failed to provide a decisive response to the question of bank shareholding regulation. Still, the evidence presented here does allow us to draw some introductory conclusions. Most notably, I feel that universal regulation of bank shareholding in Japan is not justified. Because current legislation forbids banks from holding more than 5 percent of a company's stock,[66] it can block efficient debt–equity swaps. Still, some companies may want to continue collecting funds from investors without encountering the aforementioned problem of private benefit. In these cases, companies can mitigate problems associated with private benefit through contracts or agreements. However, contracts are generally weaker than legislation.

Therefore, a one-size-fits-all rule is not an effective means for regulating bank shareholding. As outlined above, the bank shareholding regulation was intended to respond to the private benefit problem. As such, it is couched in corporate law. Therefore, for non-finance companies, legal solutions to bank shareholding are effective. Some companies may opt out of the present regulations related to bank shareholding in a format referred to as "regulatory dualism."[67]

Even if regulatory dualism is established as a viable action for a company, many problems remain. Most importantly, it is unclear as to how new types of corporations would be developed. One solution to this problem consists of creating a new format in which banks can hold stocks for individual non-finance companies without numeric limitation. Another method involves allowing companies to be fully held by a bank, or to abolish the regulations related to bank shareholding altogether. Following this, a new format in which shares cannot be held by banks will be established. The choice of which method to employ is a difficult one. In addition, legislation related to private benefit is not restricted to bank shareholding. Thus, the process of constructing new rules that address private benefit represents another difficulty.

Despite these difficulties, regulatory dualism appears to be a useful starting point for stock ownership reform. In any event, it would be more useful than adhering to current legislation that is applied to all companies.

---

[66] This problem, however, has been partially resolved by the Ordinance for Enforcement of the Banking Act. Since October 1999, the Fair Trade Commission has allowed a one-year exemption from this regulation. Hirofumi Kubota, *Debt Equity Swap*, 2 Az Insight 14 (2004) *available at*, http://www.azsa.or.jp/b_info/letter/43/az02_43.pdf.

[67] Ronald Gilson et al., *Regulatory Dualism as a Development Strategy: Corporate Reform in Brazil, the United States, and the European Union*, 63 Stan. L. Rev. 475 (2011).

11.6 CONCLUSION

In this chapter, I showed that current numeric limitations on bank shareholding are not enforced to satisfy their traditional intentions. Instead, they are associated with the problem of private benefit, which is couched in general corporate law. I also demonstrated that despite a number of issues that require resolution, regulatory dualism presents a more attractive option for stock ownership regulation than those laws to which Japan currently adheres.

12. Reappraising the role of the appraisal remedy

Hidefusa Iida and Kenichi Sekiguchi

12.1 INTRODUCTION

When the Companies Act of Japan (hereafter: Companies Act),[1] came into effect on May 1, 2006, it enhanced the role of appraisal remedy in Japan by empowering the courts to distribute synergies arising from mergers to minority shareholders who exercised the appraisal right. Since then, the number of appraisal cases coming before the Japanese courts has continued to increase. A re-examination of the appraisal right and related issues is therefore warranted. In the US, a number of scholars have discussed the role of the appraisal remedy.[2] Not enough attention, however, has been paid to the problems of distributing synergies in an appraisal in order to protect minority shareholders.[3] This chapter tries to fill this gap and explores the central question the law of mergers in Japan is facing: is the current appraisal remedy under the Companies Act the ideal method of regulating the conflicts arising from mergers?

The appraisal right refers to the right given to shareholders who

---

[1] Act No. 86, July 26, 2005.

[2] *See, e.g.*, Bayless Manning, *The Shareholder's Appraisal Remedy: An Essay for Frank Coker*, 72 YALE L. J. 223 (1962); Daniel R. Fischel, *The Appraisal Remedy in Corporate Law*, 1983 AM. B. FOUND. RES. J. 875 (1983); Hideki Kanda & Saul Levmore, *The Appraisal Remedy and the Goals of Corporate Law*, 32 U.C.L.A. L. REV. 429 (1985); Mary Siegel, *Back to the Future: Appraisal Rights in the Twenty-First Century*, 32 HARV. J. ON LEGIS. 79 (1995); Robert B. Thompson, *Exit, Liquidity, and Majority Rule: Appraisal's Role in Corporate Law*, 84 GEO. L. J. 1 (1995); Peter V. Letsou, *The Role of Appraisal in Corporate Law*, 39 B. C. L. REV. 1121 (1998); Barry M. Wertheimer, *The Purpose of the Shareholders' Appraisal Remedy*, 65 TENN. L. REV. 661 (1998).

[3] Well known is that the efficient transactions are prevented if the "fair value" is overvalued in an appraisal. *See* Lucian A. Bebchuk, *Efficient and Inefficient Sales of Corporate Control*, 109 Q. J. ECON. 957, 983 (1994); Akio Hoshi, Chapter 13 in this volume. This chapter shows that including synergies in the "fair value" easily leads to the courts' overvaluation.

oppose certain proposed actions of a corporation to have the value of their shares appraised by a court and to demand that the company purchase their shares at the appraised value.[4] The appraisal right not only protects minority shareholders from controlling shareholders' opportunistic behaviors, but also provides directors and controlling shareholders with an incentive to conduct mergers on fair terms so as to avoid attracting appraisal proceedings, which cost the company both time and money, especially in transactions involving conflicts of interests of directors or controlling shareholders, such as management buyouts (MBOs) and squeeze-outs of minority shareholders. While the appraisal right provides an important mechanism for controlling the behavior of directors and shareholders, if not properly designed it could hinder or interfere with value-increasing mergers and become a barrier to efficiency.

This chapter focuses on the role of the appraisal remedy and analyses the incentive effect that the appraisal remedy may have on shareholders and directors.[5] The analysis in this chapter is confined to listed companies and does not consider private companies. While one of the most important functions of the appraisal remedy in private companies is to provide liquidity to shareholders, shareholders of listed companies can sell their shares on equity markets, and in effect this means that the appraisal right in private companies is used for a different purpose and should thus be analyzed separately.[6]

Section 12.2 highlights some distinctive characteristics of the appraisal right under the Companies Act of Japan compared to Delaware's appraisal rights in the US. Section 12.3 examines the incentives of shareholders and directors. We conclude in section 12.4.

---

4 *See* Art. 116(1) (certain amendments to the articles of incorporation or certain actions detrimental to class shareholders), Art. 469(1) (certain transfer of undertakings), Art. 785(1) and 797(1), 806 (certain mergers and other restructuring), and Art. 172(1) (where the issuing company acquires its wholly callable shares that are a type of class shares which may be acquired by the issuing company in their entirety by a special resolution of a shareholders' meeting, shareholders may demand that the court determine the price of the wholly callable shares) of the Companies Act.

5 This chapter does not consider the conflict between shareholders and creditors.

6 *See* William T. Allen et al., Commentaries and Cases on the Law of Business Organization 481 (4th ed. 2012).

12.2 APPRAISAL STATUTE IN JAPAN

12.2.1 Meaning of "Fair Value"

Hypothetical value and synergy value

Whether in Japan or Delaware, dissenting minority shareholders exercising the appraisal right are entitled to have the "fair value" of their shares determined by the court. The meaning of "fair value" is, however, different in each jurisdiction. While the appraisal right under the Delaware General Corporation Law (DGCL) excludes consideration of synergies arising from the merger,[7] "fair value" under the Companies Act includes relevant synergies.

The original Japanese appraisal right provisions were derived from similar US provisions and first enacted in 1950.[8] The Japanese provisions initially provided that dissenting shareholders were entitled to the "fair value which the shares would have had if there were no resolution" approving the merger. This wording was amended to simply "fair value" in 2005 in order to facilitate the consideration of the distribution of synergies in determining "fair value." The primary purpose of this amendment was to provide a remedy which protects minority shareholders from freeze-out mergers which were also introduced by the Companies Act of 2005. This amendment is in large part based on the argument from influential scholars that distributing appropriate synergies to minority shareholders via an appraisal remedy is fair and necessary because the controlling shareholders might implement freeze-out mergers and monopolize all synergies from such mergers.[9]

Thus, under the Companies Act, dissenting shareholders are entitled to: (1) a fair value which the shares would have had if there were no resolution approving the merger ("Hypothetical Value"); or (2) a fair value which reflects synergies arising from the merger ("Synergy Value").[10]

---

[7] *See, e.g.*, Global GT v. Golden Telecom, 993 A.2d 497, 507 (Del.Ch. 2010) ("any synergies or other value expected from the merger giving rise to the appraisal proceeding itself must be disregarded").

[8] The revision of the Japanese Commercial Code in 1950 introduced the appraisal rights into Japanese corporate law, based on the Illinois Business Corporation Act of 1933. *See* Mark D. West, *The Puzzling Divergence of Corporate Law*: *Evidence and Explanations from Japan and the United States*, 150 U. Pa. L. Rev. 527, 529, 544 (2001).

[9] *See, e.g.*, Kenjiro Egashira, *Kaisha Housei no Gendaika ni Kannsuru Youkou Ann no Kaisetu* (*5*) [*Explanation of the Proposal on the Modernization of Corporate Law* (*5*)], 1725 Shouji Houmu 4, 9 (2005).

[10] *See, e.g.*, Tomotaka Fujita, *Shin Kaisha Hou ni okeru Kabushiki Kaitori Seikyuu Kenn Seido* [*An Appraisal Right in the New Companies Act*], *in* Kigyo

Judicial precedents

One of the most controversial issues among scholars and practitioners has been when and how the courts should intervene to determine "fair value." The current prevailing view is to distinguish arm's-length transactions from transactions involving a conflict of interest.[11] In cases where the transaction has been conducted at arm's length, the court will consider the terms of the transaction fair so long as procedures generally recognized as fair (such as obtaining a valuation report from an independent valuator; approval of shareholders' meeting based on adequate disclosure) have been undertaken. Where there is a conflict of interests, the court will review the process and consider whether the conflict has been resolved or adequately mitigated through a transparent process such as obtaining a valuation report, approval by an independent committee,[12] and approval of a majority of the minority shareholders based on adequate disclosure.[13] If the court is satisfied that the conflict has been resolved or adequately mitigated, the court will generally not interfere with the price agreed by the parties.[14]

In line with this prevailing view is the Supreme Court decision in the Tecmo case, which was an appraisal case involving a share transfer (*kabushiki-iten*) between unrelated independent parties. In the Tecmo case, the Supreme Court held that: (1) where there is no synergy or other increase in the enterprise value of a corporation arising from the share transfer, a "fair value" means, in principle, the value which the shares

---

HOU NO RIRON, JOUKANN [THEORY OF ENTERPRISE LAW, VOL. 1] 261, 283 (ETSURO KURONUMA & TOMOTAKA FUJITA EDS, 2007).

[11] *See, e.g.*, Wataru Tanaka, *Soshiki Saihenn to Taika Juunann Ka* [*Mergers and Allowing Cash as a Consideration*], 304 HOUGAKU KYOUSHITSU 75, 79–80 (2006).

[12] Because there are only a few independent directors in most Japanese companies, an independent committee would normally include not only independent directors, if any, but also outside business professionals, lawyers, and certified public accountants who are not directors.

[13] In a recent decision of the Osaka District Court (Culture Convenience Club Co., Ltd v. Anonym, Osaka Dist. Ct., April 13, 2012) in which the fair value of shares in a management buyout was disputed, the Court did not consider the tender offer price accepted by more than 90 percent of the shareholders to be fair as the tender offer price was below the range of valuations based on the discounted cash flow (DCF) method prepared by independent evaluators and the target did not recommend that its shareholders tender their shares. Approval of a majority of minority shareholders alone would thus not appear to be sufficient in certain circumstances.

[14] There is, however, no concrete view on what constitutes a fair and transparent process in this regard.

would have had as at the date ("Relevant Date") on which the dissenting shareholder demands that the corporation purchase its shares (i.e., exercise of appraisal right[15]) if there were no resolution approving the share transfer (i.e., Hypothetical Value); and (2) in all other cases (i.e., where synergies would arise from the share transfer), a "fair value" will usually mean the value which the shares would have had as at the Relevant Date if the share transfer ratio was fair (i.e., Synergy Value). The Supreme Court went on to state that, if a share transfer becomes effective between unrelated companies pursuant to procedures generally recognized as fair including approval by the shareholders' meeting based on adequate disclosure, unless extraordinary circumstances exist which prevent the shareholders from making an informed decision at the shareholders' meeting, the share transfer ratio in the share transfer will be deemed fair.

The significant weight given to the procedural steps adopted by a company in a transaction provides a strong incentive to directors and controlling shareholders to adopt fair processes so as to reduce the risk posed by appraisal proceedings.

12.2.2 Absence of Market-Out Exception

As affirmed by the Supreme Court,[16] in determining the fair value of shares listed on a stock exchange, it is reasonable to use market price as a basis for the determination of the fair value unless circumstances exist that imply that the market price does not reflect the objective value of the company. Further, in determining the Hypothetical Value, the court has a discretion to refer to market prices prior to the public announcement of the merger; in order to exclude the influence of the merger, this may include consideration of the market price as of the date on which the merger was announced or an average over a certain period prior to the announcement date. The court may also correct the referred market price based on various other factors affecting the market price between the announcement date and the Relevant Date. If, however, the merger did not enhance or diminish the enterprise value of the corporation (i.e., there was no change in the equity value due to the merger) or if the court is required to determine the Synergy Value, the court has the discre-

---

[15] Under the Companies Act, dissenting shareholders wishing to exercise the appraisal right must notify their intention to do so to the corporation within a period from the day 20 days prior to the effective date to the day immediately preceding the effective date (Art. 785 (5), 806 (5)).

[16] Sup. Ct., April 19, 2011 (65 Minshu 1311), Sup. Ct., April 26, 2011 (2120 Hanrei Jiho 126), Sup. Ct., February 29, 2012 (1388 Kinyu Shoji 16).

tion to use the market price as of the Relevant Date (as opposed to the announcement date) or the average market price for a certain period immediately preceding the Relevant Date.[17]

The courts' reliance on the market price is in large part based on the premise that the market price correctly reflects the value of a corporation. Despite the reliance of the courts on the market price, however, the Companies Act does not provide a market-out exception in any form. In comparison to the Companies Act of Japan, most states in the US, including Delaware, have adopted some form of market-out exception which excludes the appraisal right where the shareholders can sell their shares in a liquid market.[18] The theory behind the market-out exception is that "if the purpose of the appraisal remedy is to provide a judicially created market for dissenting shareholders, such a device is unnecessary where there is already a substantial trading market, either through a securities exchange or the over-the-counter market – in short, a 'market-out'."[19]

12.2.3 Lack of Other Effective Remedies

In Japan, unlike Delaware where dissenting shareholders prefer to challenge the directors' decisions on mergers by bringing a fiduciary claim, the appraisal right is recognized as the major, if not the exclusive, remedy for shareholders who oppose a merger or other fundamental changes to a corporation. Theoretically speaking, under the Companies Act, shareholders may pursue other remedies. However, these alternatives are not favored by dissenting shareholders in Japan for the reasons discussed below.

Enjoinment of mergers

Except in the case of short form mergers,[20] the Companies Act does not provide shareholders with a right to an injunctive order to prevent a

---

[17] Separate consideration may be required in case of cash-out mergers or other squeeze-out transactions in which the market price will normally be fixed around the announced cash-out price.

[18] *See* Model Bus. Corp. Act Ann. §13.02 statutory comparison (2011). Thirty-eight states have adopted the market out exception.

[19] Rodman Ward, Jr., Edward P. Welch, & Andrew J. Turezyn, Folk on the Delaware General Corporation Law § 262.5 (4th ed. 1999) at § 262.2.2.

[20] In the case of short form mergers, which do not require approval from the shareholders' meeting, if the mergers violate laws and regulations or the Articles of Incorporation of the company, or consideration of the mergers is grossly improper in light of the financial status of the merging company, or the surviving company and the shareholders of the merging company are likely to suffer disadvantage, shareholders of the merging company may demand an injunctive order to prevent

merger. Thus, under the Companies Act, it is unlikely that the court orders an injunction of a merger. Also, if an acquirer uses a two-step scheme where it first acquires a substantial amount of shares via a tender offer and then conducts a squeeze-out of the remaining minority shareholders, shareholders who are not satisfied with the tender offer price do not have any statutory right to demand an injunction of the tender offer. Hence, enjoining a tender offer is almost impossible.

Setting aside the transaction

Even if the terms of a merger are unfair, that fact alone is not sufficient to invalidate the merger. The Companies Act sets a high standard for invalidating a transaction and only permits a transaction to be set aside where the resolution is grossly improper and made as a result of a person having a special interest in the resolution exercising their voting rights. Proving the gross unfairness is not an easy task for dissenting shareholders. In a recent decision of the Osaka District Court,[21] one of the key issues was whether the resolution of a shareholders' meeting approving a squeeze-out of minority shareholders subsequent to a tender offer had been grossly improper due to the acquirer's exercise of its voting rights. The court held that the purpose of squeezing out minority shareholders alone is not sufficient to set aside the resolution and it would have to be proved that the consideration was grossly insufficient compared to the fair value of the shares. The court dismissed the claim because the proposed squeeze-out price was not grossly unfair considering the premium offered to the minority shareholders, valuation of the shares based on the market approach, and comparable company analysis.

Fiduciary duty claim

Dissenting shareholders may also pursue claims based upon the directors' fiduciary duties. Under the Companies Act, it is clear that the directors owe a fiduciary duty and a duty of loyalty to the company.[22] However, it is not clear whether they have any responsibility to compensate shareholders for a loss where a decision or an act of the directors is detrimental to all or some of the shareholders, but the corporation itself does not sustain any damage from such a decision or an act of the directors. Due to the lack of

---

the mergers (Art 784 (2), 796 (2)). In practice, satisfying the burden of proof that the consideration is "grossly" unfair is not easy.

[21] Yoshimoto Kogyo Co., Ltd v. Anonym, Osaka Dist. Ct. June 29, 2012, 1973 SHOUJI HOUMU (2012) 126–127.

[22] Art. 330 and Art. 355 of the Companies Act and Art. 644 of the Civil Code of Japan.

clear specification as to the content of the duties owed (if any) by directors or controlling shareholders towards shareholders in respect of mergers, and the lack of a class action system that enables the sharing of litigation costs among shareholders, fiduciary duty claims have not been the first choice for dissenting shareholders.

The first published case addressing these issues was the Rex Holdings management buyout case where the plaintiffs pursued fiduciary duty claims. The directors of Rex Holdings (hereafter: Rex) together with a private equity fund acquired 100 percent of Rex shares through a tender offer and a subsequent compulsory acquisition of the remaining shares at ¥230 000 per share. Dissenting shareholders filed an appraisal suit with the Tokyo District Court. While the Tokyo District Court held for Rex,[23] the Tokyo High Court decided that the fair value of the Rex shares was ¥336 696.[24] After this decision was upheld by the Supreme Court,[25] shareholders who did not seek appraisal of their shares filed a lawsuit against Rex, its directors, and statutory auditors, claiming a breach of fiduciary duty and various torts and demanding the amount equivalent to the difference between the tender offer price or the compulsory acquisition price (i.e., ¥230 000) and the fair price determined by the High Court (i.e., ¥336 696).

In the Rex case, the Tokyo District Court held that directors have, as part of the duty of care and loyalty, an obligation to give due regard to the common interests of shareholders. However, the District Court found that the defendants gave due regard to the common interests of shareholders because, among other factors, the board of directors unanimously approved the management buyout offer based on the fairness opinion and the valuation report prepared by an independent financial institution. Ultimately, the District Court dismissed the plaintiffs' claim.[26] The Tokyo High Court, on appeal, affirmed the conclusion of the District Court's decision. The High Court further elaborated the duty of directors in management buyouts. It held that directors have, as part of the duty of care, an obligation to ensure that the "fair corporate value" be transferred from the acquirer to the existing shareholders upon management buyouts. The High Court found that the defendants did not breach such an obligation

---

[23] Rex Holdings Co. v. Anonym, 1283 Kinyu Shoji 22 (Tokyo Dist. Ct., Dec 19, 2007).

[24] Rex Holdings Co. v. Anonym, 1301 Kinyu Shoji 28 (Tokyo High Ct., Sep 19, 2008).

[25] Rex Holdings Co. v. Anonym, 1326 Kinyu Shoji 24 (Sup. Ct., May 29, 2009).

[26] Anonym v. Reins International Inc., 2190 Hanrei Jiho 118 (Tokyo Dist. Ct., Feb 18, 2011).

because the price approved by the directors was considered fair according to the fairness opinion and the valuation report.[27]

An important point to note from the Rex case is the difference in the nature of appraisal proceedings and fiduciary claims. Namely, even in a case where, in the appraisal proceedings, the court determines the fair value to be higher than the price agreed by the directors, this does not necessarily imply that there had been a breach of fiduciary duty of the directors. Given the relatively lax fiduciary duty under Japanese corporate law, minority shareholders have a greater incentive to file for appraisal as opposed to filing fiduciary duty claims if they think a merger is improper.

12.2.4 Distinctive Characteristics of the Appraisal Right under the Companies Act

In comparison to the appraisal right under the DGCL, the appraisal right under the Companies Act assumes a greater role. The distinctive characteristics of the appraisal right under the Companies Act are threefold. First, as "fair value" includes synergies arising from mergers, the appraisal right under the Companies Act protects minority shareholders from unfair distribution of synergies, especially when they are frozen out by the controlling shareholders. In Delaware, freeze-out mergers by the controlling shareholders are governed by fiduciary duties and subject to the entire fairness standard of review as opposed to the business judgment rule.[28] Second, there is no market-out exception applicable to the holders of publicly traded shares. Therefore, even in cases where a listed company merges with another listed company in which shareholders of the merging company are to receive shares of the surviving company, dissenting shareholders are still entitled to seek appraisal. In Delaware, appraisal rights are not available in such cases, and the directors' fiduciary duty claims would be the main arena for the battle between shareholders and directors.

---

27 Anonym v. Reins International Inc., 2190 Hanrei Jiho 96 (Tokyo High Ct., Apr 17, 2013). Although the Tokyo High Court, for the first time, made reference to the Revlon duty in Delaware, it is not clear whether the duty to transfer the fair corporate value to the shareholders is different from the Revlon duty.

28 *See, e.g.*, Allen et al., *supra* note 6, at 483. In Delaware, the business judgment rule may be applicable if, in a two-step transaction, an independent committee approves the transaction and the majority of minority shareholders tender their shares (*In re* Cox Communications, Inc. S'holders Litig, 879 A. 2d 604 (Del. Ch. 2005), *In re* CNX Gas Corp, S'Holders Litig, C.A. No. 5377-VCL (Del Ch. May 25, 2010).

Third, due to the lack of other effective remedies, the appraisal right is always the dissenter's first choice in Japan.

Noting the considerations described above, Japanese corporate law seems to position the appraisal remedy as a substitute or supplement for the fiduciary duties concerning mergers because other remedies under the Companies Act fail to effectively protect minority shareholders. Professor Kanda of the University of Tokyo describes the appraisal right primarily as a means of providing a guaranteed exit, and secondly as a means to compensate, to a certain extent, dissenting shareholders for "damages" that they suffer due to mergers conducted in breach of duty of loyalty based on the majority's decision.[29]

However, if this is the case, it is not entirely clear why the company should be responsible for compensating the damages rather than the directors or the controlling shareholders. Except for cash-out transactions, this approach results in the expenses associated with the appraisal being borne by the other shareholders in proportion to their shareholding.[30] In addition, while the existence of the appraisal right gives incentives to the management and controlling shareholders to make the terms of mergers fair, it would appear that the imposition of personal liability on those responsible, by way of fiduciary claims, would provide a much more effective incentive.[31]

12.3 INCENTIVES OF SHAREHOLDERS AND DIRECTORS

From the perspective of efficiency, the current appraisal right under the Companies Act may not necessarily be in the most appropriate form. This section elaborates on this point by examining the incentives that shareholders and directors may have under current appraisal statutes. Section 12.3.1 suggests that the minority shareholders' incentives to file an appraisal may be excessive. Section 12.3.2 argues that the effect of the appraisal remedy on the directors' incentives may be less desirable as compared with that of the fiduciary duty.

---

[29] Hideki Kanda, *Kabushiki Kaitori Seikyuu Kenn no Kouzou* [*The Structure of the Appraisal Right*], 1879 SHOUJI HOUMU 4 (2009).

[30] Hidefusa Iida, *Kabushiki Kaitori Seikyuu Kenn no Kouzou to Kaitori Kakaku Sanntei no Kouryo Youso (1)* [*The Structure of the Appraisal Right and the Factors to Determine the Fair Value (1)*], 129 HOUGAKU KYOUKAI ZASSHI 505, 507 (2012).

[31] Hidefusa Iida, *Kabushiki Kaitori Seikyuu Kenn no Kouzou to Kaitori Kakaku Sanntei no Kouryo Youso (5)* [*The Structure of the Appraisal Right and the Factors to Determine the Fair Value (5)*], 129 HOUGAKU KYOUKAI ZASSHI 1455, 1483 (2012).

12.3.1 The Incentives of Shareholders

Given the current approach adopted by the Japanese courts to the appraisal remedy described in section 12.2, the appraisal right may give shareholders an excessive incentive to file an appraisal claim. This point can be illustrated with a simple example. Suppose two listed companies are to be merged. Firm T will be merged into Firm A which holds 40 percent of Firm T's shares. Firm T's shareholders will receive a Firm A's share (which is worth $120) for each of the Firm T's share as the consideration of the merger. Prior to the announcement of the merger, the market price of Firm T's shares was $100. Immediately after the announcement of the merger, the market price of Firm T's shares increased to $120, which suggests the market price correctly reflects the value of the consideration of the merger. Consider how Firm T's shareholder S determines whether to file an appraisal or to receive the consideration of the merger. S would compare the expected "fair value" which the court would determine in the appraisal proceedings, with $120 which he will receive when he does not file an appraisal. If S predicts that the former value is greater than the latter value, he would file for appraisal, and vice versa. In this example, "fair value" depends on the court's determination of Synergy Value because Synergy Value could be $120 or more, while Hypothetical Value could be around $100 which is either the market price of Firm T's shares immediately preceding the announcement of the merger or the average market price over a certain period, both of which could be lower than $120. If the court finds that this merger is an arm's-length transaction, the court is likely to determine the Synergy Value at $120 (which is the market price of Firm T's share correctly reflecting the merger). However, because Firm A owns 40 percent of Firm T's shares, the court might find that there is a conflict of interests between a controlling shareholder and other minority shareholders, and determine the Synergy Value at a higher price of, for example, $130. Assume further that S forecasts that the court's determination of Synergy Value would be $120 with a probability of 0.7 and $130 with a probability of 0.3. Now, S finds the expected "fair value" is $123 (($120 × 0.7) + ($130 × 0.3) = $123). One can argue that, in the present example, as long as the probability of receiving a higher Synergy Value is larger than zero, S would in theory always choose to file for appraisal.

In addition, the market price on the Relevant Date (or the average market price for a certain period immediately preceding the Relevant Date) usually forms the floor price of "fair value" because, as described in section 12.2 above, the court generally relies on the market price in determining the fair value. For instance, in a merger between two listed companies, the court might determine the Synergy Value equivalent to the market price on the Relevant Date when the court finds that the merger was transacted at arm's length, increases the enterprise value and the distribution of synergy is fair. The "fair value" could be even higher than the market price on the Relevant Date if it finds that the merger decreases the enterprise value and the Hypothetical Value is higher than the market price on the Relevant Date[32] or that the synergies arising from the merger are not fairly distributed although the merger increases the enterprise value and the Synergy Value is higher than the market price of Relevant Date.[33] Thus, if S files for appraisal, he is likely to receive the value no less than the market price on the Relevant Date.

In many cases, save for the expense associated with the exercise of the appraisal right, shareholders may be better off if they file an appraisal claim. Since voting against the merger at the shareholders' meeting is one of the prerequisites to an appraisal claim, shareholders would vote against the proposal of the merger regardless of whether they believe the merger is value-increasing or not.[34]

This incentive of shareholders to file an appraisal claim is excessive because it deters not only inefficient mergers, but also efficient mergers. In theory, an appraisal right can act as a screening mechanism to deter value-decreasing mergers.[35] It is clear that, in Japan, where there is a noticeable absence of fiduciary duties which regulate the conduct of majority shareholders and directors in relation to a merger, the appraisal remedy plays an important role in deterring value-decreasing mergers, especially in situations involving a conflict of interests such as MBOs and freeze-outs. However, the inclusion of Synergy Value in the assessment of "fair value" has a greater potential to deter value-increasing mergers than would be the case if "fair value" excluded Synergy Value and only

---

32 Typically, where the market price on the Relevant Date (e.g., $120) is far below the market price before the announcement of the merger ($140), save for the exclusion of unrelated factors such as the general trend of the economy, the court would find that the merger decreases the enterprise value and the Hypothetical Value would be around $140.

33 Suppose that the market price before the announcement of the merger was $100 and the market price on the Relevant Date is $120. While it can be said the merger enhances the enterprise value, if the merger involves conflict of interest, the court might estimate Synergy Value at $130.

34 *See* Koichi Kusano, Kaisha Hou no Seigi [Justice of Corporate Law] 145 (Shoji Homu, 2011).

35 *See*, *e.g.*, Lucian Arye Bebchuk, *Limiting Contractual Freedom in Corporate Law: The Desirable Constraints on Charter Amendments*, 102 Harv. L. Rev. 1820, 1853 (1989).

included Hypothetical Value.[36] Because the Companies Act provides that a special resolution approved by two-thirds of the shareholders is required to approve a merger,[37] a merger will not be approved if more than one-third of the shareholders vote against it. In the above-stated example, even though the merger is efficient, it might be frustrated where 34 percent of Firm T's shareholders vote "no" simply to satisfy the prerequisites for an appraisal claim. This incentive to vote against mergers, regardless of its merits, also applies indirectly where the shareholders believe that a substantial number of the other shareholders will file for appraisal, in which case, in order to avoid the need to compensate the dissenting shareholders to the detriment of the remaining shareholders, the shareholders may oppose an otherwise attractive merger. Moreover, directors may also be prevented from proposing efficient mergers due to the fact that the company will be responsible for the costs of the appraisal and they will therefore lose control over the companies' cash reserves (this point is discussed in section 12.3.2 below).

In these cases, where some shareholders have excessive incentives to file for appraisal, even value-increasing mergers may be deterred because they will either not be approved by the shareholders' meetings, or not proposed in the first place by directors.

Of course, all of the above-stated examples are hypothetical and may be affected by practical considerations. For example, the cost of filing an appraisal claim might be high enough to prevent shareholders from filing it. However, as there is no strict burden of proof to establish "fair value," the Japanese courts usually rely on the market price as opposed to expensive experts' valuation opinions, and as such, the cost of filing an appraisal claim is unlikely to be prohibitively high.[38]

The excessive impact of an appraisal right whose "fair value" includes Synergy Value (that is, deterring too many value-increasing mergers) could be alleviated by changing the rules relating to the appraisal right by other means, such as introducing a market-out exception or excluding Synergy Value from "fair value". Some might argue that such a revision would worsen the problems inherent in MBOs and freeze-outs. However, if the emphasis is upon the screening function of the appraisal right, both the stock market and the appraisal remedy whose "fair value" includes only Hypothetical Value can perform the screening function and deter value-decreasing mergers.[39] Also, as described in section 12.2, issues

---

36 *See* Letsou, *supra* note 2, at 1152–1153.

37 Art. 309(2) of the Companies Act.

38 In some published appraisal cases, individual shareholders filed the claim by themselves without retaining attorneys.

39 *See* Letsou *supra* note 2, at 1144–1145, 1152.

relating to the inherent conflict in MBO transactions and freeze-out of minority shareholders by a controlling shareholder could be addressed by other means such as clarifying the substance of the fiduciary duty of the directors of a company initiating mergers, a point which is currently vague in Japan.[40] The next section explores this point in more detail.

12.3.2 The Incentives of Directors

To a certain extent, an appraisal remedy can motivate directors to behave properly and to conduct mergers on fair terms. This is because, generally speaking, directors prefer retaining their autonomy to manage the cash of the company. This is particularly so in Japanese companies as Japanese directors tend to place a high value upon maintaining cash reserves in order to secure the long-term stability of the company.[41] If a merger attracts too many appraisal claims, it will impair directors' autonomy to manage cash in the company as the company must purchase the shares held by dissenting shareholders. Hence, directors have an incentive to conduct themselves with care, so as to avoid appraisal proceedings.

The effect which the present appraisal statute has on the incentive of the directors may, however, not be sufficient and, for the reasons discussed below, it would seem that a fiduciary duty would motivate directors more effectively than the appraisal remedy. First, and most importantly, if the court holds that the directors breach their fiduciary duty, they must compensate the damages from their own property, not from the company's cash. This threat motivates directors to act more properly. Second, if the court holds that the directors breach their fiduciary duty, their reputation

---

[40] The fiduciary duty discussed in the Rex case could punish the malicious behaviors of directors if they do not pay due regard to the shareholders' interests. On the other hand, the appraisal remedy places a monetary burden upon the company itself and the shareholders who do not file for appraisal and remain shareholders of the company, but not directors.

[41] SHINICHI HIROTA, KABUNUSHI SHUKEN WO KOETE: SUTEEKU HORUDAA GATA KIGYOU NO RIRON TO JISSYOU [BEYOND THE SHAREHOLDER PRIMACY: THEORY AND EVIDENCE OF THE STAKE-HOLDER FIRMS] 109 (TOYO KEIZAI SHINPOUSHA, 2012). *See also* Raghuram G. Rajan & Luigi Zingales, *What Do We Know about Capital Structure? Some Evidence from International Data*, 50 J. FIN. 1421 (1995) (reporting the average ratio of cash to total assets of Japan's firms was 18.4 percent while that of America's firms was 11.2 percent in 1991); Amy Dittmar et al., *International Corporate Governance and Corporate Cash Holdings*, 38 J. FIN. QUANTITATIVE ANALYSIS 111 (2003) (reporting the median of the ratio of cash to net assets of Japan's firms was 15.5 percent while that of America's firms was 6.4 percent in 1998).

will be substantially damaged. Third, if the court finds that directors did not breach their fiduciary duty, no cash will flow out of the properties of the directors or the company unless appraisal is granted. This is in sharp contrast to the appraisal right where the company has to pay the fair value and the cost of this payment is ultimately borne by shareholders who voted for the merger in proportion to their shareholding ratio. If shareholders believe that the merger is profitable for them, they should be able to vote for it without the fear that a large number of shareholders will exercise the appraisal right and decrease the value of the company.

Therefore, an appraisal remedy under the Companies Act alone may not be the best mechanism and it would appear that one possible solution would be to alter the framework in Japan by clarifying and supplementing fiduciary duties. Of course, a fiduciary duty in itself is not a perfect institution because its contents are open-ended in nature and it might have other side effects. For example, an absence of clarity regarding the duty which directors owe when dealing with mergers may have an excessive chilling effect on their decision making and deter value-increasing transactions. Thus, prior to making any change, an examination of the standard of review is necessary to establish a proper and clear standard and to avoid such a chilling effect. In doing so, the Japan-specific business environment with fewer independent directors, greater monitoring by creditors, and less active shareholders, including monitoring through hostile takeovers, should be taken into consideration. In addition, reference should be made to the judicial practices and precedents developed to date in regard to the appraisal right such as the courts' practice of giving due regard to the procedural steps adopted by a company. However, this is an issue for further discussion.

12.4 CONCLUSION

The appraisal right has been and is expected to continue to be the major remedy for dissenting shareholders against mergers in Japan. However, in light of the cost associated with the existence of the appraisal right as well as its possible deterrent effect upon efficient mergers, one can argue that the Companies Act should not have enabled the courts to distribute synergies in an appraisal right. Because the directors' opportunistic behavior in the mergers with conflicts of interest would be more efficaciously regulated by other means such as fiduciary duties than by the appraisal rights, reforming the role of the appraisal right is necessary to improve the law of mergers in Japan.

13. Appraisal or injunction? Corporate takeovers under uncertain judicial valuation

Akio Hoshi

13.1 INTRODUCTION[1]

The rise of the corporate takeover market in Japan in the mid-2000s caused a great deal of attention to be drawn to hostile takeover attempts and judicial decisions regarding takeover defense strategies.[2] From outside Japan, much less attention has been paid to other areas of Japanese corporate takeover law. One such area is judicial remedy for shareholders who believe consideration for a corporate acquisition is inadequate. Since the enactment of the Companies Act of 2005 (hereafter: Japan Companies Act), the Japanese legal system has relied heavily on the appraisal remedy to relieve such shareholders. Building upon this short-lived tradition, the government has recently proposed partially expanding the scope of injunctive relief to long-form mergers and certain other types of corporate transactions. Unlike common law jurisdictions, it is generally accepted in Japan that statutory authorization is required for a court to award shareholders with injunctive relief,[3] and the choice of available remedies depends on the form of transactions rather than their substance. For these reasons, the kind of remedies which should be available for shareholders is a matter

---

[1] Citations in this chapter are limited to primary legal sources and law review articles available in English.

[2] *See, e.g.*, Ronald J. Gilson, *The Poison Pill in Japan: The Missing Infrastructure*, 2004 COLUM. BUS. L. REV. 21; Curtis J. Milhaupt, *In the Shadow of Delaware?: The Rise of Hostile Takeover in Japan*, 105 COLUM. L. REV. 2171 (2005); Sōichirō Kozuka, *Recent Developments in Takeover Law: Changes in Business Practices Meet Decade-old Rule*, 11 J. JAPAN. L. 5 (2006); Hideki Kanda, *Takeover Defenses and the Role of Law in Japan*, 2 UT SOFT L. REV. 2 (2009).

[3] *Cf.* Hideki Kanda & Curtis J. Milhaupt, *Re-examining Legal Transplants: The Director's Fiduciary Duty in Japanese Corporate Law*, 51 AM. J. COMP. L. 887, 895–896 (2003).

of legislative policy. In this chapter, I discuss, through a simple model analysis, whether the Japanese legislature should allow for injunctions against corporate takeovers. In this analysis, the effect of uncertainty[4] in judicial valuation on corporate takeover activities is evaluated under both the appraisal system and the injunction system.

My analysis reveals that the appraisal system has the benefit that once courts successfully establish public expectation that generally courts do not overvalue target shares, the possibility of a court's overvaluing a target's shares in an individual case will not frustrate individual corporate takeover attempts. In contrast to this, the injunction system has the benefit that even if courts make unwise decisions which create an expectation amongst the public that courts tend to overvalue target company shares, such expectation does not have a general deterrent effect on corporate takeovers.

The remainder of this chapter is organized as follows. Section 13.2 briefly describes the forms of corporate takeovers with a focus on cash deals under the current takeover law regime in Japan, and indicates how the appraisal remedy and injunctive relief are used as shareholder remedies. Section 13.3 conducts a simple model analysis which sheds light on how uncertainty in judicial valuation may affect the outcome of value-increasing takeovers under both the appraisal system and the injunction system. Section 13.4 discusses policy implications for future legislation in light of a trend that has appeared in judicial cases in Japan to date. Section 13.5 provides a conclusion.

13.2 FORMS OF TAKEOVERS AND REMEDIES FOR SHAREHOLDERS

In section 13.2, I briefly describe the forms of cash deals commonly used in Japan. Under Japanese law, the kind of remedies available for

---

[4] Recent behavioural law and economics articles distinguish "risk" and "uncertainty." The former refers to randomness whose probabilistic nature is extremely familiar and can be characterized with objective probabilities. The latter refers to randomness whose probabilistic behaviour is extremely unfamiliar, unknown, or perhaps even unknowable. *See, e.g.*, Eric L. Talley, *On Uncertainty, Ambiguity, and Contractual Conditions*, 34 Del. J. Corp. L. 755, 763–786 (2009). In this chapter, however, I use the term "uncertainty" without such distinction. The "uncertainty in judicial valuation" in this chapter, which is denoted as a stochastic variable in section 13.3, would be characterized as "risk" if it was used in a behavioural law and economics article.

shareholders in the takeover process depends on the form of transactions rather than their substance. This section aims to indicate how the appraisal remedy and injunctive relief are used in those forms of takeovers in preparation for the model analysis in section 13.3.

13.2.1 Tender Offer Followed by Freeze-out

The most commonly used transaction scheme for cash deals in Japan is a two-step transaction where an acquirer freezes out minority shareholders after acquiring a controlling interest[5] in the target through a cash tender offer. Since the Financial Instruments and Exchange Act, which provides for tender offer rules, does not expressly give courts the power to award injunctive relief, target-company shareholders who believe a tender offer price is inadequate can do nothing but withhold their shares at the stage of tender offer and exercise their appraisal rights at the second step of the takeover.

Under the current corporate law regime in Japan, three schemes are mainly used for freezing out minority shareholders: (1) long-form cash merger; (2) short-form cash merger; and (3) the "shares subject to call" process.[6] Among these, primarily for tax reasons, the "shares subject to call" process is the most widely used.[7] In addition to these schemes, the

---

[5] Under Japanese law it is not easy to decide what ratio of a target's shares constitutes a "controlling interest." As is common in many jurisdictions, under Japanese law a majority of voting power gives the holder thereof the right to elect and dismiss directors in a company unless the company's Articles of Incorporation provide otherwise. Among the methods of freezing out minority shareholders as described below, however, a long-form merger and a "shares subject to call" process require two-thirds of affirmative votes at a shareholders' meeting where the quorum has been met (*see* KAISHAHŌ [Companies Act] art. 309, para. 2, no. 3 and no.12). A short-form merger and a "buyout right" require a controlling shareholder have 90 percent of voting interests in the target (*see* KAISHAHŌ [Companies Act] art. 468, para. 1). For the purpose of simplifying analysis, the model in section 13.3 assumes that an acquirer obtains a controlling interest in the target by acquiring a majority of the target's shares.

[6] *See* Stephen D. Bohrer & Akio Hoshi, *Doing Deals in Japan: An Introductory Guide for US Practitioners*, M&A LAW., Oct. 2010, at 14, 20–21 (summarizing the process in detail). The 2011 amendments to the Industry Revitalization Act of 1999 made it possible to skip certain requirements if the acquirer obtains approval from the competent minister in advance of a tender offer and succeeds in acquiring at least 90 percent of voting power in the target prior to freezing out minority shareholders. These omissions significantly shorten the time required for completing a minority freeze-out.

[7] *See* Bohrer & Hoshi, *supra* note 6, at 16–17 (summarizing the requirements for tax deferral in mergers and other corporate combination transactions).

Japanese legislature has proposed creating: (4) a controlling shareholder's "buyout right" scheme. Under current law, the appraisal remedy is available in schemes (1), (2), and (3),[8] whereas injunction is expressly authorized only in scheme (2).[9] After the Japanese government's legislative proposal is passed, however, both the appraisal remedy and injunctive relief (although injunctive relief is likely to be given only in limited circumstances) are expected to become available for shareholders in all the freeze-out schemes listed above.

If a petition for the appraisal remedy is filed, a court is required to award "fair prices" to filing shareholders.[10] The meaning of "fair price" is left to a court's reasonable discretion.[11] Consequently, I express the "fair price" to be decided by a court as a stochastic variable in the model in section 13.3. In contrast, injunctive relief is provided to be given under somewhat different standards and additional statutory requirements. In the model in section 13.3, however, I use the same stochastic variable to denote the court's judgment to award injunctive relief for the purpose of comparing the appraisal system and the injunction system under the *ceteris paribus* condition.

13.2.2 One-step Cash Merger

A one-step cash merger is also available for a cash deal under the current corporate law regime.[12] A freeze-out process is not necessary in a one-step cash merger because cash is delivered to all of the target's shareholders by operation of law if the target's shareholders approve the merger at the target's shareholders' meeting. The Japan Companies Act requires that the target's shareholders who wish to exercise their appraisal rights must notify the company that they will object to the merger prior to the shareholders' meeting and vote against the merger at the shareholders' meeting.[13]

---

[8] *See* KAISHAHŌ [Companies Act] art. 116, para. 1, no. 2, art. 172, para. 1 and art. 785, para. 1.

[9] *See* KAISHAHŌ [Companies Act] art. 784, para. 2.

[10] *See* KAISHAHŌ [Companies Act] art. 116, para. 1 and art. 785, para. 1 and Sup. Ct., May 29, 2009, 1326 KINYŪ HANREI 35.

[11] *See* Sup. Ct., May 29, 2009, 1326 KINYŪ HANREI 35 and Sup. Ct., April 19, 2011, 1366 KINYŪ HANREI 9. Note, however, that unlike Delaware law, it is generally accepted in Japan that the Japan Companies Act requires that the "fair price" include any increase in corporate value arising from the success of a corporate takeover. *See* Chapter 12 in this volume.

[12] At present, however, it is not frequently used for tax reasons. *See* Bohrer & Hoshi, *supra* note 6, at 16–17.

[13] *See* KAISHAHŌ [Companies Act] art. 785, para. 2, no. 1.

Accordingly, the target's shareholders who believe that the purchase price is inadequate and wish to use the appraisal remedy must vote against the merger at the shareholders' meeting. This voting against the merger corresponds to the decision not to tender in the model in section 13.3. While the Companies Act currently in force does not expressly authorize a court to administer injunctive relief suspending a long-form merger, the Japanese legislature has proposed that injunctive relief be given in limited circumstances.

13.2.3 Summary

As discussed above, the current corporate law regime in Japan relies heavily on the appraisal remedy for protecting the interests of the target's shareholders, whereas it allows injunctions to be awarded only in limited forms of transactions. The Japanese legislature, however, attempts to expand the scope of injunctions. In section 13.3, I compare the appraisal system currently in force with the injunction system that would cover the overall takeover process, and analyze how they affect the outcome of value-increasing takeovers.

13.3 MODEL

In section 13.3, I argue that uncertainty in judicial valuation affects the outcome of takeovers in different ways, depending on whether: (1) shareholders are entitled to the appraisal remedy; or (2) they are entitled to injunctive relief in the acquisition process where the acquirer freezes out the target's minority shareholders after successfully acquiring the target's controlling interest through a cash tender offer as described in section 13.2.1 above.[14, 15] The analysis of injunctions in this section presumes that

---

[14] The choice of one-step cash merger as an acquisition method, which would require changes in explanation of technical aspects of legal institutions in the main text (e.g., shareholders vote for the merger instead of tendering their shares), would not frustrate the analysis in section 13.3.

[15] Under Delaware law, the cash transaction analyzed in section 13.3 would trigger the target directors' *Revlon* duty. Under such a regime, it is the operation of the market for corporate control that decides Acquirer's purchase price, and not a court's valuation. In Delaware, a court's valuation has an impact on corporate takeover activities only when the emergence of competing bidders cannot be expected such as the case where an existing controlling shareholder freezes out minority shareholders. A complete analysis of the Delaware system is beyond the scope of this chapter.

tender offers are also subject to a court's injunctive order beyond the scope of the recent legislative proposals in Japan.

13.3.1 Assumptions

At $t = 0$, Target's shares are dispersed and widely owned by public shareholders. Target's share price at $t = 0$ is p_0. For simplicity, I assume that Target does not owe any debt and its enterprise value is equal to its equity value, and further, that Target's share prices correctly reflect its enterprise value. At $t = 1$, Acquirer announces its plan to acquire Target through a tender offer. The acquisition price is set to be p_1 per share. The success of the takeover will increase Target's enterprise value per share to v. In order to gain a positive payoff from the acquisition, Acquirer sets the takeover price so as to meet the following condition:

$$p_0 < p_1 < v \tag{13.1}$$

Condition (13.1) ensures that the acquisition is value-increasing. For simplicity, the tender offer is assumed to be successful if the number of tendered shares exceeds 50 percent. Transaction costs and taxes are ignored in this model. At $t = 2$, Target's shareholders encounter the choice of whether to tender their shares or call for judicial appraisal or injunction. Target's shareholders' individual decisions will not affect other shareholders' decisions. At $t = 3$, the court conducts its own valuation of Target's shares in response to a petition from Target's shareholders and determines the value to be p_j. The value p_j is not known in advance, but each shareholder of Target anticipates that the value will be $\tilde{p}_j$, which is presumed to follow a normal distribution with the mean $E(\tilde{p}_j)$ and the standard deviation σ. In mathematical terms, $\tilde{p}_j$ is a stochastic variable and p_j is its realized value. The distribution is also known by Acquirer in advance of Acquirer's commencement of a takeover attempt. Acquirer is assumed to be risk-neutral and will execute the acquisition if its expected payoff from the takeover is positive and will not execute the acquisition if its expected payoff from the takeover is negative.

13.3.2 Appraisal System

At $t = 2$, if shareholders are entitled to the appraisal remedy, Target's shareholders who believe that the acquisition price exceeds their anticipated value of court valuation (i.e., $p_1 > \tilde{p}_j$) tender their shares, whereas Target's shareholders who believe that the acquisition price is below their anticipated value of court valuation (i.e., $p_1 < \tilde{p}_j$) do not tender their shares and seek the appraisal remedy when they are frozen out after the tender

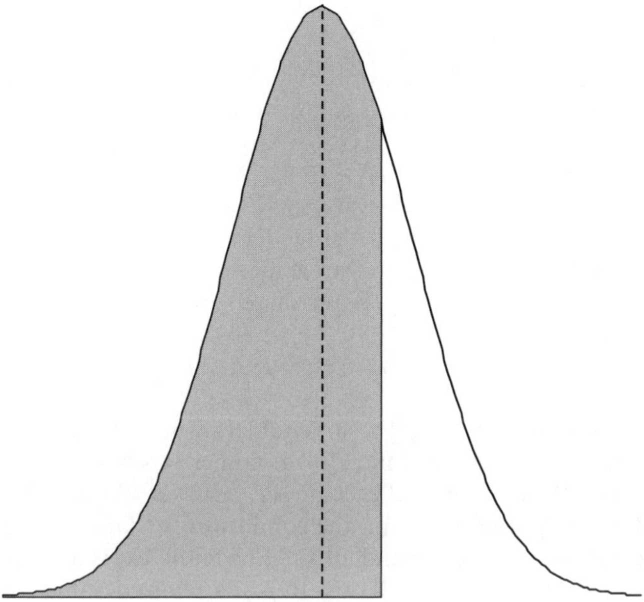

Figure 13.1 Mean of the target's shareholders' anticipation of judicial valuation and purchase price

offer is successfully completed.[16] As I posited that $\tilde{p}_j$ follows a normal distribution, Acquirer will succeed in acquiring more than 50 percent of Target's shares if Acquirer offers Target's shareholders the purchase price p_1 which exceeds $E(\tilde{p}_j)$, the mean value of $\tilde{p}_j$ (see Figure 13.1).[17] The following condition, therefore, must be met for the takeover to succeed:

---

[16] One may argue that such shareholders will engage in arbitrage transactions where they purchase Target's shares in the market and exercise their appraisal rights, and the resulting increase in Target's share prices will frustrate the tender offer. Some courts, however, suggested restricting the exercise of appraisal rights by the shareholders who purchase the shares in the market after the plan of acquisition is published. *See, e.g.*, Tokyo Dist. Ct., Oct. 11, 1983, 34 KAMINSHŪ 968 (holding that the price which may be awarded to such shareholders shall not exceed their acquisition prices for their shares in the market); Osaka Dist. Ct., Mar. 30, 2010, 314 SHIRYŌBAN SHŌJI 31 (holding that the court should take into consideration only the facts and circumstances that arise after such shareholders acquired their shares in the market). The existence of these cases will make the arbitrage transactions incomplete.

[17] Acquirer would need to set the purchase price to be $p_1 > E(p_j) + 0.44\sigma$ in a

$$p_1 > E(\tilde{p}_j) \quad (13.2)$$

Acquirer can set an acquisition price which satisfies conditions (13.1) and (13.2) at the same time only if the following condition is met:

$$v > E(\tilde{p}_j) \quad (13.3)$$

Acquirer, therefore, commences the tender offer only if condition (13.3) is satisfied. When the acquisition price meets both conditions (13.1) and (13.2), Acquirer's expected payoff per share from the takeover will be:

$$v - \alpha \cdot p_1 - (1 - \alpha) \cdot E(\tilde{p}_j) \quad (13.4)$$

where α is the ratio of Target's shareholders who believe p_1 exceeds $\tilde{p}_j$. Because the value of expression (13.4) becomes positive from conditions (13.1) and (13.2), Acquirer will execute the takeover. We should note here that, under the appraisal system, the conditions for takeover commencement and its success are dependent on $E(\tilde{p}_j)$, the expected value of the court's valuation, and are irrelevant to p_j, its realized value. Even if the court overvalued Target's shares in the process of the appraisal remedy (i.e., $p_j >> v$), and Acquirer's payoff from the acquisition ended up being negative,[18] the takeover will be successfully completed because Acquirer incurs the risk of a court's overvaluation of Target's shares.[19]

---

one-step cash merger, which requires a two-thirds majority approval in Target's shareholders' meeting. If Acquirer desires to acquire 90 percent or more of Target's shares to use a short-form merger or a controlling shareholder's buyout right, it would need to set the purchase price to be $p_1 > E(p_j) + 1.28\sigma$.

[18] The actual payoff per share will be $v - \alpha \cdot p_1 - (1 - \alpha) \cdot p_j$. The Tokyo High Court dismissed the claim by the tendering shareholders, who sought from the acquirer damages consisting of the difference between the tender offer price and the "fair price" decided by the court (*see* Tokyo High Ct., Apr. 17, 2013, 2190 HANJI 96). The payoff per share, therefore, will not be $v - p_j$ even if the court overvalued Target's shares.

[19] As I assumed that Acquirer is risk-neutral, it is the expected value of court valuation that affects *ex ante* takeover activities. If, contrary to the court's decision cited in *supra* note 18, tendering shareholders were entitled to be awarded the difference between the amount decided by the court in the appraisal process and the tender offer price, Acquirer's expected payoff per share would be $v - E(p_j)$. Because condition (13.3) ensures this value becomes positive, the success of the acquisition will not depend on whether the damages are awarded to tendering shareholders.

13.3.3 Injunction System

At $t = 2$, if shareholders are entitled to injunctive relief, Target's shareholders who believe that their anticipated value of court valuation will be between the purchase price and Target's potential enterprise value (i.e., $p_1 < \tilde{p}_j < v$) file a petition to the court for an injunctive order to suspend the acquisition.[20] At the trial, the court conducts its own valuation of Target's shares. If the court's valuation is below the purchase price (i.e., $p_j < p_1$), Acquirer is allowed to proceed with the acquisition at the purchase price p_1, whereas if the court's valuation exceeds the purchase price (i.e., $p_j > p_1$), Acquirer is required to reset its acquisition price. For simplicity, the court's valuation p_j is assumed to become known to the parties in the process of the trial, and Acquirer sets its new purchase price to be p_j. If the court's valuation exceeds Target's potential enterprise value (i.e., $p_j > v$), however, Acquirer cancels its takeover attempt. All of Target's shareholders, who also decisively get to know the court's valuation after the trial, tender their shares in response to Acquirer's new tender offer (even if some shareholders did not tender their shares, they would be frozen out at the same price as the tender offer price at the second step). The following condition, therefore, must be met for the takeover to succeed:

$$p_1 < v \tag{13.5}$$

Unlike the appraisal system, the injunction system requires that Acquirer set its acquisition price so as to meet only condition (13.1). Acquirer's expected payoff per share from the acquisition will be:

$$\beta\,(v - p_1) + \gamma\,(v - p_j) + (1 - \beta - \gamma)\,0 \tag{13.6}$$

where β is the probability of the court's deciding $p_j < p_1$, and γ is the probability of the court's deciding $p_1 < p_j < v$. Because the value of expression (13.6) is positive, Acquirer will initiate its tender offer at $t = 1$ irrespective of whether the final result of the tender offer is successful or not. The

---

[20] As discussed below, the court's valuation $p_j > v$ would prevent Acquirer from executing the takeover. Target's shareholders whose anticipated value of the court's valuation exceeds Target's potential enterprise value (i.e., $p_j > v$), therefore, do not file a petition for an injunction.

court's valuation at $t = 3$, however, may frustrate the acquisition. In other words, in contrast with the result under the appraisal system, the outcome of the takeover under the injunction system is dependent on the court's actual valuation p_j, the realized value of $\tilde{p}_j$. The risk of a court's overvaluation of Target's shares will result in the prevention of an efficient takeover.

13.3.4 Evaluation

The analysis so far has revealed that, under the appraisal system, $E(\tilde{p}_j)$, the expected value of the court's valuation, determines the outcome of a takeover, whereas, under the injunction system, p_j, the realized value of the court's valuation, determines the outcome of a takeover. Both systems have their own strengths and weaknesses. Which is the superior system depends on the magnitude relationship of $E(\tilde{p}_j)$ and v.

When $E(\tilde{p}_j)$ is smaller than v, the appraisal system is superior to the injunction system. Condition (13.3) enables Acquirer to set an acquisition price so as to meet conditions (13.1) and (13.2). As a result, a takeover will always be successful under the appraisal system. In contrast, the takeover may be frustrated under the injunction system if the realized value of the court's valuation exceeds Target's potential enterprise value (condition 13.5).

When $E(\tilde{p}_j)$ is larger than v, the injunction system is superior to the appraisal system. Failure to meet condition (13.2) under the appraisal system prevents Acquirer from commencing a takeover from the outset. In contrast, Acquirer always initiates a takeover attempt under the injunction system, and may successfully complete the takeover if the realized value of the court's valuation is below Target's potential enterprise value (condition 13.5).

The result of my model analysis in section 13.3 can be rephrased as follows for policy implications. If a court is able to keep the value of $E(\tilde{p}_j)$ below Target's potential enterprise value through the formation of appropriate case law, the appraisal system can eliminate the negative effect a court's overvaluation may have on individual corporate takeover attempts. The risk of a court's overvaluation is incurred by an acquirer and does not immediately create a general deterrent effect on value-increasing corporate takeovers. If courts create a public impression that they tend to overvalue a target's shares, however, the appraisal system would have a substantial deterrent effect on takeovers. Further, once expectation of a court's overvaluation is established, the deterrent effect might cyclically deprive courts of opportunities to correct such expectation.

In contrast, the injunction system does not have such a general deterrent effect on corporate takeovers even though improper precedents have accumulated. Even if public shareholders overly evaluated the value of $E(\tilde{p}_j)$, a wide variance in individual judicial decisions may save value-increasing corporate takeovers. On the other hand, even if a court successfully establishes a proper public expectation about a court's valuation, the injunction system may individually frustrate efficient corporate takeovers.

13.4 TREND IN JUDICIAL VALUATION AND POLICY IMPLICATIONS

In section 13.4, I discuss which is a superior legislative policy: (1) to maintain the current appraisal system; or (2) to replace the appraisal system with the injunction system (or to introduce injunctive relief into the takeover law regime)[21] in light of the judicial cases which have been decided in Japan to date. The discussion relies solely on the perspective derived from the analysis in section 13.3 and I do not intend to examine all aspects of the appraisal remedy and injunctive relief. I am fully aware of the necessity that the actual legislation would also require a thorough examination of both systems from other perspectives. The discussion in this section, therefore, is only suggestive from the single perspective obtained from the analysis in section 13.3.

13.4.1 Trend in Judicial Valuation

In Japan, case reporters have published only five cases where courts have been requested to determine the value of target shares in connection

---

[21] When the appraisal system and the injunction system coexist, the key role of protecting the interest of shareholders will move from the appraisal remedy to injunctive relief. Assuming that there is no difference in value between the court's valuation in the appraisal remedy and the court's valuation in injunctive relief, Target's shareholders who believe $p_1 < p_j < v$ holds are indifferent between exercising their appraisal rights and filing for an injunction. The filing for an injunction at $t = 2$, however, precedes the appraisal remedy procedure. Consequently, Target's shareholders may seek the appraisal remedy only when Acquirer proceeds on to its takeover attempt after the trial for an injunction is completed. In this case, the purchase price is set to be p_1 or p_j, both of which are no less than p_j. Since p_j becomes known to Target's shareholders at this stage, all of Target's shareholders will choose to tender their shares. The injunction system, therefore, overrides the appraisal system even if both systems coexist.

with the purchase of publicly traded companies for cash.[22, 23, 24] Four of them are management buyouts. Applying the model in section 13.3 to them, we can observe the following variables from the facts that appeared in the actual cases: p_0, the target's share price before the announcement of a takeover, p_1, the purchase price, and p_j, the court's valuation. In addition, the targets' potential enterprise value v can be estimated from the discounted cash flow (DCF) valuations conducted by the financial advisors which were involved in the cases. They are summarized in Table 13.1.

Table 13.1 shows first that $p_1 > p_0$ holds in every case and suggests that all the acquisitions were value-increasing. Second, it evidences that the fair prices finally determined by the courts always exceed the purchase prices. Third, it displays that the magnitude relationship between the final prices determined by the courts and the DCF valuations vary depending on the cases. Although we cannot observe the actual distribution of $\tilde{p}_j$, the fact that the target shareholders tendered 77.6 percent of their shares in *Matsuo Kyōryō*, the case where the number of tendered shares was the smallest of the five cases, suggests that the targets' shareholders had expected $p_1 > E(\tilde{p}_j)$, and then $v > E(\tilde{p}_j)$, would hold in all the cases.

The trend we have seen in those cases suggests that Japan's policy decision that it relies on the appraisal remedy for protecting the interests of shareholders in corporate takeovers was successful as initial legislative decision-making because injunctive relief might have frustrated those value-increasing takeovers in the cases where the courts' valuation exceeded or was very close to the targets' potential enterprise value v. The issue with the current takeover law regime, however, lies in the fact that courts tend to overvalue the target shares. This trend in judicial decisions is likely to give a basis for target shareholders to form an expectation that $v < E(\tilde{p}_j)$ will hold in future cases. This expectation will have a deterrent effect on value-increasing takeovers by making it difficult for potential acquirers to set an acquisition price that meets conditions (13.1) and (13.2)

22 I do not discuss individual cases in this chapter. For a discussion of individual cases, *see, for example*, Wataru Tanaka, *Going Private and the Role of Courts: A Comparison of Delaware and Japan*, 3 UT Soft L. Rev. 12 (2011).

23 I excluded the cases that clearly do not fit the takeover processes analyzed in section 13.3.

24 In Japan, an appraisal remedy is often sought in connection with stock-for-stock transactions. One reason for this phenomenon is that the Japan Companies Act, unlike the Delaware General Corporation Law, does not have a "market-out" exception. Those cases deal with fundamentally different legal issues from what is analyzed in this chapter, and are excluded from the scope of analysis in section 13.4.

Table 13.1 Appraisal remedy cases

	Pre-takeover share prices (P_0)[1]	Purchase prices (P_1)	District court decisions (P_j)	High court decisions (P_j)	DCF valuations (v)
Lex[2]	¥ 202 000	¥ 230 000	¥ 230 000	¥ 336 966	N/A[3]
Sunstar[4]	¥ 550	¥ 650	¥ 650	¥ 840	¥ 570–676 (Target)
Cybird[5]	¥ 49 026	¥ 60 000	¥ 60 000	¥ 61 360	¥ 55 657 – 68 938 (Acquirer)
Matsuo Kyōryō[6]	¥ 86	¥ 122	¥ 140	¥ 140	¥ 95–143 (Acquirer) ¥ 81–158 (Target)
Culture Convenience Club[7]	¥ 469	¥ 600	¥ 649	N/A	¥ 531–722 (Acquirer) ¥ 666–994 (Special Committee) ¥ 779–1050 (Target)

Notes:

1 I used the simple average of the closing prices during the one-month period before the announcement of the takeovers as recorded in publicly available documents.

2 Sup. Ct., May 29, 2009, 1326 Kinyū Hanrei 35; Tokyo High Ct., Sept. 12, 2008, 1301 Kinyū Hanrei 28 and Tokyo Dist. Ct., Dec. 19, 2007, 2001 Hanji 109. The Supreme Court simply dismissed the appeal from the target and did not conduct its own valuation.

3 DCF valuation is not available because the target company declined to disclose the valuation report it received from its financial advisor.

4 Osaka High Ct., Sept. 1, 2009, 1326 Kinyū Hanrei 20 and Osaka Dist. Ct., Sept. 11, 2008, 1326 Kinyū Hanrei 27.

5 Tokyo High Ct., Oct. 27, 2010, 322 Shiryōban Shōji 174 and Tokyo Dist. Ct., Sept. 18, 2009, 1329 Kinyū Hanrei 45.

6 Osaka High Ct., Jan. 31, 2012, 1390 Kinyū Hanrei 32 and Osaka Dist. Ct., Jan. 28, 2011, 1390 Kinyū Hanrei 38.

7 Osaka Dist. Ct., Apr, 13, 2012, 1391 Kinyū Hanrei 52.

at the same time. How to evaluate this trend in judicial valuation is a key to determining legislative policy for the future.

13.4.2 Choices in Legislative Policy

At the moment, we have two fundamental choices in legislative policy: (1) maintaining the current takeover law regime that relies on the appraisal remedy; and (2) adopting an injunction system that covers the entire corporate takeover process. Which to choose is dependent on how we evaluate the cases which were discussed in section 13.4.1. If we deduce from the five cases that Japanese courts are unable to form a proper public expectation concerning their valuation, then the legislature should replace the appraisal system with the injunction system because, as discussed in section 13.3, an injunction does not have a general deterrent effect on corporate takeovers even if $v < E(\tilde{p}_j)$ holds. In contrast, if we are confident that the five cases have yet to give public shareholders an expectation about overvaluation by the courts, and the courts are still capable of developing proper case law for the future, then the legislature should maintain the current appraisal system.

With respect to these legislative choices, I am of the view that the Japanese legislature should keep the current takeover law regime at this moment and wait and see how the case law will develop for a while. Unlike Delaware courts, Japanese courts are still inexperienced in litigation in respect of corporate takeovers and have paid little attention to the impact that case law will have on *ex ante* corporate takeover activities. To put it another way, due to lack of experience, Japanese courts still have much room for improving their norm-forming capabilities. Many commentators in Japan have already pointed out that the cases discussed in the section 13.4.1 may have a deterrent effect on future takeover activities. I expect that courts will listen to those arguments and pay more attention to their impact on *ex ante* corporate takeover activities. If the trend of overvaluation by courts continues in the future, however, the legislature should fully introduce injunctions to the Japanese takeover law regime at the right occasion.

13.5 CONCLUSION

In this chapter, I argued that when judicial valuation is uncertain, a key factor for the Japanese legislature to take into account when choosing either the appraisal system or the injunction system is the court's ability to establish the public expectation that they will not engage in overvaluation.

The judicial cases to date have shown a trend of overvaluation, but the view on whether the legislature should shift to an injunction system right now may vary from person to person. I expect further development of this discussion.[25]

[25] After submitting this chapter to the publisher and prior to my proofreading, three new cases were published in case reporters. They are Tokyo Dist. Ct., Sep. 17, 2013, 1427 KINYŪ HANREI 54; Tokyo Dist. Ct., Mar. 14, 2013, 1429 KINYŪ HANREI 48 ; and Tokyo Dist. Ct., Nov. 6, 2013, 1431 KINYŪ HANREI 52.

14. Stagnant Japan? Why outside (independent) directors have been rare in Japanese companies

Kenichi Osugi

14.1 INTRODUCTION

In most developed countries, listed companies usually have a board of directors that includes several outside (and independent) directors as core members. A board comprised in this way does not make decisions about day-to-day operations of the company; its main role is to supervise the management of the company. This paradigm is called the "monitoring model" of a board of directors.

In Japan, however, the vast majority of board members are insiders.[1] They are former employees who were promoted to the position of directors. To date, neither the law nor the listing rules have required listed companies to appoint outside directors, though a listing rule that urges listed companies to appoint an outside director is about to come, as will be shown in section 14.3 of this chapter.

Why are there so few outside directors in Japan? Will this change in

---

[1] Companies that appointed outside directors accounted for 48.7 percent of the 2294 companies that were listed on the Tokyo Stock Exchange (TSE) as of September 10, 2010 (comprised of 1669 companies listed on the TSE First Section, 443 companies listed on the TSE Second Section, and 182 companies listed on the TSE Mothers). The average number of outside directors per company was 0.91 for all TSE-listed companies, and of the companies that had outside directors, the average was 1.86 persons. See Tokyo Stock Exchange, Inc., *TSE-Listed Companies White Paper on Corporate Governance 2011* (March 2011), at p. 19, available at http://www.tse.or.jp/english/listing/cg/

The number of outside directors has steadily increased recently, however. In terms of the companies listed on the TSE First Section, only 30.2 percent appointed outside directors in 2004, but the rate increased to 54.2 percent in 2012. See Japan Association of Corporate Directors, *Jôjô Kigyô no Kôporeito Gabanansu Chôsa 2012* [Survey of the Corporate Governance of Listed Companies, 2012], at 3, *available at* http://www.jacd.jp/news/odid/120801_2011.html

the near future? This chapter will discuss the answers to these questions. In section 14.2, I will review best practices utilized in the United States and European countries, discovering that outside directors have become an essential component of the board even in countries that emphasize the interests of stakeholders other than shareholders. In section 14.3, I will summarize the corporate law of Japan, especially the unique system of *kansayaku*, and show that the role of the directors of Japanese companies is different from that of Western companies. In section 14.4, I will analyze institutional as well as cultural factors that seem to cause Japanese companies to hesitate to appoint outside directors. In section 14.5, I will consider whether the current practice will change along with the transformation of the factors described in section 14.4. Section 14.6 will conclude this chapter.

14.2 BEST PRACTICES IN THE UNITED STATES AND EUROPEAN COUNTRIES

14.2.1 The United States

In the United States, the percentage of independent directors in listed companies has consistently grown from 1950 through 2005, and this upward trend has been especially clear after 1970.[2] It began with the corporate scandals of the 1970s, when the Penn Central Railroad, believed to be a blue chip company, suddenly collapsed. The Special Prosecutor's investigation into the series of abuses known as "Watergate" revealed that numerous companies had been engaged in illegal domestic campaign contributions and "questionable payments" to foreign government officials. Both incidents made clear that the outside directors of the companies concerned were useless, and people believed that outside directors in other large companies were not effective either.[3]

---

[2] Jeffrey N. Gordon, *The Rise of Independent Directors in the United States, 1950–2005: Of Shareholder Value and Stock Market Prices*, 59 Stan. L. Rev. 1465 (2007). According to Gordon, *supra*, at 1475 and 1565, a rough estimate of the rate of insiders, interested but outside directors, and independent directors in the US listed companies, respectively, is as follows: 49 percent, 26 percent, and 22 percent in 1950; 43 percent, 31 percent, and 24 percent in 1960; 45 percent, 27 percent, and 28 percent in 1970; 38 percent, 23 percent, and 39 percent in 1980; 30 percent, 20 percent, and 50 percent in 1990; and 19 percent, 14 percent, and 67 percent in 2000.

[3] Gordon, *supra* note 2, at 1514ff.

Several plans aiming to improve the management of large companies were suggested. Among those plans, the *Corporate Director's Guidebook* authored by the American Bar Association and *The Role and Composition of the Board of Directors of the Large Publicly Owned Corporation* authored by the Business Roundtable (an association of chief executive officers (CEOs) of leading US companies) had much in common. Both recommended that the listed companies should spontaneously install a nominating committee, a compensation committee, and an audit committee, each of which should be mainly composed of non-management directors. In 1977, the New York Stock Exchange changed its listing rules to demand that its listed companies install an audit committee comprised exclusively of non-management directors.[4]

14.2.2 European Countries

European countries started reforming boards of directors in the 1990s. In the United Kingdom, the Cadbury Report was the first step in a series of reforms. Since then, the CEOs (as representatives of large companies), investors, the government, and academics have been called upon to form a committee at regular intervals to promulgate best-practice guidelines for corporate governance. It soon became the custom that the reports, which were prepared by governmental committees, would be incorporated into the listing rules.

Continental Europe followed the UK-led trend of reform. In France, a committee comprised mainly of the CEOs of large companies published the Vienot Report in 1995. Since then, France has updated its corporate governance guidelines, as has the United Kingdom. Germany was a latecomer in Europe in terms of corporate governance guidelines, but, as in the United Kingdom, the government called upon persons with different backgrounds to establish the German Corporate Governance Code in 2002. Since then, the code has been revised at least once every two years. The Stock Corporation Code (*Aktiengesetz*) in Germany obligates listed companies to obey the code.[5]

The corporate governance guidelines in Europe generally permit

---

[4] Gordon, *supra* note 2, at 1518f. The factors that facilitated the prevalence of independent directors in the United States are discussed in Gordon, *supra*; and Stephen M. Bainbridge, The New Corporate Governance: In Theory and Practice, at 155ff (Oxford 2008).

[5] Best-practice codes on corporate governance in countries around the world are provided on the website of the European Corporate Governance Institute, at http://www.ecgi.org/codes/all_codes.php.

companies to opt out. In other words, a listed company must disclose in detail whether it observes the guidelines, and if it does not observe them, must disclose the reason therefor ("comply or explain").[6]

14.2.3 An Analysis

In the United States and the United Kingdom, the prevailing view is that a company should be managed for the benefit of its shareholders. Yet, a different view – that corporate managers should consider the interests of employees and other stakeholders as well as those of shareholders – is more prevalent in Germany and France, as it is in Japan. However, the "monitoring model" – where outside directors supervise the corporate managers through the board of directors – has prevailed in Germany and France as well. Therefore, the difference between the views regarding "for whom a company should be managed" held by both the United States and the United Kingdom on the one hand, and those of Japan on the other, cannot independently explain the reason why outside directors are rare in Japan.

14.3 CORPORATE LAW IN JAPAN

14.3.1 History of the *Kansayaku* System

Corporate scandals occurred in Japan in the mid-1960s, as they had in the United States in the 1970s. Sanyo Special Steel Co., Ltd, a corporation listed on the Tokyo Stock Exchange (TSE), was discovered to have made misrepresentations on its financial statements, going bankrupt in March of 1965. Yamaichi Securities Co., Ltd, a large investment bank, came so close to bankruptcy that the government had to bail it out in May of 1965. These incidents highlighted the need to improve the management of large corporations.

The Ministry of Justice initiated revision of the Commercial Code in 1974, extensively overhauling the then-existing *kansayaku* system. *Kansayaku*, translated as "corporate auditor" or "statutory auditor,"[7]

---

6 Reinier Kraakman et al., The Anatomy of Corporate Law, 2nd edn, at 65ff. (Oxford 2009).

7 How to translate the word *kansayaku* into English has always been a problem. Recently, the Japan Corporate Auditors Association announced that it recommends the words *kansayaku* and *kansayaku-kai* (board of *kansayaku*) be translated as "audit and supervisory board member" and "audit and

is part of a unique system that has no equivalent in Western corporate law. A *kansayaku* is elected at the general shareholders' meeting of the company. The *kansayaku* is not engaged in the management of the company, but supervises its directors and employees. Notice that most of the "directors" in Japanese corporations are officers who engage in the day-to-day management of the company. A *kansayaku* must check whether the directors and employees are compliant with applicable laws and regulations, and whether the directors fulfill their fiduciary duties to the company. A *kansayaku*, however, only has authority to give opinions on the appropriateness of the business judgment of the board of directors; they cannot vote on board resolutions.

Since the 1974 amendments, the *kansayaku* system has been revised several times. As of fall 2012, the rules regarding the *kansayaku* system are as follows. A *kansayaku* may, at any time, request reports on the business from the directors and employees or investigate the status of operations as well as the financial status of the company. They shall attend the board of directors meetings, and shall state their opinions, if necessary. They may enjoin the directors of the company from acting in violation of the law (in practice, by filing a motion for injunctive relief). A large company shall have a board of *kansayaku* (three or more *kansayaku*), and at least half of them shall be outside *kansayaku*.[8] The board of *kansayaku* shall appoint one or more full-time *kansayaku* from among themselves. In terms of the election of *kansayaku* to serve the company, the board of directors of the company has the primary authority to nominate candidates and submit the agenda to the shareholders' meeting. However, the board of *kansayaku* has veto power over this selection and the authority to overwrite the board of directors' agenda with its own. A *kansayaku* may give their opinion on the appointment or dismissal of *kansayaku* at the general shareholders' meeting. In addition, the board of directors has the primary authority to elect an accounting firm to serve the company, but the board of *kansayaku* has veto power. Regarding the remuneration of this accounting firm, the board of directors has the primary power to determine the amount; although the board of *kansayaku* is able to invalidate the decision, it has

---

supervisory board," respectively. The background of this change is shown in the Japan Corporate Auditors Association's *New Recommended English Translation for "kansayaku" and "kansayaku-kai", available at* http://www.kansa.or.jp/en/ns121023.pdf.

[8] "Outside *kansayaku*" means a *kansayaku* of the company who has never served as a director, *kaikei-sannyo* (accounting advisor), executive officer, or employee of the company or any of its subsidiaries. Section 2, subparagraph 16 of the Companies Act.

no authority to determine a different amount which it believes to be more appropriate.[9]

The requirement for a *kansayaku* is not merely a rule on the books. There have been a few instances where the *kansayaku* of the listed company, believing that the CEO of the company was engaged in illegal acts, bravely fought against him.[10] That is, the system is not paralyzed; rather, it can fulfill a monitoring function, especially when *kansayaku* of integrity and action are present within the company.

It is believed, however, that in many companies, the nomination and compensation of both directors and *kansayaku* are in fact decided by the CEO of the company. Therefore, there is a suspicion that *kansayaku* are dependent on the executive officers of the company, either economically or intellectually. The degree of independence probably varies from one company to another. As stated earlier, a *kansayaku* can give opinions on the appropriateness of the business judgment of the management, but cannot vote on board resolutions. Thus, *kansayaku* are deemed incomplete substitutes for outside directors.

The 2002 revision of the Commercial Code enabled Japanese companies to opt out of the *kansayaku* system and adopt a "company with three committees," modeled on the practices of US-listed companies. However, only a small number (approximately 2 percent) of listed companies have adopted the latter system.[11]

---

[9] The *kansayaku* system is explained on the website of the Japan Corporate Auditors Association. *See* http://www.kansa.or.jp/en/about-corporate-auditor/about.html.

[10] In June 2008, an outside *kansayaku* of the Ebara Corporation insisted that the financial statements of the company were prepared by the management without a proper survey of possible misconduct, and refused to approve the statements. The other *kansayaku* of the company thought and behaved differently in this difficult case. Yet, the case of Kasuga Electric Works, Ltd was, without doubt, a vicious example. The company had made a questionable loan to its CEO. The full-time *kansayaku* of the company filed several lawsuits against the company and directors in order to protect the interests of the company, and the court issued injunctive relief in November 2008. *See* Toshiaki Yamaguchi, *Kansayaku no Kengen* [The Authority of Kansayaku], *in* SHINSAKU IWAHARA ET AL. (EDS), KAISHA HÔ SEKÔ 5 NEN: RIRON TO JITSUMU NO GENJÔ TO KADAI [Five Years since the Effectuation of Company Act: The Current Condition and the Agenda of Theory and Practice] Jurisuto Zôkan 37, at 38ff.

[11] Ronal J. Gilson and Curtis J. Milhaupt, *Choice as Regulatory Reform: The Case of Japanese Corporate Governance*, 53 AM. J. COMP. L. 343 (2005) at 354ff; Tokyo Stock Exchange, Inc., *TSE-Listed Companies White Paper on Corporate Governance 2011*, *supra* note 1, at 15.

14.3.2 Recent Reforms

In 2009, the TSE and other exchanges in Japan revised their listing rules to require listed companies to appoint "independent *yakuin*" (*yakuin* refers to either a director or a *kansayaku*). The TSE, however, has not mandated the appointment of outside directors to date.[12] Based on a report by foreign investors,[13] the requirement set by the TSE is the least demanding among the listing rules of stock exchanges of Asian countries.

In the deliberations leading to the revision of the Companies Act between 2010 and 2012, the pros and cons of obligating listed companies to appoint an outside director were debated. Finally, the council refrained from imposing a legal obligation. Instead, the council members reached an agreement that the issue should be dealt with through the listing rules of the stock exchanges, and a collateral resolution in favor of the agreement was passed by the Legislative Council of the Ministry of Justice in September 2012; what those listing rules will be has not been confirmed yet.

The council decided that a new system utilizing a *kansa-kantoku* committee would be introduced during revision of the Act, which will likely be passed by the Diet in 2014. Listed companies have the third option of adopting a *kansa-kantoku* committee. This committee is quite similar to the audit committee of Western countries in the sense that outside directors of the company are supposed to manage internal control and audits as members of the committee, as well as to supervise the management as members of the entire board of directors. Nobody knows how many companies will adopt the third system in the future.

14.3.3 Perceived Role of Board of Directors

Another feature of listed companies in Japan is that the board of directors tends to be involved in the decision of relatively minor matters of the company. In other words, the role of board of directors in Japan

---

[12] The TSE has worked hard to upgrade the corporate governance of Japanese companies. See its website, http://www.tse.or.jp/english/listing/cg/. The Tokyo Stock Exchange, Inc., *TSE-Listed Companies White Paper on Corporate Governance 2011*, *supra* note 1, provides comparisons to the findings of previous research and focuses on the state of implementation of new measures of the TSE's listing system, such as the independent *yakuin* system.

[13] Asian Corporate Governance Association, *Rules & Recommendations on the Number of Independent Directors in Asia* (*August 2010*), available at http://www.acga-asia.org/

is perceived not as monitoring the executives, but as participating in decision-making, as explained below.

In the United States, the traditional corporate statutes provide that the business and affairs of a corporation shall be managed by a board of directors. As early as 1945, however, it was reported that the boards of large companies did not initiate decisions on either specific matters or broad policies.[14] With this perception in mind, a proposal was made in the 1970s, assigning to the board of directors a cluster of functions which they can perform and which cannot easily be performed by any other corporate organ, including selecting, monitoring, and removing the members of the chief executive's office. In order for a board of directors to perform those functions, the proposal went on, the board should be made independent of the executives whose performance is being monitored, thus assuring a flow of adequate and objective information on the executives' performance.[15]

In Japan, the Commercial Code had a provision for the authority of a board of directors that was substantially congruent with the traditional corporate statutes. The interpretation of that provision as to the extent of matters that required board resolution was disputed, but the more influential view that significant actions of a company must be decided by such board resolution prevailed, and thus delegation of those actions to the executives was not allowed.[16] It was also a common practice at the time that significant business decisions such as the sale of important assets of the company were decided by the board.[17] This practice was codified by the 1981 revision of the Commercial Code for the sake of clarifying its interpretation.[18] After the

---

[14] See Melvin Aron Eisenberg, THE STRUCTURE OF THE CORPORATION: A LEGAL ANALYSIS (Little, Brown, 1976), at 139ff.

[15] Eisenberg, *supra*, at 169ff.

[16] *See e.g.*, Teruhisa Ishii, KAISHA-HÔ JÔ-KAN [Company Law, Vol. 1] (Keisô Shobô, 1967), at 326f.

[17] Practitioners' manuals for listed companies and other large companies at the time showed a couple of samples of rules and procedures (i.e., by-laws) that classified a sale of important assets and other similar transactions as within the board's authority. *See* Shôji-Hômu Kenkyû-Kai (ed.), TORISHIMARI-YAKU, KANSAYAKU HANDOBUKKU [Handbook for Directors and Kansayaku], (Shôji-Hômu Kenkyû-Kai, 1965), at 182, 185 & 189; Shôji-Hômu Kenkyû-Kai (ed.), TORISHIMARI-YAKU HANDOBUKKU [Handbook for Directors], (Shôji-Hômu Kenkyû-Kai, 1975), at 261.

[18] According to the account of the public officials in charge of the Commercial Code revision, the revision of the rule of the board of directors was made mainly for clarifying the ambiguous provisions at the time, and thus it seems that they did not intend to change the substance, but only to confirm the practice in those days. *See* Takeo Inaba, *Shô-Hô tô no Ichibu wo Kaisei suru Hôritsu no Gaiyô, (Chû 2)* [The Summary of the Act revising the Commercial Code and others (Part 2-1)], 909 JUNKAN SHÔJI-HÔMU 8 (1981), at 13f.

codification, however, the interpretation that a sale of even a relatively small asset requires board approval gradually became prevalent.[19]

Recently, several legal reforms have been made to facilitate an appointment of outside directors by Japanese companies. The 2002 revision of the Commercial Code introduced the system of "a company with three committees," as explained in section 14.3.1, as well as enabling the board of such a company to delegate a wide range of managerial decision-making authority to the executives of the company. The same revision also enabled a board with one or more outside directors to delegate some range of managerial decision-making power to the designated directors, who are usually a subset of the inside directors, even if the company does not opt out of the *kansayaku* system to adopt the "company with three committees" approach. The subset of inside directors was called *jûyô zaisan iinkai* (important asset committee) at first, and later, it was renamed so that the designated directors are now called *tokubetsu torishimariyaku* (special directors). However, the proportion of companies that have adopted the committee system has been quite small, and that of companies that have adopted special directors is even smaller.[20] This means that Japanese

---

[19] Two years after the revision of the code, a practitioners' manual included a proposal that was a rough standard for distinguishing the "disposal of an important asset," which requires a board resolution, from that of an unimportant asset, which does not require a board resolution, namely, the amount of the one-thousandth (1/1000) of the total assets of the company. Shôji-Hômu Kenkyû-Kai (ed.), Torishimari-yaku Handobukku, Shin-pan [Handbook for Directors, 2nd edn], (Shôji-Hômu Kenkyû-Kai, 1983), at 327.

In 1994, the Supreme Court of Japan, dealing with the case of a small-sized company, held that a sale of shares in another company by the plaintiff company which amounted to approximately 1.6 percent of the total assets of the plaintiff could fall within the "disposition of an important asset," stating: "whether a certain act constitutes a disposition of important assets as set forth in Art. 260, Paragraph 2, Subparagraph 1 of the Commercial Code, should be determined on a comprehensive basis, taking into consideration various factors including but not limited to the value of such asset, the proportion of the value of such asset to the total asset value of the company, the purpose of owning such asset, the method of disposition, and the past treatment of such asset by the company." *K.K. Naraya v. Hotta* (Supr. Ct., decided on Jan. 20, 1994), 48-1 Minshû 1.

With this judgment in mind, the latest version of the practitioners' manual explained that a rough standard for distinguishing an important sale from an unimportant one would be 1 percent of the total assets of the company. Shôji-Hômu (ed.), Torishimari-yaku, Shikkô-yaku Handobukku [Handbook for Directors and Executive Officers], (Shôji-Hômu, 2008), at 130.

[20] A survey in 2009 showed that 96.6 percent of the responding companies did not have rules and procedures (by-laws) for special directors. Bessatsu Shôji-Hômu Henshû-bu (ed.), *Kaisha-Hô Ka ni okeru Torishimari-yaku-Kai no Unei Jittai* [The

companies are not eager to make use of those systems, even if those systems exonerate a board of directors from deciding minor issues.

In this way, Japanese companies tend to stick to a board function of decision-making rather than of monitoring. In other words, it is widely believed that a board of directors is an organ of the company that appropriately makes managerial decisions. Under this belief, managers of Japanese companies often insist that outside directors are useless, and an appointment of outside directors delays decision-making, thus making it harmful. As a corollary, the idea that the board of directors monitors the executives has not become prevalent in Japanese companies. For instance, it is the common practice in Japanese companies that setting employee-director compensation is a decision delegated to a particular director, usually the director-CEO.[21] It therefore seems that board practice and the related culture of "company community" discussed in sections 14.4 and 14.5 below do not marry well with the monitoring model for a board of directors.

14.4 INSTITUTIONAL AND CULTURAL FACTORS IN JAPAN

The following paragraphs explain why rules requiring listed companies to appoint outside directors have not been adopted, and why there are not many listed companies that voluntarily appoint outside directors.

The first factor explaining these issues lies in the legal rules. As explained in the previous section, Japan's Companies Act offers the *kansayaku* system, which substitutes outside directors for other entities tasked with monitoring the management in part. The second factor is a financial matter, namely that of the main bank system and cross-shareholding.[22]

The third factor relates to career advancement (or human resources). In Japan, an employee of a company rarely quits in order to move to

---

Actual Situation of Operation of Board of Directors under the Company Act], BESSATSU SHÔJI-HÔMU 334 (Shôji-Hômu, 2009) at 60f.

[21] A recent survey showed that many listed companies delegate the decision on directors' compensation to a particular director. Bessatsu Shôji-Hômu Henshû-bu (ed.), *supra* note 20, at 61. The Supreme Court approved this practice. *Matsuo v. Ajinomoto K.K.*, (Supr. Ct., decided on Feb. 22, 1983), 138 Shûmin 201.

[22] Takeo Hoshi, *The Economic Role of Corporate Grouping and the Main Bank System*, *in* Masahiko Aoki and Ronald Dore (eds), THE JAPANESE FIRM: SOURCES OF COMPETITIVE STRENGTH 285 (Oxford 1994); Paul Sheard, *Interlocking Shareholdings and Corporate Governance in Japan*, *in* Aoki & Dore, *supra*, 310.

another company; that is, lifetime employment is common. The norm is that the CEO and the other board members of a large corporation are promoted from within as a result of ascending the corporate ladder. The external labor market for managers, employees, and outside directors is underdeveloped.[23]

The fourth factor is cultural. A company is often equated not with its shareholders, but with a "company community,"[24] which is comprised of the managers and core employees. In Japanese companies, firm-specific skills and contextual knowledge are deemed important, and attachment to manufacturing is repeatedly emphasized. Managers of a company prefer avoiding employee lay-offs to receiving additional compensation.

Most features of the second and third factors mentioned above resulted from several reforms enacted during the post-World War II period. At the time, the General Headquarters of the Allied nations (GHQ) dictated the dissolution of *zaibatsu* conglomerates, and therefore, the shares of *zaibatsu* companies were sold to citizens at a discounted price. However, members of the public were not rich enough to continue holding the shares, and thus, the shares of large corporations were sold in the market. As a result, listed companies mutually held them. This is the origin of cross-shareholding in Japan.[25] GHQ also dictated that numerous managers of large companies be purged, on the theory that they had collaborated with Japan's army in inciting World War II. The empty seats in these companies were filled with former factory managers. The promotion of inside workers to the position of CEO and to other board member seats soon became the norm. During

---

23 Masahiko Aoki, INFORMATION, INCENTIVES, AND BARGAINING IN THE JAPANESE ECONOMY (Cambridge 1988), at 49ff.; Hideshi Itoh, *Japanese Human Resource Management from the Viewpoint of Incentive Theory*, *in* Aoki and Dore, *supra* note 22, 233.

24 *See* Zenichi Shishido, *Japanese Corporate Governance: The Hidden Problems of Corporate Law and Their Solutions*, 25 DEL. J. CORP. L. 189 (2000), at 201ff.

25 Hideaki Miyajima & Fumiaki Kuroki, *The Unwinding of Cross-Shareholding in Japan: Causes, Effects, and Implications*, *in* Masahiko Aoki, Gregory Jackson, & Hideaki Miyajima (eds), CORPORATE GOVERNANCE IN JAPAN: INSTITUTIONAL CHANGE AND ORGANIZATIONAL DIVERSITY 79 (Oxford 2007), 83f.; Hideaki Miyajima, *Zaibatsu Kaitai* [The Dismantlement of Zaibatsu Conglomerates], *in* Center for Business and Industrial Research, Hosei Univ., Juro Hashimoto & Haruhito Takeda (eds), NIHON KEIZAI NO HATTENN TO KIGYÔ SHÛDAN [The Development of the Japanese Economy and Company Groups] 203 (University of Tokyo Press, 1992); Hideaki Miyajima, *Zaikai Tsuihô to Keieisha no Senbatsu* [The "Purge" and Selection of the Management of Large Companies] (hereinafter cited as "Miyajima, *Zaikai Tsuihô*"), *in* Juro Hashimoto (ed.), NIHON KIGYÔ SHISUTEMU NO SENGO-SHI [The History of the Japanese Corporate System after World War II] 43 (University of Tokyo Press, 1996), at 63f, 69f, 92f.

the high-growth period, starting around 1955, it became customary for the incumbent CEO to nominate their successor.[26]

Let me present an anecdote regarding the third factor of career advancement and the fourth factor of corporate culture. In 1975, the Ministry of Justice published inquiries for revising the Commercial Code. The list included items such as "limiting the maximum number of directors to 20," "prohibiting a director from serving also as an employee" (meaning as a subordinate to the senior executives), and "requiring large corporations to appoint a minimum number of outside directors." However, according to Professor Egashira, "nobody believed that those revisions would come true or some companies would voluntarily adopt those measures."[27] It may be that an insider-dominated board was rational and efficient at the time, able to recognize that the employees had only limited opportunities to move to another company, and that the insider board system gave them incentives to work hard and try to receive positive evaluations. Thus, the system functioned as efficient labor management.

Cross-shareholding weakened the voice of outside investors. The main bank monitored the management of debtor companies to some extent. Keeping outsiders out of the corporate board may have prompted employees to expect promotions and the management to preserve its own autonomy. In this way, the second factor of finance and the third of career advancement complement each other, and they also complement the fourth factor, that is, that a company is often equated with a "company community" consisting of the managers and core employees. As stated in section 14.3.1, however, a *kansayaku* only has authority to give opinions on the appropriateness of the business judgment of the board of directors, and cannot vote on board resolutions. This weakness of the *kansayaku* system was mitigated at the time by the following two circumstances. First, the main bank played a complementary monitoring role. Second, the autonomy given to the managers and employees motivated them to maximize company value. Therefore, the four factors stated above

---

26 Hideaki Miyajima, *Senmon Keieisha no Seiha* [The Triumph of Professional Managers], *in* Hiroaki Yamazaki and Takeo Kikkawa (ed.), Nihon Keiei-shi [The History of Company Management in Japan], Vol. 4 "Nihon-teki" Keiei no Renzoku to Danzetsu [The Continuity and Disconnection of "Japanese-style" Company Management] 75 (Iwanami Shoten, 1995), at 101; Miyajima, *Zaikai Tsuihô*, *supra* note 25, at 59–64, 78ff., 84ff.

27 Kenjirô Egashira, *Kôporeito Gabanansu no Kadai* [The Agenda in Corporate Governance], 558 Ginkô Hômu-21 4, at 8. According to Egashira, at 9, there was a joke at that time that "if anyone is bold enough to try to revise the Commercial Code as such, salary workers will riot" (i.e., commit sabotage).

complemented one another, and altogether, they constituted a unique system of corporate governance in Japan.

14.5 WILL THE APPOINTMENT OF OUTSIDE DIRECTORS BE WIDESPREAD IN JAPAN IN THE FUTURE?

Among the factors discussed in section 14.4 favoring insider-dominated boards, the second one (the financial factor) has been changing. The gradual deregulation of the financial market from 1980 through 2000 enabled many Japanese companies to utilize financing through the market, and thus, the voice of the main bank weakened. In the latter half of the 1990s, many banks in Japan experienced a financial crisis. Non-financial companies sold their stakes in banks to avoid capital losses, and banks had to sell their stakes in non-financial companies to obtain the money to write off non-performing loans, which led to a dramatic decline in cross-shareholding. The changes in accounting rules, such as the introduction of consolidated accounting and mark-to-market (current value) accounting around 2000, also spurred non-financial companies to sell their stakes in banks. The Banks' Shareholding Restriction Act, enacted in 2001, required banks to reduce their shareholdings drastically.[28]

By contrast, foreign institutional investors at that time increased their stakes in Japanese companies.[29] A positive correlation has been observed between the rate of foreign investors' stakes in a particular company and the number of outside directors at that company.[30] After 2006, the rate of cross-shareholding again increased. However, the extent of mutual shareholding between a bank and a non-financial company has not increased on average. Instead, non-financial companies increased mutual shareholdings between themselves. The increase in the cross-shareholding rate was only a fraction of the rate of its decline during the period around 2000.[31]

---

28 Miyajima and Kuroki, *supra* note 25, at 90f.

29 Miyajima and Kuroki, *supra* note 25, at 86ff.

30 Takuji Saitô, *Nihon Kigyô ni yoru Shagai Torishimari-yaku no Dônyû no Kettei Yôin to sono Kôka* [The Determinants of the Appointment of Outside Directors by Japanese Companies, and the Effect of the Appointment], *in* Hideaki Miyajima (ed.), NIHON NO KIGYÔ TÔCHI [Corporate Governance in Japan] 181, (Tôyô Keizai Shimpô-sha, 2011) at 199, 200. Concerning the investment strategy of foreign investors in Japanese companies, *see* Sanford M. Jacoby, *Convergence by Design: The Case of CalPERS in Japan*, 55 AM. J. COMP. L. 239 (2007).

31 Hideaki Miyajima and Keisuke Nitta, *Kabushiki Shoyû Kôzô no Tayôka to*

It should be noted, however, that the decline in cross-shareholding did not proceed at a similar pace across all listed companies. In companies that were profitable and had a high proportion of foreign ownership, the management tended to dissolve the cross-shareholding and succeeded in increasing market capitalization. In companies that had the opposite characteristics, the management tended to maintain cross-shareholding with banks, as they needed the bank both for financing and for the stabilization of shareholders. In a company with cross-shareholding, neither its bank nor the management has an incentive to dissolve the shareholding. In some (profitable) companies, the inertia of cross-shareholding was broken with the external shocks of the late 1990s. Other companies were locked into the traditional pattern of cross-shareholding, which generated a vicious circle of low profitability and lax governance.[32]

It is also noteworthy that domestic institutional investors may exhibit a behavioral pattern that does not contribute to the maximization of the wealth of the company in which they invest. Around the year 2000, the Pension Fund Association (PFA) in Japan tried to boost the influence of pension funds on listed companies by encouraging pension fund managers to exercise the voting rights attached to the shares they held.[33] A pension fund manager, however, did not find that interference in the governance of the company would increase their employment opportunity or bonuses. As a result, the PFA gave up its policy agenda around the fall of 2010. Life insurance companies in Japan, though holding large stakes in listed companies, hope to sell their insurance policies to businesses, and thus prevent voting in a manner hostile to incumbent managers within the company. If that is the case, they prioritize their own businesses' benefit over benefits to policyholders.[34]

The third factor, career advancement, and the fourth factor, corporate culture, both discussed in section 14.4, have been changing slowly. The latest monograph shows empirically that Japanese companies are run in a way that balances the various stakeholders' interests, and that Japanese

---

sono Kiketsu [Diversification of Share Ownership Structures and Its Consequence], *in* Miyajima (ed.), *supra* note 30, at 117, 129.

32 Miyajima and Kuroki, *supra* note 25, at 117; Miyajima and Nitta, *supra* note 31, at 142.

33 Takaya Seki, *Legal Reform and Shareholder Activism by Institutional Investors in Japan*, 13-3 CORPORATE GOVERNANCE 377 (2005), at 382f.

34 Kenichi Osugi, *Recent Reform of Japan's Corporate Law in an International Context: Who Have Participated in the Reforms, and How?* 53 JAPANESE YEARBOOK OF INTERNATIONAL LAW 320 (2010), at 337.

managers feel this is the right way to run companies.[35] This research suggests that the incentive bargaining of a Japanese firm may have shifted emphasis from a "bargaining image" to a "balancing image," in Professor Shishido's terminology.[36] Judging from the author's conversation with several managers of Japanese companies, it seems that they do not think highly of Western governance mechanisms (such as outside directors, performance-based bonuses, and so on). I am sure that they are seriously concerned about preventing corporate scandals and mishaps, but they consider the company's performance to be merely influenced by the competence and discretion of the management: they pay little attention to the need for monitoring when discussing corporate governance.

In sum, both the decline of cross-shareholding and the stable norm of "company community" act as elements that simultaneously prompt and hinder the introduction of outside directors in Japan in many ways.

14.6 CONCLUSIONS

The law, including soft law (such as listing rules), is not omnipotent. A rule that requires a company to appoint outside directors does not guarantee that they will function well. A change of rules, however, may shift the balance of power among the players in Japanese companies and society, and thus change the way actors think and behave. This scenario has occurred since the late 1990s, as shown in section 14.5. Future changes in laws and listing rules, explained in section 14.3.2, may prompt Japanese managers to utilize outside directors.

In this chapter, I demonstrated that cross-shareholdings in Japan have undergone serious change, but both the external labor market for managers and employees and the norm of "company community" have only been transformed slightly. I speculate that the number of outside directors will not increase quickly for the moment, and that two groups of companies will emerge, namely those that will utilize outside directors and those that will not.

---

[35] Shinichi Hirota, KABUNUSHI SHUKEN WO KOETE: SUTEIKU-HORUDÂ GATA KIGYÔ NO RIRON TO JISSHÔ [Beyond the Shareholder Supremacy: The Theory and Empirical Studies on Stakeholder-Oriented Corporations] (Tôyô Keizai Shimpôsha, 2012).

[36] The two images in the text are defined and explained in Shishido's "Introduction" to this volume.

Comments on Part III: the diversification of corporate governance arrangements: ownership structure and the board of directors

Hideaki Miyajima

CIII.1 COMBINING THE LAW AND EMPIRICAL STUDIES

Part III of this book addresses several critical issues, ranging from corporate ownership and the board of directors to the rule related to takeover defenses. As for the rule of takeover defenses, Sekiguchi and Iida (Chapter 12) explore whether the current appraisal remedy available under the Companies Act is an appropriate method for regulating the conflicts that arise in the context of mergers. This topic is extremely important because the conflicts of interest between directors (controlling shareholders) and minority shareholders continue to grow more serious, as the number of management buyouts (MBOs) and acquisitions by parent (controlling) firms of their listed subsidiaries have increased. Hoshi (Chapter 13) examines whether the Japanese legislature should allow for injunctions against corporate takeovers through analyzing a simple model. The key factor of his insightful analysis is the uncertainty that exists in judicial valuation of corporate takeover activities, which may influence the effectiveness of the appraisal system and the injunction system.

The rest of this chapter focuses on issues related to ownership and the board of directors. Since I have examined the evolution of corporate governance arrangements in Japan over the past decades, I would like to highlight several background facts and compiled recent empirical results on the topics at hand. The following should help facilitate understanding of the contributions made in each chapter and hopefully inspire further research.

CIII.2 FROM INSIDER DOMINATED TO "OUTSIDER DOMINATED" STRUCTURE

During the past decades, Japanese firms have experienced drastic changes to the makeup of their ownership structures. Figure CIII.1 shows the long-term evolution of ownership since the middle of the twentieth century. Outside owners are defined as shareholders whose interests are restricted to the financial performance of their investments; they do not derive "private benefits" that may conflict with financial considerations. Examples of outside owners are individuals, financial institutions (including securities houses), mutual funds and foreign investors (the main component of "Foreigner" in Figure CIII.1). On the other hand, inside owners consist of banks, insurance companies, and other companies whose interests extend beyond the pure financial performance of the company; their interests are sustained by considerations such as their employment and creditors.[1]

First, Figure CIII.1 makes clear that the turning point in the ownership structure of Japanese listed firms was in 1997, when the banking crisis happened. The insider-dominated ownership structure emerged during the high-growth era from 1950 to 1970 and, surprisingly, remained stable thereafter until the middle of the 1990s. However, since the late 1990s, the insider-dominated structure rapidly transformed into an outsider-dominated one. Inside ownership such as cross-shareholding between banks and firms is becoming less prevalent among Japanese firms. Accordingly, it is quite natural that Eguchi (Chapter 10) focuses on protecting managerial discretion rather than protecting minority shareholders; the topic itself reflects the increasing influence of outsider ownership.

However, this shift from an insider- to outsider-dominated structure seemingly stopped around 2006, when shareholding by foreign institutional investors reached its peak at 28 percent. Furthermore, this coincided with the occurrence of "widespread" hostile takeover attempts, and the introduction of takeover defenses within many Japanese firms (see Milhaupt, Chapter 9). Many pointed to a "revival" of cross-shareholding, yet it is worth noting that this practice is not common among all listed firms, and there has been no reverse trend toward inside ownership as a whole.

Second, the shift from insider to outsider ownership did not happen consistently among firms. When we divide all Tokyo Stock Exchange

---

[1] From the data provided by the Tokyo Stock Exchange, it is impossible to separate shares held by family members and directors (who should be categorized, in theory, as insiders) from shares held by "individuals."

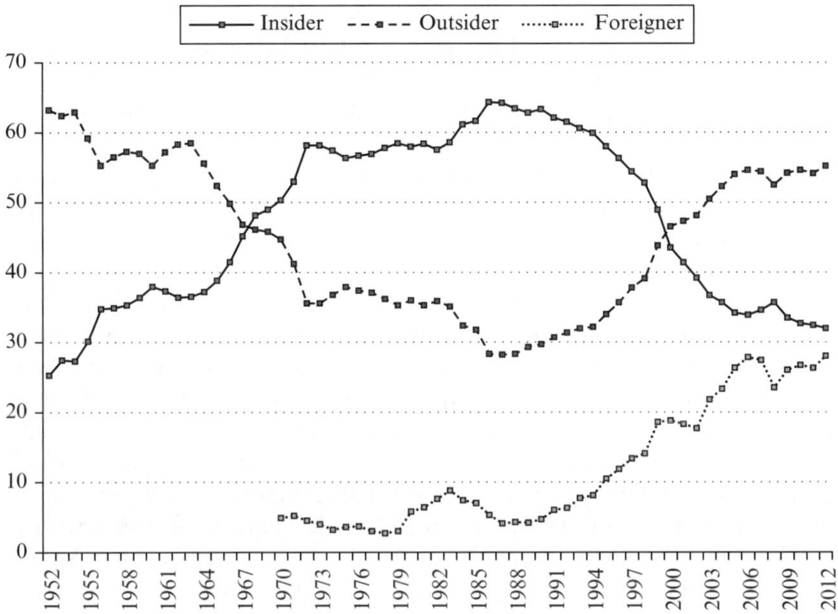

Notes: This figure shows insider and outsider ownership ratios based on the Shareownership Survey of the Tokyo Stock Exchange. Insider ratio represents the aggregated ratio of city and regional banks, life insurers, other financial institutions, and business firms. Outsider ratio represents the aggregated ratio of foreigners, individuals, investment trusts, and pension trusts. Ownership ratio is aggregated on a market capitalization basis. For data unavailable prior to fiscal year 1969, the ownership ratio data is based on the number of shares.

Source: Compiled from Tokyo Stock Exchange, *Shareownership Survey*.

Figure CIII.1 Long-term trends in ownership structure

(TSE) listed firms into five groups based on their market capitalization, the simple average percentage of shares held by outside shareholders in the group with the highest capitalization was 26 percent in the end of FY 2006, while that of the group with the lowest capitalization was only 4.8 percent.[2] The diversification of ownership structures was partly caused by uneven replacement of cross-shareholdings among Japanese firms. It is also a result of the investment bias of foreign shareholders, who prefer

[2] Miyajima, H. & Hoda, T., Henbôsuru Nihon-Kigyô no Shoyû-Kôzô wo ikani Rikai suru ka: Naigai-Kikan-Tôshika no Meigara-Sentaku no Bunseki wo Chûshin toshite [Understanding the Changing Ownership Structure of Japanese Firms: Investment Style of Foreign and Domestic Institutional Investors], Financial Research Center (FSA Institute) Discussion Paper 2011–11 (in Japanese) (2012).

firms with large assets, high liquidity, high overseas sales ratio and thus, in sum, "well-known firms." Foreign institutional investors have generally invested in companies that have their stock incorporated into the MSCI (Morgan Stanley Capital International) index, which roughly includes the largest 350–400 firms.

Third, firms that are small and have difficulty accessing the capital markets, are likely to maintain inside ownership, especially bank ownership; Tokutsu (Chapter 11) focuses on this issue. The average prevalence of bank ownership has declined from 10 percent in 1996 to 3.8 percent in 2004, a relatively high standard deviation of 5.3 percent to 3.5 percent.[3] According to the estimation results of myself and Hoda, changes in bank ownership are inversely correlated to the dividend yield of firms, and positively correlated to their leverage.[4] It is clear that banks invest in their clients for the sake of maintaining transactional relationships rather than maximizing their financial performance. Consequently, firms in which banks still kept their large ownership stakes are likely to be low performers with high leverage, and thus, also likely to need corporate restructuring. Considering these facts, deregulation of the limitations on bank shareholding – which Tokutsu proposes after examining the legitimacy of the limitations – is highly relevant, as it may lead to the realization of efficient debt–equity swaps, which would be helpful for corporate restructuring in Japan.

Last, large Japanese firms are now facing new problems such as "managerial myopia" or "short-termism." In fact, the turnover ratio (sales volume over market capitalization) of the TSE rose from 0.246 on average during 1992–1996 to 1.36 during 2007–2012. Similarly to the US, the average shareholding period has significantly declined. Noticing these changes, Eguchi proposes establishing new arrangements in order to protect managerial discretion from the volatile pressure of capital markets without depending on cross-shareholding.

However, the difficulties that should be tackled for the benefit of leading Japanese firms are not limited to those related to protecting managerial autonomy. It is also important to strengthen the incentives offered to and

---

3 Miyajima, H. & Nitta, K., Kabushiki-Shoyû-Kôzô no Tayôka to sono Kiketsu [A Diversification of Ownership Structure and its Effect on Corporate Performance: Unwinding and Resurgence of Cross-Shareholdings and the Role of Surging Foreign Investors], in Miyajima, H. ed., Nihon no Kigyô-Tôchi: Sono Saisekkei to Kyôsôryoku no Kaifuku ni mukete [Corporate Governance in Japan: Toward its Redesign and Restoring of Competitive Edge], Tôyô-Keizai-Shinpôsha (in Japanese) (2011).

4 Miyajima, H. & Hoda, T. (2012), *supra* note 2.

the capabilities of the outsiders that monitor such leading firms. The case of Olympus illustrates the problem. Despite the significant deficiencies revealed by the circumstances surrounding the resignation of Michael Woodford and the demands for change made by several foreign investors, the restructuring of Olympus proved difficult to achieve. Insurance companies and banks retained a large block of shares (39.3 percent of the total outstanding shares in 2011), while the shareholding by outsiders was fragmented, in spite of their combined shareholding being higher than that of the insurance companies and banks (44 percent). Calls for intervention and change were met by roadblocks posed by the traditional elements that have dominated Japanese corporate control in the past. The consequences are that there is now a vacuum in regard to the exercise of corporate control, even among leading Japanese firms.

Thus, the future agenda for corporate governance arrangements in Japan should be to encourage long-term shareholder commitment to firms. In addition to the cooperative engagement among institutional investors that Eguchi proposes in Chapter 10, a dual class share system would be another alternative.[5] The more influential voting rights would be given to long-term shareholders which have the long-term interests of the corporation at heart. Such arrangements could come about through initiatives by Japanese firms seeking to achieve long-term, stable shareholders and effective governance over their activities, and through Japanese institutions taking an active interest in the performance and oversight of the firms in which they invest.

CIII.3 WHAT BINDS THE JAPANESE BOARD OF DIRECTORS?

Another vital issue that Japanese firms have confronted is outside independent directors (hereafter: outside directors). The ratio of outsider directors over total directors on average among the TSE-listed firms in 2010 was approximately 10 percent, which is far lower than that in the US (74 percent), the UK (60 percent), and even South Korea (27 percent) in 2008.[6] However, considering that this ratio was almost 0 percent in the early 2000s, it is clear that the number of outside directors has been

---

[5] Bolton, P. & Samama, F., L-Share: Rewarding Long-term Investors, (working paper, 2012); Mayer, C., Firm Commitment: Why the Corporation is Failing Us and How To Restore Trust in It, Oxford University Press (2013).

[6] CFA Institute, 2009, SHAREOWNER RIGHTS ACROSS THE MARKETS: A MANUAL FOR INVESTORS.

gradually increasing. In this regard, there are a growing number of empirical studies on the determinants of board structures and the performance effect on Japanese firms, using the standard model developed in the previous studies in the US.[7]

Myself and Ogawa have also estimated the board determinants model, taking the following variables as the explanatory variables: the complexity of business, the extent of the agency problems that a firm deals with, the difficulties for outsiders to get firm-specific information, and the negotiation powers of incumbent managers over shareholders. According to our regression results, the model can explain roughly 10 percent of the determinants of the board composition among Japanese firms, although most of the variables show the expected signs that the model predicts.[8] This suggests that the determinants of Japanese boards are different from those in the US and UK, where the standard model can explain 45 percent and 25 percent, respectively.[9] We have also found that firms with high institutional shareholdings have boards which are clearly composed in accordance with firm characteristics as compared to firms with low institutional shareholdings, suggesting that influential institutional shareholders encourage firms to elect board members which are suitable in consideration of their firms' characteristics.

Furthermore, the variables related to the advisory function (the complexity of business) are more powerful in explaining board composition compared to the variables related to monitoring functions.[10] This result is consistent with the understanding that the board structures of Japanese firms are mainly determined by corporate insiders rather than outsiders. This fact is also consistent with the observations of Milhaupt (Chapter 9) and Osugi (Chapter 14) regarding the fact that corporate

---

[7] Raheja, C., *Determinants of Board Size and Composition: A Theory of Corporate Boards*, Journal of Financial and Quantitative Analysis 40, 283–306 (2005). Linck, J., Netter, J., and Yang, T., *The Determinants of Board Structure*, Journal of Financial Economics 87, 308–328 (2008).

[8] Miyajima, H. and Ogawa, R., Nihon-Kigyô no Torishimariyakukai-Kosei no henka wo ikana rikai suru ka [How to Understandchanges in the structure of Japanese corporate boards], Junkan Shôji-Hômu, No. 1973, pp. 81–95 (in Japanese) (2012).

[9] For the US, *see supra* note 7; and for the UK, see Guest, P., *The Determinants of Board Size and Composition: Evidence from the UK*, Journal of Corporate Finance 14, 51–72 (2008).

[10] Saito, T Nihon-Kigyô ni okeru Shagai-Torishimariyaku no Donyu no Kettei-yôin to sono Kôka [The determinants and effect of outside directors in Japanese Firms], in Miyajima, H. ed., *supra* note 3 (in Japanese) (2011).

boards of Japanese firms are not monitoring boards, but management boards.

As for the performance effect of outside directors, while recent empirical studies show that there is no clear evidence that introducing outside directors improves corporate performance in general, there is some evidence that the introduction of outside directors could improve corporate performance in the case where a firm faced serious agency problems such as high cash holding; where a firm was less pressured by institutional shareholders; or where a firm has characteristics that allow an outside director to acquire firm-specific information easily.[11] The results of these studies imply that while a mandatory rule requiring outsider directors might be harmful, some measures that encourage use of outside directors would be useful. Thus, it would be reasonable for government to introduce "the comply or explain principle" rather than a mandatory rule.

The results of these studies further suggest that the introduction of outsider directors may not get to the core problems that Japanese firms face. As Osugi suggests in Chapter 14, the real issue is whether or not management boards should be converted into monitoring boards. It is true that there is a group of firms that currently have management board structures which are efficient. They are young, growing firms, with relatively simple business portfolios, under the pressure of competition in their product markets. However, empirical studies also suggest that there must be another group of firms that face agency problems. They are well-established, mature firms, with ample cash holding and takeover defenses, under low pressure in their product markets. For those firms, the role of the board should be converted from a management- to a monitoring-oriented structure. Otherwise the introduction of outside directors may result in mere window dressing.

The next natural question is how to encourage these firms to move from a management board to a monitoring board. As Milhaupt suggests in Chapter 9, it is important to consider legal incentives that could encourage this functional shift. Without legal incentives, the newly drafted organizational option, the *kansa-kantoku* committee, is not likely to be chosen.[12]

Last, it should be emphasized that the mission of monitoring boards and outside directors in Japanese firms is not limited to maximizing

---

[11] Uchida, K. Shagai-Torishimariyaku-wariai no Kettei-Yôin to Pafômansu The Determinants of Outside Directors and Performance], Shôken-Anarisuto Jânaru 50(5), 8–18 (in Japanese) (2012); Miyajima and Ogawa, *supra* note 8; and Saitoh, *supra* note 10.

[12] *See* Osugi, Chapter 14 in this volume.

shareholder value. Given the governance structure of Japanese firms, in which employee commitment is strong and employee interests are critically important for value creation, the main role of monitoring boards and outside directors should be to maintain the right balance between the interests of shareholders and corporate insiders.

PART IV

The roles of governments

15. Taxation and incentives in the business enterprise

David Gamage and Shruti Rana

15.1 INTRODUCTION

Tax law is intimately connected to enterprise law.[1] In many legal practices, lawyers who serve enterprise clients regularly turn to tax lawyers for advice on structuring transactions. Often, the enterprise lawyers first devise a transaction in order to further some business-law-related end, and then turn to tax lawyers to insure that the transaction is structured in a tax-favorable manner. In other instances, tax lawyers devise transactions in order to minimize an enterprise client's tax liabilities, and then turn to the enterprise lawyers to structure the transaction in accordance with the client's non-tax goals. Enterprise lawyers and tax lawyers thus need a mutual understanding so that they can work together effectively to meet their clients' tax and non-tax goals. At a minimum, enterprise and tax lawyers need to know when to ask each other for advice and when to defer to each other's expertise to maximize client outcomes.

Similarly, anyone interested in the design of enterprise law must engage with, and understand the fundamentals of, taxation. Tax laws significantly impact all of the major incentive bargains analyzed in this volume. The agreements managers reach with employees, shareholders, and creditors are all regularly structured with an eye towards tax considerations.[2]

---

[1] *See* Dwight Drake, Business Planning: Closely Held Enterprises, at v (3rd ed., 2011); John Flood & Fabian Sosa, *Lawyers, Law Firms and the Stabilization of Transnational Business*, 28 Nw. J. Int'l L. & Bus. 489 (2008); Ronald J. Gilson, *Value Creation by Business Lawyers: Legal Skills and Asset Pricing*, 94 Yale L. J. 239 (1984).

[2] *See, e.g.*, Prakash Deo, *Cross-Border Lease Financing with Japanese Leveraged Leases*, J. Structured Finance, Winter 2008, at 36; Ronald J. Gilson & David M. Schizer, *Understanding Venture Capital Structure: A Tax Explanation for Convertible Preferred Stock*, 116 Harv. L. Rev. 874 (2003); Koji Toshima & Rintaro Shinohara, *Magic Triangles*, 27 Int'l Financial L. Rev. Guide to Japan 71 (2008).

Furthermore, tax law potentially offers policy-makers a powerful tool for influencing the incentive bargains that comprise the business enterprise.[3] Even if policy-makers do not explicitly wish to use tax law as a tool for regulating the business enterprise, tax laws will nevertheless remain an important background force that policy-makers must take into account. It is impossible to design a completely neutral tax system with respect to enterprise law's incentive bargains; taxation will inevitably impact these bargains, whether policy-makers wish it to or not. Consequently, a thorough examination of enterprise law requires substantively engaging with tax law and policy.

Section 15.2 thus elaborates the goals of taxation in order to explain the tax policy perspective on the interactions between tax law and enterprise law. Section 15.3 then outlines some of the ways in which taxation affects the incentive bargains related to enterprise law. Section 15.4 concludes with some final recommendations and insights.

15.2 THE TAX POLICY PERSPECTIVE

To understand why it is impossible to design a tax system that is neutral with respect to the incentive bargains that comprise the business enterprise, it is useful to begin by evaluating the goals of taxation. Anyone interested in the design of enterprise law must engage with the tax system and hence must understand the tax policy perspective on the interactions between taxation and enterprise law.

Nevertheless, before proceeding to evaluate the goals of taxation, we will first briefly discuss possible underlying models of government behavior. Much of tax policy scholarship adopts what might be called the beneficial dictator model.[4] This scholarship asks how a government concerned only with public welfare should design tax policy. This scholarship thus takes little account of the possibility that government actors may be influenced by goals other than promoting the general welfare.

In contrast, tax scholarship operating within the public choice tradition

---

[3] *See, e.g.*, Zenichi Shishido, *Reform in Japanese Corporate Law and Corporate Governance: Current Changes in Historical Perspective*, 49 AM. J. COMP. L. 653 (2001); James R. Hines, Jr, *Lessons from Behavioral Responses to International Taxation*, 52 NAT'L TAX J. 305, 308–19 (1999) (empirical observations of corporate behavior in response to tax policy).

[4] *See* James M. Poterba, *Public Finance and Public Choice*, *in* TAX POLICY IN THE REAL WORLD 429 (Joel Slemrod ed., 1999) (discussing critiques of the public finance tradition of tax policy scholarship).

frequently adopts what might be called the leviathan model of government behavior.[5] Under this model, governments are assumed to act so as to maximize the government's power, thus usually raising as much tax revenue as the government can get away with. Scholars who analyze tax policy based on leviathan models often focus on prescribing mechanisms for constraining the power of government actors. Questions related to determining what is the ideal tax system are viewed as less important, because a leviathan government would never enact an ideal tax system.

Between the extremes of the beneficial dictator and leviathan models, what might be called the interest group bargaining model assumes that governments sometimes pursue the general welfare and at other times attempt to reward narrow interest groups that can help politicians win re-election.[6] As a general rule of thumb, scholars often assume that governments are more concerned with broad public opinion and the general welfare when issues are highly salient, and that governments are more concerned with rewarding narrow interest groups when issues are less salient.[7]

Because our goal is to explain why it is not possible to design a tax system that is completely neutral with respect to the incentive bargains that comprise the business enterprise, we mostly adopt the beneficial dictator model in this chapter. Yet we do not mean to suggest that real-world governments operate following the beneficial dictator model. In our view, interest group bargaining models offer better predictions of real-world government behavior than do either the beneficial dictator or leviathan models. The beneficial dictator model does not sufficiently take account of the fact that politicians in democracies rely on the support of narrow interest groups whose goals do not always involve promoting the general welfare. And the leviathan model ignores that democratic governments are composed of many individual politicians facing collective action problems, such that even politicians unconcerned with the general welfare often have little incentive to prioritize expanding the government's powers. For enterprise law scholars, then, it is important to keep in mind that taxation will often affect enterprise law due to rules that governments design for

---

5 *See* Michael A. Livingston, *Reinventing Tax Scholarship: Lawyers, Economists, and the Role of the Legal Academy*, 83 CORNELL L. REV. 365, 382 (1998) (discussing the public choice tradition of tax policy scholarship).

6 For an early example of this form of scholarship, *see, e.g.*, Stanley S. Surrey, *The Congress and the Tax Lobbyist – How Special Tax Provisions Get Enacted*, 70 HARV. L. REV. 1145 (1957).

7 This idea is often called the Mancur Olson hypothesis, and is attributed to MANCUR OLSON, THE LOGIC OF COLLECTIVE ACTION: PUBLIC GOODS AND THE THEORY OF GROUPS (1965).

the benefit of particular narrow interest groups rather than for the goal of advancing the general welfare through sound tax policy.

15.2.1 The Goal of Minimizing Excess Burden

The most important reason why governments enact tax laws is to raise revenues for funding government spending. Yet a central dilemma of tax policy is that taxing any activity typically leads taxpayers to engage in less of that activity.[8] Hence, for example, taxing the income from work incentivizes taxpayers to shift from work to leisure; taxing purchased goods incentivizes taxpayers to buy less of the taxed goods; and taxing investment returns incentivizes taxpayers to make fewer taxable investments.

When taxation induces taxpayers to engage in less of a taxed activity, both the individual taxpayers and the government are made worse off. The taxpayers are made worse off because the taxpayers have shifted from a more desired activity – the activity the taxpayers would have preferred to engage in were it not for the tax – to a less desired activity. The government is made worse off because the government receives no revenue to the extent that taxpayers shift to untaxed activities. When taxation causes taxpayers to shift to untaxed alternative activities, then society as a whole is made worse off. This harm to society that results from tax-induced changes to taxpayer behavior is often called excess burden or deadweight loss.[9]

Consequently, a simple maxim for designing optimal tax policy is that governments should focus on taxing inelastic activities: activities for which taxpayers do not shift their behavior much in response to taxation. Another simple maxim is that it is usually best to make the tax base as comprehensive as possible; the more activities that are taxed at the same rate, the fewer options taxpayers have for shifting to untaxed or lower-taxed alternative activities.

Unfortunately, governments find it very difficult to tax capital income: the income that taxpayers earn from investments. Governments that rely significantly on income taxes, such as the US and Japan, thus face enormous problems in enacting a comprehensive tax base with respect to capital income.[10] Exacerbating this problem, wealthy taxpayers have developed a number of techniques for transforming the monetary compensation they

---

[8] David Gamage & Darien Shanske, *Three Essays on Tax Salience: Market Salience and Political Salience*, 65 TAX L. REV. 19, 61–63 (2011).

[9] For a more complete discussion, see *id.*

[10] *See generally* Alan J. Auerbach, *The Future of Captial Income Taxation*, INSTITUTE FOR FISCAL STUDIES ANNUAL LECTURE (2006), http://escholarship.org/uc/item/90v90406, (accessed 16/1/2014).

receive from working into a form that is taxed as capital income under an income tax rather than as labor income.[11] Hence, the difficulties governments face in taxing capital income threaten governments' ability to collect taxes from wealthy taxpayers even on their labor income. And the techniques that taxpayers use to minimize their tax liabilities, with respect to both capital income and labor income, create significant excess burden beyond the revenue loss to the government.

The transactions that wealthy taxpayers use to reduce their capital income tax liabilities, and the anti-abuse rules that governments develop in order to combat these transactions, have significant impacts on enterprise law. For instance, the income tax laws of both the US and Japan create a significant bias for debt-financing as opposed to equity financing.[12] Sophisticated taxpayers respond to this bias both by shifting from equity financing to debt financing and by creating new hybrid financial instruments that maintain some of the economic characteristics of equity while being taxed as debt. These tax-motivated transactions then significantly impact corporate governance, as equity holders and debtholders have different control rights, and as enterprise law must cope with the control rights granted to the holders of hybrid instruments.

15.2.2 The Goal of Promoting Distribution Policy

If policy-makers cared only about the goal of minimizing excess burden, then there would be a simple solution for designing the optimal tax system. Under a head tax, each citizen is taxed the exact same fixed amount; an amount that remains constant regardless of any activities or behaviors the taxpayers engages in. Hence, a head tax assesses tax liabilities based on an activity that is highly inelastic: being a citizen. The only option taxpayers have for escaping a head tax is to leave the country and renounce their citizenship.

The reason that governments do not exclusively rely on head taxes for raising revenues is distribution.[13] Even the most conservative of

---

[11] *E.g.*, Victor Fleischer, *Two and Twenty: Taxing Partnership Profits in Private Equity Funds*, 83 N.Y.U. L. Rev. 1 (2008) (analyzing one such technique).

[12] *E.g.*, Ruud A. de Mooij, *Tax Biases to Debt Finance: Assessing the Problem, Finding Solutions*, IMF Staff Discussion Note, May 3, 2011.

[13] We avoid the term "redistribution," instead using the phrase "distribution policy," because the term "redistribution" misleadingly implies a state-of-nature baseline prior to government in which taxpayers would control the entirety of their pre-tax incomes. For further discussion on this point, see Gamage & Shanske, *supra* note 8, at 79–98.

commentators generally agree that poorer citizens should not be assessed with the same tax liabilities as richer citizens. Note in this regard that even a pure flat tax is in no way a head tax. Under a pure flat tax, all citizens are assessed for tax liabilities based on the same percentage of their income or consumption. Because richer individuals have higher income and consumption than poorer individuals, a pure flat tax thus results in richer citizens paying far higher tax liabilities than poorer citizens. And conservative advocates of a flat tax rarely call for a pure flat tax. Instead, most proposals for a flat tax include an exemption amount, wherein income or consumption under a specified threshold is exempt from tax, thus making flat tax proposals even more progressive by reducing the effective tax rates on poorer taxpayers as compared to richer taxpayers.

A major reason why many support imposing taxes on corporations and large business enterprises is based on distribution. Liberals often argue that the incidence of taxes imposed on large business enterprises falls primarily on monetary capital providers, who tend to be far wealthier than workers or consumers.[14] However, the extent to which the incidence of taxes on large business enterprises actually falls on capital is not at all clear; much recent scholarship suggests that workers and consumers may bear the majority of the burden of these taxes.[15]

A simple maxim for evaluating tax incidence – who bears the economic burden of a tax – evaluates the relative elasticity of the parties that might potentially be subject to the tax.[16] With respect to corporate taxes and other taxes on large business enterprises, the question then becomes the extent to which workers are more able to switch jobs if their salaries are lowered, as compared to the extent to which consumers are more able to switch to buying alternative products if prices are raised, and as compared to the extent to which monetary capital providers are comparatively more able to switch their investment choices if the expected returns are lowered. Taxing large business enterprises reduces their profitability, which means that less money will be available to pay workers, keep prices low for consumers, and reward monetary capital providers. For distributional considerations, the question is which of these groups comparatively bears the greatest burdens from the tax.

Looking beyond taxes directly imposed on large business enterprises, distributional considerations also motivate other tax instruments that

---

[14] For a discussion of the debate over corporate tax incidence, *see* Alan J. Auerbach, *Who Bears the Corporate Tax? A Review of What We Know*, 20 Tax Policy And The Economy 1–40 (NBER, 2006).

[15] *Id.*

[16] *Id.*

significantly affect enterprise law's incentive bargains. Both the US and Japan have a progressive structure to their income taxes, wherein higher-income taxpayers face higher tax rates than do lower-income taxpayers.[17] The higher marginal income tax rates that high-income taxpayers face under a progressive income tax impact the compensation packages paid to managers and to other high-income workers, as higher marginal tax rates increase the incentives to structure compensation packages in a tax-advantaged fashion. For example, under the income tax laws of both Japan and the US, fringe benefits and performance-based compensation can often be made tax-favorable as compared to wage salaries, thus impacting the form of compensation paid to managers and workers, and thereby altering the incentive bargains reached between managers, employees, and monetary capital providers.

15.2.3 The Goal of Promoting Desirable Behavior

Beyond the goals of raising revenues while minimizing excess burden and promoting socially desirable redistribution, taxes are also used to influence taxpayer behavior. By taxing activities that generate negative externalities (harms that affect parties external to the taxpayer), or by granting tax credits or deductions for activities that generate positive externalities (benefits that accrue to parties external to the taxpayer), governments can induce taxpayers to internalize the externalities so that the taxpayer's decisions maximize social welfare rather than just the taxpayer's own welfare. Taxes designed to control externalities are sometimes called Pigouvian taxes. A classic example are taxes imposed on pollution, which if set correctly can cause the taxpayers to pollute only to the extent that the social benefit of the activity causing the pollution exceeds the harm caused by the pollution.[18]

Pigouvian taxes are less important with respect to enterprise law than are taxes designed to raise revenues and promote distribution policy. Yet both corporate and individual income taxes are filled with tax incentives designed to promote behavior that governments deem socially beneficial.

---

[17] Hiroshi Kaneko, *The Japanese Income Tax System and the Disparity of Income and Wealth Among People in Japan*, in *Proceedings from the 2009 Sho Sato Conference*, 3–4 (2009), *available at* http://www.law.berkeley.edu/files/sho_sato_tax_conf_web_paper--kaneko.pdf, (accessed 10/1/2012) (noting that the Japanese income tax has used progressive rates since its inception in the nineteenth century).

[18] For further discussion in another context, see David Gamage, *Taxing Political Donations: The Case for Corrective Taxes in Campaign Finance*, 113 YALE L. J. 1283 (2004).

These Pigouvian tax provisions can and do affect the incentive bargains of the business enterprise.

15.2.4 The Goal of Enacting Fiscal Stimulus

The final tax policy goal that we will discuss is probably the least important for enterprise law. Tax laws can play an important role in macroeconomic stabilization policy. Ideally, tax systems should be structured so as to provide fiscal stimulus during temporary economic downturns and to take away that stimulus during upturns. When government budgets do not need to be balanced in the short run, income taxes and especially corporate income taxes can provide stimulus, because these forms of taxation take far less revenue from the economy during economic downturns than during periods of strong economic growth.[19] The manner in which tax laws are designed to promote fiscal stimulus can affect enterprise law by impacting the timing of investment decisions and the attractiveness of debt as opposed to equity financing, which can affect the incentive bargains between managers and monetary capital providers. As both Japan and the US have been facing sustained periods of stagnant economic growth, the fiscal stimulus policies these governments adopt may carry significant stakes for the incentive bargains negotiated between managers and monetary capital providers.

15.3 TAXATION AND ENTERPRISE LAW'S INCENTIVE BARGAINS

Other chapters in this volume will analyze some of the specific ways in which taxation and other government activities affect enterprise law's incentive bargains. We aim in this chapter only to provide a brief overview of the goals of tax policy and how these goals inevitably lead to taxation impacting enterprise law. Our purpose is to assist readers interested in the design of enterprise law to understand the tax policy perspective so as to facilitate understanding between those interested in enterprise policy and those interested in tax policy. Having outlined the goals of tax policy, we can now analyze how managers, employees, and monetary capital providers respond to taxation.

However, as a preface, it is worth noting that while the laws governing

---

[19] *See, e.g.*, David Gamage, *Preventing State Budget Crises: Managing the Fiscal Volatility Problem*, 98 CAL. L. REV. 749, 787–88 (2010).

enterprises and taxation are often similar in the US and Japan,[20] the goals of policy-makers and other stakeholders often differ. For instance, many Japanese companies still place relatively greater emphasis on promoting the long-term welfare of their employees.[21] It is important to recognize and account for differences in legal cultures and context in considering the varied ways in which managers, employees, and monetary capital providers might respond to taxation.

15.3.1 How Managers Respond to Taxation

Individuals seek at least three rewards from their participation in the workplace: (1) monetary compensation; (2) non-monetary compensation such as fringe benefits; and (3) work-related power and prestige. Managers seek these rewards just as much as do non-managerial workers.

Within most income tax systems, monetary compensation is the most highly taxed; non-monetary fringe benefits often go only partially taxed or are not taxed at all; and work-related power and status are rarely taxed.[22] The reason for this disparity is valuation problems and concerns related to administrability. Tax agencies have no ready means for assessing the value of work-related power and status, and it is also prohibitively difficult to assess the value of many forms of fringe benefits.

Predictably, then, taxation biases managers toward seeking more untaxed fringe benefits and work-related power and prestige than they would in the absence of taxation. The higher the tax rates, the larger the bias against monetary compensation and toward these alternative workplace rewards.

Perhaps this bias plays out most powerfully in incentivizing managers to build empires through mergers and acquisitions and through investing earnings in questionable expansion projects rather than returning earnings to shareholders. Managers seek to build workplace empires partially for the rewards these empires offer in terms of work-related power and

---

[20] *See* Curtis J. Milhaupt, *A Relational Theory of Japanese Corporate Governance: Contract, Culture, and the Rule of Law*, 37 Harv. Int'l L. J. 3, 14–15 (1996) (explaining that US corporate and securities law were imported into Japan during the post-war period, and that following the war, with one major exception, the constituent organs of the Japanese corporation and the basic rules for its organization and governance took on a highly American cast).

[21] *Id.* at 26 (concern for the long-term welfare of employees serves as a major constraint on the Japanese firm).

[22] *See* Calvin H. Johnson, *An Employer-Level Proxy Tax On Fringe Benefits*, 123 Tax Notes 483, 483–86 (2009) (explaining some of the ways that fringe benefits are tax favored).

status. Were the managers to forgo these power and status-related rewards in order to focus exclusively on maximizing profits, at best the managers would receive higher monetary compensation (which is subject to taxation) in place of the foregone power and status (which is not subject to taxation).

This empire-building bias is only one of the ways in which taxation affects managers' incentives. As we noted earlier, taxation affects the forms of monetary compensation offered to managers and other employees, and this in itself can affect managers' incentives, particularly to the extent that taxation biases compensation packages toward stock options and other incentive-based forms of compensation as opposed to guaranteed salaries. Managers typically have significant power to negotiate compensation packages that are designed in a tax-favorable fashion.

15.3.2 How Employees Respond to Taxation

Employees have similar incentives to managers, although many (especially lower-income) employees may be relatively more motivated by the pursuit of monetary compensation and less by work-related power and prestige. Yet employees often have far less ability to negotiate custom compensation packages than do managers.

It is far more difficult to design tax-favored compensation packages for employees who are not able to negotiate for custom-tailored forms of compensation. These employees will typically prefer to be compensated in the form of cash wages, because receiving cash wages grants the employees flexibility in how to spend the wages. Cash wages are almost always fully taxable; providing compensation in a tax-favored form typically requires limiting employees' flexibility in how to use the compensation. Employees who are not in a position to custom negotiate a compensation package to design limitations that are not overly restrictive with respect to the employees' goals will thus often prefer to have their compensation fully taxed in order to maintain the flexibility of cash wages.

The incentive bargains managers reach with employees are also influenced by tax provisions that are regulatory in nature: tax provisions designed to encourage or discourage certain behaviors, in a Pigouvian fashion. In the US, for instance, beginning in 2014, employers may be subject to tax penalties for not providing their employees with affordable employer-sponsored health insurance.[23] US tax law also includes a number

[23] David Gamage, *Perverse Incentives Arising from the Tax Provisions of Healthcare Reform: Why Further Reforms are Needed to Prevent Avoidable Costs to Low and Moderate-Income Workers*, 65 Tax L. Rev. 669, 692–698, *available at*

of tax provisions that may penalize employers who offer fringe benefits if the employer offers the fringe benefits in a proscribed fashion.

15.3.3 How Monetary Capital Providers Respond to Taxation

Monetary capital providers are generally motivated by the desire to secure the highest possible returns to their investments. To this end, monetary capital providers sometimes also desire control rights over the business enterprises they invest in. The major influence of tax laws is to make certain forms of investments more tax-favorable than others, thus encouraging monetary capital providers to structure their investments in a tax-favorable fashion.

We have already noted that most developed-country tax systems treat debt investments more tax-favorably than equity investments.[24] This bias for debt financing both leads monetary capital providers to invest through debt instruments rather than equity investments, and encourages monetary capital providers to develop hybrid financial instruments with the tax characteristics of debt but some of the economic characteristics of equity.

Beyond the bias for debt financing, international tax rules also have a strong influence on investor behavior. It is often possible to make investments more tax-favorable by structuring the investments as cross-border transactions. The flaws in the international tax rules of the US and other nations are legendary.[25] The desire to minimize tax liabilities by exploiting gaps in the relevant international tax rules strongly influences the bargains reached between managers and monetary capital providers.

---

http://papers.ssrn.com/sol3/papers.cfm?abstract_id=2067138 (accessed on June 4, 2012).

[24] *See* de Mooij, *supra* note 12 and accompanying text. *See also* Ilma Ghouse & Humera Sultana, *Entrepreneur Activity and Statutory Tax Requirement: An Empirical Analysis for Pakistan*, Econ. Rev., Feb. 1, 2012, at 13.

[25] *E.g.*, Robert J. Dilworth, *Tax Reform: International Tax Issues and Some Proposals*, Int'l Tax J. 5 (2009) *available at* http://www.mwe.com/info/pubs/taxreform.pdf (accessed on June 11, 2014); Michael J. Graetz, *Taxing International Income – Inadequate Principles, Outdated Concepts, and Unsatisfactory Policy*, 54 Tax L. Rev. 261 (2001); Hugh J. Ault, *Taxing International Income: An Analysis of the US System and Its Economic Premises, in* Taxation in the Global Economy 28 (Assaf Razin & Joel Slemrod eds, 1990), *available at* http://www.nber.org/chapters/c7203.pdf. (As the discussion of the legal rules makes clear, implementing these general principles is far from straightforward. The present system is the result of a long process of successive efforts to close loopholes, as the tax policy-makers have discovered one way after another in which taxpayers – or foreign governments – can organize their affairs to take advantage of the US rules (accessed on 6/1/2014).

15.4 CONCLUSION

Although the goal of minimizing excess burden supports designing a comprehensive tax system that is neutral with respect to the economic decisions affecting the business enterprise, it is impossible to achieve a completely neutral tax system in practice. This is especially true in countries such as the US and Japan that rely on income taxes, as income is an inherently nebulous concept. Taxpayers find it all too easy to play tax-minimization games by restructuring transactions so as to alter the character, timing, or jurisdiction of the transaction with respect to tax laws.

To the extent that the goal of promoting distribution policy leads governments to enact progressive income tax schedules, such as in the US and Japan as well as in most other nations, the distortions created by non-comprehensive tax bases are multiplied. And, even recognizing that it is not possible to design a fully comprehensive tax base, governments fall far short of what might theoretically be possible. The goals of promoting desirable behavior and enacting fiscal stimulus often lead policy-makers to enact tax preferences or penalties in order to achieve non-tax-policy-related ends. Furthermore, politicians frequently prioritize rewarding narrow interest groups over providing for the general welfare; real-world tax laws are thus rife with special provisions intended to reward narrow interest groups.

Tax laws thus create many biases that affect the behavior of managers, employees, and monetary capital providers. Many volumes have been written analyzing subsets of these biases, and there is still considerably more to be said. In this chapter, our goal has been only to provide a high-level overview of the tax policy perspective on the interactions between tax law and enterprise law, and to sketch out a few examples of how the nature of tax law influences the incentive bargains reached between managers, employees, and monetary capital providers. It is important for those interested in tax policy and those interested in enterprise policy to understand one another's perspectives. Only through communication and collaboration can we combat the ways in which tax laws create problems for enterprise law or use tax law as a tool for correcting biases in enterprise law.

16. Income tax and incentives for corporate transactions: a Japanese perspective

Tetsuya Watanabe

16.1 INTRODUCTION

There are many transactions between a corporation and its stakeholders (i.e. shareholders, employees, creditors, directors, and so on). In many cases, the tax burden cannot be ignored.

The Companies Act is a national-level (not a state or other local) law in Japan. The Income Tax Act (ITA) and Corporate Tax Act (CTA) are also national-level laws. Accordingly, tax rules may have an effect on corporate transactions that are also governed by the Companies Act.[1] So there may be an incentive to arrange transactions in such a way that the tax burden could be mitigated.

Even if corporate law and tax law were not the same level of law, tax rules would have an effect on incentives in corporate transactions. For example, bond interest is generally deductible by the issuing corporation (CTA. Art. 22(3)) but any dividend payment is non-deductible (CTA. Art. 22(5)). Accordingly, there is an incentive to prefer debt financing for corporations compared with equity financing.

The purpose of this chapter is to consider whether the tax rules that provide an incentive or disincentive for corporate transactions are desirable or not as a matter of legislation. In other words, how should corporate law and tax law live together in the real world of business?

This chapter picks up and briefly examines several issues that may affect transaction incentives in Japan. Following a basic explanation

[1] On the other hand, the Companies Act always has a major influence on tax law. For example, the Japanese Corporation Tax Act first introduced systematic tax-free corporate reorganization rules in 2001, which was just one year after the corporation law (it was the Commercial Code at that time and was changed to the Companies Act in 2006) had introduced new corporate division rules.

of Japanese corporate taxation including the current state of national finances (section 16.2), this chapter focuses on deferral on establishing a corporation for avoiding high individual tax rates (section 16.3), shifting income from the corporation to directors or employees (section 16.4), stock options (section 16.5), dividends received, both domestic and international aspects (sections 16.6 and 16.7), and corporate reorganization, such as mergers or corporate divisions (section 16.8). Section 16.9 concludes.

16.2 BASICS OF JAPANESE CORPORATE TAXATION

Corporate tax is still an important source of revenue in Japan. In the 2012 budget, corporate tax generated the third-largest tax revenue, namely ¥7792 billion (see Figures 16.1 and 16.2).[2]

However, it may be difficult to increase tax on corporations since the tax burden of Japanese corporations is already high compared with corporations located in other developed countries. Accordingly, how to design corporate tax rules is crucial. The following provides a brief account of the current tax rules for corporations and their shareholders.

A corporation is taxable for its income under the Corporate Tax Act (in the same way as an individual under the Income Tax Act). Partnerships and trusts are basically "pass-through" entities.

The tax rate of an ordinary corporation was 30 percent before a 2011 amendment. The 2011 amendment made it 25.5 percent (CTA, Art. 66(1)). However, after the earthquake and tsunami on March 11, 2011, the corporate tax rate has become 110 percent of the normal rate, which is 28.05 percent from 2012 to 2015 (i.e. special treatment for three years) under the 2012 Revive Revenue Securing Law. Whereas the tax rate of income which does not exceed ¥8 million, for small and medium-sized enterprises (SMEs), was 18 percent before the 2011 amendment, the amendment changed it to 15 percent (CTA, Art. 66(2), Act on Special Measures Concerning Taxation (ASMT), Art. 42-3-2), but currently it has become 16.5 percent under the 2012 law for three years due to the earthquake.

For individual stockholders, dividends are included in income and subject to a withholding tax at a 20 percent tax rate (ITA, Arts. 181–182).

---

[2] However, the fact that 46.8 percent of total revenue comes from government bonds (national debt) should not be ignored.

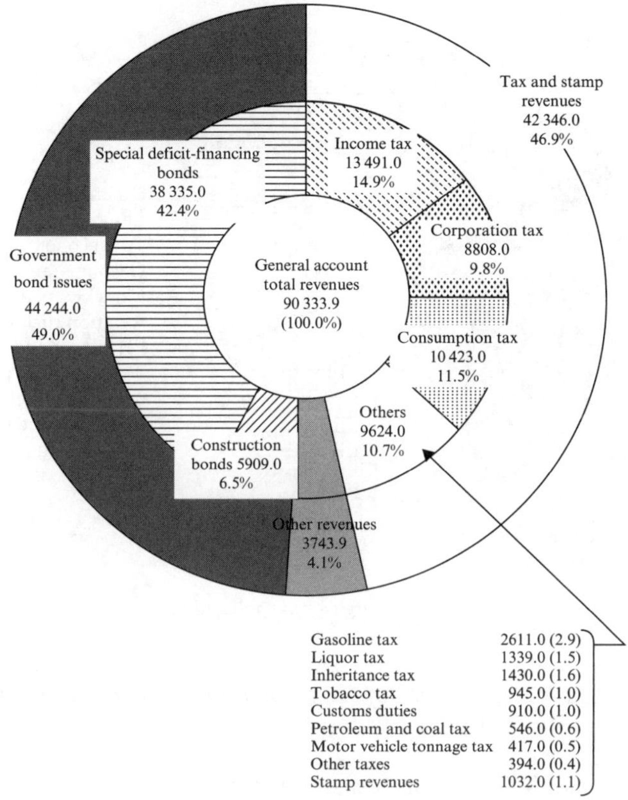

Source: http://www.mof.go.jp/english/budget/budget/fy2012/factsheet2012.pdf (last visited 2013/11/12).

Figure 16.1 Initial budget (approved by the Diet 5 April 2012) (billion yen)

Taxpayers may credit some amount of dividends received (10 percent or 5 percent, depending on dividend income) unless they elect for the separate withholding taxation (ITA, Arts 92). This "dividend credit system" is only a partial "integration" for avoiding double taxation between a corporation and shareholders.

As such, Japanese law has taken a step towards "integration." The premise of the current rule is that the nature of corporate tax is an advance payment by shareholders who will have liability for dividend income tax later. However, is this really true? Are there any other possibilities? If corporate tax increases and the corporation decreases the amount of

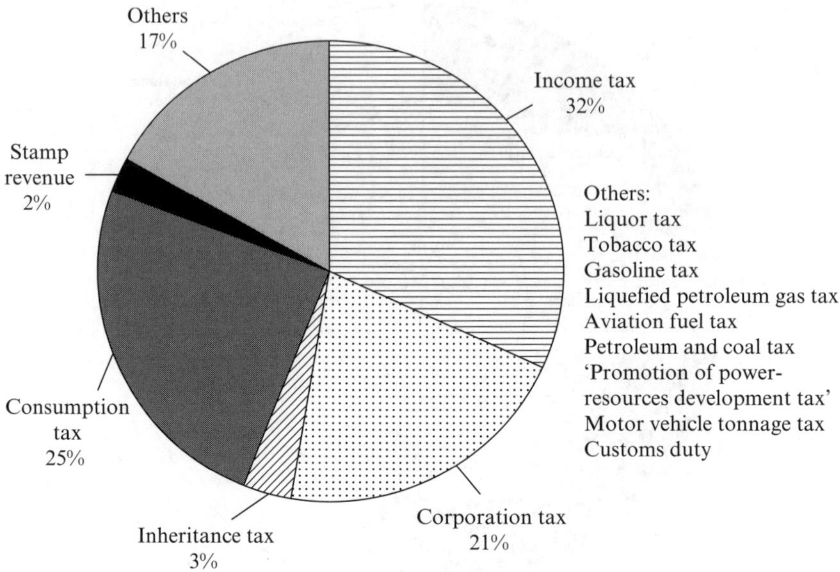

Source: Data: http://www.mof.go.jp/english/tax_policy/taxes_and_stamp_revenues/h201207e.pdf (last visited 2012/9/11).

Figure 16.2 FY 2012 Survey of the amount of tax and stamp revenues (July 2012)

dividends, shareholders may cease investment to corporations because purchasing corporate stock may not be as attractive as before.

Indeed, a corporation cannot suffer any tax burden economically since it does not have a real existence but is a fiction and cannot make consumption. Only human beings are able to suffer income tax. As such, someone else must ultimately take on the tax burden, for example a supplier selling inventory at a lower price or a consumer buying goods at a higher price than before. However, a supplier can protect himself by finding another party willing to buy his inventory at a reasonable price, and a consumer could purchase other goods.

After all, it is only people or entities who cannot escape from the pressure of a corporation, who should accept the burden. Under the incidence of corporate tax view, the ultimate payers of corporate tax might not be shareholders but employees.[3] As such, it may be necessary to rethink the integration system. This theory may be more applicable to

[3] See Daniel Shaviro, DECODING THE US CORPORATE TAX 67 (2009).

Japan than the US or Europe, since in Japan the seniority and lifetime employment system still exists and the labor market is not so open or dispersed. There are strong disincentives for employees to change their job or company.

16.3 DEFERRAL (SETTING UP A CORPORATION FOR SHELTERING INCOME FROM THE TOP INDIVIDUAL TAX RATE)

The individual income tax rate is progressive but the corporate income tax is basically flat. If local tax is included, the highest income tax bracket for an individual is 50 percent whereas it is about 35.6 percent for an ordinary corporation and from 24 percent to 26 percent for SMEs (if we ignore the special treatment due to the earthquake for three years). Accordingly, the highest income tax rate may be avoided by setting up a corporation and deferring dividends as far as possible.

There is tax preference for disposition of stock. Capital gains from stock transfer by an individual shareholder is taxed at a 15 percent flat (not progressive) rate (ASMT, Art. 37-10(1)) no matter how much income he earned.[4]

When a shareholder dies there is another preference concerning inheritance tax. The basic exemption amount for inheritance tax is quite large so that only a few heirs have tax liabilities.[5] There is also special tax treatment for unlisted stocks; that is, a tolerant estimation for inheritance tax (ASMT, Art. 70-7-2; Property Estimating Circulars 179 and 180). Accordingly, high-income-bracket taxpayers have an incentive to set up a corporation and issue stocks and later to make a succession in this stock (and not in cash).

---

[4] Generally speaking, capital loss from stock transfers cannot be offset to any other type of gain or income. It cannot be carried forward, nor carried back. Capital loss from stock transfer can offset only to the same type of gain in the same accounting year. The rest of the loss is deemed zero (ASMT, Art. 37-10(1)). However, in the case of listed stock, capital loss from stock transfer can offset to dividend (ASMT, Art. 37-12-2(1)) and also carry forward in three years (ASMT, Art. 37-12-2(6)).

[5] For example, only 4.1 percent of cases are taxable of all inheritances in 2009; http://www.mof.go.jp/tax_policy/summary/property/137.htm (last visited 2012/9/11).

16.4 SHIFTING INCOME FROM CORPORATION TO DIRECTORS

A corporation basically cannot deduct compensation payments to directors, but if the compensation is qualified salaries such as "periodic same amount salaries," that can be deductible (CTA, Art. 34 (1). On the other hand, a corporation can deduct payments of salaries to employees (CTA Art. 22(3)).

Any salaries are taxable for the directors and employees as employment income. Taxpayers apply Employment Income Deduction in figuring their employment income (ITA, Art. 28(1)).[6]

Generally speaking the amount of Employment Income Deduction is not small. It is a kind of rough estimation or standard deduction and not an itemized deduction. The amount of the deduction depends only on the amount of salary received under the statute. The more salary you receive, the more Employment Income Deduction you can use automatically. Even if a taxpayer incurs no expenses to earn his salary he can still use the Employment Income Deduction.

So there is an incentive to shift income from the corporation to directors by using Employment Income Deduction. If a taxpayer who is self-employed establishes a corporation and becomes a director in that corporation, he could use the Employment Income Deduction and the corporation could deduct the payment to him as a qualified salary ("double deduction"). In such a case, the total tax liability might decrease more than before.

The 2012 amendment creates a cap for Employment Income Deduction. After January 1, 2013, the deduction for salaries over ¥15 million is ¥2.45 million and no more (ITA, Art. 28(3)(vi)). In this case, no matter how much the salary increases, the amount of deduction is fixed. This amendment decreases the incentive to shift income from the corporation

---

[6] The amount of Employment Income Deduction depends on the amount of salary received (ITA Art. (3)). If salary does not exceed ¥1.8 million, the deduction is 40 percent of the amount of salaries. If salaries exceed ¥1.8 million but not more than ¥3.6 million, the deduction is ¥720 000 plus 30 percent of the amount of salaries minus ¥1.8 million. If salaries exceed ¥3.6 million but not more than ¥6.6 million, the deduction is ¥1.26 million plus 20 percent of the amount of salaries minus ¥1.26 million. If salaries exceed ¥6.6 million but not more than ¥10 million, the deduction is ¥1.86 million plus 10 percent of the amount of salaries minus ¥6.6 million. If salaries exceed ¥10 million, the deduction is ¥2.2 million plus 5 percent of the amount of salaries minus ¥10 million.

to directors.[7] This rule is applied to salary payments made not only to directors but also to employees. Theoretically the expense for employment income doesn't always increase in proportion to the salary increase. The amount of over ¥2.45 million as a deduction is considered to be an unnecessary preference for a high-salaried person. It also works as an "anti-double deduction" rule.

In US tax law a "publicly held corporation" is usually denied any deduction for compensation paid to a "covered employee" to the extent that the compensation for any year exceeds $1 million (IRC § 162(m)(1)).[8] The purpose of § 162(m) is a limitation on deductions for compensation received by corporate executives,[9] which seems similar to Japanese law (ITA, Art. 28(3)(vi)) to some extent. But there are two significant differences. The first is the amount of target salary, which is ¥15 million in Japan and $1 million (¥80 million) in the US. The second difference concerns the circumstances in which deduction is denied. Japanese law denies individual income tax deduction for directors or employees, but US law denies corporate income tax deduction for the corporation.

16.5 STOCK OPTIONS

There are two type of stock options: qualified and non-qualified stock options.[10] In the case of qualified stock options, employees and directors usually recognize no income at the time of grant or exercise of an option (ASMT, Art 29-2). They or their successors are taxed when the stock acquired is sold. The gain recognized on sales is treated as capital gain (ASMT, Art 37-10). Accordingly, income from a qualified stock option is never treated as employment income for a director or employee.

A qualified stock option contract must satisfy several requirements. For example, the option granted is not exercisable within two years from a shareholders' resolution, which permits the corporation to issue such

---

[7] Before the 2012 amendment, some types of "family corporation" could not deduct salary payments to their directors (former CTA, Art. 35). This was a limitation on deduction for corporations, which was a corporate income tax matter and the 2012 amendment is a limitation for a director and is an individual income tax matter. However, those corporate and income provisions both anxious about the double or excess deduction derived from Employment Income Deduction.

[8] *See generally* Bittker & Lokken, *Federal Taxation of Income, Estates and Gifts* (Current Through 2012), ¶64.6.

[9] H.R. Rep. No. 111, 103d Cong., 1st Sess. 646 (1993).

[10] *See generally* Tetsuya Watanabe, *Tax Treatment of Stock Options in Japan*, BULLETIN FOR INTERNATIONAL FISCAL DOCUMENTATION, Vol. 58 No. 1, 31 (2004).

an option to the employee or director (ASMT Art. 29-2 (1)(i)). The total amount of the option exercised does not exceed ¥12 million for a single year (ASMT, Art. 29-2 (1)(ii)).

Once a stock option becomes qualified the recipient may be treated more favorably than in the case of non-qualified stock options. However, since the issuing corporation (i.e. the employer) generally cannot deduct any expenses, paying compensation by qualified stock option is not always beneficial from the corporation's point of view.

In the case of non-qualified stock options, employees and directors are not taxed at the time of grant but are taxed when they exercise the option (Income Tax Enforcement Ordinance (ITEO), Art. 84). When an employee or director exercises an option, the income recognized is basically employment income (ITA, Art. 28) and, as such, is not treated tolerantly compared to capital gain (ITA, Art. 33) or occasional income (ITA, Art. 34).

There is asymmetrical treatment between the recipient and issuing corporation. Even if the employees or directors are taxed as the receipt of employment income when they exercise the option, the issuing corporation generally can deduct only the amount of reasonable expenses as salaries when it grants an option under the current law even if how much the value of stock increase at the time of exercise (Corporate Tax Enforcement Ordinance (CTEO), Art. 111-2 (3)). For example a corporation grants an option for which the exercise price is 10,000 yen to its employee instead of paying a reasonable expense as a salary in 100,000 yen. If the stock value is 1,000,000 yen when the employee exercises that option, he is taxed on the receipt of 990,000 yen income, whereas the corporation can deduct only 100,000 yen. So there is also a relatively small incentive for corporations to grant a stock option from the tax perspective.[11]

16.6 DIVIDENDS RECEIVED: DOMESTIC ASPECTS

Dividends received would be taxed under their own rules. For individual shareholders there is a partial integration rule that has already been mentioned. For corporate shareholders, the amount of 50 percent of dividend (not from foreign corporations) received by domestic corporations shall

---

[11] On the other hand, U.S. I.R.C. §83(h) allows an employer a deduction under §162 for the amounts employees include in gross income on grant or exercise of a non-qualified stock option. But this is not the case for qualified stock options (§421(a)(2)).

not be included in gross revenues in computing taxable income (CTA, Art. 23(1)).

In the case of qualified dividends received from a 100 percent subsidiary or from not less than a 25 percent ownership stake in a corporation, the amount of 100 percent of dividends shall not be included (CTA, Arts. 23(1) and (5)). Accordingly, whether there is a 25 percent holding or not would be a major issue for a corporate shareholder.

Before the 2002 amendment, the amount of 80 percent of dividend would not be included even if the 25 percent ownership requirement were not satisfied. Before the 1988 amendment, there was no requirement of ownership and any corporate (not individual) shareholder could receive the dividend tax-free. As a result, the tax base of dividends for corporate shareholders has gradually expanded.[12]

16.7 DIVIDENDS RECEIVED: INTERNATIONAL ASPECTS

Under a 2009 amendment dividends from a foreign subsidiary are not included as taxable income in its parent (CTA, Art. 23-2(1)).[13] In that case, the parent must hold 25 percent or more shares of such a foreign subsidiary. Since the amount of 5 percent of dividend is treated as an expense for the dividend received, the amount of 95 percent of the dividend shall be tax free (CTEO, Art. 22-4(2)).

This is similar to the case of dividends received from a domestic subsidiary where 25 percent or more ownership is held by its parent. However, if the ownership is less than 25 percent, the dividend received from a foreign subsidiary by its parent would be fully taxable.

Because dividends from foreign subsidiaries shall not be taxable, there is an incentive to convert income to dividends from other categories such as royalty or interest payments (royalty and interest are taxable in the hands of the parent). There is also an incentive to set up a foreign subsidiary, not a foreign branch.

---

[12] The 2010 amendment introduced another limitation. If a corporation acquired the stock which the issuing corporation planned to redeem, no inclusion rule for dividend can be applied (CTA, Arts. 23(1)(iv)). Before the 2010 law, such shareholders could not use an inclusion rule for deemed dividends from redemption and also report capital loss.

[13] *See generally* Yoshihiro Masui, *Taxation of Foreign Subsidiaries: Japan's Tax Reform 2009/10*, BULLETIN FOR INTERNATIONAL FISCAL DOCUMENTATION, Vol. 64 No. 4, 242 (2010).

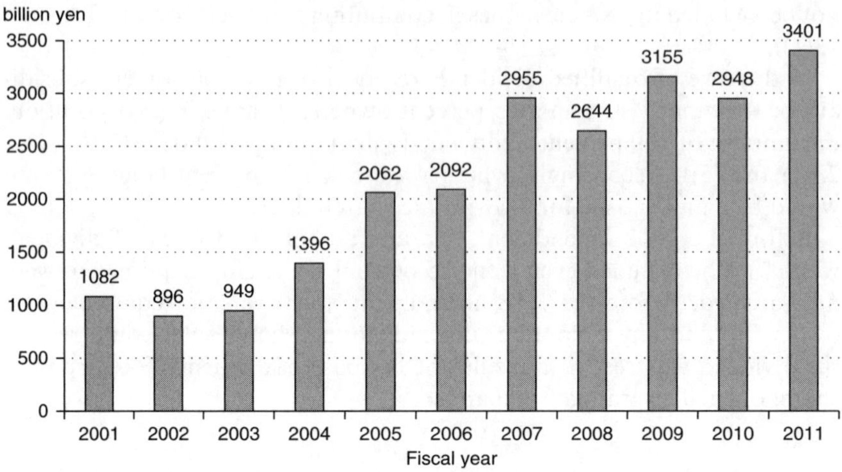

Source: Data: http://www.stat-search.boj.or.jp/index_en.html (last visited 2012/9/11).

Figure 16.3 Dividends from foreign subsidiaries

Before the 2009 amendment, dividends from any foreign subsidiaries were covered under the "Indirect Foreign Tax Credit" rule, under which a domestic corporation may be deemed to have paid foreign income taxes paid by a foreign subsidiary from which the domestic corporate shareholder receives a dividend (former CTA, 69(8), (9), (11)~(14)). But this rule has been abolished.

The 2009 law also prevents the parent claiming a foreign tax credit for withholding taxes imposed on dividends from a foreign subsidiary (CTA, Art. 69(1)) since there should be no double taxation for dividends (i.e. the dividend from a foreign subsidiary is taxed only once in the foreign country). The parent cannot deduct the withholding tax either (CTA, Art. 39-2).[14]

The 2009 amendment seems to mark a significant step towards a "territorial tax" system from a "worldwide tax" system. This represents a major change in the modern history of Japanese tax law, since Japan introduced an indirect foreign tax credit rule in 1952. According to data from the Bank of Japan (Figure 16.3), dividends from foreign subsidiaries were ¥2644 billion in FY 2008, ¥3155 billion in FY 2009, ¥2948 billion

[14] In some cases, the total tax burden of income from all foreign countries would be higher than before, since taxpayers cannot use the cross-crediting method (which is averaging foreign-source high-taxed income with foreign low-taxed income for the purpose of determining the foreign tax credit) after the 2009 amendment.

in FY 2010 and ¥3401 billion in FY 2011. Therefore after the 2009 amendment dividend increased in FY 2009 and FY 2011 but decreased in FY 2010 compared with the previous fiscal year. It may still be difficult to say that the new rule has succeeded in returning money from foreign subsidiaries.

16.8 REORGANIZATION (VERSUS DISPOSITION)

Under the current law there are several types of reorganizations; merger, corporate division, contribution in kind, distribution in kind, stock exchange and stock transfer (CTA. Arts. 2-11~2-12-17).[15]

As a general rule reorganizations are realization events.[16] For example, Corporate Tax Act, Art. 62 provides that when a corporation transfers assets or liabilities by merger or corporate division, it is treated as if that corporation transfers the assets or liabilities at fair market value (FMV), and may be taxable.

However, if the transaction falls within qualified reorganization, it is deemed a book value transfer and gains or losses are not recognized (CTA, Art. 62-2(1)).[17] That means the acquiring corporation may be taxed on a non-recognized gain or loss when it disposes of (sells) the assets or liabilities in future.

Shareholders of a merged corporation release their stock and receive acquiring corporation stock by merger. In the case of a qualified merger, such shareholders are not taxed and the basis of the acquiring corporation stock will be the same as the stock which they released (substituted basis).[18]

On the other hand, if the transaction is not a qualified merger,

---

[15] *See generally*, Tetsuya Watanabe, *Tax-Free Treatment for Corporate Reorganizations in Japan*, Proceedings from the 2009 Sho Sato Conference on Tax Law, Social Policy, and the Economy, http://www.law.berkeley.edu/files/sho_sato_tax_conf_web_paper--watanabe.pdf (last visited 2012/9/11).

[16] In Japan there is a concept of "realization" in tax law but no word or definition of it in any tax statute, unlike US law.

[17] For example, the target corporation (T corp.) merges into the acquiring corporation (A corp.) by merger. Suppose the asset's basis in T corp. is 100 and its FMV is 300, and the T stock basis in T shareholder is 50 and FMV is 150. If the transaction is qualified merger, T corp. is treated as if it transfers assets at 100 not 300. So T corp. is not taxed and the basis of the assets in A corp. will be 100 (transferred basis).

[18] Tax consequences of qualified reorganization are almost the same as US tax law under I.R.C. §§354, 358 & 361 (neither the shareholder nor the corporation are taxable and the basis of stock or assets of the target corporation are carried over).

shareholders are taxed on a deemed dividend (ITA, Art. 25(1)(i) or CTA, Art. 24(1)(i)) and also may be taxed on a capital gain (ASMT, Art. 37-10(3)(i)or CTA, Art. 22(2)).

For tax purposes there are three categories of reorganization which are: (1) 100 percent group reorganization; (2) over 50 percent group reorganization; and (3) joint business reorganization. The reason to distinguish from (1) to (3) is that the requirements for qualified reorganization applied to each category are different. To be a qualified reorganization, there are several statutory requirements that depend on the category of the transaction (CTA, Arts. 2-12-8 & 11).

There is basically one requirement for a 100 percent group reorganization. That is a "no boot" requirement. However, it should be noted that after the reorganization if the 100 percent group relationship is broken – for example in the case of a corporate division, a parent (the acquiring corporation) sells even a very small part of the subsidiary (the target corporation) stocks after reorganization – there is no longer a 100 percent group reorganization and the requirements for over 50 percent group reorganization must be applied.

For cases involving an over 50 percent group reorganization, "transfer of major assets and liabilities," "continuity of employees," and "succession of business" requirements are needed besides the "no boot" requirement. For joint business reorganization, in addition to these four requirements, there are four other requirements: the "related business," "similarity of size," "continuity of senior officers," and "continuity of shareholding" requirements. However, for the "similarity of size" and "continuity of senior officers" requirements, satisfying one requirement is enough (i.e. it is not necessary to satisfy both of them).

Finally, there is one more provision that is applicable for all categories. That is the general anti-avoidance rule for reorganization under the Corporate Tax Act, Art. 132-2. According to the *Tax Commission Paper* (the document for the second general meeting of the Tax Commission on October 3, 2000),[19] the purpose of this provision is anti-abuse, that is, disguising a sale as a qualified reorganization. However, it is still not clear what kind of avoidance would fall into this category. Though the content of the provision is ambiguous, the Tax Commission did not indicate any example transaction.

---

[19] *Kaisha Bunkatsu – Gappei tou no Kigyō Soshiki Saihensei ni kakaru Zeisei no Kihonteki Kangaekata* [*The Basic Theory for Tax System of Corporate Reorganization such as Mergers and Corporate Divisions*], at V, http://www.cao.go.jp/zeicho/siryou/a02kai_2.html (last visited 2012/9/11).

16.9 CONCLUSIONS

Since the purposes of tax laws such as the Corporate Tax Act and the Companies Act are different, tax rules may have an undesirable influence on the operation of the Companies Act. The important point is that each provision has a rationale as a tax rule.

Tax rules should not have an effect on corporate transactions unnecessarily; it is important that they should not create adverse incentives or disincentives. Needless to say, tax rules may be used as an indirect means to solve other legal problems or achieve other policy objectives. Even in such a case, however, it is important that the Diet should provide a detailed explanation and justification of the chosen policy goals. Unfortunately, this still seems to be insufficient in Japan. Establishing and articulating a clear rationale for each tax rule is crucial.

17. Tax law influences on the form and substance of equity compensation in the United States

Mark P. Gergen*

17.1 INTRODUCTION

This chapter summarizes recent scholarship on the influence of tax law on equity compensation in the United States. Following the scholarship, I focus on large publicly traded firms (for example, firms in Standard & Poor's 500), firms in the venture capital (VC) industry, including both VC firms and the start-up firms they finance, and firms in the private equity industry more generally. Success in these firms generally requires inducing individuals who are thought to have rare managerial or other talents to take risks, and to fully devote themselves, in a speculative enterprise that requires enormous amounts of other people's capital. This is done by giving them equity compensation in the form of stock, options, or a partnership profits interest.

There is little evidence or reason to believe that tax law significantly influences the substance of equity compensation in a strong systematic way. By substance I mean the mix between equity and cash compensation and the risk and term structure of equity compensation. This is particularly true with regards to publicly traded firms for tax law generally is roughly neutral in the choice between equity and cash compensation and in the structuring of equity compensation once costs and benefits to both the firm and the recipient are considered. Tax law probably also has not had much impact on the form of equity compensation in publicly traded firms. Accounting rules that understated the cost of options did create a bias in favor of options over stock or cash compensation until these rules were changed a few years ago.

Tax considerations do seem to have had an impact on the form of equity

* I thank Professor Zenichi Shishido for his advice and comments on a draft of this chapter.

compensation in the VC and private equity industries both at the start-up company level and at the fund level. It is less clear that tax considerations have had much impact on the substance of equity compensation, again meaning the choice between equity and cash compensation and choices regarding the risk and term structure of equity compensation. There is an arguable tax bias against giving founders equity compensation in the form of founders' common stock (hereafter: founders' common) in start-ups in the VC industry. And there is arguable tax bias in favor of giving fund managers equity compensation in the form of a profits interest in the private equity industry, which includes the VC industry. But there are reasons to be skeptical about whether these biases have had much of an impact on the substance of equity compensation.

Section 17.2 looks at equity compensation in publicly traded corporations. Section 17.3 looks at equity compensation in non-publicly traded corporations, focusing on the compensation of founders in the venture capital industry through a grant of common stock ("founders' common"). Section 17.4 looks at equity compensation in LLCs, which are taxed as partnerships, focusing on the compensation of fund managers in the venture capital industry and private equity more generally through a "carried interest." Section 17.5 compares founders' common and the carried interest, observing that the carried interest offers the same tax advantages as founders' common with none of the tax disadvantages. The coexistence of these two forms of equity compensation in the venture capital industry is curious. Section 17.6 concludes.

17.2 EQUITY COMPENSATION IN PUBLICLY TRADED FIRMS

17.2.1 Dominance of the Corporate Form

In the US almost all publicly traded firms are organized in corporations. This puts the firm at a disadvantage under US tax law. Unlike partnerships, corporations are subject to an entity-level tax on their income. In 2012 the top corporate tax rate (35 percent) was near the top individual tax rate (37.9 percent once the Medicare tax is added[1]) and corporations

[1] This simplifies. This was the top marginal income tax rate (35 percent) plus the 2.9 percent Medicare tax. Some taxpayers face a higher implicit marginal income rate because of phaseouts. The top individual rate was increased to 39.6 percent starting in 2013.

do not get the benefit of the capital gains preference, unlike individuals.[2] While many corporations pay a low effective tax rate because of tax preferences, most face a marginal rate at or near the top rate. It is the marginal rate that is relevant for tax planning. The entity-level tax is an important consideration in structuring compensation for typically forms of compensation that provide a tax benefit to the recipient impose an offsetting tax cost to the firm. This is true of both deferred cash compensation and equity compensation. Often these benefits and costs are in rough equipoise so there is not a strong reason to think that tax law influences the choice to use equity compensation or the structure of equity compensation.

The reasons for the dominance of the corporate form among publicly traded firms are partly historical. Until the creation of the limited liability company as a business form in the 1980s, and the advent of the "check-the-box" regulations in 1994 that made partnership classification elective, it was close to impossible to structure a publicly traded firm so that it would be taxed as a partnership. After 1994, tax treatment as a partnership remains unavailable for many publicly traded firms under a rule taxing a partnership with publicly traded interests as a corporation if a significant part of the income of the firm comes from an active trade or business.[3] Blackstone Group L.P., an investment firm, is an important counter-example. It is organized and taxed as a partnership while its interests are publicly traded. This allows it to take advantage of the unusually favorable tax treatment of equity compensation in the form of a grant of a profits interest.[4]

17.2.2 The Economics of Stock and Options

In a corporation equity compensation generally can take the form of stock or options.[5] Equity compensation tends to be through grants of restricted rights in stock or options. The recipient, usually an executive, will be

---

[2] These are 2012 tax rates. This has been the basic rate structure since 2001. The top individual rate was a bit higher than the corporate rate prior to 2001.

[3] I.R.C. § 7704(c). There is an exception for the exploration, development, processing, transportation, and marketing of mineral and natural resources. When I looked in 1997 I found few firms had taken advantage of this exception. Mark P. Gergen, *Subchapter K and Passive Financial Intermediation*, 51 S.M.U.L. Rev. 37, 44 n.2 (1997).

[4] For more on Blackstone and legislation that was proposed to strip some of these benefits *see* Victor Fleischer, *Taxing Blackstone*, 61 Tax L. Rev. 89 (2008).

[5] Stock Appreciation Rights are treated like options for tax purposes. The partnership interests most directly parallel to stock and options in a corporation are a capital interest in a partnership and an option to acquire a capital interest.

required to work for a specified term and perhaps satisfy other conditions before the right vests. On vesting the recipient can sell the stock or exercise the option and acquire the underlying stock, which they can then sell or hold.

The value of stock compensation is the price of the stock. The value of an option has two components. An option is said to have intrinsic value when the exercise price is less than the price of the underlying share. When the exercise price of an option is equal to or greater than the price of the underlying share, an option still has "option value," which is a function of the difference between the exercise price and the price of the underlying share, the volatility of the underlying share price, and the term of the option. In the US, when stock is publicly traded the exercise price of an option is almost always the underlying share price at the date of grant.

Both stock and options tie the value of a recipient's compensation to the success of the firm insofar as success is reflected in the firm's share price. The value of an option is more sensitive to changes in share price. The value of an option also is affected by the volatility of share price. These characteristics make options a cheaper way for a firm to encourage an executive to pursue risky growth opportunities. The downside is that an executive will discount the value of an option if they are risk averse. And excessive use of options may induce an executive to take excessive risks. Often equity compensation will take the form of a mix of stock and options, suggesting firms are trying to balance these competing considerations.

17.2.3 Tax Law Differences Between Stock and Options

The major tax law difference between giving an executive restricted stock and options as compensation is that a Section 83(b) election[6] is available to the executive on stock but not options.[7] This election generally should not be made when stock is publicly traded for reasons I will explain

---

These are almost never used as a form of equity compensation in partnerships because of the preferential tax treatment of a grant of a profits interest.

[6] The election is an odd feature of US tax law. Under general principles of US tax law an employee would not be taxed on contingent non-cash compensation that is subject to a substantial risk of forfeiture unless and until the contingency is eliminated. So the general rule in Section 83 provides. The election in Section 83(b) allows an employee to opt out of the general rule to be taxed at the time the employee receives property that is subject to a substantial risk of forfeiture.

[7] The election is not available for options unless the option is publicly traded. Reg. § 1.83-7. The election is not available because of the difficulty of valuing non-publicly traded options. The tax authority rightly worries that recipients of options will undervalue them to convert compensation into capital gains.

below. Absent an election both stock and options provide the tax benefit of deferral to an executive. An executive does not pay tax on the value of stock compensation until vesting. They do not pay tax on the value of an option (the difference between the exercise price and the price of the underlying share) until exercise. But there is an offsetting cost to the firm for the deduction if the expense is also deferred to the same year. At 2012 tax rates, if both parties pay the top marginal rate, then there is a small net benefit to deferral. The top individual rate is 37.9 percent and the top corporate rate is 35 percent. But this is a small net benefit and can be replicated by giving deferred cash compensation. It is not a reason to favor equity compensation over cash compensation.

The reason for giving equity compensation is to tie the eventual payoff to the executive to the firm's share price. This does not require equity compensation. A firm could pay contingent deferred cash compensation. Stock, options, and contingent deferred cash compensation are near equivalents from a tax perspective if an executive does not make a Section 83(b) election on stock. Whichever form is used, returns to the executive attributable to an increase in share price are taxed as ordinary income and not as capital gain. There is a small timing difference between options and stock that may affect character. Income is realized on stock when it vests, while it is realized on options upon exercise.

Professor David Walker has argued that equity compensation has a subtle tax advantage over cash compensation to the firm.[8] The advantage arises if a firm pursues a strategy of buying back its stock at the time of the grant. Under this strategy a firm uses the cash it would have paid as compensation to buy back its own stock. It then reissues the stock to the employee when the right to the stock vests. The source of the advantage is that the firm is not taxed on gain on an investment in its own stock. This means that compensation to the executive resulting from an increase in share price between the grant date and vesting date is paid by the firm out of tax-free dollars while providing a deduction to the firm. Professor Ethan Yale has challenged this claimed advantage.[9] Whoever may be

---

[8] David I. Walker, *Is Equity Compensation Tax Advantaged?*, 84 B. U. L. REV. 695, 743–748 (2004).

[9] Ethan Yale, *Investment Risk and the Tax Benefit of Deferred Compensation*, 62 TAX L. REV. 377 (2009). Professor Yale's argument is an extension of the general point that the pre- and post-tax return to a risky investment is the same if losses are fully deductible because the government shares in both gains and losses. One upshot of the general point is that the burden of the income tax should be expected to fall on normal risk-free returns to capital and not risky returns. Professor Yale observes: "if one accepts . . . that income taxation does not impose a significant

right, it seems clear that whatever advantage may arise from the buy-back strategy is subtle and not likely to factor significantly into the choice between equity and cash compensation.

Stock compensation does give the executive the option to make a Section 83(b) election and include the stock in income on the date of grant at the share price at that time. The election makes it possible to defer tax on any increase in share price until the stock is sold and to convert income attributable to an increase in share price into capital gains (taxed at a 15 percent rate in 2012[10]). But the election is ill-advised if stock is fairly valued on the date of grant. An executive who makes the election foregoes deferral of tax on the share price at the date of grant. If the price goes down, then the executive will have a capital loss that imperfectly offsets the ordinary income on grant. And if the stock is forfeited, then the executive gets no loss to offset the income on grant. The election also denies the firm any deduction for the increase in value.

17.2.4 Incentive Stock Options and the Cost to the Firm of Converting Compensation Into Capital Gains

Special tax rules apply to qualified Incentive Stock Options (ISOs) that make ISOs advantageous to a recipient and disadvantageous to the firm as a form of equity compensation. A recipient has no income on grant or exercise of an ISO.[11] Tax on gain is deferred until the underlying stock is sold and is taxed as capital gains. The disadvantage to the firm is that it gets no deduction for the expense.[12] Unless the firm faces a low or zero marginal tax rate the cost of foregoing the deduction will exceed the benefit to the recipient of converting ordinary income into capital gains. If firms are well advised, then they will use ISOs only if the firm faces a low or zero marginal tax rate. Otherwise firms should use conventional options or stock. If a firm faces a low or zero marginal tax rate, than there is a bias in favor of ISO compensation over cash compensation.

---

burden on capital income – then it follows that avoiding the burden through artful devices such as deferred compensation cannot yield a significant benefit." *Id.* at 380–381. More concretely, an executive who receives taxable cash compensation and invests the after-tax cash in their employer's stock has the same after-tax expected rate of return as an executive who receives tax-deferred stock compensation. Moreover, an executive who receives cash compensation can replicate the size of the tax-deferred stock position by borrowing to purchase additional stock.

10 This simplifies. In 2012 taxpayers subject to the alternative minimum tax may pay an implicit higher rate on capital gains.

11 Code § 421(a)(1).

12 Code § 421(a)(2).

The point about ISOs is of more general importance. Generally, strategies that give a recipient compensation in the form of capital gains preclude a firm-level deduction. And generally these strategies impose a higher cost on the firm than the benefit they provide to the recipient. This is because the recipient merely gets the benefit of a lower tax rate (from 37.9 percent to 15 percent in 2012) while the firm loses the full value of the expense (the top corporate rate is 35 percent).

17.2.5 Tax Law May Explain the Dearth of Discounted Options

Professor David Walker has identified a subtle way in which tax law may have influenced the form of equity compensation in publicly traded firms. Tax considerations may explain why firms issue a mix of stock and options rather than granting discounted in-the-money options, which can be comparable financially to a mix of stock and options.[13] Discounting the exercise price of an option makes the option more like stock by making the value of the option less sensitive to movements in the share price and less sensitive to the volatility of share price. At the extreme, as the exercise price of an option approaches zero, a grant of option becomes a near equivalent to a grant of stock.

Professor Walker tells a complicated story. For the period up to 2004, he attributes the dearth of discounted options to a mix of tax and accounting considerations, including the favorable accounting treatment of options more generally. The favorable accounting treatment of options is a significant part of the explanation why options dominated stock as a form of equity compensation through the 1990s and into the early 2000s.[14] Walker attributes the sharp decrease in option grants and increase in stock grants to a change in the accounting rules, as well as other factors including the burst of the dot-com bubble and options-related scandals. These developments might have created a space for discounted options were it not for the enactment of § 409A in 2004 and the issuance of implementing regulations in 2007. Under the regulations a grant of discounted options is treated as a form of non-qualified deferred compensation and subject to tax from the time of vesting (not exercise) plus a 20 percent penalty tax.[15]

---

13 David I. Walker, *The Non-Option: Understanding the Dearth of Discounted Employee Stock Options*, 89 B. U. L. REV. 1505 (2009).

14 David I. Walker, *Evolving Equity Compensation and the Limits of Optimal Contracting*, 64 VAND. L. REV. 611, 632–634 (2011).

15 David I. Walker, supra n. 13, at 1525–1526.

17.3 THE VENTURE CAPITAL INDUSTRY: FOUNDERS' COMMON

17.3.1 Tax Benefit in the Common-Preferred Structure

Tax law considerations are thought to explain the form of equity compensation given by start-ups financed by venture capital.[16] Most start-ups are formed as corporations, although, not being publicly traded, they could be formed as partnerships. This is a curious choice from a tax perspective, a point I will return to. Typically in the US the VC fund takes convertible preferred stock in a start-up. The founders take common stock. I use the term "founders" loosely to describe any participants in the start-up who receive equity compensation. The convertible preferred stock gives the fund a priority right to recover the capital invested plus a stipulated preferred dividend rate. The conversion option allows the fund to share in any additional returns if a start-up succeeds. Other financial structures could be used to achieve this pattern of payoffs while organizing start-ups as corporations. In particular, the fund could take common stock and the founders could take options. Tax considerations are thought to explain the common-preferred structure.

The tax benefit in the common-preferred structure is that it allows a founder to make a Section 83(b) election and pay a small amount of tax on grant of the stock by reporting a low value for the stock.[17] If a start-up prospers, then the gain is taxed as capital gain and tax on that gain is deferred until the founder sells the stock. Tax on the gain is avoided entirely if the stock is held until death. If a founder holds a diversified stock portfolio, then the "timing option" – meaning the power to choose when to realize gains and losses – makes it possible to take cash from a portfolio tax free by selectively realizing losses in the portfolio to shield

---

[16] Gilson & Schizer, *Understanding Venture Capital Structure: A Tax Explanation for Convertible Preferred Stock*, 116 HARV. L. REV. 874. 899 (2003). Scott Olliverre, *The Influence of Taxation on Capital Structure in Venture Capital Investments in Canada and the United States*, 68 U. TORONTO L. REV. 9 (2010), finds different capital structures dominate in Canada and that the structural differences can be explained by differences in tax law. Victor Fleischer, *Taxing Founders' Stock*, 59 UCLA L REV. 60 (2011), argues that this is a "conspicuous loophole" in the US income tax. For further detail and an interesting comparison with Japanese law, *see* Zenichi Shisido, *Sweat Equity as a Gift* (Working Paper for Sho Sato Conference at UC Berkeley Law School, March 9–10, 2009, http://www.law.berkeley.edu/files/sho_sato_tax_conf_web_paper--shishido(2).pdf).

[17] A Section 83(b) election would not be possible if the venture capitalists received common stock and the founders received options.

realized gains. The value of deferral is enhanced by the availability of tax strategies for locking in gains on appreciated stock or converting appreciated stock into cash without paying tax on gain, though these strategies tend either to be an imperfect substitute for selling the stock or to involve a tax law risk that a transaction will be treated as a sale.

Generally, it is in a founder's interest to make the Section 83(b) election and pay tax on the value of common stock only if the common stock is significantly undervalued in relationship to the preferred stock. This is for reasons previously explained. These reasons are amplified by the fact that start-ups are very risky bets. The most likely outcome is a capital loss on the stock when the start-up fails. There is a very small probability of an outcome in which conversion and deferral are of value to a recipient. Undervaluation is essential to making the strategy work, for when a start-up fails a founder has a capital loss to offset the ordinary income reported on grant. Without undervaluation a founder would be better off taking options for they create taxable income only in a successful outcome in which the option is exercised.

For most start-ups, if founders' common is valued in good faith, then its value will be a large fraction of the price of the preferred stock, for much of the expected value of the preferred stock is in the conversion feature. In a 2003 article arguing that tax law considerations explain the ubiquity of the common-preferred structure in venture capital, Professor Gilson and Professor Schizer report that many practitioners valued common stock using liquidation value, which is *de minimis*. They also report, and other sources confirm, a less aggressive convention of valuing the common stock at one-tenth the price of the preferred stock.[18] The convention may have changed in response to the enactment of Section 409A. I have been told that the convention now is to value the common stock at one-quarter the price of the preferred stock. This remains a substantial discount if most of the expected value of the preferred stock is in the conversion feature.

17.3.2 Tax Detriment to the Firm

Other tax law considerations complicate the story of founders' common. One complicating consideration is that the tax benefit to a founder from this strategy is more than offset by a tax detriment to a successful start-up

---

[18] Gilson & Schizer, *supra* note 16, at 900 n.86. Also Joseph W. Bartlett, EQUITY FINANCE: VENTURE CAPITAL BUYOUTS, RESTRUCTURINGS AND REORGANIZATIONS, 2nd edn (New York: Aspen Law & Business, 1995) at 5-4. I have heard of the same convention.

company.[19] This is for the same reason that ISOs are tax-disadvantaged. The strategy enables a founder to convert compensation into capital gain. But a start-up loses the ability to deduct the value of any compensation that is converted into capital gains. In outcomes where a start-up generates taxable income, the value of the deduction to the start-up (the top corporate tax rate is 35 percent) exceeds the value to the founder of converting ordinary income (taxed at a 37.9 percent rate in 2012) into capital gains (taxed at a 15 percent rate in 2012). The value of deferral and the timing option to a founder reduces the imbalance in value but it is unlikely to eliminate the imbalance. Many start-ups never generate taxable income in excess of their other expenses, so the lost deduction for the compensation is costless to the start-up. But a founder is better off with a grant of options in outcomes in which a start-up is unsuccessful, for the founder avoids being in the unhappy tax position of having ordinary income that is offset by a capital loss.

17.3.3 Why Not LLCs?

There is another complicating consideration. From a tax perspective start-up companies probably should be organized as limited partnerships or as limited liability companies (LLCs), which are taxed partnerships on a pass-through basis.[20] Start-up companies generate large net operating losses in the early years as they burn through their capital. The corporate form keeps these expenses within the firm. When a start-up fails, as most do, these net operating losses expire with the firm. If start-ups were organized as LLCs, then these losses would flow outside the firm and could be used to shield other income from tax, either by any investors in the fund who are in a tax position to use losses, or, if a fund holds start-ups through a "blocking corporation," then they could be used by the blocking corporation against income eventually earned by successful start-ups.

If we just compare cash compensation with equity compensation in a

---

[19] Gregg D. Polsky & Brant J. Hellwig, *Examining the Tax Advantage of Founders' Stock*, 97 Iowa L. Rev. 1085 (2012), argue that this disadvantage at the firm level justifies the advantageous tax treatment of recipients.

[20] Joseph Bankman, *The Structure of Silicon Valley Start-Ups*, 41 UCLA L. Rev. 1737 (1994), is an early treatment of the issue. Professor Bankman examines several countervailing tax and accounting considerations but finds them insufficient to explain the phenomenon. Calvin H. Johnson, *Why Do Venture Capital Funds Burn Research and Development Deductions*, 29 Va. Tax Rev. 29 (2009), concurs with Professor Bankman after considering every old and new justification. Professor Johnson also provides some useful data on success and failure rates in start-ups and on the industry structure.

start-up, assuming use of the common-preferred structure, then we would conclude that tax law is biased against equity compensation because the expected cost to a firm outweighs the expected benefit to a founder. But this disadvantage can be avoided by giving a founder options. Organizing start-ups as corporations makes the alternative of giving additional cash compensation unattractive, for the compensation expense will be added to the pile of net operating losses that expire with the majority of firms that fail. But the use of the partnership form for start-ups could make these expenses usable. The use of the partnership form also makes available a third way to give equity compensation to a founder that delivers better tax benefits to a founder while minimizing the tax cost to other participants in the enterprise. I explain this third way now.

17.4 THE PRIVATE EQUITY INDUSTRY: THE FUND MANAGER'S CARRY

17.4.1 Carried Interest

In the VC industry, capital invested in start-up companies is funneled through a VC fund.[21] The fund is established and managed by the fund manager.[22] The fund manager raises capital from a pool of investors, including institutional investors such as pension funds and universities, wealthy individuals, and corporations.[23] Typically a VC fund is organized as a limited partnership. The investors are limited partners. The

---

[21] Scholars disagree about whether this is bad policy. David A. Weisbach, *The Taxation of Carried Interests in Private Equity*, 94 Va. L. Rev. 715 (2008), defends the status quo. Andrew Metrick & Ayako Yasuda, *The Economics of Private Equity Funds* (September 8, 2008), Swedish Institute for Financial Research Conference on The Economics of the Private Equity Market. Available at SSRN: http://ssrn.com/abstract=996334, is a good source of information on the structure of a fund. This generally is consistent with Weisbach's account. *See* 94 VA. L. REV. at 720–726.

[22] The fund manager is itself an LLC. Individual managers hold interests through the LLC. The LLC bifurcates its interest in the fund. It makes any required investment in the fund and holds the profits interest through a straw entity that is the fund's general partner. The guaranteed fee is paid directly to the LLC.

[23] The same structure is used in the leveraged buyout sector of the private equity industry. The term "carried interest" has long been used in the oil and gas industry to describe the net profits interest retained by an owner of the mineral rights who conveyed production rights to another. *See*, *e.g.*, Larry L. Bean, *Taxation of Carried Interests in Oil and Gas Transactions – In Retrospect and Prospect*, 10 U. KAN. L. REV. 391 (1962).

manager is a general partner. The manager is paid a guaranteed fee set as a small percentage of total capital invested in the fund. Two percent is not unusual. The manager's equity compensation is in the form of a much larger percentage of profits once the investors recover their investment plus a stipulated "hurdle rate." This equity compensation is called a "carried interest." Typically it is 20 percent of profits.[24] Typically the manager will invest a small amount of capital in the fund. This structure is not unique to the VC industry. It is used across the private equity industry more generally, including leveraged buyout (LBO) funds and hedge funds.[25]

This structure provides significant tax advantages to fund managers when they get equity compensation.[26] Most of the cash generated by VC and LBO funds is realized in the form of capital gains. Thus a fund manager is taxed at the capital gain rate and not the ordinary rate on cash distributions with respect to a profits interest. A fund manager is not taxed on grant of the right. Unlike a founder in a start-up company, a fund manager does not need to pay tax at ordinary rates on the value of the right at the time of grant to convert later returns into capital gains. Unlike a founder in a start-up company, a fund manager does not bear whatever legal risk there may be in aggressively undervaluing the right at the time of grant

17.4.2 Absence of Entity-Level Tax Eliminates the Disadvantage of Converting Compensation into Capital Gains

A partnership is not subject to an entity-level tax. This reduces and sometimes eliminates the cost to other participants in the enterprise of structuring equity compensation to convert it to capital gain to the recipient. In the corporate context strategies that convert equity compensation into capital gain deny the firm any deduction for amounts so treated.[27] Putting aside the value of deferral and the timing option to the recipient, conversion

---

[24] Typically there is a "catch-up" provision so that the manager gets 100 percent of profits after the investors recover their investment plus the hurdle rate until profits are split 80:20. Additional profits are then split 80:20.

[25] Since most income of a hedge fund is ordinary income there is not the same tax advantage to managers.

[26] David A. Weisbach, *supra* n. 21 Noel B. Cunningham & Mitchell L. Engler, *The Carried Interest Controversy: Let's Not Get Carried Away*, 61 TAX. L. REV. 121 (2008), propose an intermediate solution. This is to treat the investors as having loaned the fund manager sufficient funds to purchase the manager's profits interest. The imputed interest on the loan would be ordinary income to the manager.

[27] There are two strategies for making the expected value of equity compensation capital gain. The straightforward strategy is to grant incentive stock options. *See* text and notes 11–12 *supra* for an explanation of the point. The duplicitous

of compensation into capital gain comes at a net cost to the firm and the participant if the firm's tax rate is greater than the difference between the ordinary income rate and the capital gain rate.

In a partnership, if a firm has capital gain income, a strategy of allocating this income to a fund manager is at worst a wash. The net tax benefit to a fund manager from converting ordinary income into capital gain equals the net tax cost to an individual investor who foregoes an ordinary compensation expense and capital gain income. There is never a net tax cost. Furthermore, the tax cost is the same with respect to individual investors in a fund.[28] And it is a wash only if the foregone compensation expense can be deducted by individual investors, which may not be the case. If the foregone expense is not deductible, then allocating a share of capital gain income to a fund manager actually reduces taxes paid by individual investors. As for tax exempt or corporate investors, there is no tax effect on them, positive or negative.[29]

17.4.3 Fee Waiver Agreements

Some private equity funds have fee waiver agreements.[30] Under these agreements the fund manager waives its right to the guaranteed fee in return for an additional profits interest. Typically this takes the form of a preferential right to any net profits in any quarter or year up to the amount of the waived fee. The tax implications to all parties are as just explained for a profits interest. The fund manager receives capital gain instead of ordinary income on the value of the guaranteed fee. There is some deferral and little risk. The deferred fee is paid even if the fund is an

---

strategy is to undervalue the right on grant. *See* text and note 19 *supra* for the same point.

[28] Chris William Sanchirico, *The Tax Advantage to Paying Private Equity Fund Managers with Profits Shares: What Is It? Why Is It Bad?*, 75 U. Chi. L. Rev. 1071 (2008). This assumes the alternative to allocating profits to the manager is to allocate the profits to the investors, pay compensation in the same amount to the manager, and give the investors an equal expense item. Professor Sanchirico concludes that under current law this expense probably is deductible against other income. If this is true, then the tax cost to the manager of taxing profits as compensation (the difference between the ordinary tax rate and the capital gains rate) will equal the tax benefit to individual investors (who will concurrently have income taxed at the capital gains rate and an equal deduction against income taxed at the ordinary tax rate).

[29] Corporations do not get a preferential tax rate on capital gains so it is the same to them. Tax-exempt investors also get no benefit from the foregone expense.

[30] Gregg D Polsky, *Private Equity Management Fee Conversions*, Tax Notes (Feb. 9, 2009), p. 743. Available at: SSRN: http://ssrn.com/abstract=1295443.

overall loser so long as there is a net profit in any quarter or year. As a consequence, fee waiver arrangements should not be considered as a form of equity compensation. It is not clear whether these arrangements will be respected for tax purposes.

One might expect the net tax benefit to participants in a fund of paying equity compensation in the form of a carried interest to create a distortion in favor of equity compensation over cash compensation. The use of fee waiver arrangements casts this effect into doubt. A fee waiver arrangement replicates the tax benefits of equity compensation for what is in substance cash compensation. Replication carries the legal risk that a fee waiver arrangement will be taxed as cash compensation. But the ubiquity of fee waiver arrangements may minimize the actual legal risk and almost certainly minimizes the perceived legal risk (which is what matters).

17.5 THE CURIOUS ABSENCE OF "FOUNDERS' CARRY"

Economically, founders' common serves essentially the same function as the fund manager's carried interest (hereafter: carry). The principal economic difference is risk. Founders make one long-shot bet. Fund managers make many such bets. Founders' common and the fund manager's carry deliver similar tax benefits to the recipients. These benefits are conversion of compensation into capital gain, deferral, and the timing option. But the carry delivers these benefits better and more purely. With the carry the recipient pays no tax on grant of the right. And with the carry there is no legal risk. The tax benefit of founders' common requires undervaluation. Further, because of the entity-level tax, use of the corporate form imposes a cost on the enterprise that is avoided by using the partnership form. Why then is the carry used at the fund level while founders' common is used at the start-up level as a form of equity compensation?

This is a twist on a question that other scholars have asked and to which they have found no good answer.[31] The comparison with the carry merely accentuates the negatives of founders' common. I do not have an answer to the question. One possible reason seems doubtful. This is that the structure of the fund at the start-up level is necessary to achieve the tax benefits at the fund and fund manager level. Forming start-ups as corporations makes it automatic that profits at the fund level will take the form of capital gains and will not be realized until investors in the fund cash out.

---

[31] *See* note 20 *supra*.

If a start-up was organized as a partnership, and a fund continued to hold a successful start-up through maturity as the start-up generated taxable income (much of which is likely to be retained by the firm), then this would be ordinary income to the fund. But this can be avoided by interposing a blocking corporation between start-ups and the fund. Or it can be avoided by converting a successful start-up into a corporation.

The existence of founders' common and the carry in the same industry is a puzzle. My reasons for concluding that tax law probably does not significantly influence the substance of equity compensation either at the start-up level or the fund level present another puzzle. My reason for expecting an absence of influence at the start-up level is that start-ups are so poorly engineered from a tax perspective that I think it unlikely that tax considerations significantly influence the economic deal struck between founders and investors. If the tax cost of founders' common was perceived as an impediment to using equity compensation, then the parties would redesign the deals to eliminate those costs. My reason for expecting an absence of influence at the fund level is that funds are so exquisitely well engineered from a tax perspective that I think the engineers will design around any tax rules that are more than a minor irritant.

17.6 CONCLUSIONS

There is little reason to believe tax law materially influences either the form or the substance of equity compensation in publicly traded corporations. Tax law does seem to influence the form of equity compensation in the private equity industry both at the start-up level and at the venture capital level. Tax considerations are thought to explain the prevalence of "founders' common" at the start-up level. But the tax benefit to the employee of converting ordinary income into capital gain is probably more than offset by the tax cost to the firm of foregoing any deduction for income so converted. There are striking tax benefits in giving fund managers equity compensation in the form of a carried interest. But the industry has contrived a way to replicate these tax benefits while paying what in essence is cash compensation through fee waiver agreements.

18. Public enforcement: an update of the literature on resource-based evidence

Howell E. Jackson*

18.1 INTRODUCTION

Several years ago, my colleague Mark Roe and I undertook an empirical study of the relationship between public enforcement and the development of robust capital markets.[1] Our paper was written in response to earlier work suggesting that private enforcement as opposed to public enforcement was the critical determinant of healthy capital markets. While we were sympathetic to the view that private enforcement could make important contributions to the depth and efficiency of securities markets, we also believed that public enforcement had a major role to play and was, in many respects, a necessary complement to and perhaps even a prerequisite of effective private enforcement. We also theorized that one of the reasons previous econometric models had not uncovered a strong relationship between public enforcement and robust capital markets was that earlier

* This chapter benefits from excellent research assistance from Hye-Sung Kim (HLS SJD Candidate), Kelley O'Mara (HLS JD '14), and Luke Martin (HLS JD '15).

1 Howell E. Jackson & Mark J. Roe, Public *Enforcement of Securities Laws: Resource-Based Evidence*, 93 J. Fin. Econ. 207 (2009). Our joint paper drew on earlier research on regulatory intensity. *See* Howell E. Jackson, *The Impact of Enforcement: A Reflection*, 156 U. Pa. L. Rev. PENNumbra 400 (2008) (available at http://www.pennumbra.com/responses/02-2008/Jackson.pdf); Stavros Gadinis & Howell E. Jackson, *Markets as Regulators: A Survey*, 80 S. Cal. L. Rev. 1239 (2007); Howell E. Jackson, *Variation in the Intensity of Financial Regulation: Preliminary Evidence and Potential Implications*, 24 Yale J. Regulation 253 (2007); Howell E. Jackson, *An American Perspective on the FSA: Politics, Goals & Regulatory Intensity*, *in* Regulatory Reforms in the Age of Financial Consolidation: The Emerging Market Economy and Advanced Countries 39 (2006) (Lee-Jay Cho & Joonkyung Kim eds) (available at http://www.kdi.re.kr/kdi_eng/database/report_read05.jsp?1=1&pub_no=00009931).

researchers had relied on formal indicia of public enforcement, such as the scope of a regulator's legal authority, indicia that might not accurately capture the actual intensity with which public authorities pursue their responsibilities. We hypothesized that the level of real resources committed to public securities enforcement – measured in the form of budgets or staffing normalized to account for the size of each jurisdiction – might provide a more meaningful proxy for public enforcement. When we employed such measures of real resources dedicated to public enforcement, we discovered that public enforcement was consistently associated with several key indicia of robust capital markets, most notably market capitalization, the number of publicly traded firms, initial public offerings, and overall trading levels. Indeed, for these indicia of robust capital markets, our measures of public enforcement intensity performed at least as well as the measures of private enforcement identified as important to capital market development in earlier research.

It has now been more than five years since preliminary versions of our study were released and our measures of real resources made available for use by other analysts. Over that period, a substantial number of researchers have employed our public enforcement variables in empirical studies of their own, and an even larger number have commented upon our approach to measuring regulatory intensity. My goal in this chapter is to review this empirical literature and to attempt to draw some preliminary conclusions as to what this subsequent body of work suggests about the role of public enforcement in the development of securities markets and the robustness of our earlier findings. I also suggest some potential paths for future data collection and research.

The bulk of my analysis appears in section 18.2, which begins with a short overview of our original paper and then organizes subsequent empirical research into five categories. Section 18.2.1 reviews papers that explore the relationship between the Jackson and Roe enforcement variables and measures of robust capital markets similar to those used in our original paper. Section 18.2.2 discusses studies that analyze interactions between a country's regulatory resources and reform efforts involving legal changes in the oversight of capital markets. Section 18.2.3 summarizes studies that attempt to link the Jackson and Roe variables to technical performance in financial markets beyond the simple metrics of market capitalization, public companies, initial public offerings, and trading volumes. Section 18.2.4 reviews work linking our enforcement variables to capital flows, valuation effects, and cross-border listings. Section 18.2.5 focuses on one particularly interesting longitudinal study of the impact of Securities and Exchange Commission (SEC) budgets on firm compliance. Section 18.2.6 reviews a number of empirical projects that extend the analysis of regulatory intensity through the development of variables related to supervisory outputs, such as sanctions and other enforcement activities. Section 18.3 then offers a cursory review of some of the emerging literature surrounding the global financial crisis and discusses potential implications for public enforcement. Section 18.4 concludes and offers some tentative suggestions for future research and the development of more comprehensive datasets on real resources and supervisory outputs.

18.2 A REVIEW OF SUBSEQUENT EMPIRICAL RESEARCH

At the outset, I should emphasize that this literature review focuses on empirical evidence regarding the efficacy or lack thereof of resource-based measures of public enforcement. I am therefore less concerned with an even larger number of scholarly papers that have either accepted the analysis that Professor Roe and I advanced in our paper,[2] or noted theoretical

---

[2] Over 100 publications and working papers have made substantive citations to our original article. *See, e.g.*, William W. Bratton & Michael L. Wachter, *The Political Economy of Fraud on the Market*, 60 U. Pa. L. Rev. 69, 72 n.1 (2011) (citing the article as representing the "consensus view" that "[t]he fraud-on-the-market (FOTM) cause of action just doesn't work"); John C. Coffee, Jr. & Hillary A. Sale, *Redesigning the SEC: Does the Treasury Have a Better Idea?*, 95 Va. L. Rev. 707, 763 n. 188 (2009) (citing article as an example of "recent academic commentary [that] has stressed the likely superiority of public enforcement over private enforcement"); Jürgen Ernstberger, Michael Stich, & Oliver Vogler, *Economic Consequences of Accounting Enforcement Reforms: The Case of Germany*, 21 Eur. Acct. Rev. 217, 223 (2012) (referring to the article as documenting a significantly positive association of strong enforcement with market capitalization, trading volume, and the number of IPOs); Luca Enriques & Matteo Gatti, *Is there a Uniform EU Securities Law After the Financial Services Action Plan?*,114 Stan. J. L. Bus. & Fin. 43, 77 n.118 (2008) (cited for the proposition that "[a]dequate funding of the relevant authorities, together with a highly motivated, sophisticated and well-paid staff, are key factors in a successful enforcement activity"); Ron Harris, *Legal Scholars, Economists and The Interdisciplinary Study of Institutions*, 96 Cornell L. Rev. 789, 805 (2011) (citing article as "hold[ing] that the level of enforcement of the rules, rather than the rules' content, can explain differences in economic outcomes"); Klaus J. Hopt, *Comparative Corporate Governance: The State of the Art and International Regulation*, 59 Am. J. Comp. L. 1, 62 n.381 (2011) (citing article for the proposition that "[t]he extent to which capital market authorities of different countries supervise and enforce corporate governance rules varies considerably"); Ross MacDonald, *Setting Examples, Not Settling: Toward a New SEC Enforcement Paradigm*, 91 Tex. L. Rev. 419, 433 n. 170 (Dec. 2012) (citing article for the proposition that "[a]n increase in the size of the Commission's

limitations to the approach to estimating the intensity of public enforcement that we employed (several of which we anticipated or acknowledged in our original work).[3] While these other lines of inquiry are interesting in their own right, my goal here is to explore whether the more than two dozen empirical studies that have made use of the Jackson and Roe enforcement variables have corroborated or conflicted with the results presented in our *Journal of Financial Economics* paper.[4]

---

budget should, by itself, have a positive effect on the overall effectiveness of the enforcement regime"); Amanda M. Rose, *The Multienforcer Approach to Securities Fraud Deterrence: A Critical Analysis*, 158 U. PA. L. REV. 2173, 2199 n.65 (2010) (citing the article as "highlighting the need to rethink fundamentally the proper allocation of securities fraud enforcement authority in the United States").

[3] For example, Bhattacharya and Daouk note that resources may possibly have only an appearance effect and may not be a credible indicator for effective public enforcement; they recommend instead *ex post* binary measures of real market interventions, such as whether prosecutions have actually taken place. *See* Utpal Bhattacharya & Hazem Daouk, *When No Law is Better than a Good Law*, 13 REV. FIN. 577, 590–594 (2009). Armour, Mayer, and Polo also argue that using the staffing and budget variables as proxy for robust public enforcement does not account for differences in which the regulatory resources are allocated to supervisory functions across different jurisdictions. *See* John Armour, Colin Mayer, & Andrea Polo, *Regulatory Sanctions and Reputational Damage in Financial Markets* 6 (Oxford Legal Studies Research Paper No. 62/2010, 2011), *available at* http://ssrn.com/abstract=1678028. In addition to the misallocation possibility, Waked argues that the level of regulatory resources does not necessarily show political and market support for public enforcement, and suggests that formal regulatory powers also need to be taken into account at the same time to make sure that regulators are authorized to exercise necessary powers for effective enforcement. *See* Dina I. Waked, *Do Developing Countries Enforce Their Antitrust Laws? A Statistical Study of Public Antitrust Enforcement in Developing Countries* 22–24 (Dec. 22, 2011), *available at* http://ssrn.com/abstract=2044047. Beyond that, Murè and Pesic point out the possibility of underestimation bias in the Jackson and Roe variables, due to the concerns about data inconsistency and incompleteness. *See* Pina Murè & Valerio Pesic, *Are Sanctions Effective in Improving Bank Performance? A Study on Supervision and Administrative Sanctions Upon Italian Banks During the 1998–2009 Period* 21 (CAREFIN Research Paper No. 23/2010, 2010), *available at* http://ssrn.com/abstract=1799882. In a similar vein, Leuz raises the possibility that the result of Jackson and Roe might understate actual enforcement differences between the United States and the United Kingdom because the measures do not account for private securities litigation and the imposition of criminal penalties, both of which tend to be more common in the United States. *See* Christian Leuz, *Different Approaches to Corporate Reporting Regulation: How Jurisdictions Differ and Why*, 43 ACCT. BUS. RES. 229, 247 (2010).

[4] Also excluded from the following discussion are empirical papers that simply utilize the Jackson and Roe public enforcement variables as robustness checks or controls that are not given substantive attention. *See, e.g.*, Douglas J.

Our principal empirical finding in that article was that higher levels of resources committed to public enforcement agencies – whether measured in terms of staff per million of national population or budgets per billion of national gross domestic product (GDP) – were positively associated with several standard measures of robust capital markets: equity market size as a percentage of GDP, trading volumes as a percentage of GDP, number of public firms per million of population, and initial public offering (IPO) value as a percentage of GDP.[5] Our research did not, however, demonstrate a consistent and statistically significant correlation with other measures of capital market development, including dispersion of ownership of shares, block premia, or technical measures of capital market performance, including efficiency and market stability.[6] Thus, while we concluded that "[w]hen measured in terms of resources, public enforcement has a consistent and robust association with four key dependent variables that measure robust external capital markets,"[7] we were more circumspect about the channels through which public enforcement effected those results: "[A]s the analysis here did not establish a consistent association between regulatory resources and technical measures of market performance, public enforcement's role in enhancing trading channels is a theoretical possibility lacking empirical validation."[8] Thus, one question of particular interest in this review is whether subsequent research has detected additional associations between our resource-based measures of public enforcement and intermediate channels through which enforcement efforts might contribute to strong securities markets.

One final preliminary note: while the following review focuses primarily on empirical findings related to the Jackson and Roe variables, the

---

Cumming, Sofia Johan, & Dan Li, *Exchange Trading Rules and Stock Market Liquidity*, 99 J. FIN. ECON. 651 (2011); Douglas J. Cumming, Feng Zhan, & Michael J. Aitken, *High Frequency Trading and End-of-Day Manipulation* (Sept. 12, 2012), *available at* http://ssrn.com/abstract=2145565; Larry Fauver, Xi Li, & Alvaro Taboada, *The Impact of International Governance Reforms: A Multi-Country Examination* (July 2012), *available at* http://www.fma.org/Atlanta/Papers/InternationalGovernanceReforms.pdf; Xi Li, *An Examination of the Impact of the Sarbanes–Oxley Act on Cross-Listed Foreign Private Issuers and the Legal Bonding Hypothesis* (Mar. 5, 2011), *available at* http://ssrn.com/abstract=952433; Amir N. Licht, Christopher Poliquin, Jordan I. Siegel, & Xi Li, *What Makes the Bonding Stick? A Natural Experiment Involving the US Supreme Court and Cross-Listed Firms* (Harvard Business School Strategy Unit Working Paper No. 11-072, 2011), *available at* http://ssrn.com/abstract=1919805.

[5] *See* Jackson & Roe, *supra* note 1, at 217–223 (tables 4 and 5).

[6] *Id.*, at 227–233 (tables 8 and 9).

[7] *Id.*, at 235.

[8] *Id.*

papers reviewed do not themselves have such a specific focus. Rather, each of these papers investigates a distinctive hypothesis and as part of that analysis utilizes one of the Jackson and Roe variables or some variant thereon to determine whether enforcement intensity has a bearing on the other variables of interest. Often times, this aspect of the analysis is a relatively minor piece of the overall paper. The goal of this exercise is to bring together these disparate lines of research to present a larger picture of the extent to which the expenditure of real supervisory resources has been found to have a consistent and significant association with important indicia of financial market performance.

18.2.1 Papers Exploring the Relationship Between the Jackson and Roe Variables and Measures of Robust Capital Markets Similar to Ones Used in Our Original Paper

At least two subsequent empirical studies explore the relationship of the Jackson and Roe resource-based enforcement variables to dependent variables similar to the one we employed in our original paper, albeit in somewhat different functional forms.

In a 2010 working paper, Echeverri-Gent and Bloom focus their attention on the relationship between politics and financial development.[9] In a model that incorporated controls for electoral competitiveness, federalism, and checks on executive power, they conceptualize regulatory budgets and staffing as reflections of political choices and thus also included our public-enforcement variables in several sets of regressions. The dependent variables in their regressions are quite similar to the four measures of robust financial markets that we used in our original paper, though they added a measure of private bond market capitalization that we did not utilize in our study. They report statistically significant and positive coefficients for regressions in functional forms similar to ones in our original paper, but do not find consistent or statistically significant correlations between our enforcement variables and private bond markets. The authors conclude: "[W]e find support for those who argue that the well-endowed government regulators play an important role in promoting financial market development."[10]

---

[9] *See* John Echeverri-Gent & Benjamin J. Bloom, *Do Competitive Politics Produce Competitive Markets? Politics of Financial Market Development* (APSA 2010 Annual Meeting Paper, 2010), *available at* http://ssrn.com/abstract=1644631.

[10] *Id.*, at 1 (quoting abstract). *See also id.*, at 23 ("Using measures of resources available to regulators, we found a positive and significant association between two of four dimensions of financial market development and standardized measures of regulatory budgets and staff.").

In a 2011 working paper, Cumming, Knill, and Richardson[11] explored the influence of public and private enforcement on securities issuances utilizing a research strategy that distinguishes between the size of issuers and the level of economic development of countries, differentiating between G10 jurisdictions and non-G10 jurisdictions. Their analysis exploits a newly assembled dataset of 42,337 firms across 46 countries and spanning the years 1996 to 2007, thus generating approximately 175,000 firm-year observations, and considerably more statistical power than the 47-country cross-sectional sample upon which our original paper was based. In two sets of regressions – one utilizing the Jackson and Roe public enforcement variable and the other employing an alternative measure of public staffing reported in La Porta, Lopez, and Schliefer (LLS)[12] – the Cumming, Knill, and Richardson paper concludes as follows:

> Consistent with Jackson and Roe (2009), we find evidence that the staffing levels increase the probability of equity access. At the same time, our initial findings are substantiated by the inclusion of resource-based measures. Public enforcement significantly increases the probability of equity issuance by 72.1 percent and 58.6 percent for small G10 firms when the LLS and Jackson and Roe variables are included, respectively. Large firm access to equity in G10 countries is significantly hindered by public regulation, reducing issuance by approximately 50.1 percent (for LLS in Panel A) to 87.2 percent (for Jackson and Roe in Panel B) and reducing the amount raised by $4.024 million in Panel A.[13]

Beyond providing additional evidence that resource-based measures of enforcement are associated with robust capital markets in a different functional form, the Cumming, Knill, and Richardson paper suggests that the impact of enforcement may vary in a consistent manner across firm size and national economic development, with the most pronounced effects being for smaller firms in developed economies.[14]

---

[11] *See* Douglas Cumming, April Knill, & Nela Richardson, *Firm Size, Institutional Quality and the Impact of Securities Regulation* 18 (Jan. 24, 2011), *available at* http://ssrn.com/abstract=1572655.

[12] Rafael La Porta, Florencio Lopez-de-Silanes, & Andrei Shleifer, *What Works in Securities Laws?*, 61 J. FIN. 1 (2006).

[13] Cumming, Knill, & Richardson, *supra* note 11, at 18. In their principal presentations, the authors utilized the LLS formal measures of public enforcement, which we criticized in our 2009 paper, and obtained comparable results. Accordingly, this aspect of the authors' analysis is inconsistent with our assertion that resource-based measures of enforcement offer more informative correlates with robust capital markets than do formal measures of public enforcement.

[14] In our original research, we did report robustness checks on non-Organisation for Economic Co-operation and Development (OECD) countries

18.2.2 Papers Investigating Interactions Between Levels of Real Resources Dedicated to Capital Market Oversight and the Success of Reform Efforts

Another group of studies utilize our resource-based measures of public enforcement to examine whether countries that dedicated more resources to regulatory reform behave differently in some areas of regulatory reform or market activities. While the results of these studies are not uniform in their findings, in many contexts, greater resources have been found to have a statistically significant association with the dependent variable of interest. Several of these studies explore technical measures of financial market performance similar to the ones with which we could not document a correlation with real resources in our original paper.

For example, in a 2011 working paper, Christensen, Hail, and Leuz conducted an empirical study of the changes in the market liquidity and the cost of capital to firms in each of the 27 countries in the European Union as the countries implemented the Market Abuse Directive and the Transparency Directive on a staggered basis between 2001 and 2009.[15] Their work shows that the implementation of the two directives was significantly correlated with the increase of market liquidity (measured by bid–ask spreads and percentage of zero-return days) and the decrease of cost of capital (measured by implied cost of capital and dividend yields). Of particular interest here, the paper's examination of liquidity effects segments countries based on both their prior level of supervisory staffing and also the amount by which the countries increased their staffing at the time of implementation of the directives.[16] The study concludes: "[T]he countries that exhibit the largest liquidity improvements are those that already had relatively well-staffed supervisory authorities to begin with, but further increase the supervisory staff around the introduction of the new directives."[17]

---

and did not find differential effects. *See* Jackson & Roe, *supra* note 1, at 237 n.13. We did not explore the relationship between firm size and public enforcement as our model analyzed effects at the national level.

15 *See* Hans B. Christensen, Luzi Hail, & Christian Leuz, *Capital-Market Effects of Securities Regulation: Hysteresis, Implementation, and Enforcement* (Nat'l Bureau of Econ. Res., Working Paper No. 16737, Jan. 2011), *available at* http://www.nber.org/papers/w16737.

16 The authors developed their own measures of real-resource levels and growth by utilizing a technique quite similar to the one employed in Jackson & Roe, *supra* note 1.

17 Christensen, Hail, & Leuz, *supra* note 15, at 33. As discussed below, causality between real resources and robust capital markets is potentially bi-directional.

The Christensen, Hail, and Leuz results are informative on multiple dimensions. First, they provide evidence of a positive relationship between supervisory resources and a technical measure of market performance (bid–ask spreads), which might reasonably be thought to contribute to robust capital markets. Second, at least in this context, they isolate the source of this improvement as coming largely from countries that already had substantial supervisory staffing and increased that staffing at the time of implementation of the directives. In other words, the gains did not come from traditionally low-supervisory jurisdictions that contemporaneously increased supervisory resources. The authors conclude with the following interpretation:

> The liquidity effects of the two directives are stronger in countries with a history of higher regulatory quality and with traditionally stronger securities regulators. Stricter implementation and enforcement of the two directives also result in larger liquidity effects, but these effects stem largely from countries with strong prior regulatory quality and with already relatively well staffed securities regulators. One explanation for these findings is that countries that have put more resources into securities regulation and that have a better track record of implementing and enforcing regulation are more willing and better able to implement the new EU directives. Put differently, the same forces that limited the strength of past regulation appear to be at work when new rules are introduced. It is important to note that these forces could span a wide range, including institutional fit, resource constraints, inefficient bureaucracies, and political pressures, and that our tests cannot distinguish between these forces. In sum, our findings support a causal link between stricter securities regulation and market liquidity. They also support the notion that the success of regulation depends critically on how regulation is implemented and enforced. Thus, policy debates should pay close attention to implementation and enforcement issues if regulation is to have the intended effects. Our finding that countries with weaker securities regulation do not catch up with stronger countries illustrates the difficulty of harmonizing capital markets through regulatory reforms. It highlights that prior regulatory conditions matter and that imposing the *same* regulation on countries with disparate initial conditions can have the effect of making countries diverge more, not less.[18]

In a subsequent 2012 working paper also exploring the effects of adoption of the European Union (EU) Market Abuse Directive (MAD), Dubois, Dumontier, and Frésard document changes in another technical

---

See *infra* text accompanying notes 46–51. Findings such as the Christensen, Hail, and Leuz results, which establish links between regulatory intensity and improvements in technical measures of market quality, offer additional evidence that causation runs from resources to robustness.

[18] *Id.*, at 34–35.

measure of stock market performance: biased research advice from the sell-side equity research industries in 13 European countries between 1997 and 2007. Utilizing both Jackson and Roe variables and LLS formal indices of formal powers, the paper reports more rapid declines in biased research from jurisdictions with higher levels of real resources dedicated to securities supervision.[19] The Dubois, Dumontier, and Frésard paper also includes proxies for actual legal sanctions and finds further positive effects. They conclude:

> [U]sing the heterogeneity that exists in legal sanctions and enforcement practices across European countries, we find that the curbing effect of MAD largely depends on countries' institutional traits. In particular, we estimate that the impact of MAD is significantly stronger in countries where the sanctions applicable in cases of violations of MAD's rules are severe.[20]

18.2.3 Other Papers Exploring the Relationship Between the Jackson and Roe Variables and Other Technical Measures of Financial Market Performance

A 2012 working paper by Amiram and Owens studied another technical measure of capital market performance, the relationship between income smoothing in financial statements and the cost of firm debt.[21] In an empirical study based on 1817 facility-level debt observations for 639 non-US borrowers across 20 countries from 1996 to 2009, the authors concluded that income smoothing is associated with lower costs of debt in countries where it is more difficult for managers to extract private benefits of firm value and is associated with higher costs of debt in jurisdictions where it is easier to extract private benefits. In alternative specifications, the authors segment jurisdictions substituting the Jackson and Roe variables as a proxy for restraints on private benefits and report "qualitatively consistent" results.[22] Accordingly the paper offers additional evidence that increased investments in public enforcement can be associated with lower costs of capital.

---

[19] *See* Michel Dubois, Pascal Dumontier, & Laurent Frésard, *Regulating Conflicts of Interest: The Effect of Sanctions and Enforcement* (Working Paper, Jan. 2012), *available at* http://ssrn.com/abstract=1786523.

[20] *Id.*, at 34.

[21] *See* Dan Amiram & Edward Owens, *Private Benefits Extraction and the Opposing Effects of Income Smoothing on Private Debt Contracts* (Oct. 19, 2011), *available at* https://community.bus.emory.edu/Faculty/Events%20Documents/Owens_paper.pdf.

[22] *Id.*, at 23.

Another paper investigating technical measures of performance is Kerl and Ohlert's 2012 working paper on the accuracy of forecasts by star analysts.[23] Using three separate measures of forecast accuracy, the authors explore a number of hypotheses, including the question of whether the quality of corporate governance affects the accuracy of analysts' forecasts. In distinguishing among corporate governance regimes, they use several different proxies, including one that is based on the Jackson and Roe staffing variable. In jurisdictions with higher levels of supervisory staffing, Kerl and Ohlert report, the forecasts of all analysts are more accurate and the relative merits of star analyst forecasts are especially pronounced.[24] The paper concludes: "[B]etter corporate governance and stronger investor protection positively influences the forecasting accuracy of star-analysts."[25]

In a similar vein, Arand, Kerl, and Walter have undertaken a 2013 study into the informativeness of 600,000 sell-side analyst reports in eight leading capital markets.[26] The authors explored whether the regulatory environment of both issuers and institutional investors influences the informativeness of analyst reports, measured by both short-term market reactions and an *ex post* assessment of report accuracy. The study uses several different measures of the quality of the regulatory environment, one of which is the Jackson and Roe staffing variable.[27] In a variety of model specifications, the authors found higher levels of informativeness for analyst reports in jurisdictions with larger Jackson and Roe staffing levels: "the information value of target price and earnings forecast revisions, as proxied by the level of market reaction, increases with the level of investor protection."[28] Similarly, "forecast errors are negatively associated

---

23 *See* Alexander Kerl & Martin Ohlert, *Star-analysts' Forecast Accuracy and the Role of Corporate Governance* (Dec. 2012), *available at* http://papers.ssrn.com/abstract=2195909.

24 *See id.*, at 38, Table 5, Panel D. The authors also use the LSS public enforcement index as a separate measure of corporate governance and find similarly positive though somewhat less consistent effects. *See id.*, Panel C

25 *Id.*, *at* 5.

26 *See* Daniel Arand, Alexander G. Kerl, & Andreas Walter, *When Do Sell-Side Analyst Reports Really Matter? Shareholder Protection, Institutional Investors and the Importance of Equity Research* (Feb. 2013), *available at* http://ssrn.com/abstract=2044548.

27 As its primary proxy for investor protection, the paper uses common law origins. As alternative measures, in addition to the Jackson and Roe staffing variable, the study uses a measure of anti-self dealing and the LSS public enforcement index. The results reported in the text are largely comparable for alternative specifications.

28 *Id.*, at 17.

with the respective investor protection measure and highly significant at the 1% level."[29] The study also found that report informativeness was influenced by whether institutional investors came from jurisdictions with higher Jackson and Roe staffing variables, suggesting that enforcement intensity might have positive extra-territorial effects.[30]

To be sure, not all intervening studies have reported robust effects of supervisory resources on capital market performance. In a 2012 working paper, Cumming, Imad'Eddine, and Schwienbacher test various law and enforcement proxies in connection with the degree of spread of Undertakings for Collective Investment in Transferable Securities (UCITS) equity funds and bond funds to other countries.[31] While the authors find a statistically significant correlation between the level of UCIT spread and host countries with better anti-director rights or with better creditor rights, they fail to indicate any association between the regulatory budget and staffing level of host countries and the spread of UCITS funds.

Similarly in a 2009 working paper, Frijns, Gilbert, and Tourani-Rad developed datasets of the scope, sanctions, and enforcement of insider trading laws for a sample of 1432 firms from 30 countries to examine their efficacy in decreasing informational asymmetry and the incidence of insider trading.[32] In their analysis, they failed to find any statistically

---

[29] *See also id.*, at 24.

[30] *See id.*, at 18–22 & n.22; 24–26 & n.28. In a separate study on stock market manipulation, Comerton-Forde and Putniņš devise a measure of regulatory budgets normalized by the number of stocks for which market regulators in a country are responsible, a variant on the Jackson & Roe measure of real resources. See Carole Comerton-Forde & Tālis J. Putniņš, *Stock Price Manipulation: Prevalence and Determinants* (May 17, 2013) (Review of Finance first published online March 4, 2013 doi:10.1093/rof/rfs040). The authors report: "We find that government regulatory budget has a strong effect on both manipulation and detection. Across all three models, larger government regulatory budgets increase the probability of detecting and prosecuting manipulation and also decrease the probability of manipulation." *Id.* at 16. In *The Deterrence Effect of SEC Enforcement Intensity on Illegal Insider Trading* (May 13, 2013), available at http://papers.ssrn.com/so13/papers.cfm?abstract_id=1784528, Diane Del Guercio, Elizabeth R. Odders-White and Mark J. Ready present similar evidence showing that increases in regulatory budgets of the SEC reduce the level of insider trading in the United States.

[31] *See* Douglas J. Cumming, Gael Imad'Eddine, & Armin Schwienbacher, *Legality and the Spread of Voluntary Investor Protection* (Dec. 15, 2011), *available at* http://papers.ssrn.com/sol3/papers.cfm?abstract_id=1990477.

[32] *See* Bart Frijns, Aaron B. Gilbert, & Alireza Tourani-Rad, *Elements of Effective Insider Trading* (Finance and Corporate Governance Conference 2010 Paper, Aug. 3, 2009), *available at* http://ssrn.com/abstract=1443597.

significant association of the size of the regulatory budget and staffing and the deterrence of insider trading.

At least one 2011 working paper identified an association between supervisory resources and reform outcomes that might be viewed as having negative implications. In a study exploring the speed with which national authorities adopted International Financial Reporting Standards (IFRS), Pownall and Wieczynska found that a higher level of regulatory budget and staff, as measured by the Jackson and Roe variables, was negatively associated with the likelihood that a firm in the European Union adopted IFRS.[33] However, when assessing their results involving other proxies for enforcement, the authors conclude: "We find little evidence that cross-country enforcement conditions or mechanisms are associated with IFRS adoption during our period."[34]

18.2.4 Studies Exploring the Relationship between Jackson and Roe Variables and Capital Flows, Valuations, and Cross-Listing Decisions

A separate strand of research investigates the impact of cross-border flows of capital, valuation effects, and cross-listing decisions by corporate issuers. While some of the studies find statistically significant correlations with the Jackson and Roe public enforcement variables, the results are mixed. On balance, however, the evidence available to date suggests a possible impact of real resources dedicated to enforcement activities on cross-border capital flows.

In a 2012 paper published in the *Journal of International Money and Finance*, Eichler examined a dataset measuring equity home bias of US investors toward 38 countries from 2003 to 2008 with the goal of exploring the influence of the quality of corporate disclosure in each country on mitigating the equity home bias of US investors – a bias which generally leads investors to overinvest in the United States at the expense of what are thought to be more desirable levels of international diversification.[35] After determining that the quality of corporate disclosure in foreign jurisdictions is associated with a statistically significant reduction in home-country bias

---

[33] *See* Grace Pownall & Maria Wieczynska, *Deviations from the Mandatory Adoption of IFRS in the European Union: Implementation, Enforcement, Incentives, and Compliance* (Working Paper, 2011), *available at* http://ssrn.com/abstract=1919805.

[34] *Id.*, at 34.

[35] Stefan Eichler, *Equity Home Bias and Corporate Disclosure*, 31 J. INT'L. MONEY FIN. 1008 (2012).

on the part of US investors,[36] the author then expanded his analysis to consider the marginal impact of supervisory intensity, using the Jackson and Roe staffing variable. He concludes: "I find that more comprehensive de facto corporate disclosure significantly reduces the equity home bias of US investors only if the staff of the domestic securities supervisory agency exceeds 5.28 employees per million of a country's population."[37] The Stefan analysis thus corroborates a hypothesis advanced in our original article: that one of the channels through which public enforcement benefits capital markets is through its interaction with disclosure standards.[38]

In a further exploration of the relationship between disclosure and public enforcement in a cross-border context, Loureiro and Taboada have presented a 2011 working paper exploring the relationship between stock market informativeness and the adoption of IFRS of 18,762 firms across 32 countries from 1999 through 2009.[39] While their primary investigation concerned the positive effect on stock market informativeness of voluntary adoptions, they also investigated whether higher public enforcement levels were associated with greater informativeness where issuers were mandated to adopt IFRS. Using both a variant of the LLS public enforcement index and the Jackson and Roe variable for regulatory budgets, the authors reached the following conclusion:

> The results show that mandatory adopters in countries with better enforcement exhibit a more significant increase in stock price informativeness following IFRS adoption. These results are both statistically and economically significant. In model 1, for mandatory adopters, a one standard deviation increase in the 19 public enforcement index (0.392) is associated with an 8.8 percentage point increase in [stock price informativeness] for mandatory adopters, which constitutes about 7.2 percent of its standard deviation. The results using the regulatory budget variable confirm our findings.[40]

The authors interpret these results to suggest that, when an issuer is forced to adopt IFRS as the result of a government mandate, stock market

---

[36] Interestingly, the paper finds this effect only when using a measure of de facto disclosure and not when using the LLS disclosure index based on formal legal requirements. *Id.*, at 1021.

[37] *Id.*, at 1024. The paper also finds marginal improvements in home bias reduction when countries have higher scores on the LLS liability measure, although the effect is not as significant as the effect for the Jackson and Roe variable.

[38] *See* Jackson & Roe, *supra* note 1, at 236.

[39] Gilberto R. Loureiro and Alvaro G. Taboada, *The Impact of IFRS Adoption on Stock Price Informativeness* (Oct. 31, 2011), *available at* http://papers.ssrn.com/sol3/papers.cfm?abstract_id=1952593.

[40] *Id.*, at 18–19.

pricing rewards that adoption only when the jurisdiction maintains robust systems of supervisory oversight; in lax jurisdictions, the authors reason, mandatory IFRS adoption does not send a credible market signal.[41]

Studies regarding the cross-listing of securities are more mixed in their findings with respect to enforcement intensity. In a 2012 working paper, Sarkissian and Schill explored the importance of law enforcement in explaining foreign listing premium in 2838 listings on 32 foreign stock exchanges from 69 home markets during the period 1985–2006.[42] From the Jackson and Roe variables, they create a dummy variable that takes the value of one when a host market's enforcement level is higher than that of a home country. However, they fail to find any statistically significant correlation between the intensity of public enforcement and foreign listing premium, other than in a small positive effect in the cases of US firms listed overseas.[43]

In contrast, Samarasekera, Chang, and Tarca present a study of the accounting quality of 495 UK-listed firms which implemented IFRS, including 246 cross-listed firms (mostly from Germany and the US).[44] Finding that accounting quality improves for only cross-listed firms, the authors conclude that changes in regulatory scrutiny (by cross-listed countries) had a material effect on the quality of accounting reporting, reasoning that the additional scrutiny imposed on firms listed in multiple jurisdictions contributed to these improvements. While the study did not utilize Jackson and Roe variables in their analysis, they concluded: "Consistent with the view of Jackson and Roe (2009) that public enforcement is a key mechanism for promoting protection of investors and growth of securities markets, our evidence shows benefits from activity

---

41 *Id.*, at 22.

42 *See* Sergei Sarkissian & Michael J. Schill, *The Nature of the Foreign Listing Premium: A Cross-Country Examination* (Darden Business School Working Paper No. 1639848, Jan. 29, 2012), *available at* http://ssrn.com/abstract=1639848.

43 *Id.*, at 17–18. The study also found insignificant effects for rule of law variables and LLS disclosure indices. See also Robert P. Bartlett, *Do Institutional Investors Value the 10b-5 Private Right of Action? Evidence from Investor Trading Behavior Following Morrison v. National Australia Bank Ltd.* (Oct. 22, 2012), *available at* http://papers.ssrn.com/id=2171006 (in a study finding no evidence of a statistically significant shift to ADR trading following the Supreme Court's 2010 Morrison decision, the analysis also determines that trading also did not shift from foreign securities listed in jurisdictions with low scores on Jackson and Roe enforcement variables).

44 *See* Nelly Samarasekera, Millicent Chang, & Ann Tarca, *IFRS and Accounting Quality: The Impact of Enforcement* (Dec. 1, 2012), *available at* http://ssrn.com/abstract=2183061.

by public bodies to promote the quality of audit and compliance with accounting standards."[45]

18.2.5 One Longitudinal Study on the SEC Budgets and Estimates of Corporate Compliance

As Professor Roe and I acknowledged at the time, one of the potential weaknesses of our original paper was its reliance on cross-sectional analysis, which is poorly suited to deciphering causality. While we made some attempts to employ instrumental variable to tease out the causal relationship between greater resources and more robust capital markets,[46] we recognized that causation might plausibly run in the other direction with more robust capital markets leading to greater resources. As we noted at the time, longitudinal studies offered a promising solution for unpacking causation, but we lacked the necessary data to undertake such a study. At least one team of researchers has undertaken to rectify this shortcoming.

In a 2013 working paper, Lohse, Pascalau, and Thomann assembled a dataset containing SEC funding and enforcement between 1946 and 2010 to investigate whether increases in SEC resources improved compliance with securities market rules.[47] Following Jackson and Roe, these investigators used SEC budgets as a proxy for public enforcement. Their paper is noteworthy because it expands on our original analysis in two important ways. First, it presents a longitudinal view that explores the impact of SEC resources in one period on future events, thus addressing potential concerns of reverse causation. Second, the paper links real resources to enforcement actions, a regulatory output, and then goes on to interpret from the incidence of enforcement actions the level of industry compliance: a goal of any well-functioning system of supervision.[48] The authors summarize their findings as follows:

---

[45] *Id.*, at 8.

[46] *See* Jackson & Roe, *supra* note 1, at 233–234.

[47] Tim Lohse, Razvan Pascalau, & Christian Thomann, *Public Enforcement of Securities Market Rules*: *Resource-Based Evidence from the Securities Exchange Commission* (Jan. 29, 2013) (on file with author). Note that the Comerton-Forde and Putniņš paper and the Del Guercio et al. paper, discussed above in note 30, also made use of longitudinal data on changes in regulatory budgets over a series of years.

[48] The paper also differs from our prior work in that it focuses on the impact of resources within a single jurisdiction over time, thus eliminating confounding problems of heterogeneity across countries. *See id.*, at 4.

> In a theoretical model, we characterize a corporation's compliance decision with the securities laws under the SEC's supervision. The model predicts, first, that increases in the regulator's resources deter firms from misbehaving (compliance hypothesis). Second, the model predicts that an increase in the SEC's budget leads to a (temporary) decrease of observed compliance. Given that the SEC may even police past misbehavior, this decrease reflects the delayed adjustment of corporations' compliance behavior (adjustment hypothesis). We test these hypotheses by using data on the SEC's funding and the reported cases of current noncompliance (injunctions). We find supportive evidence for our theory: Our empirical results show that the increases in the SEC's budget lead to a higher compliance by financial market participants. First, using Granger-causality tests we establish that there is a significant link between the SEC's resources and corporations' contemporaneous misbehavior. Second, we show that an increase in the SEC's budget leads to a (temporary) decrease of observed compliance. This is reflected in a temporary increase in the number of injunctions that the SEC brings against the securities industry. Third, the longer-term effect of an increase in the SEC's resources is a decrease in (reported) ongoing misbehavior. The results from the VAR analysis suggest that a positive budget shock leads to an aggregate decrease in the number of ongoing misbehavior [sic], reflected by a decrease in the number of injunctions by 10% within five years and by 18% . . . within ten years, respectively. This is clear evidence for higher firm compliance.[49]

Though limited to the United States, Lohse, Pascalau, and Thomann offer perhaps the most compelling evidence to date of the causal relationship between public enforcement and capital market behavior. Utilizing empirical techniques developed to unpack similar problems of causality in criminology, the paper offers a much more sophisticated approach to causality than the one that Professor Roe and I attempted in our original work.

In addition, the study documents the impact of real resources on an intermediate outcome: firm compliance. As the authors explain:

> [N]either [Jackson and Roe nor LLS] models how resources available for enforcement directly influence firms' decisions to comply with securities market rules. Instead, both studies investigate how enforcement affects financial market development. While financial market development is likely to be the longer-term result of enforcement it is not directly affected by this. In practice, before enforcement can lead to better financial markets, i.e. markets where investors demand a relatively low return on their capital as they do not have to be afraid of being defrauded, it must initially influence firms' decisions to comply with securities market rules. By analyzing the incentives for firms' disclosure provided by the SEC's enforcement, our study closes this gap. It is those changes in compliance that – over time – can lead to improved financial markets.[50]

---

49 *Id.*, at 6.
50 *Id.*, at 3.

Thus the paper presents additional evidence of a channel through which real resources could lead to more robust capital markets.

Finally, the paper is noteworthy through its effort to expand the analysis to include public enforcement variables. While Lohse, Pascalau, and Thomann utilize enforcement outcomes – specifically injunctions – as the dependent variable in their analysis,[51] one could imagine further lines of inquiry that employ such enforcement levels as explanatory variables for various kinds of market activities. Admittedly, the collection of data of this sort presents significant challenges in cross-country analyses as enforcement tools and utilization rates differ considerably from jurisdiction to jurisdiction. But when used in time series for a single jurisdiction, as Lohse, Pascalau, and Thomann have in their paper, the approach is tractable and holds considerable promise.

18.2.6 Other Studies Exploring the Impact of Sanctions and other Regulatory Outputs

Although our original paper did not attempt to analyze the impact of actual enforcement actions on the development of robust capital markets, we did note the potential for this form of analysis,[52] and several subsequent papers have started to explore the impact of enforcement actions on various outcomes of interest, a number of which specifically cite our 2009 article as a point of departure for their efforts.[53]

For example, Delis and Staikouras, identifying their work as "inspired

---

[51] This functional form makes the authors' interpretations of rising and then falling levels of enforcement actions a critical component of their analysis. In particular, the authors' inference that lower levels of enforcement actions reflect greater private compliance might be resisted on the grounds that other factors – such as an evolution of enforcement priorities – are not associated with changes in private compliance. The authors' interpretation is, however, entirely plausible and strengthened by the longitudinal approach of their analysis.

[52] *See* Jackson & Roe, *supra* note 1, at 237.

[53] Another 2011 working paper not discussed in the text but very much drawing on the same tradition is Dina I. Waked, *Do Developing Countries Enforce Their Antitrust Laws? A Statistical Study of Public Antitrust Enforcement in Developing Countries* (Dec. 22, 2011), *available at* http://ssrn.com.ezp-prod1.hul.harvard.edu/abstract=2044047, which presents a unique database of 20 antitrust enforcement variables for 50 developing countries, including both regulatory inputs (such as staffing and budgets) as well as regulatory outputs (including numerous variables related to sanctions). The paper demonstrates that these measures of enforcement based on actual regulatory inputs and outputs are not consistently correlated with enforcement proxies that researchers have traditionally used in academic research. *Id.*, at 81–87.

by the works" of Jackson and Roe (as well as that of Professor John Coffee of Columbia Law School), developed a new dataset measuring two enforcement outputs in the context of bank supervision: on-site audits and sanctions.[54] The authors summarize their findings as follows: "Our results show an inverted U-shape relationship between on-site audits and bank risks, while the relationship between sanctions and risk appears to be linear and negative."[55] While this paper deals with a special aspect of bank risk, the work suggests that collection data on supervisory outputs can produce important, objective analysis as to the efficacy of different supervisory tactics.

Work in a similar vein, also following lines of analysis suggested in our original article, is Brogi's 2011 working paper exploring the efficacy of Bank of Italy administrative sanctions in disciplining bank board members.[56] After presenting a comprehensive overview of Bank of Italy sanctions between 1998 and 2009, the paper concludes as follows:

> Results confirm that the Bank of Italy has been increasingly active in its supervisory role as concerns both inspections and sanctions . . . However, Bank of Italy sanctions do not seem to be effective in disciplining board members or banks. Recidivism is extremely widespread (37% of sanctioned banks and 22% of sanctioned persons are sanctioned more than once in the twelve-year period). The fact that most people sanctioned more than once are sanctioned again in the same entity after 3 years of the first sanction suggests that administrative sanctions do not prevent re-election of bank board members[57]

Based on these findings, the author goes on to suggest a number of different options that might increase the efficacy of Bank of Italy sanctions in the future, thus illustrating that even evidence of ineffective enforcement activity can generate potentially valuable insights for supervisory authorities.

In an even more extensive review of sanctioning policy, Gadinis published an important study in 2012 exploring the relationship between SEC enforcement actions against broker-dealers and the kinds of firms and

---

54 *See* Manthos D. Delis & Panagiotis K. Staikouras, *Supervisory Effectiveness and Bank Risk*, 15 Rev. Fin. 511, 511 (2011).

55 *Id.*

56 *See* Marina Brogi, *Once Bitten Twice Shy? A Study on the Effectiveness of Administrative Sanctions to Discipline Bank Board Members* (June 14, 2011), *available at* http://www.efmaefm.org/0EFMAMEETINGS/EFMA%20ANNUAL%20MEETINGS/2011-Braga/papers/0289.pdf.

57 *Id.*, at 22.

levels of sanctions imposed.[58] After constructing an extensive new dataset of SEC administrative and judicial enforcement actions between 2005 and April 2007, Gadinis proceeded to consider whether the SEC employs comparable enforcement practices between large and small firms and concluded that on many critical dimensions the Commission treats large firms more favorably in terms of imposing fewer sanctions on individuals, relying to a greater extent on administrative as opposed to judicial proceedings, and imposing less stringent penalties on employees of large firms. The Gadinis article demonstrates how empirical analysis of sanctioning practices can help monitor enforcement practices and potentially identify inconsistent treatment of similarly situated regulated firms and individuals.

Another interesting illustration of the empirical investigation of administrative sanctions is a 2012 working paper by Bengtsson, Dai, and Hensen, which documents the effects of SEC enforcement actions on the structure on the private investment in public equity (PIPE) markets in 2002.[59] Employing a series of alternative specifications, the authors demonstrate a number of significant changes in the structure of PIPE transactions after the SEC's 2002 enforcement. While the authors reserve judgment on whether the effects served to enhance shareholder value, their work offers further empirical validation of the impact of supervisory actions on market behavior.[60]

Yet another recent example of work exploring the relationship between enforcement strategies and market outcomes is Cumming, Johan, and Li, a 2011 empirical study of market integrity regulation (market manipulation, insider trading, and broker-agency conflict from the World Federation of Exchanges) across 42 exchanges during the period of 2006–2008. [61] The goal of the paper is to consider whether differences in regulations in these

---

[58] *See* Stavros Gadinis, *The SEC and the Financial Services Industry: Evidence from Enforcement Against Broker-Dealers*, 67 Bus. L. 679 (2012).

[59] *See* Ola Bengtsson, Na Dai, & Clifford Chad Henson, *SEC Enforcement in the PIPE Market: Actions and Consequences* (April 2012), *available at* http://papers.ssrn.com/abstract=2033950 (finding effects on securities terms but reserving judgment on whether changes enhanced value).

[60] *See also* Dharmapala Dhammika & Vikramaditya S. Khanna, *Corporate Governance, Enforcement, and Firm Value: Evidence from India* (June 23, 2011), *available at* http://ssrn.com/abstract=1105732 (finding increased levels of sanctioning to be associated with higher firm value in Indian companies). *See also* John P. Preiato, Philip P. Brown, & Ann Tarca, *Mandatory Adoption of IFRS and Analysts' Forecasts: How Much Does Enforcement Matter?* (May 23, 2010), *available at* http://ssrn.com/abstract=1499625 (finding that a staffing enforcement variable based on the Jackson and Roe variable is associated with lower forecast errors but does not enhance accuracy when interacted with IFRS adoption).

[61] *See* Douglas J. Cumming, Sofia A. Johan, & Dan Li, *Exchange Trading Rules and Stock Market Liquidity*, 99 J. Fin. Econ. 651 (2011).

areas significantly affect market liquidity of national markets (velocity, volatility, and bid–ask spread). While the analysis centers on the relationship between specific regulations and market liquidity, the authors also consider whether enforcement intensity contributes to improved liquidity. Although the authors failed to detect any material impact on their analysis from including the Jackson and Roe enforcement variables, they did find that the inclusion of a surveillance index – a different measure of enforcement based on the monitoring practices of stock exchanges – had a positive effect on liquidity.[62] Thus, the Cumming, Johan, and Li paper offers another illustration of a recent empirical paper drawing connections between enforcement practices and market outcomes.

18.3 IMPLICATIONS OF EMPIRICAL RESEARCH ON THE GLOBAL FINANCIAL CRISIS

The global financial crisis has been the dominant event of the past five years and considerable academic work has already been done exploring the causes of the financial crisis and the characteristics of countries that were particularly hard hit by the crisis. From my review of the literature, none of this work has focused precisely on the question of whether real resources for supervisory activities are positively or negatively correlated with the economic performance of countries in the aftermath of the crisis. Casual empiricisms, however, suggest that the effect is unlikely to have been strong and consistent. The United States and the United Kingdom both dedicate high levels of resources to supervisory functions but both were at the epicenter of the crisis. Australia and Canada, on the other hand, also expend high levels of resources to supervision and both are regarded as having weathered the crisis particularly well.[63] Nevertheless, the extensive body of empirical investigation into the causes of the financial crisis does offer some potentially intriguing insights into the study of public enforcement. While a complete review of this literature is beyond

---

62 *Id.*, at 669.

63 *See* Andrew K. Rose & Mark M. Spiegel, *Cross-Country Causes and Consequences of the 2008 Crisis*: *An Update*, 55 EUR. ECON. REV. 309, 324 (2011). *See also* Jennifer G. Hill, *Why Did Australia Fare So Well in the Global Financial Crisis*, *in* Eilís Ferran et al., *In* THE REGULATORY AFTERMATH OF THE GLOBAL FINANCIAL CRISIS 203 (Cambridge University Press 2012); Donald J.S. Brean, Lawrence Kryzanowski, & Gordon S. Roberts, *Canada and the United States*: *Different Roots*, *Different Routes to Financial Sector Regulation*, 53 BUS. HIST. 249 (2011).

the scope of this chapter and much of the analysis focuses on the substance of regulatory requirements as opposed to the allocation of supervisory resources,[64] two general points merit emphasis here.

18.3.1 Correlations between Certain Supervisory Activities and Financial Stability

Some empirical papers on the financial crisis explore relationships between the allocation of public enforcement efforts – particularly in the area of bank supervision – and the severity of the impact of the financial crises, including the global financial crisis, on particular jurisdictions. While the body of research is unwieldy and susceptible to a variety of interpretations, there does seem to be compelling evidence that the allocation of supervisory resources played a role in the capacity of countries to weather financial distress.

For example, in a 2012 article reviewing 124 banking crises from 65 advanced and developing countries during the period 1976–2005, Amri and Kocher find that the official powers of banking regulators to conduct on-site examinations, surveillance, set rules, and impose sanctions has a significantly negative relationship with the probabilities of the incurrence of banking crises.[65] While the paper utilizes variables based on formal

---

[64] For example, in a 2011 article focusing on the global financial crisis, Ahrend, Arnold, and Murtin examined various indicators of banking regulation on-the-book as collected by the World Bank and their associations with the damage to each country during the crisis, as measured either by the degree of equity value destruction in the banking sector or by the fiscal cost of financial sector rescue. *See* Rüdiger Ahrend, Jens M. Arnold, & Fabrice Murtin, *Have More Strictly Regulated Banking Systems Fared Better During the Recent Financial Crisis?*, 18 APPLIED ECON. LETTERS 399 (2011). Their results reveal that moderately stronger prudential regulation, stricter regulatory requirements with respect to accounting and provisioning, and stricter restrictions on entry rules and ownership structures were associated with better stock prices and a lower expected rescue cost. Stricter requirements for capital were also found to be correlated with a lower expected cost for the financial crisis. *Id.*; *see also* Gerard Caprio, Jr, Vincenzo D'Apice, Giovanni Ferri, & Giovanni Walter Puopolo, *Macro Financial Determinants of the Great Financial Crisis: Implications for Financial Regulation* (Oct. 21, 2010), *available at* http://ssrn.com/abstract=1695335 (drawing on datasets on 83 countries over the period 1998–2006, this study documents that the incidence of the financial crisis was lower for countries with higher levels of restrictions to bank activities and private monitoring structures, but higher for those countries having higher levels of credit deposit ratio).

[65] *See* Pupsa Delima Amri & Brett Matthew Kocher, *The Political Economy of Financial Sector Supervision and Banking Crises: A Cross-Country Analysis*, 18 EUR. L. J. 24 (2012).

powers rather than actual supervisory outcomes or resources dedicated to supervision, the Amri and Kocher analysis documents potential benefits from investment in supervisory services particularly in the area of on-site examination. The authors conclude:

> We have shown that, in line with our expectations, effective financial sector supervision significantly contributes to reducing the probability of a country experiencing a banking crisis. Because bank supervision is primarily measured by the scope and legal framework for supervisors to conduct bank examination, there is strong support that supervisory effectiveness is largely proportional to the scope of official power.[66]

Other recent work has explored the relationship between the organization of financial market oversight and stability in the global financial crisis. For example, in a 2011 International Monetary Fund (IMF) working paper, Masciandaro, Pansini, and Quintyn focus on the supervisory structure by studying the correlation between the macroeconomic performance of 102 countries during the financial crisis in 2008–2009 and their supervisory unification, degree of central bank involvement in supervision, and supervisory governance (in terms of independence and accountability) in 2007.[67] Contrary to expectations, their analysis result suggests that the high levels of supervisory governance as well as supervisory unification were negatively associated with economic resilience, with central bank involvement in supervision having little effect on outcomes.[68]

While much more remains to be done on the subject, this line of research suggests that financial stability and the ability to withstand global financial distress are important variables of interest and should be part of future work on the effects of public enforcement.

---

66 *Id.*, at 38. *Cf.* Delis & Staikouras, *supra* note 54 (documenting linkage between on-site audits and reductions in bank risk).

67 *See* Donato Masciandaro, Rosaria Vega Pansini, & Marc Quintyn, *The Economic Crisis: Did Financial Supervision Matter?* (Nov. 2011), *available at* http://ssrn.com/abstract=1961908.

68 *Cf.* Andrea Beltratti & René M. Stulz, *Why Did Some Banks Perform Better During the Credit Crisis? A Cross-Country Study of the Impact of Governance and Regulation* (July 2009), *available at* http://www.nber.org/papers/w15180 (finding a negative correlation between power of supervisory authorities and financial performance of banks in 2008, but suggesting that some of the effect may be the product of supervisory orders to raise capital and dilute existing shareholders). See also K.J. Hopt, *Corporate Governance of Banks and Other Financial Institutions After the Financial Crisis*, 13 J. Corp. L. Studies 219, 241–243 (Oct. 2013) (discussing role of shareholder control over bank risk-taking).

18.3.2 Potentially Troubling Associations with Robust Capital Markets

A somewhat more troubling strain of empirical research into the global financial crisis concerns the potentially destabilizing relationship between robust capital markets in ordinary times with the performance of national economies in times of financial stress. For example, several studies have drawn a connection between bank reliance on short-term credit and the severity of the financial crisis.[69] Particularly to the extent that banks moved away from deposit funding to reliance on short-term capital market funding, those institutions appear to have been more vulnerable in times of financial turmoil. Strong reliance on depository funding is one of the factors that researchers have cited as explaining the relatively strong performance of Canadian[70] and Australian[71] banks in the financial crisis.

A negative correlation between capital market funding for banks and poor results in financial crisis is relevant to the study of public enforcement and the law and finance approach more generally in that it suggests some potentially undesirable consequences of robust capital markets. In prior work, including the Jackson and Roe paper itself, higher levels of market capitalization and trading volumes were implicitly accepted as unambiguously desirable outcomes. The possibility that some capital market expansions might have negative ramifications in times of financial distress suggests that more nuanced analysis may be needed in the future.[72]

---

69 *See, e.g.*, Rüdiger Ahrend & Antoine Goujard, *Drivers of Systemic Banking Crises: The Role of Bank-Balance-Sheet Contagion and Financial Account Structure* (June 5, 2011), *available at* http://www.oecd-ilibrary.org/economics/drivers-of-systemic-banking-crises_5kg3k8ksgglw-en.

70 *See* Lev Ratnovski & Rocco Huang, *Why Are Canadian Banks More Resilient?* (IMF Working Paper No. 09/152, July 2009), available at http://ssrn.com/abstract=1442254 (a higher share of depository funding in liabilities was identified as a strong indicator of resilience to the financial crisis of Canadian banks).

71 *See* Alison Lui, *Macro and Micro Prudential Regulatory Failures amongst Financial Institutions in the United Kingdom: Lessons from Australia* (Apr. 27, 2011), *available at* http://ssrn.com/abstract=1716264 (noting that, among other things. Australian banks had better loans-to-deposits ratios than the UK banks).

72 *See also* Beltratti and Stulz, *supra* note 68 (noting that banks located in shareholder-friendly regimes may have been encouraged to take on excessive risks before the financial crisis and therefore suffered greater losses when the crisis occurred).

18.4 CONCLUSION

In the years since Professor Roe and I initially presented our work on public enforcement, a large number of independent researchers have adopted our variables to explore a wide range of hypotheses. As described above, this work has done much to corroborate our claim that the investment of real resources into public enforcement can have significant positive effects on capital market outcomes. While the effects are not universal, a large number of subsequent papers do report statistically significant effects. Many of these results reveal effects on technical measures of financial performance, like measures of liquidity and the informativeness of disclosures and analyst reports, effects that we were unable to document in our original work. Important work has also been done to establish that causality runs from real resources to market outcomes and not in the opposite direction, an issue not fully resolved in our original work. Finally, a number of papers have begun to extend our research by exploring the impact of sanctions and other supervisory outputs on market behavior. While much work remains to be done – and the global financial crisis suggests some important ways in which future work might be refined – the intervening body of work confirms our starting hypotheses: real resources can offer an important metric for estimating the efficacy of public enforcement; and regulatory intensity, when measured in terms of real resourses, is associated with important indicia of robust capital markets.

Another important lesson of the large and growing body of subsequent work is the appetite that the academic community has for data on public enforcement. Were public authorities to be more forthcoming in collecting and disseminating consistent information about key variables of public enforcement – budget, staffing, allocation of resources, and supervisory outputs – a large body of talented researchers would put that information to immediate use and develop even more helpful insights into the most efficient and effective ways to deploy public resources in financial supervision. The global financial crisis has demonstrated how important it is to maintain effective supervision of financial markets and financial institutions. Researchers stand ready to aid the cause as soon as new datasets are made available.

19. Transparency and corporate governance

Benjamin E. Hermalin

19.1 INTRODUCTION

We are suspicious of what goes on behind closed doors. This is especially true when the doors are to the boardroom and the offices of senior management of the corporations in which we invest. And, in light of scandals such as Enron and Worldcom, we would appear to have good reason to be suspicious. But even before those events, economists and other commentators on corporate governance have long expressed concern and, consequently, called for greater transparency.[1]

It is, in fact, difficult at times to imagine reasons why we would not wish for the corporations in which we invest to be maximally transparent. As I will argue in this chapter, however, that view can be short-sighted: some opaqueness could ultimately be to investors' advantage. Moreover, even if we believe that transparency is generally to be promoted, that does not necessarily justify legally mandating greater transparency, as for instance was a goal of the United States Sarbanes–Oxley legislation and similar legislation in Japan and other nations.

19.2 THE CASE FOR TRANSPARENCY

The case for transparency may seem self-evident, but it nonetheless warrants a quick review. An obvious advantage to transparency is that it presumably makes it harder for managers to engage in outright fraud and theft: crime is less prevalent on well-lit streets than in dark alleyways. Another, related, advantage is that models of optimal responses to

---

[1] *See e.g.*, Adam Smith, Wealth of Nations, Book V, Part III, Article I (1776); William Z. Ripley, Main Street and Wall Street (1927); Adolph A. Berle & Gardiner C. Means, The Modern Corporation and Private Property (1932).

moral-hazard problems show that improving the informativeness of the public information upon which incentive contracts are contingent leads to better contracts.[2] This is because better information, in a statistical sense, makes it easier to separate managers' contributions to firm performance from factors beyond their control.

Another rationale for better transparency is that it can facilitate trade in a firm's securities: fear of trading against those with superior information reduces investors' willingness to trade in the firm's securities.[3] The more illiquid a firm's securities, the greater premium investors will demand to hold them, which limits a firm's ability to issue securities, raises its cost of capital, or both. A related point is that initial public offerings are also adversely affected if investors worry that they may be trading against better-informed insiders.[4]

A number of arguments have also been put forth in favor of greater transparency having to do with the effects a given firm's transparency may have on other actors in the broader economy; that is, a given firm's greater transparency could generate positive externalities. For instance, various contagion effects have been hypothesized to exist, such that distorted information from one firm could lead to distorted or inefficient decisions by other actors.[5]

19.3 THE COSTS OF TRANSPARENCY

There are no free lunches, so the benefits of transparency must come at a cost. An obvious, but non-trivial cost is the need to collect and disseminate information. For example, a recent survey of firms found that the average annual per-firm cost of complying with §404 of the Sarbanes–Oxley Act is $2.3 million.[6]

---

[2] *See e.g.*, Bengt Holmstrom, *Moral Hazard in Teams*, 13 BELL J. ECON. 74 (1982); Sanford J. Grossman & Oliver D. Hart, *An Analysis of the Principal–Agent Problem*, 51 ECONOMETRICA 7 (1983); Son Ku Kim, *Efficiency of an Information System in an Agency Model*, 63 ECONOMETRICA 89 (1995).

[3] For a survey of the accounting, economics, and finance literature on disclosure, *see* Christian Leuz & Peter Wysocki, *Economic Consequences of Financial Reporting and Disclosure Regulation: A Review and Suggestions for Future Research* (2008), *available at* http://papers.ssrn.com/sol3/papers.cfm?abstract_id=1105398. Christian Leuz & Robert E. Verrecchia, *The Economic Consequences of Increased Disclosure*, 38 J. ACCOUNT. RESEARCH 91 (2000), document that firms' cost of capital decreases when they voluntarily increase disclosure.

[4] *See* Leuz & Wysocki, *supra* note 3, at §2.

[5] *See id.*, at §2.

[6] Office of Economic Analysis, US Securities and Exchange Commission,

Transparency can disadvantage a firm by providing information to product-market rivals or other parties (e.g., unions or government regulators).[7] Obviously, a firm does not wish to be transparent about its trade secrets, its research and development (R&D), or its strategy. But even information about expenditures or revenues can provide a rival with a strategic edge (e.g., an incumbent firm would not wish for a potential entrant to be able to infer that demand was strong or the incumbent had high costs).

Another issue – well known to social scientists – is that observation can change behavior. The way one acts when guests are visiting tends to be different than how one behaves when alone or with just the family. At some level, this is precisely the goal of transparency: knowing the light is on them, managers behave better than they would if they could operate in the shadows. Yet, it is alleged that too much transparency can distort behavior in ways that are at odds with a firm's best interests: managers are induced to behave in ways that merely look good rather than in ways that are truly good.[8] For instance, a claim is that passage of the Sarbanes–Oxley Act has led to managers becoming too timid.[9] Although, as a matter of economic theory, it is also possible that greater transparency, if it reveals the risk attributes of projects *ex ante*, could lead to excessive risk-taking.[10] Finally, greater transparency could ironically also increase the incentives of managers to directly manipulate information (there is no motive to distort information unless it will be made public).[11]

Study of the Sarbanes–Oxley Act of 2002 Section 404 Internal Control over Financial Reporting Requirements (2009), Table 8.

7 For a discussion, *see* Leuz & Wysocki, *supra* note 3, for one model of this issue. *See* Alfred Wagenhofer, *Voluntary Disclosure with a Strategic Opponent*, 12 J. ACC. & ECON. 341 (1990)

8 For formal modeling of this concept, *see e.g.*, Jeremy C. Stein, *Efficient Capital Markets, Inefficient Firms: A Model of Myopic Corporate Behavior*, 104, Q. J. ECON., 655 (1989); Bengt Holmstrom, *Managerial Incentive Problems: A Dynamic Perspective*, 66 R. ECON. STUDIES 169 (1999); Benjamin E. Hermalin & Michael S. Weisbach, *Information Disclosure and Corporate Governance*, 67 J. FINANCE 195 (2012). The last is particularly germane as discussed *infra*.

9 For studies documenting that the passage of the Sarbanes–Oxley Act has led to a reduction in risk-taking, *see e.g.*, Leonce Bargeron et al., *Sarbanes–Oxley and Corporate Risk Taking*, 49 J. ACC. & ECON. 34 (2009) and Kate Litvak, *Defensive Management: Does the Sarbanes–Oxley Act Discourage Corporate Risk-Taking? available at* http://ssrn.com/abstract=1120971. For a broader analysis of the role of financial reporting in managerial behavior, *see* John Graham et al., *The Economic Implications of Corporate Financial Reporting*, 40 J. ACC. & ECON. 3 (2005).

10 For details *see* Benjamin E. Hermalin, *Managerial Preferences Concerning Risky Projects*, 9 J. L. ECON. & ORG. 127 (1993).

11 For a related model of managers seeking to distort information, *see*

In a recent article, Michael Weisbach and I provide a general exploration of how better disclosure regimes can aggravate agency problems and related costs, including executive compensation.[12] Among the article's findings are that greater transparency can lead to an increase in executive compensation: more transparency (1) makes executives' jobs less desirable, for which they will require compensation; and (2) executives will be able to capture some of the financial benefits of greater transparency. Although point (1) can arise through a number of channels, one channel is the following. If shareholders and directors learned no information that helped them to assess the ability and competence of the executives, then they would have never have grounds to dismiss the executives. If they learn information, then they may learn information that leads to dismissal. From the executives' perspective, then, more information serves to increase the risk of job loss. Executives will require additional compensation to bear this risk. [13]

As shown in the aforementioned article, there is another potential link between greater transparency and greater executive pay: the former can induce, as discussed above, executives to expend effort on looking good (regardless of whether they are actually doing good). Even if such Potemkin efforts are not directly harmful to firm value, the executives will need to be compensated for the disutility that such efforts impose on them. In equilibrium, their compensation will be greater.[14]

19.4 LEGAL REQUIREMENTS FOR DISCLOSURE AND TRANSPARENCY

Corporate transparency generates both benefits and costs. Presumably, an optimal amount of transparency exists that balances benefits and costs; that is, an increase in transparency on a given dimension would increase benefits no more than it would raise costs, and a decrease in transparency would generate cost savings that do not exceed the lost benefits. If one thinks of a firm's "transparency regime" as part of the overall "contract" that defines the firm, then one imagines that the parties to that contract (i.e., management and investors) would desire a regime that maximized

---

Benjamin E. Hermalin and Michael L. Katz, *Corporate Diversification and Agency*, *in* INCENTIVES, ORGANIZATION, AND PUBLIC ECONOMICS: PAPERS IN HONOUR OF SIR JAMES MIRRLEES (P. Hammond & G. Myles eds, 2001).

12 Hermalin & Weisbach, *supra* note 8.

13 *See* Hermalin & Weisbach, *supra* note 8, at §§ I.B, I.C., and II.B.

14 *See* Hermalin & Weisbach, *supra* note 8, at 208.

their joint welfare. A role for legal mandates on disclosure and other aspects of transparency policy would exist only if the parties would otherwise be unable to maximize their joint welfare or if the regime that maximized their joint welfare was for some reason at odds with broader social goals.

In an article written with Michael Katz, he and I established that there are only three justifications for the state to interfere or otherwise limit private parties' contracting:[15]

1. Because of asymmetric information that exists at the time the parties approach the bargaining table, the parties would benefit from limitations on the contract space to restrict inefficient signaling via distortion of the contractual terms proposed.[16]
2. The state has access to better contracting methods than the private parties, including more efficient means of bargaining.
3. The contract to which the private parties would agree imposes externalities on third parties excluded from the contractual bargaining.[17]

To the best of my knowledge, no model invoking rationale #1 has been set forth to justify disclosure or similar transparency requirements. It is, however, straightforward to build a model in which regulation barring costly information revelation would be useful to avoid inefficient costly revelation due to a standard unraveling story.[18]

---

[15] Benjamin E. Hermalin & Michael L. Katz, *Judicial Modification of Contracts between Sophisticated Parties: A More Complete View of Incomplete Contracts and Their Breach*, 9 J. L. ECON, & ORG. 230 (1993). For a recent survey on the economics of contracting, *see* Benjamin E. Hermalin, Avery W. Katz, & Richard Craswell, *Contract Law*, *in* HANDBOOK OF LAW & ECONOMICS, §2 (A. Mitchell Polinsky & Steven Shortell eds, 2007).

[16] The possibility of this rationale for contractual restrictions was first put forth by Philippe Aghion & Benjamin E. Hermalin, *Legal Restrictions on Private Contracts Can Enhance Efficiency*, 6 J. L. ECON. & ORG. 381 (1990). To an extent, this rationale might be captured by the second Hermalin–Katz rationale (Hermalin & Katz, *supra* note 15).

[17] To the extent one views this rationale at odds with Ronald Coase, *The Problem of Social Cost*, 3 J. L. & ECON. 1 (1960), one could appeal to the difficulty of fitting many disparate and potentially anonymous stakeholders around the same bargaining table; that is, there is an argument that this rationale is subsumed by the second rationale.

[18] An earlier model of "unraveling" is Sanford J. Grossman, *The Informational Role of Warranties and Private Disclosure about Product Quality*, 21 J. L. & ECON. 461 (1981). As a simple example, suppose that a founder of a firm must sell it to investors via auction. The founder knows the firm's value, v, but investors know

Rationale #2 provides a somewhat stronger case for laws governing disclosure and transparency: the costs of coordinating many investors in their negotiations with management suggest that welfare would be enhanced by the state providing a set of default disclosure rules. Although true that avoiding bargaining could enhance efficiency, such an observation only indicates that the state can aid welfare by providing default rules – it does not establish that those rules should be mandatory. In other words, it is not immediately evident that firms should be barred from choosing alternative transparency regimes if they wish (i.e., among other factors, were willing to incur the bargaining costs). For rationale #2 to justify mandatory rules requires establishing why subsequent bargaining could be inefficient or flawed. A possibility along that line would be to note that shareholder democracy is plagued by the same free-riding problems as political democracy: if management can exploit shareholder inattentiveness, it might be able to put in place transparency regimes that the shareholders, were they truly able to act as one, would have blocked.[19]

The possibility that one firm's transparency regime imposes externalities (rationale #3) has already been discussed.[20]

A question related to the preceding discussion is: what are the political motives for legislatively dictated reforms to corporate governance and transparency, such as the Sarbanes–Oxley Act? Potential externalities are one explanation: those adversely affected by the current state of transparency successfully lobby their legislators to impose a different set of standards. Another possibility is simply that outrage over various scandals leads to legislative pandering to the masses through the passage of seemingly punitive legislation.[21] Yet another possibility is that investors seek to obtain through legislation what they are unable to obtain

---

only that the value was drawn from a uniform distribution on the unit interval. At a cost c, $0 < c < ½$, the founder can credibly disclose v. It is readily shown that, in equilibrium, a founder whose firm is worth $2c$ or more discloses, and a founder whose firm is worth less does not. But disclosure is not productive in this simple model (recall that the founder must sell), so it is simply a wasted expenditure; welfare would, in this simple mode, be enhanced if the law forbade disclosure. *See also* Aghion & Hermalin, *supra* note 16.

[19] Sanford J. Grossman & Oliver D. Hart, *Takeover Bids, the Free-Rider Problem, and the Theory of the Corporation*, 11 Bell J. Econ. 42 (1980) is an early model illustrating the potential problem of free-riding *vis-à-vis* efficient governance. *See also* Hermalin et al., *supra* note 15, at §2.3.1; Ernesto Dal Bó, *Bribing Voters*, 51 Amer. J. Pol. Sci. 789 (2007).

[20] In a governance context, an important exploration of such externalities is Jean Tirole, *Corporate Governance*, 69 Econometrica 1 (2001).

[21] *See* Hermalin & Weisbach, *supra* note 8, at 217, for a discussion.

in bargaining with management. Given that investors constitute many voters, and managers few, it is conceivable – especially when a scandal focuses public scrutiny on the topic – that legislators seek to give investors what they were unable to achieve in direct negotiations with management.[22] Such legislative largesse is not, however, necessarily to investors' long-term benefit: anticipating that the legislature might impose greater transparency, management bargains harder initially (e.g., obtains even greater compensation than it might otherwise); in equilibrium, investors are thus worse off than they would be if the legislature committed never to change the law (or, alternatively, the investors could commit not to try to subsequently lobby the legislature for change).

19.5 CONCLUSION

Some amount of transparency is essential for the corporate system to work. Yet there are costs associated with transparency. The optimal transparency regime needs to balance costs and benefits. In particular, a view that more transparency is always to be welcomed is likely mistaken. Especially given that, as detailed above, some of the costs of transparency are subtle, they may fail to have the salience that the benefits of transparency possess; consequently, caution is warranted before advocating even "obvious" reforms.

Moreover, before advocating reform, one needs to ask: why are things the way they are? In light of the limited scope for the state to improve on private contracting, one must be wary about claims of money left lying on the sidewalk. Even when there are strong proponents for change (e.g., investors), one needs to ask whether even they would be better off, in equilibrium, if the state committed to a more "hands-off" attitude.

At the same time, recent experience suggests that one should be cautious about adopting a completely laissez-faire approach. The bottom line, then, is that the issue of transparency is tricky: although one should not fear to tread there, one should do so with caution and humility.

---

22 For an analysis along these lines, *see id.*, at 217–219.

20. Reverse engineering SOX versus J-SOX: a lesson in legislative policy

Zenichi Shishido and Sadakazu Osaki

20.1 INTRODUCTION

Although both the US and Japan recently introduced similar corporate governance regulations, respectively the Sarbanes–Oxley Act of 2002 (SOX) and the Financial Instruments and Exchange Act of 2006, known as "J-SOX" because of its similarity to SOX, there is an interesting discrepancy between the first-year reports in regard to the discovery of "material weakness" of internal controls by US companies (16.9 percent) and Japanese companies (2.1 percent). What does this discrepancy mean and why does it exist? In order to answer these questions, this chapter attempts to reverse engineer SOX and J-SOX by focusing on how these regulations affect the incentive bargain among the key players complimentarily with the pre-existing laws, practices, markets, and social norms in both jurisdictions.[1]

SOX and J-SOX have similar origins, purposes, and substance. They were both enacted after major fraudulent disclosure scandals by legislatures that were forced to react to increasing social criticism.[2] Both the US Congress and the Japanese Diet intended to remedy what was perceived to be defective corporate governance regulations through active intervention in the internal controls of publicly traded companies. Four years after the enactment of SOX, the Japanese Diet transplanted SOX into the corporate governance regulatory system of Japan after making some modifications to its provisions. Although these two regulations were nearly identical upon implementation, each has evolved differently due mainly to the distinctions between the relevant environments in the US and Japan.

SOX strengthened the bargaining power of monitors and may have

[1] This chapter aims to apply the framework of the legislative policy of enterprise law through backward induction to SOX and J-SOX as explained in the "Introduction" to this volume.

[2] *See* Roberta Romano, Chapter 21 in this volume.

improved the corporate governance of publicly traded American companies. However, both an increase in defensive management and out-of-pocket costs resulted as serious side effects. On the other hand, J-SOX did not strengthen the bargaining power of monitors nor did it substantially improve the corporate governance of publicly traded Japanese companies; it also did not lead to serious side effects, except for a substantial increase in auditing fees. The rates at which US companies (16.9 percent) and Japanese companies (2.1 percent) reported material weakness may symbolize the management and auditors' level of seriousness in finding and disclosing deficiencies in their companies' internal controls. These differences result from the existing complementarities among the laws, practices, markets, and social norms in each country.

Section 20.2 describes the political backdrops related to the implementation of SOX and J-SOX, and argues that both were typical policy push legislation.[3] This section further explains that both legislatures attempted to change actual corporate behavior to desirable corporate behavior in accordance with the multitude of social criticism that gained strength in response to the well-covered corporate scandals. Section 20.3 compares the substantive rules and enforcement systems of SOX and J-SOX, while section 20.4 focuses on non-legal infrastructure, in particular the markets and social norms in both countries and their influence on SOX and J-SOX. Section 20.5 provides an analysis on how all of the infrastructures, new rules and enforcement systems created by SOX and J-SOX, existing laws, existing practices, stock markets, labor markets, and social norms influence the incentive bargain that plays out among key players of the firm, and as a result, how SOX and J-SOX changed the corporate governance practices in both the US and Japan. Sections 20.6 and 20.7 summarize statistical studies and empirical data to support the analysis set forth in the previous sections. The conclusions of this analysis are laid out succinctly in section 20.8.

20.2 BACKGROUND OF SOX AND J-SOX

20.2.1 Major Fraudulent Disclosure Scandals

SOX, enacted in response to major corporate and accounting scandals in 2001 including those that involved Enron Corporation and WorldCom, is considered the most important regulatory reform in the 70-plus-year

---

[3] *See* Zenichi Shishido, "Introduction" to this volume.

history of US federal regulation of securities transactions. Similarly, after the fraudulent disclosure scandals that occurred in 2004 including the Seibu and Kanebo scandals, Japan implemented the Financial Instruments and Exchange Act in 2006 (J-SOX); among other things, J-SOX required public companies to report on the effectiveness of their internal controls to a specific government entity.

20.2.2 Policy Push Legislation

SOX and J-SOX are typical policy push legislation. In other words, through the enactment of these regulations, the legislatures attempted to establish a norm that facilitates accurate disclosure through perfect corporate governance and replaces the reality of firms having leeway to make fraudulent disclosures due to imperfect corporate governance. More specifically, in order to strengthen trust in the market, the governments of both countries intervened in the internal control mechanisms of the corporations within their jurisdictions.[4]

It is important to note that the legislatures of both countries were forced to react to the populist sentiment developed after several major corporate scandals. Although such legislation tends to create both visible and invisible social costs,[5] SOX and J-SOX provide an interesting comparison of the way in which such social costs are imposed.

20.3 SUBSTANTIVE RULES AND ENFORCEMENT

20.3.1 Common Rules

SOX and J-SOX require that internal control disclosures be certified by management and attested to by independent auditors. Section 302 of SOX requires chief executive officers (CEOs) and chief financial officers of public companies to attest to the effectiveness of internal controls as well as the adequacy of financial statements. Furthermore, Section 404 requires

---

4 In the US, governmental intervention started with the Foreign Corrupt Practices Act of 1977, which requires that public companies keep accurate books and records. SOX is a considerable expansion of this requirement, with detailed instructions for audit committees, most importantly the executive certification and audit attestation requirements.

5 *See* Roberta Romano, *The Sarbanes–Oxley Act and the Making of Quack Corporate Governance*, 114 YALE L. J. 1521 (2005). *See also* Roberta Romano, *Does the Sarbanes–Oxley Act Have a Future?*, 26 YALE J. ON REG. 229 (2009).

that management assess the effectiveness of internal controls over financial reporting and requires the external auditor to attest to and report on such assessments. "Significant deficiencies" must be reported by management and by an independent auditor. In principle, J-SOX is nearly identical to SOX in this regard. Under J-SOX, all publicly traded companies are required to submit a report that evaluates the company's internal controls over financial reporting and have the report independently audited.

20.3.2 Differences

Some differences in the substantive rules of J-SOX, as compared to SOX, are due to the Japanese legislature's ability to learn from the US's experience with SOX. As J-SOX was implemented four years after SOX, Japanese legislators had time to examine the US experience, particularly the criticism of the high cost of Section 404(b), the internal controls auditor attestation provision. In an attempt to significantly reduce such costs, Japan elected not to require direct certification of management's reports on the effectiveness of internal controls and instead only requires a simple review of such reports by the external auditor.[6]

Another important difference is related to reporting lines for external auditors. While there is only a single reporting line from external auditor to audit committee in the US, there are three reporting lines in Japan: from external auditor to management, board of directors, and statutory auditors (*kansayaku*).[7]

Although Japanese legislators tried to decrease the cost of J-SOX by adapting its provisions, interestingly, the scope of J-SOX is broader than that of SOX. First, J-SOX applies to all publicly traded companies, including companies listed on initial public offering (IPO) markets, while SOX Section 404, that is, the external auditor attestation requirement, does not apply to the 44 percent of listed companies with a public float under $75 million.[8] Second, J-SOX applies to both subsidiaries of publicly

---

6 Although the rule is complicated, J-SOX takes an indirect approach.

7 Statutory auditors (*kansayaku*) are specialized compliance monitors, elected through shareholder meetings; these statutory auditors are considered quasi board members as they do not have voting rights but only the right to voice an opinion. Although they could potentially be powerful monitors by utilizing their inspection and veto-type rights, in practice they have not used these powers effectively. *See e.g.* Olympus case (section 20.7.2). *But see* Kenichi Osugi, Chapter 14 in this volume.

8 When J-SOX was enacted, these smaller firms were permanently exempted from the provision in Section 989G of the Dodd–Frank Wall Street Reform and Consumer Protection Act of 2010, Pub. L. No. 111-203, 124 Stat. 1376 (2010).

traded companies and "affiliated companies," that is, entities in which the relevant publicly traded company owns more than 20 percent of the voting rights or entities over which the relevant publicly traded company is deemed to have a substantial influence. SOX only applies to subsidiaries, not to affiliated companies.

20.3.3 Enforcement Systems

The more significant differences between the regulatory schemes, which affect the incentives of management and auditors, lie in their enforcement systems, rather than the substantive rules. First, public enforcement through the monitoring of external auditors is much stronger in the US. While SOX created the Public Company Accounting Oversight Board (PCAOB), a new quasi-governmental entity tasked with overseeing the auditing of firms, only a traditional peer review by the JICPA (Japanese Institute of Certified Public Accountants) exists in Japan.[9]

Second, there is a stronger private enforcement system for monitoring outside directors, management, and, to a lesser extent, auditors, in the US. While class action lawsuits and shareholder derivative actions with extensive discovery are available in the US, there is no class action mechanism and the discovery system is very limited in Japan,[10] although shareholder derivative actions do play an important role.

20.4 MARKETS AND SOCIAL NORMS

Other than laws, markets and social norms are an important part of the infrastructure of the incentive bargain among firm participants. Their interaction affects the incentives of key players and affects actual firm practices.

Moreover, Section 103 of the Jumpstart Our Business Startups Act enacted in 2012, Pub L. No. 112-105, 126 Stat. 306 (2012), exempted emerging growth companies – that is, companies with total annual gross revenues under $1 billion – from the attestation requirement.

9 The PCAOB is a non-profit corporation organized under the laws of the District of Columbia; its board members are appointed by the SEC, which also has oversight authority over the PCAOB (e.g., approves the PCAOB rules, standards, and budget). Japan has established the Certified Public Accountants and Auditing Oversight Board (CPAAOB), a government body equivalent to the PCAOB. However, the CPAAOB conducts on-site inspections on CPAs only after receiving quality control review reports from the JICPA.

10 It is much harder for shareholders to inspect the books and records of corporations in Japan.

20.4.1 US Environment

US stock markets mostly consist of "genuine shareholders," whose investment objective is rate of return maximization. Few investments are made by trading partners or the issuing company's banks. Among such genuine shareholders, institutional investors, such as pension funds, are particularly influential and push for comprehensive disclosure.[11]

The US has liquid external labor markets not only for white-collar and blue-collar employees, but also for management, including outside directors.[12] In addition, CEO turnover is high, especially for CEOs that perform poorly.[13]

In regard to social norms that affect the incentive of human capital providers, which include both employees and management, the individualism norm, which allows human capital providers to pursue their own interests instead of company's interest, predominates in the US.

20.4.2 Japanese Environment

The contrast between the two nations is vivid. Considering Japanese stock markets, the more influential "trading partner shareholders" coexist with genuine shareholders.[14] Most trading partner shareholders are cross-holding shareholders that reciprocally agree to follow a policy of non-intervention in regard to the issuing company's management decisions.

External labor markets in Japan are illiquid for both employees and management. Conversely, internal labor markets are well developed and

---

[11] *See* Hollis Ashbaugh-Skaife, Daniel W. Collins, & William R. Kinney Jr, *The Discovery and Reporting of Internal Control Deficiencies prior to SOX-Mandated Audit*, 44 J. ACCT. & ECON. 166 (2007).

[12] *See* Jeffrey N. Gordon, *The Rise of Independent Directors in the United States, 1950–2005: Of Shareholder Value and Stock Market Prices*, 59 STAN. L. REV. 1465 (2007).

[13] Steven N. Kaplan & Bernadette A. Minton, *How Has CEO Turnover Changed?*, 12 INT'L. REV. FIN. 57 (2012) (average CEO tenure was less than seven years with an annual turnover rate of 15.6 percent from 1992 to 2005, due to board-driven turnover related to stock performance, particularly post-1998); Dirk Jenter & Katharine Lewellen, *Performance-Induced CEO Turnover* (Working Paper 2010) (CEO turnover is highly sensitive to performance, and especially so for firms with strong boards). As discussed in section 20.6 below, US corporate boards differ substantially from Japanese boards, consisting almost solely of outsiders, whereas Japanese boards are composed primarily of insiders.

[14] *See* Paul Sheard, *Interlocking Shareholdings and Corporate Governance*, *in* THE JAPANESE FIRM: THE SOURCE OF COMPETITIVE STRENGTH 310 (Masahiko Aoki & Ronald Dore eds, 1994).

most members of management teams are core employees promoted from within the same company. Management, most board members, and core employees create their own "company community," which provides a *raison d'être* for its members.[15]

In contrast to the US, the individualism norm is not influential in Japan. Instead, the company community norm has the most influence on the incentive of the firm's human capital providers. In the minds of Japanese employees, members of the company community owe their loyalty to both the company community itself and fellow employees. According to this norm the company community is always considered independent, and other companies, even if they are major shareholders, should not intervene in the company community's decision-making process.[16] In addition to the company community norm, the "solidarity norm," by which managers and employees make decisions in consideration of the actions of their peers, also plays an important role.

20.5 THE INFLUENCE OF SOX AND J-SOX ON THE INCENTIVE BARGAIN AMONG THE KEY PLAYERS

SOX and J-SOX have different effects on the incentive bargain of the key players of the firm when considering them complementarily with existing laws, practices, markets, and social norms.

20.5.1 SOX Influence

SOX strengthened the bargaining power of monitors, both external auditors and independent directors, by increasing their duties and liabilities. It also strengthened employees' ability to monitor, through the inclusion of provisions designed to protect whistleblowers.[17]

The internal controls auditor attestation requirement encourages external auditors to insist that deficient internal controls be corrected. The

---

[15] *See* Zenichi Shishido, *Japanese Corporate Governance: The Hidden Problems of Corporate Law and Their Solutions*, 25 Del. J. Corp. L. 189, 202 (2000).

[16] *See id.*, at 204.

[17] The Dodd–Frank Act considerably strengthened SOX's whistleblower protection provisions and included incentive provisions adopted in May 2011, requiring the SEC to implement rules to pay awards to whistleblowers. SEC, Final Rule, Implementation of the Whistleblower Provisions of Section 21F of the Securities Exchange Act of 1934, Rel. No. 34-64545, 17 CFR Parts 240 and 249 (2011).

PCAOB exerts a significant deterrent effect on external auditors, through the sanctioning powers provided for in regard to failures identified during audit reviews. External auditors are forced to be vigilant in identifying weaknesses in internal controls; some would contend that this process is overly cautious and technical as well as inordinately expensive.

A single reporting line from external auditor to audit committee gives independent directors a more important role in corporate governance. Prior to SOX, although the boards of directors of publicly traded companies in the US were already substantially independent of management, auditors were typically hired by management. SOX emphasized the role of the independent audit committee of the board, placing the authority to select auditors in its hands. Through the independent directors' exclusive responsibility in the internal auditing process, such directors are forced to be more active in monitoring company management.

As a result, management not only has a more difficult time persuading auditors to accept aggressive accounting choices, but is also likely to become more defensive. Examples of defensive management include: restructuring business in a way that makes it look more familiar and thus less suspicious to auditors; avoiding novel management techniques and compensation arrangements; retaining inefficient business practices because new practices call for new internal controls; moving away from flexible, decentralized decision making toward slower, more bureaucratized procedures; and discouraging entrepreneurialism and initiative.[18]

When internal control problems are found, the players, including employees, have less of an incentive to accept the legal risk of concealment. Due to highly liquid external labor markets, human capital providers do not necessarily stick with the same company, and the individualism norm influences them to move on to pursue their own interests.

20.5.2 J-SOX Influence

In contrast to SOX, J-SOX has not necessarily strengthened the bargaining power of monitors, including statutory auditors. The indirect reporting system, which simply requires external auditors to review management's reports, in effect allows insiders to consult with external auditors while

---

[18] Kate Litvak, *Defensive Management: Does the Sarbanes-Oxley Act Discourage Corporate Risk-Taking?* (Working Paper, 2008); Leonce Bargeron, Kenneth Lehn, & Chad J. Zutter, *Sarbanes–Oxley and Corporate Risk-Taking*, 49 J. ACCT. & ECON. 34 (2010).

drafting management reports. This practice makes it psychologically difficult for external auditors to refuse to give an unqualified opinion to the final report. These auditors are not subject to the same liability concerns as US auditors, were they to overlook deficiencies in a company's internal controls, given the fact that both public and private enforcement is weak in Japan.

Under J-SOX, neither statutory auditors nor outside directors are expected to play an important role. It is not clear who is responsible if the external auditor reports a problem in the tripartite reporting line system. In practice, the boards of directors of Japanese publicly traded companies are not as independent as their US counterparts. There are very few companies with a majority of outsiders on the board. Instead, the boards are dominated by home-grown directors and many of the publicly traded companies still do not have any outside directors. Although statutory auditors have substantial monitoring power under the law, it is very rare to see such legal monitoring power exercised.

As a result, it is not difficult for management to persuade monitors to accept the decision-making and accounting practices of management, which in turn reduces the need to be defensive seen in the US scenario. The J-SOX experience illustrates that internal control regulation by itself does not affect the incentive bargain or result in defensive management without including the existence of an independent board in the calculus.

In any event, due to the solidarity norm, Japanese management does not voluntarily disclose its companies' material weaknesses, as long as other companies also refuse to do so.[19] If internal control problems are found, most players choose to accept the legal risk of concealment, partly because the enforcement system, both public and private, is not an effective deterrent, and partly because the lack of liquid external labor markets forces human capital providers to remain at the same firm. The company community norm also discourages management from revealing identified problems.

---

[19] Companies that disclosed material weaknesses in the first J-SOX reporting in 2009 were, in most cases, forced to do so either because certain problems had already been revealed, or because it was obvious that almost no internal control systems were in place. For a comparison with US material weakness reports, *see* Jeffrey T. Doyle, Weili Ge, & Sarah E. McVay, *Determinants of Weaknesses in Internal Control over Financial Reporting*, 44 J. ACCT. ECON. 193 (2007).

20.6 AFTER SOX

Considerable empirical research has been undertaken on how SOX has affected publicly traded companies.

20.6.1 Improvement of Corporate Governance

There are some signs which show that the corporate governance of US publicly traded companies may have improved. One study suggests that SOX's internal control requirements resulted in improved earnings quality, because levels of unexpected accruals increased during the year that the internal control weaknesses were disclosed and decreased in the year of the first effective internal control reports.[20] Another study suggests that there was also a decline in the frequency of just meeting or beating analysts' earnings expectations in the aftermath of the 2001–2002 accounting scandals and the passage of SOX.[21]

Two studies point to positive stock market reactions to the corporate governance improvement by SOX. One study found abnormal stock returns related to SOX legislation events and the extent of a corporation's earnings management to be significantly and positively related, and claims that research results suggest that investors anticipated SOX would increase the constraint on earnings management and enhance the quality of financial information.[22] The other study detected that market liquidity measures improved significantly after the passage of SOX and the establishment of the Securities and Exchange Commission's (SEC) implementation rules, and also suggests that these regulatory actions were successful in restoring market participant confidence in corporate governance, financial reports, and audit functions.[23]

Another study examined specific, disclosed material weaknesses and found that corporations that report account-specific weaknesses tend to be larger, older, and financially healthier corporations than those

---

[20] Jean Bedard, *Sarbanes Oxley Internal Control Requirements and Earnings Quality* (Working Paper 2006).

[21] Eli Bartov & Daniel Cohen, *The "Numbers Game" in the Pre- and Post-Sarbanes–Oxley Eras*, 24 J. Acct. Auditing & Fin. 505 (2009).

[22] Haidan Li, Morton Pincus, & Sonja Olhoft Rego, *Market Reaction to Events Surrounding the Sarbanes–Oxley Act of 2002 and Earnings Management*, 51 J. Law & Econ. 111 (2008).

[23] Pankaj K. Jain, Jang-Chul Kim, & Zabihollah Razaee, *Trends and Determinants of Market Liquidity in the Pre- and Post-Sarbanes–Oxley Act Periods* (Working Paper 2006).

corporations that report company-level weaknesses; although in general, material weaknesses in internal controls are more likely to exist in corporations that are smaller, less profitable, more complex, growing rapidly, or undergoing restructuring.[24] Another study models pre-SOX 404 internal control deficiency disclosures as a function of internal control risk factors and incentives of managers and auditors to discover and disclose internal control deficiencies. This study found that corporations disclosing internal control deficiencies have faced more prior SEC enforcement actions and filed more financial restatements, are more likely to use a dominant auditing firm, and have more concentrated institutional ownership.[25] These studies taken together suggest that the fact that 17 percent of companies made material weakness disclosures in the first year of 404 reports can be taken as a proxy of the seriousness of management and auditors to find and disclose problems with the relevant company's internal controls.

The stock markets take the information provided through SOX internal control disclosures seriously. One statistical study examined the market's reaction to internal control weakness disclosures and the characteristics of these disclosures under Section 302 and found size-adjusted returns on the days that weaknesses are disclosed to be significantly negative, and that the magnitude of the market reaction is related to the severity of the disclosed weakness. This suggests that information contained in internal control weakness disclosures is informative and used by investors to revise their expectations in regard to firm value.[26] Another statistical study also found a significant adverse market impact related to disclosure of unaudited material weaknesses under Section 302. The same study, however, detected no market response to Section 404 audited material weakness disclosures and suggests that the reason for this is that accelerated filers (large firms that are required to file under Section 404) operate in richer information environments.[27]

---

24 Doyle et al., *supra* note 19, at 220.

25 Hollis Ashbaugh-Skaife, Daniel W. Collins, & William R. Kinney Jr.,*The Discovery and Reporting of Internal Control Deficiencies Prior to SOX-Mandated Audits*, 44 J. Acct. & Econ. 166 (2007).

26 Jacqueline S. Hammersley, Linda A. Myers, & Catherine Shakespeare, *Market Reactions to the Disclosure of Internal Control Weaknesses and to the Characteristics of those Weaknesses under Section 302 of the Sarbanes Oxley Act of 2002*, 13 Rev. Acct. Stud. 141 (2008).

27 Messod D. Beneish, Marry B. Billings, & Leslie D. Hodder, *Internal Control Weaknesses and Information Uncertainty*, 83 acct. rev. 665 (2008). *See also* Maria Ogneva, K.R. Subramanyam, & K. Raghnandan, *Internal Control Weakness and Cost of Equity: Evidence from SOX Section 404 Disclosures*, 82 Acct. Rev. 1255 (2007).

20.6.2 Increased Costs

Roughly, compliance costs have more than doubled; this increased cost has a significant impact on small corporations, despite the small-company exemption. A statistical study shows that SOX disproportionately burdens small firms by finding that the propensity of small public American targets to be acquired by private acquirers rather than public ones increased substantially in the first year after the enactment of SOX.[28]

Between 2001 and 2006, average audit fees increased by 311 percent ($1.044 million) for Standard & Poor's (S&P) small-cap companies, 251 percent ($1.82 million) for S&P mid-cap companies, and 189 percent ($5.789 million) for S&P 500 companies.[29] Since the enactment of SOX, the average cost of compliance for companies with under $1 billion in annual revenue has increased by 171 percent ($1.7 million) to approximately $2.8 million.[30]

Director compensation and directors' and officers' liability (D&O) insurance premiums have also increased in accordance with the increased duties and liabilities of independent directors. Furthermore, median pay per director increased by more than 50 percent ($38 000), and median D&O insurance premiums increased by more than 150 percent during the period from 2001 to 2004. Both increases fall especially hard on smaller companies.[31] Such data clearly demonstrates that SOX has increased the duties and liabilities of independent directors.

20.6.3 Side Effects

Several statistical studies show that management has become more defensive, particularly in already well-governed corporations. One study shows that several risk-taking measures, such as capital expenditures, research and development (R&D) expenditures, and standard deviation of returns, declined significantly for US versus non-US corporations after SOX was implemented.[32] Another study shows that the risk of SOX-exposed foreign

---

[28] Ehud Kamar et al., *Going-Private Decisions and the Sarbanes–Oxley Act of 2002: A Cross-Country Analysis*, 25 J. L. Econ. & Org. 107 (2008).

[29] Thomas E. Hartman, *The Cost of Being Public in the Era of Sarbanes-Oxley* (Foley & Lardner LLP 2006), www.foley.com/. . ./Foley2007SOXstudy.pdf.

[30] *Id.*

[31] James S. Linck, Jeffry M. Netter, & Tina Young, *The Effects and Unintended Consequences of the Sarbanes–Oxley Act on the Supply and Demand for Directors*, 22 Rev. Fin. Stud. 3287 (2009).

[32] Bargeron et al., *supra* note 18, at 39.

companies declined significantly after SOX in three areas: volatility of returns, financial leverage, and cash hoarding. The same study also found that corporations with high Tobin's Q values suffered larger declines in risk, and corporations that were riskier before SOX lost more of their value after SOX than less risky corporations.[33] A third study found that the rate at which US company managers apply to discount investment projects ("hurdle rate") rose significantly after 2002, while the discount rate for UK companies remained unchanged. This study also shows that well-governed companies, companies with credit ratings, and accelerated filers under Section 404 have become more cautious investors.[34]

Two studies found indirect data showing that US companies became more defensive after the enactment of SOX. One study shows that pay-for-performance sensitivity of CEO compensation has declined.[35] Another study shows that after SOX, board committees have increased the number of meetings and D&O insurance premiums have doubled. Further, it has been shown that directors are now more likely to be lawyers, consultants, financial experts, or retired executives, and less likely to be individuals currently acting as executives, and also that boards today are larger and more independent. Others have also pointed out a significant increase in director pay and overall director costs, particularly among smaller corporations.[36]

20.6.4 Cost–Benefit Balance

Although the results of these statistical studies are a bit mixed, most studies show that the stock market response to SOX was negative, particularly for smaller corporations. Various event studies focusing on US stock markets found significantly positive and abnormal stock returns subsequent to SOX legislative events,[37] while others found significantly negative abnormal returns.[38]

As such, US-based studies have difficulty separating the effects of contemporaneous events; some studies incorporate data from cross-listed

---

33 Litvak, *supra* note 18.

34 Qiang Kang, Qiao Liu, & Rong Qi, *The Sarbanes–Oxley Act and Corporate Investment: A Structural Assessment*, 96 J. Fin. Econ. 291 (2010).

35 Daniel A. Cohen, Aiyesha Day, Thomas Z. Lys, The Sarbanes Oxley Act of 2002: Implications for Compensation Contracts and Managerial Risk-Taking (Working Paper 2007).

36 James S. Linck et al., *supra* note 31, at 3302.

37 Haidan Li et al., *supra* note 22, at 111.

38 Ivy Xiying Zhang, *Economic Consequences of the Sarbanes–Oxley Act of 2002*, 44 J. Acct. Econ. 74 (2007).

foreign companies. One study's findings show that the stock prices of foreign companies subject to SOX declined significantly in response to key announcements indicating that SOX would fully apply to cross-listed issuers, as compared to cross-listed companies not subject to SOX and non-cross-listed companies.[39] Another study shows that abnormal returns around delisting and deregistration announcements by cross-listed foreign companies were negative before the passage of SOX but positive after passage.[40]

20.7 AFTER J-SOX

Although there are far fewer statistics available regarding the costs and benefits of J-SOX in comparison to SOX, this section presents an image of Japanese publicly traded companies after J-SOX through referencing available data and anecdotes.

20.7.1 Improvement of Corporate Governance

There are few signs showing that corporate governance has improved after the enactment of J-SOX. The fact that only 2 percent of corporations reported material weakness can be seen as a result of the superficial efforts by management and auditors to discover material weaknesses.

A statistical study shows that J-SOX material weakness disclosures have no noticeable impact on stock price, which suggests that the stock market does not recognize the informative value of material weakness. The same study shows that companies that conduct international transactions and companies with high growth rates tend not to disclose material weakness.[41]

Another statistical study shows that young firms that have promising growth prospects, firms that operate in a volatile environment, firms that are financially constrained, and firms with weak governance structures were found to be more likely to suffer material weakness, and suggests that these findings echo findings of studies that focus on the

---

[39] Kate Litvak, *The Effect of the Sarbanes–Oxley Act on Non-US Companies Cross-Listed in the US*, 13 J. Corp. Fin. 195 (2007).

[40] Xi Li, *An Examination of the Impact of the Sarbanes–Oxley Act on Cross-Listed Foreign Private Issuers and the Legal Bonding Hypothesis* (Working Paper 2011).

[41] Kenichi Yazawa, *Why Don't Japanese Companies Disclose Internal Control Weakness?: Evidence from J-SOX Mandated Audits* (Working Paper 2010).

US market.[42] The same study also shows that material weakness is more likely to exist in firms with stronger links to their main banks. Although this statistical study and its interpretation is interesting in that a company's strong tie to its main bank correlates to its financial weakness,[43] it is easy to be skeptical about the suggested symmetry in regard to SOX and J-SOX material weakness reports, because of the doubtful premise that the meaning of material weakness disclosures in the US and Japan is the same.[44]

20.7.2 Olympus Case

The recent accounting fraud case involving Olympus exemplifies the fact that even seemingly perfect adherence to J-SOX does not necessarily result in an accurate financial disclosure.[45] Olympus concealed a huge investment loss which had been hidden away since the Japanese bubble era of the early 1990s, even though Olympus had more outside directors than the average Japanese company. Olympus's adherence to J-SOX procedures was perfect on paper and no internal control material weaknesses were found after 2009, the first year that J-SOX reporting requirements were in effect. Furthermore, the independent third-party committee that Olympus organized after the scandal pointed out that the company's J-SOX assessment had overlooked the following: the risk of fraudulent disclosure by top management, the fact that the financial department was headed by the same persons for a long period, a faulty whistleblower system, problems regarding the independence and capability of

---

42 Anna Chernobai & Yukihiro Yasuda, *Disclosures of Material Weaknesses by Japanese Firms after the Passage of the 2006 Financial Instruments and Exchange Law*, 37 J. BANKING & FIN. 1524 (2013).

43 *See* Gregory Jackson & Hideaki Miyajima, *Introduction*: *The Diversity and Change of Corporate Governance in Japan*, *in* CORPORATE GOVERNANCE IN JAPAN: INSTITUTIONAL CHANGE AND ORGANIZATIONAL DIVERSITY 1 (Masahiko Aoki et al. eds., 2007).

44 *See* Yazawa, *supra* note 41.

45 *See* Floyd Norris, *Deep Roots of Fraud at Olympus*, NEW YORK TIMES (Dec. 8, 2011), http://www.nytimes.com/2011/12/09/business/deep-roots-of-fraud-at-olympus.html?_r=1; Kenichi Osugi, *Can Corporate Scandal be Prevented by the Companies Act Reform?*, DAILY YOMIURI ONLINE (Jan. 5, 2012), http://www.yomiuri.co.jp/adv/chuo/dy/research/20120105.htm; *The Third Party Committee of Olympus Corporation*, *Investigation Report Summary* (Dec. 6, 2011), http://www.olympus-global.com/en/info/2011b/if111206corpe.pdf.

the statutory auditors, and problems regarding the independence of the internal audit department.[46]

There are three events related to the Olympus case that are particularly symbolic of how J-SOX is not effective within the Japanese corporate environment. The first is that, when its former auditor reported a possible accounting problem to Olympus's board of statutory auditors (*kansayaku-kai*), of which a majority of the members were "independent," the board of statutory auditors obtained a third-party expert opinion that included several reservation clauses, stating "[W]e did not find any serious problems within the limited time of the investigation and the limited information provided;" this ended the investigation into the accounting problem. The second is that, when former CEO Michael C. Woodford tried to point out the problem to the board of directors, which included more than the average number of independent directors for Japanese companies, the board removed him from his position as the CEO through a unanimous vote. The final event is that, after everything had been revealed, when Woodford attempted to return to his CEO position through a proxy fight, a majority of Olympus's shareholders, including banks and insurance companies, did not support Woodford, forcing him to abandon his endeavor.

20.7.3 Increased Costs

Although compliance costs have significantly increased as a result of J-SOX, the magnitude of the increase has been much smaller than in the US. Moreover, there are two interesting differences in the respective cost increases. First, most of the increased cost (in Japan) comes in the form of increased audit fees, and neither director's compensation nor D&O premiums have increased. Second, the rate of the increase in audit fees is higher for bigger corporations.

Average audit fees increased by 51 percent (¥16.6 million) for all publicly traded companies to ¥48.9 million from 2008 to 2010. It should also be noted that an abnormal increase in audit fees started from 2006, the year that J-SOX was enacted. From 2006 to 2010, the average audit fees for all publicly traded companies increased by 103 percent (¥24.8 million), but for companies with more than ¥1 trillion in annual revenue the increase was 155 percent.[47] The reason for the larger increase in audit

---

46 The Third Party Committee of Olympus Corporation, *Investigation Report* (*Summary*) (Dec. 6, 2011), http://www.olympus-global.com/en/info/2011b/if111206corpe.pdf.

47 Figures are calculated based on data provided by the Japan Institute of Certificated Public Accountants (http://www.hp.jicpa.or.jp).

fees for bigger companies is likely based on the fact that bigger companies have more subsidiaries and affiliated companies to which J-SOX applies. The audit fees for IPO firms also jumped by 65 percent from 2007 to 2008, which likely discourages initial public offerings because there is no small-firm exemption under J-SOX.

20.7.4 Side Effects

There have been no statistical studies on J-SOX's effect on management risk-taking. Nor has there been concern in regard to defensive management mentioned in business circles or by the media. Anecdotally, corporate group management has become more bureaucratic and the autonomy of subsidiaries has weakened.

20.7.5 Cost–Benefit Balance

Neither a positive nor a negative stock market reaction to J-SOX has been statistically observed.

20.8 CONCLUSIONS

Although the basic structure of SOX and J-SOX is the same, the related regulatory schemes have led to completely different results. While SOX fundamentally changed the make-up of the incentive bargain of the corporation, J-SOX had no such effect. The discrepancy between the first-year reports of "material weakness" in the US and Japan symbolize the different results. These divergent results are based not only on the various differences in the substantive rules of SOX and J-SOX, but also on the differences in the prevailing enforcement systems, existing corporate governance practices, stock markets, labor markets, and social norms in the two countries.

The cost–benefit balance is an important issue for the creation of legislation. Even when legislatures successfully accomplish their purpose, side effects inevitably occur. SOX and J-SOX demonstrate an interesting comparison of the cost–benefit balance of the two pieces of legislation; both have been unsuccessful, but for completely different reasons.

It appears that SOX improved the corporate governance of US listed companies by strengthening the bargaining power of the monitors, complementarily with the pre-existing independent boards, influential institutional investors, liquid external labor markets, and so on. At the same time, however, this increased monitoring strength has led to the serious side effect of increased defensive management, along with the huge out-of-pocket costs associated with SOX compliance.

On the other hand, J-SOX has failed to improve the corporate governance of publicly traded Japanese companies. It has not strengthened the bargaining power of monitors. Its indirect reporting system and incomplete enforcement mechanism, complementarily with the prevalence of insider-dominated boards, cross-holding shareholders, illiquid external labor markets, and the company community norm, allow management and auditors to formally comply with the rules while concealing the real problems. Ironically, however, J-SOX has created few side effects, other than the substantial increase in audit fees.

21. Regulating in the dark

Roberta Romano*

21.1 INTRODUCTION

How should one regulate in the midst of a financial crisis? This is a fundamental question for financial regulation, and it is not readily answerable, as the issues implicated are truly complex, if not intractable. Yet foundational financial legislation tends to be enacted in a crisis setting,[1] and over the past decade, when confronted with this question, the US Congress has answered it reflexively by enacting legislation massively increasing the scope and scale of the regulation of business firms, and especially financial institutions and instruments, in a manner seemingly oblivious to the cost and consequences of its actions. By tending to enact comprehensive financial legislation only in reaction to an immediate financial crisis, Congress acts most swiftly precisely when greater deliberateness is called for, given the paucity of information available to produce a high-quality decision.

In order to understand financial regulation undertaken in a crisis, we need to take account, as Frank Knight put it, of "human nature as we know it."[2] Human nature in this context is that legislators will find it impossible not to respond to a financial crisis by "doing something," that is, by ratchetting up regulation, instead of waiting until a consensus understanding of what has occurred can be secured and a targeted solution

---

* A fuller discussion may be found in my chapter "Regulating in the Dark" in the volume REGULATORY BREAKDOWN: THE CRISIS OF CONFIDENCE IN US REGULATION (University of Pennsylvania Press, 2012), edited by Cary Coglianese. The chapter appears here with the Press's permission. I would like to thank Alain Pietrancosta for suggesting what became the title of this chapter; Cary Coglianese, Jill Fisch, Jonathan Macey, Andrew Verstein, and participants at the Penn Program on Regulation conference, the Quinnipiac University School of Law Federalist Society Student Chapter Lunch Lecture, and the Yale Law School Graduate Student Seminar for helpful comments; and Aaron Ferner for editing the chapter for reproduction in this volume.

1 *See e.g.*, Roberta Romano, *The Sarbanes–Oxley Act and the Making of Quack Corporate Governance*, 114 YALE L. J. 1521, 1591–1594 (2005).

2 FRANK H. KNIGHT, RISK, UNCERTAINTY AND PROFIT 270 (1965).

then crafted, despite the considerable informational advantage from such an approach, which would, no doubt, improve the quality of decision-making. Compounding the problem, Congress tends not to move nimbly to rework financial legislation when it becomes widely acknowledged as flawed or seriously deficient. For instance, it took decades to repeal the Glass–Steagall Act's separation of commercial and investment banking; 11 years to make relatively small revisions to accounting and bribery provisions of the Foreign Corrupt Practices Act; and eight years to amend the Sarbanes–Oxley Act to exempt only the smallest firms from the requirement of auditor attestation of the effectiveness of internal controls, despite substantial consensus regarding the statutes' problems.

In addition, financial firms operate in a dynamic environment in which there are many unknowns and unknowables and state-of-the-art knowledge quickly obsolesces.[3] In such a context, even the most informed regulatory response – which Congress's reaction in the recent crises was not – will be prone to error, and is likely to produce backward-looking regulation that takes aim at yesterday's perceived problem, rather than tomorrow's, for regulators necessarily operate under considerable uncertainty and at a lag behind private actors. Further, institutions and individuals adapt their behavior in response to regulation, and their reactions change over time, interacting with the regulatory environment, in non-linear, often unpredictable ways, greatly complicating analysis. Accordingly, the unintended consequences of crisis-driven financial legislation are legion.

This chapter contends that the best means of responding to the typical pattern of financial regulation – legislating in a crisis atmosphere under conditions of substantial uncertainty followed by status quo stickiness – is for Congress and regulators to include as a matter of course, in financial legislation and regulation enacted in the midst or aftermath of a financial crisis, procedural mechanisms that require automatic subsequent review and reconsideration of those decisions, along with regulatory exemptive or waiver powers that create flexibility in implementation and encourage, where possible, small-scale, discrete experimentation to better inform and calibrate the regulatory apparatus. Such an approach, in my judgment, could mitigate, at least at the margin, errors which invariably accompany financial legislation and rule-making originating in a crisis atmosphere. Given the fragility of financial institutions and markets, and their centrality to economic growth and societal well-being, this is an area in which it

---

3 *See* Francis X. Diebold et al., *Introduction, in* THE KNOWN, THE UNKNOWN, AND THE UNKNOWABLE IN FINANCIAL RISK MANAGEMENT 3 (Francis X. Diebold et al. eds, 2010).

is exceedingly important for legislators, acting in a crisis with the best of intentions, to not make matters worse.

21.2 IMPROVING THE QUALITY OF CRISIS-BASED FINANCIAL REGULATION

There are two key components that should be included in financial regulation to mitigate the adverse effects of crisis-based financial legislation: (1) a sunset requirement that the legislation and implementing regulation be reviewed and reconsidered within a fixed period after enactment (e.g., five to six years) to stay on the books; and (2) a structure that is hospitable to regulatory experimentation wherever possible. By permitting legislators and regulators to incorporate new information into the decision-making process, and simultaneously increasing the likelihood that new information will be generated from the regulatory variety generated by experimentation, the quality of decision-making has a better chance of being improved.

21.2.1 Sunsetting Financial Regulation

Sunsetting – providing that a statute expires on a specified date unless re-enacted – is a time-honored legislative tool.[4] It has been used by Congress and state legislatures since the US's founding, although its use as a law-making strategy has ebbed and flowed over time. For instance, in the late 1970s, sunset legislation rapidly coursed through the states, with 35 legislatures enacting sunset laws to review administrative agencies, widely perceived to be ineffective and wasteful.[5] At the same time, Congress considered, but did not enact, a broad sunset statute, yet it still followed

---

[4] For an overview of the use of temporary legislation, of which sunset statutes are one variety, *see* Jacob Gersen, *Temporary Legislation*, 74 U. Chi. L. Rev. 247 (2007). The US income tax code is, in fact, rife with time-delimited provisions, often referred to as "extenders" (because typically they are automatically rolled over), rather than "sunsets." For a critical appraisal of the political dynamics of tax sunsets, which, being related to evasion of restrictive budgetary rules, is orthogonal to the issues concerning the use of sunsets in this chapter's context of crisis-driven legislation, *see* Rebecca M. Kysar, *The Sun Also Rises: The Political Economy of Sunset Provisions in the Tax Code*, 40 Ga. L. Rev. 335 (2005–2006).

[5] Lewis Anthony Davis, *Review Procedures and Public Accountability in Sunset Legislation: An Analysis and Proposal for Reform* 33 Admin. L. Rev. 393 (1981); Dan R. Price, *Sunset Legislation in the United States*, Baylor L. Rev. 401 (1978).

the trend in sunsetting the newly created Commodity Futures Trading Commission (CFTC) in the Commodity Futures Trading Commission Act of 1974.

By 1990, enthusiasm for administrative agency sunsetting waned, given the time and cost of reviews, but over 20 states still have some form of active sunset review, and in recent years, as states' fiscal situations have deteriorated, states have once again adopted or reinvigorated the process.[6] Articles discussing the effectiveness of state sunset reviews in their heyday in the 1970s indicate that they were on balance successful, resulting in the termination of agencies (although no major entities were terminated), and improvements in agency operations, even in states that discontinued sunset reviews.[7]

Sunsettting is particularly well suited for crisis-driven financial legislation. Of the rationales for adopting a sunsetting strategy, the key justification in the financial regulatory domain is that sunsetting mitigates the predicament of legislating with minimal information, and therefore running the risk of getting things seriously and, for all practical purposes, permanently wrong. Congress can, of course, in principle modify crisis legislation that turns out to be misplaced. But the US political system's organizing principles of separation of powers and checks and balances create numerous veto points throughout the legislative process (e.g., approval of both chambers, then presidential approval, or approval by a supermajority of both chambers) that make repealing a statute extremely arduous. Sunsetting loosens the institutional stickiness of the status quo, by putting a statute in play with a need for affirmative legislative action at a specific date to remain in effect.

But more importantly, in the financial regulation context, sunsetting sets in motion a process by which post-enactment information can be incorporated into the regulatory regime. For instance, by the time of a statute's sunset review, several years after enactment, there should be a better understanding of the causes of the crisis that the legislation sought to

---

[6] Richard C. Kearney, *Sunset: A Survey and Analysis of the State Experience*, 50 Pub. Admin. Rev. 49 (1990); Sarah Weaver, *Sunset Review in the States* (Report for the California Legislature Joint Sunset Review Committee, June 8, 2011), http://docs.google.com/viewer?a=v&q=cache:2gej2r5F638J:www.assembly.ca.gov/acs/Committee/C501/Hearings/060811/Sunset%2520Review%2520in%2520the%2520States.pdf+%22richard+kearney+sunset+survey%22&hl=en&gl=us&pid=bl&srcid=ADGEEShCFqIkO2zC0eoleRDmjwSvqVc5l3NeXIG31jaPNxGx9Fq_4zHKkM2M3A9QB6_GImdPRqLtUMVgauIDZyvYjfQYxD5aVuIUeVdel5XTcc08ucoBmjmkLJNHMBsMJm0S4vMzME6B&sig=AHIEtbQyr2I6CKax7O-onS_NCoAl24VnBA.

[7] *See* Kearney, *supra* note 6, at 52–55; Price, *supra* note 5, at 440.

address, along with knowledge of the enacted legislation's consequences: information indispensable for getting regulation right, but unavailable when a crisis necessitates a response. In addition to permitting a more clear-eyed assessment, with the benefit of hindsight, of the crisis-enacted regulation, economic and technological conditions may have dramatically changed in the interim, with financial innovation occurring apace, and that information can also be taken advantage of in the legislative "second look," for the most appropriate regulatory responses will undoubtedly have shifted as well.

To be effective, it is important that the sunsetting process be crafted in light of the states' experiences with what works. To guide the collection and analysis of information in a sunset review, and hence the reassessment of whether legislation should be retained or revised, evaluative criteria for the sunset review, and not simply an expiration date, need to be specified in the statute responding to the crisis. Otherwise, a review will lack focus and may become a pro forma process, as legislators will often have more immediate concerns that they wish to pursue rather than undertake a serious reassessment, especially if, as is probable, constituent concerns in a crisis that motivated the statute in the first place have drifted to new matters.[8] The evaluative criteria will, of course, vary depending on the specific legislation.

The availability of new information at the time a second vote on a statute is required for it to remain in force of course does not guarantee that legislators will engage in a serious reassessment, rather than a pro forma review.[9] To increase the likelihood that new information will be conscientiously acted upon, there is another component that should be included in a sunset provision, in addition to an expiration date and evaluative criteria: establishment of a sunset review panel to perform the review along with a timetable for action.[10] A sunset review panel should be tasked to recommend what action – repeal, re-enactment, revision – Congress should take, and a timetable should set out the interval in which a panel recommendation would be considered by the House and Senate committees with jurisdiction over the legislation, after which the panel's recommendation would be automatically discharged as a bill for a floor vote if the committees do not themselves bring it, or an amended version, to the floor.[11]

---

[8] Lewis Anthony Davis, *supra* note 5, at 394, 396–401.

[9] Stephen G. Breyer, Regulation and Its Reform 365 (1982).

[10] *See id.*, at 366.

[11] I am advocating a modified version of a proposal of Justice (then Professor) Breyer, for review of federal regulatory programs for waste and inefficiency. *See*

The sunset review panel should consist of independent experts, who are neither government employees nor officials, and be empowered to obtain information from relevant regulatory agencies and firms to undertake its review. The advantage of independent experts is that they tend to self-identify more strongly with professional norms and are more concerned about reputational damage if peers perceive them to be doing the bidding of interest groups or party politics, than government employees who are in a hierarchical chain of command. For the review panel to be both politically accountable and independent, it should be appointed by Congress and the President, paralleling the practice used for creating blue ribbon government panels. Although Congress could establish a standing blue ribbon review panel, which would reduce the cost to future Congresses of forming a panel, reviews would be more effective if undertaken by panels created specifically for the legislation to be evaluated, as the relevant expertise is likely to vary with a statute's focus. For example, expertise in macroeconomics would be pertinent for reviewing much of Dodd–Frank, but not Sarbanes–Oxley.

To ensure that the sunset process is meaningful, the authorizing legislation would need to include adequate funding for a review. Budgets of prior congressionally appointed blue ribbon investigatory panels could be used to provide guidance. Given budgetary concerns, Congress could impose a fee on the relevant sector affected by the legislation to cover a review panel's operating cost. It could also mandate that governmental research organizations, such as the Congressional Research Service or General Accounting Office, and the relevant regulatory agencies, provide evaluations of the sunsetting regulations to the panel, for use in its review. But that would probably not substantially reduce the expense of a sunset review, as the panel would likely want to seek to conduct its own evaluation *de novo*.

The rationale for this review mechanism, an expert panel and a timetable, is that the threat of a required floor vote on a recommendation

---

id., at 366–367. Breyer rejected a sunset approach because he was concerned that a congressional minority could "destroy" an existing program by preventing a bill from coming out of a committee or by filibustering or otherwise blocking a floor vote to reapprove a majority-supported program. *See id.*, at 367. His proposal therefore would continue a program were Congress not to adopt a recommendation. Breyer's proposed automatic discharge eliminates the issue of committee blocking, but not, of course, minority blocking on the floor. But sunset could be retained and the latter issue eliminated with a rule for sunset review analogous to the reconciliation process applicable to budget legislation, which limits debate and bypasses filibusters.

made by outside experts would compel a higher-quality reassessment of a statute by all concerned, and in particular by congressional committee members who know they cannot prevent a vote on a recommendation they might otherwise be able to oppose merely by inaction. It should also better incentivize review panel members, as they would know that a floor vote on their work product is assured. The use of a review panel has a further benefit, of reducing the time required by legislators and their staff to engage in a sunset review, for the panel would collect data and perform the analyses necessary for the legislature's reassessment. It would thereby mitigate a key operational problem experienced by states in their 1970s sunset reviews and that led several states to abandon the procedure: legislators, particularly in states where they were part-time, did not have the time or resources to engage in the demanding process of reviewing numerous state agencies.[12]

A variant of legislative sunset, which would reduce even further demands placed on Congress of a required review, would be to impose the sunset review on agencies implementing the legislation. In this alternative, crisis-driven financial legislation would mandate agency reassessment of regulations implemented under the statute, with an automatic expiration in five years unless they are found to be cost-effective, and with the technical analysis undertaken by independent experts, rather than agency staff, to minimize potential bias from an agency's being too closely involved in the rules it administers to evaluate them objectively.[13] Further, to guard against an agency's inherent bias in interpreting the independent experts' analysis in support of the regulatory status quo or its agenda, a congressional vote on the agency's determination should be required in an administrative sunset review regime.

21.2.2 Opening Financial Legislation Up to Experimentation

An additional means of increasing the available information, and hence improving the quality of crisis-based legislative decision-making, is to incorporate experimentation into financial legislation. It is the genius of the federal organization of the US government that makes it quite amenable to such an approach.[14] Moreover, structuring financial regulation to be more hospitable to experimentation is consistent with a contemporary

---

12 *See* Kearney, *supra* note 6, at 55.

13 Cary Coglianese, *Let's Review the Rules*, L. A. Times, Apr. 29, 2011, at A23. *See* Romano, *supra* note 1, at 1601.

14 Roberta Romano, The Genius of American Corporate Law (1993).

trend in economics to introduce experimentation into policymaking, as the gold standard for policy evaluation.[15] Michael Greenstone advocates implementing regulatory initiatives through a proccss that either starts with small-scale randomized experiments or permits states to implement different regulatory approaches.[16] The expectation is that coverage would be expanded nationwide were these initial experiments successful, essentially on a cost–benefit metric. Although this approach, as he notes, is most feasible for environmental, health, labor market, and safety regulations, where discrete programs can be implemented using randomized trial experiments or "quasi" experiments, on the model of Food and Drug Administration testing requirements for new drugs, there is, I think, an analogue in the financial setting. That could be done by providing agencies with expanded exemptive and waiver power and an accompanying directive to use the authority to permit individual or classes of institutions to operate under different regulatory arrangements.[17]

Congress has, in fact, used such an approach in crisis-driven financial legislation, but it has been limited in scope. For example, Sarbanes–Oxley's mandate of independent audit committees (by requiring the SEC to direct stock exchanges to prohibit the listing of any firm without an independent committee), states that the SEC can establish exemptions to the statutory criteria of director independence (Sarbanes Oxley Act § 301). Such an approach could be more broadly applied, and agencies instructed to implement rules along the lines of a small-scale experiment, with incremental expansion only after a cost–benefit analysis undertaken by independent experts.

One means by which experimentation could be implemented within a waiver setting is by permitting a firm or class of firms to request a regulatory waiver, and by not leaving the matter solely up to an agency's initiative. The standard for approval of an exemption could be an assessment

---

[15] Michael Greenstone, *Toward a Culture of Persistent Regulatory Experimentation and Evaluation*, *in* New Perspectives on Regulation, 111–126 (David A. Moss & John A. Cisternino eds, 2009).

[16] *See id.*, at 118.

[17] This chapter advocates congressional directives to agencies to use existing exemptive authority in implementing emergency regulation. I consider explicit instruction necessary because history teaches that the SEC will not voluntarily use its exemptive powers to remedy flawed rules that it has adopted in implementing emergency legislation. The well-known cognitive bias to favor the status quo aids in explaining why agency exemptive power alone is not an effective means of revising flawed legislation and sunsetting is critical. *See* William Samuelson & Richard Zeckhauser, *Status Quo Bias in Decision Making*, 1 J. Risk & Uncertainty 7 (1988).

of minimal adverse impact on the statutory objective (for example, on reducing systemic risk or financial statement fraud; objectives, respectively, of Dodd–Frank and Sarbanes–Oxley). Because an agency could be expected to be predisposed to believe that whatever regulation exists is good and hence to oppose exemptions, it could be required to accept, or at least to have to rebut in a meaningful way, an analysis of the proposed waiver provided by independent experts. Maintenance of the statutory purpose would be safeguarded by having the agency engage in ongoing monitoring and review of approved waivers, to make sure no adverse impact developed. And paralleling Greenstone's contemplated regulatory reform process, were the waivers deemed successful, the agency would be expected to extend them to more, or all, firms or sectors.[18] Where the proposed waiver is a private sector initiative, the firms could be required to cover the agency's cost of evaluating and administering the experiment.

The interaction between statutory experimentation through waivers and required sunset reviews can, however, be complicated. When exempted firms are non-random, one cannot evaluate properly either the impact of the waiver with an eye to generalization, or the efficacy of the regulation under sunset review, for the analysis would be subject to selection bias, as covered and excluded firms would not be comparable. For instance, firms that request a waiver would most likely be those that would be most adversely affected by a rule. This difficulty could be addressed if regulatory waivers were constructed as natural experiments, in which firms receiving a waiver were selected by lot.[19] But such an approach would, in my judgment, in many instances be politically infeasible and inappropriate, as it could seriously interfere with market competition, where the exempted firms' operating cost would be less than that of the regulated firms. In addition, if the exemption was for a limited time frame – for instance, until the "experiment" was evaluated by the agency for its effectiveness

---

[18] *See* Greenstone, *supra* note 15, at 111–126.

[19] The Securities and Exchange Commission (SEC) undertook a random experiment to investigate the effect of relaxing restrictions on short selling in 2004. U.S. Securities & Exchange Comm'n, Office of Economic Analysis, Economic Analysis of the Short Sale Price Restrictions under the Regulation SHO Pilot (2007), http://www.sec.gov/news/studies/2007/regshopilot020607.pdf. The experimental results led the agency to repeal the uptick rule restricting short sales. *SEC Votes on Regulation SHO Amendments and Proposals: Also Votes to Eliminate 'Tick' Test* (2007), http://www.sec.gov/news/press/2007/2007-114.htm. Despite the change in policy's grounding in a "gold standard" natural experiment, in the wake of the financial crisis, pressed by opponents of the rule change, the SEC reinstated a limited version of the rule. Final Rule. Amendments to Regulation SHO, Release No. 34-61595, 75 Fed. Reg. 11,232 (2010).

– then firms' behavior may not represent how they would respond to a permanent rule, as they strategize to affect the outcome. In short, there is an inherent tension between sunset reviews and experimentation. But I do not believe the potential conflict is sufficient to reject the proposed dual-pronged regulatory approach.[20] Given the sunset review panel's expertise, it should be well attuned to the selection issue and able to recalibrate the analysis when undertaking its regulatory evaluation in the context of experimental data.

21.3 CONCLUSION

Congress typically legislates on financial matters in a crisis environment, which is not conducive to high-quality decision-making. Although Congress is not about to restrain itself from acting in a crisis and increasing financial regulation, there are procedural mechanisms that can be systematically employed to mitigate the unintended consequences likely to accompany those legislative decisions.

First, sunsetting is a useful legislative tool that could mitigate legislative failure in the field of financial regulation. Second, one could make headway in improving the quality of decision-making by incorporating experimentation and regulatory diversity into the legislative process, by Congress's directing agencies to use regulatory exemptive and waiver powers to foster such objectives. In tandem with sunsetting, the greater flexibility arising from the use of such tools would facilitate timely updating of the legislative and regulatory architecture, offsetting the woefully inadequate information environment in which crisis-based legislation is enacted.

---

[20] Greenstone, it should be noted, recommends automatic sunsets along with experimentation in his regulatory reform agenda and does not view them to be in tension. This is most likely because he envisions experiments undertaken on a randomized, small-scale basis, which would not be likely to interfere but rather would assist in the cost–benefit evaluation of the sunset review he contemplates. In addition, he advocates automatic sunset for all regulations, many of which would not have been subjected to experimentation. Greenstone, *supra* note 15, at 121.

Comments on Part IV: the political economy of legislation

Noriyuki Yanagawa

Part IV is a collection of seven informative chapters mainly focused on the (various) roles of government. The first half of Part IV examines the relationship between tax law and corporate law. Obviously, both types of law have a significant effect on corporate behavior, but the relationship between the two has not been examined in detail. The first three chapters in Part IV make an attempt to do so.

Chapter 15, "Taxation and incentives in the business enterprise" by David Gamage and Shruti Rana, explores the fact that tax laws tend to create many biases which affect the behavior of managers, employees, and monetary capital providers. Gamage and Rana provide an overview of the interactions between tax law and corporate law, and outline a few examples of how the nature of tax law influences the incentive bargains reached between managers, employees, and monetary capital providers.

Chapter 16, "Income tax and incentives for corporate transactions: a Japanese perspective" by Tetsuya Watanabe, considers an important legislative problem, that is, whether or not tax rules should provide an incentive or disincentive for corporate transactions. This chapter picks out and carefully examines several examples of tax law that may affect the incentive bargains in Japan.

Chapter 17, "Tax law influences on the form and substance of equity compensation in the United States" by Mark P. Gergen, focuses on tax laws that affect the form and/or substance of equity compensation schemes used in publicly traded corporations in the United States. By examining this specific problem, Gergen has succeeded in providing highly detailed information on the relationship between tax law and transactions of firms.

These three chapters help to elucidate that tax laws materially affect corporate behavior in both the United States and Japan, and that tax laws may change some of the incentive effects within a corporation. However, a clear picture about the interrelationship between corporate law and tax law is still lacking. Whether tax law and corporate law should be coordinated, and how such a task could be accomplished, are questions that still need answering. Furthermore, if one country's corporate law is different from another's, should the tax laws of these countries also be different?

From an economic theory perspective, some degree of coordination between corporate law and tax law is desirable since both affect the interactions of a corporation related to incentives. In reality, however, the philosophies behind these two types of law seem to be quite different. Hence, it is difficult to answer the above questions, but by accumulating important pieces of information, such as the results of these three chapters, a new theory combining tax law and corporate law may be seen in the near future.

In the second half of Part IV, four chapters present some of the demerits and costs associated with legal regulation. Chapter 18, "Public enforcement: an update of the literature on resource-based evidence" by Howell E. Jackson, reviews the seminal paper by Jackson and Roe, and their claim that the investment of real resources into public enforcement can have significant positive effects on capital market outcomes. Jackson shows that a large number of subsequent papers report statistically significant effects. Furthermore, he suggests some potentially undesirable consequences of robust capital markets by showing several studies about a negative correlation between capital market funding for banks and poor results in a financial crisis

Chapter 19, "Transparency and corporate governance" by Benjamin E. Hermalin, clearly shows that there is no so such thing as a free lunch; that is, the benefits of the transparency realized through legal rules come at a cost. This chapter explores the costs of the Sarbanes–Oxley Act (SOX) in a way that makes the issue easy to understand.

Chapter 20, "Reverse engineering SOX versus J-SOX: a lesson in legislative policy" by Zenichi Shishido and Sadakazu Osaki, carefully comes to the conclusion that the Financial Instruments and Exchange Act (J-SOX) did not strengthen the bargaining power of monitors, nor did it substantially improve the corporate governance of publicly traded Japanese companies. Shishido and Osaki show that while the basic structure of the Sarbanes–Oxley Act (SOX) and J-SOX is the same, the related regulatory schemes have led to completely different results.

Chapter 21, "Regulating in the dark" by Roberta Romano, argues that the US Congress typically legislates on financial matters in response to crises, which is not conducive to high-quality decision making. This chapter points out some of the risks of legislating in response to a crisis in addition to suggesting meaningful mitigation for these risks.

These chapters help to demonstrate that applying a legal rule might lead to critical side effects which may not be well understood during the legislation process. One reason behind this phenomenon is limited information or bounded rationality in regard to the future. Another reason may be the "political neglect" involved in the legislation process. If one political goal is (implicitly or explicitly) the impetus of legislation, Congress might tend to underestimate the de-merits of the newly legislated legal rule. Political decision-making processes are usually very complex. Hence, it may be desirable to examine political decision-making problems more rigorously in order to understand corporate law more deeply. Recently, political economic theory and theoretical and empirical analysis of bounded rationality have advanced rapidly. Introducing these new insights on economic theory might be a fruitful future research topic.

General comments: afterword

J. Mark Ramseyer

What does one say about a book this thoughtful and diverse? A book this thoughtful raises issues to which one cannot respond summarily. A book this diverse one cannot summarize at all.

Professor Zenichi Shishido carefully captures the gist of the project. In firms, shareholders and creditors provide financial capital, and managers and employees provide human capital. The task they face is (Professor Shishido nicely outlines it with much more subtlety and sophistication) to assemble a bargain that gives each of them an incentive to maximize the value of the firm. The task of the law (again, Professor Shishido outlines it with more subtlety and sophistication) is to provide the set of default terms that best facilitates those bargains.

It is a good thing for the corporate university community when scholars this talented contribute such sharply analytical chapters. It is a good thing when the best scholars from Japan and the United States contribute together. In both countries, we face the task of understanding how and why managers, investors, and workers organize their productive enterprise the way they do. In both countries we benefit from the cross-national comparisons that a project like this engenders.

It is a good thing when the best scholars across different legal subfields contribute together toward a project like this. Judges do not enforce securities law separately from tax or bankruptcy or labor law, and corporate managers do not plan securities strategies separately from those for tax or bankruptcy or labor law. Across the many subfields, we face the task of understanding why and how people organize their firms the way they do. Across the many subfields, we benefit from the cross-field comparisons that this book engenders.

And it is a good thing when scholars work together across divergent interpretive strategies. We in the academy approach our work from a wide range of perspectives: whether economics, finance, law and economics, psychology, or sociology. Across these many perspectives, we benefit from the interdisciplinary conversations that a collaboration such as this engenders.

* * *

Whatever else one says about this book, we can hope that the collaboration continues. The scholars who participated have begun an immensely promising project, and we can only pray that they continue to collaborate across multiple volumes in the future. It would be a crying shame if this were the end now. And as the scholars continue their collaboration, let me urge them to remember three principles:

1. Talk to each other.
   As talented as the scholars who contributed to this project are, I could not read some of the chapters without wishing that they had talked with each other more. The chapters present a beguiling diversity, but in that very diversity they also embody an odd "disconnect." Several of the authors seem to have "done their thing" and moved on.
   The "disconnect" represents an opportunity foregone. Had the authors talked to each other, they would not have made some of the claims that they did. Scholars as talented as these would not have let some of the less felicitous statements among the other chapters lie. Focus more sharply on a common problem, and future volumes will be the better for it.
2. Check your facts.
   Several of the authors take facts as given in stylized form, and focus on explaining them. In effect, they take their facts from the conventional wisdom. Unfortunately, that conventional wisdom only haphazardly captures anything that actually happens in practice. By its very nature, the conventional wisdom represents what people say they do. Sometimes, they do indeed do what they say they do. But often they do not. Anthropologist Napoleon Chagnon devoted his life to studying the Yanomamo Indians in the Venezuelan Amazon. In his account of his "life among two dangerous tribes – the Yanomamo and the anthropologists," he captures the essence of conventional wisdom:[1]

   > Field-working cultural anthropologists are (or should be) aware of two kinds of "truth" that they eventually report from their field studies: (1) what the natives say they do, and (2) what the natives actually do. Sometimes these are nearly identical, but more often the discrepancy between them is very large.

---

[1] Napoleon A. Chagnon, NOBLE SAVAGES: MY LIFE AMONG TWO DANGEROUS TRIBES – THE YANOMAMO AND THE ANTHROPOLOGISTS 232 (New York: Simon & Schuster, 2013).

Explain the stylized facts in the conventional wisdom, and sometimes an author can help us understand what happens. But not always. Sometimes he merely helps us understand why the sun revolves around the earth.

Take some examples. Several of the authors premise their analysis on a claim that Japanese firms swap extensive stock in each other through cross-shareholding agreements. Unfortunately, none of the authors checks how many firms "cross-hold" how many shares in which industries. Several years ago, economist Yoshiro Miwa and I checked exactly that. We studied the cross-shareholding patterns at the firms that – by the conventional wisdom – maintained the most extensive cross-shareholding arrangements: the firms in what scholars called the *keiretsu* groups at their height in the 1960s and 1970s.

Miwa and I found virtually no cross-shareholding. The point is crucial: we did not find "much less" cross-holding than usually claimed; we found almost none.[2] Given that Japanese law did not impose a Glass–Steagall ban on stock ownership at banks, the large Japanese financial firms held stock in Tokyo Stock Exchange-listed firms. As part of that portfolio, they also held shares of firms in their so-called *keiretsu*. But in 1965, the non-financial firms slotted by observers into the Sumitomo *keiretsu* collectively held 6.1 percent of the stock of the member firms; those slotted into the Sanwa *keiretsu* held 2.1 percent. In 1975, the non-financial firms classed in the Sumitomo *keiretsu* collectively held 9.5 percent of the stock of the member firms; those in the Sanwa *keiretsu* held 3.5 percent (Table A.1).

In fact, the usual claims about "cross-shareholding" involve much more: that pairs of firms swap stock in each other. Miwa and I found virtually no such arrangements. In 1965, 11 pairs of firms classed in the Sumitomo *keiretsu* held at least a 1 percent stake in each other. Among firms classed in the Mitsui and Sanwa *keiretsu*, six pairs of firms held at least 1 percent stakes in each other. Among those classed in the Mitsubishi *keiretsu*, four pairs of firms held at least 1 percent stakes; among the Fuji firms three such pairs; and among the Daiichi firms two pairs.[3]

The conventional wisdom about "main bank" arrangements captures a similar factual vacuum. The wisdom posits that Japanese firms agree that one bank will serve as its "main bank." As such, the bank

---

[2] Yoshiro Miwa & J. Mark Ramseyer, *The Fable of the Keiretsu*, 11 J. ECON. & MGMT STRATEGY 169 (2002).

[3] Miwa & Ramseyer, *supra* note 2.

Table A.1 Percentage (weighted average) of shares in non-financial firms held by other keiretsu members

A. 1965						
Held by	Mitsubishi	Mitsui	Sumitomo	Fuji	Sanwa	Daiichi
All firms	16.5	8.6	17.6	9.1	7.6	9.4
Non-financial firms	4.9	3.5	6.1	2.0	2.1	4.7
B. 1975						
Held by	Mitsubishi	Mitsui	Sumitomo	Fuji	Sanwa	Daiichi
All firms	25.2	15.3	22.6	17.7	11.0	17.4
Non-financial firms	9.2	5.3	9.5	4.6	3.5	7.9

Source: Yoshiro Miwa & J. Mark Ramseyer, *The Fable of the Keiretsu*, 11 J. ECON. & MGMT STRATEGY 169 (2002).

will monitor the firm on behalf of the other banks. It will send personnel to help the firm. It will lend extra funds to rescue the firm should it fall into distress.

Miwa and I found no evidence that any of this happens.[4] No bank ever agrees to serve as "main bank" to any firm, and no firm ever asks it to be a "main bank." No bank ever monitors a debtor on behalf of another bank, and no sensible bank would ever trust a competitor to monitor any firm on its behalf anyway. No bank ever agrees to lend a firm extra money should it blow the funds it has.

Several authors in this volume build substantial models on claims about cross-shareholding arrangements and main bank contracts. They would do well to check whether any of this ever happens first.

3. Remember Demsetz–Lehn.

In 1985, Harold Demsetz and Kenneth Lehn asked whether the ownership concentration of US firms correlated (as often claimed) with their economic performance.[5] They found no evidence that it did. The

---

[4] Yoshiro Miwa & J. Mark Ramseyer, *Does Relationship Banking Matter? The Myth of the Japanese Main Bank*, 2 J. EMPIRICAL LEGAL STUD. 261 (2005); Yoshiro Miwa & J. Mark Ramseyer, *The Myth of the Main Bank: Japan and Comparative Corporate Governance*, 27 LAW & SOCIAL INQUIRY 401 (2002).

[5] Harold Demsetz & Kenneth Lehn, *The Structure of Corporate Ownership*, 93 J. POL. ECON. 1155 (1985); see Yoshiro Miwa & J. Mark Ramseyer, *Does Ownership Matter? Evidence from the Zaibatsu Dissolution Program*, 12 J. ECON. & MGMT STRATEGY 67 (2003).

reason, however, did not lie in the irrelevance of ownership concentration. Instead, it lay in its endogeneity. At some firms, high ownership concentration levels contributed to firm performance; at others, it did not. Given competitive capital, product, and labor markets, firms tended to choose their firm-specifically optimal levels of ownership concentration on their own, for the simple reason that they otherwise went out of business. Firms that benefited from high levels of concentration tended to have them; firms without high levels probably would not have found them helpful. Given the resulting firm-specifically optimal levels of ownership, any regression of firm performance on ownership concentration necessarily showed no effect.

The principle applies far beyond ownership concentration. Would firms benefit from outside directors? Probably some firms would, but most of them will already have outside directors. In 1985, Miwa and I found that 56.7 percent of Tokyo Stock Exchange (TSE)-listed firms had a director who had earlier worked at another firm, and 44.2 percent had someone concurrently working at another firm.[6] Firms without outside directors disproportionately will be those at which such directors would not be helpful, and any statute requiring their appointment will necessarily be counter-productive. Would firms benefit from the Japanese *kansayaku* auditors? If any would, they would appoint such auditors on their own. Would they benefit from employee stock ownership arrangements? Again, the same principle applies.

* * *

Professor Shishido has organized an enormously insightful project. Across national boundaries, across subfields, across disciplinary perspectives, he has enlisted the finest scholars. They have given us a volume both thoughtful and diverse. We can only hope that they follow it with more.

---

6 Yoshiro Miwa & J. Mark Ramseyer, *Who Appoints Them, What Do They Do? Evidence on Outside Directors from Japan*, 14 J. ECON. & MGMT STRATEGY 299 (2005).

Table of references

Addison, John T. & Jean-Luc Grosso, *Job Security Provisions and Employment: Revised Estimates*, 35 INDUS. REL. 585 (1996)

Addison, John T. & Paulino Teixeira, *The Economics of Employment Protection*, 24 J. LAB. RES. 85 (2003)

Addison, John T., Paulino Teixeira, & Jean-Luc Grosso, *The Effect of Dismissals Protection on Employment: More on a Vexed Theme*, 67 SOUTHERN ECON. J. 105 (2000)

Adler, Barry E., Vedran Capkun, & Lawrence A. Weiss, *Destruction of Value in the New Era of Chapter 11* (Working Paper, 2008)

Adler, Barry E., *Financial and Political Theories of American Corporate Bankruptcy*, 45 STAN. L. REV. 311, 315 (1993)

Aghion, Philippe & Benjamin E. Hermalin, *Legal Restrictions on Private Contracts Can Enhance Efficiency*, 6 J. L. ECON. & ORG. 381 (1990)

Ahrend, Rüdiger & Antoine Goujard, *Drivers of Systemic Banking Crises: The Role of Bank-Balance-Sheet Contagion and Financial Account Structure* (June 5, 2011), *available at* http://www.oecd-ilibrary.org/economics/drivers-of-systemic-banking-crises_5kg3k8ksgglw-en

Ahrend, Rüdiger, Jens M. Arnold, & Fabrice Murtin, *Have More Strictly Regulated Banking Systems Fared Better During the Recent Financial Crisis?*, 18 APPLIED ECON. LETTERS 399 (2011)

Allen, William T., *The Corporate Director's Fiduciary Duties of Care and the Business Judgment Rule Under US Corporate Law*, *in* COMPARATIVE CORPORATE GOVERNANCE: THE STATE OF THE ART AND EMERGING RESEARCH 307 (Klaus J. Hopt et al. eds., 1998)

ALLEN, WILLIAM T. ET AL., COMMENTARIES AND CASES ON THE LAW OF BUSINESS ORGANIZATION (4th ed. 2012)

Amiram, Dan & Edward Owens, *Private Benefits Extraction and the Opposing Effects of Income Smoothing on Private Debt Contracts* (Oct. 19, 2011), *available at* https://community.bus.emory.edu/Faculty/Events%20Documents/Owens_paper.pdf

Amri, Pupsa Delima & Brett Matthew Kocher, *The Political Economy of Financial Sector Supervision and Banking Crises: A Cross-Country Analysis*, 18 EUR. L. J. 24 (2012)

AOKI, MASAHIKO, INFORMATION, INCENTIVES, AND BARGAINING IN THE JAPANESE ECONOMY (1988)

Aoki, Masahiko, *The Japanese Firm as a System of Attributes: A Survey and Research Agenda*, *in* THE JAPANESE FIRM: SOURCES OF COMPETITIVE STRENGTH 11 (Masahiko Aoki & Ronald Dore eds, 1994)

Aoki, Masahiko, *Monitoring Characteristics of the Main Bank System: An Analysis and Development View*, *in* THE JAPANESE MAIN BANK SYSTEM: ITS RELEVANCE FOR DEVELOPING AND TRANSFORMING ECONOMICS (Masahiko Aoki & Hugh Patrick eds., 1994)

AREEDA, PHILIP & LOUIS KAPLOW, ANTITRUST ANALYSIS § 201 (6th ed. 2004)

ARAKI, TAKASHI, LABOR AND EMPLOYMENT LAW IN JAPAN (2002)

Araki, Takashi, *Corporate Governance Reforms, Labor Law Developments, and the Future of Japan's Practice-Dependent Stakeholder Model*, 2-1 JAPAN LABOR REVIEW 26 (2005)

Arand, Daniel, Alexander G. Kerl, & Andreas Walter, *When Do Sell-Side Analyst Reports Really Matter? Shareholder Protection, Institutional Investors and the Importance of Equity Research* (Feb. 2013), *available at* http://ssrn.com/abstract=2044548

Arikawa, Yasuhiro & Hideaki Miyajima, *Relational Banking in Post-Bubble Japan: Co-existence of Soft-and Hard Budget Constraint*, *in* CORPORATE GOVERNANCE IN JAPAN: INSTITUTIONAL CHANGE AND ORGANIZATIONAL DIVERSITY 51 (Masahiko Aoki et al. eds., 2007)

Armour, John, Jack B. Jacobs, & Curtis J. Milhaupt, *The Evolution of Hostile Takeover Regimes in Developed and Emerging Markets: An Analytical Framework*, 52 HARV. INT'L L. J. 219 (2011)

Armour, John, Colin Mayer, & Andrea Polo, *Regulatory Sanctions and Reputational Damage in Financial Markets* (Oxford Legal Studies Research Paper No. 62/2010, 2011), *available at* http://ssrn.com/abstract=1678028

Aronson, Bruce E., *Reconsidering the Importance of Law in Japanese Corporate Governance: Evidence from the Daiwa Bank Shareholder Derivative Case*, 36 CORNELL INT'L L. J. 11 (2003–2004)

Ashbaugh-Skaife, Hollis, Daniel W. Collins, & William R. Kinney Jr, *The Discovery and Reporting of Internal Control Deficiencies prior to SOX-Mandated Audit*, 44 J. ACCT. & ECON. 166 (2007)

Auerbach, Alan J., *The Future of Captial Income Taxation*, INSTITUTE FOR FISCAL STUDIES ANNUAL LECTURE (2006), http://escholarship.org/uc/item/90v90406 (last accessed 10/1/2012)

Auerbach, Alan J., *Who Bears the Corporate Tax? A Review of What We Know*, 20 TAX POLICY AND THE ECONOMY 1 (NBER, 2006)

Ault, Hugh J., *Taxing International Income: An Analysis of the US System and Its Economic Premises*, *in* TAXATION IN THE GLOBAL ECONOMY 28 (Assaf Razin & Joel Slemrod eds., 1990), *available at* http://www.nber.org/chapters/c7203.pdf

Autor, David, John Donohue, & Stewart Schwab, *The Employment Consequences of Wrongful Dismissal Laws: Large, Small or None at All?*, 94 AM. ECON. REV. PAPERS & PROC. 440 (2004)

Autor, David, John Donohue, & Stewart Schwab, *The Costs of Wrongful-Discharge Laws*, 88 REV. ECON. & STAT. 211 (2006)

BAINBRIDGE, STEPHEN M., THE NEW CORPORATE GOVERNANCE: IN THEORY AND PRACTICE (2008)

BAINBRIDGE, STEPHEN M., CORPORATE GOVERNANCE AFTER THE FINANCIAL CRISIS (2012)

Baird, Douglas G. & Thomas H. Jackson, *Corporate Reorganizations and the Treatment of Diverse Ownership Interests: A Comment on Adequate Protection of Secured Creditors in Bankruptcy*, 51 U. CHI. L. REV. 97 (1984)

Baird, Douglas G. & Robert K. Rasmussen, *The End of Bankruptcy*, 55 STAN. L. REV. 751 (2002)

Baird, Douglas G. & Robert K. Rasmussen, *Chapter 11 at Twilight*, 56 STAN. L. REV. 673 (2003)

Baird, Douglas G. & Robert K. Rasmussen, *Private Debt and the Missing Lever of Corporate Governance*, 154 U. PA. L. REV. 1209 (2006)

Bank, Steven A. & Brian R. Cheffins, *The Corporate Pyramid Fable* (Working Paper, 2011)

Bankman, Joseph, *The Structure of Silicon Valley Start-Ups*, 41 UCLA L. REV. 1737 (1994)

Bargeron, Leonce L. et al., *Sarbanes–Oxley and Corporate Risk-Taking*, 49 J. ACCT. & ECON. 34 (2010)

BARTLETT, JOSEPH W., EQUITY FINANCE: VENTURE CAPITAL BUYOUTS, RESTRUCTURINGS AND REORGANIZATIONS, (2nd ed., New York: Aspen Law & Business 1995)

Bartlett, Robert P., *Do Institutional Investors Value the 10b-5 Private Right of Action? Evidence from Investor Trading Behavior Following Morrison v. National Australia Bank Ltd.* (Oct. 22, 2012), *available at* http://papers.ssrn.com/id=2171006

Bartov, Eli & Daniel Cohen, *The "Numbers Game" in the Pre- and Post-Sarbanes–Oxley Eras,* 24 J. ACCT. AUDITING & FIN. 505 (2009)

Bean, Larry L., *Taxation of Carried Interests in Oil and Gas Transactions – In Retrospect and Prospect*, 10 U. KAN. L. REV. 391 (1962)

Bebchuk, Lucian A., *Limiting Contractual Freedom in Corporate Law: The Desirable Constraints on Charter Amendments*, 102 HARV. L. REV. 1820 (1989)

Bebchuk, Lucian A., *Efficient and Inefficient Sales of Corporate Control*, 109 Q. J. ECON. 957 (1994)

Bebchuk, Lucian A., *The Case for Increasing Shareholder Power*, 118 HARV. L. REV. 848 (2005)

Bebchuk, Lucian A. & Howard F. Chang, *Bargaining and the Division of Value in Corporate Reorganizations*, 8 J. L. ECON. & ORG. 253 (1992)

Bebchuk, Lucian A. & Jesse Fried, *The Uneasy Case for the Priority of Secured Claims in Bankruptcy*, 105 YALE L. J. 857 (1996)

BEBCHUK, LUCIAN A. & JESSE M. FRIED, PAY WITHOUT PERFORMANCE: THE UNFULFILLED PROMISE OF EXECUTIVE COMPENSATION (2004)

Bebchuk, Lucian A. & Zvika Neeman, *Investor Protection and Interest Group Politics*, 23 REV. FIN. STUD. 1089 (2010)

Bebchuk, Lucian A. & Randal Picker, *Bankruptcy Rules, Management Entrenchment, and Firm Specific Human Capital* (Working Paper, 1993)

Bebchuck, Lucian & Mark Roe, *A Theory of Path Dependence in Corporate Governance and Ownership*, 52 STAN. L. REV. 127 (1999)

Bebchuk, Lucian A. et al., *Stock Pyramids, Cross-Ownership and Dual Class Equity: The Mechanism and Agency Costs of Separating Control From Cash-Flow Rights*, in CONCENTRATED CORPORATE OWNERSHIP 295 (Randall Morck ed., 2000)

Bedard, Jean, *Sarbanes Oxley Internal Control Requirements and Earnings Quality* (Working Paper, 2006)

Beltratti, Andrea & René M. Stulz, *Why Did Some Banks Perform Better During the Credit Crisis? A Cross-Country Study of the Impact of Governance and Regulation* (July 2009), *available at* http://www.nber.org/papers/w15180

Beneish, Messod D., Marry B. Billings, & Leslie D. Hodder, *Internal Control Weaknesses and Information Uncertainty,* 83 ACCT. REV. 665 (2008)

Bengtsson, Ola, Na Dai, & Clifford Chad Henson, *SEC Enforcement in the PIPE Market: Actions and Consequences* (April 2012), *available at* http://papers.ssrn.com/abstract=2033950

BERLE, ADOLF A. & GERDINER C. MEANS, THE MODERN CORPORATION AND PRIVATE PROPERTY (1932)

Bermant, Gordon & Ed Flynn, *Bankruptcy by the Numbers: Outcomes of Chapter 11 Cases: US Trustee Database Sheds New Light on Old Questions*, AM. BANKR. INST. J., FEB. 1998

Bhattacharya, Utpal & Hazem Daouk, *When No Law is Better than a Good Law*, 13 REV. FIN. 577 (2009)

Black, Bernard S. *Shareholder Passivity Reexamined*, 89 MICH. L. REV. 520 (1990)

Black, Bernard S. & John C. Coffee, Jr, *Hail Britannia?: Institutional Investor Behavior under Limited Regulation,* 92 MICH. L. REV. 2002 (1994)

Blanchard, Oliver & Justin Wolfers, *The Role of Shocks and Institutions in the Rise of European Unemployment: A First Pass*, 6 J. EUROPEAN ECON. ASSOC. 45 (2008)

Blasi, Joseph R. & Douglas Kruse, *The Court's Views On Employee Ownership Research*, OHIO EMPLOYEE OWNERSHIP CENTER, *available at* http://www.oeockent.org/library/doc/304/raw (last modified Jul. 16, 2009)

Blasi Joseph R. et al., *Creating a Bigger Pie? The Effects of Employee Ownership, Profit Sharing, and Stock Options on Workplace Performance*, *in* SHARED CAPITALISM AT WORK: EMPLOYEE OWNERSHIP, PROFIT AND GAIN SHARING, AND BROAD-BASED STOCK OPTIONS 139 (Douglas L. Kruse et al. eds., 2010)

Blasi, Joseph R. et al., *Risk and Lack of Diversification under Employee Ownership and Shared Capitalism*, *in* SHARED CAPITALISM AT WORK: EMPLOYEE OWNERSHIP, PROFIT AND GAIN SHARING, AND BROAD-BASED STOCK OPTIONS 105 (Douglas L. Kruse et al. eds., 2010)

Bolton, Patrick & Frederic Samama, *L-Share: Rewarding Long-term Investors* (Working Paper, 2011)

Booth, Richard A., *Stockholders, Stakeholders, and Bagholders (or How Investor Diversification Affects Fiduciary Duty)*, 53 BUS. LAW. 429 (1998)

Bradley, Michael & Michael Rosenzweig, *The Untenable Case for Chapter 11*, 101 YALE L. J. 1043 (1992)

Bratton, William W. & Michael L. Wachter, *The Political Economy of Fraud on the Market*, 60 U. PA. L. REV. 69 (2011)

Brean, Donald J.S., Lawrence Kryzanowski, & Gordon S. Roberts, *Canada and the United States: Different Roots, Different Routes to Financial Sector Regulation*, 53 BUS. HIST. 249 (2011)

BREYER, STEPHEN G., REGULATION AND ITS REFORM (1982)

Briggs, Thomas W., *Corporate Governance and the New Hedge Fund Activism: An Empirical Analysis*, J. CORP. L. 681 (2007)

Brogi, Marina, *Once Bitten Twice Shy? A Study on the Effectiveness of Administrative Sanctions to Discipline Bank Board Members* (June 14, 2011), *available at* http://www.efmaefm.org/0EFMAMEETINGS/EFMA%20ANNUAL%20MEETINGS/2011-Braga/papers/0289.pdf

Brubaker, Ralph & Charles Jordan Tabb, *Bankruptcy Reorganizations and the Troubling Legacy of Chrysler and GM*, 2010 U. ILL. L. REV. 1375 (2010)

Brudney, James, *To Strike or Not to Strike*, 1999 WISC. L. REV. 65 (1999)

Brügeman, Björn, *Employment Protection: Tough to Scrap or Tough to Get?* 117 ECON. J. F 386 (2007)

Brynjolfsson, Erik & Paul Milgrom, *Complementarity in Organizations*, *in* THE HANDBOOK OF ORGANIZATIONAL ECONOMICS 11 (Robert Gibbons & John Roberts eds., 2012)

Buchanan, Bonnie, Jeffry M. Netter, Annette B. Poulsen, & Tina Yang,

Shareholder Proposal Rules and Practice: Evidence from a Comparison of the US and UK, 49 Am. Bus. L. J. 756 (2012)

Buchanan, John et al., Hedge Fund Activism in Japan: The Limits of Shareholder Primacy (2012)

Cai, Hongbin, *Delay in Multilateral Bargaining Under Complete Information*, 93 J. Econ. Theory 260 (2000)

Cai, Hongbin, *Inefficient Markov Perfect Equilibria in Multilateral Bargaining*, 22 Econ. Theory 583 (2003)

Cappelli, Peter, The New Deal at Work: Managing the Market Driven Workforce (1999)

Caprio, Gerard Jr, Vincenzo D'Apice, Giovanni Ferri, & Giovanni Walter Puopolo, *Macro Financial Determinants of the Great Financial Crisis: Implications for Financial Regulation* (Oct. 21, 2010), *available at* http://ssrn.com/abstract=1695335

Comerton-Forde, Carole & Tālis J. Putniņš, *Stock Price Manipulation: Prevalence and Determinants*, Rev. Fin. (May 17, 2013) (first published online March 4, 2013 doi:10.1093/rof/rfs040)

Carlson, David Gray, *Bifurcation of Undersecured Claims in Bankruptcy*, 70 Am. Bankr. L.J. 1 (1996)

Chamberlain, Neal, A General Theory of Economic Process (1955)

Charness, Gary, Peter Kuhn, & Marie Claire Villeval, *Competition and the Ratchet Effect*, 29 J. Lab. Econ. 513 (2011)

Cheffins, Brian R., Corporate Ownership and Control: British Business Transformed (2008)

Cheffins, Brian R., *The Stewardship Code's Achilles' Heel*, 73 Mod. L. Rev. 1017 (2010)

Chernobai, Anna & Yukihiro Yasuda, *Disclosures of Material Weaknesses by Japanese Firms after the Passage of the 2006 Financial Instruments and Exchange Law,* 37 J. Banking & Fin. 1524 (2013)

Choi, Albert & George Triantis, *Market Conditions and Contract Design: Variations in Debt Contracting*, 88 N.Y.U.L.Rev. 51 (2013)

Choi, Stephen, *Proxy Issue Proposals: Impact of the 1992 SEC Proxy Reforms*, 16 J. L. Econ. & Org. 233 (2000)

Choper, Jesse H., John C. Coffee, Jr & Ronald J. Gilson, Cases and Material on Corporations (7th ed. 2008)

Christensen, Hans B., Luzi Hail, & Christian Leuz, *Capital-Market Effects of Securities Regulation: Hysteresis, Implementation, and Enforcement* (Nat'l Bureau of Econ. Res., Working Paper No. 16737, Jan. 2011), *available at* http://www.nber.org/papers/w16737

Chuma, Hiroyuki, *"Kaikoken Ranyo Hori" no Keizai Bunseki* [*Economic Analysis of the "Doctrine of Abusive Dismissal"*], *in* Kaishaho no

KEIZAIGAKU [THE ECONOMICS OF CORPORATE LAW] 425 (Yoshiro Miwa et al. eds., 1998)
CLARK, ROBERT, CORPORATE LAW (1986)
Coase, Ronald, *The Problem of Social Cost*, 3 J. LAW & ECON. 1 (1960)
Coffee, John C. Jr, *Unstable Coalitions: Corporate Governance as a Multiple-Player Game*, 78 GEO. L. J. 1495 (1990)
Coffee, John C. Jr, *The Future as History: The Prospects for Global Convergence and Its Implications*, 93 NW. U. L. REV. 641 (1999)
Coffee, John C. Jr, *The Rise of Dispersed Ownership: The Role of Law and the State in the Separation of Ownership and Control*, 111 YALE L. J. 1 (2001)
Coffee, John C. Jr & Hillary A. Sale, *Redesigning the SEC: Does the Treasury Have a Better Idea?*, 95 VA. L. REV. 707 (2009)
Cohen, Daniel A., Aiyesha Day, Thomas Z. Lys, *The Sarbanes Oxley Act of 2002: Implications for Compensation Contracts and Managerial Risk-Taking* (Working Paper, 2007)
Cools, Sofie, *The Real Difference in Corporate Law between the United States and Continental Europe: Distribution of Powers*, 30 DEL. J. CORP. L. 697 (2005)
Cumming, Douglas J., Gael Imad'Eddine, & Armin Schwienbacher, *Legality and the Spread of Voluntary Investor Protection* (Dec. 15, 2011), *available at* http://papers.ssrn.com/sol3/papers.cfm?abstract_id=1990477
Cumming, Douglas J., Sofia Johan, & Dan Li, *Exchange Trading Rules and Stock Market Liquidity*, 99 J. FIN. ECON. 651 (2011)
Cumming, Douglas J., April Knill, & Nela Richardson, *Firm Size, Institutional Quality and the Impact of Securities Regulation* 18 (Jan. 24, 2011), *available at* http://ssrn.com/abstract=1572655
Cumming, Douglas J., Feng Zhan, & Michael J. Aitken, *High Frequency Trading and End-of-Day Manipulation* (Sept. 12, 2012), *available at* http://ssrn.com/abstract=2145565
Cunningham, Noel B. & Mitchell L. Engler, *The Carried Interest Controversy: Let's Not Get Carried Away*, 61 TAX. L. REV. 121 (2008)

Dal Bó, Ernesto, *Bribing Voters*, 51 AMER. J. POL. SCI. 789 (2007)
Dau-Schmidt, Kenneth G., *A Bargaining Analysis of American Labor Law and the Search for Bargaining Equity and Industrial Peace*, 91 MICH. L. REV. 419 (1992)
Dau-Schmidt, Kenneth G., *Employment in the New Age of Trade and Technology: Implications for Labor and Employment Law,* 76 IND. L.J. 1 (2001)
Dau-Schmidt, Kenneth G., *The Changing Face of Collective Representation: The Future of Collective Bargaining*, 82 CHI. KENT L. REV. 903 (2007)

Dau-Schmidt, Kenneth G., *Promoting Employee Voice in the American Economy: A Call for Comprehensive Reform*, 94 MARQ. L. REV. 765 (2011)

DAU-SCHMIDT, KENNETH G., M.H. MALIN, R.L. CORRADA, C.D. RUIZ CAMERON, & C.L. FISK, LABOR LAW IN THE CONTEMPORARY WORKPLACE (2009)

Dau-Schmidt, Kenneth G. & Arthur R. Traynor, *Regulating Unions and Collective Bargaining*, in LABOR AND EMPLOYMENT LAW AND ECONOMICS (Kenneth G. Dau-Schmidt et al. eds., 2009)

DAVIES, PAUL, INTRODUCTION TO COMPANY LAW (2nd ed. 2010)

Davis, Lewis Anthony, *Review Procedures and Public Accountability in Sunset Legislation: An Analysis and Proposal for Reform* 33 ADMIN. L. REV. 393 (1981)

de Mooij, Ruud A., *Tax Biases to Debt Finance: Assessing the Problem, Finding Solutions* (IMF Staff Discusssion Note, May 3, 2011)

Degryse, Hans et al., *Corporate Governance: A Review of the Role of Banks* (Working Paper, 2008)

Del Guercio, Diane, Elizabeth R. Odders-White, & Mark J. Ready, *The Deterrence Effect of SEC Enforcement Intensity on Illegal Insider Trading* (May 13, 2013), available at http://papers.ssrn.com/so13/papers.cfm?abstract_id=1784528

Delis, Manthos D. & Panagiotis K. Staikouras, *Supervisory Effectiveness and Bank Risk*, 15 REV. FIN. 511, 511 (2011)

Deo, Prakash, *Cross-Border Lease Financing with Japanese Leveraged Leases*, J. STRUCTURED FIN. (2008)

Dhammika, Dharmapala & Vikramaditya S. Khanna, *Corporate Governance, Enforcement, and Firm Value: Evidence from India* (June 23, 2011), *available at* http://ssrn.com/abstract=1105732

Diebold, Francis X. et al., *Introduction*, *in* THE KNOWN, THE UNKNOWN, AND THE UNKNOWABLE IN FINANCIAL RISK MANAGEMENT 3 (Francis X. Diebold et al. eds., 2010)

Dilworth, Robert J., *Tax Reform: International Tax Issues and Some Proposals,* INT'L TAX J. 5 (2009) *available at* http://www.mwe.com/info/pubs/taxreform.pdf

Dittmar, Amy et al., *International Corporate Governance and Corporate Cash Holdings*, 38 J. FIN. QUANTITATIVE ANALYSIS 111 (2003)

Doyle, Jeffrey T., Weili Ge, & Sarah E. McVay, *Determinants of Weaknesses in Internal Control over Financial Reporting*, 44 J. ACCT. ECON. 193 (2007)

DRAKE, DWIGHT, BUSINESS PLANNING: CLOSELY HELD ENTERPRISES (3rd ed. 2011)

Dubois, Michel, Pascal Dumontier, & Laurent Frésard, *Regulating*

Conflicts of Interest: The Effect of Sanctions and Enforcement (Working Paper, Jan. 2012), *available at* http://ssrn.com/abstract=1786523

Easterbrook, Frank H. & Daniel R. Fischel, *The Corporate Contract*, 89 COLUM. L. REV. 1416 (1989)

EASTERBROOK, FRANK H. & DANIEL R. FISCHEL, THE ECONOMIC STRUCTURE OF CORPORATE LAW (1991)

Echeverri-Gent, John & Benjamin J. Bloom, *Do Competitive Politics Produce Competitive Markets? Politics of Financial Market Development* (APSA 2010 Annual Meeting Paper, 2010), *available at* http://ssrn.com/abstract=1644631

Edelman, Lauren B., Howard S. Erlanger, & John Lande, *Internal Dispute Resolution: The Transformation of Civil Rights in the Workplace*, 27 LAW & SOC'Y REV. 497 (1993)

EGASHIRA, KENJIRO, KAISHAHŌJINKAKUHININ NO HŌRI [PIERCING THE CORPORATE VEIL] (1980)

Egashira, Kenjiro, *Kôporeito Gabanansu no Kadai* [*The Agenda in Corporate Governance*], 558 GINKÔ HÔMU-21 4 (1999)

Egashira, Kenjiro, *Kaisha Housei no Gendaika ni Kannsuru Youkou Ann no Kaisetu (5)* [*Explanation of the Proposal on the Modernization of Corporate Law (5)*], 1725 SHOUJI HOUMU 4 (2005)

EGASHIRA, KENJIRO, KABUSIKI KAISHA HO [LAWS OF STOCK CORPORATIONS] (4th ed. 2011)

Eichler, Stefan, *Equity Home Bias and Corporate Disclosure*, 31 J. INT'L. MONEY FIN. 1008 (2012)

EISENBERG, MELVIN A., THE STRUCTURE OF THE CORPORATION: A LEGAL ANALYSIS (1976)

Eisenberg, Melvin A., *The Divergence of Standards of Conduct and Standards of Review in Corporate Law*, 62 FORDHAM L. REV. 437 (1993)

Enriques, Luca & Matteo Gatti, *Is there a Uniform EU Securities Law After the Financial Services Action Plan?*, 114 STAN. J. L. BUS. & FIN. 43 (2008)

Enriques, Luca, Henry Hansmann, & Reinier Kraakman, *The Basic Governance Structure: The Interests of Shareholders as a Class*, *in* THE ANATOMY OF CORPORATE LAW (Reiner Kraakman et al. eds., 2nd ed. 2009)

Ernstberger, Jürgen, Michael Stich, & Oliver Vogler, *Economic Consequences of Accounting Enforcement Reforms: The Case of Germany*, 21 EUR. ACCT. REV. 217 (2012)

Estreicher, Samuel, *Unjust Dismissal Laws: Some Cautionary Notes*, 33 AM. J. COMP. L. 310 (1985)

Fauver, Larry, Xi Li, & Alvaro Taboada, *The Impact of International Governance Reforms: A Multi-Country Examination* (July 2012), *available at* http://www.fma.org/Atlanta/Papers/InternationalGovernanceReforms.pdf

Fischel, Daniel R., *The Appraisal Remedy in Corporate Law*, 1983 AM. B. FOUND. RES. J. 875 (1983)

Fisher, Eric B. & Andrew L. Buck, *Hedge Funds and the Changing Face of Corporate Bankruptcy Practice*, 25 AM. BANKR. INST. J. 24 (2007)

Fleischer, Victor, *Taxing Blackstone*, 61 TAX L. REV. 89 (2008)

Fleischer, Victor, *Two and Twenty: Taxing Partnership Profits in Private Equity Funds*, 83 N.Y.U. L. REV. 1 (2008)

Fleischer, Victor, *Taxing Founders' Stock*, 59 UCLA L REV. 60 (2011)

Flood, John & Fabian Sosa, *Lawyers, Law Firms and the Stabilization of Transnational Business*, 28 NW. J. INT'L L. & BUS. 489 (2008)

Fortgang, Chaim J. & Thomas M. Mayer, *Trading Claims and Taking Control of Corporations in Chapter 11*, 12 CARDOZO L. REV. 1 (1990)

FREEMAN, RICHARD B., AMERICA WORKS: CRITICAL THOUGHT ON THE EXCEPTIONAL US LABOR MARKET (2007)

Freeman, Steven F., *Effects of ESOP Adoption and Employee Ownership: Thirty Years of Research and Experience* (Organizational Dynamics Programs, University of Pennsylvania, Working Paper #07-01, 2007), *available at* http://repository.upenn.edu/cgi/viewcontent.cgi?article=1001&context=od_working_papers

Frijns, Bart, Aaron B. Gilbert, & Alireza Tourani-Rad, *Elements of Effective Insider Trading* (Finance and Corporate Governance Conference 2010 Paper, Aug. 3, 2009), *available at* http://ssrn.com/abstract=1443597

Fujimura, Hiroyuki, *Japan's Labor Unions: Past, Present, Future*, 9 JAPAN LAB. REV. 6 (2012)

Fujita, Tomotaka, *Shin Kaisha Hou ni okeru Kabushiki Kaitori Seikyuu Kenn Seido [An Appraisal Right in the New Companies Act]*, *in* KIGYO HOU NO RIRON, JOUKANN [THEORY OF ENTERPRISE LAW, VOL. 1] 261 (Etsuro Kuronuma & Tomotaka Fujita eds., 2007)

Gadinis, Stavros, *The SEC and the Financial Services Industry: Evidence from Enforcement Against Broker-Dealers*, 67 BUS. LAW. 679 (2012)

Gadinis, Stavros & Howell E. Jackson, *Markets as Regulators: A Survey*, 80 S. CAL. L. REV. 1239 (2007)

Gamage, David, *Taxing Political Donations: The Case for Corrective Taxes in Campaign Finance*, 113 YALE L. J. 1283 (2004)

Gamage, David, *Preventing State Budget Crises: Managing the Fiscal Volatility Problem*, 98 CALIF. L. REV. 749 (2010)

Gamage, David, *Perverse Incentives Arising from the Tax Provisions of Healthcare Reform: Why Further Reforms are Needed to Prevent Avoidable Costs to Low- and Moderate-Income Workers*, 65 Tax L. Rev. 669 (2012), *available at* http://papers.ssrn.com/sol3/papers.cfm?abstract_id=2067138

Gamage, David & Darien Shanske, *Three Essays on Tax Salience: Market Salience and Political Salience*, 65 Tax L. Rev. 19 (2011)

Gergen, Mark P. *Subchapter K and Passive Financial Intermediation*, 51 S.M.U.L. Rev. 37, 44 (1997)

Gersen, Jacob, *Temporary Legislation*, 74 U. Chi. L. Rev. 247 (2007)

Ghouse, Ilma & Humera Sultana, *Entrepreneur Activity and Statuary Tax Requirement: An Empirical Analysis for Pakistan*, Econ. Rev. (Feb. 1, 2012)

Gilson, Ronald J., *Value Creation by Business Lawyers: Legal Skills and Asset Pricing*, 94 Yale L. J. 239 (1984)

Gilson, Ronald J., *Globalizing Corporate Governance: Convergence of Form or Function*, 49 Am. J. Comp. L. 329 (2001)

Gilson, Ronald J., *The Poison Pill in Japan: The Missing Infrastructure*, 2004 Colum. Bus. L. Rev. 21 (2004)

Gilson, Ronald J. & Curtis J. Milhaupt, *Choice as Regulatory Reform: The Case of Japanese Corporate Governance*, 53 Am. J. Comp. L. 343 (2005)

Gilson, Ronald J. & Mark J. Roe, *Understanding the Japanese Keiretsu: Overlaps Between Corporate Governance and Industrial Organization*, 102 Yale L. J. 871 (1993)

Gilson, Ronald J. & Mark J. Roe, *Lifetime Employment: Labor Peace and the Evolution of Japanese Corporate Governance*, 99 Colum. L. Rev. 508 (1999)

Gilson, Ronald J. & David M. Schizer, *Understanding Venture Capital Structure: A Tax Explanation for Convertible Preferred Stock*, 116 Harv. L. Rev. 874 (2003)

Gilson, Ronald J. et al., *Regulatory Dualism as a Development Strategy: Corporate Reform in Brazil, the United States, and the European Union*, 63 Stan. L. Rev. 475 (2011)

Goegen, Marc & Luc Renneboog, *Strong Managers and Passive Institutional Investors in the UK*, *in* The Control of Corporate Europe (Fabrizio Barca & Marco Becht eds., 2001)

Goldman, Alvin L., Labor and Employment Law in the United States (1996)

Goldschmid, Paul M., *Note, More Phoenix than Vulture: The Case for Distressed Investor Presence in the Bankruptcy Reorganization Process*, 2005 Colum. L. Rev. 191 (2005)

Gordon, Jeffrey N., *The Rise of Independent Directors in the United States,*

1950–2005: Of Shareholder Value and Stock Market Prices, 59 STAN. L. REV. 1465 (2007)

Graetz, Michael J., *Taxing International Income – Inadequate Principles, Outdated Concepts, and Unsatisfactory Policy*, 54 TAX L. REV. 261 (2001)

Graham, John et al., *The Economic Implications of Corporate Financial Reporting*, 40 J. ACC. & ECON. 3 (2005)

Grant, Jeremy & Thomas Kirchmaier, *Who Governs? Corporate Ownership and Control Structures in Europe* (Working Paper, June 2004)

Greenstone, Michael, *Toward a Culture of Persistent Regulatory Experimentation and Evaluation, in* NEW PERSPECTIVES ON REGULATION 111 (David A. Moss & John A. Cisternino eds., 2009)

Grossman, Sanford J., *The Informational Role of Warranties and Private Disclosure about Product Quality*, 21 J. L. & ECON. 461 (1981)

Grossman, Sanford J. & Oliver D. Hart, *Takeover Bids, the Free Rider Problem, and the Theory of the Corporation*, 11 BELL J. OF ECON. 42 (1980)

Grossman, Sanford J. & Oliver D. Hart, *An Analysis of the Principal–Agent Problem*, 51 ECONOMETRICA 7 (1983)

Guest, Paul, *The Determinants of Board Size and Composition: Evidence from the UK*, 14 J. CORP. FIN. 51 (2008).

Hansmann, Henry & Reinier Kraakman, *The End of History for Corporate Law*, 89 GEO. L. J. 439 (2001)

Hamada, Michiyo, *Kaishaho to Mochikabugaishkisei* [*Corporate Law and the Regulation for Holding Companies*], 17 KEIZAIGAKKAI NENPO 48 (1996)

Hammersley, Jacqueline S., Linda A. Myers, & Catherine Shakespeare, *Market Reactions to the Disclosure of Internal Control Weaknesses and to the Characteristics of those Weaknesses under Section 302 of the Sarbanes Oxley Act of 2002,* 13 REV. ACCT. STUD. 141 (2008)

HANAMI, TADASHI A., LABOUR LAW AND INDUSTRIAL RELATIONS IN JAPAN (1979)

HANAMI, TADASHI A. & FUMITO KOYAMA, LABOUR LAW IN JAPAN (2011)

Hanks, James J. Jr, *Playing with Fire: Nonshareholder Constituency Statutes in the 1990s*, 21 STETSON L. REV. 97 (1991)

Hara, Masato, *Rodo Joken Henkoji niokeru Jugyoin-Keieisha kan Kosho no Igi* [*The Significance of Bargaining between Employees and Management in Determining the Fairness of Modified Labor Agreements*] *in* "KIGYOU-HO" KAIKAKU NO RONRI: INSENTHIBU SHISUTEMU NO SEIDO SEKKEI [THE LOGIC OF "ENTERPRISE LAW" REFORMATIONS: INSTITUTIONAL DESIGN OF THE INCENTIVE SYSTEM] 102 (Zenichi Shishido ed., 2011)

HARDIN, PATRICK & JOHN E. HIGGINS, EDS. THE DEVELOPING LABOR LAW:

THE BOARD, THE COURTS, AND THE NATIONAL LABOR RELATIONS ACT, VOL. 1 (2006)

Harris, Ron, *Legal Scholars, Economists and The Interdisciplinary Study of Institutions*, 96 CORNELL L. REV. 789 (2011)

HART, OLIVER, FIRMS, CONTRACTS, AND FINANCIAL STRUCTURE (1995)

Hart, Oliver & John Moore, *Debt and Seniority: An Analysis of the Role of Hard Claims in Constraining Management*, 85 AM. ECON. REV. 567 (1995)

HASHIMOTO, RYUGO, DOKUSENKINSHIHO TO WAGA KOKUMINKEIZAI [ANTI-MONOPOLY LAW AND OUR NATIONAL ECONOMY] (1947)

Heckman, James J. & Carmen Pagés-Serra, *The Cost of Job Security Regulation: Evidence from Latin American Labor Markets*, 1 ECONOMIA 109 (2000)

Hellwig, Martin, *On the Economics and Politics of Corporate Finance and Corporate Control, in* CORPORATE GOVERNANCE: THEORETICAL AND EMPIRICAL PERSPECTIVES (Xavier Vives ed., 2000)

Hermalin, Benjamin E., *Managerial Preferences Concerning Risky Projects*, 9 J. L. ECON. & ORG. 127 (1993)

Hermalin, Benjamin E., *The Firm as a Noneconomy: Some Comments on Holmstrom*, 15 J. L. ECON. & ORG. 104 (1999)

Hermalin, Benjamin E. & Michael L. Katz, *Judicial Modification of Contracts between Sophisticated Parties: A More Complete View of Incomplete Contracts and Their Breach*, 9 J. L. ECON & ORG. 230 (1993)

Hermalin, Benjamin E. & Michael L. Katz, *Corporate Diversification and Agency, in* INCENTIVES, ORGANIZATION, AND PUBLIC ECONOMICS: PAPERS IN HONOUR OF SIR JAMES MIRRLEES (P. Hammond & G. Myles eds., 2001)

Hermalin, Benjamin E. & Michael S. Weisbach, *Information Disclosure and Corporate Governance*, 67 J. FIN. 195 (2012)

Hermalin, Benjamin E., Avery W. Katz, & Richard Craswell, *Contract Law, in* HANDBOOK OF LAW & ECONOMICS, §2 (A. Mitchell Polinsky & Steven Shortell eds., 2007)

Hill, Jennifer G., *Why Did Australia Fare So Well in the Global Financial Crisis, in* IN THE REGULATORY AFTERMATH OF THE GLOBAL FINANCIAL CRISIS 203 (Eilis Ferran et al. eds., 2012)

Hines, James R. Jr, *Lessons from Behavioral Responses to International Taxation*, 52 NAT'L TAX J. 305 (1999)

Hirota, Shin-ichi, *Nihon no Main Bank Kankei* [*The Relationship of Main Bank in Japan*] (RIETI Discussion Paper 09-J-023, 2009), *available at* http://www.rieti.go.jp/jp/publications/dp/09j023.pdf

HIROTA, SHIN-ICHI, KABUNUSHI SHUKEN WO KOETE: SUTEEKU HORUDAA GATA KIGYOU NO RIRON TO JISSYOU [BEYOND THE SHAREHOLDER

PRIMACY: THEORY AND EVIDENCE OF THE STAKE-HOLDER FIRMS] (Toyo Keizai Shinpousha, 2012)

Hirota, Shin-ichi & Kohei Kawamura, Managerial Control inside the Firm, 21 J. JAPANESE & INT'L ECONOMIES 324 (2007)

Hirsch, Jeffrey M., *A Comparative Perspective on Unjust Dismissal Laws*, *in* GLOBAL LABOR AND EMPLOYMENT LAW: REPORTS FROM LAW OFFICES WORLDWIDE (Samuel Estreicher ed., 2012)

Hiwatari, Nobuhiro, *Employment Practice and Enterprise Unionism in Japan*, *in* EMPLOYEES AND CORPORATE GOVERNANCE 275 (Margaret M. Blair & Mark J. Roe eds., 1999)

Holmstrom, Bengt, *Moral Hazard in Teams*, 13 BELL J. ECON. 74 (1982)

Holmstrom, Bengt, *Managerial Incentive Problems: A Dynamic Perspective*, 66 R. ECON. STUD. 169 (1999)

Hopt, Klaus J., *Comparative Corporate Governance: The State of the Art and International Regulation*, 59 AM. J. COMP. L. 1, 62 (2011)

Hopt, Klaus J., *Corporate Governance of Banks and Other Financial Institutions After the Financial Crisis*, 13 J. CORP. L. STUD. 219 (2013)

Hoshi, Takeo, *The Economic Role of Corporate Grouping and the Main Bank System*, *in* THE JAPANESE FIRM: THE SOURCE OF COMPETITIVE STRENGTH 285 (Masahiko Aoki & Ronald Dore eds., 1994)

Hoshino, Ei-ichi, *Minpo-Kaisyakuron Josetsu* [*Isagogics of the Interpretation of Civil Law*], *in* EI-ICHI HOSHINO MINPO RONSHU [THE COLLECTION OF PAPERS ABOUT CIVIL LAW, VOL.1.] 11 (1970)

Hu, Henry T.C. & Bernard Black, *Hedge Funds, Insiders, and the Decoupling of Economic and Voting Ownership: Empty Voting and Hidden (Morphable) Ownership*, 13 J. CORP. FIN. 343 (2007)

Iida, Hidefusa, *Kabushiki Kaitori Seikyuu Kenn no Kouzou to Kaitori Kakaku Sanntei no Kouryo Youso (1)* [*The Structure of the Appraisal Right and the Factors to Determine the Fair Value (1)*], 129 HOUGAKU KYOUKAI ZASSHI 505 (2012)

Iida, Hidefusa, *Kabushiki Kaitori Seikyuu Kenn no Kouzou to Kaitori Kakaku Sanntei no Kouryo Youso (5)* [*The Structure of the Appraisal Right and the Factors to Determine the Fair Value (5)*], 129 HOUGAKU KYOUKAI ZASSHI 1455 (2012)

Ikeda, Hisashi, *Saiken-gata Tosan Tetsuduki ni okeru Rodoho Kihan no Tekiyou (Go)* (The Application of Labor Law in Corporate Reorganization and Rehabilitation (5)), 128 HOUGAKU KYOUKAI ZASSHI 2837 (2011)

IMAMURA, SHIGEKAZU, DOKUSENKINSHIHO [ANTI-MONOPOLY LAW] (2nd ed. 1985)

Inaba, Takeo, *Shô-Hô tô no Ichibu wo Kaisei suru Hôritsu no Gaiyô, (Chû 2)*

[*The Summary of the Act revising the Commercial Code and others (Part 2-1)*], 909 JUNKAN SHÔJI-HÔMU 8 (1981)

Ippolito, Richard A., *Bankruptcy and Workers: Risks, Compensation and Pension Contracts*, 82 WASH. U. L. Q. 1251 (2004)

ISHII, RYOZO, DOKUSENKINSHIHO-KEIZAISHUCHUHAIJOHO [ANTI-MONOPOLY LAW AND ECONOMIC DECENTRALIZATION LAW] (1947)

ISHII, TERUHISA, KAISHA-HÔ JÔ-KAN [COMPANY LAW, VOL. 1] (1967)

Itoh, Hideshi, *Japanese Human Resource Management from the Viewpoint of Incentive Theory*, *in* THE JAPANESE FIRM: THE SOURCE OF COMPETITIVE STRENGTH 233 (Masahiko Aoki & Ronald Dore eds., 1994)

Itoh, Hideshi, *Kosho niokeru Kachi no Soshutsu-Bunpai to Hoseido no Hokansei* [*Value Creation and Allocation by Bargaining and Complementarities of Law*], *in* "KIGYOU-HO" KAIKAKU NO RONRI: INSENTHIBU SHISUTEMU NO SEIDO SEKKEI [THE LOGIC OF "ENTERPRISE LAW" REFORMATIONS: INSTITUTIONAL DESIGN OF THE INCENTIVE SYSTEM] 132 (Zenichi Shishido ed., 2011)

Iwahara, Shinsaku, *Ginko no Kessaikino to Kawase Gyomu no Haitasei* [*The Finality Function of Banks and the Exclusiveness of the Business of the Money Order*], *in* GENDAIKIGYORIPPO NO KISEKI TO TENBO [THE ORBIT AND THE HORIZON OF THE MODERN LEGISLATION OF THE ENTERPRISE LAW] 529 (Seiichi Ochiai, Kenjiro Egashira, & Tomonobu Yamashita eds., 1995)

IWAHARA, SHINSAKU, DENSHIKESSAI TO HO [ELECTRONIC CLEARING AND LAW] (2003)

IZUMOI, MASAO, SHINDOKUSENKINSHIHO NO KAISETSU [COMMENT ON NEW ANTI-MONOPOLY LAW] (1953)

Jackson, Gregory & Hideaki Miyajima, *Introduction: The Diversity and Change of Corporate Governance in Japan*, *in* CORPORATE GOVERNANCE IN JAPAN: INSTITUTIONAL CHANGE AND ORGANIZATIONAL DIVERSITY 1 (Masahiko Aoki et al. eds., 2007)

Jackson, Howell E., *An American Perspective on the FSA: Politics, Goals & Regulatory Intensity*, *in* REGULATORY REFORMS IN THE AGE OF FINANCIAL CONSOLIDATION: THE EMERGING MARKET ECONOMY AND ADVANCED COUNTRIES 39 (Lee-Jay Cho & Joonkyung Kim eds., 2006), *available at* http://www.kdi.re.kr/kdi_eng/database/report_read05.jsp?1=1&pub_no=00009931

Jackson, Howell E., *Variation in the Intensity of Financial Regulation: Preliminary Evidence and Potential Implications*, 24 YALE J. ON REG. 253 (2007)

Jackson, Howell E., *The Impact of Enforcement: A Reflection*, 156 U. PA. L. REV. PENNUMBRA 400 (2008)

Jackson, Howell E. & Mark J. Roe, *Public and Private Enforcement of Securities Laws: Resource-Based Evidence,* 93 J. FIN. ECON. 207 (2009)

Jackson, Thomas H., *Bankruptcy, Non-bankruptcy Entitlements, and the Creditors' Bargain*, 91 YALE L. J. 857 (1982)

Jackson, Thomas H. & Anthony T. Kronman, *Secured Financing and Priorities Among Creditors*, 88 YALE L.J. 1143 (1979)

JACOBY, SANFORD M., THE EMBEDDED CORPORATION: CORPORATE GOVERNANCE AND EMPLOYMENT RELATIONS IN JAPAN AND THE UNITED STATES (2005)

Jacoby, Sanford M., *Convergence by Design: The Case of CalPERS in Japan*, 55 AM. J. COMP. L. 239 (2007)

Jain, Pankaj K., Jang-Chul Kim, & Zabihollah Razaee, *Trends and Determinants of Market Liquidity in the Pre- and Post-Sarbanes–Oxley Act Periods* (Working Paper, 2006)

Jensen, Michael C., *Agency Costs of Free Cash Flow, Corporate Finance, and Takeovers*, 76 AM. ECON. REV. 323 (1986)

Jensen, Michael C., *Takeovers: Their Causes and Consequences*, 2 J. ECON. PERSP. 21 (1988)

Jensen, Michael C. & William H. Meckling, *Theory of the Firm: Managerial Behavior, Agency Costs and Ownership Structure*, 3 J. FIN. ECON. 305 (1976)

Jenter, Dirk & Katharine Lewellen, *Performance-Induced CEO Turnover* (Working Paper, 2010)

Johnson, Calvin H., *An Employer-Level Proxy Tax On Fringe Benefits*, 123 TAX NOTES 483 (2009)

Johnson, Calvin H., *Why Do Venture Capital Funds Burn Research and Development Deductions*, 29 VA. TAX REV. 29 (2009)

Jones, Derek C. & Takao Kato, *The Productivity Effects of Employee Stock-Ownership Plans and Bonuses: Evidence from Japanese Panel Data*, 85 AM. ECON. REV. 391 (1995)

Kamar, Ehud et al., *Going-Private Decisions and the Sarbanes–Oxley Act of 2002: A Cross-Country Analysis*, 25 J. L. ECON. & ORG. 107 (2008)

Kanda, Hideki, *Kabushiki Kaitori Seikyuu Kenn no Kouzou* [*The Structure of the Appraisal Right*], 1879 SHOJI HOMU 4 (2009)

Kanda, Hideki, *Takeover Defenses and the Role of Law in Japan*, 2 UT SOFT L. REV. 2 (2009)

Kanda, Hideki & Saul Levmore, *The Appraisal Remedy and the Goals of Corporate Law*, 32 U.C.L.A. L. REV. 429 (1985)

Kanda, Hideki & Curtis J. Milhaupt, *Re-examining Legal Transplants: The Director's Fiduciary Duty in Japanese Corporate Law*, 51 AM. J. COMP. L. 887 (2003)

Kaneko, Hiroshi, *The Japanese Income Tax System and the Disparity of Income and Wealth Among People in Japan* (Proceedings from the 2009 Sho Sato Conference, 2009), *available at* http://www.law.berkeley.edu/files/sho_sato_tax_conf_web_paper--kaneko.pdf (last accessed 10/1/2012)

Kang, Qiang et al., *The Sarbanes–Oxley Act and Corporate Investment: A Structural Assessment*, 96 J. FIN. ECON. 291 (2010)

Kaplan, Steven N. & Bernadette A. Minton, *How Has CEO Turnover Changed? Increasingly Performance Sensitive Boards and Increasingly Uneasy CEOs* (NBER Working Paper No. 12465, 2006)

Kaplan, Steven N. & Bernadette A. Minton, *How Has CEO Turnover Changed?,* 12 INT'L REV. FIN 57 (2012)

Kaplow, Louis, *Why (Ever) Define Markets?*, 124 HARV. L. REV. 437 (2010)

Karmel, Roberta S., *Implications of the Stakeholder Model*, 61 GEO. WASH. L. REV. 1156 (1993)

Kato, Takahito, *Riekikyoyo Kinshi Kitei to Kabushiki Mochiai: Kabunushi no Insenthibu Kozo no Kanten kara* [*Corporate Law Statute to Prohibit Giving Benefit for the Exercise of Shareholder Rights and Cross-shareholding: From the Point of View of the Shareholders' Incentive Structure*], *in* "KIGYOU-HO" KAIKAKU NO RONRI: INSENTHIBU SHISUTEMU NO SEIDO SEKKEI [THE LOGIC OF "ENTERPRISE LAW" REFORMATIONS: INSTITUTIONAL DESIGN OF THE INCENTIVE SYSTEM] 159 (Zenichi Shishido ed., 2011)

KAUFMAN, BRUCE E. & JULIE L. HOTCHKISS, THE ECONOMICS OF LABOR MARKETS (7th ed. 2006)

Kawahama, Noboru, *Beikoku ni okeru Ginko no Kabushikihoyukisei no Hensen* [*The Transformation of the Regulation Related to Bank Shareholding*], 152 HOGAKU-RONSO 21

KAWAKITA, HIDETAKA, NIHON GATA KABUSHIKI SHIJO NO KOZO HENKA: KINYU SHISUTEMU NO SAIHENSEI TO GABANANSU [STRUCTURAL CHANGE OF THE JAPANESE -STYLE STOCK MARKET: RESTRUCTURING OF THE FINANCIAL SYSTEM AND CORPORATE GOVERNANCE] (1995)

Kearney, Richard C., *Sunset: A Survey and Analysis of the State Experience*, 50 PUB. ADMIN. REV. 49 (1990)

Keating, Daniel, *Why the Bankruptcy Reform Act Left Labor Legacy Costs Alone*, 71 MO. L. REV. 985 (2006).

Keating, Daniel, *Automobile Bankruptcies, Retiree Benefits, and the Futility of Springing Priorities in Chapter 11 Reorganization*, 96 IOWA L. REV. 261 (2010)

Kennan, John & Robert Wilson, *Bargaining with Private Information*, 31 J. ECON. LITERATURE 45 (1993)

Kerl, Alexander & Martin Ohlert, *Star-analysts' forecast accuracy and the role of corporate governance* (Dec. 2012), *available at* http://papers.ssrn.com/abstract=2195909

Kim, E. Han & Paige Ouimet, *Employee Capitalism or Corporate Socialism? Broad-Based Employee Stock Ownership* (AFA 2010 Atlanta Meetings Paper, 2008), *available at* http://ssrn.com/abstract=1107974

Kim, Pauline, *Bargaining With Imperfect Information: A Study of Worker Perceptions of Legal Protection in an At-Will World*, 83 CORNELL L. REV. 105 (1997)

Kim, Pauline, *Norms, Learning, and Law: Explaining the Influences on Workers' Legal Knowledge*, ILL. L. REV. 447 (1999)

Kim, Son Ku, *Efficiency of an Information System in an Agency Model*, 63 ECONOMETRICA 89 (1995)

Kitazawa, Masahiro, *Ownership/Management/Control of Business Corporation* (in Japanese), *in* GENDAI HO TO KIGYO [CONTEMPORARY LAW AND FIRM] (Makoto Yazawa ed., 1966)

Klass, Gregory & Kathryn Zeiler, *Against Endowment Theory: Experimental Economics and Legal Scholarship* (Georgetown Public Law and Legal Theory Research Paper No. 13-01, 2013)

KLEIN, WILLIAM A. & JOHN C. COFFEE, JR, BUSINESS ORGANIZATION AND FINANCE: LEGAL AND ECONOMIC PRINCIPLES (10th ed. 2007)

KNIGHT, FRANK H., RISK, UNCERTAINTY AND PROFIT (1965)

Korobkin, Russell, *Wrestling with the Endowment Effect, or How to Do Law and Economics without the Coase Theorem*, in OXFORD HANDBOOK OF BEHAVIORAL ECONOMICS AND THE LAW (Oxford University Press, forthcoming)

KOYAMA, YOSHIAKI, GINKOHO [BANKING ACT] (2nd ed. 2012)

Kozuka, Sōichirō, *Recent Developments in Takeover Law: Changes in Business Practices Meet Decade-old Rule*, 11 J. JAPAN. L. 5 (2006)

KRAAKMAN, REINIER ET AL., THE ANATOMY OF CORPORATE LAW: A FUNCTIONAL AND COMPARATIVE ANALYSIS (2nd ed. 2009)

Kruse, Douglas et al., *Motivating Employee-Owners in ESOP Firms: Human Resource Policies and Company Performance* (Nat'l Bureau of Econ. Research, Working Paper No. 10177, 2003), *available at* http://www.nber.org/papers/w10177.pdf

Kubo, Katsuyuki, *Haito Seisaku to Koyo Chosei* [*Dividend Policy and Employment Adjustment*], *in* NIHON NO COPORETO GABANANSU [JAPANESE CORPORATE GOVERNANCE] 409 (Hideaki Miyajima ed., 2011)

Kubota, Hirofumi, *Debt Equity Swap*, 2 AZ INSIGHT 14 (2004) *available at*, http://www.azsa.or.jp/b_info/letter/43/az02_43.pdf

Kuroki, Masanori, *The Deregulation of Temporary Employment and Workers' Perceptions of Job Insecurity*, 65 ILR REV. 560 (2012)

KUSANO, KOICHI, KAISHA HOU NO SEIGI [JUSTICE OF CORPORATE LAW] (2011)

Kusunoki, Shigeki, *Shaping an Anti-Monopoly Law Sanction Regime Against Cartels or Bid Collusion: A Perspective on Japan's Choice*, 79 U. DET. MERCY L. REV. 399 (2001–2002)

Kuwahara, Yasuo, *Employment Relations in Japan*, *in* INTERNATIONAL AND COMPARATIVE EMPLOYMENT RELATIONS 249 (Greg J. Bamber & Russell D. Lansbury eds., 1998)

Kysar, Rebecca M., *The Sun Also Rises: The Political Economy of Sunset Provisions in the Tax Code*, 40 GA. L. REV. 335 (2005–2006)

La Porta, RafaeI, Florencio Lopez-de-Silanes, & Andrei Shleifer, *Corporate Ownership around the World*, 95 J. FIN. 471 (1999)

La Porta, Rafael, Florencio Lopez-de-Silanes, & Andrei Schleifer, *What Works in Securities Laws?*, 61 J. FIN. 1 (2006)

La Porta, Rafael, Florencio Lopez-De-Silanes, Andrei Shleifer, & Robert W. Vishny, *Legal Determinants and External Finance*, 52 J. FIN. 1131 (1997)

Lazear, Edward, *Job Security Provisions and Employment*, 105 Q. J. ECON. 699 (1990)

Lemmon, Dennis P. & Karl V. Lins, *Ownership Structure, Corporate Governance, and Firm Value: Evidence from the East Asian Financial Crisis*, 58 J. FIN. 1445 (2003)

Letsou, Peter V., *The Role of Appraisal in Corporate Law*, 39 B. C. L. REV. 1121 (1998)

Leuz, Christian, *Different Approaches to Corporate Reporting Regulation: How Jurisdictions Differ and Why*, 43 ACCT. BUS. RES. 229 (2010)

Leuz, Christian & Robert E. Verrecchia, *The Economic Consequences of Increased Disclosure*, 38 J. ACCOUNT. RESEARCH 91 (2000)

Leuz, Christian & Peter Wysocki, *Economic Consequences of Financial Reporting and Disclosure Regulation: A Review and Suggestions for Future Research* (2008), *available at* http://papers.ssrn.com/sol3/papers.cfm?abstract_id=1105398

Levine, David I., *Just-Cause Employment Policies in the Presence of Worker Adverse Selection*, 9 J. LAB. ECON. 294 (1991)

Levmore, Saul, *Monitors and Freeriders in Commercial and Corporate Settings*, 92 YALE L. J. 49 (1982)

Li, Haidan, Morton Pincus, & Sonja Olhoft Rego, *Market Reaction to Events Surrounding the Sarbanes–Oxley Act of 2002 and Earnings Management*, 51 J.L. & ECON. 111 (2008)

Li, Xi, *An Examination of the Impact of the Sarbanes–Oxley Act on Cross-*

Listed Foreign Private Issuers and the Legal Bonding Hypothesis (Mar. 5, 2011), *available at* http://ssrn.com/abstract=952433

Licht, Amir N., Christopher Poliquin, Jordan I. Siegel, & Xi Li, *What Makes the Bonding Stick? A Natural Experiment Involving the US Supreme Court and Cross-Listed Firms* (Harvard Business School Strategy Unit Working Paper No. 11-072, 2011), *available at* http://ssrn.com/abstract=1919805

Linck, James S., Jeffry M. Netter, & Tina Yang, *The Effects and Unintended Consequences of the Sarbanes–Oxley Act on the Supply and Demand for Directors,* 22 Rev. Fin. Stud. 3287 (2009)

Lincoln, James R. & Masahiro Shimotani, *Whither the Keiretsu, Japan's Business Network: How were they structured? What Did They Do? Why Are They Gone?* (Working Paper, 2009)

Litvak, Kate, *The Effect of the Sarbanes–Oxley Act on Non-US Companies Cross-Listed in the US*, 13 J. Corp. Fin. 195 (2007)

Litvak, Kate, *Defensive Management: Does the Sarbanes–Oxley Act Discourage Corporate Risk-Taking?* (Working Paper, 2008)

Livingston, Michael A., *Reinventing Tax Scholarship: Lawyers, Economists, and the Role of the Legal Academy*, 83 Cornell L. Rev. 365 (1998)

Lohse, Tim, Razvan Pascalau, & Christian Thomann, *Public Enforcement of Securities Market Rules: Resource-Based Evidence from the Securities Exchange Commission* (Jan. 29, 2013) (on file with author)

LoPucki, Lynn, *The Nature of the Bankrupt Firm: A Response to Baird and Rasmussen's* The End of Bankruptcy, 56 Stan. L. Rev. 645 (2003)

LoPucki, Lynn M. & Joseph W. Doherty, *Bankruptcy Fire Sales*, 106 Mich. L. Rev. 1 (2007)

Loureiro, Gilberto R. & Alvaro G. Taboada, *The Impact of IFRS Adoption on Stock Price Informativeness* (Oct. 31, 2011), *available at* http://papers.ssrn.com/sol3/papers.cfm?abstract_id=1952593

Lui, Alison, *Macro and Micro Prudential Regulatory Failures amongst Financial Institutions in the United Kingdom: Lessons from Australia* (Apr. 27, 2011), *available at* http://ssrn.com/abstract=1716264

MacDonald, Ross, *Setting Examples, Not Settling: Toward a New SEC Enforcement Paradigm*, 91 Tex. L. Rev. 419 (Dec. 2012)

Macey, Jonathan R., *An Economic Analysis of the Various Rationales for Making Shareholders the Exclusive Beneficiaries of Corporate Fiduciary Duties*, 21 Stetson L. Rev. 23 (1991)

Maeda, Shigeyuki *Wagakuni niokeru Ginkokantokuho to sono Ripporontekikadai – Jorontekikousatsu* [*The Law of Supervising Banking and the Issue of its Legislation in Japan—Isagogics*], *in* Gendaikigyorippo no Kiseki to Tenbo [The Orbit and the Horizon of the Modern

LEGISLATION OF THE ENTERPRISE LAW] 469 (Seiichi Ochiai, Kenjiro Egashira, & Tomonobu Yamashita eds., 1995)

Maeda, Tatsuaki, *Ho-Kaishaku ni tsuite* [*On the Interpretation of Law*], 64 HOSO-JIHO 1 (2012)

Makman, David, *Japanese Market Reform Sputters*, 31 NAT'L L. J. 13 (2008)

Mann, Ronald J., *The Role of Secured Credit in Small-Business Lending*, 86 GEO. L. J. 1 (1997)

Manning, Bayless, *The Shareholder's Appraisal Remedy: An Essay for Frank Coker*, 72 YALE L. J. 223 (1962)

Masciandaro, Donato, Rosaria Vega Pansini & Marc Quintyn, *The Economic Crisis: Did Financial Supervision Matter?* (Nov. 2011), *available at* http://ssrn.com/abstract=1961908

Masui, Yoshihiro, *Taxation of Foreign Subsidiaries: Japan's Tax Reform 2009/10*, 64 BULL. FOR INT'L FISCAL DOCUMENTATION 242 (2010)

Mayer, Colin, FIRM COMMITMENT: WHY THE CORPORATION IS FAILING US AND HOW TO RESTORE TRUST IN IT (2013)

Metrick, Andrew & Ayako Yasuda, *The Economics of Private Equity Funds* (Swedish Institute for Financial Research Conference on The Economics of the Private Equity Market, Sept. 8, 2008), *available at* http://ssrn.com/abstract=996334

Milhaupt, Curtis J., *Managing the Market: The Ministry of Finance and Securities Regulation in Japan*, 30 STAN. J. INT'L L. 423 (1994)

Milhaupt, Curtis J., *A Relational Theory of Japanese Corporate Governance: Contract, Culture, and the Rule of Law*, 37 HARV. INT'L L. J. 3 (1996)

Milhaupt, Curtis J., *The Lost Decade for Japanese Corporate Governance Reform?: What's Changed, What Hasn't, and Why* (Working Paper, 2003)

Milhaupt, Curtis J., *In the Shadow of Delaware?: The Rise of Hostile Takeover in Japan*, 105 COLUM. L. REV. 2171 (2005)

Miller, Harvey R. & Shay Y. Waisman, *Does Chapter 11 Reorganization Remain a Viable Option for Distressed Businesses For the Twenty-First Century?*, 78 AM. BANKR. L. J. 153 (2004)

Mimori, Jin, *Annotation to §31*, in SHIN CHUSHAKU MINJI SAISEI HO JO [NEW ANNOTATION TO CIVIL REHABILITATION ACT] 145 (Chiharu Saiguchi & Makoto Ito eds., 2011)

Mimura, Osamu, *Jugyōin Mochikabu Seido <Jō>* [*Employee stock purchase plans <Vol. 1>*], 430 SHŌJI HŌMU KENKYŪ 2 (1967)

Miwa, Yoshiro & J. Mark Ramseyer, *The Fable of Keiretsu*, 11 J. ECON. & MGMT. STRATEGY 169 (2002)

Miwa, Yoshiro & J. Mark Ramseyer, *The Myth of the Main Bank*, 27 LAW & SOC. INQUIRY 401 (2002)

Miyajima, Hideaki, *Zaibatsu Kaitai* [*The Dismantlement of Zaibatsu Conglomerates*], *in* NIHON KEIZAI NO HATTENN TO KIGYÔ SHÛDAN [THE DEVELOPMENT OF THE JAPANESE ECONOMY AND COMPANY GROUPS] 203 (Juro Hashimoto & Haruhito Takeda eds., Center for Business and Industrial Research, Hosei Univ., 1992)

Miyajima, Hideaki, *Senmon Keieisha no Seiha* [*The Triumph of Professional Managers*], *in* NIHON KEIEI-SHI [THE HISTORY OF COMPANY MANAGEMENT IN JAPAN], VOL. 4 "NIHON-TEKI" KEIEI NO RENZOKU TO DANZETSU [THE CONTINUITY AND DISCONNECTION OF "JAPANESE-STYLE" COMPANY MANAGEMENT] 75 (Hiroaki Yamazaki & Takeo Kikkawa eds., 1995)

Miyajima, Hideaki, *Zaikai Tsuihô to Keieisha no Senbatsu* [*The "Purge" and Selection of the Management of Large Companies*], *in* NIHON KIGYÔ SHISUTEMU NO SENGO-SHI [THE HISTORY OF THE JAPANESE CORPORATE SYSTEM AFTER WORLD WAR II] 43 (Juro Hashimoto ed., 1996)

Miyajima, Hideaki. & Takaaki Hoda, *Understanding the Changing Ownership Structure of Japanese Firms: Investment Style of Foreign and Domestic Institutional Investors* (in Japanese) (Financial Research Center (FSA Institute) Discussion Paper 2011-11, 2012).

Miyajima, Hideaki & Fumiaki Kuroki, *The Unwinding of Cross-Shareholding in Japan: Causes, Effects, and Implications*, *in* CORPORATE GOVERNANCE IN JAPAN: INSTITUTIONAL CHANGE AND ORGANIZATIONAL DIVERSITY 79 (Masahiko Aoki et al. eds., 2007)

Miyajima, Hideaki & Keisuke Nitta, *Kabushiki Shoyû Kôzô no Tayôka to sono Kiketsu* [*Diversification of Share Ownership Structures and Its Consequence*], *in* NIHON NO KIGYÔ TÔCHI [CORPORATE GOVERNANCE IN JAPAN] 117 (Hideaki Miyajima ed., 2011)

Miyajima, Hideaki & Ryo Ogawa, *How to Understand the Changing Board Composition in Japanese Firms* 1973 SHOJI-HOMU 81 (in Japanese) (2012).

Morck, Randall, *How to Eliminate Pyramidal Business Groups: The Double Taxation of Inter-Corporate Dividends and Other Incentive Uses of Tax Policy* (Working Paper, 2004)

Morck, Randall & Masao Nakamura, *Banks and Corporate Control in Japan*, 54 J. FIN. 319 (1999)

Morck, Randall et al., *Banks, Ownership Structure, and Firm Value in Japan*, 73 J. BUS. 539 (2000)

Morito, Hideyuki, *Jigyo Saisei to Kigyo Nenkin* (*Business Restructuring and Corporate Pensions*), 1401 JYURISUTO 38 (2010)

Murè, Pina & Valerio Pesic, *Are Sanctions Effective in Improving Bank Performance? A Study on Supervision and Administrative Sanctions Upon Italian Banks During the 1998–2009 Period* 21 (CAREFIN

Research Paper No. 23/2010, 2010), *available at* http://ssrn.com/abstract=1799882

Nakagawa, Takehisa, *Administrative Informality in Japan: Governmental Activities Outside Statutory Authorization*, 52 ADMIN. L. REV. 175 (2000)

NEGISHI, AKIRA ET AL., DOKUSENKINSHIHO NYUMON [THE INTRODUCTION OF ANTI-MONOPOLY LAW] (1983)

Ochiai, Seiichi, *Kigyo Ho no Mokuteki: Kabunushi Rieki Saidaika Gensoku no Kento* [*The Object of Corporate Law: Consideration of the Shareholder Value Maximization Rule*], *in* KIGYO TO HO (GENDAI NO HO 7) [ENTERPRISE AND LAW (CONTEMPORARY LAWS, VOL. 7)] 23 (Masahiko Iwamura et al. eds, 1998)

OGAWA, GOTARO, SHIN-GINKOHORIYU GE (THE LEGISLATIVE PURPOSE OF NEW BANK ACT) (1930)

Ogneva, Maria, K. R. Subramanyam, & K. Raghnandan, *Internal Control Weakness and Cost of Equity: Evidence from SOX Section 404 Disclosures,* 82 ACCT. REV. 1255 (2007)

Ohkusa, Yasushi & Fumio Ohtake, *The Productivity Effects of Information Sharing, Profit Sharing, and ESOPs*, 11 J. JAPANESE & INT'L ECONOMIES 385 (1997)

Okazaki, Tetsuji, *Development of Corporate Governance in Japan: A Historical Perspective (in Japanese)*, 13 BANK OF JAPAN MONETARY & ECON. STUD. 62 (1994)

Okazaki, Tetsuji, *The Japanese Firm under the Wartime Planned Economy*, *in* JAPANESE FIRM: SOURCES OF COMPETITIVE STRENGTH (Masahiko Aoki & Ronald Dore eds., 1994)

Okazaki, Tetsuji, *Nihon ni okeru Koporeto Gabanansu no Hatten* [*The Development of Corporate Governance in Japan*], *in* SHISUTEMU TOSHITENO NIHON KIGYO [JAPANESE ENTERPRISES AS A SYSTEM] 456 (Masahiko Aoki & Ronald Dore eds., 1995)

Olliverre, Scott, *The Influence of Taxation on Capital Structure in Venture Capital Investments in Canada and the United States*, 68 U. TORONTO L. REV. 9 (2010)

OLSON, MANCUR, THE LOGIC OF COLLECTIVE ACTION: PUBLIC GOODS AND THE THEORY OF GROUPS (1965)

Olubunmi, Faleye et al., *When Labor Has a Voice in Corporate Governance*, 41 J. FIN. & QUANTITATIVE ANALYSIS 489 (2006)

Orts, Eric W., *Beyond Shareholders: Interpreting Corporate Constituency Statutes*, 61 GEO. WASH. L. REV. 14 (1992)

Osaki, Sadakazu, *Tairyo Hoyu Houkoku-seido no Haseikoka to Kinofuzen* [*Spillover Effects and Malfunction of the Large Stockholding Report*

Regulation], *in* "KIGYOU-HO" KAIKAKU NO RONRI: INSENTHIBU SHISUTEMU NO SEIDO SEKKEI [THE LOGIC OF "ENTERPRISE LAW" REFORMATIONS: INSTITUTIONAL DESIGN OF THE INCENTIVE SYSTEM] 272 (Zenichi Shishido ed., 2011)

OSANO, HIROSHI, KŌPORĒTO GABANANSU TO JINTEKI SHIHON [CORPORATE GOVERNANCE AND HUMAN CAPITAL] (2005)

Osugi, Kenichi, *Transplanting Poison Pills in Foreign Soil: Japan's Experiment*, *in* TRANSFORMING CORPORATE GOVERNANCE IN EAST ASIA 36 (Hideki Kanda, Kon-Sik Kim, & Curtis J. Milhaupt eds., 2008)

Osugi, Kenichi, *Recent Reform of Japan's Corporate Law in an International Context: Who Have Participated in the Reforms, and How?* 53 JAPANESE YEARBOOK INT'L L. 320 (2010)

OTA, YO ET AL., ATARASHĪ MOCHIKABU-KAI SETSURITSU UN'EI NO JITSUMU [PRACTICE OF ADOPTION AND OPERATION OF NEW EMPLOYEE STOCK PURCHASE PLANS] (2011)

Pagano, Marco & Paolo Volpin, *Managers, Workers, and Corporate Governance*, 60 J. FIN. 841 (2005)

Partnoy, Frank & David Skeel, *The Promise and Perils of Credit Derivatives*, 75 U. CINN. L. REV. 1019 (2007)

Pascale, Richard & Thomas P. Rohlen, *The Mazda Turnaround*, 9 J. JAPANESE STUD. 219 (1983)

Peek, Joe & Eric S. Rosengren, *Unnatural Selection: Perverse Incentives and the Misallocation of Credit in Japan*, 95 AM. ECON. REV. 1144 (2005)

PINDYCK, ROBERT S. & DANIEL L. RUBINFELD, MICROECONOMICS §12.7 (7th ed. 2008)

Polsky, Gregg D., *Private Equity Management Fee Conversions*, TAX NOTES (Feb. 9, 2009), *available at* http://ssrn.com/abstract=1295443

Polsky, Gregg D. & Brant J. Hellwig, *Examining the Tax Advantage of Founders' Stock*, 97 IOWA L. REV. 1085 (2012)

Poterba, James M., *Public Finance and Public Choice*, *in* TAX POLICY IN THE REAL WORLD 429 (Joel Slemrod ed., 1999)

Pownall, Grace & Maria Wieczynska, *Deviations from the Mandatory Adoption of IFRS in the European Union: Implementation, Enforcement, Incentives, and Compliance* (Working Paper, 2011), *available at* http://ssrn.com/abstract=1919805

Preiato, John P., Philip P. Brown, & Ann Tarca, *Mandatory Adoption of IFRS and Analysts' Forecasts: How Much Does Enforcement Matter?* (May 23, 2010), *available at* http://ssrn.com/abstract=1499625

Price, Dan R., *Sunset Legislation in the United States*, BAYLOR L. REV. 401 (1978)

Puchniak, Dan W. & Masafumi Nakahigashi, *Japan's Love for Derivative Actions: Irrational Behavior and Non-Economic Motives as Rational Explanations for Shareholder Litigation*, 45 VAND. J. TRANSNAT'L L. 1 (2012)

Pugh, William N. et al., *The Effect of ESOP Adoptions on Corporate Performance: Are There Really Performance Changes?*, 21 MANAGERIAL & DECISION ECON. 167 (2000)

Raheja, Charu G., *Determinants of Board Size and Composition: A Theory of Corporate Boards*, 40 J. FIN. & QUANTITATIVE ANALYSIS 283 (2005)

Rajan, Raghuram G. & Luigi Zingales, *What Do We Know about Capital Structure? Some Evidence from International Data*, 50 J. FIN. 1421 (1995)

Ramseyer, J. Mark, Are Corporate Governance Systems Converging? (Working Paper, 1998)

RAMSEYER, J. MARK, BUSINESS ORGANIZATION (2012)

RIPLEY, WILLIAM Z., MAIN STREET AND WALL STREET (1927)

Ratnovski, Lev & Rocco Huang, *Why Are Canadian Banks More Resilient?* (IMF Working Paper No. 09/152, July 2009), available at http://ssrn.com/abstract=1442254

Rock, Edward B. & Michael L. Wachter, *The Enforceability of Norms and the Employment Relationship*, 144 U. PA. L. REV. 1913 (1996)

Roe, Mark J. & David Skeel, *Assessing the Chrysler Bankruptcy*, 108 MICH. L. REV. 727 (2010)

Romano, Roberta, *The Shareholder Suit: Litigation without Foundation?*, 7 J. L. ECON. & ORG. 55 (1991)

ROMANO, ROBERTA, THE GENIUS OF AMERICAN CORPORATE LAW (1993)

Romano, Roberta, *The Sarbanes–Oxley Act and the Making of Quack Corporate Governance*, 114 YALE L. J. 1521 (2005)

Romano, Roberta, *Does the Sarbanes–Oxley Act Have a Future?*, 26 YALE J. ON REG. 229 (2009)

ROMANO, ROBERTA, FOUNDATIONS OF CORPORATE LAW (2nd ed. 2011)

Rose, Amanda M., *The Multienforcer Approach to Securities Fraud Deterrence: A Critical Analysis*, 158 U. PA. L. REV. 2173 (2010)

Rose, Andrew K. & Mark M. Spiegel, *Cross-Country Causes and Consequences of the 2008 Crisis: An Update*, 55 EUR. ECON. REV. 309 (2011)

Rosen, Corey, *An Overview of How ESOPs Work*, *in* UNDERSTANDING ESOPs 1 (Corey Rosen & Scott Rodrick eds., 2010)

Rudy, Jesse, *What They Don't Know Won't Hurt Them: Defending Employment-At- Will in Light of Findings that Employees Believe They Possess Just Cause Protection*, 23 BERKLEY J. EMP. & LAB. L. 307 (2002)

Saitô, Takuji, *Nihon Kigyô ni yoru Shagai Torishimari-yaku no Dônyû no Kettei Yôin to sono Kôka* [*The Determinants of the Appointment of Outside Directors by Japanese Companies, and the Effect of the Appointment*], *in* NIHON NO KIGYÔ TÔCHI [CORPORATE GOVERNANCE IN JAPAN] 181 (Hideaki Miyajima ed., 2011)

Samarasekera, Nelly, Millicent Chang & Ann Tarca, *IFRS and Accounting Quality: The Impact of Enforcement* (Dec. 1, 2012), *available at* http://ssrn.com/abstract=2183061

Samuelson, William & Richard Zeckhauser, *Status Quo Bias in Decision Making*, 1 J. RISK & UNCERTAINTY 7 (1988)

Sanchirico, Chris William, *The Tax Advantage to Paying Private Equity Fund Managers with Profits Shares: What Is It? Why Is It Bad?*, 75 U. CHI. L. REV. 1071 (2008)

Santella, Paolo, Enrico Baffi, Carlo Drago, & Dino Lattuca, *A Comparative Analysis of the Legal Obstacles to Institutional Investor Activism in the EU and in the US* (working paper, 2009), published as *Legal Obstacles to Institutional Investor Activism in the EU and in the US,* 23 EUR. BUS. L. REV. 257 (2012)

Santos, Alvaro, *Labor Flexibility, Legal Reform, and Economic Development*, 50 VA. J. INT. L. 43 (2009)

Sarkissian, Sergei & Michael J. Schill, *The Nature of the Foreign Listing Premium: A Cross-Country Examination* (Darden Business School Working Paper No. 1639848, Jan. 29, 2012), *available at* http://ssrn.com/abstract=1639848

Saunders, Robert S., *Why Majority Voting in Director Elections Is a Bad Idea*, 1 VA. L. & BUS. REV. 117 (2006)

Scholes, Myron S. & Mark A. Wolfson, *Employee Stock Ownership Plans and Corporate Restructuring: Myths and Realities*, 19 FIN. MGMT. 12 (1990)

Schwab, Stewart J., *Life-Cycle Justice: Accommodating Just Cause and Employment At Will*, 92 MICH. L. REV. 8 (1993)

Schwartz, Alan, *Security Interests and Bankruptcy Priorities: A Review of Current Theories*, 10 J. LEGAL STUD. 1 (1981)

Schwartz, Alan, *A Contract Theory Approach to Business Bankruptcy*, 107 YALE L. J. 127, 183 (1997)

Seki, Takaya, *Legal Reform and Shareholder Activism by Institutional Investors in Japan*, 13-3 CORP. GOVERNANCE 377 (2005)

Shaviro, Daniel, DECODING THE US CORPORATE TAX (2009)

Sheard, Paul, *The Main Bank System and Corporate Monitoring and Control in Japan*, 11 J. OF ECON. BEHAVIOR & ORG. 399 (1989)

Sheard, Paul, *Interlocking Shareholdings and Corporate Governance*, *in* THE JAPANESE FIRM: THE SOURCE OF COMPETITIVE STRENGTH 310 (Masahiko Aoki & Ronald Dore eds., 1994)

Sheard, Paul, *Reciprocal Delegated Monitoring among Delegated Monitors: Principal–Agent Aspects of the Japanese Main Bank System*, 8 J. JAPANESE & INT'L ECONOMIES 1 (1994)

Sheehan, Dennis P., *Comment*, *in* CONCENTRATED CORPORATE OWNERSHIP 315 (Randall Morck ed., 2000)

SHIRAISHI, TADASHI, DOKUSENKINSHIHO [ANTI-MONOPOLY LAW] (2006)

Shishido, Zenichi *Japanese Corporate Governance: The Hidden Problems of the Corporate Law and Their Solutions*, 25 DEL. J. CORP. L. 189 (2000)

Shishido, Zenichi, *Reform in Japanese Corporate Law and Corporate Governance: Current Changes in Historical Perspective*, 49 AM. J. COMP. L. 653 (2001).

SHISHIDO, ZENICHI, DOKIZUKE NO SHIKUMI TOSHITENO KIGYO: INSENTHIBU SHISUTEMU NO HOSEIDO RON [THE FIRM AS AN INCENTIVE MECHANISM: THE ROLE OF LEGAL INSTITUTIONS] (2006)

Shishido, Zenichi, *The Turnaround of 1997: Changes in Japanese Corporate Law and Governance*, *in* CORPORATE GOVERNANCE IN JAPAN: INSTITUTIONAL CHANGE AND ORGANIZATIONAL DIVERSITY 310 (Masahiko Aoki et al. eds., 2007)

Shishido, Zenichi, *Sweat Equity as a Gift* (Working Paper for Sho Sato Conference at UC Berkeley Law School, March 9–10, 2009), *available at* http://www.law.berkeley.edu/files/sho_sato_tax_conf_web_paper--shishido(2).pdf

Shishido, Zenichi, *A Response to John Armour, Jack B. Jacobs and Curtis J. Milhaupt,* HARV. INT'L L. J. (2011)

Shishido, Zenichi, *The Law and Practice of the Venture Industry in Japan: A Period of Transition*, *in* THE JAPANESE LEGAL SYSTEM: AN ERA OF TRANSITION 193 (Tom Ginsburg & Harry N. Scheiber eds., 2012)

Shishido, Zenichi & Takaaki Eguchi, *The Future of Japanese Corporate Governance: Internal Governance and the Development of Japanese-Style External Governance through Engagement*, *in* RESEARCH HANDBOOK ON SHAREHOLDER POWER (Randall Thomas & Jennifer Hill eds., forthcoming)

Siegel, Mary, *Back to the Future: Appraisal Rights in the Twenty-First Century*, 32 HARV. J. ON LEGIS. 79 (1995)

SIEMS, MATHIAS M., CONVERGENCE IN SHAREHOLDER LAW (2008)

Skeel, David A., *Creditor's Ball: The "New" New Corporate Governance in Chapter 11*, 152 U. PA. L. REV. 917 (2003)

Skeel, David A., *The Past, Present and Future of Debtor-in-Possession Financing*, 25 CARD. L. REV. 1905 (2004)

Smith, Adam, WEALTH OF NATIONS (1776)

Smith, Clifford W. Jr & Jerold B. Warner, B*ankruptcy, Secured Debt, and Optimal Capital Structure: Comment*, 34 J. FIN. 247 (1979)

SOLOMON, JILL & ARIS SOLOMON, CORPORATE GOVERNANCE AND ACCOUNTABILITY (2004)

Sonoo, Ryuji, *Minji saisei tetsuzuki to saisei keikaku no jitsujo to kadai* [*Real State and Issues of the Civil Rehabilitation Proceedings and Rehabilitation Plans*], 736 NBL 8 (2002)

Spamann, Holger, *The "Antidirector Rights Index" Revisited*, 23 REV. FIN. STUD. 467 (2010)

Springer, Jonathan D., *Corporate Constituency Statutes: Hollow Hopes and False Fears*, 1999 ANN. SURV. AM. L. 85 (1999)

Stein, Jeremy C., *Efficient Capital Markets, Inefficient Firms: A Model of Myopic Corporate Behavior*, 104 Q. J. ECON., 655 (1989)

Stretcher, Robert et al., *The ESOP Performance Puzzle in Public Companies*, 18 J. EMP. OWNERSHIP L. & FIN. 3 (2006)

Stulz, Rene M. & Herb Johnson, *An Analysis of Secured Debt*, 14 J. FIN. ECON. 501 (1985)

Sugeno, Kazuo, JAPANESE EMPLOYMENT AND LABOR LAW 486 (Leo Kanowitz trans., 2002)

Sugiura, Ichiro, *Kyodai-na Keizaikenryoku no Shakaitekiseigyo toshiteno Mochikabugaishakisei* (*The Regulation for Holding Companies as a Social Control Giant Economic Power*), 17 KEIZAIHO GAKKAI NENPO 30 (1983)

Summers, Clyde W., *Worker Dislocation: Who Bears The Burden? A Comparative Study of Social Value in Five Countries*, 70 NOTRE DAME L. REV. 1033 (1994–1995)

Sunstein, Cass R., *Human Behavior and the Law of Work*, 87 VA. L. REV. 205 (2001)

Surrey, Stanley S., *The Congress and the Tax Lobbyist – How Special Tax Provisions Get Enacted*, 70 HARV. L. REV. 1145 (1957)

Suzuki, Kentaro, *DIP-gata Kaisha Kosei to Jigyo Saisei ADR* [*Debtor-in-Possession Type Reorganization and Business Rehabilitation ADR*], *in* "KIGYOU-HO" KAIKAKU NO RONRI: INSENTHIBU SHISUTEMU NO SEIDO SEKKEI [THE LOGIC OF "ENTERPRISE LAW" REFORMATIONS: INSTITUTIONAL DESIGN OF THE INCENTIVE SYSTEM] 176 (Zenichi Shishido ed., 2011)

Takizawa, Miho, Kotaro Tsuru & Kaoru Hosono, *Baishu Boeisaku Donyu no Doki: Keiei Hoshin Kasetsu no Kensho* [*Takeover Defense Measures: Testing of Entrenchment Hypothesis for Corporate Managers*] (RIETI Discussion Paper, 2007)

Talley, Eric L., *On Uncertainty, Ambiguity, and Contractual Conditions*, 34 DEL. J. CORP. L. 755 (2009)

Tanaka, Wataru, *Extinguishing Security Interests: Secured Claims in*

Japanese Business Reorganization Law and Some Policy Implications for US Law, 22 EMORY BANK. DEV. J. 427 (2006)

Tanaka, Wataru, *Soshiki Saihenn to Taika Juunann Ka* [*Mergers and Allowing Cash as a Consideration*], 304 HOUGAKU KYOUSHITSU 75 (2006)

Tanaka, Wataru, *Going Private and the Role of Courts: A Comparison of Delaware and Japan,* 3 UT SOFT L. REV. 12 (2011)

TATSUTA, MISAO, KAISHA HO TAIYO [BUSINESS CORPORATION LAW] (2007)

Thompson, Robert B., *Exit, Liquidity, and Majority Rule: Appraisal's Role in Corporate Law*, 84 GEO. L. J. 1 (1995)

Tirole, Jean, *Corporate Governance*, 69 ECONOMETRICA 1 (2001)

TIROLE, JEAN, THE THEORY OF CORPORATE FINANCE (2006)

Toichi, Takashi, *Kaikoken Ranyo Hori no Motarasu Insenthibu Koka to Hasei Mondai* [*Incentive Effects of the Abusive Dismissal Doctrine and Their Spill-over Effects*] *in* "KIGYO HO" KAIKAKU NO RONRI [LOGICS OF "ENTERPRISE LAW" REFORM] 59 (Zenichi Shishido ed., 2011)

Tokutsu, Akira, *Mochiaikabushiki no Hoteki-chii, vol.1.* [*The Legal Status of the Stock in the Cross-shareholding, Vol.1.*], 125 HOGAKU KYOKAI ZASSHI 455 (2008)

Tokutsu, Akira, *Mochiaikabushiki no Hoteki-chii, vol.5.* [*The Legal Status of the Stock in the Cross-shareholding, Vol.5.*], 126 HOGAKU KYOKAI ZASSHI 2027 (2009)

Toshima, Koji & Rintaro Shinohara, *Magic Triangles*, 27 INT'L FIN. L. REV. GUIDE TO JAPAN 71 (2008)

Triantis, George G., *Secured Debt under Conditions of Imperfect Information*, 21 J. LEGAL STUD. 225 (1992)

Triantis, George G., *A Theory of the Regulation of Debtor-in-Possession Financing*, 46 VAND. L. REV. 901 (1993)

Triantis, George G., *A Free Cash-Flow Theory of Secured Debt and Creditor Priorities*, 80 VA. L. REV. 2155 (1994)

Triantis, George G., *Debt Financing, Corporate Decision Making and Security Design*, 26 CAN. BUS. L. J. 93 (1995)

Triantis, George G., *Financial Slack and the Laws of Secured Transactions*, 29 J. LEGAL STUD. 35 (2000)

Triantis, George G., *Exploring the Limits of Contract Design in Debt Financing*, 161 U. PA. L. REV. 2041 (2013)

Triantis, George G. & Ronald J. Daniels, *The Role of Debt in Interactive Corporate Governance*, 83 CALIF. L. REV. 1073 (1995).

Tsuneki, Atsushi & Manabu Matsunaka, *Labor Relations and Labor Law in Japan*, 20 PAC. RIM L. & POL'Y J. 529 (2011)

Tung, Frederick, *Confirmation and Claims Trading*, 90 NW. L. REV. 1684 (1996)

Uchida, Konari, *Shagai Torishimariyaku Wariai no Ketteiyoin to Pafomansu* [*The Determinants of Outside Directors and Performance*], 50 SHOKEN ANALYST J. 8 (2012)

Ume, Kenjiro, *Horitsu no Kaishaku* (*The Interpretation of Law*) 9 TAIYO 61 (1903)

Utset, Manuel A., *Towards a Bargaining Theory of the Firm*, 80 CORNELL L. REV. 540 (1995)

Verkerke, J.H., *An Empirical Perspective on Indefinite Term Employment Contracts: Resolving the Just Cause Debate*, 1995 WISC. L. REV. 837

Verkerke, J.H., *Employment Contract Law*, *in* THE NEW PALGRAVE DICTIONARY OF ECONOMICS AND THE LAW (1998)

Verkerke, J.H., *The Story of Woolley v. Hoffmann-La Roche: Finding a Way to Enforce Employee Handbook Promises*, *in* EMPLOYMENT LAW STORIES (Samuel Estreicher & Gillian Lester eds., 2007)

Verkerke, J.H., *Discharge*, *in* LABOR AND EMPLOYMENT LAW AND ECONOMICS (Kenneth G. Dau-Schmidt, Seth Harris, & Orly Lobel eds., 2009)

Wachter, Michael L., *Theories of the Employment Relationship: Choosing between Norms and Contracts*, *in* THEORETICAL PERSPECTIVES ON WORK AND THE EMPLOYMENT RELATIONSHIP (Bruce E. Kaufman ed., 2004)

Wagenhofer, Alfred, *Voluntary Disclosure with a Strategic Opponent*, 12 J. ACC. & ECON. 341 (1990)

Waked, Dina I., *Do Developing Countries Enforce Their Antitrust Laws? A Statistical Study of Public Antitrust Enforcement in Developing Countries* (Dec. 22, 2011), *available at* http://ssrn.com/abstract=2044047

Walker, David I., *Is Equity Compensation Tax Advantaged?*, 84 B. U. L. REV. 695 (2004)

Walker, David I., *The Non-Option: Understanding the Dearth of Discounted Employee Stock Options*, 89 B. U. L. REV. 1505 (2009)

Walker, David I., *Evolving Equity Compensation and the Limits of Optimal Contracting*, 64 VAND. L. REV. 611 (2011)

WARD, RODMAN JR, EDWARD P. WELCH, & ANDREW J. TUREZYN, FOLK ON THE DELAWARE GENERAL CORPORATION LAW (4th ed. 1999)

Warren, Elizabeth & Jay Westbrook, *Secured Party in Possession*, 2003 AM. BANKR. INST. J. 150 (2003)

Watanabe, Tetsuya, *Tax Treatment of Stock Options in Japan*, 58 BULL. FOR INT'L FISCAL DOCUMENTATION 31 (2004)

Watanabe, Tetsuya, *Tax-Free Treatment for Corporate Reorganizations in Japan* (Proceedings from the 2009 Sho Sato Conference on Tax Law,

Social Policy, and the Economy), *available at* http://www.law.berkeley.edu/files/sho_sato_tax_conf_web_paper--watanabe.pdf (last visited 2012/9/11)

Weaver, Sarah, *Sunset Review in the States* (Report for the California Legislature Joint Sunset Review Committee, June 8, 2011), *available at* http://docs.google.com/viewer?a=v&q=cache:2gej2r5F638J:www.assembly.ca.gov/acs/Committee/C501/Hearings/060811/Sunset%2520Review%2520in%2520the%2520States.pdf+%22richard+kearney+sunset+survey%22&hl=en&gl=us&pid=bl&srcid=ADGEEShCFqIkO2zC0eoleRDmjwSvqVc5l3NeXIG31jaPNxGx9Fq_4zHKkM2M3A9QB6_GImdPRqLtUMVgauIDZyvYjfQYxD5aVuIUeVdel5XTcc08ucoBmjmkLJNHMBsMJm0S4vMzME6B&sig=AHIEtbQyr2I6CKax7O-onS_NCoAl24VnBA

Weisbach, David A., *The Taxation of Carried Interests in Private Equity*, 94 VA. L. REV. 715 (2008)

Weiss, Lawrence A., *Bankruptcy Resolution: Direct Costs and Violation of Priority of Claims*, 27 J. FIN. ECON. 285 (1990)

Wertheimer, Barry M., *The Purpose of the Shareholders' Appraisal Remedy*, 65 TENN. L. REV. 661 (1998)

West, Mark D., *The Puzzling Divergence of Corporate Law: Evidence and Explanations from Japan and the United States*, 150 U. PA. L. REV. 527 (2001)

West, Mark D., *Why Shareholders Sue: The Evidence from Japan*, 30 J. LEGAL STUD. 351 (2001)

Xu, Peng & Wataru Tanaka, *Baishu Boeisaku in za Shado obu Mochiai: Jirei Kenkyu* [*Anti-Takeover Measures in the Shadow of Cross-Shareholding: A Case Study*], 1885 SHOJI HOMU 4 (2009)

Yale, Ethan, *Investment Risk and the Tax Benefit of Deferred Compensation*, 62 TAX L. REV. 377 (2009)

YAMABE, TOSHIFUMI, CHUSHAKU DOKUSENKINSHIHO [A COMMENRARY ON THE ANTIMONOPOLY LAW OF JAPAN] (Akira Negishi ed., 2009)

Yamaguchi, Toshiaki, *Kansayaku no Kengen* [*The Authority of Kansayaku*], *in* KAISHA HÔ SEKÔ 5 NEN: RIRON TO JITSUMU NO GENJÔ TO KADAI [FIVE YEARS SINCE THE EFFECTUATION OF COMPANY ACT: THE CURRENT CONDITION AND THE AGENDA OF THEORY AND PRACTICE] Jurisuto Zôkan 37 (Shinsaku Iwahara et al. eds., 2011)

Yamakawa, Ryuichi, *New Wine in Old Bottles: Employee / Independent Contractor Distinction Under Japanese Labor Law*, 21 COMP. LABOR L. & POL. J. 99 (1999)

Yamakawa, Ryuichi, *Changing Aspects of Japanese Dismissal Law*, *in* LAW IN JAPAN: A TURNING POINT 483 (Daniel H. Foote ed., 2007)

Yamamoto, Kazuhiko, *Nihon ni okeru Honkakuteki na Jizen Chosei Gata Kaisya Kosei Tetsuduki no Makuaki he* [*The Beginning of a Full-Scale Prepackaged Corporate Reorganization Procedure in Japan*], 128 JIGYO SAISEI TO SAIKEN KANRI 4 (2010)

Yamamoto, Keiko, *Saikosho niyoru Kigyo no Saiken: Kaisha Kosei Tetsuzuki niokeru Saikenshakan no "Kosei-Kohei" na Kenri Bunpai no Arikata wo Fumaete* [*Restructuring of Companies by Renegotiation: "Fair and Equitable" Sharing of Interest among Creditors in Corporate Reorganization Procedure*], *in* "KIGYOU-HO" KAIKAKU NO RONRI: INSENTHIBU SHISUTEMU NO SEIDO SEKKEI [THE LOGIC OF "ENTERPRISE LAW" REFORMATIONS: INSTITUTIONAL DESIGN OF THE INCENTIVE SYSTEM] 159 (Zenichi Shishido ed., 2011)

Yazawa, Kenichi, *Why Don't Japanese Companies Disclose Internal Control Weakness?: Evidence from J-SOX Mandated Audits* (Working Paper, 2010)

YAZAWA, MAKOTO, KIGYOHO NO SHOMONDAI [PROBLEMS IN ENTERPRISE LAW] (1981)

Zeiler, Kathryn & Charles R. Plott, *The Willingness to Pay – Willingness to Accept Gap, the "Endowment Effect," Subject Misconceptions, and Experimental Procedures for Eliciting Valuations*, 95 AM. ECON. REV. 530 (2005)

Zeiler, Kathryn & Charles R. Plott, *Exchange Asymmetries Incorrectly Interpreted as Evidence of Endowment Effect Theory and Prospect Theory?*, 97 AM. ECON. REV. 1449 (2007)

Zhang, Ivy Xiying, *Economic Consequences of the Sarbanes–Oxley Act of 2002,* 44 J. ACCT. ECON. 74 (2007)

Index

absolute priority 23
abusive dismissal doctrine 13, 15, 71–75, 77–78, 79
accounting 302
accounting quality 331
accounting rules 264
acquisitions 237, 241–46, 248, 250
administrative informality 45
administrative sanctions 336
adverse selection 63
affiliated companies 353, 365
agency model 8
American Bar Association (ABA) 254
anti-abuse rules 281
anti-competition regulations 42
antitrust law 206, 210
appraisal remedy/rights/system 29, 34, 222–36, 237–51
asymmetric information 61, 62
at-will employment contracts 54
audit attestation 351
audit committees 352, 356
automatic stay (US) 153
autonomy 235

backward induction 48
bad worker signaling 62, 63
balance between autonomy and monitoring 4, 25, 33, 36, 47, 49
balancing image 6, 14
bank ownership 270
bank shareholding 205
bank supervision 338
Banking Act (Japan) 206
banking law 205
bankruptcy 20, 47, 125
Bankruptcy Code (US) 163
bankruptcy judge 132
banks 134
Banks' Shareholding Restriction Act (Japan) 264
bargaining image 9
bargaining power 13, 15–16, 24–55, 27–29, 44, 81–86, 90, 92, 94–95, 349, 356, 365
bargaining relationships 4, 7, 8, 10
behavioral economics 53, 68
behavioral law and economics 66, 68
beneficial dictator model 278–79
Berle and Means 7
best practices 254
boards 271–3
  determinants model 272
  management boards 272
  monitoring boards 272
  performance effect of boards 272
board primacy 193–94
board systems 27
bonuses 102
bounded rationality 66, 379
boycotts 81, 84, 89–90, 98
Bulldog Sauce case (Japan) 38, 186, 189
business judgment rule 27, 31, 38, 230, 254

Cadbury Report (UK) 254
capital income 280–81
capital market performance 328
capital markets 9
career advancement 263, 265
Chapter 11 of the Bankruptcy Code (US) 152
chilling effects 31, 236
Civil Code (Japan) 168
Civil Rehabilitation Act (Japan) 151
class actions 353
coalitions 4, 6, 7, 10, 12, 14, 16, 32, 46, 83, 94, 97, 99
Coasean invariance 58
collateral 126

collective action 83–84, 89–90, 92, 94, 97, 98–99
collective bargaining 16, 81, 83–85, 87–91, 93, 94, 97–99
collective bargaining agreements 164
commitment 75
common law 59
community of shared fate 94
Companies Act (Japan) 237, 239–41, 248
company community 10, 14, 15, 28, 71, 77–78, 262–63, 265–66, 355
company with three committees (Japan) 257
complementarities 48–49, 71, 78–80, 105, 118–21, 263, 349, 350, 365
complementary institution 97
comply or explain 255, 273
comprehensive tax base 280, 288
confirmation bias 66
conflicting interests 3, 6, 19, 33–34, 47
conflicts of interest 133
constitution (constitutional) 89
contingent workers (employees) 95
control rights 281, 287
controlling shareholder 219
convergence of corporate governance 5
corporate auditors (*kansayaku*) 255
corporate control market 12, 32, 36, 178
corporate culture 105
corporate governance 101, 125, 134, 271, 281, 327, 349–50, 358, 362, 365
Corporate Governance Code (Germany) 254
corporate governance guidelines (Europe) 254
corporate income tax *see* tax
corporate personality 44
Corporate Reorganization Act (Japan) 152n13, 164
corporate scandals (Japan) 255
corporate scandals (US) 253
corporate tax incidence 282
corporate taxes on large business enterprises 282
Corporate Value Study Group (Japan) 183–85, 187–88
corporations 303–08
covenants 19, 126, 130, 132, 136
cramdown (US) 24, 153, 157–58
credit default swap 134
creditor control 125
creditor priority 128
creditors 12, 18, 75
creditors' committees 135
crisis or crisis-driven financial legislation 367–68, 370, 376
cross-border capital flows 329
cross-border transactions 287
cross-country comparisons 60
cross-listing of securities 331
cross-shareholding 10, 33, 35, 38, 197–98, 262–65, 268, 383–84

D&O insurance 31, 360–61, 364
deadweight loss 280
debt contracts 125
debt–equity swap 220
debt-financing 281, 287
debt overhang 128, 130
debtor-in-possession (DIP) 20
debtor-in-possession (DIP) financing 131–32
deemed dividends 300
default 125, 127, 130
defense regulations 33
defensive management 357, 360, 365–66
deferring 293
defined benefit pension plans 161, 165–66, 170
defined contribution pension plans 161, 165, 170
defined contribution retirement plans 109
delegation 259–60
deregulation of financial markets 264
design of enterprise law 278
director primacy 36
director's responsibilities to third parties 20, 30
discharge 57
disclaimers 65
disclosure 329
disclosure regimes 345
disclosure regulations 19, 29, 43, 44
discovery 29, 353
discrimination 57

dismissal 70, 72
  reorganizational 72
dismissal right 193–94, 196–97
disposition of an important asset 260
dispute acts 90–92
dissolution of *zaibatsu* conglomerates
    see zaibatsu
distribution policy 281, 288
distributional considerations 282
diversity of stock ownership 5–6
dividend restrictions 20
dividends 25, 70
dividends from a foreign subsidiary
    297
dividends received 296–97
double taxation 40–41
dual class share system 271
duty of care 30
duty of loyalty 30

earnings management 358
economic weapons 81, 83, 91–92, 94, 98
efficiency (efficient) 223, 231, 233, 236
empire building 7, 41
empirical analysis 53
empirical results 58
employee commitments 273
employee ownership 100–06, 111, 114,
    115–17
employee stock purchase plan (ESPP)
    100, 107
employees 12, 80–83, 84–99
employers (or management) 81–99
employment-at-will 15, 54, 66, 70, 73
employment contract 58
employment income deduction 294
employment protection law (EPL) 10,
    14, 53, 58
end-game 20, 46
endowment effect 66–68
enforcement 42
  private 43, 317, 353, 357
  public 43–44, 317, 353, 357
engagement 37, 195–97, 201–04
engagement, regulations 196–97, 202–03
Enron 342
enterprise law 1
enterprise law's incentive bargains
    283–84
entire fairness 230
entrenchment 37, 105, 116
equity financing 281, 284
ERISA 166
ESOP 109
ex ante incentives 22–23
ex ante constraints 131
ex post discipline 131
excess burden 280–81
exclusive representation 82, 87, 88, 98
executive certification 351
executive compensation 9, 345
exemption amount 282
exit 25
experiment *see* regulation,
    experimentation
external auditors 352, 356
external labor markets 71, 73, 77–78,
    79, 354
extinguishing security interests (Japan)
    152, 154–59

fair value 35, 224–26
fiduciary duties 15, 27, 29, 34, 71,
    75–77, 79, 228–30
financial crisis 264, 337
Financial Instruments and Exchange
    Act (Japan) 202
financial statements 351
firing costs 54, 57, 58, 61
firm-specific human capital 74, 78
firm-specific information 272, 273
firm-specific investment 6, 10, 23, 33,
    46
fiscal stimulus 284, 288
five percent rule 26, 33
flexibility (flexible) 95, 97
Foreign Corrupt Practice Act (US) 351
foreign shareholders 269
framing effects 66
free cash flow 25, 32
free-rider problem 104
freedom to conduct operations 91
freeze-out 239–41
fringe benefits 283, 285, 287

general concentration 210
General Motors 161–62, 165, 171
GHQ 199
global economy (or global trade)
    82–83, 85, 86, 90, 92, 94–96, 98

goals of taxation 278
good faith 89
government 11, 40

head tax 281–82
healthcare benefits 161, 163
hold-up problem 16
holding companies 216
hostile takeovers 31, 79, 178–90, 268
human capital providers 1, 9, 12
hypothetical value 224

implied contract exception 59
important asset committees 260
incentive bargain 1, 12, 18, 24, 40, 44–45, 47, 48–49, 277–79, 283–84, 286, 288, 349, 355, 365
incentive mechanism 3
incentive patterns 4, 6, 45
incentives of employees 162, 170, 171
income tax 280–81, 283–85, 288
income tax law (Japan) 280–81, 283, 288
income tax law (US) 280–81, 283, 288
independent directors 27, 39, 44
independent directors (US) 253
independent *yakuin* 258
indirect foreign tax credit 298
indirect reporting 356
individual income tax 283
industry regulations 45
inelastic activities 280–81
information forcing rules 64
information technology (or information age) 82–83, 86, 94–96, 98
informational asymmetry 328
injunctions 238, 240–42, 245–47, 250–51
injunctive relief 29
inside owners 268
insider-dominated boards 252, 263
insider-dominated ownership structure 268
insider trading 328
insider trading regulations 112
insolvency 20, 125
institutional investors 195–96, 202–03, 265, 268, 270, 271, 328
institutional investors, as catalysts 203–04
institutional investors, forum 203–04
insurance 61
integration 291
interactions between taxation and enterprise law 278
interactive governance 126, 136
interest group bargaining model 279
internal control 349, 351–52, 355, 358–59
internal labor markets 95
international tax rules 287

J-SOX 349–52, 355–57, 362–66
Japan (Japanese) 82–3, 85, 87, 89–94, 97–99
Japan Airlines 161–62, 167, 170–71
job security 62, 64, 68
just-cause contracts 53, 56, 66
just-cause norm 65
justifiable acts 89
justifications for state interference in contracting 346–47

kansayaku see corporate auditors, statutory auditors
kansa-kantoku committee 258
Kay Review (UK) 202
keiretsu 35, 383–84
  horizontal 35
  vertical 35

La Porta, et al. 28
labor income 281
labor law 54
labor market efficiency 61
labor markets 9–10, 15, 28, 46
labor relations 84–85, 88
Labor Union Act (Japan) 86
labor unions 13–14, 16
later-in-time priority 131
law 81–90, 92–93, 97–98
law in action 60
legacy cost 161
legal-information-forcing default rule 64, 68
legislation 47
  crisis-driven 47

demand pull 47
policy push 48
sunsetting 369–73, 375–76
Legislative Council of the Ministry of Justice (Japan) 258
leveraged ESOP 110
leveraged ESPP 116
leviathan model of government behavior 279
lifetime employment 14–15, 93, 262
Livedoor case 183
lockout 91–92, 98
loss aversion 66

macroeconomic stabilization policy 284
main bank 9, 18, 218, 264, 384
management 12, 73, 81–83, 85, 93, 94, 97–99, 351
management boards 272–3
management buyouts 223
management control 7, 26
management–shareholder relations 193, 195–96, 197–204
managerial autonomy 270
managerial myopia 270
managers, compensation 302
manipulation of information 344
market failure 63
market for corporate control *see* corporate control market
market out 226–27
market price 232, 234
material weakness 349, 359, 365
maximization of shareholder value 71, 75–76
maximize client outcomes 277
measurement and modeling issues 59, 60
mergers 237, 239–41
mergers and acquisitions (M&A) 75
minority protections 24, 28, 34
Miwa, Yoshiro 383–85
monetary capital providers 1, 9, 18, 24
monitoring boards 272–73
monitoring image 7, 15
monitoring model 252, 255
monitors 349, 356, 365
moral hazard 23, 61

National Center for Employee Ownership (US) 102
National Labor Relations Act (NLRA) (US) 84–85, 87, 89
negative externalities 283
nomination of CEOs 263
non-covered workers 56
non-performing loans 264
non-recognition rule of corporate reorganization 41
non-recognized gain or loss 299
norms 57

Olympus case 270–71, 363
on-the-job training 78
opportunistic behavior 19, 35, 74
optimal tax policy 280
optimism bias 66
options 304–08
outside directors 271–73, 385
outside directors, numbers and ratios in Japan 252
outside *kansayaku* 256
outside owners 268
outsider-dominated ownership structure 268
overinvestment 128, 130
ownership 268–70
bank ownership 270
insider ownership 268
outside ownership 268
ownership structures 194, 196, 198–200

partnerships 311–15
payers of corporate tax 292
Pension Fund Association (Japan) 265
performance-based compensation 283
permanent replacement 82, 84, 91, 98
periodic repayment 126
Pigouvian taxes 283–84, 286
piercing the corporate veil 208
plural unions 88, 98
poison pill 33, 36, 37
policy push legislation 350–51
political neglect 379
positive externalities 283
pre-petition lenders 133
preferential transfer 127

priority of claims in bankruptcy 66, 168, 170
private benefits 7, 101, 216–17, 219, 220, 268
private equity 309–16
private information 62
product markets 12
productivity 100–03, 105, 115, 117
profit-sharing 102
prohibition on property benefits 113
proxy 25–26, 28
public choice 278
Public Company Accounting Oversight Board (PCAOB) (US) 353, 356
pure flat tax 282
principal–agent relationships 61
purge of corporate managers 262

rational ignorance 65
reciprocal fairness 66
reduction in force (RIF) 56
reference shareholders 194–95, 198
regulation
  exemptions 374–76
  experimentation 373–76
  sunsetting 373, 375–76
  waivers 374–75
regulatory dualism 220
relation-specific investment 35
relational bank lending 136
relational creditors 125
relevant date 226
renegotiation 16, 20–21, 46
reorganizations 299
repeat play 65
repeated game 45
reporting line 352, 356, 357
repurchase regulations 113
reputation 65
residual claimant 18, 20, 24
retirees 21
Revlon case (US) 180–81
Rex Holdings case (Japan) 229–30
risk 3, 25, 46
risk-averse 18–20
risk-based capital standard 207
risk-neutral 18–19, 24
role of board of directors (Japan) 258–61
roll up 133
screening 233–34
secondary boycott 84, 89–90, 98
secured claims in bankruptcy 151
secured credit 128
secured DIP lenders 136
securities regulation 42, 112
security interests 130, 136
senior creditor control 24
severance pay 57, 58
shareholder activism 25–26, 29, 37
shareholder class actions 27, 30
shareholder derivative actions 20, 27, 30, 353
shareholder, empowerment 195–97
shareholder, influence 193, 195, 198
shareholder information rights 29
shareholder meeting 28
shareholder value maximization 14
shareholders 1, 75, 92, 242
sharing control 4, 32, 45–46
sharing value added 4, 32, 45–46
shark repellent 13, 33
shirking 61
short-termism 270
signaling 62, 346
Silicon Valley model 9
small and medium sized enterprises 290
social norms 8–10, 14, 28, 46, 57, 65, 71–72, 80, 353–54
SOX (Sarbanes–Oxley Act of 2002) (US) 20, 43, 342–44, 347, 349–53, 355–56, 358–64, 365–66
  compliance costs of 343
special directors 260
staggered board 33
stakeholder coalitions *see* coalitions
stakeholder statutes 27, 79
stakeholders 255
start-up companies 309–12, 315–16
status quo bias 66
statutory auditors (*kansayaku*) 27, 255–57, 352, 357, 364
statutory labor rights 60
stock 304–07
stock majority rule 25
stock option 8, 295
stock pyramids 216
strikers 91–92
strikes 81–82, 84, 86, 90–91
structuring transactions 277, 288

successor nomination 263
sunset *see* legislation, sunsetting; regulation, sunsetting
supervisory staffing 324
squeeze out 223
synergies 222, 230
synergy value 224

takeover defenses 268
Takeover Guidelines (Japan) 184–85, 187
takeovers 237–39, 241–50
tax 40
  corporate income 41, 283–84
  individual income 41
tax (US) 302 *passim*
tax benefits 110
tax credits 283
tax deductions 283
tax-favorable 277, 283, 286–87
tax-favored compensation packages 286
tax incentives 280, 283
tax incidence 282
tax-induced changes to taxpayer behavior 280, 283, 286
tax law 277–78, 280, 287–88
tax lawyers 277
tax-motivated transactions 281
tax penalties 286, 288
tax policy 278–79, 280–81, 284, 288
  central dilemmas of 280
  incentives of 280
  optimal 280
  scholarship 278–79
tax salience 279
tax subsidies 105
tax rate 290
taxation 277–80, 284–86
taxing large business enterprises 282
taxpayer behavior 283
tax-qualified ESPP 109
Tecmo case (Japan) 225
temporary stay (Japan) 153
tender offers 239, 241–45
territorial tax 298
theoretical speculation 63
TOB regulations 26, 33, 47
Tobin's Q 361
Tokyo Stock Exchange (TSE) 185, 188–89,258
transparency
  arguments against 343–45
  arguments for 342–43
  associated agency problems 345

uncertainty 238, 241, 250
underinvestment 128
union workers 63
unions (or employee organizations or organized labor) 81–84, 86–94, 97–98
United States (or America or American) 82–83, 85, 87–88, 90–98
unjust termination 54
Unocal case (US) 180–81, 183
unraveling 346

valuation 238, 241–42, 244–50
venture capital firms 312–16
venture capital industry 309–16
venture capitalists 9
Vienot Report (France) 254
voice 25
voting rights 24–25, 101, 108

wages 73–74
Wal-Mart 96
whistleblowers 66, 355, 363
white squires 13, 33
Williams Act (US) 179
workers 82–83, 86–92, 94, 96–98
workplace norms 57
Worldcom 342
worldwide tax 298
written disclaimers 64
wrongful termination 56

zaibatsu 198–99
  dissolution of 262